SOCIAL PSYCHOLOGY

An Introduction

Bernard Seidenberg
Alvin Snadowsky

*Both of Brooklyn College
of The City University of New York*

With Teresa Amabile, Alvin L. Atkins, Robert Brannon,
Thomas J. Crawford, Samuel L. Gaertner, Albert H. Hastorf,
Irma Hilton, Bruce Kleinhans, John M. Levine, Barry McLaughlin,
Arthur G. Miller, Dean G. Pruitt, Karl E. Scheibe, Dalmas A. Taylor,
Elaine Walster, G. William Walster, Norman C. Weissberg,
and Richard H. Willis

THE FREE PRESS
A Division of Macmillan Publishing Co., Inc.
NEW YORK

Collier Macmillan Publishers
LONDON

Copyright © 1976 by The Free Press
              A Division of Macmillan Publishing Co., Inc.

All rights reserved. No part of this book may be reproduced or transmitted in any form or by any means, electronic or mechanical, including photocopying, recording, or by any information storage and retrieval system, without permission in writing from the Publisher.

The Free Press
A Division of Macmillan Publishing Co., Inc.
866 Third Avenue, New York, N.Y. 10022

Collier Macmillan Canada, Ltd.

Library of Congress Catalog Card Number: 75-9236

Printed in the United States of America

printing number

1 2 3 4 5 6 7 8 9 10

Library of Congress Cataloging in Publication Data
Main entry under title:

Social psychology.

    Includes bibliographies and index.
    1. Social psychology--Addresses, essays, lectures.
I. Seidenberg, Bernard. II. Snadowsky, Alvin M.
HM251.S672   301.1   75-9236
ISBN 0-02-928050-8

COPYRIGHT ACKNOWLEDGMENTS

The authors gratefully acknowledge permission to reprint from the following:

Chapter 4. Excerpts and poster number 6 of Laws of the Pioneers, "A Pioneer Develops Courage and Does Not Fear Difficulties," from *Two Worlds of Childhood: U.S. and U.S.S.R.*, by Urie Bronfenbrenner, with the assistance of John C. Condry, Jr., © 1970 by Russell Sage Foundation. Also with the permission of George Allen & Unwin Ltd., London.

Chapter 4. From *Principles of Behavior Modification* by Albert Bandura. Figure 3-16, p. 190. Copyright © 1969 by Holt, Rinehart and Winston, Publishers. Reprinted by permission of Holt, Rinehart and Winston, Publishers.

Chapter 4. From "Moral and Religious Education and the Public Schools," by Lawrence Kohlberg, in *Religion and Public Education,* edited by Theodore R. Sizer. Table 1, p. 171. © 1967 by Houghton Mifflin Co. Used by permission.

Chapter 7. Figure 2, Figure 4, and an unnumbered illustration (p. 349) appeared in "Modes of Resolution of Brief Dilemmas," by Robert P. Abelson, *Journal of Conflict Resolution*, Vol. 3, No. 4 (Dec. 1959), pp. 345–349, and are reprinted by permission of the Publisher, Sage Publications, Inc.

Chapter 8. Illustration adapted from Figure 6, p. 62, from "A Study of a Neglected Portion of the Field of Learning—the Development of Sensory Organization," by Robert Leeper, *The Journal of Genetic Psychology, 46,* 1935, pp. 41–75. Copyright 1935 by The Journal Press.

Chapter 8. From M. Karlins, T. L. Coffman, and G. Walters, "On the Fading of Social Stereotypes: Studies of Three Generations of College Students," *Journal of Personality and Social Psychology, 13,* 1969. Table 1, pp. 4–5. Copyright 1969 by the American Psychological Association. Reprinted by permission.

Chapter 8. From H. H. Kelley, "The Process of Causal Attribution," *American Psychologist, 28,* 1973. Figure 7, p. 114. Copyright 1973 by the American Psychological Association. Reprinted by permission.

Chapter 11. From J. Horai and J. T. Tedeschi, "Effects of Credibility and Magnitude of Punishment on Compliance to Threats," *Journal of Personality and Social Psychology, 12,* 1969. Figure 1, p. 166. Copyright 1969 by the American Psychological Association. Reprinted by permission.

Chapter 11. From R. M. Liebert, W. P. Smith, J. H. Hill, and M. Keiffer, "The Effects of Information and Magnitude of Initial Offer on Interpersonal Negotiation," *Journal of Experimental Social Psychology, 4,* 1968. Tables 1, 2, and 3, pp. 432–437. Copyright 1968 by Academic Press.

Chapter 11. From R. B. Mogy and D. G. Pruitt, "The Effects of a Threatener's Enforcement Costs on Threat Credibility and Compliance," *Journal of Personality and Social Psychology, 29,* 1974. Figure 2, p. 176. Copyright 1974 by the American Psychological Association. Reprinted by permission.

Chapter 11. From D. G. Pruitt and S. A. Lewis, "Development of Integrative Solutions in Bilateral Negotiation," *Journal of Personality and Social Psychology, 31,* 1975. Table 1, p. 623. Copyright 1975 by the American Psychological Association. Reprinted by permission.

Chapter 12. From I. Steiner, *Group Process and Productivity*. Figure 4.3, p. 96. Copyright 1972 by Academic Press.

Chapter 12. From *FIRO: A Three-Dimensional Theory of Interpersonal Behavior* by William C. Schutz. Figure 8-7, p. 166. Copyright © 1958 by William C. Schutz. Reprinted by permission of Holt, Rinehart and Winston, Publishers.

Contents

Preface ix

About the Authors xi

PART ONE *Introduction* 1

   CHAPTER 1 ***The Field of Social Psychology*** by Bernard Seidenberg and Alvin Snadowsky 3

   Introduction/Theories of Social Psychology/The Empirical Approach/Summary/ Suggested Readings

   CHAPTER 2 ***The Social Psychology of the Research Situation*** by Arthur G. Miller 23

   Introduction/Portraits of the Human Subject in Psychological Research/The Subject's View of Psychological Research/Deceiving the Experimental Subject/The Role of the Experimenter in Research/Epilogue/Summary/Suggested Readings

PART TWO *Determinants of Social Behavior* 49

   CHAPTER 3 ***Social Motivation*** by Alvin L. Atkins and Irma Hilton 51

   Introduction/Primary Sources of Motivation/Secondary Sources of Motivation/ Instrumental Responses/Social Goals/Implications for Social Motivation/Summary/ Suggested Readings

   CHAPTER 4 ***Socialization: The Formation of Identity*** by Karl E. Scheibe 81

   Introduction: What Is Socialization?/Some Conceptual Distinctions/Socialization Through Observation/Socialization to National Identity/In Conclusion/Summary/ Suggested Readings

   CHAPTER 5 ***Situational Determinants of Hurting and Helping Behavior*** by Samuel L. Gaertner 111

   Introduction/Hurting and Helping/Instrumental Aggression/Angry Aggression/Helping Behavior/Summary/Suggested Readings

PART THREE *Attitudes and Attitude Change* 143

   CHAPTER 6 ***Attitudes and the Prediction of Behavior*** by Robert Brannon 145

   Introduction: The Challenge of Attitudes/Attitude Theory/Attitude Measurement/ Attitude and Behavior/Where Do We Go from Here?/Summary/Suggested Readings

CHAPTER 7 *Theories of Attitude Change* by Thomas J. Crawford — 199

Introduction/The Inductive Approach: Studies of Source, Message, and Audience Effects/The Functions and Structure of Belief Systems/The Dynamics of Change in Belief Systems: Cognitive Consistency Theories/Summary/Suggested Readings

PART FOUR *Interpersonal and Group Processes* — 237

CHAPTER 8 *Person Perception* by Teresa Amabile and Albert H. Hastorf — 239

Introduction/Perception:Objects and Persons/The Judgment of Nonverbal Behavior/Impression Formation/Attribution Theory/Future Trends in Person Perception Research/Summary/Suggested Readings

CHAPTER 9 *Interpersonal Attraction* by Elaine Walster and G. William Walster — 279

Introduction/Interpersonal Attraction: A Definition/The Reinforcement Model of Interpersonal Attraction/Equity Theory/Current Status of Interpersonal Attraction/Theoretical Applications and Future Research Directions/Summary/Suggested Readings

CHAPTER 10 *Interpersonal Influence and Conformity* by Richard H. Willis and John M. Levine — 309

Introduction/What Is Conformity?/What Are the Alternatives to Conformity?/Why Conformity and Why Deviation?/When Conformity and When Deviation?/Conformity—Good or Bad/Summary/Suggested Readings

CHAPTER 11 *Power and Bargaining* by Dean G. Pruitt — 343

Introduction/Forms of Personal Power/Threats and Promises/Influence Through Allies/The Power of the Group/Bargaining/Summary/Suggested Readings

CHAPTER 12 *Group Development and Structure* by Dalmas A. Taylor and Bruce Kleinhans — 377

Introduction/Group Formation and Development/Group Structure/Perception of Structure/Summary/Suggested Readings

CHAPTER 13 *Group Processes, Productivity, and Leadership* by Bruce Kleinhans and Dalmas A. Taylor — 407

Introduction/Group Processes/Group Performance/Leadership/Summary/Suggested Readings

PART FIVE *Social Issues and Applications* — 435

CHAPTER 14 *Social Movements* by Barry McLaughlin — 437

Introduction/The Study of Social Movements/Three Contemporary Social Movements/Conclusion/Summary/Suggested Readings

CHAPTER 15 *Applied Social Psychology* by Norman C. Weissberg 463

Introduction/Poverty/The Black-White Thing/Black-White Interactions and Social Change/Summary/Suggested Readings

References 499

Name Index 543

Subject Index 553

Preface

"What the world needs most" is probably not another social psychology textbook. Most users of such books would agree that new books or new editions of older books are somewhat justifiable on the basis of being "up-to-date." And although all new books are so for a while, the simple fact of being the newest book on the block simply does not stand up as a sole reason for such a costly endeavor. In addition, this principle hardly explains the fondness that many teachers of social psychology have for certain older books of "character" such as those of Asch, Brown, and Kretch and Crutchfield's first edition.

Being up-to-date is not enough. What qualities are required in addition may be disputed and may ultimately boil down to a question of taste. What the three examples cited have in common is that they are individual positions strongly identified with their eminent authors. They represent positions that may be supported or disputed but which, in either case, provide a basis for engaging some of the critical issues in the field. It would seem, however, that the growth in the scope and quantity of social psychological research over the last twenty years makes it increasingly difficult to produce such a book even if any book must, through the process of including and excluding material, inevitably reflect the orientation of the author.

Initially, we intended to do the entire book by ourselves. Very early on we were impressed and chastened by some interesting barriers. Even our combined interests did not begin to encompass the field as we saw it. Particular enthusiasms resulted in some good chapter outlines but also in some rather bland and boring ones. Neither of us felt that our intuitive notions of how the field should or would be were quite ready for public scrutiny now, if ever.

It then occurred to us that a true sense of participation and involvement frequently absent from textbooks could be cultivated by seeking out workers in each area and asking them to survey the area and, where appropriate, to focus on some particularly noteworthy aspect of the field.

The results, we feel, confirm that our decision to change our role from authors to editors was the right one. Each of the chapters represents a view of an area of research as seen by a person intimately involved in it rather than a bird's eye view or a distillation or a simplification or an homogenization of a complex area.

Throughout, we have tried to exercise a light editorial hand. Each author was encouraged to exercise maximum freedom in the selection and presentation of material within the guidelines we provided for format and topic treatment. We were particularly pleased that some of the problems arising from such a multi-authored venture—problems of overlap and jurisdiction—led to informal contact among the contributors and to a community zeal that grew and mushroomed as we worked.

We have, we believe, a book that surveys a major portion of the field of social psychology. We believe that the various chapters survey particular areas and focus on both the major findings and problems in those areas in an involving and exciting way. Finally, we think that our contributors have incorporated much relevant and current material into the corpus of their work without being "trendy" or superficial. We hope that teachers and students of social psychology will agree.

We want, first of all, to express our deep appreciation to each contributor. They worked hard to follow our guidelines and were professional and patient in dealing with editorial suggestions. We appreciate that they have subjugated some personal preferences to the superordinate goal, and we know that they had important suggestions that proved helpful to us. Their dedication and enthusiasm were important ingredients in finishing the task.

We are particularly grateful to Robert Wallace of The Free Press for his continuing support and editorial guidance. Robert Harrington of The Free Press was the very able overseer of the manuscript through the production process. Colleagues who provided useful comments and discussion at various points were William De Jong, Glen Hass, Harry Jagoda, Gudmund Smith, and Michael Wolff. Special thanks are due to Barbara Braden, Vikki Del Pellegrino, Leslie Felsher, Judy Greener, Gertrude Leon, Gerry Mason, Ethelreda Seidenberg, Deleri Springer, Judy Steinberg, Lenore Weissberg, and Bonnie Weinstein for their support and dedication to the task of preparing this book for publication.

Bernard Seidenberg

Alvin Snadowsky

About the Authors

Teresa Amabile is completing her Ph.D. in Social Psychology at Stanford University. She is coauthor of "Attribution Theory" in the *Encyclopedia of the Social Sciences* (in press). Her research interests include attributional errors and biases, the maintenance of intrinsic interests, and the psychology of creativity.

Alvin L. Atkins is Associate Professor of Psychology at the Ferkauf Graduate School, Yeshiva University, where he has taught since receiving his Ph.D. from Columbia University. He coauthored *Clinical and Social Judgment* and is currently conducting research in the social and clinical aspects of aggression as well as in the field of community psychology.

Robert Brannon received his Ph.D. from the University of Michigan. He is a member of the faculty at Brooklyn College of The City University of New York. His interests are attitude measurement and predictive validity, accuracy of person perception, prejudice and intergroup relations, and sex-role attributions.

Thomas J. Crawford received his Ph.D. from Harvard University and is currently Associate Professor of Social Ecology at the University of California, Irvine. His paper "Sermons on Racial Tolerance and the Parish Neighborhood Context" was awarded the Gordon W. Allport Intergroup Relations Prize by the Society for the Psychological Study of Social Issues (SPSSI). His research interests include race relations, family planning, and police work.

Samuel L. Gaertner received his Ph.D. in Psychology from The City University of New York and is currently Associate Professor at the University of Delaware. He is also a consultant for the Public Defender's Office of the State of Delaware. His research interests include the study of racial attitudes (particularly among those who view themselves as unprejudiced), helping behavior, and aggression.

Albert H. Hastorf received his Ph.D. from Princeton University and is currently Professor of Psychology at Stanford University. At Stanford he has served also as Chairman of the Psychology Department and as Dean of the School of Humanities and Science. He is coauthor of *Person Perception*. His research interests are concerned with the relation of cognitive processes and social interaction.

Irma Hilton received a Ph.D. from the Department of Social Psychology at Columbia University. She is Associate Professor of Psychology at Ferkauf Graduate School, Yeshiva University. Her current research is on the social and developmental causes of dependency and aggression.

Bruce Kleinhans received his Ph.D. in Social Psychology from the University of Maryland. He is presently an Associate in Research, Addiction-Prevention Treatment Foundation, New Haven,

Conn. His research interests, in addition to groups, include attribution processes, self-disclosure, interpersonal attraction, and environmental psychology.

John M. Levine received his Ph.D. from the University of Wisconsin and is currently Associate Professor of Psychology at the University of Pittsburgh. His research interests include reaction to attitudinal deviance, determinants of conforming and nonconforming behavior, nonverbal communication, and animal social behavior.

Barry McLaughlin received his Ph.D. from Harvard University and is currently Associate Professor of Psychology at the University of California, Santa Cruz. He is editor of *Studies in Social Movements* and author of *Learning and Social Behavior.* His research interests include the study of social movements and the social psychology of communication.

Arthur G. Miller received his Ph.D. from Indiana University and is currently Associate Professor of Psychology at Miami University (Ohio). He edited *The Social Psychology of Psychological Research,* which was an earlier treatment of the issues raised in his chapter. His research interests are in attribution theory and interpersonal attraction.

Dean G. Pruitt received his Ph.D. from Yale University and is currently Professor of Psychology at the State University of New York, Buffalo. He coedited *Theory and Research on the Causes of War.* He does research on social conflict and bargaining and is working also on a series of case studies of campus crises of the late 1960's.

Karl E. Scheibe received his Ph.D. from the University of California at Berkeley and is currently Professor and Chairman of the Department of Psychology at Wesleyan University. He was a Senior Fulbright Fellow at the Catholic University of Sao Paulo, Brazil, and is author of *Beliefs and Values.* His research interests are in the area of socialization processes.

Bernard Seidenberg received his Ph.D. from New York University and is currently Professor of Psychology at Brooklyn College of The City University of New York. He was Fulbright Lecturer at the Catholic University of Nijmegen in Holland and is coeditor of *Basic Studies in Social Psychology.* His research interests include moral conflict resolution and factors in the maintenance and channeling of social interaction.

Alvin Snadowsky received his Ph.D. from The City University of New York and is currently Associate Professor of Psychology at Brooklyn College. He is editor of *Social Psychology Research: Laboratory-Field Relationships* and *Child and Adolescent Development: Laboratory-Field Relationships.* His research includes empirical analyses of communication structures, impact studies of social problems, and assessments of human potential groups.

Dalmas A. Taylor received his Ph.D. from the University of Delaware and is currently Professor of Psychology at the University of Maryland, College Park. He is the author of several books, including an introductory textbook in psychology. His major research interests in addition to groups are self-disclosure, person-perception, and personality.

Elaine Walster received her Ph.D. from Stanford University and is currently Professor of Psychology and Sociology at the University of Wisconsin. She is coauthor of *Interpersonal Attraction*. Her main research interest is Equity Theory.

G. William Walster received his Ph.D. from the University of Minnesota and is currently Associate Professor of Sociology at the University of Wisconsin. His main research interest is in developing inferential statistical decision-making techniques for the Social and Behavioral Sciences.

Norman C. Weissberg received his Ph.D. from the University of Michigan and is currently Associate Professor of Psychology at Brooklyn College of The City University of New York. He is completing work on a general readings book in social psychology. His research interests include race relations, attitudes, and poverty.

Richard H. Willis received his Ph.D. from the University of Wisconsin and is currently Professor of Psychology at the University of Pittsburgh. He held a Fulbright Lectureship in Finland and was Rockefeller Visiting Professor at the University of the Philippines. His research interests include social influence processes, cognitive dynamics, and intrapsychic and social conflict.

PART ONE

Introduction

1. **THE FIELD OF SOCIAL PSYCHOLOGY**
   Introduction
   Social psychology defined? / Applications of social psychology
   Theories of Social Psychology
   Simple and sovereign theories / Broader orientations
   The Empirical Approach
   Data collection techniques / Research settings
   Summary
   Suggested Readings

2. **THE SOCIAL PSYCHOLOGY OF THE RESEARCH SITUATION**
   Introduction
   Portraits of the Human Subject in Psychological Research
   Historical developments / The subject as powerless / Preserving self-esteem and dignity / A more positive view / Conclusion

2 Introduction

The Subject's View of Psychological Research
 Conceptions of the subject's role / Research illustration / Current assessment of subject roles / Conclusion / Who are the subjects?
Deceiving the Experimental Subject
 How prevalent is deception? / What are the effects of deceiving subjects? / Alternatives to deception: role playing / A summarizing research report
The Role of the Experimenter in Research
 Experimenter effects / Experimenter expectancy effects / What produces the expectancy effect? / Recent applications of the expectancy research / Summary of Rosenthal's work
Epilogue
Summary
Suggested Readings

1
The Field of Social Psychology

Bernard Seidenberg and Alvin Snadowsky

INTRODUCTION

A traditional way of beginning a textbook is to define the subject matter. About here we should write, "Social psychology is the...." Such a definition has a calming effect as it enables the student to learn something tangible in the first paragraph and to master the answer to one of the many and inevitable multiple-choice test items that will be encountered during the semester. The sense of well-being persists despite the fact that the definition is violated throughout the remainder of the book.

A similar state of affairs holds here. The very act of writing a definition of the field may provide a sense of mastery and completeness that will be contradicted repeatedly by the subject matter of the book, if the author has taken any but the most narrow of stances. In addition, although it may escape the novice, his instructor will realize that any definition may be violated more by what is not in the book than by what is covered. No introductory social psychology textbook could possibly include even brief allusions to every topic that social psychologists would consider part of the field.

The entire issue could be sidestepped, of course, by not attempting a formal definition, and the authors of some more recent texts have taken this tack. Obviously, there remains an implicit definition in terms of the contents of the book.

In our opinion modern social psychology defies meaningful definition, although it is possible to note certain themes that seem to characterize the field. For example, social psychology has been defined as the scientific study of interpersonal behavior events (Krech, Crutchfield, & Ballachey, 1962). Another definition points to it as the study of behavior as influenced by the implied or actual presence of other persons (Allport, 1968). Both of these definitions pay homage to the influence of John

B. Watson in that they focus on behavior. As is pointed out in Chapter 6, this attempt at objectivity and precision is more apparent than real. However, it is in keeping with a long tradition in American psychology and supports a sense of scientism if not of science.

The important aspect of both definitions is the focus on how the social context or persons influence the behavior of people. It is this focus on the effects of persons, concrete social situations, or symbolic representations of both on the behavior of persons or groups that seems to be the crux of the social psychological orientation.

Social Psychology Defined?

It might be instructive to take a closer look at a recent reasonable definition to see what the impact and implications are of what is said and what is not said in the definition: "Social psychology is the *scientific* study of *individual behavior as a function of social stimuli*" (Shaw & Costanza, 1970, p. 3).

Scientific is a deceptively simple word that has acquired a specialized meaning in recent years. For many social psychologists—and a quick perusal of the major journals would confirm this—it means the use of the laboratory experimental paradigm. As we shall see later, the laboratory experiment is only one of the approaches available for the scientific study of behavior; its use is not always feasible and in some instances is perhaps not preferable. However, almost no psychologist would argue against the use of the term in its broadest meaning of controlled observations. Social psychology must reach beyond the frequently biased observational habits of the man-in-the-street, but it is not confined to the laboratory.

Individual is another innocuous word that makes for problems. It highlights the limitations of social psychology and even its primitive state of development. Thus, despite the fact that the study of group phenomena has always been part of the subject matter of social psychology, there is a paucity of concepts and measurement based on organic properties of groups per se. Inevitably, such measures as are used are derived from the summation or averaging of measures based on the behavior of all the individuals in the group. Although this kind of derived score is frequently useful, workers in nascent areas such as family therapy and those interested in how dyadic and group interaction are maintained are struggling with the problem of finding concepts and developing observational indices based on mutual interaction and emergent features not readily indexed by summating or averaging the responses of the observed individuals.

There is another sense, too, in which the term *individual* is misleading. Social psychologists often make no pretense of understanding why a particular individual behaves as he does in a social situation. We may measure the behavior of single individuals, but we then usually analyze these measures with a variety of statistical techniques to provide general statements of behavioral trends in a given situation. Thus, we can and do make statements that a certain proportion of people with certain characteristics will behave a certain way in a given situation, while we have no way of predicting the behavior of a given person in that situation.

Of course, some social psychologists have insisted on the lawfulness of the single case, that is, the necessity to predict the behavior of the individual and not lose the person in the "average." Kurt Lewin (1951) was the most notable social psychologist espousing this view. In practice, most social psychologists have opted to pursue the generation of statistical or "average"-type laws, some because they believe that is the task of a scientific social psychology and others because they believe such laws may be all our current knowledge permits us to say.

We have previously alluded to the implications of the word *behavior* to psychologists. The reader may remember from introductory psychology courses that Watson's extreme emphasis on measuring behavior as the focus of psychology seemed necessary to save psychology from the subjective and increasingly solipsistic morass into which the excesses of Wundt, Titchener, and their followers had plunged the field. A question of some importance is whether the baby has been thrown out with the bath water.

All of you are aware of the richness and variety of your inner experiences. You have a succession of moods, feelings, thoughts, perceptions, fantasies, daydreams, and dreams that certainly enhance your sense of individuality and that you believe influence your behavior in a variety of situations. That social psychologists seem indifferent to these aspects of the "real you" may surprise you and even offend you. However, they have reasons.

Many social psychologists attempted to follow the lead of Lewin, who stressed the importance of the *psychological field*. By this he meant that behavior must be described in terms of the situation as it exists for the individual at a given time. The situation must be described from a subjective or phenomenological viewpoint, that of the behaving person. In practice this approach has proved extremely time-consuming at best and is considered unnecessary by most social psychologists. Many researchers frequently use their own phenomenology to guide them in the initial stages of the formulation of a research problem. Others obtain detailed interviews from some small number of respondents to provide insights about a particular situation. Many more gather some additional information from their subjects during or after an experiment to check on any unforeseen reactions or interpretations of the research situation. In Chapter 2, there is an insightful analysis of the factors present in a research situation that may affect the behavior of subjects.

In any case, the subjective and phenomenological aspects of a person's reaction to a situation have probably been eschewed not so much for reasons of ideological disagreement as for pragmatic reasons. It is simply easier to set up a situation, make certain reasonable assumptions about what that situation means to the subjects, and record one or more objectively available responses to the situation. This procedure has proven effective in terms of the current level of development of social psychology.

The next term of significance is *function,* in accord with one view of the scientific enterprise that holds that the task of science is to establish a series of causal or functional statements of the form "A is a function of B" or, to put it another way, "B causes A." This part of our definition aptly describes what many social psychologists believe is the goal of social psychology and what still others believe is all we can do considering the current state of our art.

For another perspective, we turn again to that brilliant pioneer, Kurt Lewin. Lewin (1951) espoused the notion of the *field,* a state of forces in dynamic equilibrium. Changes in any portion or portions of the field more or less immediately give rise to new dynamics. The focus is always on the current dynamic properties of the field rather than any attempt to note simple correspondences between any two elements. This mode of analysis has in fact been widely used in physics for many years and has proved to be a powerful conceptual tool when more simplistic functional notions have failed. However, if the experience of physics is a useful guideline, it would seem that a superior measurement technology and sophisticated mathematics are necessary to insure that a field approach is something more than a futile exercise.

The functional approach has yielded modest success to this point, considering the complicated phenomena that social psychologists study and the relatively primitive conceptual and measurement tools developed at this stage in our history. However, the functional approach seems most productive when research situations are deliberately structured, as are most experiments, to simplify interaction situations and to measure end products rather than processes.

The functional approach is not particularly helpful in dealing with real-life situations, which are more complex. In addition, it ignores two important features of behavior that are increasingly being emphasized by a new approach to social phenomena, *ethnomethodology* (Garfinkel, 1967). First of all, behavior is reflexive. That is, current interaction, for example, depends on what immediately preceeded it. In turn, what is happening now leads to new elements in the immediate future. One can observe and describe such sequences, but they elude a functional analysis in the traditional sense.

For example, in a course taught by one of the authors, students were videotaped interacting spontaneously in pairs or triads. In one instance, a male and two females were interacting when the male and one of the females discovered that they had a common interest and began discussing it while excluding the other female. As they continued conversing they started to lean toward each other, and each crossed his legs so that each top leg pointed toward the other, establishing a "bridge"—a term Sheflin (1973) coined for this type of physical human connection. After some minutes of this conversation during which the other female was not a conversational participant and also "seemed" to be excluded physically, she seized an opportunity to ask the male a question about the topic. He began to answer and spent some time doing so. Slowly the female he had been talking to uncrossed her legs and started to lean as far back in her chair as possible. The male then shifted his body toward his new conversational partner while uncrossing his legs, and she shifted her body, leaning toward him.

These phenomena and similar ones occurred frequently during the course of the recorded interaction. Other investigators have noted similar events occurring in the process of interaction and are convinced that any increase in our understanding of how interaction is maintained and directed depends upon our ability to conceptualize and interpret these kinds of observations. Yet attempts to do so within a functional paradigm have proved elusive.

The second important but frequently overlooked property of interaction is that meanings of events and sequences of events are emergent through the process of interaction. The ethnomethodologist holds that almost any act or utterance is ambiguous in the sense that many possible meanings or interpretations could be placed on it. Two septuagenarians might have been born into poverty. The one who is now a millionaire may very well place a certain value on the role such influences had on his character formation and on his later success in life. The other, his poverty now aggravated by extreme age, may very well attribute his current situation to the damaging effects of that early poverty.

In a similar vein, we have all had the experience of revising or confirming an interpretation of an event because of subsequent information. If a good friend returns a greeting in a perfunctory manner we may be puzzled, hurt, or angry. We may also conjure up a variety of explanations for this unusual event. Later information that our friend is home with a temperature of 102°, has failed an exam, or gone to a rock concert with some other people can confirm a suspicion or provide us with the experience of, "Aha, now I understand!" In any case, it is clear that phenomena such as we have been discussing fit into a functional paradigm with difficulty, if at all.

The preceding discussion also highlights some problems with the final phrase in the definition we have been dissecting, *social stimuli*. Clearly, social stimuli refers to other people. But just as clearly the term must refer to them whether or not they are physically present. The meaning of social stimuli then must be expanded to include symbolic representations of people and other social products, along with less tangible aspects of social life such as our knowledge of normative or expected behavior. In addition, we must be able to account for apparent inconsistency as in the storied cases of aristocrats able to pursue all sorts of intimate interactions in the presence of servants or, a much more mundane example, the motorist stopped for a red light who picks his nose as if he were shielded from view by solid walls rather than by car windows. It is not always clear how a person sees himself in a social situation, and his symbolic representations of social situations are certainly not directly available to us. Frequently, in terms of clarity, specificity, and even awareness, they may not be available to him.

Thus, our attempt to present a definition of the field of social psychology has raised many questions and answered none. At this point we should recognize that we have probably raised the reader's anxiety level by presenting a whole series of problems and issues without any solutions. The student, with some justification, may be wondering whether there is a subject matter to be studied.

Applications of Social Psychology

Despite the importance of the issues raised and the absence of ready answers, there are thousands of social psychologists busily engaged in both research and the application of research findings. The necessity of taking concrete action goads them into making certain decisions which may not be ideal but which advance our knowledge of human social behavior. Science involves compromises between what is ideal and what is possible no less than do all other human activities.

Perhaps the best overview of social psychology would be obtained by leafing through a few volumes of the *Journal of Personality and Social Psychology*. You would find that the great majority of the reports are of laboratory experiments of a wide variety of topics. Studies of factors affecting helping behavior, attitude change, liking for others, and the attribution of personal characteristics to others are likely to make up a large proportion of the reports in any issue.

Surprisingly, one will find relatively few studies of group processes in this journal. In part this is a reflection of the current interests of social psychologists. Twenty-five years ago there was a great flurry of activity in this area, but the absence of developing theories of group processes seems to have held up research in this field. Two other journals, *Sociometry* and *Human Relations,* are slightly more specialized toward groups and are likely to have a higher proportion of such studies. Social psychologists also study cross-cultural differences of all kinds, and some are interested in social movements.

Although many people might believe that social psychologists should address themselves to applied problems, relatively few do so. The *Journal of Social Issues* publishes many of these studies. The reasons are many but understandable. Such research requires many resources—money, cooperation from authorities, and large staffs, for example. Also, this kind of research is very difficult to do elegantly—it is called "dirty" in the trade—and the researchers must have great experience and diplomatic skill to carry out their projects.

The work of social psychologists does not procede *in vacuo*. The contributions of past generations of psychologists and other social scientists has yielded a tradition that provides a framework for contemporary social psychologists to extend, modify, or rebel against. This tradition comprises a variety of theoretical approaches to human behavior, a range of settings in which observations generally are made, and a variety of data-gathering tools. We shall discuss each of these facets of the tradition in turn.

THEORIES OF SOCIAL PSYCHOLOGY

For a number of reasons, it is very easy to overestimate the prevalence and coherence of theorizing in social psychology. First of all, there seems to be a strong predilection or need for scholars in a field to attempt to impose coherence or, if that proves impossible, at least the semblance of coherence. Second, there is a clearly discernable trend in the history of science toward the development of broader, more inclusive, and more powerful theories. This gives rise to a status hierarchy within science so that the older sciences such as physics, chemistry, and astronomy, in which powerful predictions based on well-developed theories can be made, have a higher status than the newer sciences such as sociology and psychology. This leads inevitably to a status differential within any science in which theorizers are usually accorded higher status than the data-gatherers or empiricists.

The end result of all of these forces in social psychology is a great deal of confusion concerning the status of theory. For example, Tedeschi and Bonona (1972, p.1) take the stand that "social psychological theory as such does not exist." They agree with Kuhn (1962), who has postulated that it is possible to subdivide the development of any science into two phases. In the pre-paradigm stage there is almost-random activity, emphasizing rival but diverse and unorganized subfields of inquiry and a lack of theoretical or empirical direction. In the paradigm stage the accumulation of knowledge is reorganized logically and theoretically to define a coherent integrated new approach to the field.

"The state of the art of social psychology is quite evidently in the pre-paradigm phase of development . . . (Tedeschi & Bonona, 1972, p. 1). There are many small theoretical models in competition, each of which provides a degree of order or explanation for a small portion of the data within specific subfields. The use of common-sense language and trial-and-error approaches into research areas and the generation of disconnected and ambiguous hypotheses has resulted in a large number of seemingly unrelated concepts and undigested mountains of empirical data.

If this is true, how can we speak of theories in social psychology? We can if we agree immediately that there is no one theory under which all social psychological phenomena can be placed or explained. Of course, construction of such a theory has been attempted. One kind of attempt has been to explain all sorts of complex events in terms of a single principle. You are all probably familiar with friends and relatives who use a pet principle of motivation or behavior to "explain" the behavior of other people. This frequently emerges as "nothing but," that is, all behavior is nothing but a love for power, money, or sex, to give three common examples. These reductionist views have been used by very famous social philosophers in attempts to fathom the social behavior of man.

Simple and Sovereign Theories

In his excellent chapter in *The Handbook of Social Psychology,* Gordon Allport (1968) described the powerful tendency of nineteenth-century social psychologists to explain human behavior in terms of overriding principles or motives. Hedonism, egoism, sympathy, gregariousness, imitation, and suggestion were some of the concepts that various theorists saw as the central theme or motive underlying all human behavior. Although modern social psychologists are too sophisticated to fall into the *simplistic fallacy* in an obvious fashion, Allport cautioned against another variety of unitary explanation.

> Yet even today we find authors who favor some one predominant factor to the *relative* neglect of others. Among these factors are such favorites as *conditioning, reinforcement, anxiety, sexuality, guilt, frustration, cognitive organization, role, identity, alienation* and *social class.* Thus, it is difficult for even a modern author to keep a balance of explanations in his repertoire. The reason seems to be that every writer aspires to a coherent system of explanation and wishes to reduce the number of variables in his system to a minimum. (p. 10).

Broader Orientations

If "simple and sovereign" theories are not the answer, what other theoretical solutions are available? In the early history of psychology a number of orientations or schools arose which were characterized by certain views of human nature and by certain philosophical preferences as to how the task of studying behavior should be undertaken and what principles were necessary to accomplish the task. These viewpoints have been labeled theories, but we must understand that they are not theories in the same powerful way that Newton's laws of motion constitute a theory. However, they do provide views and concepts that enable social psychologists to construct small theories or models, that is, a conceptual scheme designed to pull together the facts we have about some limited area of behavior and to provide the basis for making further predictions in that limited area.

Gestalt Orientation. "Gestalt" is the German word for form or figure. This term became the symbol for the orientation put forward by a group of German researchers (e.g., Wertheimer, 1923; Kohler, 1929; Koffka, 1935) who were studying perception, the experiencing of forms and patterns being one of their areas of interest. Their thesis was set forth as a reaction to the elementistic schools of thought (i.e., Structuralism and Associationism) which explained perception as a combination of sensations and stimulus–response associative bonds. Taking a *molar* rather than a *molecular* approach, the Gestalt psychologists argued that because the whole is greater than the sum of its parts, one does not get the true picture of a phenomenon by studying it only in terms of its apparent elements. They suggested that perceptual experience is organized and that the organization, rather than being random, is directed toward the "best conditions" of order and simplicity in accordance with the current situation. Unfortunately, these researchers did not define precisely the characteristics of the best conditions and the processes through which they are achieved.

The implication of the Gestalt orientation for the social psychologist is that an individual's major interest is to evolve an organized and meaningful conception of the environment. Research by Asch (1946) on impression formation is illustrative of this approach. In one experiment, each of two groups of students was read a list of personal characteristics attributed to a hypothetical individual. For the first group the list contained the words intelligent, skillful, industrious, warm, determined, practical, and cautious. The second list was identical to the first with the exception that "cold" was substituted for "warm." Subjects then were asked to write an impression of the person. It was found that the two lists significantly influenced the tone of the impressions, so that the individual who was described as warm was seen in a more positive light. In a second experiment the words warm and cold were replaced by the words polite and blunt in lists presented to two new groups. The observed differences between groups were weaker than those found in the first experiment.

A further analysis of the data led Asch to conclude that (1) an individual strives to form a complete impression even when the information is meager; (2) the characteristics attributed to the same person are viewed as interactive in that the "industriousness" of a "cold" individual is seen differently from the "industriousness" of a "warm" individual; and (3) traits belonging to the same person do not have equivalent weight, in that some characteristics are central, providing direction (e.g., "warm" and "cold" in this experiment) while others are peripheral and dependent (e.g., "intelligent" and "industrious" here).

Some of the spirit if not the substance of the Gestalt orientation has influenced aspects of social psychology. For example, Heider's theory of interpersonal relations and many aspects of attribution theory show Gestalt influences (see Chapter 8).

Field Theory. The most important influence of Gestalt psychology on social psychology has been somewhat indirect and through a derivative system called Field Theory. Kurt Lewin, a student of the founders of Gestalt psychology, was the developer of Field Theory; through his students and writings, he has had an important influence on social psychological thought.

According to Deutsch (1968), Field Theory has certain important properties, some of which we shall briefly summarize.

1. The psychological approach: Lewin emphasized the importance of understanding behavior in terms of the psychological meaning of the situation for the person. This did not mean to him a subjective approach but that we may understand someone else's behavior not in terms of our interpretation of a situation or some "objective" standard but only in terms of the psychological reality of the person.

2. Emphasis on the total situation: For Lewin, the distinction between person and environment is erroneous and misleading. The person-in-a-situation is a system (the life space), and what occurs in that system can be understood only by recognizing the systemic attributes of the total psychological field for the individual. This view, of course, runs counter to the very usual notion of abstracting the relationship of two or three measurable variables in a situation.

3. Systematic versus historical causation: Because of his emphasis on the life-space as a field, Lewin believed that it is the present condition of the field that must be considered in dealing with changes. For Lewin, past events cannot directly have caused present events but only find a place in a complex chain of events that led to the present situation.

4. The dynamic approach: Lewin, as did Freud, eschewed a static view of human behavior and focused on the notion that a situation at any particular time is an equilibrium based on a resolution of all the dynamic forces present, including motives and tensions within the person and forces acting on him in the field.

Lewin's theoretical notions have not provided the theoretical umbrella he and his followers hoped for, but his orientation has led to some fruitful middle-range theories, including Heider's theory of interpersonal relations and Deutsch's theory of cooperation and competition (Shaw & Costanza, 1970 p. 137). In addition, it is very likely that his thinking has influenced many other social psychologists in more subtle and pervasive ways.

Reinforcement Theory. The very important orientation of reinforcement theory is based on the core notion, probably known since men domesticated animals and each other, that reward and punishment can influence the learning process. At the turn of the century both Thorndike in America and Pavlov in Russia were studying these effects systemtaically. Thorndike's work (1913) led to his famous law of effect: If behavior is followed by a satisfying state of affairs it is stamped in, and if followed by a dissatisfying state of affairs it is stamped out. Pavlov determined the basic laws of conditioning, including the need for reinforcement (the availability of a strong unconditioned reflex) to maintain the new response.

This work paved the way for Watson's behavioristic revolution against the essentially introspective brands of psychology then extant. Although Watson (1919) saw reinforcement only as maintaining behavior learned by mere contiguous relationships between stimuli and responses, his system provided the groundwork for further theoretical positions. Both Guthrie (1935) and Tolman (1932), assigned reinforcement a secondary role in their systems. For Guthrie reinforcement played a role much like its role for Watson, maintaining stimulus–response associations. Tolman saw reinforcement as not playing a role in learning per se but rather as facilitating performance. Tolman's position and opposition to Hull (1943), another pioneer who emphasized the importance of reinforcement in cementing S–R bonds, turned the 1930s and 1940s into an exciting ongoing contest between these two giants. Many novel experiments were conducted as proponents of one theory sought to refute important points of the other theory and were in turn attacked. Tolman's system later provided a base for cognitive theory, which we will discuss shortly.

The reinforcement position as it evolved through the efforts of Hull and then Skinner has a common core of concepts. The starting point for our purposes is a *stimulus,* some event internal or external to the organism that leads to an alteration in behavior, called the *response.* Thus, stimulus and response are logically inseparable from each other. A third concept, *reinforcement,* refers to any stimulus that strengthens a response when present (positive reinforcer) or that strengthens a response when removed (negative reinforcer).

The richness of the system is further enhanced by additional concepts. For example, *generalization* refers to the fact that responses can be elicited by stimuli that resemble the original stimuli but have never before been paired with the response. *Extinction,* or the progressive weakening of a response under conditions of nonreinforcement, provides an explanation of the weakening or disappearance of responses. *Drive,* for some reinforcement theorists, describes internal states either innate or learned that act as strong stimuli. Skinnerians (Skinner, 1953), less prone to make inferences about unobservable processes, see drive as expressing the relationship between some antecedent operations and the strength of the organism's response.

These concepts and others have been used to construct a wide assortment of related models stemming from the reinforcement orientation and applied to a variety of situations and phenomena. Attitudes (Bem, 1967; McGuire, 1964), social learning (Bandura, 1962), and interactions in terms of social exchange theory (Homens, 1961; Thibaut & Kelley, 1959) are examples of areas in which reinforcement models have been used. In general, such models have the advantage of apparently objectively and precisely defined terms that seem subject to relatively simple measurement and observation. In addition, there is an apparent ease in specifying functional relationships among the concepts to such a degree that mathematical relationships can sometimes be worked out and predicted.

On the debit side we must consider that real-life social situations frequently bear only a superficial resemblance to the very simplified situations that give rise to such models and are used to test the models. The apparent rigor of the models is bought at the cost of simplifying—some would say overly much—their assumptions, and many people feel that this approach ignores the richness of human social life. Perhaps the controversy generated by the reinforcement orientation centers about whether it goes to the heart of social behavior or cuts the heart out of it.

The Cognitive Orientation. The cognitive orientation has evolved from a number of different sources. Interestingly, one major precursor has been Tolman's behaviorism, a theoretical system that was originally built on animal studies. Tolman conceived learning as involving organization or reorganization of environmentally contiguous stimuli. Explaining these connections led Tolman and his students to posit certain ongoing psychological processes such as cognitive maps and expectancies. Thus, Tolman's rats seem to have been endowed with an enormous variety of inferred mental activity.

The other major contributors to cognitive theory have been Gestalt and Lewinian psychology. With the latter two systems it shares a nonmechanistic orientation that focuses on the organization and differentiation of conscious experience and on processes such as thinking and perception.

Basic to this orientation is the concept of *cognition*. This term seems to indicate some bit of sensory input that has been processed and stored by the individual. It seems to refer to some item of knowledge, very broadly taken. These cognitions are organized into *cognitive structures,* which seems to mean "any form of interdependence among cognitive elements which has motivational, affective, attitudinal, behavioral or cognitive consequences" (Zajonc, 1968b, p. 321). Cognitive structures have certain organizational properties, and Zajonc (1969) has enumerated four:

1. differentiation: the number of attributes constituting a given cognitive structure
2. complexity: the degree of interrelatedness of attributes
3. unity: the degree to which attributes are functionally dependent upon each other
4. organization: the extent to which one attribute or cluster of attributes dominates the whole

This rather simple-appearing orientation has given rise to an enormous body of research. One line of research has explored cognitive organization or entities in terms of attributes, dimensions, categories, concepts, and schemata. A more fruitful approach, however, has been the exploration of cognitive dynamics, that is, the study of changes that occur in cognitive systems when they are exposed to attack, strain, or conflict.

Considering the vagueness (or broadness) of the definition of cognition, it should come as no surprise that phenomena as diverse as person perception (Heider, 1958), interpersonal relations (Newcomb, 1961), and attitude change (Osgood & Tannenbaum, 1955; Festinger, 1957) have been approached from a cognitive viewpoint. In addition, cognitive dissonance theory, one of this family, has instigated a huge volume of research in the area of attitude change, primarily, but also in areas such as norm internalization.

In general, the models belonging to the cognitive orientation have been very productive and provocative. In addition, they are more satisfying from a humanistic point of view to many people because these theories seem to recognize the complexity of human behavior, the importance of the "silent processes" inside one's head, and principles such as organization and relatedness. However, cognitive theories tend to oversimplify or not to consider many potentially relevant variables (e.g., unconscious processes). Also, the theories tend to be very broad and to utilize concepts that are not precisely defined. All in all, however, these approaches seem to be among the most useful and promising available to social psychologists currently.

The Psychoanalytic Orientation. It will probably come as a surprise to many students that the psychological theory that many of them have viewed as almost synonymous with psychology does not play an especially prominent role in modern social psychology. We shall review briefly some of the central ideas of psychoanalysis and then examine some of its applications to social psychology.

The cornerstone of Freud's theory is that each individual is endowed with psychic or mental energy. This energy, *libido,* is sexual in nature. For Freud this meant a general kind of pleasure-seeking quality that was expressed in a variety of ways depending on the developmental stage of the individual and the outlets available to him.

This expression of libido is facilitated by a property of the mental apparatus, *cathexis,* which refers to an investment of energy in a mental representation of an object. It is the ebb and flow of mental energy and the pattern and nature of its cathexes that determine personality formation and behavior. In addition, anticathexes or forces inhibiting the expression of instinctual aims are generated, leading to a blocking of instinctual urges, as in the case of repression, or to a delay, as in the case of planning or thinking.

From this beginning psychoanalysis becomes an extraordinary complex system difficult to explain in summary form. A number of major views can be derived from Freud's writing, a few of which we will list here:

1. The empirical viewpoint asserts that the subject matter of psychoanalysis is behavior, which for Freud included thoughts, feelings, symptoms, dreams, and unconscious wishes.
2. The holistic viewpoint asserts that all behavior is the multidetermined outcome of a field of forces, in a way similar to Lewin's view.
3. The genetic viewpoint encompasses the well-known progressive shift of drives and objects through the oral, anal, phallic, and genital stages of development.
4. The structural viewpoint refers to the id, ego, and superego as organized structures of personality having differing yet interacting contributions to the channeling and investment of psychic energy.
5. The dynamic viewpoint stresses that all behavior is based on a dynamic interplay of conscious and unconscious forces.

In point of fact only a very few investigators have applied psychoanalytic theory or derivations of it to social psychological research in a systematic way. Most famous is the research flowing from *The Authoritarian Personality* (Adorno, Frenkel-Brunswik, Levinson, & Sanford, 1950). These researchers showed that social attitudes toward social and religious groups can be traced to dynamic factors of personality within a psychoanalytic framework. Others (Sarnoff, 1960) have attempted to show how other social attitudes can be related to a variety of ego-defensive functions.

Two of the most interesting applications of psychoanalytic theory to social phenomena have been made by a social philosopher (Marcuse, 1955) and a classicist (Brown, 1959). These writers have creatively utilized Freudian theory, particularly the relationship between culture and repression, to present powerful social criticism.

Clearly, Freud provided a rich legacy of concepts derived from extensive experience, both general and with patients. These theories provide a rich texture for intensive analysis of individual behavior and for extensive analysis of history and culture. However, psychoanalytic concepts have yet to yield a return in the hands of social psychologists whose behavioristic and experimental biases are not receptive to them.

Role Theory. Role theory is an orientation stemming from Sociology that has given rise to a very large body of research on topics ranging from conformity to family dynamics to hypnosis. Basically, it is not a theory, but rather a conceptual language and set of descriptive categories for analyzing social behavior.

Biddle and Thomas (1966) have provided a framework for classifying the many constructs of role theory into a few basic categories:

1. Some terms such as *actor* (the individual who is the focus of the analysis) and *other* (the target of behavior) refer to participants in an interaction.
2. Other terms such as *norms* or *role expectations* refer to behavioral expectations operating in a situation. *Role performance* refers to an actor's actual behavior, and *sanction* refers to the fact that the actor may be rewarded or punished depending on the adequacy of his performance.
3. Finally, *status* represents a position in the social system and behaviors associated with that position and thus defines the actor and his actions.

A classic example of the use of role concepts occurs in a study by Gross, McKeachie, and Mason (1965). They studied, by questionnaire, the various role expectations that different segments of the population held toward school superintendents and how these conflicting expectations resulted in cross-pressures on the superintendents. They then studied the variety of resolutions available to the superintendents and the factors leading to each one.

Other Approaches. More and more social psychologists are paying attention to the work of Goffman (1959), who has provided a whole range of concepts, insightful analyses, and brilliant observations of interpersonal interaction that have enriched our notions of the interaction process. A number of studies have been inspired by Goffman's work, but it has yet to yield programmatic research.

Another impetus from sociology has been the work of the ethnomethodologists. Garfinkel (1967), McHugh (1968), and others address themselves to uncovering the silent yet very basic assumptions that enable us to construct our conceptions of social reality. The ethnomethodologists have developed some simple yet interesting methods for revealing these assumptions. Their work depends heavily on observation and interpretation and is not easily adapted to an experimental approach. However, because the ability of people to interpret and attribute meaning to social events plays an important role in this viewpoint, it would seem inevitable that social psychologists, particularly those with a cognitive orientation, will soon become increasingly interested in this approach.

These correspondences between what is

known as microsociology and social psychology emphasize the critical interdependency between the two disciplines. Social psychology stands in a unique position. On the one hand, the field of general psychology strives to establish functional relationships between the properties of the physical world and man's basic psychological processes. On the other hand, sociology is primarily concerned with social processes as a function of groups. Social psychology and adjacent areas of sociology (ethnomethodology) play the critical role of exploring how the basic psychological processes operate on the social world and, indeed, whether still other complexities arise from man's integration in the social nexus.

THE EMPIRICAL APPROACH

At this point the student might, with some justification, wonder about these theoretical musings of social psychologists. After all, in what way, except perhaps in terms of language and pedantry, are these formulations superior to his own explanations of behavior or very different from the speculations that philosophers and wise men have been making for centuries about human nature? If these theories were derived in the same way as were the armchair inquiries of the past, the reservations would have a firm basis. For indeed, dogmatic assertions about human behavior have been with us for millenia. In part, this is based on the traditional weight given rational analysis since the time of the Greeks. The powers of the mind could approach any question and determine answers through reason, analysis, and synthesis. A second influence may well have been the familiarity of the subject matter. It would seem obvious that a person, particularly a wise and intelligent person, must be an expert at analyzing human thinking and behavioral processes. The biases inherent in this view are not readily apparent, or the ease with which our personal views of our own behavior can be distorted.

Modern social psychology departs from tradition not because it lacks theoretical explanations of and speculations about human social behavior but because such explanations and speculations are based on a certain type of empirical observation. Ultimately every theory is based on data, and the fit between them determines the viability of the theory. But, so too were the theorizings of the ancients and many social philosophers. Clearly, it would be ridiculous and erroneous to assert that men such as Aristotle, St. Augustine, Hobbes, and Shakespeare made less use of self-study and observation of other people than did Freud, William James, Kurt Lewin, or any contemporary social psychologist. Additionally, to deny that these great commentators on the human condition attained useful and cogent insights into human motivation and behavior would also be begging the issue.

However, we can profit from these great thinkers while recognizing some serious defects in their *modus operandi* in gathering their data. Basically, all operated without realizing the necessity for making unbiased or controlled observations and developing techniques for doing so. The necessity for awareness is highlighted by our knowledge that various internal factors influence what data or events we notice and what interpretations we make of these events. Thus, not only may bias intrude in terms of how well we sample but also in terms of what we do observe.

For example, suppose you were interested in the coordination of movement between motorists and pedestrians. Of course, we all know (common knowledge) that there are formal regulatory rules as indicated by traffic lights and traffic signs. In addition, you may have had the experience as a motorist of waving a pedestrian across a street or as a pedestrian of holding up your hand in the time-honored way of the Boy Scout or traffic policeman while you or someone you were helping walked safely across the street. Would you conclude on the basis of the hand signals you have given or observed that all drivers and pedestrians communicate and in just the ways specified? Clearly, one would want to observe many potential motorist–pedestrian interaction situations over a wide variety of conditions involving different types of people to determine to the fullest extent the variety of interaction that does occur.

In addition to trying to set up procedures for making unbiased observations, the technology available becomes an important factor. For example, in studying driver–pedestrian interaction we do not have to depend only on the eyes of the observers. We can film or videotape the situations. It may be that the kind of gestures we have described play a minor role in such interactions. Detailed viewing of the interactions made possible by recording and perhaps slow-motion viewing may reveal aspects of communication where none could be seen before.

We have seen that ultimately our theories of social psychology can be no better than the data on which they are based. It becomes essential, then, to take any necessary steps to insure that the data are unbiased. That, at least, is the theoretical ideal. However, the process of collecting data in the real world must involve compromise. One can see this most clearly in the simple fact that data cost time and money to collect. As both are limited, one must almost always end up with fewer data than one would like. We must also remember that there are no automatic rules for eliminating bias, which by its very definition means not knowing all aspects of the situation. For example, we may randomly sample some behaviors we think are important for answering some question. Our sampling procedure may insure against some biases, but we have had to decide which behaviors to observe, as we cannot observe everything. This decision itself, although based on our best judgment, is itself a reflection of our biases about what may be important.

Data Collection Techniques

Essentially, there are but a few sources of research data available to the investigator. Each source involves specialized techniques, advantages, and disadvantages. In practice most researchers have used all these sources at one time or another, although many have preferences for or interests in a particular one. The complete researcher will use any technique that promises to be helpful.

Observing Behavior. Perhaps the most prevalent mode of data collection is to observe the behavior of people. As the techniques and methods may vary greatly in subtlety, complexity, and overtness, a full exposition is beyond the scope of this chapter. Some examples will illuminate this procedure.

Sometimes, particularly in the initial stages of research, one may simply find situations in which a pattern of behavior occurs and observe and record it. This record of free behavior may then be studied to see if meaningful and identifiable patterns emerge.

Very often the researcher has some idea of the range of behaviors that will occur in a situation (based on pilot studies using free behavior) and uses trained observers to rate the behaviors on rating scales or, more frequently, to categorize certain behaviors. Basically, categorization involves defining certain behaviors as relevant and counting the occurrence of those units.

Most often, the researcher, particularly in laboratory situations, has decided to study the effect of his manipulations on certain selected behaviors. He then constructs a situation in which the subjects must respond in terms of the behaviors he has selected to observe. He frequently ignores most other responses that occur. The researcher then records the frequency or magnitude of the chosen responses, which may be button pressings, physiological reactions, choices, activity, ratings, or even various types of self-reports.

Asking Questions. It has been remarked that if you want to know how someone feels about something or someone, ask the person. Generally, many psychologists are skeptical of self-reports for two major reasons. First, it is believed that people may not always tell the truth. However, some studies on voting behavior indicate that voters accurately report their intentions as born out by election results (see Chapter 6). Kinsey's (1948) studies of sexual behavior show that people will talk about intimate sexual behavior and, despite extensive criticism of his methodology, his work remains a landmark of its type.

Perhaps the most important criticism of asking questions about behavior is that people frequently do not know what they do or why they do it. That is, there may be an important difference between how people view what they do and why they do it and the actual what and why as the psychologist views it.

Despite these misgivings, a wide variety of devices have been developed to tap verbal behavior. Two basic types may be distinguished. One type is the *interview*. Here a skilled interviewer asks questions of a respondent and records the answers which are analyzed in any of a variety of ways. Sometimes the focus may be on a description of an internal state or on the phenomenology of the respondent. Just about any verbalization or aspect of feelings, philosophy of life, or behavioral-event descriptions can be tapped. *Questionnaires,* a written list of questions with space for the respondent to write free answers or to choose among fixed alternative answers, are similar to interviews except that they are self-administering.

The second major type of verbal instrument is seen by many as belonging to behavioral observation, although such subtle distinctions need not concern us. Here an instrument is designed to elicit an indication of agreement or ratings which can be scored according to a set procedure; the instrument may be a precoded quantative device simply scored. Attitude scales are a prime example of this type of instrument. Various devices designed to elicit information about interpersonal choices and attraction such as sociometric questionnaires fall into this category also.

The Analysis of Communications. Certain cultural material of a verbal or symbolic nature such as books, magazines, newspapers, and movies and personal documents such as letters can be analyzed by means of a variety of techniques called *content analysis*. This method generally calls for a system of rules for selecting the material, definitions of categories, and the unit of analysis. Content analysis has been used to determine the authorship of anonymous materials or suspected misattribution of authorship, effects of propaganda, cultural differences as reflected in popular songs, and social class differences in language behavior.

The Analysis of Records. One aspect of human culture is that it is a way of passing on information across generations. Sometimes the informational content is minimal, as in the case of flint fragments whose past use physical anthropologists try to puzzle out. On a more substantial level there are the commercial transactions that come to light from ancient written records. Such papyri and clay tablets increase our understanding of daily life in those times and may even be used to bolster modern psychological theories, as McClelland (1958) has done in the use of ancient Greek commercial records to support his theories of achievement motivation development.

Perhaps the most famous use of records and statistics was Durkheim's *tour de force* (1951) in which he systematically presented various theories of suicide and then used such records first to demolish each theory in turn and finally to demonstrate his own views of the causes of suicide. In our chapter on applied social psychology (Chapter 15), many examples of the use and misuse of records and statistics are given to support or refute social hypotheses of various types.

Research Settings

Although the analysis of communications and public records is best done in archives or research workrooms, there are a number of settings in which the researcher can observe behavior or ask questions of respondents. The research setting has an important influence on the outcome of the research and the conclusions drawn.

Campbell (1957) makes a distinction between internal and external validity. Internal validity refers to the impact of the experimental variation or treatment, that is, the internal logic of the experiment within the experimental situation, whereas external validity refers to the generalizability of the effect to other populations and settings. Campbell believes that the optimal design for an experiment in a social setting is one that maximizes both internal and external validity. The problem for the researcher, then, is to select the best setting possible for his research, one in which both internal and external validity will be maximized.

The Laboratory Experiment. For many social psychologists the preferred method or setting is the laboratory experiment. Aronson and Carlsmith (1968) argue eloquently that this setting, despite its many shortcomings, maximizes internal validity and, if an experiment is constructed with care and verve, can also have high external validity. In this setting the experimenter, generally guided by hypotheses or theory, selects one or more independent variables or conditions that he can control or modulate and exposes subjects to these conditions. He then notes the effect of this exposure on some preselected response or responses, the dependent variable(s). Through a combination of the structure of the experiment and the rather sophisticated analyses available to him in this format, he can make cause-and-effect statements about the relationship of the independent and dependent variables. In addition, in experiments one usually achieves better control over extraneous variables. As this, of course, is exactly the nub of the meaning of internal validity, it is usually assumed that internal validity is maximized in the laboratory experiment.

Critics, however, have argued that the laboratory experiment is so contrived and unreal that it has little or no external validity. Aronson and Carlsmith counter this argument by making a distinction between experimental realism and mundane realism. "An experiment is realistic if the situation is realistic to the subject, if it involves him, if he is forced to take it seriously, if it has impact on him" (p. 22). They further argue that many events in the real world are trivial and even boring. In any event, they feel that experiments can be designed that are high in both experimental and realistic impact.

The Field Study. Almost the direct opposite of the laboratory experiment is the field study or naturalistic study. Here the focus is on persons or groups in natural settings. The researcher must take what comes in the sense that he has almost no control over the situation except, of course, in terms of his selection of what situations to study. As he cannot vary any of the conditions, causal relationships can never quite be pinned down; consequently, internal validity is low. Certainly mundane realism is high, but whether external validity is enhanced in such settings is a moot point.

Certainly, field studies are consonant with the growing acceptance of ethological research methods over the last quarter century. Much has been made of the fact that animals behave differently and more variably in natural settings than in zoos and laboratories. By analogy, many researchers have argued that the laboratory study of man yields only a psychology of laboratory man and that the richer natural environment provides a fuller picture of behavior potentialities in man that can never be revealed in the laboratory.

The Natural Experiment. Interesting compromises between laboratory and field studies would seem to be the natural experiment and the field experiment. In the natural experiment, some change in policy or a critical event in the community or social system provides the investigator an opportunity to study the effect of the change on the persons or groups in question. This change is natural; the investigator does not introduce it, and he must attempt to institute appropriate controls to be sure that the observed effects are really the result of the naturally instituted change. If he is really lucky, the investigator may come across a situation in which only a segment of the population is at first exposed to the change; the rest of the population then constitutes a naturally occurring control group.

An example of this type of study is presented by Silverman and Shaw (1973). Following a court order, the junior and senior high schools in Gainsville, Florida, underwent massive racial integration. The investigators took advantage of this naturally occuring social and political event to measure social interaction after the event. In this particular case, the absence of a control condition was unimportant since, of course, black and white students could not interact socially in a segregated school.

As you might imagine, the researcher interested in such research must strive to be up on current events in order to anticipate such a situation and must have at his disposal a trained and mobile research team able to take immediate advantage of such events.

The Field Experiment. In the field experiment, the primary disadvantage of the natural experiment, unpredictability, is circumvented; the experimenter deliberately introduces change into a natural setting with the cooperation of those in authority. Of course, every attempt is made to ensure conditions that permit necessary controls to be used in the comparison of properly equated groups. The field experiment combines the advantages of laboratory control with the realism inherent in a field study.

In the following chapters, you will encounter all the data collection techniques we have discussed applied in all the research settings we have described. Some social psychologists believe that any study not able to be conducted as an experiment is simply a waste of time because causal statements cannot be made with precision. Others, just as sincere, believe that only naturalistic research can reveal the true dimensions of human behavior and that what emerges from laboratory experiments is artificial.

The view taken here is simply that, at this stage of development, it behooves social psychologists to utilize any technique and setting in the pursuit of greater understanding of human behavior. Some problems simply cannot be studied in the laboratory, and therefore the alternative to experimentation otherwise would be to give up all hope of collecting data and perhaps to deal with these problems as philosophical issues only. Other phenomena, although well established in laboratory settings, might not occur as clearly when studied in natural settings. Additionally, their validity could certainly be enhanced if it were found that the same or similar effects did occur in natural settings.

Clearly, dogmatic assertions about the ideal methods for pursuing knowledge are not helpful and can have stultifying effects on the advancement of the scientific knowledge of behavior. Perhaps the best solution is to encourage trained social psychologists to take a very pragmatic view of their craft and to be conversant with all its techniques. Most important is some sense of what is the most useful technique to use at a particular stage in the development of a research program. The strongest arguments for the effects of a particular variable probably emerge when it is studied in a variety of ways in a variety of laboratory and field settings and the results flow together into an articulated and meaningful whole.

SUMMARY

In this chapter we have attempted to introduce the reader to the field of social psychology in a variety of ways.

In one direction we pointed out the difficulties inherent in any definition of the field. One definition was selected for detailed analysis, in which it was pointed out that each term presented problems in definition. Social psychology is scientific, not in the narrow restricted sense of being confined to the laboratory but in the broad sense of being based on controlled observation. It focuses on the individual both because of its historical antecedents and because of the lack of concepts based on collectivities. In addition, it uses groups of individuals to generate generalizations about behavior rather than attempting to understand the individual case. Although the focus of study is behavior, many of the data collected refer to reports of internal states; indeed, social psychologists have never been bashful about making inferences about internal mental states. This fact certainly seems to reflect a lack of unanimity about what should be studied.

Although most social psychologists view their goal as establishing functional relationships among variables, the complex subject matter of social interaction may be more amenable to concepts based on emergence and field properties. These, however, have not yet evolved to the point of usefulness.

Finally, it was shown that social stimuli is a term indicating a wide range of complex meanings. Primarily, it alerts us to the need to take man's ability to deal with his world symbolically into account in analyzing social behavior.

These difficulties in definition do not prevent social psychologists from studying a wide variety of phenomena. Attitude change, helping behavior, the attribution of personal characteristics, and small group behavior are some of the areas studied. Social psychologists also study social attitudes, cross-cultural differences in behavior, and large-scale organizations and social movements.

In the past, social theorists attempted to explain social behavior in terms of simple and sovereign theories. Gradually, certain broad theoretical systems evolved, each with a unique approach, view of man, and emphasis on a certain central feature. In turn the Gestalt, field, cognitive, reinforcement, Freudian, role-theory, and ethnomethodological orientations were discussed. Although these orientations have been very influential, it was pointed out that most social psychologists construct rather circumscribed models designed to deal with a focused area of behavior rather than calculated to encompass broad areas.

However, it is not theory as such but the empirical approach that separates modern social psychology from earlier social philosophy.

Social psychologists observe behavior, ask questions, collect ratings and scales, and analyze communications and public records. In collecting data in these ways, they attempt to ensure that various sources of bias will be controlled. These techniques are applied in a variety of settings. Most preferred is the laboratory experiment in which the investigator has maximum control and in which many social psychologists believe both internal and external validity are maximized. However, depending upon the problem to be studied and the resources available, social psychologists also use field studies, natural experiments, and field experiments. These techniques for data collection were seen as all being necessary and useful in building a meaningful and viable body of social psychological data.

SUGGESTED READINGS

Asch, S. E. *Social psychology*. Englewood Cliffs, N.J.: Prentice-Hall, 1952.

A classic text that not only presents a Gestalt-orientated view of social psychology but raises many of the philosophical issues involved in building a science of social man.

Brown, R. W. *Social psychology*. New York: Free Press, 1965.

A delightfully written text that presents one distinguished psychologist's view of social psychology. It is different enough in viewpoint to provide a valuable supplement to any other social psychology text.

Deutsch, M. & Krauss, R. M. *Theories in social psychology*. New York: Basic Books, 1965.

This is an integrated presentation and critical analysis of the major theoretical approaches and theories in social psychology.

Lindzey, G., & Aronson, E. (Eds.). *The handbook of social psychology* (5 Vols., 2nd ed.). Reading, Mass.: Addison-Wesley, 1968.

Although these five volumes are written for the graduate student and the professional, the beginning student might find browsing through them interesting and instructive. Allport's chapter (Vol. 1, chap. 1) is particularly recommended.

2
The Social Psychology of the Research Situation

Arthur G. Miller

INTRODUCTION

Within the last decade, a substantial area of inquiry has developed that might be termed the *social psychology of psychological research*. The focal concern is with those factors of the research situation that affect research outcomes. A major effort has been directed at examining the social roles of *subject* and *experimenter* and the nature of the social interaction between these participants in the research process. There has also been pronounced interest in certain research practices, in particular the use of deception. The ethics of research have become a central issue facing psychological researchers, largely as a result of the increased awareness of the social properties of research. An immense challenge is inherent in research on human social behavior, which can be understood by reflecting that the psychological experiment often consists of certain human beings attempting to obtain scientific information from others.

Research methods and research ethics are closely related in social psychological research, particularly when the goal is to study antisocial or dysfunctional behavior (e.g., aggression) inside an experimental laboratory. One sees a recurrent conflict between vigorous scientific inquiry and human values seemingly opposed to such intrusion. Increasing the methodological rigor of the research operations often produces ethical losses in terms of the subject's (temporary) discomfort and vulnerability. As research procedures are "watered down" (e.g., in role playing), the external validity of the research becomes suspect, raising the question of whether the findings may be generalized or applicable to corresponding behaviors in more natural contexts. Within the confines of the experimental situation, a precise understanding of the subject's and the experimenter's views of events is a prerequisite for establishing the internal validity of the research, the degree to which the experimenter's operationally defined independent variables or treatments are, in fact, the real causes of the subject's behavior. Thus, to appraise the validity of research requires an appreciation of the social nature of research (Campbell & Stanley, 1966).

As one investigates the research situation, one achieves substantive knowledge about social behavior. In viewing the experimenter as an unintended determinant of his own data (Rosenthal, 1966), one is sensitized to design subsequent research to minimize this artifact. At the same time, however, one is learning about the transmission of expectancies, nonverbal communication, self-fulfilling prophecies, and the like. Analyses of the subject's reaction to the laboratory setting have increased substantive knowledge about the responses to the social influence and situational demands characteristic of that social setting, with implications for other contexts sharing the interpersonal structure of the laboratory (e.g., Orne, 1970). Psychotherapy and hypnosis, for example, have interesting parallels to social psychological experiments. Specifically, these are social occasions where one individual (higher status) will administer some form of treatment to another, both individuals having expectations about what will occur. Assessing the scientific status of the treatment itself may become extremely complicated in view of the immensely powerful social psychological forces (e.g., trust, obedience, anticipation) operating in these contexts. Thus, an examination of the research situation produces a twofold dividend: increased sophistication in terms of procedure or method, and substantive data about behavior relevant not only to the laboratory but to a surprisingly large number of other places which share important features with the laboratory.

Experimentation is a social psychological phenomenon. The organisms need not be human, nor the object of study a traditional social psychological phenomenon. Rosenthal's early research on experimenter expectancy effects, for example, utilized maze learning in rats as the illustrative case (1966, chap. 10). Operant and classical conditioning models of human learning have had, as their primary methodological obstacle, the very social matter of the subject's awareness of the experimental operations and hypotheses. The development of signal detection theory in psychophysics was a recognition that a subject's report of a visual or auditory stimulus occurs in a social context with determinants of its own, in addition to characteristics of the stimuli and receptor organs. Any encounter between an investigator and a data-producing organism is a social event. It is true, however, that experiments in human social psychology raise, and make especially salient, the fundamental issues to be discussed in this chapter. What follows, then, is social psychology as it studies itself, as it experiments on its methods of experimentation.

This chapter is divided into four sections. The first considers the image of the research subject from the perspective of the researcher. The issues discussed here are ethical or quasi-philosophical, and they should sensitize the reader to problems that are taken up later in the chapter. There have been sharply divergent views regarding the propriety of the subject's position in the laboratory and what is done to him in that setting. How the subject is viewed may be expected to influence the subject's own view of the research enterprise. The second section focuses upon the subject's reactions to being a research subject. At issue is the social role of the subject and how different perceptions of that role will be manifested in behavior. There are serious consequences if the experimenter is unaware of the subject's precise view of things, and there are forces at work in the situation to make this a genuine possibility. The third section will deal with the matter of deception. This procedural strategy attempts to defuse the subject's potential for extracting the experimenter's intentions and expectations and in turn "helping" or hindering the researcher for reasons which are detrimental to his scientific pursuits. The aim of the third section will not be toward a moral resolution of the contesting arguments, but rather on issues that have been approached empirically: How effective is debriefing? What are the long-term effects of deception? Are there viable procedural alternatives? The fourth section considers the experimenter's own involvement in his endeavors. This will feature the problem of the experimenter "leaking" his expectation to his subjects. Recent extensions of the original methodological work to the fascinating area of teacher expectancies will be described, a digression into the social psychology of the classroom.

PORTRAITS OF THE HUMAN SUBJECT IN PSYCHOLOGICAL RESEARCH

Historical Developments

In the late nineteenth and early twentieth centuries, the research subjects in psychological experiments were highly trained and skilled in the task of introspecting about their reactions to stimuli. They were viewed as rather special people and were endowed with about as much role prestige as were their experimenters. They were the observers as much as the observed; in fact, subjects were called "observers" (Schultz, 1969). It was recognized that the "contents of consciousness" could be adversely influenced by social forces in the research setting, but overcoming these biasing influences was to be achieved by professionalizing the subject. It was apparently the intrinsic subjectivity involved in deciding when the subject's verbal reports were accurate reflections of experience that weakened the introspectionist strategy and prompted different views of the research subject.

Subsequent traditions in the history of psychology tended to increase the social distance between the researcher and his subject. One emphasis was on individual differences, with the individual subject assuming the character of a statistic. No longer skilled introspectionists, the subjects were untrained and naive, from college and general populations. The parallel developments of behaviorism and psychoanalytic theory had the effect of legitimizing the view of the subject as "the one to be observed." The relationship between the experimenter and his subject became highly differentiated. The subject was no longer said to observe; rather, he behaved: "Almost anyone can behave—children, the mentally ill, animals, and even the college sophomore!" (See Schultz, 1969, p. 217.) The reasons for this transition are complex, but certainly one was the model of the natural sciences which psychology was emulating. It seemed effective, and became prestigious, to treat their human subjects as if they were analogous to chemicals, pulleys, animals, and organs. The prediction and control of behavior became the psychologist's credo, and objectivity in the form of operational definitions and replicability of results assumed high priority in the developing science of behavior.

The zest for experimentation was applied initially to learning, memory, and perception; and it came somewhat later to social psychology in Allport's investigations of social facilitation (1920) and Sherif's research on norm formation (1936). As of the middle 1970s, the dominant theme in social psychology, without question, is experimentation, very much in the tradition of the earlier, behavioristically inspired experimental psychology. The reader will notice, however, that social psychology, despite its quest for scientific rigor, pays considerable homage to a kind of introspectionism in its use of the ubiquitous questionnaire and rating scale, which are among the most frequently used measures in social psychology. The reasons for this are numerous, but one for certain is the domination of the concept of attitude throughout the history of social psychology (see Chaps. 6 and 7).

Current approaches to verbal reports as psychological data (Buchwald, 1961) caution against a testimonial interpretation of such utterances as indications of true experience, but the subject's report of things in the laboratory is very much a part of social psychology. The postexperimental inquiry period has been of major interest in the social psychology of research, and it is here that the most hardened, behaviorally oriented social psychologist must somehow find it within himself to ask the subject what he thought about during the experiment. Verbal and written statements turn out to be a continuous thorn in the social psychologist's side. They are often more feasible and economical to obtain in the research setting than are nonverbal behaviors. In addition, what people think, feel, and say are often the behaviors of interest, for example in bargaining, in conformity, in aggression, or in opinion change. Unfortunately, this form of human behavior is most susceptible to social psychological influences and, from the experimenter's perspective, bias.

Saul Rosenzweig alerted psychologists to the social dynamics of the research process as early as 1933 in a paper aptly titled "the experimental situation as a psychological problem." He touched upon most of the issues with which this chapter is concerned. Regarding the subject, Rosenzweig noted that "he entertains opinions about the experiment—what its purpose is and what he may reveal in it—instead of simply reacting in a naive manner" (p. 343). A remarkable paper, but it was not the "in thing" to be concerned about these matters in 1933, and it did not become so for another 30 years. Adair (1973) points out that the leading figures in the development of the social psychology of research were themselves involved in areas which suffered from a rigorous application of behavioristic ideology (e.g., no unobservable constructs). Experimental research in such areas as clinical psychology (Rosenthal, 1966), attitude change (Rosenberg, 1965), and hypnosis (Orne, 1970) inevitably produced a concern with the subjects' awareness of the experimenter's purposes. The uses of misinformation, accomplices, or cover stories—what perhaps unfortunately came to be termed deception—were efforts to solve this problem of the transparency of the researcher's design and expectancies. Another provocative point is that the climate of the 1960s (concern about civil rights, Vietnam) fostered a questioning attitude with respect to anything, and within the academic halls psychological methods and topics were fair game for this skepticism.

The Subject as Powerless

Herbert Kelman, a leading voice of dissent within social psychology (1967), has discussed the power deficiency of the subject in social research (1972). The subject is seen as powerless within the social system at large and within the research situation itself. Who are the subjects? Children, old people, minority groups, welfare recipients, military recruits, the physically and mentally ill, the college undergraduate—all relatively powerless in terms of age and socioeconomic status. They may be studied because they are the target population of interest. These individuals are also more available to the researcher. Students in introductory psychology courses have provided the data for a large amount of the research reported in this text. The subjects' lack of freedom in terms of their role in the research process is a central pillar in any discussion of research ethics, a matter which will be returned to in the section on deception.

The subject has inherent power in that his cooperation is vital to the enactment of the research, but Kelman notes that the subject perceives himself as lacking the capacity and right to question the procedures. The subject's lack of information is one factor, but also relevant are the investigator's real or perceived expertise (Ph.D. degree, white coat), the aura of legitimacy of the university, government, or hospital agency housing or funding the research, and the cultural image of science as a virtuous and beneficent enterprise. Voluntary and informed consent, often cited as a prerequisite for truly ethical research, becomes an awkward and unrealistic burden for social psychological reasons. The social position of most subjects makes their participation rarely voluntary in any strict sense, and their lack of information about what is to come is often crucial to an unbiased research outcome. Kelman concludes his argument with a well-reasoned plea for procedures to increase the subject's relative power. Although it may not be for everyone to voice moral alarm with Kelman's conviction, his sensitizing value to the research community is beyond cavil.

Preserving Self-Esteem and Dignity

Major research programs in experimental social psychology often attend to man in his less glorious moments (obedience, conformity, aggression, deindividuation), whether in terms of the behaviors at issue or in terms of the experimental conditions or treatments that are administered to subjects. Milgram's research, wherein subjects were instructed to shock a 50-year-old man who allegedly had a heart condition (see Chapter 5), has stimulated ethical misgivings in behalf of the subjects, who appeared greatly distressed in their dilemma in this obedience situation. Kelman (1967) noted that "subjects in these experiments may well have emerged with lowered self-esteem, having to live with the realization that they were willing to yield to destructive authority to the point of inflicting extreme pain on a fellow human being" (p. 4). Baumrind's (1964) published reaction to Milgram's work, with its extremism in defense of the subject's self-concept, has been a focal point in debates on research ethics. She suggested that research with the kind of effects produced in Milgram's subjects should simply not be pursued. Her analysis included a tenuous thesis that the relevance of research should dictate the legitimacy of noxious treatments. Although relevance may be a perception to begin with, it is difficult to assess before the work is done. Her point, however, that there is a threshold of manipulation and emotional insult beyond which research should not be undertaken has been well received.

Baumrind focused on the importance of the debriefing of subjects after their experimental episode, which has become a major issue in the social psychology of research. Here the experimenter can establish an altogether different form of relationship with his subject in order to ameliorate residual distress. The subject also can further enlighten the experimenter by retrospecting on the experiment itself. The subject is portrayed as a forgiving individual, one who can be made to understand the need for what has been done. This solution itself has been controversial (e.g., Campbell, 1969; Stollak, 1967), for there are those who question the comforting effects of the "truth" lavished on subjects at the end. Debriefing at present constitutes the most general solution to ethical problems in psychological research. Data on its effectiveness will be examined later in the chapter.

A More Positive View

Aronson and Carlsmith (1968) have authored the chapter on research methodology for the *Handbook of Social Psychology,* a source which both reflects upon and influences perceived standards of rigor and propriety in research. Their chapter, which argues for the joys and rewards of research in social psychology, is considered traditional and "hard-nosed" in terms of the premium on experimental realism:

> ... an experiment is realistic if the situation is realistic to the subject, if it involves him, if he is forced to take it seriously, if it has impact on him.... It is the major objective of a laboratory experiment to have the greatest possible impact on a subject within the limits of ethical considerations and requirements of control. (p. 22)

The subject, however, is never likened to an object, a depersonalized machine, or any of the metaphors noted by the critics. These authors are particularly concerned about the sensitivity of the researcher and the importance of a compassionate attitude, especially after the experiment is over. Aronson's dual career as an experimentalist and as a devotee of humanistic encounter groups (1972, chap. 8) adds to the credibility of his statements on this issue.

Aronson and Carlsmith argue for the experimenter–subject "contract" as an implicitly understood set of norms governing the boundaries of permissable activities in the laboratory: "The occasional use of deception can be considered one of the implicit clauses in this contract" (p. 35). They contrast this with the example of a therapeutic contract, where the use of deception by a clinician or physician would be totally unconscionable. Not all agree, however, that experiments should have their own special ethics. Kelman (1967) voiced the opposing view:

> We seem to forget that the experimenter-subject relationship—whatever else it is—is a *real* interhuman relationship, in which we have responsibility toward the subject as another human being whose dignity we must preserve.... We tend to regard it as a situation that is not quite real, that can be isolated from the rest of life like a play performed on a stage, and to which, therefore, the usual criteria for ethical interpersonal conduct become irrelevant. (p. 5)

This is the essential controversy regarding the human subject's position in research. Regarding the experiments reported in this volume, the reader should consider the Aronson and Carlsmith arguments vis-à-vis those of Kelman. Could the social psychologist achieve significant knowledge and apply, strictly, the values Kelman and others advocate? This is an important question.

Others have spoken out in similar spirit. McGuire, a leading theorist in the area of attitude change, recognizes the moral price of knowledge in social psychological research, but he sees it as preferable to ceasing research activity: "Were we to list the moral problems of psychology, we would cite those who are doing experiments which involve deception far below those who are doing too few experiments or none at all as a source of ethical concern" (1969b, p. 53). McGuire (1967) has emphasized research quality and the attractive features of research in nonexperimental settings. He expresses the assurance that the discipline will provide needed correctives for research practices that become dangerously overemphasized.

Gergen (1973a) questioned whether those critical of research are accurate in their charges. He asked for empirical evidence documenting the harmful effects of research participation. A rigid set of research ethics based on unconfirmed presumptions would pose unnecessary hardships for the researcher. Reflecting the situational ethics of Aronson and Carlsmith, he makes a strong case for the semantic basis of many criticisms of research. The very words manipulation and deception take on pejorative connotations which are an arbitrary and dysfunctional view of reality.

It would be amiss to conclude this section without a word in behalf of knowledge! Kaufmann, in an eloquent defense of Milgram's work, has put it this way:

> While the discussion of possible aftereffects remains academic, a plausible case can be made for the positive side: Perhaps the realization of one's flaws leads to a useful and constructive examination of oneself. . . . A social theory of evil may be distressing and humiliating to the stature of man, but then, learning to know oneself is seldom a gratifying experience, yet one which few of us would forgo. (1967, p. 322)

It has been argued that the research context is not designed for, nor does it legitimize, correctives in self-awareness and insights into the defects of one's character. Yet, in observing Nazi films showing the shooting, hanging, and gassing of countless men, women, and children (e.g., ABC-TV, *World at War,* July 14, 1974), one wonders how anyone—let alone social scientists—could argue with conviction against the pursuit of research which in any reasonable way would increase the understanding of this phenomenon. If this be naive sentimentality, so be it!

Conclusion

The views of the research subject are diverse, the issues disturbing, and the solutions not clear. A commitment to experimentation, with its yield of causal statements, and to the value of rigorous tests of hypotheses characterizes social psychology at this time. Recent enthusiasm for research in less contrived settings (McGuire, 1973) will soften objections regarding the arbitrary assignment of noxious conditions to human subjects, but it will raise concern about the unobtrusive invasion of privacy. The most significant development has been the widespread interest in these issues. Empirical inquiry on ethical issues that is being undertaken will have the ultimate effect of instilling in researchers, particularly in their graduate training, a sophisticated appreciation for the sources of strain and possible shortcomings in their interaction with research subjects. Intellectual awareness and sensitivity in actual practice should produce the most viable compromise between ethical and scientific considerations.

THE SUBJECT'S VIEW OF PSYCHOLOGICAL RESEARCH

How do individuals react to being research subjects? The significance of this question relates to the basic strategy of experimental research, which is to present one or more levels of some variable or treatment and measure the subjects' reaction. Although there are procedural rules to permit the conclusion that the subjects' responses were caused by the experimental conditions (e.g., random assignment), there are nonetheless sources of resistance to the experimenter's ability to instill within subjects the psychological state called for by his theory. To illustrate, consider Festinger and Carlsmith's (1959) verification of a prediction from cognitive dissonance theory that subjects would change their attitude in the direction counter to their initial opinion more for less money ($1) than for a large reward ($20). Their reasoning was that the difference in money operationally defined more ($1) or less ($20) cognitive dissonance in subjects. The money has had different implications for other theorists (Bem, 1967; Rosenberg, 1965). Rosenberg (1965) contended that the different payments varied the subjects' sensitization to being evaluated by the experimenter, specifically that a $20 payment would alert subjects to the psychologist's probable interest in their responses to such a large payment. Hence, any resulting "attitude change" (or lack thereof) could justifiably be related to that variable as opposed to variations in cognitive dissonance.

One notices the high priority given to establishing the most plausible interpretation of subjects' behavior. Given that subjects' reactions to a study may differ in important and systematic ways from that view which the experimenter intended them to have, it becomes vital to understand the subject's potential for becoming a creative force in his own behavior within an experiment. Subject behavior is termed artifactual when it results in performance which, although at first glance supportive of the investigator's prediction, can just as readily be attributed to other systematic determinants, typically overlooked by the investigator. Thus, the investigator may hypothesize the existence of a "hypnotic trance," when it is in reality the subject's active willingness to obey the hypnotist; the psychotherapist may advocate his technique for inducing personality change, when it is the client's own effort to validate his presence in the therapeutic situation that is producing his "new look"; the learning theorist may pronounce Pavlovian conditioning principles as generalizable to human adults, when it is the subjects' awareness of the hypothesis or procedures that is feigning what the experimenter terms conditioning.

Conceptions of the Subject's Role

The "Good" Subject. Martin Orne's 1962 paper in the *American Psychologist* was the first major publication dealing with the human subject to have a pronounced influence on researchers. The seminal features of his paper were two: a characterization of the motivation of subjects as they enter the research setting, and a contextual analysis of the laboratory—in particular, a recognition of the *total stimulus complex* confronting the research subject. Regarding the motivational issue, Orne offered this view: "We might well expect then that as far as the subject is able, he will behave in an experimental context in a manner designed to play the role of a 'good subject,' or . . . to *validate the experimental hypothesis*" (p. 778). The subject's beneficence required that he be active in his role, that he be a problem-solver, and that he deduce for himself the purpose of the research to guide his behavior. The cues that would serve this function were termed the *demand characteristics* of the experiment. Rarely would the experimenter's precise hypothesis be so transparent as to constitute the demand characteristics per se (although there are instances where this appears to be true). It was the invention by the subject of a guiding hypothesis that was Orne's fundamental contribution. He gave this example, which has received considerable attention from researchers (Lana, 1969): "If a test is given twice with some intervening treatment, even the dullest college student is aware that some change is expected, particularly if the test is in some obvious way related to the treatment" (p. 779). The significant threat was that demand characteristics would be systematically associated with experimental conditions, and be as (or even more) plausible a determinant of behavior.

Orne stressed the social control in the laboratory, citing numerous examples of subjects performing tasks requiring considerable patience or "courage." He viewed the subject as modeling the experimenter's own purposes in conducting scientifically valid research, that his role was to facilitate this worthy venture. One of Orne's continuing concerns has been with the *ecological validity* of laboratory findings (1969, 1970), the degree to which data can be generalized to nonexperimental contexts. He noted that while all settings have demand characteristics, those inside the laboratory may differ radically from those outside. Experimental behaviors are context specific. A particularly interesting application of this line of reasoning was based on the assertion that one of the salient demand characteristics of the research laboratory is the unwritten guarantee that no harm or genuine danger will befall the subject (Orne & Holland, 1968). The consequences of viewing the laboratory as a benign environment will be pursued later in the chapter.

The "Socially Desirable" Subject. Rosenberg (1965, 1969) has emphasized the subject's concern about the psychological implications of their behavior, a manifestation of the layman's perception of psychology as inherently a clinical or mental health enterprise:

> In experiments the subject's initial suspicion that he may be exposing himself to evaluation will usually be confirmed or disconfirmed in the early stages of his encounter with the experiment . . . the typical subject will be likely to experience *evaluation apprehension;* that is, an active, anxiety-toned concern that he win a positive evaluation from the experimenter, or at least that he provide no grounds for a negative one. (1969, p. 281)

Although applicable, in principle, to almost any experiment in psychology, the evaluation apprehension concept is particularly congenial to personality–social research, where the phenomena in question—aggression, attraction, cooperation—have a readily perceived dimension of social desirability. This matter of a bias in the form of favorable self-presentation has, of course, long been of concern to psychologists, particularly in the field of psychological testing.

The "Faithful" Subject. Fillenbaum (1966) suggested another dispositional attribute of research subjects. He presented two experiments, in sequence, to his subjects. After the first (an impression-formation task), half of the subjects were thoroughly informed about the deceptive aspects of the experiment. The performance on the second, involving the incidental learning of material in a word-cancelling task, was the criterion. There were no significant differences in performance on this task between the deception-aware and deception-unaware groups of subjects, nor were there differences in the amount of suspiciousness about the second experiment voiced during postexperimental inquiry (about 55% in both groups). A replication of this experiment, in which an effort was made to "force" the deception-aware subjects to be sensitive to the criterion experiments, again failed to show performance differences. Fillenbaum concluded that it is difficult to raise substantially, even by deception-revealing experiences, the percentage of suspicious subjects and that it is only a minority of suspicious subjects who act on their suspicions.

The "Negativistic" Subject. Masling (1966), Argyris (1968), and others have suggested that the subject may react to his subordinate social position by misbehaving in the laboratory, giving responses which he sees as contrary to the experimenter's purposes and intentions. Numerous factors could produce this stance, e.g., the method of recruiting the subject and the personal style of the researcher, but it turns out to be a ticklish problem in proving that the motive was in fact negativism. Cox and Sipprelle (1971), in a complex study involving the operant conditioning of heart rate, were only able to replicate previous results using volunteer subjects. They apparently perceived the coerced (nonvolunteer) subject as a negativistic one: "It would appear that the practice of using coercion, however mild and disguised, to secure research subjects should come under scrutiny as a possible error in the design, conduct, and generality of research" (p. 728). It would seem questionable to equate negativism with not giving the experimenter what he wants. Argyris (1968) suggested that subjects may cooperate in an ingratiating or manipulative manner, to fulfill the onerous obligation of being a subject in the most trivial but conforming manner. Before summarizing these various concepts of subject roles, it should be instructive to describe an actual research program in which the subjects' perception of the laboratory may have influenced their behavior.

Research Illustration

Berkowitz's "Weapons Effect." In 1967, Berkowitz and LePage published a finding which had a startling quality in terms of being a laboratory experiment with ramifications for a pressing social problem, in this case gun control:

> An experiment was conducted to test the hypothesis that stimuli commonly associated with aggression can elicit aggressive responses from people ready to act aggressively. . . . Students received either 1 or 7 shocks, supposedly from a peer, and were then given an opportunity to shock this person. In some cases, a rifle and revolver were on the table near the shock key. These weapons were said to belong, or not to belong, to the available target person. In other instances, there was nothing on the table near the shock key, while for a control group 2 badminton racquets were on the table near the key. The greatest number of shocks were given by the strongly aroused subjects (who had received 7 shocks) when they were in the presence of the weapons. The guns had evidently elicited strong aggressive responses from the aroused men. (p. 202)

This study, by a leading aggression theorist, emphasized arousal within potential aggressors and contextual stimuli likely to elicit pronounced aggressive responses. The key word is *elicit,* for it was Berkowitz's intention to deal with "stimulus-elicited impulsive reactions" (p. 202), a kind of conditioned, automatic reaction—not planned or consciously enacted. This is crucial because, while there is no disputing *what* Berkowitz's subjects did, what has become an issue is *why* they did it. The authors stated that "none of the subjects voiced any suspicions of the weapons, and, furthermore, when they were queried generally denied that the weapons had any effect on them" (p. 206). These investigators also reasoned that the demand characteristic analysis could not explain why it was that only the angered subject showed a weapons effect and moreover that the behavior was socially undesirable, contrary to what might be expected in terms of the apprehensive-subject role. Thus, Berkowitz and LePage argued for the stimulus-control properties of aggressive stimuli, with implications for gun control and the validity of the application of a classical conditioning model to human social behavior.

Page and Scheidt (1971) applied a demand-characteristic analysis to Berkowitz and LePage's experiment. A central concern of Page (in his own research) has been the postexperimental interview, crucial in obtaining the subject's retrospective view of the experiment. The postexperimental phase has its own social psychological dynamics. Orne (1962), for example, spoke of the *pact of ignorance*—that after the experiment, both subject and experimenter are partners to a silent agreement not to reveal, or probe for, suspicions and insights that might ruin the experiment, e.g., "blowing" the cover story. Page insists that only an extensive and funnel-type (increasingly specific) interview will pin the subject down and extract his critically important recollections; one or two questions will not suffice (e.g., Levy, 1967). The Berkowitz and LePage study apparently used the casual, short-form inquiry.

Page and Scheidt performed three partial replications of the Berkowitz and LePage study, the first two of which did not produce the weapons effect. The second attempt, in fact, showed a reverse effect, with subjects in the weapons condition giving significantly *fewer* shocks than those in the no-weapons condition. Page and Scheidt did not report separately the behaviors of those who were (50%) or were not (50%) later classified as having been aware of the purpose of the weapons. This experiment did involve the use of social psychology students as subjects, however, in an effort to match more closely the nature of the subject pool used by Berkowitz and LePage at Wisconsin. (Berkowitz has stated that subjects participate in many experiments, hence many may be sophisticated or "experiment-wise.") Page and Scheidt noted the likely evaluation apprehension experienced by these subjects, hence their dominant motive being that of "looking good" (i.e., non-aggressive) rather than one of cooperating with the experimenter (i.e., emitting shocks).

With modifications in procedure, the weapons effect was obtained in a third experiment but only in subjects who had prior experience in a deception experiment. A strong relationship between the subject's post experimental interview responses and experimental behavior was shown, with subjects aware of the weapons hypothesis and motivated to cooperate producing significantly more shocks than those unaware or not motivated to cooperate. The investigators concluded that "what appeared to be aggressive behavior . . . seems to have been a sham or artifact. Demand awareness and cooperation gave a better account of the data" (p. 315).

Berkowitz's rebuttal (1971b) emphasized what has been a standard contention among researchers who have been confronted with similar critiques (e.g., Staats, 1969), namely, that the postexperimental interview is itself a reactive instrument, producing what it attempts to measure:

> If subjects are so responsive to demand cues in the experiment, why isn't the repeated probing at the end of the session a strong demand in its own right? Isn't it likely that the interview crystalizes the subject's suspicions, focusing and steering their doubts in the direction of the questions, and ultimately putting words in their mouths? . . . Here is the most serious weakness of the Page and Scheidt paper: Their argument rests on correlational evidence, and we cannot be sure about the dirction of causation. (pp. 335–336)

Berkowitz cited a variety of evidence suggesting that awareness should be associated with noncompliance and that his data are nonartifactual because they counter results that would be predicted from conceptions of the apprehensive or negativistic subject roles. He expressed amazement at the widespread acceptance of Orne's view of the compliant subject when "time and time again we have seen that our subjects' awareness of the deceptions practiced on them tends to be inversely related to the strength of their aggressive reactions to the experimentally presented stimuli" (p. 336). The story is by no means at an end. Buss, Booker, and Buss (1972) failed to confirm the aggression-eliciting properties of weapons in five related experiments and expressed serious reservations about accepting the conclusions of Berkowitz and LePage. Berkowitz, in a recent theoretical paper (1974), counters with supportive evidence from other laboratories, including an important study by Turner and Simons

(1974) in which manipulations of awareness and evaluation apprehension were performed in the context of the Berkowitz and LePage procedure. The weapons effect appeared only in subjects who were *unaware* of the hypothesis and who were low in evaluation apprehension. Schuck and Pisor (1974), however, could find no differences in "aggression" between real subjects and a group of simulators (Orne, 1969) using a design similar to that of Berkowitz and LePage.

The point of all of this should be clear. Because of the genuine importance of aggression as a social issue, it is essential to recognize the potential limitations imposed on the data by the social nature of the research setting.

Current Assessment of Subject Roles

Subjects will always have motives or dispositions of some sort in an experiment. The experimenter's goal is to design his research so that one particular motive does not prevail and, more specifically, so that it does not result in behavior which is artifactual or ambiguous. It is often difficult to determine which motivation might give rise to a specific experimental response. Yielding to a verbal conditioning procedure might signify a desire to appear intelligent (in line with apprehensiveness) or to be helpful in confirming the apparent hypothesis. If it appears that attitude change is called for, subjects who do not change may be presenting themselves as independent (apprehensive) or negativistic, i.e., counter-reacting to perceived pressure. It may be the case, of course, that the experimental variables do not produce attitude change, regardless of subject roles. Changing one's position or opinion could signify flexibility and openness, or gullibility and dependency. In short, the presence or absence of a given experimental response can be the result, logically, of more than one motive or can be relatively independent of any systematically biasing motive.

The evidence to date favors evaluation apprehension as the most predictable stance of the research subject. Sigall, Aronson, and Van Hoose (1970) conducted an experiment which ingeniously pitted the apprehensive and helpful roles against one another. Subjects were led to believe that the experimenter expected an increase or decrease in the task of copying numbers. In both instances, subjects increased their performance, presumably to appear high in achievement potential. When a third group was told that the expected performance was a decreased output and that an increased output had been previously associated with an obsessive–compulsive personality, the subjects showed a radical decrease. Thus, the experimenter's hypothesis was confirmed, but only when it served to enhance the subject's self-concept.

Various reviewers of the effects of subject roles (Rosnow & Aiken, 1973; Weber & Cook, 1972) agree that where a hypothesis is clearly available, subjects will use it to guide their behavior, hence introducing bias. If evaluation apprehension is not at issue, the directionality of subject-induced bias will vary with the experimental behaviors or topics involved. Attitude change experiments will typically produce compliant behaviors (Silverman & Shulman, 1970). Silverman (1968) performed an experiment in which half of the subjects (class members) were not told that it was an experiment (but thought it was a project). Significantly more attitude change occurred for subjects who perceived it to be an experiment (a finding consistent with Orne, 1962). Conditioning studies also support the idea of a compliant subject (e.g., Page's research), but the apprehensive role is plausible as well (viewing compliance as insight and noncompliance as independence). Subjects in conformity studies generally do not produce the expected behavior if they are aware of the hypothesis, a finding consistent with the apprehensive or negativistic roles (e.g., Stricker, Messick, & Jackson, 1969).

Some minimize the issues. McGuire, a prolific attitude researcher who has noted the prevalence of deception in his research and carefully outlined the potentially disrupting effects of suspicion in subjects (1969b), notes that about 15% of his subjects can verbalize a fairly accurate statement of the study's purpose. Partitioning subjects into those who can and cannot verbalize the hypothesis does not, however, produce differential data patterns. Silverman and Shulman (1970), however, state that the susceptibility of attitude-change research to subject effects and the fact that these influences may direct the subject into a flexible or resistant posture have made replication of results difficult and added to the barriers involved in relating attitudes measured in the lab to behaviors outside it (cf. Chapter 6). These writers argue in defense of experimentation, but with an emphasis upon measures that are better disguised (e.g., Webb et al., 1966).

Conclusion

The desirability of hypotheses being successfully camouflaged is obvious from the previous discussion, but of course that is an endorsement of deception. Again, the ethical–methodological issue is joined! There is general support for using procedures to assess whether subjects could guess the hypothesis and produce the predicted data without even participating as real subjects, in particular Orne's (1969) discussion of quasicontrol groups (e.g., simulators, role playing). Hypothesis learning may be less of a problem because of the sheer complexity of many research designs. The crucial problem is that subject roles, in particular evaluation apprehension, may be correlated with treatments.

Who Are the Subjects?

Documentations of subject selection practices in psychological research (e.g., Jung, 1969) indicate an overwhelming reliance on college students, many of whom are introductory psychology students. There also appears to be a preponderance of male subjects (Carlson, 1971). Because the subject's view of the laboratory and his subsequent behavior could be influenced by the very rationale for being there, attention has been given to the recruitment procedures, specifically the problem of the so-called volunteer subject. Are the individuals who come to experiments willingly, even enthusiastically, different from those who do not come similarly disposed or refuse to come altogether?

Personality and demographic characteristics of volunteers and nonvolunteers have been investigated by first administering a variety of questionnaires, en masse, to a large captive audience—a class, for example. The data are then "in." Afterwards there is a call for volunteers for a fictitious experiment. The questionnaire data are then examined, comparing the results of those who did and did not volunteer. Reviews of this literature (Rosenthal & Rosnow, 1969) show volunteers to be better educated, higher in occupational status, in need for social approval, and in intelligence (for males only), and lower in authoritarianism. While differences between volunteers and nonvolunteers could be important, the data are sparse concerning actual behavioral differences. In an experiment involving visual motor dexterity, volunteers were more accurate and persistent than coerced subjects (Black, Schumpert, & Welch, 1972). The study by Cox and Sipprelle (1971), showing a failure to obtain heart-rate conditioning in coerced subjects, could be similarly categorized. Hood and Back (1971) observed that male subjects volunteering for research indicated more self-disclosure in their past behavior than nonvolunteers. Volunteers may perceive experiments as self-disclosing events; and to the extent that this behavior is relevant to the research problem, the volunteer status of the subject could interact with the experimental variables. Adair (1973) cogently points out that "we should be cautious in interpreting failure to find with coerced subjects effects that have been demonstrated with volunteers as an indication that one sampling procedure is more valid than another" (p. 54).

The term "volunteer" is a generic one, signifying numerous possible motivations for coming to a research project. There is no evidence that it constitutes a pervasive source of bias (Kruglanski, 1973), although it can become absolutely critical in certain instances. Green (1963), for example, found that the Zeigarnik phenomenon (greater recall for incompleted tasks) related theoretically to the subject's volunteer status, with higher achievement motivation characterizing the volunteers. A number of commentators have argued that representative sampling is important (Campbell, 1969; Kruglanski, 1973) when the subject characteristic is meaningful to the research per se. It would not be meaningful to take any experimental effect and proceed, anthropologically through space and time, to present it to every variety of mankind for the sheer sake of thorough sampling. Of course, in less theory-oriented research contexts—a voting opinion poll, for example—representative sampling could be mandatory because the explicit purpose is to estimate accurately, from a sample, the behavior of a population. Representative sampling (of college students, firefighters, janitors, and so on) paradoxically could work against the idea of experimentation because it would increase variability in the responses and thus decrease the statistical likelihood of demonstrating an experimental effect. Researching possible differences between volunteers and nonvolunteers is hardly the most glorious of ventures, but the work should not be belittled in value. Such data provide a very useful background for investigators who may need to know, before beginning their research, whether or not to attend to subject variables in their design.

DECEIVING THE EXPERIMENTAL SUBJECT

If deception were not an issue in human research, many of the concepts and problems with which this chapter is concerned would evaporate. Suspicion, demand cues, awareness, apprehension—these would be minimized or made irrelevant. The ethical quandary in endeavoring to learn about man and yet relate to him with basic dignity would certainly be mitigated. Thus, when Weber and Cook advise that "all experiments should be designed so that the hypotheses are difficult to learn . . . this should be the sine qua non of experimentation" (p. 291), to follow such advice is to follow a hellish course in the service of a fundamental set of values and beliefs. The rationales for using deception are all variations on the theme that behavior will lose its realistic or natural quality to the extent that subjects react to the very fact of being observed or studied. As Allen Funt captured spontaneous and informative reality with the *Candid Camera,* so do experimenters in social psychology seek undistorted, unbiased behavior—and for many, in a seemingly unsuitable place, the laboratory. Deception, in the form of diversionary cover stories, instructions, confederates, equipment, and the like, has been the recognized answer to this quest for naturalness in an unnatural place. Aronson and Carlsmith (1968) have stated it best: "It is an apparent paradox that experimental *realism* can be achieved through *falsehood,* but it is nevertheless the case" (p. 26).

How Prevalent Is Deception?

A review by Stricker (1967) indicated widespread use of deception in many areas of social psychological research: 81% of conformity studies, 72% of cognitive dissonance research, 50% of decision-making experiments, and 40% of attitude-change studies. Were one to include deception by omission—that is, what the experimenter could not say to subjects even if asked—the percentage would rise beyond these figures. Earlier commentaries noted with alarm the apparent prestige and legitimacy which deception methodologies were attaining within the research establishment (Kelman, 1967; Ring, 1967), and a recent survey by Menges (1973) indicates that this trend has become more pronounced. Menges observed a large percentage of experiments to involve deception (80%), with only half of these reporting specific debriefing procedures. He could document no marked changes in research practices despite the influx of critical commentary in the past half decade.

What Are the Effects of Deceiving Subjects?

Two features of this question will be considered. First, what are the effects of deception on experimental behaviors, either in the immediate experiment or in future research participation? Second, are there deleterious effects of deception upon the subjects and can these be ameliorated by postexperimental debriefing procedures?

Performance Effects. There have been a number of investigations on the performance effects of deception (e.g., Brock & Becker, 1966; Holmes & Bennett, 1974). A typical procedure is to expose subjects to two experiments, but with only half of the subjects informed about the deception after the first study. Performance on the second study then becomes the behavior of interest. Brock and Becker (1966) observed that extensive debriefing, even immediately prior to a criterion experiment, did not influence performance unless there was a strong perceived relationship between the criterion experiment and the prior debriefed study. Since this condition would not ordinarily hold for many laboratories, it was an encouraging report which suggested that naive subjects may not be, in fact, a necessary selection factor in many experiments.

What about attitudes toward research participation? Holmes and Appelbaum (1970) exposed subjects to either a positive, a negative, or no prior experience in research condition, and then examined their performance on a verbal conditioning criterion task. They concluded that "the positive history of experience in experiments enhanced the subjects' subsequent experimental performance while the negative history . . . did not cause a significant decrement in the subjects' subsequent performance" (p. 201).

The Ethics of Deception: Empirical Evidence. Many commentators (e.g., Baumrind, 1971; Jourard, 1968; Kelman, 1967) have construed experimental deception as an ethically corrupt practice which dehumanizes the research enterprise. Some of these considerations were described earlier in the chapter. Is it possible to resort to evidence on these moral perspectives of the use of deception?

In view of Kelman's (1967) thesis that "a subject ought not to leave the laboratory with greater anxiety or lower self esteem than he came with" (p. 8), Walster, Berscheid, Abrahams, and Aronson (1967) investigated the effectiveness of debriefing following deception. In a study that itself required massive deceptions, subjects were first primed to be concerned or not concerned about the quality of their interview performance, after which they were led to believe that they did very well or poorly. Self-esteem ratings after the final debriefing compared to premeasures, served as the criterion. There were no noticeable effects for the prior-concern variable, and although some effects of the self-esteem manipulation lasted for a short period after debriefing, there was evidence that these eventually dissipated. In a study by Lowin, Walsh, Klieger, Sandler, and Wilkes (1968), deception was viewed as a message and debriefing as a countermessage in an attitude-change study. As in the Walster et al. study, this experiment involved an emotionally severe deception regarding self-esteem. Short-term effects of deception were noted, but no lasting ones, measured in terms of days and months after the experiment. On the basis of available evidence, there currently is no justification for abolishing deception and related "offensive" manipulations in the context of social-psychological research. Not all would agree that this issue is solely an empirical one, however, to be resolved with data.

How do subjects actually feel about research practices? Sullivan and Deiker (1973) compared the views of 400 psychologists and 357 undergraduate psychology students. They responded to a number of questions after reading one of four detailed descriptions of experiments varying in stressful procedures and deceptions. In 18 of 20 response categories, the psychologists gave more strict interpretations of the ethical issues than did the students. In all of the experiments, a majority of students judged the use of deception as ethical and justified, whereas the reverse was true for psychologists. Both groups indicated that having a course grade be contingent on participating in research was coercive and unethical.

In a unique study, Resnick and Schwartz (1973) used ethical standards as an independent variable in a verbal conditioning study. One group, termed nonethical, was run in a traditional manner involving mild but necessary deceptions. The second, "ethical" group was recruited from a large class, where the experimenter discussed in candid detail the nature of the experiment he was conducting—why he was doing it, the actual hypothesis, previous findings, and so on. Subjects in the nonethical procedure produced the usual conditioning effect, increasing the reinforced response over trials. Only 3 of the 14 subjects were categorized via postexperimental inquiry as aware of the reinforcement contingency, and no subject voiced complete awareness of the experimenter's purpose. In contrast, the "ethical" group showed significant negative conditioning, with 12 of 14 subjects categorized as aware. Thus, being related to in what might be termed a "compulsively ethical" manner produced negativism. A variety of evidence indicated that the ethical condition was reacted to with suspicion, boredom, and disbelief. The real surprise is the form of the data, since extensive investigations of the social psychology of the verbal conditioning paradigm have invariably shown illusory profiles of positive conditioning in aware subjects (e.g., Levy, 1967; Page, 1972). Subjects thus did not react favorably to the ethical prebriefing, as if it violated their conception of what psychological research "should be like."

A related study by Epstein, Suedfeld, and Silverstein (1973) investigated the subject's view of the "experimental contract." Very few subjects demanded honesty from experimenters, but they did view as very desirable that the experimenter be competent and provide for the subject's welfare. Subjects saw their own obligations in terms of being cooperative and honest. Subjects thus seem willing to participate for a worthy and cordial experimenter, treatment they would demand from a physician, a lawyer, or a clergyman. They acknowledge the need for specific procedural aspects, e.g., deception, although they do not view it as desirable in absolute terms. All of these recent investigations are encouraging for the researcher in terms of the basic tenets of contemporary methodology. They corroborate Aronson and Carlsmith's (1968) sage advice that it is the manner in which experimenters relate to subjects that is crucial, perhaps more than what the experimenter does—particularly during the postexperimental session. Harrassed and busy students, graduate and undergraduate, (and faculty as well) are often the experimenters. To the extent that they violate the commonsense aspects of relating to their subjects with confidence and realistic gratitude, ethical codes and inquiry will be superfluous.

Alternatives to Deception: Role Playing

The most frequently mentioned alternative to laboratory deception has been some form of role playing. Kelman outlined one rationale for role playing (1967):

> The kind of techniques that I have in mind would be based on the principle of eliciting the subject's positive motivations to contribute to the experimental enterprise. They would draw on the subject's active participation and involvement in the proceedings and encourage him to cooperate in making the experiment a success—not by giving the results he thinks the experimenter wants, but by conscientiously taking the roles and carrying out the tasks the experimenter assigns to him. (p. 9)

The enthusiasts for role playing argue that it would bypass the defects introduced by various subject roles (previously described) and would raise the status of the subject from a subordinate to a more equal collaborator in the research effort. A precise definition of role playing is not available. All variations of it are characterized by the subject realizing that the situation is not real, or not as it is designed to appear. Subjects asked to role play the Asch conformity situation would be told that the others present were confederates (e.g., Horowitz & Rothschild, 1970). Role-playing subjects must be immunized from the ethical pitfalls exposed to real subjects, which usually requires their being informed of the crucial deceptions involved in the experiment. It would not necessitate being informed of the experimenter's hypothesis, although this seems to be an inherent possibility in many role-playing experiments.

Reactions of a majority of social psychologists to role playing as an alternative to deception have been negative, despite Kelman's well-reasoned position (e.g., Miller, 1972). Social psychologists might be expected to resist the idea of role playing since the influence of real situations is the very cornerstone of their discipline. How people think or predict they would respond to emergencies, to authoritative commands, or to witnessing violence is not, in principle, the same as how they in fact respond. Sometimes there will be correspondence, sometimes not. There is no substitute for actual behavior as the final criterion (Freedman, 1969). A number of investigators (Latane & Darley, 1970; Milgram, 1974) have patently shown that subjects cannot "armchair" the behavior of genuinely involved subjects.

Mixon (1971, 1972) suggests, however, that role playing has not been fully explored. Specifically he argues that it is only the passive role-playing model that has been compared to deception, i.e., where subjects, in the comfort of their armchairs, are given a description of a study and are asked what they would do. Mixon is correct in stating that this is a pale shadow of what could be a truly active, involved role-playing experience (for example, with genuine props). The epistemological fact, however, that no matter how realistic the situation seemed to be, the behaving subjects would always know that the context was, in fact, false, seems to be an inevitable shortcoming of any role-playing effort.

Role playing does occupy, however, a vital niche in research methods in social psychology, for example in theoretical developments in attitude change (Elms, 1969), simulation (Guetzkow et al., 1962), and self-perception (Bem, 1967). Orne (1969) has developed control procedures by using role-playing variants to detect how much of a given experimental effect (hypnosis, psychotherapeutic, sensory deprivation) could be attributed to subjects' seeing through the hypothesis and providing artifactual evidence confirming the experimenter's prediction (e.g., Schuck & Pisor, 1974). It is only as an alternative to deception, then, that role playing is inadequate.

A Summarizing Research Report

A recent study by Holmes and Bennett (1974) addressed the issues of role playing, debriefing effectiveness, and informed consent in a single research effort. Subjects were randomly assigned to one of five experimental conditions after being attached to blood pressure and respiration recording instruments and told that the experiment dealt with stimulation, emotion, and physiological responses. The basic condition was a stress group, told that they would receive painful electric shocks. None were actually given, but self-ratings of mood and physiological measures of emotional arousal were obtained at various times before and after subjects were debriefed as to the true nature of the study. Other conditions included: a role-play group (told that no shocks would actually be given), a debriefed group (debriefed immediately before shocks were to be given), an informed group (told that the experiment might involve some form of deception, unspecified), and a no-stress group (no mention of electric shocks).

The dependent measures were changes in reports of anxiety and changes in pulse and respiration rate. The results, in general, did not support the effectiveness of role playing, did support the effectiveness of debriefing, and showed that merely informing subjects of the possibility of deception did not bias or affect the behavior of these subjects. Role-playing subjects were able to simulate the verbal rating behavior of deceived subjects, but not their actual physiological arousal. Subjects in the debriefed group were very similar in their arousal pattern to subjects in the no-stress control group. The final debriefing for those in the stress condition also was effective. Holmes and Bennett boldly concluded that "these findings would seem to eliminate the two major ethical objections to the use of deception in psychological research" (p. 366), that is, that (1) debriefing is an effective antidote in "returning" subjects to their pretreatment psychological state and (2) informing (truthfully) subjects that deception is a possible feature of the experiment does not influence their subsequent behavior, even when that behavior is physiological activation. Thus, the frank admission, beforehand, that illusion or incomplete information may be necessary in an experiment could serve as a more straightforward way to handle the "informed consent" problem in psychological research.

THE ROLE OF THE EXPERIMENTER IN RESEARCH

That the experimenter could contribute illicitly, if unknowingly, to the data he obtains has been a sensational issue in psychology since the early 1960s, when Robert Rosenthal performed numerous experiments on this problem and collected his data and thoughts in *Experimenter Effects in Behavioral Research* (1966). The scientist's role would seem to be a virtuous and noble one in contemporary society. To demonstrate a bias in the form of self-serving experimental results is no minor event. It is corruption from on high—understandable perhaps in the subordinate; exploited subject population, but unforgivable and unconscionable in the researcher himself. In contrast to the varied portraits of the research subject, the researcher's motivation would seem more readily comprehended, namely, to execute a rigorous experiment according to the rules of scientific method. There should be no question about the experimenter being good, helpful, faithful, cooperative, apprehensive, or negativistic. To be an experimenter is to elevate oneself above these baser human conditions! Yet the evidence clearly shows that the experimenter may seriously interfere with his own proceedings.

Most of the conceptualizations of the role of subject presume that the subject is "tuned in" to the experiment, that he is active, curious, concerned about what is going on, what will be asked of him, and how he will be evaluated. The subject focuses upon the experimenter as a likely source of information. In Orne's terms, the experimenter is a major source of demand characteristics. He knows the experimental hypothesis, and the subject knows that he knows it. As with mystery writers, experimenters usually have a precise view of the outcome before things even begin. Enacting many social psychological experiments is particularly difficult because, in addition to the rudimentary aspects of scientific preparation in terms of design, random assignment, and subject selection, the experimenter may have to step on stage as an actor himself. He may have to deceive subjects, a difficult task irrespective of its ethical status. In short, the experimenter has many operations that must be performed intentionally. What are the possibilities for unintentional slippage? Rosenthal has isolated two facets of the experimenter's social-psychological functioning in the laboratory, experimenter effects and expectancy effects (1966, 1969).

Experimenter Effects

There are a variety of experimenter characteristics which can influence how he behaves toward subjects and, in turn, how they respond to him. Biosocial factors (Rosenthal, 1966) such as age, sex, and race may influence interpersonal exchange in the laboratory. Rosenthal (1967) has found male experimenters to be more friendly to their subjects than females.

Harris and Masling (1970) observed female investigators to obtain similar performances from male and female subjects in a Rorschach personality test situation, whereas male examiners elicited more responses from female subjects. In earlier and ingenious research, Masling (1966) demonstrated the effects of subject behavior on experimenters. Warm, accepting female subjects (confederates) obtained more flattering personality interpretations from male examiners than did subjects acting cold and aloof, despite almost identical test responses. Deutsch, Canavan, and Rubin (1971) noted that an attractive female experimenter "evoked more competitive behavior from our male undergraduates than our male experimenter . . . it appears to us that our subjects were most competitive when they and the experimenter were opposite in sex and most cooperative when they were the same sex" (p. 266).

Rosenthal also discussed what he terms psychosocial effects. The experimenter's need for approval, anxiety, warmth, and social status may produce different responses in subjects (1966, chap. 5). There are insufficient data in terms of consistent directional effects to warrant broad generalizations concerning these variables.

Experimenter Expectancy Effects

The major interest in terms of the experimenter has been the potential for communicating hypotheses to subjects (Rosenthal, 1966, 1974). There are, of course, a variety of pressures for the experimenter to want the hypothesis confirmed. Officially, these relate to his role as a theoretician and an academician. There are also personal motives, however—career advancement, salary, grant requests—that place a premium on successful experimentation. Traditional scientific methodology has by no means totally ignored this problem. The experimenter's role is often "standardized" or "objectified" in terms of removing possible biases (e.g., random assignment of subjects to conditions, reading or tape recording experimental instructions, maintaining certain constants in the experimenter's behavior and position inside the laboratory). These important procedures may not, however, be enough. Rosenthal (1969) contends that the danger of experimenter expectancy effects is that they are not public matters. They may easily escape detection, and by definition, they relate to the specific experimental conditions or independent variable levels of the experiment. There is considerable generality to this concept. Many social relationships involve one person having an expectation about the behavior of another—doctors and patients, teachers and students, parents and children, clergy and congregants, one nation for another, and animal trainers and their beasts (e.g., Pfungst, 1911, cited in Rosenthal, 1966). Recent approaches to the problem have analyzed the difficult question of how the experimenter actually conveys his hypothesis and have extended expectancy research into nonexperimental locales. Before describing these developments, some of the demonstrational experiments are worth noting.

In an often-cited early study, Rosenthal and Fode (in Rosenthal, 1966) told a group of experimenters (a class in experimental psychology) that their rats were maze-bright or maze-dull according to their genetic strain. After subsequent training, a variety of measures—the rat's movement, speed, attitudes of experimenters toward their animal, their handling behavior—reflected these randomly assigned, fictitious trait labels. Another experiment involved person perception. Student experimenters were assigned to test their subjects' empathy by having them rate a series of photographs in terms of the degree to which the person in the photograph had been experiencing success or failure (using a scale of -10 to $+10$). The photographs previously had been scaled by an independent sample of raters as approximately neutral on this dimension. By means of a deceptive cover story, Rosenthal instructed the real subjects in all of these experiments, namely the student experimenters, that their subjects should produce a mean rating of $+5$ or (in half of the experimenters) -5. Rosenthal was blatant in terms of "demanding" the effect. He stressed the fact that the previous results on the picture-rating task were conclusive and should be replicable if the experiment was run well. All experimenters read a standard set of instructions to their subjects. Significantly higher ratings were obtained by experimenters expecting their subjects to perceive success in the photos.

What Produces the Expectancy Effect?

Barber and Silver (1968), in a scathing critique of Rosenthal's work, have suggested that cheating and recording errors were responsible in many instances for the false assertion that experimenters unintentionally communicate their hypotheses to subjects—in short, that the expectancy effect itself is an artifact. Rosenthal (1969) countered this critique with a variety of experiments in which the possibility of this source of the effect was removed or strongly inhibited. Johnson and Adair (1970, 1972) have provided support for Rosenthal's version of the effect by comparing the observations of tape-recorded behavior by experimenters who did or did not have expectancies. Clear evidence for expectancies was shown, beyond the matter of recording errors.

Analyses of filmed interactions between experimenter and subject—without the experimenters' knowledge—have attempted to discover the source of expectancy transmission. These have not been conclusive. Auditory cues, alone, however, may produce the effect. Adair and Epstein (1967) used audio recordings of the instructions read by experimenters who expected and had previously obtained biased results. These tape recordings were sufficient to produce the expectancy effect on the picture-perception task. Research on the auditory transmission of the experimenter's expectancy (Duncan, Rosenberg, & Finkelstein, 1969) has substantiated the role that auditory cues play in this phenomenon. Apparently there are paralinguistic or voice-quality cues that are particularly salient when the hypothesis is being signaled. These investigators replicated Minor's (1970) finding that apprehensive subjects are particularly "on guard" for these cues and will subsequently make use of them.

Recent Applications of the Expectancy Research

Without question, the most noteworthy recent interest in the problem of expectancy was stimulated by the report of Rosenthal and Jacobson (1968), *Pygmalion in the Classroom*. Children in an elementary school in a lower socioeconomic neighborhood were administered a test purported to predict intellectual "blooming." Within three existing tracks (low, average, high) at each of six grade levels, approximately 20% of the students were randomly designated as likely to show dramatic intellectual growth by the end of the following year. The names of these students were given to their teachers. An IQ test, involving picture vocabulary and reasoning, was administered eight months later. The evidence was clear that in certain instances, the expectancies were translated into growth, particularly for the abstract reasoning part of the test. Children at the highest level within each grade showed the strongest effects. Those children from whom the effect was expected were rated by their teachers as having greater potential, as being more interesting, curious, and happy. They were perceived by their teachers as more intellectually promising and stimulating. Those children who in fact gained intellectually but who had not been predicted to do so were perceived much less glowingly by their teachers, as if the teachers did not relish unexpected positive outcomes! This was true specifically of the slow track children. A replication of this research in a Midwestern middle-class school setting produced generally similar findings (Rosenthal & Evans, cited in Rosenthal, 1969), but with some differences involving sex of subjects. Rosenthal and Jacobson (1968) were unable to specify how the effect was produced, although it was apparent that time spent with the students was not a major factor. They speculated that: "by what she said, by how she said it, by her facial expressions, postures, and perhaps by her touch, the teacher may have communicated to the children of the experimental group that she expected improved intellectual performance" (p. 429). The evidence is that the teachers soon forgot who the "special" children were, suggesting that the effects of the expectancy were mediated (or initiated) early in the academic year. Thus, the possibility that the children were treated differently only at the time of the retaking of the IQ test, which would produce the test effects but not other relevant interactional data, was not considered likely.

Two investigations by Rubovits and Maehr (1971, 1973) have analyzed the Rosenthal and Jacobson phenomenon. In the first, the interaction-quality hypothesis was tested, the idea that it was a subtle interchange in form rather than sheer quantity of interaction that produced the effect. The subjects were student teachers who were given a fictitiously high IQ score for one student in the group of four they were working with. Trained observers, blind to the deceptively labeled "gifted" student, recorded various dimensions of the teacher's behavior (attention, encouragement, elaboration, ignoring, praise, and criticism). Student teachers were not more attentive to the "gifted" students, nor did these students initiate more interaction than their (actually equally gifted) peers. The teachers did, however, request more statements from the "gifted" students, and the statements of these students were praised significantly more often. These were the only significant effects, and they constitute partial support for the Rosenthal and Jacobson interpretation. These investigators were sensitive to the credibility of their situation and reported no suspicions of their hypothesis from their student-teacher subjects. Of course, in this study, the expectancy effect itself was not at issue, only the manner in which it might be actuated in terms of teacher–pupil interaction.

Rubovits and Maehr (1973) extended their research to the domain of race relations, where the idea of a self-fulfilling prophecy has been an influential explanatory construct (Clark, 1965a). There is evidence, for example, that black students perceive white teachers to have low expectancies for their ability, and there is evidence that teachers in fact have such differential expectations (Brown, 1968). In a study based on their earlier (1971) procedure, Rubovits and Maehr had student teachers interact with a group of four students involving a discussion on the topic of television. Students were selected from the same ability-grouped class unit, two being white and two black. One white student and one black were randomly assigned a high IQ (130, 135) and labeled gifted; the other two students were given IQs of 98 and 102 and labeled nongifted. The teachers had a seating chart, with the names of the students, their IQs, and the labels, and were instructed to be attentive to this information and alert to individual student behaviors and performance. Observers rated the teachers' interaction with the four students.

Numerous significant differences in interaction quality were observed, favoring the white students. Black students were praised less, for example, and criticized more. These effects were teacher-produced; there were no differences in actual spontaneity or student-initiated verbosity between white and black students. Black students labeled "gifted" were criticized more, and more was requested of them. Of particular importance were the effects of the labels given the race of the students. A general pattern of bias emerged:

> . . . the expectation of giftedness is associated with a generally positive response of teachers—*if* the student is white. For the black students, if anything, a reverse tendency is evident, in which the expectation of giftedness is associated with *less* positive treatment. (p. 215)

Again, post-inquiry supported the expectancy manipulation with no indication of suspicion of the hypothesis. In view of the liberal, idealistic public stance (presumed, that is) of the student teachers, the bias should have been in the direction of equanimity and ingratiation toward the black students, in the manner of the evaluation apprehension construct noted earlier. The results again are supportive of the Rosenthal and Jacobson thesis.

Summary of Rosenthal's Work

As with any research program in social psychology attracting a great deal of interest and stimulating considerable research, Rosenthal has been resoundingly criticized by several methodologists, in terms of his research on the experimenter-expectancy phenomenon in general (Barber & Silver, 1968) and the teacher-expectancy effect in particular (Snow, 1969). The themes of these critiques have dealt with the possible artifactual bases of expectancy effects (e.g., they might not be unintentional), the allegedly biased use of statistical analyses to inflate the appearance of these effects, and the weaknesses of the dependent measures used in the Rosenthal and Jacobson research. A thorough perusal of the criticisms as well as the predictable rejoinders (Rosenthal, 1968, 1974) would be a major scholastic undertaking in itself.

Most reactions have been respectful and complimentary. Aronson and Carlsmith (1968), for example, acknowledge the importance and extensive nature of Rosenthal's evidence. They react somewhat skeptically to Rosenthal's notion regarding keeping experimenters blind to the hypothesis (as in the double-blind placebo control in drug research where the experimenter does not know who the treated and nontreated subjects are). One reason is that the experimenters are, in actuality, subjects in these experiments. Rosenthal's research, in fact, deals with subject effects. The subjects in this case are given the role of experimenters, but they in fact are subjects to the real experimenter, namely, Rosenthal himself. Thus, the blind experimenters (subjects) might deduce the hypothesis or respond to demand characteristics as noted in the previous section. There is evidence that a research director will communicate what he expects his experimenters to obtain even when he does not directly instruct them (Rosenthal, Persinger, Vikan-Kline, & Mulry, 1963). Also, since many experimenters are graduate students, keeping them blind would be an anti-intellectual approach that would be counterproductive from a number of points of view. Aronson and Carlsmith point out that many experiments in social psychology require the participation of the experimenter as an integral part of the experiment, e.g., research in aggression and cognitive dissonance. He is not merely a reader of instructions, but is active. He may well be aware of the hypothesis, but he should try to keep himself blind to the specific conditions of the independent variable as much as possible and for as long as possible. If, for example, he is to induce failure or success in subjects, he should turn up a card indicating which condition to run at the last possible moment, rather than know it far in advance and possibly treat subjects differently in the waiting room. Recent texts in experimental methodology in social psychology acknowledge in detail the potential significance of the issues Rosenthal has raised (e.g., Hendrick & Jones, 1972, chap. 3).

EPILOGUE

The purpose of this chapter has been to document the social psychological character of the experimental situation. Some have been inclined to use the evidence reviewed here as a justification for leaving the laboratory. There is no question that there is an emerging legitimacy and fashion for experimental research in more natural contexts. The gain in this venture is that the subjects will be less self-conscious about being studied; they may be totally unaware that they are subjects. This self-awareness issue has been a major theme in the present chapter. Laboratory experimentation will continue, however, to be a dominant mode of analysis in social psychology. The gains in precision and control are beyond comparison. Unfortunately, the same is true for the potential for social-psychologically induced artifact! The resolution? Campbell's (1969) thesis, that "experiments cannot prove theories, but only probe them," (p. 377) is a useful one. He postulates that because no single research method can prove a hypothesis to be true, there is no justification for considering one research context to be, in principle, superior to another. The plausibility of a given interpretation for a social psychological hypothesis is arrived at by ruling out alternative hypotheses and interpretations through research in a variety of contexts. When there has been amassed sufficient data, the pattern of which is present in varied contexts and observed through different methods and measurements, only then can one begin to have confidence in the truth value of the relationship.

What is the evidence regarding the potential damage to subjects or data in the experimental situation? McClintock (1973) best summarized things when he said: "Where there is smoke, there's smoke!" (p. 261). The evidence is certainly not condemning with respect to subjects' reactions to being experimented upon or with respect to experimenters' abilities to cope with the social nature of research, but there are caution lights at every turn in the road. What is encouraging is that the important questions are being asked, and they are being answered. The following quote from Rosenberg (1969) is a fitting choice for a finale:

> When the critics suggest that the experimental God is dead, they appear to have missed the point implicit in all research on the social psychology of the experiment. That point is that the experimental method can readily be used to perfect, or at least to significantly improve itself. Any experimental demonstration of some source of systematic bias and of the process by which it operates immediately suggests procedures for the control and elimination of that source of bias. (p. 347)

SUMMARY

This chapter examines the social interaction between the psychological researcher and his human subject. The validity of the research may be impossible to assess without a clear appreciation for the operation of social dynamics in the laboratory. The practice of deception is a pivotal issue in the chapter, illustrating the close interplay between ethical and methodological dimensions. There may often be a conflict between vigorous scientific inquiry and certain human values. The simple fact that there are human beings at both the administrative and receiving stations of the psychological experiment seems to generate a social psychology of the research situation.

Historically the roles of experimenter and subject have become increasingly differentiated. The subject is the "object of study," one whose behavior is to be predicted. Critics speak in terms of the depersonalization and sterility of the experimenter–subject relationship, viewing it as counterproductive to the goals of psychological research. Social psychological experiments frequently expose subjects to stressful manipulations. The behaviors under study may be unpleasant or antisocial. To learn about man seems to require invasions of privacy and dignity. In testing theories, researchers must contend with their subjects' natural inclinations to be self-conscious and to shape their own behaviors to save face or to help the investigator. The use of deception and other manipulative procedures, without informed consent, in the eyes of some casts a shadow on the research enterprise. They are concerned about the subject's welfare and the public image of psychological research. The subject is acknowledged to be in a vulnerable position in the laboratory. Reactions to the critics, however, recognize the moral costs in research, advocate precautions in the treatment of subjects, and ask for empirical evidence regarding harmful after-effects of research involvement.

Subjects are not inert reactors, but are creative forces in their own behavior. They are potentially responsive to numerous cues in the laboratory. Their definition of the research situation may depart significantly from that intended for them; and the unknowing experimenter may, as a result, make misleading interpretations of his data. Subjects generally wish to appear normal or adjusted and to cooperate with the experimenter. To satisfy these goals requires that the subject discover (to his satisfaction, at least) the experimenter's purpose or hypothesis. The researcher must therefore be careful that the behavior of interest does not systematically reflect these subject motives, at the expense of whatever psychological variables and treatments are at issue in his research. The detection of the subject's awareness is both necessary and extremely difficult. The form of the behavior itself is often insufficient to indicate clearly what psychological conditions actually caused the behavior. Research in the area of aggression illustrates how the social nature of the research situation has produced controversy in the interpretation of laboratory behavior. One answer (a mixed blessing to say the least) to this host of issues has been the effective use of deception.

Deception is used to create illusions in the laboratory, e.g., the perception that the subject is shocking another person. Deception is also used to present to subjects a rationale for their presence in the experiment, thereby fulfilling their need to have such a rationale in the first place and, more critically, diverting their attention from the experimenter's true purpose or hypothesis. The evidence regarding the effects of deception does not appear to validate the critics' fears. Knowing about deception, or having experienced it previously, does not invariably lead subjects to be unusually suspicious or disruptive in later experiments. There is no indication, moreover, that subjects experience psychological damage from participating in stressful research. Sensitive researchers appear effective in debriefing their subjects. Nevertheless, there is not total acceptance of the means-to-an-end ideology that, for many, justifies deception in research. Role playing, cited as an alternative to deception, has received endorsement from a number of social psychologists but is not viewed here as an effective solution.

The experimenter himself may depart from his position of objectivity and convey unintended directives to his subjects. The experimenter's social role in the laboratory is one of high status. He is an authority figure who holds special information, usually concealed from his subjects, in the form of an expectancy or prediction. There is substantial evidence that most individuals desire confirmation of their expectancies, and the experimenter is no exception. Experimental data must not in principle reflect these (understandable) hopes and aspirations of the experimenter, yet there is abundant evidence that experimenters are capable of such intrusion in their own affairs. They have a receptive audience for their unintentional communications, as noted previously in characterizing the human subject as an active and curious laboratory animal. There are interesting extensions of this analysis into educational settings, where teachers, given expectancies, appear to bias the behavior of their students. Thus, the experimenter is a "loaded gun" in his own laboratory. He has precious information, scientifically speaking; and in many social psychological experiments, he has a demanding set of duties to execute. He must guard against the unintentional slippage of information that might produce falsely supportive data for his theory or prediction.

SUGGESTED READINGS

Campbell, D. T., & Stanley, J. C. *Experimental and quasi-experimental designs for research.* Chicago: Rand McNally, 1966.

A definitive primer of methodology showing in precise detail the relationship between social determinants and problems of design and interpretation. A variety of control groups and examples, in addition to sage discussion, are to be found in this important work.

Ethical principles in the conduct of research with human participants. *American Psychologist,* 1973, *28,* 79-80.

Ten principles of the revised code of research ethics, following an extensive period of review and numerous predrafts. These principles constitute the first code of ethics to appear after the widespread interest in the social psychology of research.

Miller, A. G. (Ed.). *The social psychology of psychological research.* New York: Free Press, 1972.

A collection of conceptual and experimental papers dealing with the social psychology of research. Featured is an extensive consideration of Milgram's obedience experiments—criticisms and rebuttals dealing with the ethical and methodological aspects of this research.

Rosenthal, R., & Rosnow, R. (Eds.). *Artifact in behavioral research.* New York: Academic Press, 1969.

An important textbook containing essays by the leading figures in this area (McGuire, Orne, Rosenberg, Rosenthal). Contains reviews of research on a variety of subject role artifacts and experimenter effects. Especially recommended is the concluding chapter by Donald T. Campbell.

Willems, E. P., & Raush, H. L. (Eds.). *Naturalistic viewpoints in psychological research.* New York: Holt, Rinehart, & Winston, 1969.

An important collection of papers by enthusiasts for research in contexts other than formally designated laboratories. Provides an important perspective on an emerging research trend in social psychology.

PART TWO

Determinants of Social Behavior

3. **SOCIAL MOTIVATION**
   Introduction
   Primary Sources of Motivation
   Secondary Sources of Motivation
   Anxiety-fear / Frustration / Guilt
   Instrumental Responses
   Aggression and sex roles / Dependency and birth order
   Social Goals
   Nurturance / Achievement
   Implications for Social Motivation
   Summary
   Suggested Readings

4. **SOCIALIZATION: THE FORMATION OF IDENTITY**
   Introduction: What Is Socialization?
   Some Conceptual Distinctions
   Mechanisms / Socialization as process / The content of socialization / That which socialization is not

Socialization Through Observation
Socialization as role learning
Socialization to National Identity
Socialization in the Soviet Union / Contemporary problems in socialization in the United States
In Conclusion
Summary
Suggested Readings

5. **SITUATIONAL DETERMINANTS OF HURTING AND HELPING BEHAVIOR**
Introduction
Hurting and Helping
Definitions / Research strategies
Instrumental Aggression
Obedience / Evaluation of the frustration-aggression hypothesis
Angry Aggression
Frustration-aggression: revisited / The long hot summer / The victim's behavior during and prior to the attack
Helping Behavior
The presence of other bystanders / Characteristics of the victim and helping
Summary
Suggested Readings

3
Social Motivation

Alvin L. Atkins and Irma Hilton

INTRODUCTION

This chapter traces the development of the notion of "motives" from simple forms of behavior to more complex forms of social interaction. Starting with the question of why the concept arose initially, we focus on how the efforts to satisfy our basic needs like hunger, thirst, and sex lead us to engage in certain acts, while our inability to do so or our frustration over not being able to satisfy such needs prompts us to undertake other actions. Thus, it is important to examine how interference with our efforts to satisfy primary need states elicits anxiety, fear, frustration, and guilt (called secondary sources of motivation) and, in turn, how we cope with these feeling states. Among the responses to such feeling states are various types of aggressive behavior and forms of dependency and, subsequently, strivings for achievement and group membership.

Naturally, observing how we display aggression and dependency raises certain questions. Do we all handle aggressive feelings and dependent yearnings in similar ways, or do socialization processes that operate differently from culture to culture play a role? Certainly we have witnessed dramatic changes in our own culture in how men and women respond both in terms of aggression and dependency.

Extending these questions, the chapter goes into issues dealing with more intricate social goals. Acquired social motives may affect the ways in which we seek nurturance, power, and achievement. Although initially we may respond aggressively when our primary needs are frustrated, we may also see ourselves using aggressive means to achieve power and status. Similarly, our early needs for nurturance may reflect an initial primary motive tied to the need for satisfaction of hunger, thirst, and sex. Yet as we grow and change, the motive may take on different forms, where groups and social interaction are essential in order to satisfy affiliative tendencies. Thus, the interplay of primary and secondary sources of motivation becomes a very complex topic to analyze. This chapter is directed at examining the origins, development, and extensions of the issues that such an analysis requires.

PRIMARY SOURCES OF MOTIVATION

The concept of "motive" is one of the most controversial ones in the field of psychology (Appley, 1970). Frequently, motives are discussed in terms of drives and instincts. Having been introduced into the psychological literature by Woodworth at least as early as 1918 (Woodworth, 1918), the drive concept has occupied a position of prominence among both learning theorists as well as psychoanalytic theorists (Appley, 1970). As such, the concept generally implied a set of internal conditions arising out of biological needs which impel or energize the organism towards behavior directed at satisfying these needs. Hunger, thirst, and sex are among such basic biological needs, all of which facilitate one's self-preservation and survival. Accordingly, primary needs for water, food, air, and sex reflect a general, undifferentiated drive state leading to increased activity making the organism "more likely to encounter whatever was necessary to satisfy its need" (Berkowitz, 1969). At the same time, the organism would be expected to demonstrate "need-specific stimulation which would give rise only to the responses that were associated with it, either innately or through prior learning" (Berkowitz, 1969).

Central to the operation of such basic or primary drive states is the underlying deprivation of tissue requirements, tending to automatic need-satisfying activity. Despite the fact that early research supported the notion that prolonged deprivation of food, for example, led to heightened food-seeking activity (Berkowitz, 1969), it was also observed that anticipation of the discomfort produced by an organic need also operated as a general drive state (Mowrer, 1950). Extending this work, it was observed that organisms do not necessarily function to reduce internal tension but may, indeed, independently seek external stimulation (Berlyne, 1960). Thus, if various forms of behavior are not clearly an outgrowth of the supposed primary drives, a much more comprehensive formulation of motivation is required.

It is to this issue that our attention is directed when we begin to focus upon the drives "acquired" in the course of social behavior. Perhaps one of the clearest distinctions between primary and acquired drives can be found in the work of the Harlows (1958), who constructed surrogate mothers for isolated monkeys. Both equipped with a nursing bottle attached to the upper thoracic region, the mothers differed in that one was constructed of wire mesh while the other consisted of sponge rubber covered in terrycloth. Thus, while both mothers provided milk, one also provided something to cling to. The preference for the cloth mother might be interpreted as innate contact comfort, or even as the result of a conditioned response to cloth associated with the availability of food. More elaborate observation, however, suggests that security, affection, and nurturance-seeking were operating as goals and sources of satisfaction for the monkeys (Brown, 1965). Thus, what may have originally functioned to impel the monkey to seek milk (primary drive) is linked with the social contact (acquired drive) generated by the array of satisfactions derived from the more lifelike cloth mother.

Further evidence that external factors impinge on internal primary states can be observed in the sexual behavior of rats. Wilson, Kuehn, and Beach (1963) observed copulation between male and female rats until a point of sexual exhaustion was reached. Although removing and replacing the original female partner did not stimulate renewed sexual activity by the male rats, a new partner rearoused sexual behavior. Thus, a novel external stimulus activated an otherwise satiated primary drive. However, if primary drives cannot account for all basic activity, how do we explain such phenomena as achievement orientation, power seeking, and affiliative tendencies when basic need states are satisfied? Clearly a broader conceptualization is needed to explain such behavior.

SECONDARY SOURCES OF MOTIVATION

It is obvious that the satisfaction of basic drives can involve conflict. Do I eat when I am hungry if others are hungry and cannot eat? Do I lust after that which belongs to another? If the answer is "no," then the basic drive remains unsatisfied. I may feel frustrated and anxious. If the answer is "yes," than I may feel guilty.

The inability to satisfy or conflict about having satisfied the primary motive or drives leads to feelings of discomfort and uneasiness. The ensuing need to relieve this discomfort then acts as a secondary source of motivation. The goal of this motivation, however, may not necessarily be that which aroused the activity initially. Deprivation of a specific goal-seeking behavior (drive) need not necessarily lead to behaviors oriented towards alleviating the particular deprivation, but may lead to activity arousal without specific goal satisfaction. If the deprivation itself is stressful, e.g., elicits anxiety, the goal which is sought after may be unrelated to the original deprivation. It may, in fact, be related to the cognitive restructuring of the source of the anxiety. For example, if arousal occurs because of deprivation of food or sex, it may make one hypersensitive to other formerly neutral stimuli and eager to remove any noxious component in the present stimulus. The goal is transferred from the satisfaction of the primary need to the resolution of the perceived difficulty with the stimulus currently present in the environment.

What determines the feelings of a particular person after attaining a goal he has sought? The same objective circumstances can lead one person to feel satisfied, another frustrated, and a third guilty. Conversely, the same instigation can lead to quite different reactions in different people. How one feels seems to be an interaction of cognitive and physiological stimuli. Schachter and Singer (1962) conducted a fascinating series of experiments to illustrate this point. The formulation is summarized in the following major propositions:

1. Given a state of physiological arousal for which an individual has no immediate explanation, he will label this state and describe his feelings in terms of the cognitions available to him. The same physiological state could be labeled "fear," "joy," "anger," or otherwise, depending on the situation as defined by the individual.

2. If the individual has an appropriate explanation for his aroused bodily state (for example, "I feel aroused because I have taken a drug which makes my heart beat faster"), there will be no need to label his feelings in terms of the alternative cognitions available (for example, "I feel aroused because I am amused by this comic scene").

3. Given the same situation the individual will react emotionally or describe his feelings as emotional only to the extent that he experiences a state of physiological arousal.

These hypotheses were tested in an experiment in which an injection of epinephrine (a commercial form of adrenaline) was used to produce autonomic excitation. One group of subjects received the injection and was told that they had received an emotion-arousing injection (Epi-Informed). Another group received the injection and was not told anything of the presumed effects (Epi-Ignorant). A third group received an injection and was given misleading expectations as to the effects of the injection (Epi-Misinformed). A fourth group received an injection of saline solution which presumably would not stimulate the autonomic nervous system (Placebo).

A stooge isolated with the subject behaved in either an angry or a euphoric way. According to the theory, the subjects who had been artificially aroused by epinephrine ought to have the greatest need to label their emotions and would be most likely to reflect the behavior demonstrated by the stooge if they had no accurate interpretation of the feelings to fall back upon (Epi-Ignorant and Epi-Misinformed). They could not attribute their arousal to the presumed effects of epinephrine and were most likely to report feeling euphoric or angry and to imitate the behavior of the stooge. The results supported the predictions.

The experiment illustrated that motivational states are not always fixed by either personal (internal) or environmental (external) stimuli. The blocking of basic drives leads to feelings of tension. The blockage may be due to internal sanctions, e.g., guilt (one ought not) or external inhibition (prohibitions) against satisfaction. The perception of the meaning of this tension, that is, the label one places upon it, varies from person to person as a function of an interaction between internal and external states.

We will refer to as secondary sources of motivation these conditions which arise when there is interference with the satisfaction of primary drives. Three variables will be considered here: anxiety-fear, frustration, and guilt. These sources can be viewed as outcomes of deprivation as well as sources of motivation for further action. Although in some instances it is difficult to separate one from the other—and it is possible that one could subsume them under a general anxiety construct—they will be considered independently to maximize the kinds of predictions about social behavior that can be made. Clearly the perception of one's feeling as a function of deprivation will affect the subsequent behaviors in such a way that anxiety will probably lead to different behaviors from either frustration or guilt.

Anxiety-Fear

The distinction between fear and anxiety has not always been made, and it is not always clear when made. Essentially, according to psychoanalytic theory, fear is the real, touchable, objective component, with anxiety considered to be the vague, repressed, subjective component. In fear, the individual's concern is drawn to the threat arising from a specific object. Anxiety arises from a threat to an individual's security. In his early work with the notion of anxiety, Mowrer (1950) saw anxiety as a conditioned form of reaction to pain. Consequently, it was a strong motivating force for behavior, since the organism sought to reduce the level of anxiety and reinforced any behavior serving that purpose.

In whatever way one chooses to define it, however, it is clear that anxiety is a potent social motivator (Teichman, 1974). Currently, there is controversy over the value of fear as a social motivator. Nevertheless, Solomon (1964) and others have indicated that the use of physical punishment can be a much more effective means of social control than has generally been believed, that is, if it is applied correctly. Physical punishment can effectively prevent the occurrence of disapproved behavior even when the punishing agent is not on the scene, if the punishment has been administered earlier and if alternative modes of behavior are readily available to the punished individual. In Mowrer's terms the anticipation of this pain or anxiety would serve to dissuade the person from a negatively sanctioned activity, providing that another outlet were available.

Although for most of us anxiety and fear have a pejorative tone, invoking something to be avoided, there is evidence that mild forms of anxiety and fear serve a useful function in alerting the system to relevant dangers and galvanizing it into action. Janis and Feshbach (1953) investigated the effects of three different intensities of fear appeal in a study of the optimal utilization of appeals in mass communication. A 15-minute talk was prepared in three versions which contained the same essential information about causes of dental disease and the same recommendations for proper care of teeth, but which differed in the amount of fear-arousing material. Version 1 used a strong fear appeal emphasizing the painful consequences of tooth decay and showed illustrative slides on diseased gums and other results of poor dental hygiene. Version 2 used a moderate appeal in which the dangers were presented in a milder form. Version 3 used a minimal fear appeal in which more neutral material appeared. Both the verbal material and the accompanying slides varied in the degree to which they contained threats concerning the consequences of not conforming to the recommended course of action concerning dental-hygiene.

The freshman class of a large high school was divided into four groups—three experimental groups (one for each of the appeals) and one control. Evidence that the three appeals differed in the amount of emotional tension they aroused was obtained from questions asked of the audience concerning their worry about the condition of their own teeth. A clear progression appeared, with 74% of the strong fear group, 60% of the moderate fear group, and 50% of the minimal fear group reporting feeling "some worry" during the presentation.

The principal results of the experiment bear on the extent to which the recommendations were accepted and followed. The greatest change was obtained in the minimal fear-arousal condition. This was in line with the authors' expectation that fear arousal, if intense, may lead to adverse effects, such as hostility toward the communicator and subsequent rejection of the message the communication was intended to convey. It is interesting to speculate about the impact of warnings about cigarette smoking in relation to the degree of fear in the message. Recent newspaper articles have reported that the rise in smoking is the steepest in the decade. Can it be that the statement, "Warning: The Surgeon General Has Determined That Cigarette Smoking Is Dangerous to Your Health," which appears on every cigarette package constitutes too strong a fear appeal?

If anxiety or fear become sufficiently severe so as to become disruptive, what are the alternatives to antisocial behavior? If one introspects on one's own reactions it seems that anxiety might produce lashing-out or disoriented behavior or possibly withdrawal, all reactions designed to alienate one from others and, above all, from the source of anxiety itself. But, in addition, one might seek to be with other people, possibly to reduce the anxiety or to distract oneself from it or to find a way to identify the cause and thereby eliminate it.

Rats, young monkeys, and young human beings have been shown to become less fearful when in the presence of someone who is similar to them or at least familiar. Davitz and Mason (1955) showed that the presence of an unfrightened rat reduced the fear responses displayed by other rats in an open field situation. Arsenian (1943) reported that frightened children become less anxious when a familiar adult draws near. Mason (1960) deliberately frightened young rhesus monkeys and found there was less emotional disturbance when they were in the presence of a same-age peer than when an unfamiliar adult monkey or a rabbit was nearby.

Perhaps the most definitive study of the relationship between anxiety and affiliation was the series done by Schachter, entitled *The Psychology of Affiliation* (1959). On the basis of autobiographical data and observations of subjects in an exploratory study of experimentally induced isolation, Schachter postulated that anxiety is a frequent companion of isolation and that consequently affiliative tendencies should be increased under anxiety-inducing conditions. In Schachter's studies undergraduates who were made anxious by a threat of shock chose to await the anticipated painful stimulation in the company of others rather than alone. This preference was exhibited even when communication during the waiting period was restricted, provided that the group members were presented as being all in the same predicament. Further analyses of the data indicated that the relationship between anxiety and affiliative response held only for subjects who were first-born and only children and that later-born children did not exhibit affiliative tendencies when placed under stress. First-born subjects were more anxious and frightened when faced with a standard anxiety-evoking situation than were later-born subjects. Anxious early-born subjects manifested more dependent responses in the form of seeking the company of others than did equally anxious later-born subjects. Schachter attributed this affiliative response to anxiety on the part of first-borns to a greater need for evaluation, that is, a greater reliance on others for definition of the anxiety. The effect of this social comparison was to lower the level of reported anxiety. Whatever adverse effects might occur from anxiety, therefore, might be lessened through possibilities for affiliation and/or social comparison (Teichman, 1973). It would be possible, however, to postulate that whatever pro-social effects (e.g., greater needs for excellence) which have been activated by anxiety might similarly be reduced by excessive social interaction.

Frustration

It seems likely that the first reaction to a sense of deprivation of the primary goals would be feelings of frustration. A frustration, according to the definition employed by Dollard, Doob, Miller, Mowrer, and Sears in their now-classic monograph *Frustration and Aggression* (1939), is an "interference with the occurrence of an instigated goal response at its proper time in the behavior sequence." To translate this technical terminology into simpler language, they present an illustration of a boy, James, who, on hearing an ice-cream vendor's bell, wants an ice cream cone. He runs towards his mother thinking of the delights of the ice cream and calls to her. When he reaches his mother, he pleads for the cone, pulling her to the front door. If he gets the cone and eats it, the goal-oriented activities will be terminated. But suppose that James does not get the ice cream. His mother may insist, for example, that he wait until dinnertime. The series of responses leading to the consumption of the cone is interrupted. There is an interference with the occurrence of the instigated goal response, and James cannot eat the ice cream. This interference is the frustration.

The thrust of the early empirical research focused on frustration as the antecedent condition for aggression (Dollard et al., 1939). Frustration appeared to be necessary for aggression to occur, and aggression would not occur without a frustrating antecedent. (This concept is discussed at greater length in Chapter 5.) Although later writers (Miller, 1941) disputed the inevitability of this relationship, much evidence has been amassed as to its power. Azrin, Hutchinson, and Hake (1968) taught pigeons to peck at a key by reinforcing them with food every time they carried out the action. Then after the key-pressing response was well established, the investigators suddenly stopped giving the birds food for their behavior. If another pigeon was in the cage at the time, the thwarted animals would attack it, even to the extent of pulling out feathers from the target bird.

Research with young children (Mallick & McCandless, 1966) also testifies to the aggressive consequences of at least some frustrations. Eight- and nine-year-old boys and girls had to perform a simple construction task in order to earn money. Even though their peers' (experimental confederates') "inadvertently clumsy" behavior prevented some of the subjects from completing their assignment, the frustrator coupled his interference with sarcastic remarks. Various aggression measures were obtained in the three investigations carried out by the researchers: the number of electric shocks administered to the peer, the number of presses on a button that supposedly would interfere with the peer's work, and questionnaire ratings of like or dislike for him. For each of these measures, the frustrated subjects exhibited stronger aggression than did the nonfrustrated controls.

Aggression, however, is not an inevitable consequence of frustration. Barker, Dembo, and Lewin (1941) showed that children when frustrated may regress to earlier forms of behavior. Davitz (1952) showed that children reacted to frustration with aggression or with constructive activity, depending on the type of training they had received. Depression and withdrawal may also be reactions to frustration.

The choice of response to frustration is in some instances dependent on the situation (e.g., a two-year-old cannot reach a lollipop on the mantel) and in other instances on personality factors. Some will cry for help, some will go for a stool to climb up on, some will take it out on their younger siblings, and some will ignore it. In this way, the particular choice may be a question of prior conditioning, a personality factor, or a situational cue.

Guilt

Much attention has been focussed by social psychologists on the functions of anxiety and frustration. Considerably less is known about guilt. However, it is clear that not all people experience guilt to the same degree or react to the experience of guilt in the same manner.

Although the more frequent function of guilt is that of inhibition and control, the activation of feelings of guilt can also lead to the increased likelihood of a goal-seeking response. The experience of guilt may lead one to try harder to please the one who has induced guilt, thereby increasing dependent ties; or it may lead one to try to understand one's feelings and rid oneself of them (e.g., confession or psychotherapy). Altruistic behavior may often be a reaction to guilt or anxiety. Guilty persons may expiate their guilt by punishing themselves or by doing something good (Freedman, Wallington, & Bliss, 1967; Wallington, (1973). Thus, Darlington and Meeker (1966) showed that individuals who believed that they had harmed another were more apt to agree to donate blood to a local hospital. The results of Freedman et al. (1967) indicate that the motive to compensate for harm done to another person is not so much an attempt at making restitution to the victim as to expiate guilt.

Perhaps the most frequent function of guilt in a nonviolent society or subculture is as an inhibitor before aggression. Psychoanalytic theory as well as clinical experience provide ample evidence that aggressive feelings often do not find direct release (Freud, 1949, 1953; Miller, 1948; Geen, Stonner, & Kelley, 1974). The repression of aggressive impulses may take the form of misperception of the individual who performs an act that creates hostile feelings. Similarly, selective inattention may often obscure the actual source of frustration, thus making direct aggressive responses less likely. Such factors, together with the evidence that many individuals actually report tendencies to restrain the outward display of aggressive acts, support the notion that strong culturally induced negative sanctions (strong internalized superego controls) provide a barrier to the open expression of aggression. Whether such restraints have a deeper unconscious origin or are the product of consciously suppressed feelings, it is suggested that the reminder of previous feelings, as well as anticipation of future feelings, blocks the direct aggression. The most frequent function of guilt, therefore, is one of restraint before an aggressive act is performed. Clearly, however, aggressive acts do occur. What is the role of guilt under such circumstances?

Inasmuch as we have been particularly interested in the relationship between guilt and aggression, let us consider the possible causes for such a response to the induction of guilt. Presumably, most people can feel remorse without subsequent feelings of aggression. One has observed people, however, who when confronted with an antisocial behavior, escalate the animosity rather than show the expected restraint. Various distortions of interpersonal acts occur, for example, denial, attribution of evil intentions to the other party, and unrealistic justification of one's own behavior (Janis & Katz, 1959).

It is suggested here that if an aggressive action arouses guilt, it is necessary for the individual to handle this feeling of remorse for such behavior. Whereas for some people guilt is accepted and handled adequately by the functioning ego, for others guilt cannot be handled adequately as a controlling mechanism. It is inferred in the latter case (Bandura & Walters, 1959) that superego controls are ineffective as a result of early dependency conflicts wherein the absence of adequate reinforcement of dependency needs results in aggressive behavior whenever dependency is activated. Guilt over this aggression must be repressed because the need to overcome the feelings of dependency is so strong. In order to dissipate the guilt, further aggressive actions are committed, presumably meant to undo the earlier action but developing into a continuous pattern of aggressive action and aggressive reaction. Thus, an "aggressive personality," characterized by aggressive actions, remorseful feelings, and aggressive reactions, emerges where internal superego controls do not function as inhibitory mechanisms. For these people, particularly, appeals to social conscience or human dignity will be singularly ineffective in restraining further aggressive behavior because the guilt aroused will trigger a further aggressive response.

Berkowitz and Holmes (1960) noted that some people with relatively strong predispositions to aggressive behavior may actively display inordinately intense hostility on one occasion and then only fairly weak aggression soon afterward, perhaps because their first hostile responses had provoked anxiety and/or guilt (Hokanson, 1961). Once an aggressive act has been performed, one frequently observes a marked tendency toward the inhibition of further aggressive acts. Furthermore, such inhibition need not be solely a response to external restraint or punishment.

For example, if one examines the nature of student unrest and campus disturbances so prevalent in the late 1960s, it is interesting to note that a relatively calm atmosphere currently prevails. It may be that the inhibitions against the expression of aggression were overcome for many students by the emergence of a new social norm and press for activity and peer-group affiliation. Following these outbursts, however, internal restraints against further displays of aggression took precedence as salient and controlling factors over these external pressures. Further violence would have necessitated even more powerful social pressure to overcome the restrictions of conscience experienced and reported by many students as a function of having participated in the first wave of violence. Thus internal controls, overcome at one point by social forces, are reactivated and serve to block the continued display of aggressive actions.

It may be postulated that when the internalization of negative sanctions is not strong enough to inhibit aggression in the first place, the expression of aggression may occur but will not develop into a pattern or style because of the guilt that ensues once the act has been performed. In such cases, the perception of the aggressive act has aroused sufficient guilt so as to activate the internal control against further expression at that time. Whereas individuals who are more prone to overriding superego sanctions would not be expected to engage in any such actions, these individuals can be engaged but suffer ensuing superego sanctions which inhibit immediate repeated aggression. In this instance, the congruence between the perception of one's act with the basic predispositional tendency strengthens the already-existing prohibitions against aggression. These individuals will be susceptible to group pressure again when the guilt aroused by the specific act has dissipated.

INSTRUMENTAL RESPONSES

It has been shown that the experience of any secondary motivator could lead to a variety of instrumental responses. For example, anxiety, frustration, or guilt can lead to aggression, but any one of these may also lead to affiliation or dependency. And furthermore, any one can lead to greater responsiveness and productivity. What are the determinants of a choice of a particular response? How can we encourage pro-social versus antisocial responses? It is suggested that in part the choice of a particular response will reflect variations in the socialization process. In discussing the possible outcomes of the induction of guilt, we have emphasized the role of personality development in the link between guilt and aggression and between guilt and dependency. Certain role categories prescribe role-linked responses. Because of the current interest in the changing roles of women, let us consider sex as an example of a category which seems to be tied to the choice of a response.

Aggression and Sex Roles

In the casual observation of parents and young children it can be seen that parents modify their expectations of social behavior as a function of the sex of the young child. We have all heard it said in praise of some little boy "He's all boy!" or in praise of some little girl "She's all girl!" Whereas there is growing interest in equal treatment under the law, equal opportunities and unisex clothing, the pattern persists of a "man's man" who goes off to war and drinks with the boys while the "real" girl remains at home pregnant with his child hoping that he will remain true to her. The relationship between the characters in the rock musical *Hair* is not that far from that of Penelope and Ulysses.

Nevertheless, much attention has been focussed on the possibility that role relationships between men and women are not biologically based but reflect differences in cultural patterning. The now classic studies by Margaret Mead of sex and temperament in New Guinea (1935) led her to conclude that the polarity of the aggressive male and the passive female did not reflect an innate dimension, but rather an adaptation to the needs of a particular culture.

There has been very little experimental evidence relevant to the effects of cultural learning on role patterning. The studies tend to support one's suspicion that males are taught to be aggressive and females passive and dependent. A study by Hilton and Singer (1972) illustrates this point. In their research, they conceptualized the problem in terms of Berscheid's (1968) suggestion that an act of aggression produces a social situation which calls for some further action from one of the participants, either (1) justification of the aggression through further hostility and/or compensation by the aggressor or (2) retaliation by the victim. The aggressor's justification of his initial hostility through further aggression increases the probability of the victim being harmed again. It is clearly beneficial, from the victim's point of view, to take steps to have equity restored before the aggressor is able to justify his aggression. The victim's retaliation can be considered, then, an attempt to "master the environment" by seizing control of an inequitable situation which demands a next move.

Locus of control (Rotter, 1966) is a personality dimension related to an individual's attempt to "master the environment." The construct extends from Internals (individuals who believe that they control fate) to Externals (individuals who believe that they are controlled by fate). Studies have shown that in civil rights activism (Gore & Rotter, 1963), conformity (Crowne & Liverant, 1963), and attitude change (Phares, 1965), Internals are likely to attempt to improve their environment and are apt to be effective agents of such changes. It was, therefore, hypothesized that Internal subjects would be more likely to retaliate than External subjects. Although sex differences in locus of control have not always been significant, in view of our culture's sex-role standards—particularly the stereotype of the passive female—it seems likely that males would show a greater tendency to "master the environment." Consequently, it was hypothesized by Hilton and Singer that male subjects would be more likely to retaliate than female subjects. The subjects were the three eighth-grade sections of a New York City private school. Forty-three subjects, 24 boys and 19 girls, participated in the experiment. Thirty-two subjects were of white, upper-income and middle-income families, and 11 were of nonwhite, lower-income and middle-income families. Boys and girls were equally distributed in the two socioeconomic groups.

A series of ten scenarios, depicting a central character in a possible retaliatory position against a sibling or a peer who had aggressed against them, was constructed. The scenarios were prepared in booklet form with male characters for boys and with female characters for girls. The subject's task was to choose one of the two offered story-endings, either a retaliatory or a nonretaliatory ending. A retaliation score, equal to the total number of retaliatory endings chosen, was computed for each subject.

Although the stories represented a range of possible initial aggressions and retaliations from minor insults and rejections to direct physical attack, for only one of the ten scenarios was the proportion of girls retaliating greater than the proportion of boys retaliating. The obtained sex differences are consistent with previous studies in differences in aggression and with studies in child-training practices in sex typing of aggression (Sears, Maccoby & Levin, 1957; Kohn, 1959). Boys are permitted—even encouraged—to express aggression in response to provocation, while girls are required to inhibit such behavior.

Although suggestive, the results did not exclude the possibility, however, that girls might retaliate in ways which were not overt, since no systematic attempt had been made to sample the forms of retaliation. Feshbach (1970) had proposed that females do not retaliate less than males but rather that females

TABLE 3-1
Sample Stories—Scenarios for Aggressive Response

FORM OF AGGRESSION IS OVERT-PHYSICAL:

It was a beautiful day and Johnny decided to ride his bicycle in the park. While he was riding he saw Billy, who lived on his block, playing ball. As he rode past, Billy threw a ball at Johnny and hit him in the back. Johnny was mad but kept on riding. The next day, Johnny went to the grocery store for his mother. He saw a wallet on the ground and he looked inside of it. He found an identification card with Billy's name on it. Johnny remembered how Billy had hurt him the day before. Johnny didn't know whether he should return the wallet to Billy or whether he should throw the wallet in the garbage to make sure that Billy wouldn't get it back. Johnny finally decided to . . .

   I. return the wallet to Billy.
   II. throw the wallet in the garbage.

WHY DID YOU CHOOSE THAT STORY ENDING?

(a) Because Johnny should return the wallet because Billy would feel bad.
(b) Because Johnny was afraid that Billy would get even with him if he found out that Johnny threw his wallet away.
(c) Because Billy deserved some punishment.
(d) Because Billy did something wrong to Johnny doesn't mean that Johnny has to do something bad to Billy.
(e) Because he would feel bad about throwing Billy's wallet in the garbage.
(f) Other.

FORM OF AGGRESSION IS REJECTION:

It was the first day of school. Dick was talking with his friends when he saw a boy come in whom he had seen at the beach. This was the boy's first year at the school. Dick. . . .

   I. calls him over and introduces him to his friends.
   II. pretends not to see him and continues talking with his friends.

WHY DID YOU CHOOSE THAT STORY ENDING?

(a) Because he would feel badly if the boy would be lonely.
(b) Because he hoped that someone would do the same for him sometime.
(c) Because he would feel embarrassed to interrupt the group's discussion.
(d) Because the boy would know that it was because of Dick that he hadn't met the other boys.
(e) Because he liked the group the way it was.
(f) Other.

choose to retaliate in a covert fashion, especially through rejection. In constrast, McIntyre (1972) in a study with preschoolers, found that boys are more physically aggressive than girls, whereas for girls the aggression is primarily verbal. For both sexes, however, the form was direct. Preschoolers may not have learned the ways in which to express indirect aggression. Accordingly, Hilton, Paul, Wajsman, Herscovic, Loew, and Chaplan (1974) decided to study this issue more fully. Additional stories were written so that the retaliations would fall into five categories—physical overt, physical covert, verbal overt, verbal covert, and rejection. Examples of the stories appear in Table 3-1. In addition, the stories were ranked by a panel of independent judges as to the severity of their consequences.

The subjects were all eighth graders at a New York City private school. Twenty-six boys and 26 girls participated in the study. This study took place two years after the original one. As before, however, males retaliated more than females. To 11 out of 17 stories, males gave more retaliatory responses. To only 4 of the 17 stories, females gave more retaliatory responses. In addition, for the four stories where females retaliated more, the consequences were relatively less serious. The four stories for which females retaliated more did not cluster in any single category; there was one in each category except verbal overt.

It would seem, therefore, that there is good evidence to believe that males really do learn to retaliate more. Contrary to the popular expectation that females will retaliate when the means are indirect or covert, males show a greater tendency to retaliate regardless of the mode of the response. Further investigation is necessary to clarify whether cultural prohibitions against the expression of aggression in females not only inhibit responses of a direct and overt nature but also inhibit those responses which lead to mastering or coping with the environment.

Another study by Kaleta (1973) demonstrates that the perceived femininity of the victim will affect aggression intensity. Previous studies have shown that males not only aggress more but are more likely to be aggressed against than females. These findings have been explained on the basis of gender stereotypes. We all are taught at a very early age that girls are more fragile and delicate than boys and therefore should be treated with greater care. In contrast to this, boys are depicted as being tougher than females and able to "take more." To follow this train of thought further, Kaleta reasoned that women who appeared less feminine would receive more aggression than feminine women. Femininity was varied by manipulating the victim's (confederate's) appearance and behavior, with femininity defined in terms of this society's traditional women's roles. Three moderately attractive women served as confederates. When dressed in a feminine fashion, they appeared neat and fastidious. They wore some make-up, and their dresses were colorful and frilly. When dressing in an unfeminine fashion, the confederates were not very neat; they wore no make-up, and their dresses were plain and loose-fitting.

Among the characteristics traditionally associated with femininity are sympathy, empathy, passivity, lack of assertiveness, and lack of confidence. These were the characteristics varied in the behavioral manipulations. There were four opportunities for the confederates to act feminine or unfeminine. When acting feminine the confederates were not assertive, lacked confidence in their ability, and showed sympathy when given an opportunity to do so. When acting unfeminine the women were assertive, confident, and did not show any sympathy when they could have. While the confederates behaved confidently and assertively in the unfeminine condition, they were not rude, obnoxious, or aggressive.

The aggression was measured by means of the Buss Aggression Machine (Buss, 1961). The subjects were to teach a concept to the confederate, shocking her whenever she gave a wrong response. They were told to press one of 10 shock buttons to let the confederate know that she was wrong; these buttons were graded in intensity, with 1 being the last intense shock and 10 the most intense. Having sampled the shock, they knew that shock 5 was clearly painful. The confederate was not actually receiving the shock, but she was recording the shock intensities.

The results showed that the least shock was given when the confederates were feminine in both appearance and behavior, and the most shock was given when the confederates were unfeminine in both appearance and behavior.

The other two conditions, feminine appearance–unfeminine behavior, and unfeminine appearance–feminine behavior, produced shock intensities between those found in the extreme conditions.

These two studies tend to support the picture of the unretaliatory female painstakingly appearing to be feminine in order to avoid aggression. What about the new breed of woman, however? How will her changing attitudes towards her role affect her predispositions to aggression? A paper by Hymer and Atkins (1973) directs itself to this question. In addressing this issue, they observed that two dominant views have influenced theoretical and empirical work on sex differences. Freud (1933) accounted for his male activity–female passivity thesis primarily in terms of genetic and constitutional differences between the sexes. The learning viewpoint is represented by the cultural stereotyping theories of Bandura, Buss, and Berkowitz (Feshbach, 1970). These theorists maintain that boys and girls learn to use different types of aggression as a result of socialization experiences that channel the sexes into socially appropriate roles. Boys learn that it is acceptable and appropriate to use physical aggression. Girls learn to inhibit physical aggression and rely on more "indirect" forms of aggression, sometimes in the form of depression.

Becker (1964) notes, however, that resocialization forces in adulthood can result in new attitudes and behaviors that overturn assimilations made during childhood socialization. The Women's Liberation Movement has been successful in changing sex-typed attitudes regarding traits, occupations, and abilities deemed appropriate for women. Whether attitudes toward such a social movement can contribute to changes in sex-typed behaviors (such as aggression) is at issue. A Women's Liberation Movement Scale (Hymer, Berman, Galper, & Fekete, 1972) was developed to compare women strongly adhering to the goals and beliefs of the Movement with women subscribing to more traditional beliefs regarding women's roles. Further, Hymer and Atkins assumed that fewer sex-typed aggressive responses would be obtained from women subscribing to the Movement as revealed in a forced choice measure to aggressive content scenarios. Thus, Hymer and Atkins predicted that high female scorers on the Women's Liberation Movement Scale will show higher frequencies of direct (verbal, institutionalized, physical) aggressive responses to scenarios than low scorers. Second, low scorers would be expected to show higher frequencies of indirect (fantasy, depression, displaced) aggressive responses than high scorers.

The original subject pool ($N=79$) consisted of three female undergraduate groups and a group of noncollege office workers. Twenty-six scenarios were developed to assess the modes of aggression used by women subscribing to different views regarding the Women's Liberation Movement. Each scenario involved an interpersonal aggressive content story in which subjects were given the opportunity to retaliate against the scenario aggressor by responding to one of six possible fixed alternative aggressive choices. Three choices involved direct aggression (physical, verbal, institutionalized), which is operationally defined to include all aggression in which the subject herself (or another) directs harm against the object of aggression. Institutionalized aggression is a mode in which the subject uses an authority figure (police, parents, and the like) to do harm to the object of aggression. The three indirect aggression choices (fantasy, depression, displaced) involve aggression in which harm does not accrue to the object of aggression but rather to other sources (for example, aggression directed against the self, like depression). This direct–indirect dimension falls roughly into the traditional masculine (direct)–feminine (indirect) aggression stereotypes. See Table 3-2 for examples of the scenarios.

TABLE 3-2
Sample Scenarios—Alternative Modes of Responses

1. You and your next-door neighbor have known each other on a "hello-how-are-you" basis for the past five years. Lately, your neighbor is getting a little irritated about your weeping willow tree that is overflowing into her yard. You tell her that there is nothing that you can do about it, but she threatens to take action if you leave things the way they are. Next day, while hanging out your clothes, you notice that half the branches have been cut.

Check *one*.

	Very Weak	Weak	Neutral or Undecided	Strong	Very Strong
I would insult my neighbor.	——	1	2	3	4	5
I would take my anger out on the kids.	——	1	2	3	4	5
I would slap her.	——	1	2	3	4	5
I would imagine all the possible ways of getting back at her.	——	1	2	3	4	5
I would call the police and have them take action against her.	——	1	2	3	4	5
There would be nothing I could do.	——	1	2	3	4	5

2. You and a school acquaintance are both applying for the same prestigious position in a large company. Both of you have excellent qualifications and credentials, and have an equal chance of getting the job. This company also insists that their employees have the highest moral standards. Your friend starts a rumor about your personal life that has now reached the upper echelons of the company. Coincidentally, shortly thereafter, she is given the job.

Check *one*.

	Very Weak	Weak	Neutral or Undecided	Strong	Very Strong
There would be nothing I could do.	——	1	2	3	4	5
I wouldn't do anything.	——	1	2	3	4	5

TABLE 3-2 (*Continued*)

I would make an appointment with the president to plead my case against the girl.	——	1	2	3	4	5
I would insult her.	——	1	2	3	4	5
I would imagine all the possible ways of getting back at her.	——	1	2	3	4	5
I would slap her.	——	1	2	3	4	5
I would take my anger out on the kids.	——	1	2	3	4	5

Significant differences between the means of high-scoring and low-scoring subjects in four modes of aggression were found. High scorers showed more verbal aggressive responses than low scorers. A significant difference between the means of high-scoring and low-scoring subjects was obtained for the depression mode. Differences between high-scoring and low-scoring subjects on fantasy aggression were also significant in the predicted direction. The displaced-aggression category yielded results, but in the opposite direction from that predicted; that is, high-scoring subjects showed more displaced aggressive responses than low-scoring subjects. High scorers did not, however, show more physical aggression than low scorers, and there were no significant differences in the extent to which institutionalized others were called upon to do harm to the aggressor. These results suggest that sex-typing of aggressive responses no longer uniformly exists among females. Adult socialization forces, such as the Women's Liberation Movement, seem to provide alternative values and goals that often run counter to those acquired during childhood socialization.

Drawing upon prior research (e.g. Hilton and Singer, cited earlier) there is good reason to assume that physical aggression is a mode of aggression used by males significantly more frequently than females. It is possible that females may not find physical aggression as productive, but the socialization issue is why they do not. Although the same test was not given to a comparable male population, male scoring patterns were assumed based on existing research.

That physical aggression did not yield significant results may be explained in terms of a cultural lag theory in which attitudes become acceptable far in advance of their behavioral correlates. Although women express favorable attitudes toward the Movement, corresponding changes in sex-typed behaviors such as aggression are often slower in surfacing. The "institutionalized" category, although operationally defined as a direct form of aggression, is somewhat ambiguous, since in the traditional family the woman often threatens the child with punishment from the father (an authority figure). It is possible that institutionalized aggression may indeed be a more "female-oriented" aggression mode.

One reason for the consistent findings in sex differences in past studies may be that the great majority of these were carried out on children still undergoing childhood socialization by parents transmitting traditional sex-typed attitudes and behaviors. It now appears that adult socialization forces, such as Women's Liberation, offer alternative models de-emphasizing sex-typing. The probability that males, when anxious, frustrated, or guilty, will respond with greater aggression than females appears to be, at least in part, learned. These illustrations were intended to demonstrate that sex-role stereotyping can influence the likelihood of an aggressive response. Naturally, other characteristics will influence the likelihood of a choice of instrumental response. Another such illustration is the relationship between dependency and birth order.

Dependency and Birth Order

Since the publication in 1959 of Schachter's *Psychology of Affiliation* there has been considerable interest in birth order as a predictive variable. With some minor exceptions the general trend of the data is as follows:

> First-borns affiliate more when anxious (Schachter, 1959).
>
> First-borns are more susceptible to suggestion, particularly when anxious (Staples & Walters, 1961).
>
> First-borns have higher need achievement (Sampson, 1962).
>
> First-borns choose more popular people (Schachter, 1963).
>
> First-borns are overrepresented in graduate schools and in colleges—although there do not seem to be any consistent ordinal position differences in intelligence (Schachter, 1963).

As Hilton (1967) pointed out, however intriguing as these findings are in and of themselves, ordinal position is not a psychologically meaningful concept. It was scientifically challenging, therefore, to try to determine some causal factor which might account for this diversity of first-born linked behaviors, some child-rearing patterns responsible for these ordinal position effects. The emphasis must no longer be merely with the "what" of ordinal position differences but with the "why" of these differences.

Common sense would suggest that the first birth is an event of profound psychological importance for the parents and that later births are events of considerably less moment. One expects, therefore, that the parents would be considerably more involved with their first-born child. The study by Hilton (1967) involved the systematic observation of mother-child interaction in either one of two independent experimental conditions, a condition in which a child failed badly at a presumed test of creativity and independent thinking (failure) and a condition in which the child did beautifully on this test (success). Although the major purpose of the experiment was to understand differences in mother treatment of first-born and later-born children, some only children were included as a separate condition to illuminate the possible effects of a second child on the behavior of the mother and the first-born child. The children were approximately four years old; half were boys, half girls; 20 were only children, 20 first-borns, and 20 later-borns. The first-borns and later-borns were from two-child families with siblings of the same sex to control for the mounting evidence that one behaves less like a later-born if one is born second but still the first of his own sex.

Throughout the entire period of the experiment the mother's behavior was coded and evaluated for indications of interference, extremity of reaction, and inconsistency. The child's behavior was coded and evaluated for indications of dependency. The results indicated that first-born and only children were significantly more dependent than later-borns and that mothers with their first-borns were significantly different from mothers with their later-borns:

1. They were more likely to interfere with or direct their children's activities.
2. They were more extreme in their affect towards the children.
3. They were more inconsistent in their attitudes towards the children.

On theoretical grounds, interference or inconsistency could both lead to dependency, as they both undermine the child's opportunities to develop reference points for internal evaluation. Festinger (1954) has pointed out that when there are no objective or internal standards to use as reference points, one is more likely to be influenced by the attitudes of others. When the parent is inconsistent, there is no stable guideline for internalizing the correct course of action. The child cannot predict outcomes on the basis of past performance and must continue to ask for evaluation because the same behavior will elicit a varying response.

The effect of excessive interference is to create standards that the child must fulfill. He does not set his own goals, but rather achieves the ones set for him. He learns to ask for praise for his activities, and the evidence on excessive support is that if he achieves he gets it. Because he does not set his own goals, he cannot determine whether they have been adequately met.

His satisfaction must come from pleasing others.

The first-born therefore becomes more socially dependent because his mother treats him in ways which lead to the development of dependency. It is not one's birth order as such which predisposes one to dependency, but rather that in a particular birth order one is more likely to be exposed to the kinds of attitudes which create dependency.

These two examples were intended to show that the choice of a particular response—either aggression or dependency—can be influenced by the socialization processes. Similarly, the translation of these responses into social behaviors is affected by the social milieu.

SOCIAL GOALS

The analysis of such instrumental responses as aggression and dependency requires further study into more broadly based social goals. We have already indicated various ways in which acquired social drives or motives may have both energizing and directive properties which can be manifested in specific and discrete acts of behavior. Thus, frustrating, anxiety-producing, and guilt-arousing situations may induce an aggressive response, just as inadequate fulfillment of the dependency motive may elicit nurturant counterresponses or aggression. Can we extend this analysis to an understanding of social motivation where, for example, nurturance and achievement have developed from simpler forms into more complex forms of social organization? Are the primary and secondary sources of motivation evident in these more intricate patterns of interaction?

Nurturance

If we examine the work on nurturance, or attachment behavior, it is obvious that the means by which we achieve affiliative and supportive interpersonal contact varies from the more traditional dyadic situation to the current "communal" structure among youth today. It is perhaps less obvious that the content of the social motivation, that is, nurturance, remains the constant while the forms for satisfying this motive have varied. If we turn to the primate literature for "our beginnings," we find that the basic dilemma is portrayed most graphically. The infant's search for nurturance originates with the mother and later transfers to the peer group. Similarly, as we shall see, this transition is mirrored in human social relationships as the more traditional family arrangement is challenged as a source of nurturance by the peer culture, sometimes a deviant subculture or "gang."

The primate literature has given us insight into the varying forms that nurturance-seeking may take. In the growth of the young primate, the mother comes to play a central and pivotal role in the life of the youngster. "She is sought when danger threatens, and her presence is a source of comfort and emotional security. It is these effects above all that characterize the filial attachment" (Mason, 1964, p. 283). As described earlier in this chapter, artificial mothers were provided for young monkeys in an experiment in which some monkeys were exposed to one model constructed of wire mesh (wire mother) and some to one made of sponge rubber and covered in terry cloth (cloth mother). It was reasoned that if affection (which legitimately may be classed as a motive) derived from the feeding or caretaking function alone, then the type of mother would be irrelevant. In other words, according to this notion, the monkeys ought to have clung to whichever mother fed them and perhaps ought to have shown affection for that mother. That the nursing function did not direct the monkeys' clinging and affection not only discredited the notion that nursing was central but pointed to a strong finding. Clinging to the cozier cloth mother reflected that contact comfort was a source of emotional security. Not only was the cloth surrogate mother an effective incentive for lever-pressing and for the solution of simple, mechanical puzzles (Mason, 1964), but this cloth mother was sought when the monkey was frightened or upset.

The experimental demonstration of this phenomenon is particularly significant in demonstrating the importance of filial attachment in the formation of early social bonds. However, the development of later social attachments seems to require more elements in the process. As Brown (1965) points out, "terry cloth will release clinging and induce affection and security but it is not enough to produce a normal monkey." After three to five years of contact with a cloth mother but deprived of contact with peers, these monkeys displayed socially and sexually aberrant behavior. By contrast, monkeys reared with a cloth mother as well as active age-mates showed a gradual social and psychological development that eventually paralleled that of the normal group.

The opportunity to have contact with peers seems crucial enough to the development of such primates that the deprivation of such contact may actually result in conditions somewhat analogous to those observed among monkeys raised in total isolation. At this juncture, we must stop and examine the impact of these findings. Clearly, filial attachments are crucial, but so are peer attachments. And if we are subject to similar conditions of growth, where does this line begin and end for humans?

Perhaps a most telling and fascinating example of the relative importance given to the family as opposed to the peer culture is seen in still another animal study, the story of Patty Cake. A baby gorilla, Patty Cake, was the subject of much debate when a controversy arose over whether this gorilla should be housed in the Central Park Zoo or in the Bronx Zoo in New

York City (*New York Times,* June 6, 1973). Having been reared in continuous contact with her parents in the Central Park Zoo for the first six months of her life, the baby gorilla was removed to the Bronx Zoo's animal hospital for recuperation following an accident in which her arm was broken. Following her recovery, the controversy centered on whether to return Patty Cake to her parents or to allow her to remain in the company of other young gorillas at the Bronx Zoo. In determining to return her to her parents, it was stated that "early separation of young primates from their mothers results in serious and long-lasting deficits in the social orientation of the offspring." Apparently the foundation that filial attachment provides for normal adult functioning was considered essential for Patty Cake.

The conflict that is posed for man by seeking nurturant and affiliative responses in the family organization as opposed to varieties of peer-group formations has been described by a number of writers. Riesman's (1950) study of the changing American character points to the transitions that our culture has experienced in its evolution of social character and concomitant social changes. Drawing upon a definition of character proposed by Fromm (1944), he quotes:

> In order that any society may function well, its members must acquire the kind of character which makes them want to act in the way they have to act as members of the society or of a special class within it. They have to desire what objectively is necessary for them to do. Outer force is replaced by inner compulsion, and by the particular kind of human energy which is channeled into character traits. (p. 382)

Riesman's analysis of these character types includes three basic distinctions. The "tradition-directed" type is reflected in a society in which early life experiences encourage conformity to tradition; in the "inner-directed" type, social character is insured by "their tendency to acquire early in life an internalized set of goals." Of more relevance to our concerns, however, is the third distinction drawn, namely, the "other-directed" type. Tracing the development of these "character types" in relation to changes in family patterns and in socialization practices, Riesman draws attention to the role of peer-group pressures in shaping and reinforcing personality. As he indicates,

> What is common to all the other-directed people is that their contemporaries are the source of direction for the individual. . . . this source is of course internalized in the sense that dependence on it for guidance in life is implanted early. The goals toward which the other-directed person strives shift with that guidance: it is only the process of striving itself and the process of paying close attention to the signals from others that remain unaltered throughout life. (Riesman, 1950, p. 37)

What is the relationship between peer-group orientation, other-directedness, and nurturance? Although it would be reductionistic to claim that the striving for nurturance may account for the many types of peer-group activities observed today, it is important to examine the links that actually may be found. Let us focus upon communal living, for example. It has been observed that the emergence and growing emphasis on communal living may, indeed, represent efforts to change existing patterns in order to combat a pervasive sense of personal alienation (Keniston, 1965). As Erikson has pointed out, the "identity crisis" may well be a necessary developmental stage in the life cycle "when each youth must forge for himself some central perspective and direction, some working unity" (Erickson, 1958). It is perhaps most characteristic of our present-day society that the practices and traditions of the time-honored family arrangements are no longer considered to be as relevant or instrumental in meeting the needs of youth. In order to meet this challenge, various social arrangements have been established that attempt to abolish the hierarchical structure inherent in the traditional family organization. One of the earliest modern utopias to be outlined according to principles derived from Skinnerian learning theory was *Walden Two* (Skinner, 1948). Designed to apply a scientific technology to human conduct, Walden Two has since been used as a model for such communes as Twin Oaks (Kinkade, 1972) where efforts are made at equalization of labor and at a decision-making procedure that is noncompetitive. Similarly, Bettelheim's *Children of the Dream* (1969) describes communal child-rearing among second- and third-generation children of the Israeli kubbutzim. Here the explicit purpose of the child-rearing practices was to reduce the extremely close family ties that had been present in prior generations.

If a central purpose served by such peer affiliations is the development of personal identity, why the strong emphasis on a group milieu for the enhancement of individual growth (Steiner, 1974)? How do you account for the interest in encounter groups, for example (Schutz, 1967)? There seems to be strong motivation for the individual to establish a sense of self through relating to other people, primarily peers. Perhaps in the writings of Fromm there is a clear statement that helps account for this tendency, for, as he notes, in his quest for individuality man strives "to transcend his separateness and relate himself to his world" (Landis & Tauber, 1971). In *The Art of Loving,* Fromm states:

> This awareness of himself as a separate entity, the awareness of his own short life span, of the fact that without his will he is born and against his will he dies, that he will die before those whom he loves, or they before him, the awareness of his aloneness and separateness, of his helplessness before the forces of nature and of society, all this make his separate, disunited existence an unbearable prison. He would become insane could he not liberate himself from his prison and reach out, unite himself in some form or other with men, with the world outside. . . . the deepest need of man, then, is the need to overcome his separateness, to leave the prison of his aloneness. (Fromm, 1956, p. 8)

It would appear, then, that the motive for group involvement, whether it be a product of "other-directedness" or the affiliative tendency described earlier in this chapter, is the manifestation of a need for support, direction, and contact which can be viewed as different facets of nurturance. To seek a social setting in which to "find oneself" or "to encounter" is merely a statement of our interdependency on one another. Although empirical data are not available to unequivocally support the idea that this can be traced ultimately to inadequate fulfillment of the dependency motive in early parent-child relations, the field is open for such speculation. Perhaps the controversy over Patty Cake can be extended to her relatives as well!

Achievement

The motive to attain standards of excellence has been studied as "the achievement motive" by McClelland (1953, 1961), Atkinson (1958), Sorrentino (1973), and other researchers. Drawing upon the Thematic Apperception Test (TAT), a projective technique consisting of twenty pictures wherein a respondent describes what he feels is "being thought" and "being felt" in each scene, they developed a means of scoring individual need states. Since the respondent is believed to be reacting to the picture out of his own motivational substance, the researchers began by investigating traces of hunger in stories. Groups of male subjects were deprived of food for varying periods of time and then TAT stories were scored for such categories as "need for food." Not only did the mean scores for "need for food" increase as the period of deprivation increased, but the researchers were usually able to make a correct assessment of the group to which a particular subject belonged. Judging from the use of the TAT, "hunger is detectable in the stream of imagination as well as in the blood stream" (Brown, 1965, p. 429).

To apply this approach to the study of achievement required more elaborate analysis, however. Achievement states cannot be as readily manipulated as can hunger states. A system for coding categories of levels of achievement imagery has been developed which the researchers attempted to validate against a number of important criteria. For example, people who have high scores perform better in terms of long-term occupational and academic goals and also do better on tasks where the objective is to satisfy some standard of excellence and not just to accomplish some uninteresting routine.

> High scorers have better memory for tasks they have left incompleted, and so presumably are more motivated to finish something once begun (Atkinson, 1955); they are more active in college and in their communities (McClelland, 1961); when asked to choose working partners they prefer successful strangers to unsuccessful friends (French, 1956); and they are more prone to volunteer as subjects for psychological experiments (Burdick, 1955). The measure appears to be drawing upon something that corresponds with our intuitive understanding of achievement motivation. (Brown, 1965, p. 441)

What do we know of the origins of the achievement motive? Are there any connections between the development of this motivational state and dependency and aggression? In an effort to study the prevalence of this motive cross-culturally, McClelland and Friedman (1952) scored popular folktales as reflective of the culture's ethos and socialization practices. In their analysis of eight cultures, they found a significant positive relationship between the amount of stress on early independence training and the level of achievement motivation in the folktales. In a far-reaching cross-cultural study involving 23 countries, McClelland (1961) sought to establish a link between two large-scale social movements. Drawing upon Weber's *Protestant Ethic and the Spirit of Capitalism* (1904), he saw in the Protestant ethic of work and the acquisition of good deeds for salvation the underpinnings for the entrepreneurial drive. McClelland reasoned that the Protestant ideology should be manifested in parental stress on achievement, self-reliance, and self-denial. Since such stress and training varies from country to country, variations were also to be found in indicators of economic development. Using as an economic indicator the amount of electricity produced in kilowatt-hours per capita, the level of achievement motivation (as analyzed through themes in stories) was found to be predictive of an increase in the rate of economic growth when the period of 1929 is compared to 1950.

It is not as clear, however, as to what dimensions of child rearing are related to achievement motivation, especially since early independence training did not show a consistent trend in all studies. If we examine other sources of data for clues to the origins of the achievement motive, a number of intriguing possibilities emerge. In an analysis of birth order, eminence, and higher education, Schachter (1963) reports that scholars "derive from a college population in which first-borns are in marked surplus." Stimulated by the apparent empirical observation that there is a preponderance of first-born or only children among samples of creative or eminent scholars, as listed in such sources as *American Men of Science and Who's Who,* he undertook to document the consistency of this observation. In 1959 and in 1961, birth-order data were gathered on students enrolled in the introductory course in psychology at the University of Minnesota. The trend for these college students paralleled that found earlier by Cattell and Brinhall (1921), namely, that for every family size there is a significant overrepresentation of first-borns among those receiving higher education. That this trend appears to persist through time is supported by Schachter's further inquiries into the Columbia College population at Columbia University. In an examination of a 10% sample of all undergraduates who entered Columbia between 1943 and 1962, he discovered that there has been a steady predominance of first-borns at Columbia over the past 20 years.

How do we explain such trends? Certainly a number of possible explanations can be offered, but if we consider the data on birth order and dependency described earlier in this chapter do we not have an exciting possibility for integrating the work on achievement? If, as Schachter wonders, there is "something in the makeup of the first-born that drives or leads him to fame," is it not plausible that the link between birth order and the motivation to achieve lies in the dependency needs which are inconsistently met in the first-born? As Hilton (1967) has reported, observations of mother–child interactions have revealed that first-borns show greater dependency strivings than do later-borns. If inadequate fulfillment of dependency needs contributes to greater affiliative tendencies, greater willingness to volunteer, and greater nurturance seeking, might it not also be likely that dependency needs play a major role in achievement orientation? Thus, first-borns may well be more prone to aggressively seek out educational routes to eventual positions of eminence and social power. In such a conceptualization, the motive of power and prestige is not the energizing force but rather the derivative or outcome of dependency–achievement strivings. In this way, frustration of dependency needs may well be a central underpinning for the motivation to attain excellence and to achieve power and praise.

But this may be only part of the story! The recent concern with women's roles and cultural stereotyping has brought to our attention that much of the work on achievement motivation has concentrated on males, with the strong likelihood that there may be some glaring differences. As Horner (1968, 1969) has indicated, "The result of all this research is an impressive and a theoretically consistent body of data about the achievement motive—in men." Because the results on females, when included, were contradictory or at least confusing, she undertook to explore the basis for sex differences in achievement motivation. As a starting point, she considered a number of factors. Included were consistent empirical findings indicating higher test-anxiety scores for women, interpreted by many as an outgrowth of the defiance of "conventional standards" for the girl who aspires to achieve. Further, not only has Margaret Mead (1967) suggested that "intense intellectual striving can be viewed as competitively aggressive behavior," but Freud (1965) considered the essence of femininity to be the repression of aggressiveness and intellectualism.

Thus, as Horner (1968) notes, intellectual achievement is equated for women with loss of femininity and competitiveness. She posited, therefore, that for women the desire to achieve is often contaminated by the "motive to avoid success," which she claims reflects a "stable disposition within the person, acquired early in life along with other sex-role standards." She administered the standard TAT achievement motivation measures to a sample of 90 women and 88 men, all undergraduates at the University of Michigan. Each respondent was asked to tell a story based on the following clue:

"After first-term finals, John (Ann) finds himself (herself) at the top of his (her) medical-school class." The women wrote about Anne, the men about John (Horner, 1968).

The stories were scored for "motive to avoid success" if any of the imagery elicited expressed concern about doing well. Such imagery tended to fall into three categories. The most frequent Ann story "reflected strong fears of social rejection as a result of success," with the women displaying anxiety about becoming unpopular and lonely. In the second category, the women expressed less concern over social disapproval but they did express guilt and despair over success and their femininity. Finally, in the third category the women used mechanisms of denial and distortion to avoid confronting the possibility that a woman could be so successful.

Over 65% of the women told stories that fell into one or another of these three categories, as opposed to less than 10% of the men who displayed any such motive to avoid success. In further extensions of her research on sex differences, Horner found that significantly more males performed more successfully in competitive situations involving verbal and arithmetic tests. Seventy-seven percent of the women who feared success did better when alone (and where less anxiety was aroused) than in a competitive situation.

It seems clear that while there is support for the motive to achieve, the fulfillment of one's strivings may depend on a number of complex factors. The influences of socialization practices that make one motive acceptable for men and threatening for women cannot be underestimated. To view one's sex as a predictor of performance and achievement may be less a function of actual ability than what social and cultural factors have permitted us to learn. Or better still, it may be a function of what we are permitted to reveal of what we truly know!

We no longer feel that men and women are born with innately different social goals. Earlier psychologists, such as Brown (1956), DeLucia (1963), and Hartup and Zook (1960), accepted the traditional sex roles of this society as given and regarded children whose behavior did not conform to the cultural norms as immature or deviant. Implicit in their discussions of sex-role development were the assumptions that it is psychologically healthier for children to develop stereotyped sex roles, that there is one correct pattern of sex roles, and that children learn their sex roles in a relatively benign social context. These assumptions were accepted in spite of the fact that "cross-sex" identification in girls had been found to be more beneficial than a "feminine" identification on many dimensions. For instance, Maccoby (1966) found that a "masculine" identification in girls is consistently related to high IQ and creativity; Milton (1957) found that a "cross-sex" identification was related to superior problem-solving ability in girls; and many psychologists such as Broverman, Broverman, Clarkson, Rosenkrantz, and Vogel (1970) and Heilbrun (1962) have related "masculine" interests in females to positive psychological adjustment.

In recent years, it has been recognized that sex-typing stunts the goals and expectations of both women and men. Rigid sex roles serve the needs of a masculine-oriented culture by giving the men status and power. The results of psychological research strongly support this viewpoint. Brown (1956) and Kohlberg (1966) have both shown that boys clearly prefer "masculine" toys and activities more than girls prefer "feminine" toys and activities. Wylie (1963) found that junior high school children consistently underrated the scholastic abilities of girls. S. Smith (1939) and Baldwin, Baldwin, Hilton, and Lambert (1969) found that with increasing age, both girls and boys had a progressively better opinion of boys and a progressively poorer opinion of girls. Kohlberg (1966) concludes: "Although the extent to which power and status are sex-typed differs widely among cultures, whatever sex-typing does exist favors the male. A review of early gender stereotypes indicated that by age five to six, children award greater power, strength and competence (and consequently more status) to the male."

Sex-role stereotyping must be distinguished from individual preference (Taynor & Deaux, 1973). If a girl chooses to play with dolls, it does not necessarily mean that she has been trained to fit a sex-role stereotype. On the other hand, if all of the girls in a group choose dolls, none choose trucks, and many even comment when they see a "masculine" toy, "That's for my brother," it can be assumed that these children have incorporated the many overt and covert cues of the culture which dictate what is proper for girls. The possibilities for growth, intellectual and emotional development and achievement of children in such a sex-role stereotyping society must be more limited than in a culture where children have a greater range of choices and no opportunity is unavailable to them because of their sex. Selcer and Hilton (1972) undertook to investigate what causes these differential motivations. Specifically, three questions were investigated in the study:

1. Will children's preferences for activities vary as a function of the cultural stereotypes to which they are exposed?
2. Will children's perception of appropriate activities for females and males vary as a function of the cultural stereotypes to which they are exposed?
3. Is the degree of differences between females and males perceived by children a function of the cultural stereotypes to which they are exposed?

The subjects were 12 girls and 12 boys from a traditional culture, Orthodox Judaism, and 12 girls and 12 boys from a nontraditional culture. They ranged in age from 3 years 9 months to 5 years 6 months.

The values of both groups of children were supported by strong societal norms. The Orthodox Jewish tradition clearly favors males. Zborowski and Herzog (1952), anthropologists who intensively studied Orthodox Jewish family life, conclude: "Despite the recognition of interdependence between the man and the woman, the culture is clearly male-oriented." The traditional children attended an Orthodox Jewish primary school which differentiated male and female roles very overtly.

The children in the nontraditional group either attended a cooperative nursery with a nonauthoritarian, fairly unstructured orientation (10 girls and seven boys) and/or had mothers actively involved in the Women's Liberatoin Movement (seven girls and eight boys). Their parents shared a common set of values which included the idea that stereotyping of female and male roles harms women and men and the relationship between them.

Observation of the children indicated that those from a traditional culture played in a very sex-typed manner; the girls played in the kitchen corner and the boys played with tools and trucks. At the nontraditional schools, there were no kitchen corners or boys' side of the room. Boys and girls constantly played with each other, and it was very rare to see a group made up exclusively of boys or girls.

In a task where boys and girls were asked to select their favorite four toys out of a possible 24, where degree of masculinity and femininity had been assessed in a previous study (DeLucia, 1963), it was found that the toy preferences of the traditional boys and girls were significantly more stereotyped than the choices of children reared in a less traditional environment.

TABLE 3-3
Incomplete Stories

1. A child is seated on the floor with blocks. A woman and a man are seated on a couch in the background. The subject was told:
    a. Leslie is playing and would like someone to play with her. Who does she ask to come and play?
    b. This child has made a mess on the floor. Who is she going to ask to help clean up the mess?
    c. Leslie is hungry. Who does she ask for something to eat?
    d. Now it is the time for the child to go to bed. Who tells the child: "Leslie, time for bed"?
    e. Who tucks the child in and gives her a good night kiss?
2. A boy and girl are shown fighting:
    a. These children are fighting. Who do you think started the fight?
    b. One of the children starts crying. Which child?
    c. One of the children is going to run home to tell what happened. Which child?
    d. Whom does the child want to tell—Mommy or Daddy?
3. A small child (A) is shown running to her mother. A boy and girl are playing in the foreground:
    a. This child (point to A) was playing in the yard when one of these children got mean and pushed the child down. Which child do you think pushed Leslie down?
    b. Which child is going over to see if she is all right?

In addition the children were asked to respond to stories of role fulfillment (such as those in Table 3-3) by pointing to a picture of a man and a woman. Significant differences in stereotyping were found between the responses of traditional and nontraditional children on nine of the 21 questions. A stereotyped response occurred when the children in the group agreed as to the sex of the person fitting the role; less stereotyped responses occurred when the female responses approached 50%. The nontraditional children were more likely to see the father cleaning the house; boys playing house, teacher, nurse, and with dolls; girls playing cowboys and indians, doctor, and with trucks.

Thirty-one of the 48 children said they did not know the difference between girls and boys. Seventeen children named characteristics such as differences in hair, clothing, toys, physical strength, and anatomy. The traditional children were significantly more likely to differentiate betwen the sexes than the nontraditional children. The ability to abstract differences between the sexes was also closely related to age: 14 of the 17 children who differentiated were over the median age of 4½ years.

It was concluded that the results support the theory that sex-role attitudes and behaviors are molded by socialization practices and that they can be changed when the values of the culture and child-rearing practices are changed. Further research needs to be conducted in order to more specifically investigate the extent to which socialization factors can influence the performance of sex-related roles and the effects of such modifications on traditional cultural structures.

IMPLICATIONS FOR SOCIAL MOTIVATION

It has been suggested in this chapter that secondary sources of motivation can be ultimately traced to the interference or disruption in satisfying primary sources of motivation. We mentioned in our introduction a discomfort with the familiar "drive" concept because often the goal which is sought is not traceable to a single source, for example, a physiological deficit.

The work of Schachter (1962) on labelling of emotional states was cited earlier as evidence of the interaction of cognitive and physiological factors in emotions. This work has illustrated the intricate way in which internal bodily conditions and external environmental factors may ultimately account for one's behavior.

Extending this work, Schachter has more recently examined the effects of experimental manipulations of one of the most elementary of motives, hunger (Schachter, 1971). In this research he has questioned the time-honored assumption that one eats when hungry and when satiated one no longer eats. This assumption has been challenged by analysts who have worked with obese patients, who have observed that obese people do not necessarily know when they are physiologically hungry. It has been proposed, in fact, that for such people early childhood behavior did not provide opportunities to discriminate between hunger and other states like fear, anger, and anxiety. If this is indeed the case, an individual may be labeling virtually any state of arousal as hunger, or conversely attaching a label when no internal arousal state exists. Among the intriguing studies conducted, Schachter, Goldman, and Gordon (1968) directly manipulated food deprivation so that some subjects entered the experimental situation, designed to evaluate the "taste" of different crackers, with "empty" stomachs and some with "full" stomachs. Subjects were classified according to whether they were obese or normal, as determined by norms provided by an insurance company. Having been asked not to eat the meal preceding the experimental appointment, all subjects presumably entered the experiment in a relatively similar state. Although the experimental manipulations were rather involved they can be summarized as follows: (1) One group was given an opportunity to eat as many roast beef sandwiches as they would like before the taste experiment began ("full" stomach). (2) One group was not given any food before the experiment began ("empty" stomach). (3) A third group was told that in order to measure the effect of tactile stimulation on taste, electrical stimulation of skin receptors would be used. However, this group was given to expect only a slight tingle sensation (low fear). (4) A fourth group, given the same rationale as the third for the use of electrical stimulation, was told to expect very painful sensations (high fear). Combinations of these conditions were, of course, included.

The use of fear was introduced, in addition to the availability of food, because evidence indicates that fear inhibits gastric motility (Carlson, 1916) and that fear leads to the suppression of gastric movement and the liberation of sugar into the blood (Cannon, 1929). Thus, Schachter and his cohorts reasoned that if obese subjects do not respond accurately to internal, visceral cues they should eat as much when their stomachs are full as when they are empty, and just as much when they are frightened as when they are calm. In contrast, however, it was expected that normal subjects should be directly affected by such manipulations, eating less when full and eating more when calm. Their predictions were supported, with the subjects in the low fear and "empty"-stomach conditions eating more than twice the number of crackers consumed by those in the high fear, "full"-stomach condition.

Thus, again, the interplay of internal or primary states with external conditions is glaring. In fact, further research reported by Schachter (1971) on the manipulation of other external factors like time (expecting that it is dinner time when that is not the case) has a significant impact on obese people, who again show failure to discriminate internal physiological states by eating more when they believe it is dinner time. Rather, their susceptibility to environmental factors, which are manipulated, lends additional evidence to the proposition that such internal states of arousal (primary drives) are often redirected through secondary sources of motivation as means of achieving psychological satisfaction.

To test directly the notion that such external factors like "time" can actually significantly affect eating behavior, Schachter and his researchers studied obese and normal subjects under conditions where clocks were "gimmicked" to run at twice the normal speed, thus creating the illusion of different time periods. In this study Schachter and Gross (1968) instructed subjects that by attaching electrodes to them they would be able to obtain base-line reaction levels to two physiological processes, heart-rate and sweat-gland activity in a completely neutral situation. Presumably, these reactions would be correlated with personality and other data. Thirty minutes after the electrodes were attached, the experimenter returned, administered a version of the Embedded Figures Test, and offered the subject some crackers. Following this, the experimenter again left the room, this time leaving the crackers while specifically telling the subject it was permissible to eat some crackers if he felt like doing so. Unbeknown to the subjects, however, during the initial 30-minute period of time when the base-line reactions were being taken, the clocks were adjusted by a 15-minute period.

Those in the "slow" condition were given to believe that the time was 5:35 instead of 5:20. In the "fast" condition the subjects were supposedly in the experimental room at 6:20 instead of 6:05. Thus, only a 15-minute period of time constituted the external variable which was manipulated; yet for some subjects this was intended to create the illusion that dinner time had come. And so it did! The obese subjects in the "fast" condition ate almost twice as much as obese subjects in the "slow" condition. For them, "the impression that it is roughly dinner time is a spur to the eating behavior." On the other hand, for normal subjects the effect of manipulated time was actually the reverse, with eating in the "slow" condition actually being greater than in the "fast" condition (presumably in order to wait for dinner and not spoil the appetite). Thus, the "hunger" seems to have been subordinated by cognitive factors directed through the simple manipulation of an external factor, time.

This past section was intended to illustrate the interplay between primary and secondary sources of motivation, wherein the satisfaction of a primary drive (hunger) may be the result of a stimulus heretofore considered as secondary (anxiety). We had mentioned earlier that one of the failures of the drive concept is its inability to deal in a one-to-one fashion with drives and their reduction. For example, feelings of hunger are not necessarily stimulated by prior conditions of not eating, as Schachter et al. (1968) point out. External factors may well trigger the primary drives by activating secondary sources of motivation, making the link between primary and secondary motives quite intricate.

Similarly, social goals are not always sought after for obvious reasons. Social conditions may stimulate the desire for nurturance in the form of group memberships and social interaction. Power, for example, may be a logical outgrowth of an instrumental response (aggression) insofar as one may seek ways of influencing others and asserting control over others. At the same time, as we have observed, groups in power may be comprised of people whose primary source of satisfaction is social affiliation, not social influence. To achieve may also reflect strong "aggressive" tendencies, but the achievement may serve to enhance one's position vis-à-vis another and to satisfy needs for meeting social approval, as well as keeping up with one's "reference group" of other achieving people.

Thus, to single out any one primary "drive" or "motive" obviously does not explain the many underpinnings of the observed behavior.

Indeed, the more complex this final behavior, the more difficult it becomes to speak in terms of any single explanatory factor.

SUMMARY

Although the varieties of social goals available to man are many, the particular blend of motives will vary from person to person and in relation to the sociocultural context. What is common to man's functioning is the sequence of behaviors which can be traced from such primary sources of motivation as the need for water, food, and sex through secondary sources such as anxiety, frustration, and guilt to the choices of actual instrumental responses.

Anxiety arises from a threat to a person's security. Research indicates that mild anxiety may move a person to realistic attempts to deal with the source of the anxiety but that stronger levels may disrupt goal-oriented behavior and lead to evasive or defensive maneuvers. Under certain circumstances the arousal of anxiety may lead to affiliative tendencies, particularly if there is a great need for others to define or evaluate the anxious response—a condition apparently more prevalent in first-born individuals.

Frustration arises from the blockage of goal-directed behavior and has attracted much attention as the antecedent condition for aggression. Frustration, however, may have other consequences, including withdrawal, regression, and even creative problem solving.

Relatively little empirical research has centered on guilt. Most frequently, guilt functions as an inhibitor and a control mechanism, but its activation may also increase the likelihood of goal-seeking responses such as altruism and alternatives to aggression.

A wide variety of instrumental responses may flow from primary and secondary motivational states. Learning, environmental supports, and cultural factors such as sex role interact to determine the specific form. Thus, in our culture males learn to retaliate with aggressive behavior more than do females. However, adult socialization forces such as the Women's Liberation Movement may offer alternative behavioral models.

Other evidence indicates that dependency behaviors vary with birth order. Evidently first-time mothers interfere more with the child's activities and show greater variability in mood and attitude toward their first child. These maternal responses seem to instigate greater degrees of dependency behavior.

Consideration of instrumental responses such as aggression and dependency leads inevitably to the question of how such social motives become manifest in complex social goals. A clear example of this stems from Harlow's work. One can follow the contact preferences of infant monkeys through the opportunity for peer contact and its effect on social behavior. These behaviors in turn seem to have implications for group involvement and social orientations, such as other-directedness.

Similarly, some of the threads leading to achievement-oriented behavior have been teased out. Firstly, achievement behavior seems related to being first-born, which in turn seems tied to increased amounts of dependency behavior. One basis for achievement behavior, then, may be compensatory for the frustration of dependency needs. However, this path seems culturally acceptable only for males, and culturally available sex-role stereotypes again act to channel and direct energy toward different social goals.

Social goals are not always clearly related to underlying motivational states, and underlying states may be expressed in a great variety of social activities. For example, Schachter's work demonstrates that arousal states are not always identifiable and distinct but may be differentially labeled, depending on what environmental or cognitive factors may be available.

Thus, how we interpret the many social situations around us is a very complex issue. Similarly, how we establish the priorities of our goals and strivings is dependent on both our need states and the means available in our environment for satisfying our primary and social motives.

SUGGESTED READINGS

Harlow, H. *Learning to love*. New York: A Ballantine Walden Edition (paper), 1971.

The development of affectional systems in monkeys is traced through five areas: maternal love, infant love, age-mate or peer love, heterosexual love, and paternal love. Applications to human relationships are evaluated in terms of promises and pitfalls.

Johnson, R. *Aggression in man and animals*. Philadelphia: Saunders, 1972.

A broad and comprehensive review of the conceptions of aggression ranging from ethological to biological and learning proponents. Attention is also given to the inhibition and control of violence in society.

Maccoby, E. E., and Jacklin, C. N. *The psychology of sex differences*. Stanford: Stanford University Press, 1974.

The current focus on sex differences is given a historical perspective, with attention especially given to areas deemed to be crucial in development, namely, attachment and dependency. Research is cited in support of theoretical statements.

Schachter, S. *The psychology of affiliation*. Stanford: Stanford University Press, 1959.

A classic monograph in the field of social psychology on the sources of gregariousness in man. The studies are ingeniously designed and provide a model for the logical development of critical thinking in experimentation.

4
Socialization: The Formation of Identity

Karl E. Scheibe

INTRODUCTION: WHAT IS SOCIALIZATION?

Texts and handbooks on human development offer their most assured generalizations about neonates and very young children. As behavior patterns and problems are discussed for each succeeding age level, generalizations become more and more highly qualified. The relative frequency of words like "if," "may," and "perhaps" increases markedly as puberty is discussed, and most texts give up the task of offering generalizations by age levels somewhere in the middle of adolescence. Parents are often amazed at the accuracy of description provided by Dr. Spock (1957). Young psychologists are equally amazed at how well Piaget's (1952) generalizations about cognitive development seem to fit what is occurring in their own children. But no book on adolescence has the surety of Dr. Spock's book on baby care, and at adolescent stages of cognitive development—particularly the stage of "formal operations"—psychologists begin to bicker with Piaget about possible cultural or idiosyncratic restrictions in his generalizations about mental functioning. Age-bound generalizations about psychological functioning make a tentative appearance again at senescence. Geriatric psychology, properly a part of developmental psychology, begins to recapture some of the descriptive assurance of neonatal psychology, one end of life being as certain and simple as the other.

But in the midrange of life the possibilities for variation are enormous. No single volume—indeed, no library—could provide a comprehensive description of the psychological possibilities associated with the thirtieth year of human life. A large part of the task of psychology is to render an account of how developmental differentiation occurs. Used most abstractly, socialization refers to the developmental differentiation occurring in the individual as a result of the way that person is treated by the representatives of the society into which he is born. In common usage, the term is more limited, referring primarily to the evaluative dispositions which the individual develops as a result of interactions in society. Thus, becoming a Yankee fan may be thought of as a result of socialization, while learning who the Yankees are, although clearly a socially mediated process, is not ordinarily considered to be an example of socialization.

The intent of this chapter is to discuss the mechanisms, process, and content of socialization. Particular reference will be made to the development of valued loyalties to institutions such as the nation. Passions and politics are evidently closely connected, especially in times of national crisis. A major component of a person's identity is formed by the development of values about the political institutions of which he is a part.

What socialization is defined to be can be made clearer by referring to the common distinction between beliefs and values (see Scheibe, 1970). Beliefs refer to questions of fact, questions about that which exists, what happened in history, or what might happen in the future. The term *belief* can be used as the broadest generic label for a whole class of cognitive dispositions—expectations, hypotheses, or subjective probabilities. In the aggregate, a person's beliefs amount to his functional knowledge about the way the world is put together and his own place in that world. Future-oriented beliefs (expectations) act as guides to behavior, as operative behavior maps which tell the person what leads to what and what is likely to be the consequence of a contemplated course of action.

If beliefs answer to questions of fact or possibility, values answer to questions of preference or desirability. What is good? What do I want or like? What is right (in a moral rather than a factual sense)? The term *value* can be used as the broadest generic label for human motivational dispositions—wants, desires, needs, preferences, loves, and hates. Functionally, values also operate in the direction of behavior, not as maps but rather as forces which attract and repel an individual with respect to the regions in the mapped portion of the world. To have a goal is to have a positive evaluative disposition toward some particular identifiable object or state of being.

A moment's reflection is sufficient to note that a number of values might be connected with a simple act, such as eating an apple. These values might include the positive value of acquiring nourishment, providing beneficial gum stimulation, "keeping the doctor away," providing employment to fruitpickers, or demonstrating solidarity with a new back-to-nature political movement whose chosen symbol is the apple. As a further complication, we note that values do not exist in a vacuum but refer to the contents of knowledge or beliefs.

In a general way, a person's decisions may be considered to be consequences of beliefs and values, of what is considered to be true or likely and what is considered to be best or preferable. This paradigm is common to a wide variety of behavioral theories and is not a flagrant departure from common sense. It is thought that people do what they want to do if they think they can. Of course, finding out what people want and what they think are formidable problems.

A good deal of psychological theory has been written and research done on the mechanisms by which the cognitive and emotional dispositions of the person combine with the configuration of influences presented in a particular behavior setting in such a way as to produce behavior. In fact, this may be considered to be one of the two major problems in psychology. The other problem, by no means secondary, is the developmental one to which reference has been made: How does the person come to have the particular cognitive and motivational dispositions which influence behavior? How are beliefs and values acquired? The problem of the development of beliefs is the problem of cognitive learning. The problem of the acquisition of values is that of socialization. Socialization may also be seen as a form of learning, but one in which the product is not knowledge but changed evaluations of persons, things, or events.

Surely there is a hidden supposition in this particular use of socialization. The supposition is that most behaviorally operative values have social origins, that they are acquired in some way from the social milieu of the developing person. This is why one rarely sees discussions of the so-called primary drives—hunger, thirst, and other tissue needs—in discussions of socialization, for it does not seem plausible that these operative values are social in origin. As we shall see later in this chapter, the sorts of values generally discussed under the heading of socialization are of a "higher" sort—moral values, or values that are relevant to forms of human interaction.

Socialization is responsible for dramatic differences in moral standards over cultures. In a recent book comparing patterns of socialization in the Soviet Union and the United States, Bronfenbrenner (1972) describes an example of a kind of moral socialization which would seem very peculiar by American standards.

The schoolroom poster shown in Figure 4-1 depicts a youthful Pioneer (sort of a Boy Scout) publicly exposing a bit of misbehavior of an unfortunate colleague:

> As the drawing indicates, being truthful includes, as one Soviet educator preferred to put it, "expressing one's opinion publicly about a comrade's misconduct." (Note that the shamed seatmate had carved his name on the desk.) But there is a poster within the poster. It depicts a serious-faced Pioneer named Pavlik Morozov. Although the name is

FIGURE 4-1 A Pioneer tells the truth and treasures the honor of his unit.

> unfamiliar to most Westerners, it is a household word in the U.S.S.R. A young Pioneer during the period of collectivization, Pavlik denounced his own father as a collaborator with the Kulaks and testified against him in court. Pavlik was killed by people of the village for revenge, and is now regarded as a martyr in the cause of communism. A statue of him in Moscow is constantly visited by children, who keep it bedecked with fresh flowers, and many collective farms, Pioneer palaces, and libraries bear his name. (1972, p. 47)

The reported anecdote about Pavlik Morozov allows the inference that he had been socialized to value loyalty to the new collectivity more than he valued loyalty to his father. Somehow, the series of social events to which Pavlik had been exposed in his development led to this particular ordering of values, an ordering not shared by the unregenerate folk of his village who took vengeance on him and is not shared by contemporary citizens of the United States, who would see this act of betrayal as base and immoral. But, happily, for Pavlik Morozov's good name, his supreme loyalty to the collectivity above family is the dominant pattern in the Soviet Union. Now the legend of Pavlik serves as one of the mechanisms for socialization to that ideal.

If one is socialized to one set of value standards and is judged by another set, then the consequence is sharp moral conflict—a profound disagreement about what course of action is right or makes sense in a given situation. Another example, this one drawn from G. B. Shaw's fictionalized account of Christian martyrdom, illustrates this point from a slightly different perspective. In the play *Androcles and the Lion*, the following conversation occurs between Lavinia, one of the Christian martyrs, and a Roman Captain, who is speaking to a group of Roman legionnaires and their Christian prisoners:

> Lavinia: Captain, is there no hope that this cruel persecution. . . . Captain: (unmoved and somewhat sardonic) Persecution is not a term applicable to the act of the Emperor. The Emperor is the Defender of the Faith. In throwing you to the lions he will be upholding the interests of the religion in Rome. If you were to throw him to the lions, that would no doubt be persecution. . . . I call the attention of female prisoner Lavinia to the fact that as the Emperor is a divine personage, her imputation of cruelty is not only treason, but sacrilege. I point out further that there is no foundation for the charge, as the Emperor does not desire that any prisoner should suffer; nor can any Christian be harmed save through his or her own obstinacy. All that is necessary is to sacrifice to the gods; a simple and convenient ceremony effected by dropping a pinch of incense on the altar, after which the prisoner is at once set free. Under such circumstances you have only your own perverse folly to blame if you suffer. I suggest to you that if you cannot burn a morsel of incense as a matter of conviction, you might at least do so as a matter of good taste, to avoid shocking the religious convictions of your fellow citizens. I am aware that these considerations do not weigh with Christians; but it is my duty to call your attention to them in order that you may have no ground for complaining of your treatment or of accusing the Emperor of cruelty when he is showing you the most signal clemency. Looked at from this point of view, every Christian who has perished in the arena, has really committed suicide. (1962, p. 437–38)

This is an unfortunate sort of conflict, for everyone involved seems to be acting from the best of motives, according to the kinds of values to which they have been socialized. The example is particularly useful because it illustrates the generalizability of values within a particular social role. Becoming a Christian is a transformation in identity, a taking on of a new role, with an accompanying shift in regulative norms. Similarly, becoming a Roman Captain or a Roman Emperor is a transformation of identity entailing the acceptance by those who take these roles of the kinds of values that are considered to be appropriate. Also, this example illustrates the effect of certain cosmological beliefs on the evaluation of behavioral options. The decision of the martyrs not to forsake Christianity is a rational one if they believe the teachings of Christianity about the way this world is related to the next. As the Romans do not share this belief, they are continually astounded at the courage and almost jovial mood of the Christians. The behavior of the Romans also seems silly to the Christians, who do not believe there is anything divine about the Emperor and hence feel that there is no value in being loyal to him or his officially sanctioned religion.

Much of the human conflict we see about us can be understood as the direct consequence of contact between individuals or sets of individuals who have been socialized to differing versions of what is truly valuable in the world. From a partisan point of view, wars are almost always seen as conflicts between Good and Evil. From a more detached perspective, the same wars can be seen as conflicts between two different versions of Good. But there is no perspective, however detached, which does not carry with it norms or values which may be applied to persons, events, and ideas. One may be socialized, for example, to the role of Scientist, which is supposed by many to be a value-free sort of identity. It may be value-free in the sense that the ideal scientist may have a greater respect for the quest of scientific truth than he does for any political ideology or religious creed. However, he has his own creed, his own ethic: that it is good to know things, that it is good to exchange information freely, that human beings must continually strive to know more and more about nature, and that anything which competes with Science for scarce resources is suspicious. It turns out that this is also a form of parochialism, increasingly recognized as such as the era of magical enamoration with science passes into history.

The root problem for socialization theory and research is to develop an understanding of how individuals come to adopt the values which guide their behavior. Necessarily, this involves a consideration of the person's social identity, the configuration of roles with which he has become associated in the process of development. Necessarily also, this entails a consideration of creeds and political ideologies, because these seem to form bases in beliefs about the real world from which important value judgments are drawn.

The content of the values to which human beings can be socialized is enormous. In some cultures, people can eat snails; in others, dogs and monkeys; and in others, people become sick at the idea of cooking beef to eat. In some cultures, infanticide is practiced without moral compunction (Neel, 1970); in others, euthanasia is practiced for old people; and in others, aborting a one-month-old fetus is considered to be a mortal sin. But whatever their content, it is obvious that human societies are dependent upon the continual transmission from one generation to the next of value standards. Socialization occurs and, indeed, must occur in order for human societies to survive and prosper.

The anthropologist LeVine (1969) has argued that the norms transmitted through socialization practices have survival value for societies in the Darwinian sense, although the understanding of a particular norm within a culture may have no relation to the function it serves. LeVine cites as an example the post-partum taboos on sexual intercourse, which are often considered in ancient societies to be based on the possibility that semen might contaminate the milk of a nursing mother or that evil spirits can enter the nursing infant as a result of intercourse with a lactating mother. From a scientific perspective, it makes more sense to view the post-partum taboo as a way of insuring a longer period of nursing which enhances the child's chance of survival. Of course, it is perfectly possible that a social norm which has evolved in this functional way may lose its significance as conditions in the world change. For example, it may be that the strong veneration most societies have evolved for the nuclear family may no longer make the same sense in the modern technological world as it once did, when the means of production and distribution of goods and services on the face of the earth were in a more primitive condition.

It is clear that a significant portion of adult activity is devoted to attempts at influencing the course of development of their offspring. The continuity of human society seems dependent upon a constant effort of adult members to mold and shape new members of society. The object of socialization is to instill (or install) behavioral controls in each succeeding generation. This process begins at birth and probably continues throughout almost the entire lifetime of a person. As a person emerges from one stage of life into another, new values are assumed as appropriate to the new stage. Examples of such human developmental stages are childhood, puberty (menarche), adolescence, adulthood, old age (menopause), and senescence. To some extent, the enumeration and description of these stages is a matter of established cultural convention. Aries (1962) suggests that children were once regarded as miniature adults rather than as a separate category of beings, as is currently the case. Keniston (1970) has suggested that recently a new phase of life has been created in the modern world between adolescence and adulthood—a phase of life which he calls "youth." What makes a stage of life distinguishable are the particular kinds of social norms which are associated with it; whatever these are, they must comprise the evaluative content toward which succeeding generations of entrants are socialized.

Intriguing psychological problems can be identified for all these levels of consideration of socialization. The special focus of this chapter will be upon the kind of socialization represented in the examples of Pavlik Morozov and of the characters in Shaw's *Androcles and the Lion*. More specifically, the interest will center upon the way in which a political or quasipolitical system determines the values to which individuals are socialized. But before embarking on a discussion of the mechanisms of socialization and the process of political socialization, it will be appropriate to make a few additional conceptual distinctions and to sketch in some of the history of socialization theory and research in psychology.

SOME CONCEPTUAL DISTINCTIONS

Socialization can be studied and described on the level of mechanisms, processes, contents, and—by way of contrast—compared with other kinds of psychological development.

Mechanisms

The mechanisms of socialization refer to the means by which changed evaluative dispositions occur in the individual. For example, the social psychologist Zajonc (1968a) has stated that familiarity with social stimuli increases the judged attractiveness of those stimuli. He has shown that frequency of exposure determines the judged attractiveness of human faces. (See also Saegert, Swap, & Zajonc, 1973; Heingartner & Hall, 1974.) Generalizing from this principle, one might suggest that at least one of the mechanisms for socialization involves the frequency of exposure of stimulus materials to the developing person. Alternatively, the classic stimulus–response (S–R) position on mechanisms of socialization gives central importance to the principle of reinforcement, whereby stimuli come to acquire attractive properties by being paired in presentation with other stimuli such as food or water which have primary drive-reducing properties.

Still another mechanism is suggested by Harlow's (1971) work on the development of "love" in infant monkeys. Harlow finds that the provision of nutriment has little to do with the developing affectional bond between a mother monkey and her infant. Instead, such properties of the mother as softness and warmth are instrumental to the development of positive affective bonds. In Harlow's experiments, surrogate mothers made of terry cloth drew more affectionate regard than surrogate mothers made of wire, even though the latter devices were fitted with bottles for feeding and the former were not. Although Harlow does not name the mechanism responsible for the diversification of affectional responses in monkeys, he has demonstrated the presence of a natural maturational sequence for the species. Because development to the successive stages of this sequence is dependent upon the presence of specific conditions or stimulus configurations, the mechanism might be referred to as "conditional maturation," with the understanding that the conditions necessary for progressive affectional development are specific to a given species.

Yet another kind of socialization mechanism is described by Freud and those in the psychoanalytic tradition. Freud considers the basic relationship between the individual and the society into which he is born to be one of enmity. Civilization prohibits the individual from directly satisfying his instinctual urges. But in the course of development a person becomes "civilized" through the introjection of the standards of civilization. The basic mechanism for the acquisition of these standards is identification, whereby the child takes as his own such values as are presented to him by the agents of society, most notably, his parents. In *Civilization and Its Discontents* (1930), Freud (1961, Strachey translation) speculates on the manner in which civilization is built up as a cumulative effect of the renunciation of individual instincts. The individual is forced to identify with society in order to maintain his psychic economy. Through his social learning the individual is transformed into an agent of society.

Modern social learning theorists consider one of the major mechanisms of socialization to be imitation, a concept which has much in common with identification (see Mussen, 1967, for a discussion of the distinction between these terms). In the course of development, a child is exposed to a set of models who exhibit their values in their behaviors. Bandura (Bandura & Walters, 1963) has shown that behaviorally operative values are acquired through direct observation of models, without the implication that the children have identified with the models, in the psychoanalytic sense of that term.

Finally, role playing is widely regarded as a means by which socialization is accomplished. A child playing with imaginary playmates or enacting a make-believe role comes to recognize the legitimacy of particular kinds of social norms in the regulation of social behavior (Sarbin & Allen, 1968).

It is unlikely that any one mechanism of socialization is responsible for the acquisition of the entire range of social values. Also, it should be clear that the use of the term "mechanism" is metaphoric. No one has ever observed the details of the mechanical or chemical process, presumably on the neurological level, which is associated with what we may observe as a shift in values. One observes, instead, certain regular associations of antecedent conditions with subsequent shifts in behavior. A "mechanism" is described in a way that fits this observed association. Familiarization, reinforcement, conditional maturation, identification, imitation, and role playing are examples of such terms.

Socialization as Process

If several or many mechanisms are involved in the socialization of an individual and if innumerable events have socializing consequences for the person, then socialization may be described as a long-term process, the evolution or development of values in the person. The anthropologist views the process of socialization as enculturation. The sociologist sees it as the acquisition of social norms, and the psychologist as the learning of values. Of course, all refer to different aspects of the same general process, which goes on no matter what it is called and regardless of how badly it is understood. A good sense of the process of socialization can be gained from extended case studies of individuals. Good psychological biography achieves a convincing description of how a person's values took their characteristic form. Some examples of this form are Erikson's *Young Man Luther* (1958) and *Ghandi's Truth* (1969). Additional examples are George and George's (1956) study of Woodrow Wilson or Freud's (1916, Tyson translation, 1964) study of Leonardo da Vinci. Collective case descriptions offer descriptions of the developmental history of classes of individuals. For example, MacKinnon offers the following composite picture of the background of creative architects:

> . . . an extraordinary respect by the parent for the child, and an early granting to him of an unusual freedom in exploring his universe and in making decisions for himself; an expectation that the child would act independently but reasonably and responsibly; a lack of intense closeness between parent and child so that neither overdependence was fostered nor a feeling of rejection experienced, in other words, the sort of interpersonal relationship between parent and child which has a liberating effect upon the child; a plentiful supply in the child's extended social environment of models for identification and the promotion of ego ideals; the presence within the family of clear standards of conduct and ideas as to what was right and wrong; but at the same time an expectation, if not requirement, of active exploration and internalization of a framework of personal conduct; an emphasis upon the development of one's own ethical code; the experience of frequent moving within a single community, or from community to community, or from country to country which provided an enrichment of experience, both cultural and personal, but which at the same time contributed to experiences of aloneness, shyness, isolation, and solitariness during childhood and adolescence; the possession of skills and abilities which, though encouraged and rewarded, were nevertheless allowed to develop at their own pace; and finally the absence of pressures to establish prematurely one's professional identity. (MacKinnon, 1965, p. 280)

Of course, more careful, controlled, and exhaustive observations can be made on other species of animals. As Harlow (1971) and Goodall (1971) have shown, primates are rewarding to watch, since they resemble man in many ways but have a relatively short developmental period.

Harlow's recent book, *Learning to Love,* is a composite description of the process of socialization as it occurs for groups of rhesus monkeys raised in his laboratories at the University of Wisconsin. Harlow notes that the affectional responses of monkeys develop through four distinct periods, which he refers to as maternal love, age-mate or peer love, heterosexual love, and paternal love. Harlow emphasizes the dependency of this progression on specific social events and circumstances in the development of the young monkey. For example, if a young monkey does not have a fair amount of contact and interaction with a mothering monkey, its heterosexual affectional responses do not emerge properly later in development. The process of socialization for monkeys—and most assuredly for human beings—is well described as a progression of stages. The way in which one stage of development is realized determines the potential for socialization at the next stage.

The Content of Socialization

Socialization, then, is a process which occurs over the developmental history of the person and is accomplished by one or more of a set of mechanisms for transforming social influences into changed dispositions of the person. But what is the content of socialization? How might the range of evaluative dispositions which are the product of socialization be described?

According to anthropologists (Ford & Beach, 1956), the taboo against incest is universal. If we presume that individuals are not born with an automatic repulsion toward sexual relations with near relatives, then this norm must be the product of socialization. Through some mechanism—whether it be accounted for in terms of the Oedipus complex, conditioning theory, or role theory is of little importance for the present—a process occurs whereby individuals come to hold negative values toward incest. This does not mean, of course, that incest does not occur in human society; it most certainly does. But part of the universal content of socialization is the incest taboo.

Undoubtedly, other universal contents of socialization could be enumerated—prohibitions against ingroup aggression, nurturance and support for helpless infants, norms for protection from out-group aggression, and so on. But the known range of cultural diversity in social norms means that the process of socialization can produce fantastically diverse contents. Even within a given society, the content of socialization varies tremendously. Consider a brief list of social types in our own society: the playboy, the ambitious executive, the middle-American, the hippie, the artist, the dope addict, the revolutionary, the healer, the preacher, the wise old man, the prostitute, the politician, the professor, the groupie. Each of these labels evokes an idea of the content of socialization. The content of the rules by which people in these categories live varies enormously, but all of them live by rules of some kind, that is, by regular, recurrent evaluative standards which are invoked as ways of deciding upon possible courses of behavior.

A substantial contribution to research and theory on socialization has been made in recent years by Kohlberg and his co-workers at Harvard University who have attempted to develop a characterization of the process of socialization by describing, at a somewhat abstract level, the content of socialization at various stages of development. Kohlberg's characterization of moral development is based largely on the logical features of Piaget's theory of cognitive development. Specifically, Kohlberg has proposed that " . . . universal and regular age trends of development may be found in moral judgment, and these have a formal-cognitive base. Many aspects of moral judgment do not have such a cognitive base, but these aspects do not define universal and regular trends of moral development" (Kohlberg, 1969, p. 375). The stages which Kohlberg believes are universal and general are listed in Table 4-1.

Kohlberg has gathered evidence from long-term studies in the United States which show that this sequence of moral development is, in fact, characteristic. A child at an early stage of development will apply moral standards that derive from immediate consequences, whether punishment or praise is likely to follow from a given action. At an intermediate stage of development, the child will obey rules which are general and attempt to "live up to standards." At the latter stages of moral development, the child questions arbitrary standards according to general principles of justice and morality which he has evolved. It is important to note two things about this progression: First, the content of morality becomes more and more abstract, general, and "decentered," as development occurs. Second, the general progression of development is considered by Kohlberg to be in a positive moral direction, that is, he

TABLE 4-1
Classification of Moral Judgment into Levels and Stages of Development

Levels	Basis of moral judgment	Stages of development
I	Moral value resides in external, quasi-physical happenings, in bad acts, or in quasi-physical needs rather than in persons and standards.	Stage 1: Obedience and punishment orientation. Egocentric deference to superior power or prestige, or a trouble-avoiding set. Objective responsibility.
		Stage 2: Naively egoistic orientation. Right action is that instrumentally satisfying the self's needs and occasionally others'. Awareness of relativism of value to each actor's needs and perspective. Naive egalitarianism and orientation to exchange and reciprocity.
II	Moral value resides in performing good or right roles, in maintaining the conventional order and the expectancies of others.	Stage 3: Good-boy orientation. Orientation to approval and to pleasing and helping others. Conformity to stereotypical images of majority or natural role behavior, and judgment by intention.
		Stage 4: Authority and social-order maintaining orientation. Orientation to "doing duty" and to showing respect for authority and maintaining the given social order for its own sake. Regard for earned expectations of others.
III	Moral value resides in conformity by the self to shared or shareable standards, rights, or duties.	Stage 5: Contractual legalistic orientation. Recognition of an arbitrary element or starting point in rules or expectations for the sake of agreement. Duty defined in terms of contract, general avoidance of violation of the will or rights of others, and majority will and welfare.
		Stage 6: Conscience or principle orientation. Orientation not only to actually ordained social rules but to principles of choice involving appeal to logical universality and consistency. Orientation to conscience as a directing agent and to mutual respect and trust.

approves of the higher stages of development. The implication is that procedures should be devised to encourage as much development of abstract morality as possible.

By no means is development to the highest stages of morality inevitable. Since development through stages is dependent on a complex series of social interactions within each stage, development may be retarded or arrested at any point. Kohlberg notes that development to the higher stages of moral development is faster and more frequent in the United States than in the other cultures he has studied, such as Taiwan, Turkey, and Mexico. Also, middle-class children show a faster rate of moral development than do lower-class children. But rate of moral development is no respecter of religious faith: Christians, Buddhists, Jews, Moslems, and atheists are not found to have different rates of progress through Kohlberg's stages.

In order to clarify the kind of moral content that is characteristic of Kohlberg's progression, it is instructive to consider an example from the early work of Piaget (1932), who is the acknowledged inspiration for the extensive research and theory accomplished by Kohlberg. Piaget undoubtedly spent many hours as a boy playing the game of marbles. Later, he was to make systematic observations of the way little children play marbles, and he noticed a fascinating progression in the way in which the children seemed to regard the rules of the game at different ages. The very youngest children had to be taught the rules, and their adherence to the rules of the game had to be constantly enforced. This is, they seemed to be operating on a moral system that depended upon constant external provision of rewards and punishments in order to keep their behavior within legal bounds. Somewhat older children did not have to be constantly sanctioned in order for them to play by the rules. They knew the rules and adhered to them strictly without threat of punishment for infractions and without special incentives for playing honestly. But for these children, the rules seemed absolutely given; they were presumed to be the only legitimate rules, permitting of no modification or questioning. Still older children were able to realize that rules made by men can be changed by men and frequently made modifications of the rules to suit particular occasions or to increase the variation and interest in the game. All the while, the content of the moral rules used by children pertained, in this case, to the playing of the game of marbles. But the nature of that content was seen by Piaget to have exhibited a characteristic evolution or development in the direction of "decentration." For example, in the cognitive domain, Piaget showed that children become able, at a certain stage, to imagine what a landscape would look like from another geographic perspective. In the moral domain, he was able to show a similar progression. The higher stages of moral development, for both Piaget and Kohlberg, consist of an ability to shift perspectives and imagine consequences, to treat various concrete situations with great flexibility but with a consistency of application of general abstract principles of morality.

Kohlberg's theory of moral development was taken as an example of the content of socialization. Kohlberg takes pains to point out that the content of socialization is much broader than consistently applied moral rules. Most of the value judgments which individuals make, even though they are at the highest level of moral development, are not systematically derived from some consistent set of principles, of whatever kind. In fact, one of the best-documented facts about the contents of socialization is that such contents are not terribly consistent over time. Individuals who are honest in one situation, for example, simply may not be depended upon to be honest in a different situation. The conclusion of a classical series of studies by Hartshorne and May (1928–1930) was that honesty is not a general trait. In ordinary academic situations, for example, a large proportion of college students will cheat on an examination when given the opportunity to do so. Such an opportunity arises, for example, when students are allowed to grade their own exams; when the teacher has surreptitiously corrected them previously, but without making any marks on the paper, this cheating can be detected.

Referring again to the example cited at the beginning of this section, the taboo against incest may very well be universal. But the observance of this taboo is not universal, that is, behavior does not follow unequivocally from general social norms. Still earlier in this chapter, it was emphasized that many values are commonly involved in the execution of a very simple action. The same individuals who protest that they would not voluntarily hurt other people for no reason are willing accomplices in an experimental situation in which they are required to administer what appears to be severe punishment to another person (Milgram, 1963). Persons who would not think of themselves as killers of other men can be made to kill other men by first being initiated and trained into the role of soldier. And soldiers who think of themselves as honest and uncorrupted can still be made to falsify documents in order to cover up some unsavory incident if it appears that the orders for falsification come from legitimate sources.

That Which Socialization Is Not. The point of these last examples is to demonstrate that no unequivocal relation exists between general socialization and behavior. It is a mistake, albeit a very inviting mistake, to think of the process of socialization taking place in a cumulative and directed way, so that at any given point in time the person is what he is and will behave in such a way as to give clear expression to the values he has evolved. But such a conception overlooks the tremendous effect that variations in roles play in modifying the behavior potential of the person. Also, this conception greatly oversimplifies the relation between values and behavior. We must admit that socialization is not the only, or even the major, antecedent to social behavior.

Other qualifications should be placed on the concept of socialization. Certainly socialization should be considered subsidiary to psychological development; the terms are not synonymous. The kind of unfolding or maturational development described by Gesell (1954), for example, is not appropriately called socialization. The neuromuscular maturational sequence which leads to head-lifting, rolling over, sitting up, crawling, standing, and walking is certainly influenced to some extent by the way in which the infant is handled. However, this sequence is relatively invariant over cultures and is in no clear way related to later evaluative dispositions of the person. Similarly, it would be strained usage to think of language acquisition as a product of socialization, even though the particular language learned is clearly a function of social stimuli and even though language, as an abstract symbol system, undoubtedly plays a very large role in the mechanisms, process, and content of socialization. Of course, how a person speaks, to whom he addresses commands and requests, whether he speaks at all in certain circumstances, and the forms of speech and types of inflection used in social settings is very much a matter of socialization. That a child speaks is not a matter of socialization; that he does not speak in the company of certain elders or during certain ceremonies is definitely a result of socialization.

It is important to note that this way of talking about socialization presumes no specific position on the question of the genetic determination of behavior. It is not necessary to assume, as the early behaviorists did or as Skinner (1971) would, that any well-formed baby can be brought up to be just about anything its enlightened trainer wanted it to be. Indeed, strong presumptive evidence exists that the development of both cognitive and motivational dispositions in the person are conditional upon the form of the given genetic stuff.

To recapitulate this section, socialization refers to a part of psychological development. It is accomplished by mechanisms, such as identification, conditioning, familiarization, or role learning. The mechanisms of socialization result in a process by which the individual comes to incorporate in some unique way a set of evaluative possibilities which are displayed to him or taught to him by the social host in which he develops. The result is a set of constantly evolving evaluative standards, consisting partly of stable principles, partly of a medley of constantly fluctuating preferences and tastes. Socialization does not produce a sharply defined set of constant values in the individual, though the individual might evolve some principles which he adheres to quite consistently. Some theorists, such as Piaget and Kohlberg, have suggested that the general direction of development of such principles is away from egocentrism and toward general principles of evaluation such as justice, equity, and consistency.

The next two sections of this chapter are devoted to a consideration of examples of the mechanisms and process of socialization. First, attention will be directed to the best-developed series of empirical studies on socialization mechanisms, that of Albert Bandura and his colleagues at Stanford University. Then the process of political socialization, alluded to already several times in this chapter, will be discussed.

SOCIALIZATION THROUGH OBSERVATION

Yogi Berra, the well-known baseball figure, is credited with the remark, "You can learn a lot just by watching." This simple idea has the germ of common sense. But it would have been derided by most orthodox psychologists a generation ago, because the accepted position was that nothing is learned by mere observation. Indeed, it was thought that practice and reward were necessary conditions for the occurrence of learning. Any learning occurring without practice or reward was referred to as "incidental." Fortunately, modern psychologists are likely to give Mr. Berra due credit for his wisdom on how to learn.

While Freud certainly recognized the imitation by children of value standards of their parents, modern experimental confirmation of imitation learning was provided slightly more than ten years ago at Stanford University (Bandura & Walters, 1963). This research, initiated by Albert Bandura, is based on a very simple experimental paradigm. The subject, usually a nursery school child, is allowed to observe the behavior of a model (the experimenter, in the role of "teacher") in some novel circumstances. The model displays a carefully prepared set of critical behaviors or expressions when engaged in some activity. A control group of children is given preliminary experience with the activity, but without the critical set of behaviors shown by the model. Later all subjects are given an opportunity to engage in the activity by themselves, not in the presence of the model. Performances are scored by observers for the number of critical behaviors exhibited by the model which are imitated by the children. For example, a model may hit an inflated doll with a bat, while uttering the appropriate expressions, "Biff!" "Take that," and so on. Bandura found that the children who had seen these behaviors tended to exhibit the same behaviors when given an opportunity to do so. Clearly, the relationship of the child to the model is of some importance, since it is obvious that children don't go around imitating every bit of behavior they see when given the opportunity to do so. Also, characteristics of the model are important. Baron (1970) performed a replication of the Bandura experiment, but he varied the attractiveness and the competence of the model. His results showed that both of these variables were important in eliciting imitative responses from observing children.

Throughout his research, Bandura has maintained the distinction between acquisition by the child of the potential to behave in a particular way and the actual execution of that behavior. It seems plausible that the process of acquisition is silent and does not require motoric participation from the subject. Performance occurs only when the occasion arises and when other aspects of the situation are favorable to the evocation of the bit of observed behavior. The implication of this distinction should be clear: A child does not have to practice the social performances he is observing in order to come to recognize their appropriateness. Over time he sees a great deal of social behavior from teachers, parents, older children, television characters, and actors. Role-learning takes place in this way, and children acquire in this fashion a huge quantity of impressions about what kinds of behaviors are appropriate in what kinds of situations. Then, when similar situations arise for them, they draw upon this stock of understandings as a way of guiding their own behavior.

Bandura has extended his research to show that imitation learning takes place when models are observed not directly but on television or film. In one experiment, children were shown films of other children being introduced to an inflated Bobo doll by the aggressive model. In another condition, children were shown aggressive episodes of an animated cartoon figure. The experimenters conclude, "Subjects who viewed the aggressive human and cartoon models on film exhibited nearly twice as much aggression than did subjects in the control group who were not exposed to the aggressive film content" (Bandura, Ross & Ross, 1963, p. 370).

In addition to showing that aggressive responses can be imparted via imitation, Bandura and his colleagues have demonstrated similar effects with a number of other types of content. For example, children with strong phobic reactions to dogs were allowed to observe other children interacting successfully with dogs. In this case, the model was a child, who engaged in a graduated series of more and more courageous interactions with a dog. Initially the model just looked at the dog and occasionally patted it. At the end of the series he had climbed in the pen with the dog, allowed it to eat out of his hand, and rested his head on it. Observation of the films of these events effectively reduced the displayed avoidance reactions of the initially phobic children to dogs. In an even more dramatic demonstration of the same kind of effect, Blanchard (1969) showed that observations of films in which models handled snakes were effective in reducing the strength of snake phobias in a group of adult subjects who had for many years been troubled by an irrational fear of snakes. Blanchard included four conditions in his experiment, as illustrated in Figure 4-2. In the three experimental conditions (there was also a control condition), visual modeling of snake handling was present. In one of these conditions, verbal information was added to the visual modeling, and in the third, the subject participated more directly in graduated approach toward the snakes. It may be seen from the

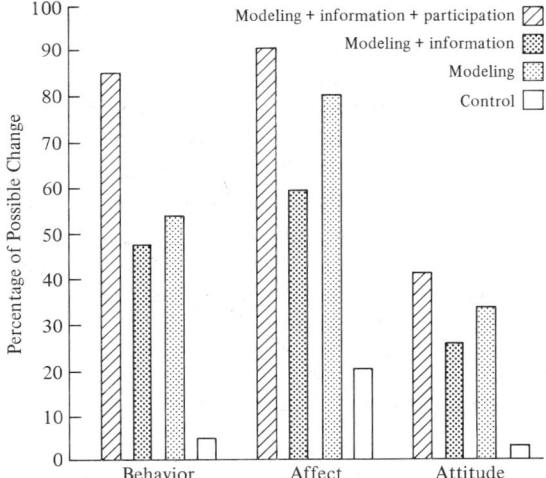

FIGURE 4-2. Percentage of change in approach behavior, fearfulness, and attitudes displayed by subjects who received different components of the modeling-guided participation treatment (Blanchard, 1969; Figure from Bandura, 1969).

figure that by far the largest effect on changes in approach behavior, affective response, and measured attitude were attributable to the effects of visual modeling alone.

While caution should be exercised in the interpretation of these findings, they constitute at least a dramatic illustration of the way an individual's evaluative behavior may be modified by observation and imitation. In these experiments, the salience, attractiveness, and competence of the model is assuredly high; and because of the nature of the experimental contract, the subject's attention is necessarily directed in the proper way. Under such conditions, the subject is in a perfect situation for vicarious learning. It is as if the subject himself were engaged in the modeled behavior and may easily observe that no negative consequences are forthcoming. Gradually, as this kind of observation is repeated and extended, the subject acquires confidence in his own ability to control his fear reactions in the presence of the formerly dreaded object.

The significance of studies of the effects of mere observations on the shaping of aggression and approach-avoidance behaviors is potentially very great in our society. We seem to assume implicitly that nothing which children see has any effect on them. The average 6 year-old child in the United States spends an estimated 21 hours per week in commercially sponsored observational learning, via television (Bailyn, 1959). Certainly a fair amount of what the child sees, if translated into actual behavior in the appropriate circumstances, would not meet with the approval of parents, who spend far fewer hours per week with the child than do his televised companions and models. Bronfenbrenner (1972) has suggested that parents in the United States seem to have abdicated their role as the main socializing agent for children. In a cross-cultural survey involving several nations, only the English were found to spend less time with their children or to express less concern over the child's development and activity.

The recent controversy on the relation between televised violence and aggression in children should be something of an embarrassment to social psychology, for the results should have appeared far less controversial in terms of determining the factual character of the relationship. The study by Bandura, Ross, and Ross on the effect of filmed aggression has already been cited. Additional studies showing the instigating effects of vicarious aggression have been performed by Berkowitz (1964) and by Berkowitz, Corwin, and Heironimus (1963). While these are all laboratory studies which might be criticized because they do not reproduce natural viewing conditions, a recently published nonexperimental study by Eron, Lefkowitz, Huesman, and Walder (1972) shows a strong relation between amount of violence observed on television and later aggression. This study was based upon a longitudinal survey of over 400 teenagers, in which viewing habits were assessed over a 10-year period of time. The main dependent variable was peer-rated aggression. This variable was strongly related to the preference for watching violent television programs. As to the enduring quality of this effect, the authors conclude, "It was found that the violence of programs preferred by the male subjects in Grade 3 was even more strongly related to aggression ten years later" (Eron et al., 1972, p. 263).

The relation between observed violence and aggressive behavior is not, however, a settled issue in psychological research. Feshbach and Singer (1971) have published a major experimental study which showed no such effect, except as reflected in the fantasies, not the behaviors, of the TV-exposed subjects. A study by Geen and Stonner (1973) has shown that the aggression-instigating effect of observed violence is dependent on both the state of the subject (attacked or nonattacked) and the particular meaning of the depicted violence (vengeance, "professional" violence, or unexplained). The position taken here is that some relation exists between observed violence and aggressive behavior and that TV is thus implicated in the causal chain for at least some aggressive acts. The details of this relationship are not well established. It is a good bet that future research will indicate more clearly how and when observed violence performs its modeling function.

The implications of socialization through imitation are not all negative. Evidence is in hand that altruism as well as aggression is influenced by observational learning. Bryan and Test (1967) have provided a series of illustrations that behaviors such as contributing to beggars and Salvation Army pots are positively influenced by the priming behaviors of models. Probably auctioneers and hustlers of all varieties have known of this phenomenon for ages. The "shil" is someone who wins conspicuously at a gambling house, eagerly makes the first purchase of a worthless lot in Florida, or bids with happy abandon at an Atlantic City sidewalk auction parlor.

Experimental evidence also shows that subjects can be induced to dissent from participation in an apparently noxious procedure by observing models initiate the breaking of the experimental contract (Feldman & Scheibe, 1972). When no models exhibited dissent behavior, no subjects dissented from participating in a procedure which was perceived as being very unpleasant.

Socialization as Role Learning

These observations on the imitation mechanism of socialization can be readily accommodated in the language of social-role theory. While the classical study of learning mechanisms and processes has had only the most distant potential application to the problem of social learning, the kind of research just described is clearly related to what is meant by role learning. Sarbin and Allen assert,

> In role learning, the importance of persons enacting complementary roles, the importance of teachers, models, and coaches, and the importance of relevant audiences cannot be overemphasized. In fact, this role relationship itself deserves careful analysis. . . . Research on role learning must deal with the particular kind of learning that occurs in interactional settings and must recognize the complexity of the content of the learning, the pervasiveness of the influence of other persons, and the crucial importance of the role relationship itself. (1968, p. 545)

The metaphor of the drama employed by role theory encourages us to think of the child as a fledgling actor, someone who is actively trying to learn the parts he will later be called upon to play. Traditionally, a distinction is made within role theory between roles which are granted or ascribed to a child immediately, through no exercise of option on the child's part, and roles which are attained or achieved. Occupational roles and professional attainments are not ascribed but are achieved as a result of choice and of confirming, validating actions. Sex, kinship, race, and sometimes religion are ascribed to the child. But even though these are granted components of the child's identity, he or she must learn the kinds of behaviors appropriate for that which the child already is. Sex-role training begins at a very early age, perhaps as soon as the child is born (see Kagan, 1964). Similarly, the child must learn all the rules of behavior that go with being a member of a particular family, church, race, or social class. Socialization accomplishes an accomodation of the child to the requirements of each of these ascribed roles. In this process, it is clear that the function of individuals in complementary role positions—parents, teachers, nurses, coaches, and trainers—is of critical importance. While the acquisition of labels for ascribed components of identity is automatic, learning the behaviors proper to those components of identity requires considerable time and involvement. Moreover, very strong negative sanctions are administered for failing adequately to discharge one's duty or responsibility as a son, a member of the family, or a citizen in the community.

Some authors prefer to use the word "enculturation" to describe the learning of achieved or attained roles and to reserve the term socialization for the acquisition of granted roles. While this usage will not be maintained here, it is of interest to consider the distinction which prompted it. Once the skills associated with granted roles are learned, one may behave in society in such a way as to avoid embarrassment or trouble. However, in order to gain special recognition, power, and responsibility in society, it is necessary for special instruction to be given in preparation for the assumption of achieved roles. This latter kind of instruction is much more likely to be considered formal education—primarily verbal presentation of information which is necessary for the assumption of achieved roles. Handbooks, manuals, courses, and degree programs are offered in a prepackaged way so that a person might gain access to achieved positions such as doctor, lawyer, politician, or truck driver. At the same time, it seems to be considered necessary to impart to the person all sorts of information which will be of no use whatever in the discharge of achieved responsibilities. One must learn about wars, kings, composers, artists, architectural styles, grammatical conventions in various languages, styles of dress in ages gone by, customs of remote tribes, styles of ancient and contemporary authors, and details of the careers of remote culture heroes, who are probably dead. All this "enculturation" may be seen as a forced effort to make one's identity seem to be a great achievement. While the process of socialization to granted components of identity takes place naturally and without great difficulty on the part of the sharply observant child, the process of formal education for achieved components of identity is often characterized as onerous and labored.

In the composite, a person's social identity is a combination of that which was granted and that which is attained. A birthright—a life charter—is implicitly granted to a person upon the event of birth. The most powerful lessons to be learned about identity consist in a discovery by the developing child of the terms of his birthright: Who am I? What is my name? What am I given? What are my rights and obligations as a person? Most of the early part of socialization is a matter of the child's becoming that which was called for in the birthright. The evolution of identity continues as the child is taught the requisite skills for entry into achieved roles. For both kinds of role learning, social mediators in complementary role positions are of critical importance.

This conception of socialization as role learning and the earlier description of socialization as moral development (viz., Kohlberg) may be brought together by considering some aspects of the thought of George Herbert Mead, who is critically important to the history of both of these traditions. The title of Mead's (1934) major work is *Mind, Self, and Society.* Mead's radical thesis is that mind, self, and society come into existence only in relation to each other. Human individuals come into self-consciousness only through social interaction. Mind is social both in origin and effect. Mind and self emerge from the interaction of the protean individual with society. Mead considers socialization, then, to be the essential process by which human beings become human beings. A few quotations from Mead will provide a clearer sense of these ideas:

> The individual enters as such into his own experience only as an object, not as a subject; and he can enter as an object only on the basis of social relation and interaction, only by means of his experiential transactions with other individuals in an organized social environment. (quoted in Pfeutze, 1954, p. 92)

> The individual is there only through cooperative interaction with others in the community. (quoted in Pfeutze, 1954, p. 57)

Socialization is identity formation as a consequence of social interaction. As the individual acquires roles, he also comes to acquire some conception of himself. In time, the person is able to see himself from outside himself, to view himself as an object. Similarly, the person becomes able to take a broad social perspective when regarding other people or social events. Like Piaget, Mead considers the person to become increasingly capable of attaining a decentered perspective as development proceeds through stages of interaction with others. Social training and moral training are seen as having similar roots.

> That which creates the duties, rights, the customs, the laws and the various institutions in human society, as distinguished from the physiological relationships of an ant hill or a beehive, is the capacity of the human individual to assume the organized attitude of the community toward himself as well as toward others. (Mead, 1938, p. 625)

The process of role taking is considered to be essential to psychological development and also essential to the development of a mature moral perspective, the kind of perspective represented in the highest stages of Kohlberg's schematization. Playing with other children, playing at imaginary games, and continued involvement with games is moral training, for the individual learns the meaning of social control both as operator and subject and comes to appreciate the norms of justice. "[The self] is constituted by an organization of the social attitudes of the generalized other or the social group as a whole to which he belongs" (quoted in Pfuetze, 1954, p. 87).

Mead's social psychology is one of the few systems of thought within psychology in which acts of altruism seem sensible and nonparadoxical. The broad social collectivity not only contributes individuality to the person, but it also becomes incorporated into the person. Mature moral judgments are made from the perspective of the "generalized other." This is not an alien perspective to the person, but rather one which he has incorporated as his own. Of course, the extent to which the person has internalized this perspective depends very much on the way in which social interactions take place at the various stages of development. Programs for moral education can be devised in such a way as to maximize the likelihood of a swift attainment of the highest stages of moral development. But now a fundamental problem has been touched: A system of moral education is based on certain premises about human rights and responsibility, indeed, on a particular conception of the idealized nature of man. The practice of socialization by each distinct human collectivity is dictated by two kinds of premises: first, by what sorts of techniques are most effective in forming children into the kinds of beings we idealize and, second, by what kinds of beings we idealize. Disagreements on the first score can presumably be settled by the appropriate research on developmental psychology. Disagreements about what people should become, however, are not resolvable by research of any kind, but are ground-level disputations over values.

It is for this reason that political ideologies become conditions of fundamental importance in understanding the process of human socialization. Aside from such technical ideas about child-rearing as may spring from a political ideology, it is sure that the ideology will define the limits of the moral dimensions of socialization. Since political regimes usually control the educational process for children, it is reasonable to suppose that the explicit or implicit ideology of the political regime will be translated into practice through the schools. The modern nation-state, as a definer of the law for its people, is also the most potent moral force in society, either implicitly or explicitly. But the importance of the body politic as an institution of socialization is so fundamental that it is often overlooked.[1] The next section is addressed to this issue.

---

[1] An exception to this neglect is provided in the work of Adelson and his coworkers, which is descriptive of the significance of political ideas in the process of moral development. (See Gallantin & Adelson, 1971; Adelson & O'Neil, 1966.)

SOCIALIZATION TO NATIONAL IDENTITY

> We hold these truths to be self-evident, that all men are created equal, that they are endowed by their Creator with certain inalienable rights, and among these are Life, Liberty, and the pursuit of Happiness.—That to secure these rights, Governments are instituted among Men, deriving their just powers from the consent of the governed.—*The Declaration of Independence*

If the history of mankind were compressed to a day, the time elapsed since 1776 would amount to no more than an eyeblink. Although the truths in the first sentence quoted from the Declaration of Independence are laid down as self-evident, it is a good bet that it was not always thus. These truths are the product of a rather highly evolved line of European philosophical thought, the Enlightenment. Two centuries ago they may have seemed arbitrary or debatable assertions, but they are more nearly self-evident now, for their statement has constituted a kind of moral ideal to which succeeding generations in the United States, as well as in other parts of the world, have been socialized.

The second sentence in the excerpt is less frequently quoted than the first, but it is very much to the point of this section. Truths once stated do not prevail by themselves. Governments must be established in such a way as to make them prevail. The Declaration of Independence is, after all, a document for the justification of a fraternal war. The justification is drawn from what are set up to be universal moral principles. If those principles are accepted, the justification is very successful indeed. Of course, after the war was won the principles were sanctified by blood and remain as a proud expression of the highest ideals of the nation, and the government remains an entity dedicated to the continual securing of these rights. If its initial job was to gain political independence from England in order to implement its ideals, its continuing job is to maintain that independence from all foreign powers and at the same time to socialize succeeding generations of its own people to these ideals, so that the nation is not subverted from within. Clearly, socialization has failed to achieve its objectives if individuals come to challenge the principle of human equality and the right to life, liberty, and the pursuit of happiness. Subject to their history of socialization, it is very difficult for Americans to realize that these ideals do not stand at the moral foundations of all nations and that a different set of self-evident truths may be made to prevail by a different government.

Because international comparisons are likely to impinge upon high passions, it is best to begin with an easier case as an illustration of what socialization to collective ideals entails. A good example is provided by a legal case (State of Wisconsin vs. Yoder, 1972) which was recently decided in Wisconsin regarding the right of a religious sect, the Amish, to maintain complete control over the education of their children. While the Amish are hardly a nation, their insistence on religious and cultural autonomy makes them a kind of self-contained and unique enclave within the United States.

The Supreme Court case centered on the conviction of three Amish parents by a state court for failing to send their children to school beyond the eighth grade, as is required by law in Wisconsin. The Amish provide their own schools for their children, but they do not continue formal school beyond the eighth grade, when the child is from 13 to 15 years old. After this, the young adolescent continues to learn the skills which are considered necessary within the community, but these are imparted in the informal setting of barnyard, house, or shop. The State of Wisconsin considered that it had an obligation, in the words of its chief prosecutor, "to liberate the children from oppression. . . . to expose them to the good things in life which the outside world has to offer."

For over two hundred years the Amish have been a self-sufficient segment of society in the United States. Their fundamentalist religious beliefs lead them to avoid contact with the modern world; electricity, automobiles, telephones, and the like are looked upon as unnecessary and corrupting. In the same way, science is not regarded as an activity worthy of human effort, and learning of a non-Biblical variety is looked upon with suspicion. "The social unit is small, communal, and enforced by strict shunning of those who violate community values. Their life-style and daily lives are the expression of their religious worship" (Arons, 1972, p. 52). Their educational system is efficient for their purposes. No problems of unemployment, poverty, juvenile delinquency, or crime plague them. Evidently, the socialization techniques they have evolved are quite effective, completely without the aid and advise of child psychologists.

But without question, the children in the Amish society are denied a certain access to "Life, Liberty, and the pursuit of Happiness." In the *Brown* decision of 1954 the Supreme Court held that separate education of minority groups is inherently unequal. Not only are the Amish children completely segregated from other minorities and the dominant majority in Wisconsin, they are also subject to an unusually strict and well-controlled regime in all phases of their life—at home, at school, or in the community.

A strong argument in favor of the Amish was their long success as an independent community. If certain rights were denied their children, the Court effectively decided on balance that the greater virtue lay in the preservation of their distinctness and affirmed their right to be different. But the Court pointed out that this exclusion would not apply to all. "Chief Justice

Burger took pains to exclude from the ruling, 'a group (presumably non-religious) claiming to have recently discovered some progressive or more enlightened process for rearing children for modern life'" (*New York Times,* May 14, 1972).

It is an open question as to whether the Amish could survive as a distinct subculture in the United States without jealous protection of their right to maintain complete control over the socializing regime to which their children are exposed. But doubtless their survival is facilitated by the maintenance of control. Compulsory education was established in the middle of the nineteenth century in the United States, in part as a way of assuring the continued loyalty of the populace. Doubtless the Amish see the same kind of advantage in the control of their educational system.

The greatest example of control of socialization in the twentieth century is undoubtedly that of China since the revolution of 1948. China's population of over 700,000,000 has been, and is being, socialized to a single set of cultural ideals, which is being accomplished by a single set of educational and re-educational procedures. Little emphasis is placed on such ideals as freedom of choice and the autonomy of the individual. But great emphasis is given to the idea that China must be independent and completely self-reliant. It is China, rather than Communism, which is the most fundamental object of loyalty for the Chinese. Ross Terrill comments on this fact as follows:

> The Chinese are a rooted and a continental people.... Their cultural memories run the length of the dynasties. They possess effortless assurance of their own cultural identity. This does not negate the fact that Peking sees the world through the spectacles of Communist ideology. But something in the Chinese way damps down the lust and swagger of Marxism. They take a very long view of things. Long dwelling amidst the mountains and waters of ancestors ten times as ancient as the Pilgrim Fathers has given the Chinese a patience of the ages. They do not, in fact, go around the world lighting fires of revolution, for they are genuinely skeptical that one nation can ignite another. And they believe in their hearts that few others, if any, can follow the epic Chinese way to revolution and socialism. (1972, p. 58)

A good deal of information is becoming available about the socialization techniques utilized by the Chinese. However, discussion of these techniques should wait on the availability of a much greater quantity of reliable and systematic information about the theory and practice of the Chinese educational and political indoctrination systems.

A good systematic study of political socialization on Taiwan was recently published (Wilson, 1970). This book, somewhat ironically entitled *Learning to Be Chinese,* makes it clear that the state in Taiwan uses the schools as a way of instilling a hatred for the regime on the mainland. But the task of socializing all children to a single-minded loyalty to the Chiang government appears to be complicated by a deep conflict between the native Taiwanese, who are the majority of the population and who were native to the island, and the mainlanders, who are residents of only 25 years' standing but who control most of the political positions of importance. Nevertheless, the regime appears to be generally successful at using the schools as a means of instilling loyalty to the nation. The difficulty comes in creating enthusiasm for the idea of invading the mainland and ousting the Communists.

The common theme in all these examples is that the school functions as the primary mechanism by which political socialization is acccomplished. Extensive studies on political socialization in the United States (Hess & Torney, 1968) yield the same general conclusion. The school, here and elsewhere, has the double function of developing the cognitive skills of children and at the same time inculcating in them a veneration for the moral ideals which are held to be fundamental to the nation. What are the techniques by which the child acquires an identification with the nation? And why does this process sometimes not work?

Doubtless most of the readers of this chapter are familiar with the means by which schools in the United States attempt to accomplish an identification of the child with the nation and with the "principles for which it stands." No point would be served by a recitation of the familiar here. It is likely that the process of political socialization can be seen more clearly at a distance. However, for comparative purposes it would be useful to consider one's own experience of political socialization in relation to the account presented in the next section of this process in another culture.

Socialization in the Soviet Union

" . . . in the collective, by the collective, for the collective" is a slogan coined by Makarenko, the most widely read and highly regarded authority on the upbringing of children in the Soviet Union. As an ideal for the socialization of children, this slogan represents a bridge between the theoretical ideals of the Soviet state and the actual techniques used to rear children. This slogan also epitomizes a difference in cultural ideals between the Soviet Union and the United States, where the emphasis on individual freedom and liberty conflicts sharply with the ideal of collectivization. The study by Bronfenbrenner of childhood socialization in the Soviet Union and the United States will be instructive, as we examine this work in more detail to develop a better idea of how socialization to these diverse ideals is implemented.

According to Bronfenbrenner (1972), the primary objective of early socialization in the Russian family is to teach the child obedience and self-discipline. The idea is to get the child to obey parents willingly, " . . . fulfilling the wishes of adults not as commands from without but as internally motivated desires" (p. 12). Bronfenbrenner quotes a leading authority on child development on the question of independence training: "What about developing independence in children? We shall answer: if a child does not obey and does not consider others, then his independence invariably takes ugly forms. Ordinarily this gives rise to anarchistic behavior, which can in no way be reconciled with laws of living in Soviet society" (p. 13). Obviously, socialization toward the norm of self-discipline requires effective techniques. Those most frequently employed by Soviet parents appear to be withdrawal of love, encouragement and praise, and for older children, verbal persuasion and explanation. Physical punishment is viewed as potentially harmful and is generally avoided. While the technique of withdrawal of love is given great importance, it takes place in the context of very close and affectionate contact between parent and child. Bronfenbrenner reports that the amount of physical contact of children with their parents and with other adults is far greater in the Soviet Union than it is in the United States. Also, Soviet parents spend more of their nonworking hours with their children. Solicitousness towards children appears very general in the Soviet Union, not only from parents but also from adolescents and other adults.

In the schools, the norm of collective responsibility is the constant theme, and a method analogous to withdrawal of love, public criticism or, in extreme cases, ostracism, is the primary mechanism for punishing deviations from the norm. Children who attend nursery schools begin immediately to play in groups and are taught to perform socially useful acts, such as feeding pets, watering plants, or cleaning floors. Many collective games and activities are organized. All children in the Soviet Union begin primary school at age seven. The opening of school is the occasion for happy celebrations, and the teachers are regarded with admiration and respect. In primary school, great emphasis is given to cooperation and group competition. The objective is to teach children to rely on each other and, reciprocally, to assume responsibility for the behavior of others in the group.

The relationship between cooperation and competition as norms of socialization are illustrated in a quotation from a Soviet school manual:

> It is not difficult to see that a direct approach to the class with the command, "All sit straight," often doesn't bring the desired effect since a demand in this form does not reach the sensibilities of the pupils and does not activate them. . . . (instead the teacher should say), "Let's see which row can sit the straightest."
>
> The children not only try to do everything as well as possible themselves, but also take an evaluative attitude toward those who are undermining the achievement of the row. If similar measures arousing the spirit of competition in the children are systematically applied by experienced teachers in the primary classes, then gradually the children themselves begin to monitor the behavior of their comrades and remind those of them who forget about the rules set by the teacher, not to forget what needs to be done and what should not be done. The teacher soon has helpers. (quoted in Bronfenbrenner, 1972, pp. 54–55)

The competition for approval is continuous and the emphasis is always on self-monitoring.

The example of Pavlik Morozov, the heroic boy who betrayed his father, sets the high ideal for Soviet children of placing loyalty to the collectivity above all else, so that the collectivity will prosper. Teachers seem to be quite successful in delegating their authority to classroom monitors, who take their responsibility for controlling infractions very seriously.

Bronfenbrenner and his colleagues performed a study in which various kinds of social misdemeanors were described to children. The children were asked what action they would take in relation to an infraction such as stealing something, cheating on an examination, and so on. The answers of children in the United States were found to depend greatly on who they thought would see their responses; they tended to show little or no conern with the infraction if they thought their responses would be seen by their peers. Soviet children, by contrast, showed no such differential. Their classmates were just as effective as parents or teachers in controlling misbehavior.

Apparently, the techniques for controlling misbehavior are quite effective. Incidents of antisocial behavior in the schools appear to be very rare by our standards. Of course, the techniques used to enforce good behavior would also appear to be morally repugnant by standards in the United States.

For example, a fifth-grade boy who is having difficulty with his mathematics is made the subject of a class discussion. After considerable debate, a girl proposes that two students be assigned to the struggling student to help him. He protests:

> "I don't need them. I can do it by myself. I promise."
>
> But Lyolya is not impressed. Turning to Vova, she says quietly, "We have seen what you do by yourself. Now two of your classmates will work with you and when *they* say you are

ready to work alone, we'll believe it. (Bronfenbrenner, 1972, p. 65)

Another example is provided in a description of a third-grade classroom, drawn from a Soviet school manual:

> Class 3-B is just an ordinary class; it's not especially well-disciplined nor is it outstandingly industrious. It has its lazy members and its responsible ones, quiet ones and active ones, daring, shy, and immodest ones.
>
> The teacher has led this class now for three years and she has earned the affection, respect and acceptance as an authority from her pupils. Her word is law for them.
>
> The bell has rung, but the teacher has not arrived. She has delayed deliberately in order to check on how the class will conduct itself.
>
> In the class all is quiet. After the noisy class break, it isn't so easy to mobilize yourself and to quell the restlessness within you! Two monitors at the desk silently observe the class. On their faces is reflected the full importance and seriousness of the job they are performing. But there is no need for them to make any reprimands: the youngsters with pleasure and pride maintain scrupulous discipline; they are proud of the fact that their class conducts itself in a manner that merits the confidence of the teacher. And when the teacher enters and quietly says to be seated, all understand that she deliberately refrains from praising them for the quiet and order, since in their class it could not be otherwise. . . .
>
> "What are you fooling around for? You're holding up the whole link," whispers Kolya to his neighbor during the preparation period for the lesson. And during the break he teaches her how to organize better the books and pads in her knapsack.
>
> "Work more carefully," says Olya to her girl friend. "See, on account of you, our link got behind today. You come to me and we'll work together at home." (quoted in Bronfenbrenner, 1972, pp. 59–60)

In a recent article, Kohlberg (1971) quotes this incident as an example of socialization to the norm of fundamental group loyalty. But Kohlberg is critical of the line of philosophic thinking, identified with Durkheim as well as Marx, which leads to the justification of these techniques.

> We see . . . that when this line of thinking is carried to its logical conclusion, it leads to a definition of moral education as the promotion of collective national discipline which most of us feel is consistent neither with rational ethics nor with the American constitutional tradition. What I am arguing is that the trouble with (this approach) is not that (it) starts from a conception of moral development, but rather that (it) starts from an *erroneous* conception of moral development. (p. 28) (my emphasis)

To be sure, this kind of collective control does seem to be inconsistent with the norms of individual autonomy so prevalent in the United States. Also, Kohlberg's implied suggestion that these techniques are inconsistent with American constitutional liberties certainly seems plausible. But in what sense may this be described as deriving from "an erroneous conception of moral development?" Certainly not in a technical or factual sense is the conception erroneous: It stands the pragmatic test of giving just about the kind of results its administrators intend to produce. But in a moral sense, it does deviate from the norms to which Americans have been socialized. The hottest place in the American version of Hell would be reserved for the likes of Pavlik Morozov. Anyone who has taken a realistic view of the way "honor systems" function in American institutions must conclude that students do not assume a great deal of responsibility for the success or honesty of their peers. "Do your thing" is a modern American motto, and privatism a way of life.

In their introduction to a volume of essays on "Moral Education," Sizer and Sizer (1970) summarize the modern American morality in this fashion:

> ... The moralisms of the prairie have a strong hold on the large remnant of Middle America. Nixon's "forgotten American" learned much from simple sermonizing. For a class of people it worked; it took hold. *But was it moral!*. ... The answer is a qualified no; sermonizing denies individual autonomy, which, with justice, lies at the heart of a new morality. (p. 3)

Later these authors describe the new morality as follows:

> Moral autonomy, the independent arrival at a conviction of one's accountability toward one's fellow men, the rational and emotional acceptance of justice as the most proper atmosphere in which all individuals can flourish, including even one's secret self—this is the "new morality" toward which we are to guide ourselves and other people. (p. 4)

Although this is not the place to enter a critique of the meaning of justice as an abstract moral principle, it is sufficient to recall the speech of the Roman Captain in response to Shaw's Lavinia, wherein he made it clear that the determination of what is just rests upon prior suppositions about who is divine.

The moral autonomy part of the "new morality" is given clearer expression in a quotation attributed to the late Fritz Perls, founder of the Gestalt therapy movement:

> I do my thing, and you do your thing. I am not in this world to live up to your expectations, and you are not in this world to live up to mine. You are you, and I am I; if by chance we find each other, it's beautiful. If not, it can't be helped. (Perls, 1969, p. 4)

This is certainly a far cry from the Soviet slogan, "Mine is ours, ours is mine." Soviet children are socialized to the idea that they are responsible to the expectations of their peers. If they fail to live up to these expectations, the result is public criticism and perhaps rejection by the group. It is a good bet that children raised in the United States would make poor citizens of the Soviet Union, and vice versa. The former would be ostracized socially for their individualism, and the latter would be pilloried for acting as finks for the system.

Speculations on the consequences of technological advance, migration to the city, and the decline of religious institutions have their place in discussions of the evolution of contemporary moral standards in Western society. Human institutions and the moral force carried by them are not fixed entities but are constantly in flux. However, our concern here is not with the cultural history of current moral standards but with the ways in which those standards come to influence the process of socialization for individuals. Those interested in the cultural history of current moral standards might consult the previously cited set of essays edited by Sizer and Sizer (1970) or the collection of essays by Lifton (1971). In the next section, attention is directed to some of the consequences for individuals of contemporary moral standards in the United States.

Contemporary Problems in Socialization in the United States

If primary socialization is performed by those institutions which grant to the individual the ascribed components of his identity, then concern is justified about how well the task of primary socialization is being performed in the United States. The United States is increasingly a securlarized society; organized religions maintain very little of the authority they once held. It is no secret that the nuclear family is breaking down: one out of every three marriages ends in divorce (see *The Death of the Family,* Cooper, 1970). Those families which do remain together do not set permanent roots in the community: One out of every five families in the United States may be expected to move each year. Book titles in the social sciences are clues to this condition: in *The Temporary Society* (Bennis & Slater, 1968) Americans are engaged in a *Collective Search for Identity* (Klapp, 1969). Americans are becoming a nation of existential nomads, restlessly trying on new life styles and new identities with the aid of the therapeutic and the cosmetic industries.

One institution which might continue as the ultimate definer of individual birthrights is the United States. But the nation seems somehow to have squandered its legitimacy in the eyes of many of its youth (cf. Keniston, 1968, *The Young Radicals*).

Several studies have appeared recently on the psychological histories of men of draft age who chose to go to prison or to Sweden or Canada in preference to serving in the armed forces (Gaylin, 1970; Borgida, 1972). Between 1965 and 1971, between 60,000 and 70,000 men have emigrated to Canada alone, as a way of avoiding or escaping military service.

Borgida (1972) interviewed a number of draft dodgers and deserters in Toronto:

> For the draft dodgers and deserters, the draft and military service created a role conflict between the national role demands for supreme loyalty to nation and the salience of other social roles, primary group ties, or moral and ethical principles. . . . For example, one twenty-five-year-old draft dodger from the Midwest did not define his obligation to the nation as a military obligation: "My obligations to society are that I be a productive member of it in some respect. But to fight a battle for the government—no!—especially if I don't agree with the end or aims." Similarly, a draft dodger who had completed one year of graduate study before he left the United States and came to the Toronto area, felt that his only "supreme loyalty" was to himself: "I didn't feel that I had to serve in the Army to fulfill the obligation to my country. I didn't feel it was a necessary obligation to do something like that for my country." . . . Most of the dodgers and deserters interviewed strongly believe that the government has no right to impose the draft on a man's life and, in effect, demand that he fight in a war which he regards as particularly illegitimate and immoral. "I had decided that the government law is immoral," said a dodger whose father is a Southern Baptist deacon. (pp. 8–9)

Of course, these individuals and those like them who found other solutions to the problem of avoiding military service are still a small minority of their age group. At the peak of youth protests against the war in Vietnam, a Survey Research Institute study of attitudes among high school students showed the overwhelming majority to be in support of their government's position and expressing a willingness to serve in the armed forces if called (Johnston & Bachman, 1970). But it is quite clear that all the emphasis placed on the development of the morally autonomous individual in our society is bearing fruit. A growing number of the young people in the United States are simply not going to march to the nation's drums.

The problem of understanding how the nation operates as an institution of socialization is vastly complicated by the factor of size. The generalizations offered above about patterns of socialization in China, the United States, and the Soviet Union, are undoubtedly inappropriate to large numbers of individuals in those countries and should be based on far more evidence than is available.

IN CONCLUSION

This chapter has construed the process of socialization basically as the evolution and development of values in the individual. From a slightly different perspective this amounts to the formation of a social identity. At this stage of our knowledge about the way in which developmental changes are encoded in the human organism, it is inappropriate to consider this process to be the result of a single, identifiable mechanism. Among the mechanisms by which socialization occurs are familiarization, identification, imitation, and the direct administration of social sanctions—punishments and rewards. At each stage of his development, the individual has an operative set of values which function for him both as a way of choosing among possible courses of action and as a way of defining himself in relation to other people and social institutions.

Most of the research and thinking within psychology in the past on the topic of socialization has been oriented around the question of mechanisms. While these are problems of fundamental significance, they are no more fundamental than the question of the relation of socializing institutions to the developing individual. While considerable concern has centered on the institution of the family as a socializing influence, very little work has been done within psychology on the effect of broader social institutions such as political collectivities on socialization. Yet these institutions effectively set the ground conditions for the objectives of socialization within a society. The examples cited in this chapter are meant to be invitations to further inquiry along these lines rather than assured generalizations about the character of socialization in the Soviet Union, the United States, or any other country.

In the context of contemporary conditions within the United States, it makes sense to reaffirm the obvious proposition that experiences and examples to which developing individuals are exposed will have consequences on their moral development. It makes sense to say this, because implicitly we have believed the contrafactual proposition that the influences to which children are exposed don't much matter. The null hypothesis has been that the observation of violence on television will have no consequences, that the shift of the custody of the child from the parent to the television set will have no consequences, that the break up of marriages and the disruption of community stability encouraged by modern corporate emphasis on mobility will have no consequences, that allowing cities to become overpopulated and decrepit will have no consequences, that the destruction of venerable landmarks and places of quiet beauty in the interest of progress will have no consequences, that avoiding our children will have no consequences. In all of these cases the null hypothesis is most certainly false. However, the alternative hypothesis which describes the true relation between each of these manipulations or events on the process of human socialization is in most cases not known. But it is very perilous to assume, because the precise effects are unknown, that no negative effects are likely to occur. Just as the changes wrought by man in the physical environment produce readjustments in the ecology which extend over hundreds of years, so will changes in the social developmental milieu for human beings produce unanticipated consequences which will continue to be realized for a considerable period of time.

Bronfenbrenner has suggested as one measure of the moral development of a civilization the amount of concern one generation has for the next generation. Even given the enormous cultural differences in the content of social norms, the constant factor of directed concern of parents for the upbringing of their young continues to produce a modicum of humanization for each generation of our species. Perhaps the specific direction of socialization is less important than the fact that it is directed. The care devoted to children will determine the extent to which those children, as adults, will be capable of caring.

SUMMARY

Socialization refers to the developmental differentiation occurring in the individual as a result of the way he is treated by the representatives of the society into which he is born. More specifically, it refers to the development of personal values as a result of social interaction.

The root problem for socialization theory and research is to develop an understanding of how individuals come to adopt the values which guide their behavior. The major concern of this chapter is the way in which a political system or quasipolitical systems determine the values to which individuals are socialized.

Three analytically distinct aspects of socialization are mechanisms, processes, and contents of socialization. The mechanisms of socialization refer to the means by which changed evaluative dispositions occur in the individual. Examples of mechanisms are familiarization, conditioning, identification, imitation, and role-playing. Socialization may be described as a long-term developmental process. The anthropologist describes this process as enculturation, the sociologist as acquisition of social norms, the psychologist as the learning of values. The contents of socialization display an enormous range of cultural diversity. Some psychologists have suggested that there is a general process of human social development which may be described as a progression of stages, in which the content of moral rules changes systematically.

A great deal of recent research has centered on the role of imitation in social learning. Aggressive responses can be learned by children as a direct result of the observation of models or through the observation of aggressive behavior on films or television. Also, irrational fears (phobias) can be reduced by the observation of models who show no signs of fear in a potentially threatening situation. The significance of studies of the effects of mere observations on the shaping of aggressive and approach-avoidance behaviors is potentially very great.

Another important perspective on socialization is provided by role theory. The metaphor of the drama employed by role theory encourages us to think of the child as a fledgling actor, as someone who is actively trying to learn the parts he will later be called upon to play. As the individual acquires roles, he also comes to acquire some conception of himself. In time, the person is able to see himself from outside himself, to view the self as an object. Similarly, the person becomes able to take a broad social perspective when regarding other people or social events. The broad social collectivity not only contributes individuality to the person, it also becomes incorporated into the person. It is from this perspective that political ideologies are seen as fundamentally important in understanding the process of human socialization.

Socialization is best approached without the constraints of any single theory or narrowly disciplined point of view. Indeed, perhaps the most important lessons to be learned about socialization can be derived from a reading of history, including current history. The range of possible outcomes of the process of human socialization is suggested, but not defined, by the examples of history. History's catalog of heroes, villains, and knaves represents a set of realized outcomes of human socialization.

Quite obviously, some of the individuals in this catalog turned out in ways which greatly surprised the social milieu which nurtured the formation of their identities. These surprises will continue to occur—sometimes to our joy, sometimes to our horror. The advantage of knowing as much as we can know about the mechanisms, processes, and contents of human socialization is that such knowledge might maximize our joyful surprises and minimize the horrible ones.

SUGGESTED READINGS

Bandura, A., & Walters, R. H. *Social learning and personality development*. New York: Holt, Rinehart & Winston, 1963.

This is a standard text on personality from the standpoint of social learning theory. Considerable attention is given to studies of imitation as a mechanism of social learning.

Bronfenbrenner, U. *Two worlds of childhood: U.S. and U.S.S.R.* New York: Clarion, 1972.

This book presents a good summary of Bronfenbrenner's extensive comparative observations on socialization in Soviet and American schools. The observational detail is far richer for the former than the latter.

Hess, R.D., & Torney, J. V. *The development of political attitudes in children*. New York: Doubleday, 1968.

Data and conclusions from a large-scale research project on political socialization are here summarized. This is the best current source on the role of schools as vehicles of political socialization in the United States.

Goslin, D. A. (Ed.). *Handbook of socialization theory and research*. Chicago: Rand-McNally, 1969.

This is the standard reference for current research and theory on socialization within psychology. All of the classical positions are represented.

Mead, G. H. *Mind, self and society*. Chicago: University of Chicago Press, 1934.

This is the classical presentation of Mead's seminal ideas on social development, one of the foundations of modern role theory. It is difficult, but worth the effort.

5
Situational Determinants of Hurting and Helping Behavior

Samuel L. Gaertner

INTRODUCTION

Amid discussions of My Lai, Watergate, and B. F. Skinner's *Beyond Freedom and Dignity* (1971), a familiar question arises: To what extent are a person's actions the result of internal forces (i.e., innate capacities, personality, moral fiber) as opposed to immediate external forces (i.e., environmental factors such as social pressure, reinforcement contingencies)? In many cases the answer to this question determines the extent of the person's legal and moral culpability for his actions. It seems more likely that the cause of a person's behavior would be attributed to external forces if it is believed that most people would have behaved identically under similar circumstances. In addition, increased confidence in the effectiveness of external determinants would be gained if it could be demonstrated that predictable changes in behavior occur when the magnitude of these forces are varied systematically.

The focus of the material discussed here is limited to the research literature which speaks to the facilitating and inhibiting effects of the immediate situational context on hurting and helping behavior. Discussion of these variables will be limited to those present immediately before or during the execution of the aggressive or helpful act. Influential factors within the situational context may include, for example, the number of other persons present, the proximity to the victim, the apparent similiarity to the victim, and the victim's behavior, as well as the larger situational context such as the institutional setting, the social norms, or the population density of the region.

The approach taken in this chapter suggests that if you were a member of Charlie Company at My Lai on March 16, 1970, you would probably have fired upon the helpless civilians. Yet it also acknowledges that some people may be more inclined than others to hurt or to help across a variety of situations. That is, it does not expect situational factors to explain or control the behavior of every individual. In fact, it would not offer a precise prediction about the behavior of any single individual. Most students upon initial exposure to this approach are disturbed by this failure to make predictions for individuals. The value of the situational perspective is that it, in many cases, seems to account for the behavior of a sizeable portion of the population without benefit of additional individual information. In fact, in studies which attempted to determine whether personality variables or situational factors were better predictors of a person's behavior, the latter was a more powerful factor (Larsen, Coleman, Forbes, & Johnson, 1972; Mangelsdorff, 1973). Nevertheless, systematic knowledge of the internal determinants such as personality is invaluable. Without an individual difference or a personality perspective, differences in behavior within a particular situational context would be unexplained.

This chapter, then, acknowledges the classic formula proposed by Kurt Lewin, $B = f(P,S)$. Lewin asserted by this means that behavior (B) is always a function of, or caused by, some complex interaction between the personal qualities of the individual (P) and the situational context in which he acts and is embedded (S). Ideally, a full explanation of any behavior would encompass an understanding of both kinds of factors. However, it would seem that one set or the other might predominate, that is, be more influential, in certain cases to the almost total exclusion of the other. Thus, a person with a phobia can be expected to react fearfully to whatever the phobia object is, no matter how pleasant the context may be in other respects. Similarly, a situation such as an earthquake may be so compelling that almost everyone may be expected to display panic.

Although a complete specification in terms of Lewin's formulation would seem the ultimate goal of social psychological research, there are legitimate reasons for focusing on either set of determinants for strategic reasons. For example, some observers believe that contextual forces can reach a magnitude capable of completely altering a person's state of consciousness to the extent that usual personality dispositions become irrelevant determinants of behavior. Indeed, it appears that new personality dispositions emerge. Usually, situational forces are relatively weak, thereby permitting the great diversity in personality or behavior we observe (and often enjoy) among our acquaintances each day. However, as the magnitude of situational forces increase there seems to be a reduction in this diversity among people; these forces tend to push us universally in a common direction.

Zimbardo (1969) has described the process of deindividuation whereby antecedent situational factors dramatically transform an individual's consciousness and behavior. Zimbardo writes:

> Deindividuation is a complex, hypothesized process in which a series of antecedent social conditions lead to changes in perception of self and others, and thereby to a lowered threshold of normally restrained behavior. Under appropriate conditions what results is the "release" of behavior in violation of norms of appropriateness.
>
> Such conditions permit overt expression of antisocial behavior, characterized as selfish, greedy, power-seeking, hostile, lustful, and destructive. However, they also allow a range of "positive" behaviors which we normally do not express overtly, such as intense feelings of happiness or sorrow, and open love for others. Thus emotions and impulses usually under cognitive control are more likely to be expressed when the input conditions minimize self-observation and evaluation as well as concern over evaluation by others. (1969, p. 251)

The situational factors postulated to lead to the state of deindividuation include, among others: anonymity, the opportunity to diffuse or share responsibility for one's actions, the opportunity to concentrate primarily on the here and now (while the past and future remain less salient), novel or unstructured situations (i.e., those which lack clear prescriptions for appropriate behavior), and the opportunity to rely on noncognitive (i.e., physical) interactions and feedback.

In a dramatic demonstration of the process of deindividuation, Zimbardo (1972) and his colleagues introduced normal, physically healthy, decent, reasonably rational and humane student volunteers to a simulated prison located in the basement of the Stanford University psychology building. Arbitrarily, some participants were assigned the role of guard and others the role of prisoner. Guards were provided with identical khaki uniforms, silver reflector sunglasses, billy clubs, handcuffs, and keys to the barred cell doors. These guards were told to maintain law and order in the prison and were given considerable latitude with regard to their strategies for prisoner management. The prisoners were given smocks and nylon stocking caps to wear and were housed in the barred cells.

Within a few days dramatic transformations began to appear among these otherwise "normal, middle-class, highly educated people." Many guards became sadistic, capricious, and tyrranical in their arbitrary use of power. Other guards were regarded as tough but fair and would occasionally do small favors for the prisoners. However, these tough but fair guards never intervened in behalf of the prisoners when the sadistic guards were issuing arbitrary commands or unfair and often brutal treatment to the prisoners.

Among the prisoners some were released because they suffered from hysterical crying, distorted thinking, and severe depression. Other prisoners became servile, selfish, hostile, and anxious only to escape or to be paroled. Although this "prison" experience was to last for two weeks, Zimbardo and his colleagues were forced to terminate the project after only six days and nights because:

> We were no longer dealing with an intellectual exercise in which a hypothesis was being evaluated in the dispassionate manner dictated by the canons of the scientific method. We were caught up in the passion of the present, the suffering, the need to control people, not variables, the escalation of power and all of the unexpected things that were erupting around and within us. (Zimbardo, Banks, Haney & Jaffe, 1973, p. 56)

Thus, the situational context, in this case the institutional pressures of a "prison environment," radically transformed the behavior of its constituents.

HURTING AND HELPING

All definitions of aggression specify an act that results in (or was intended to result in) pain, injury, or death to another organism. However, acts of aggression may serve various underlying motives. More important for this discussion is the seemingly paradoxical fact that the same situational context (as viewed by an observer) may facilitate or inhibit the aggressive act, depending upon the behavior's motivational basis. To place in perspective the various types of aggressive acts please consider the following simplifying definitional scheme.

Definitions

Angry Aggression. The primary goal of an angry aggressive attack (verbal or physical) is to inflict injury or pain upon the victim or that personal property which will indirectly affect his well-being. The attack may be initiated by hostility felt towards the victim's person or towards what he represents, or a desire for retribution and revenge. The attack, however, need not necessarily be accompanied by rage or obvious anger. A behavioral definition of angry aggression is a response which is reinforced by the pain or injury inflicted (Buss, 1961).

Instrumental (nonangry) Aggression. The primary goal of an instrumental aggressive attack (verbal or physical) is to obtain some personal or social good (e.g., money, excitement, or peace) or to fulfill role expectations (e.g., the security guard's wounding the thief). The victim's well-being, however, is rather inconsequential. Often the anticipated pain and injury to the victim may even be considered unfortunate but necessary. The extent of pain and injury inflicted does not exceed the minimum believed by the attacker to be necessary to obtain the goal or to fulfill his role obligation.

The assumption that one type of aggression is any more desirable, justifiable, or pathological than the other is often invalid. It is sometimes difficult for the observer of a simple act to distinguish an angry from an instrumental attack. Furthermore, during the course of an instrumental attack, there may be a transition to angry aggression. For example, the soldier firing at his faceless enemy in the name of Democracy or because he is following orders is utilizing a nonhostile attack. Suddenly his buddy is fatally wounded. His next shot, in the name of revenge, represents a transition to angry aggression. For further illustration, the case of the police officer using excessive force suggests that he is not impersonally following his role prescription. Any force which exceeds that which the officer perceives as really necessary to the situation would be an angry attack.

In spite of these limitations imposed upon an observer, the separation of angry and instrumental aggression provides a useful scheme for the classification of aggressive behavior examined in the social psychological literature. Similarly, as in the treatment of aggression, a distinction between two types of helping is valuable academically.

Altruism. Macaulay and Berkowitz (1970) succinctly defined "altruism" as behavior carried out to benefit another without anticipation of external rewards. The ultimate form of the act as defined here would be the performance of a helping response in which neither the victim nor anyone else was aware of the helper's identity (i.e., where material compensation would be impossible).

Instrumental Helping. The second kind of helping is behavior which helps another but whose primary intention is the attainment of external rewards (e.g., social recognition, the victim's gratitude). Obviously, it would be difficult to discern altruism from instrumental helping by merely observing a single instance of helping behavior.

There are interesting similarities between hurting and helping which were instrumental in the decision to discuss both phenomena in the same chapter. Both areas have stimulated great interest among researchers, students, and the general population. The notions of instrumental helping and instrumental aggression suggest that the same motive may lie behind these two quite different behaviors. Another link is the possibility that, in some instances, refusal to aggress is based upon altruistic concern for the victim. Similarly, a refusal to help may be based upon a desire to perpetuate the victim's suffering. That is, purposely remaining passive and refusing to help (e.g., as in emergencies, or through passive acceptance of sociopolitical policy that disables a particular group) is perhaps a "civilized" expression of aggression toward disliked victims. By doing nothing, the victim suffers, while this passive bystander avoids many of the distasteful consequences of actively expressed aggression (e.g., legal penalties or possible physical injury).

Research Strategies

The experimental psychologist's most conclusive test of his theoretical analysis of some behavior rests on his ability to control the occurrence of the phenomenon by systematically varying the antecedent conditions suggested by his theory. Following the manipulation of these specified conditions, the researcher awaits corresponding predictable changes in behavior. When the behavior is related to hurting or helping, however, special practical and ethical problems arise (considerably more for hurting than for helping). For example, how would you test the validity of the argument posed by proponents of strong gun control legislation that the mere presence of a gun, not to mention its lethality, instigates violence? Obviously, a full-fledged experimental test (important as it may be) is out of the question.

Nevertheless, with some modifications, this question has been addressed in the laboratories of Leonard Berkowitz (Berkowitz and Lepage, 1967) and Arnold Buss (Buss, Booker, and Buss, 1972). The laboratory context and the type and degree of aggression elicited (i.e., relatively intense levels of electric shock delivered to the victim in the context of a task evaluation) do not totally mirror reality, but the situations contained the essential features of the situation posed by the original question. In general, the research in aggression has been confined to laboratory situations in which the experimenter is assured that "real" injury is unlikely.

INSTRUMENTAL AGGRESSION

Obedience

Consider for a moment the number of things you do each day, not because you really want to, but because someone (e.g., a parent, instructor, employer, friend, or physician) tells you to. These people whom you obey may derive their social power from their ability to reward or to punish, their attractiveness, their expertise, or their perceived legitimacy. Although these people obviously influence your behavior (e.g., with regard to demonstrating gratitude, working inconvenient hours, or watching your diet), you might be unwilling to admit that they could successfully influence you to obey their command to subdue and possibly kill a likeable 50-year-old man. During childhood, we have been taught the importance of respecting and obeying authority, as well as respect for the value of human life. To what extent, however, can we as normal, socialized adults detach ourselves from the commands of legitimate authority when obedience requires inflicting pain and suffering upon a helpless victim? Under what situational circumstances would our moral values and our concern for the victim compel us to obey these destructive commands? An experiment was carried out to test one such situation.

General Procedure. Subjects in a series of experiments designed and run by Stanley Milgram (1963) were recruited through local newspaper and direct mail solicitation and represented a variety of ages and occupational types. In each experimental session a single naive subject was joined by a 50-year-old male employee of the project posing as a naive subject and by an experimenter. The experimenter paid each participant $4.50 for coming to the laboratory and explained that the purpose of the experiment was to study the effects of punishment on human learning. Specifically, the aim of the experiment was to determine how much punishment is best for human learning and also whether an adult learns best from a person younger or older than himself.

The learning task required one of the participants to be the teacher and the other to be the learner. A rigged drawing ensured that the naive subject was always the teacher and the confederate always the learner. To prepare the learner for receiving punishment a shock electrode was attached to his wrist, and the experimenter gave his assurance that "although the shocks can be extremely painful, they cause no permanent tissue damage."

The instrument panel of the shock generator consisted of a horizontal series of 30 switches, each clearly labeled as to its voltage. These switches proportedly increased the intensity of the shock by 15-volt increments ranging from 15 to 450 volts. In addition, each group of four switches was consecutively labeled: "slight shock," "moderate shock," "strong shock," "very strong shock," "intense shock," "extreme intensity shock," and "danger: severe shock." The last two switches bore the designation "XXX."

As teacher the subject was to read a series of word pairs to the learner (e.g., blue book, white house). Following this initial training trial, he was to read the first member of each word pair followed by three additional words plus the word originally paired with the stimulus word. The learner was then to indicate which of the four words was the correct paired associate by depressing an appropriate finger switch, which in turn signaled the teacher's box.

The subject was told to administer a shock each time the learner gave an incorrect response; furthermore, he was instructed to "move one level higher on the shock generator each time the learner flashes a wrong answer." Before delivering each punishment, the subject was to announce the correct word and also the numerical voltage designation of the impending shock. This procedure was to continue until the learner had learned all the word pairs.

According to plan the learner provided many incorrect answers (about three wrong for each correct answer) which, during the course of the experiment, would have required the teacher to use the maximum level on the shock generator. Of course, the learner never actually received any shock. If at any time the subject expressed doubts about continuing the experiment, the experimenter delivered a standard sequence of prods to bring the subject into line. Each particular prod was used only if the preceding one failed to obtain the subject's obedience.

Prod 1: "Please continue," or "Please go on."

Prod 2: "The experiment requires that you continue."

Prod 3: "It is absolutely essential that you continue."

Prod 4: "You have no other choice; you must go on."

Thus, the subject was placed in a situation in which he was expected to inflict increasing levels of pain upon a helpless victim for the sake of a scientific enterprise.

Given this basic situation, Milgram asked a number of intriguing questions regarding the extent to which immediate situational factors would affect the subjects' level of obedience. For example, Milgram questioned the importance of the immediacy of the victim in terms of both his proximity to the teacher and his overheard screams of pain and protest.

An initial series of experiments were conducted almost exactly as just described, the victim providing no protest or agonizing screams upon the delivery of punishment. Milgram (1965a) reported: "It was thought that the verbal and voltage designations on the control panel would create sufficient pressure to curtail the subject's obedience. However, this was not the case." When the learner was located in a room adjacent to the teacher, only to be dimly perceived through a glass window, virtually all subjects, once commanded, went blithely to the end of the board, seemingly indifferent to the verbal designations ("extreme shock" and "danger: severe shock"). " . . . subjects frequently averted their eyes from the person they were shocking, often turning their heads in an awkward and conspicuous manner. One subject explained, 'I didn't want to see the consequences of what I had done'" (Milgram, 1965a, p. 61).

In a second series of experiments, Milgram (1965b) varied the severity of the victim's protests by manipulating both the victim's physical proximity to the teacher and the nature of his screams and protests. Milgram expected that obedience to the experimenter's commands would decrease, as the subject became psychologically "closer" to his victim.

In the "remote feedback" condition the victim, located in an adjacent room, was not visible to the subject. When the voltage reached 300 volts (switch 20), the victim audibly pounded on the wall in protest. After 315 volts, he was not heard from again, nor did he provide answers on the learning task. In this "remote feedback" condition approximately 66% of the subjects (26 out of 40 males) obeyed the experimenter's commands fully and proceeded to the last switch labeled "XXX :450-volts." The mean maximal shock delivered by the subjects in the "remote feedback" condition was approximately 405 volts ("danger: severe shock").

The "voice feedback" condition was identical to the "remote feedback" except that voice protests ranging from groans to shouts from the victim were added to the situation. From 300 volts on, he no longer responded to the multiple-choice task but shrieked in agony upon the delivery of each shock up through 450 volts.

In this condition 62.5% of the subjects continued to administer punishment through the 450-volt level. The mean maximal shock for subjects in this condition was approximately 375 volts (labeled "danger: severe shock").

Milgram reported that obedient subjects experienced tremendous tension and anxiety. They continuously protested to the experimenter and verbally expressed deep concern for the victim's well-being. However, "many subjects cannot find the specific verbal formula that would enable them to reject the role assigned to them by the experimenter. Perhaps our culture does not provide adequate models for disobedience (1965b, p. 68)."

In a slight variation of this condition in which the victim claimed to have a slight heart condition and was not heard from following the 330-volt shock, 50% of the subjects continued to 450-volt shock.

In the "proximity" condition the learner was moved to the same room as the subject and was seated 1½ feet from him. The victim's protests were similar to those in the "remote feedback" condition. Under these circumstances 40% of the subjects were completely obedient. Here the mean maximal shock was approximately 315 volts ("Extreme Intensity Shock").

In a "touch proximity" condition, the victim could only receive a shock when his hand rested on a shock plate. At the 150-volt level he refused to ever again place his hand on this shock plate, whereupon the experimenter ordered the subject to force the victim's hand onto the plate. In this condition 30% of the subjects continued to physically force the victim's hand onto the shock plate against his protests through the 450-volt level. The mean maximal shock for all subjects in this condition was approximately 270 volts ("intense shock").

As the experimental situation changed from the "remote feedback" condition to that of "touch proximity," the proportion of obedient subjects declined from 66% to 30%. Milgram's "immediacy" manipulation did combine the independent factors of physical proximity, visual cues, and auditory cues; nevertheless, the general manipulation clearly demonstrated the importance of the victim's conspicuousness upon our tendency to inflict pain and suffering upon command from legitimate authority. Further support for this idea comes from Arnold Buss (1966) who, in examining instrumental (nonhostile) aggression, also found that the victim's feedback in the form of moans and groans significantly decreased the intensity of punishment administered.

One hypothesis for the decrease in obedience as the conspicuousness of the victim increased is that the subject becomes increasingly aware of the intensity of the victim's suffering as psychological distance decreases. However, Milgram reported that when subjects were asked during a post-experimental interview to estimate on a 14-point scale the pain experienced by the victim, there were no consistent differences across the various conditions. Milgram's explanation for these findings was that, at greater psychological distances, the attacker is aware of the victim's suffering in an abstract or conceptual rather than emotional sense. The bombardier, for example, fully realizes that his actions will result in pain and suffering, but he escapes the emotional experience that would result from his observing the final consequences. Such an emotional reaction might instigate the termination of the attack because of a greater empathic or altruistic concern for the victim or because the unpleasant emotional reaction itself could be diminished by termination of the attack.

In a related series of experiments Milgram varied the spacial relationship between the subject and the experimenter. The effectiveness of the experimenter's commands was less when he delivered his orders from another room over a telephone (only 22.5% of subjects were obedient) than when he sat just a few feet from the subject (66% of subjects were obedient). Clearly then, proximity to either the victim or to the legitimate authority significantly affects the performance of a nonhostile attack initiated by the command of legitimate authority.

Disregarding the variations caused by the proximity manipulations, the absolute level of obedience throughout was surprisingly high. Forty psychiatrists given a detailed description of the *Voice feedback* condition (in which the experimenter was present) expected only .1% of subjects to continue through the 450-volt level.

To account for the surprisingly high level of obedience, Milgram claimed that his subjects experienced an altered state of consciousness which permitted partial escape from the conflicting demands of authority and conscience. In the altered state of consciousness, labeled the state of "agency," subjects concentrated on the narrow performance of their task and believed that the experimenter rather than themselves bore responsibility for the victim's welfare. In one experiment Milgram decreased the subject's responsibility by assigning him a subsidiary task while another "teacher" (actually a confederate of the experimenter) pressed the shock button. Here over 90% of the subjects continued their participation to the end.

In other experiments (Milgram, 1963, 1965b) the subject responsible for pressing the shock button was joined by two additional teachers (actually confederates of the experimenter). In one condition, in which the confederate teachers refused to continue, 90% of the subjects similarly defied the experimenter's authority.

In a second condition, the confederate teachers suggested that the shock level be increased despite the victim's protests and the absence of any command from the experimenter to do so; only 17.5% of the subjects carried out this suggestion. Apparently, disobedient models can effectively liberate us from the destructive commands of legitimate authority; destructive models, however, are less effective influencers than the commands of legitimate authority.

Obviously, the results of Milgram's study of obedience are disturbing. Variations in the situational context, however, significantly affected the level of obedience, in this case the proportion of subjects willing to administer painful, potentially lethal electric shocks to an innocent victim. The parallels between Milgram's research and real-life events are disturbingly tangible. Apparently, in some situations, many normal, decent people faced with the commands of legitimate authority tend to obey, regardless of the content of the act. Such findings have been supported by additional research. For example, obedience has recently been studied in Munich, West Germany (Mantel, 1971). A replication of Milgram's "remote feedback" condition yielded 85% obedience, not significantly different from the 65% reported by Milgram.

Obedience Research and the Critics. Alongside ethical criticism over placing subjects in extremely stressful situations, some critics have disagreed with Milgram regarding the content of his subjects' actions. Masserman (1968) and Orne and Holland (1968) have argued that the experimental context of obedient behavior prohibits generalization and commentary about our society at large. Specifically, these critics have taken issue with Milgram's report that obedient subjects truly believed they were inflicting pain upon the helpless learner. This interpretation emphasizes the point that subjects participating in experiments have implicitly signed a contract with the experimenter in which they agree to do what is asked of them in return for which the experimenter promises that no injury will befall them and that their participation will be scientifically meaningful. Given the subjects' belief that trained experimenters are reputable, the callous behavior of Milgram's experimenter is too incongruous to be taken seriously. The experimenter's apparent calmness and lack of concern for the learner, supposedly writhing in pain, cued the subject to the true state of affairs, that the learner was not really being injured. Subjects then continued the performance of their role in the experiment without revealing their knowledge of the experimenter's deception because (1) they perceived that the experimenter expected them to continue and (2) they wanted the record of their performance to be used rather than discarded because they were wise to the experimenter's deception. Thus, subjects continued their performance, providing the experimenter with protests and nonverbal evidence that they were suitably disturbed by the experimental procedures.

On the basis of viewing Milgram's filmed report of his obedience research (*Obedience,* New York University Film Library, 1965) and further experimental evidence concerning people's behavior in psychological experiments, this author tends to agree with Milgram's account of his subjects' behavior.

Orne (1962) argues that, in a psychological experiment, the subject uses the experimenter's behavior and other cues in the experimental situation to uncover the experimenter's hypothesis to determine how he is expected to behave in the situation. Applying Orne's approach to Milgram's situation, we might examine the nature of the hypotheses obedient subjects might reasonably derive, assuming that they are aware of the true state of affairs regarding the learner's apparent pain. It seems likely that subjects would conclude that the experimenter wished to test what kind of person he was by measuring how long he would continue to inflict pain on the victim. Would the subject then go on to shock the victim severely, perhaps fatally?

Additional research on the effects of participating in psychological experiments has revealed that subjects are not singularly concerned with behaving according to the experimenter's apparent hypothesis. They are concerned with creating a favorable impression upon the experimenter regarding their personal characteristics, however. In fact, Siegal, Aronson and Van Hoose (1970) have demonstrated that when subjects are given the choice of behaving in a manner supportive of the experimenter's apparent hypothesis or presenting themselves in a favorable light, subjects chose the latter alternative. If subjects were aware of Milgram's deception, they would therefore be expected to discontinue shocking. It seems unlikely to this author, that subjects, seeing through the deception, chose instead to continue their participation.

Orne and Holland's criticism assumes that the experimental context increases the level of destructive obedience because subjects were assured of the learners well-being by the unspoken contract between experimenters and their subjects. Destructive obedience, however, has been observed in a hospital setting in which subjects were unaware of their participation in an experiment (Hofling, Brotzman, Dalrymple, Graves & Pierce, 1966). Acting in violation of hospital and professional regulations, 21 of 22 nurses prepared to administer twice the recommended daily dose of a medication which did not appear on the hospital's list of approved drugs when ordered to do so over the telephone by an unknown physician. When additional nurses were asked on a questionnaire what they would have done given the irregularities of the physician's order, 10 out of 12 claimed they would have refused to administer the medication.

Given the appropriate social structure, the commands of legitimate authority are apparently more persuasive than personal or social regulators of conduct. All too often, subordinates are either incapable of or unwilling to risk the censure and confrontation that they fear would result from their defiance of unethical destructive commands.

Evaluation of the Frustration-Aggression Hypothesis

One of the famous doctrines of American psychology has been the frustration-aggression hypothesis formulated by Dollard, Doob, Miller, Mowrer, and Sears (1939) at Yale University. Originally, the hypothesis stated that "aggression is always a consequence of frustration" and that the "occurrence of aggressive behaviors always presupposes the existence of frustration and, contrariwise, the existence of frustration always leads to some form of aggression." Frustration was defined as a "condition which exists when a goal response suffers inteference." Miller (1941) later clarified the Yale group's position by claiming that frustration instigates a number of responses, one of which is aggression. Furthermore, he reemphasized that the instigation to aggress could be suppressed by factors in the environmental context, i.e., punishment or inhibitions imposed by learning.

In one of an extensive series of experiments, Buss (1966) attempted to demonstrate the relative ineffectiveness of frustration alone as an instigator of aggression. Buss reasoned that frustration could lead to aggression only if the aggressive response was instrumental in dealing with the frustration. That is, if someone is annoying you to the extent that you could not complete a task and thus frustrating you, you would aggress against that person only if you believed that your aggression would terminate this person's annoying behavior. If aggression would not reduce the frustration, then only minimal levels of aggression could be expected. In the context of this chapter, we might conceptualize the instrumental value of aggression in goal achievement as (1) a motivational base for aggression and (2) a contingency established within the situational context.

To study aggression Buss also used the "learning experiment: shock box" paradigm which he developed simultaneously with, but independently of, Milgram's research. Buss' shock generator, however, contained only 10 shock intensities with "painful" shocks supposedly beginning with depression of button 3. As in Milgram's experiments the "learner" was preprogrammed to make several errors during the learning study.

In the condition in which subjects were to believe that aggression was to be instrumental in goal attainment, the experimenter informed them that previous research had established that the more intense were the shocks administered for wrong answers, the faster the learner would master the list. Thus, subjects' success as teachers would be facilitated by increasing the level of punishment. When aggression was to lack instrumental value, the experimenter simply did not report the fabricated findings about increased levels of punishment leading to faster learning.

Frustration was induced in half of these subjects within the instrumental and noninstrumental conditions by the learner's apparent inability to learn the list in the number of trials claimed by the experimenter to be normal for college students. In the "frustration" condition subjects were also told either (1) that previous research showed that the ability of the teacher was a major determinant of learning and that more capable teachers were getting faster learning or (2) that the "teacher's" professor was interested in the results and would use them to help determine borderline grades.

In the "low frustration" condition the subjects' motivation to fulfill role obligations was minimized by deleting information regarding his capability as a teacher or grade improvement. Also, the "low frustration" subjects were not told the number of trials usually necessary for learning. Thus, one would expect "frustration" subjects to have been more highly motivated to teach effectively and consequently more frustrated than the "low frustration" subjects by the learner's inability to learn.

The results indicated that when aggression was portrayed as instrumental, regardless of the level of frustration, greater intensities of pain were administered to the learner than in those conditions in which aggression had no instrumental value. However, "frustration" subjects for whom aggression was portrayed as instrumental were no more aggressive than "low frustration" subjects for whom aggression was instrumental. In the present study frustration simply did not lead to aggression. However, the instrumentality of aggression was clearly shown to be an important factor in determining the level of pain administered. In addition, Buss replicated Milgram's finding that lower-intensity shocks were administered when the learner provided audible cues to his suffering.

One of the major difficulties in evaluating the frustration-aggression hypothesis has been the number of meanings ascribed to the fundamental terms. Buss, for example, specifically defines frustration as the blocking of an ongoing instrumental response that has in the past led to a reinforcer. Buss believes that frustration alone is at best a weak antecedent of aggression. However, anger aroused upon the reception of noxious stimuli (attack) is considered to be of major importance in eliciting aggression.

While the definition of frustration preferred by Berkowitz (1962) does not really distinguish between attack and the blocking of instrumental responses, it is instructive. Laboratory analogues of the anger-arousal process usually required the subject to be insulted by the experimenter or by confederates posing as naive subjects. Berkowitz considered an insult or the reception of other noxious stimuli as interfering with subjects' feelings of well-being, security, self-esteeem, and the like and thus frustrating the attainment of these goal states.

When pure frustration (i.e., blocking of instrumental responses) is experimentally differentiated from attack (Buss, 1966; Geen, 1968), it is apparent that pure frustration alone is a weaker antecedent to aggression than attack.

Evidence regarding the frustration-aggression hypothesis is not decisive. We might conclude, however, that sometimes frustration leads to aggression, although aggression can be instigated in its absence.

To deal more effectively with the apparent complexity of aggression arousal, Berkowitz (1962; 1965b) reformulated the frustration-aggression hypothesis. According to this revised model, frustration leads to an arousal state or a state of "readiness" for aggressive behavior. However, unless this arousal state is severely high, aggression will be elicited only if the situational context includes stimulus cues (external triggers) which have previously been associated with aggression. In addition, aggression can be elicited by relatively lower levels of arousal if the external stimulus cue(s) are extremely potent. The strength of the aggressive response is thus a function of (1) the aggressive cue value of the external stimulus, determined by the degree of association between this cue and previous aggression in related situations and (2) the degree of aggression readiness, or the strength of aggressive responses in the organism's behavior repertoire.

ANGRY AGGRESSION

Frustration-Aggression: Revised

The discussion of Berkowitz's revision of the frustration-aggression hypothesis is included under the topic of angry aggression because, for the most part, the direct empirical tests of the reformulation have employed personalized attacks (e.g., noxious stimuli or verbal insults) rather than pure frustration manipulations. The initial tests of the revised frustration-aggression model were embedded in studies which sought to gauge the effects of witnessing fictional film violence on aggression. A previous study by Berkowitz and Rawlings (1963) employed film violence (a 7-minute segment from the motion picture *Champion,* in which film star Kirk Douglas, portraying a boxer named Midge Kelley, receives a brutal beating in the ring at the hands of "Johnny Dunne") described as justified aggression, in the sense that the victim was receiving his "just desserts." After viewing this justified aggression, angered subjects were found to engage in more hostile verbal behavior than when the film sequence was prefaced by the inference that such violence was unjustified.

The first study directly testing the reformulated hypothesis (Berkowitz, 1965c) attempted to vary the aggressive cue value of the victim by manipulating the degree to which he was associated with a previously viewed film depicting justified aggression. Theoretically, victims with higher cue value for aggression should elicit greater aggressiveness than victims unassociated with previously witnessed aggression, particularly if the person was previously angered by his potential victim. In one condition of this initial experiment male subjects were insulted by a confederate of the experimenter posing as a naive subject and identified as either a physical education major interested in boxing or as a speech major. In the second condition the "physical education major" or "speech major" was not insulting. In both conditions subjects then viewed either an aggressive film sequence (*Champion,* prefaced by the unjustified-aggression plot summary) or a neutral film sequence about English canal boats.

Following the viewing session, the subjects were given a socially sanctioned opportunity to aggress against the experimenter's confederate. In the context of an experiment supposedly studying "physiological reactions to various tasks," the subject was given the role of evaluating the imaginativeness of the confederate's solution to a problem involving space arrangement. The subject carried out the evaluation by delivering one electric shock to the confederate if he thought the solution was very good or as many as 10 shocks if he thought it was bad. The confederate's solution was the same in all conditions of the study, and the subject was assured that the shocks would not do any physical harm.

The results generally supported the revised hypothesis in that the strongest attack (in terms of the number of shocks and/or the duration of the shock) was directed against the confederate interested in college boxing by insulted subjects viewing the prize-fight film. However, the overall results were not perfectly consistent with expectations since even those subjects not previously angered by the confederate directed more aggression toward the boxer than toward the speech major, regardless of the film sequence viewed. Berkowitz offered two explanations for this unexpected finding. First, the boxer's association with fighting could have generally increased his cue value for aggressive behavior; second, subjects could have disliked him to some extent because he expressed interest in boxing.

In a second study Berkowitz and Geen (1966) once again varied the victim's association with previously viewed violence, this time by varying the confederate victim's name rather than his interest in aggression-related activities. In the prize fight film used in previous studies Kirk Douglas, portraying "Midge Kelley," received a terrible beating. Taking advantage of the well-known actor's name, half of the subjects in the present study were introduced to a confederate victim who identified himself as "Kirk" Anderson, while for other subjects he said his name was "Bob" Anderson. The expectation was that angered subjects viewing the prize-fight film would engage in more aggressive behavior when the victim was associated with previously viewed violence (i.e., when his name was Kirk as opposed to Bob).

In this second study the "anger" condition was determined by having the confederate first evaluate the subject's solution to a creative problem solving task. In the "nonangry" condition the confederate delivered only one electric shock, indicative of a very favorable rating, while in the "anger" condition the subject received 7 shocks, indicating a relatively poor evaluation. Mood ratings immediately following the anger manipulation attested to the effectiveness of the manipulation: subjects receiving 7 shocks reported that they felt more angry than the one shock (nonangry) group. This general method for manipulating anger has become typical of many studies of aggression.

As expected, angered subjects viewing the prize-fight film administered a greater number of shocks to the confederate victim Kirk than to Bob. However, angered subjects viewing a nonaggressive track race sequence, for whom association between the name Kirk and aggression had not been established, failed to distinguish between the anger-instigating confederates in the number of shocks administered. Nonangered subjects, however, shocked the confederate victims reliably less than angered subjects and, across all conditions, failed to distinguish between the two confederate victims. Thus, as expected, angered subjects aggressed more intensively when an aggression-eliciting cue was present in the situational context.

A further test of the cue-eliciting hypothesis (Berkowitz & Lepage, 1967) asked whether weapons would serve as aggression-eliciting stimuli, causing an angered person to display stronger violence than he would have shown in the absence of such weapons. Following the usual anger manipulation (i.e., 1 shock vs. 7), male subjects in turn evaluated the confederate victim's creative solution using the shock apparatus. Lying on a table adjacent to the subject's shock administration button were (1) a 12-gauge shotgun and a .38-caliber pistol or (2) no object or (3) badminton racquets. As expected, the angered subjects gave the greatest number of shocks in the presence of the weapons. The presence of the weapons, however, did not boost the intensity of aggression for non-angered subjects. Although these particular findings are striking, some investigators have been unable to replicate them (Buss, Booker, & Buss 1972) or explain these findings in terms of demand characteristics, subject sophistication, and evaluation apprehension (Page & Scheidt, 1971).

In summary, then, apart from the attempted replications of the weapons study, the evidence basically supports Berkowitz' revised frustration-aggression model: Angry persons will aggress against their victims to a greater degree when the situational context contains aggression-eliciting cues than in the absence of such cues.

The Long Hot Summer

According to the U.S. Riot Commission report (1968), at least 75% of inner city disorders occurred at the end of a day in which the temperature had reached a high of at least 79 degrees. Thirty-eight percent of the disorders occurred on days in which the temperature reached 90° or higher. Many have come to believe that there is a direct cause-effect relationship between high ambient temperature and human violence, besides the fact that high temperatures increase the number of people to be found outdoors.

An initial laboratory test of this hypothesis, however, suggested that greater degrees of violence are elicited under comfortable temperatures than under uncomfortably hot conditions (Baron, 1972). In this study Baron used the same anger manipulation and aggression opportunity procedures used by Berkowitz and Geen (1966). In addition, the ambient temperature in the laboratory was 75° for subjects in the "cool" condition and approximately 93° for subjects in the "hot" condition.

Baron's second attempt to study the effects of ambient temperature on aggression (Baron, 1972) used only angered subjects but permitted half of these subjects to first witness another person (actually a second confederate of the experimenter) aggress quite severely (i.e., using buttons 8, 9, and 10 on the shock generator) against the confederate victim. This second experimental attempt specifically investigated whether high ambient temperatures indirectly increase the level of human violence by enhancing the degree to which people are susceptible to influence from an aggressive model. The results strongly supported the hypothesis.

In the "no model" condition the results closely paralleled those of the first study: higher levels of aggression were elicited in the "cool" than in the "hot" condition. However, all subjects were reliably more aggressive following exposure to an aggressive model, and more aggression was here elicited under uncomfortably hot conditions than under cool conditions. Thus, ambient temperatures may act to enhance human aggressiveness indirectly by facilitating the aggression-eliciting influence of aggressive models.

The Victim's Behavior During and Prior to the Attack

Pain Cues Emitted by the Victim. As part of the situational context, the victim's behavior just prior to and during an aggressive encounter may be considered potential regulators of the intensity of an aggressive attack. Milgram (1965a;b), Buss (1966), and Tilker (1970), for example, demonstrated that screams from the suffering victim reduced the level of shock administered by non-angered subjects. Baron (1971b) conducted a theoretically provocative study in which non-angered as well as angered subjects were exposed to pain cues emitted by their suffering victims. If aggression were instrumental, Baron reasoned that pain cues emitted by a suffering victim should inhibit subsequent aggression by an unangered aggressor, as in Milgram's study. If the victim had previously angered the aggressor, however, these pain cues might actually increase the intensity of the attack. Since the victim's suffering is theoretically the desired goal state of angry aggression, such pain cues should reinforce this aggressiveness.

Although the design of this study was somewhat more complicated, the results showed that pain cues from the victim tended to inhibit further attacks from unangered subjects but failed to exert such restraining effects, or actually tended to facilitate subsequent aggression, when subjects had previously been angered by the victim.

These results are important theoretically because they demonstrate that the conceptual distinction between instrumental and angry aggression is more than a matter of semantics; it has been shown empirically that they have different operating characteristics in the presence of identical stimuli. In addition, these different operating characteristics are theoretically consistent with expectations derived from the semantic distinction.

Eye-Balling the Attacker. Ethologists have noted that members of only a few animal species engage in aggressive behavior which results in severe injury or death with members of their own species. Attacks are generally terminated when the weaker or more submissive animal displays appeasement gestures. A wild dog, for example, generally ends his attack upon a conspecific when his opponent rolls over, revealing his vulnerable throat and stomach region.

Among primates, eye contact seems to be an important regulator of aggressive behaviors. A steady, direct stare seems to be an essential component of the threat display, while facing away or looking down or away seem to serve as effective appeasement gestures and generally result in a diminution of aggression (Bolwig, 1964; Exline, 1969; & Van Hooff, 1967). Would such a gaze-aversion temper aggression in a human being? According to Zimbardo's theory of deindividuation (1969), a victim's gaze-aversion should actually facilitate human aggressive behavior; it would be easier for the attacker to treat his victim as an object rather than as a person and therefore easier to overcome inhibitions to hurting him. Milgram's (1965) findings regarding the increase in obedience as the distance between the "teacher" and "learner" increases support such a prediction.

Patrons of local taverns and public transportation facilities might claim that it is the steady stare that provokes aggressive displays and encounters. Once aggression is underway, however, ethologists and social psychologists might make different predictions regarding the effects of gaze aversion and steady stares upon the continuation of human aggressiveness.

Thus, to test these opposing predictions, Ellsworth and Carlsmith (1973) permitted previously angered and nonangered subjects to aggress by means of electric shock upon confederate victims who maintained one of three eye-contact relationships with their aggressors just before each attack. In the "angry" condition the confederate was generally obnoxious and administered to the subject more than the amount of stressful stimulation (white noise) recommended by the experimenter. In Phase II of the study the confederate victim either looked the subject in the eye, looked down, or varied these looking patterns according to a random sequence, just as the subject was about to depress one of three shock buttons labeled as low, medium, and high intensity.

In an experiment supposedly studying anticipatory stress reactions, male subjects were to choose the frequency and intensity of shock to be administered to the confederate victim, while noting his anticipatory reactions. As expected, subjects shocked the confederate victim more frequently and intensively when he had previously angered them. Among angered subjects, the frequency and intensity of attacks were greater when the confederate victim consistently looked down, averting eye contact, than when he consistently looked his attacker in the eye prior to each attack. The consistent visual behavior of the confederate victim, however, had no effect upon the shocking behavior of non-angered subjects.

Because a baseline is lacking, we cannot discern whether, among angry subjects, gaze-aversion increased the level of aggression or whether looking inhibited aggression. Ellsworth and Carlsmith suggested that the condition in which the victims of angered subjects sometimes looked and sometimes looked down be used as the best available baseline. They report that victims who always look down are not shocked reliably more than victims who varied their looking behavior, but they are shocked more than victims who consistently maintain eye contact. Thus, that eye contact played an inhibitory role appears more likely than that gaze-aversion facilitated aggressive responses.

In contradiction to the data when victims maintained a consistent pattern of visual behavior throughout the experiment, angered subjects whose victims both looked and looked down randomly actually gave more frequent and intense shocks to the victim when he looked than when he looked away. Here, gaze-aversion resulted in less aggression, whereas when visual behavior was constant, gaze-aversion was associated with more aggression. Ellsworth and Carlsmith sought a unifying concept to explain this conflicting pattern of results. Subjects' reports suggested to these authors that eye contact in this situation was aversive for subjects and that their behavior across conditions may be explainable in terms of the subject's motivation to minimize or terminate eye contact with the confederate victim.

When confederate victims consistently looked prior to shocking, the subject could avoid eye contact simply by reducing the number of shocks, since victims only looked upon a warning signal from the subject that shock was about to be delivered. When the victim's looking was variable, however, subjects may have punished the victim for looking by increasing the shock level in an attempt to minimize the victim's looking.

The anger manipulation in the Ellsworth and Carlsmith study (similar to most other attempts) appears to have been relatively weak; subjects apparently were more concerned with avoiding the unpleasantness of eye contact with their victims than with inflicting pain and injury upon their anger instigator. When aggression was of instrumental value in reducing their unpleasantness, aggression increased. When aggression did not control the victim's visual behavior, however, subjects chose to shock less frequently rather than endure the personal discomfort associated with inflicting pain and injury upon a victim who refused to avert his gaze. Successful attempts to systematically study the behavior of angered people may have to await the development of anger-arousal procedures that are both ethical and effective in a laboratory context.

Although there are many inhibitions against expressing aggression in an experimental laboratory, it is surprising that in not one experimental paper does the investigator report having to restrain an angered subject from physically attacking his anger-instigator. For the most part, subjects do not become extremely angry, perhaps because the meaning ascribed to the confederate's behavior is also affected by the experimental context. Usually, the accomplice's anger-provoking behavior is well within the bounds sanctioned by the rules of his experimental task and therefore would not be perceived by the subject as a perfectly arbitrary or unnecessary attack. Although such anger-manipulations undoubtedly arouse mild degrees of anger and dislike towards the accomplice, such feelings are far from those probably necessary to arouse the desire to brutalize him actively.

Researchers in the area of aggression are well aware of these problems but continue their research with mildly angered subjects, assuming that a linear relationship exists between the degree of anger aroused and the intensity of aggression elicited under various experimental conditions. That is, if the variables in the situational context (e.g., the presence or absence of weapons, or of pain cues from the victim) reliably affect the intensity of aggression in mildly angered people, it is assumed that these effects would simply be exaggerated among the extremely angered. However, some extremely influential variables (e.g., eye contact, the presence of weapons, or pain cues from the victim) may not begin operating until the anger level reaches a threshold beyond that which can be aroused by traditional laboratory procedures.

HELPING BEHAVIOR

A recent advertisement of the Firestone Tire and Rubber Company, encouraging the purchase of their "trouble-free" steel-belted tire, warned that other motorists cannot be relied upon to help those needing roadside assistance. Appearing in this advertisement were the responses of eight people living in various cities in the U.S., apparently asked if they would stop to help someone on the road having tire trouble. Below are the eight responses included in the advertisement:

> "No. I keep my nose out of other people's business."
>
> "No. I'm afraid. Maybe if it's a woman alone."
>
> "No. Why should I?"
>
> "No. I just don't, I'm usually too busy."
>
> "I wouldn't stop for anyone, period."
>
> "No. I might cause an accident."
>
> "No. I used to, but not anymore."
>
> "No. I don't really want to get involved."

Generally, these responses reflect unconcern for others, fear of strangers, concern for personal needs first, alienation, callousness, a feeling that the world is becoming more dangerous, and general apathy. Surely at least some of these represent valid reasons why people often fail to help others in a wide variety of situations. It is interesting to speculate upon additional reasons as well as upon those factors in the immediate situational context which might affect whether help will be forthcoming, perhaps in spite of these inhibiting reasons.

In 1964 in New York City, a young woman, Kitty Genovese, on her way home from work at 3 o'clock in the morning, was attacked for over 30 minutes and eventually murdered by a knife-wielding lunatic. During her attempts to ward off the attacker and flee, Miss Genovese screamed continuously to her neighbors residing in the apartments above, "Please help me!" "Please help me!" "I'm dying."

Police reports later indicated that at least 38 of Miss Genovese's neighbors were aware of some disturbance on the street. Not one intervened personally or telephoned the police in time to report the attack. Alienation, apathy, fear, selfishness, and hardheartedness may be sufficient explanations for the failure of Miss Genovese's neighbors to intervene. The following research, however, suggests others.

The Presence of Other Bystanders

Amid the controversies over our apparent loss of human-heartedness, the research program of Latane and Darley turned toward the situational context for an additional perspective on the unresponsive bystander. Specifically, they focused on the presence of other bystanders as a factor possibly influencing intervention and helping behavior.

The Latane and Darley (1969) model of bystander intervention assumes that the bystander makes a number of decisions before helping. He must notice that something unusual is happening, he must decide that something is wrong and that help is needed, and he must determine the extent to which he has a responsibility to act. Once resigned to action, he must then decide upon the form of assistance he should offer and finally upon the implementation of his choice of action. At each decision point the presence of other bystanders is assumed to profoundly affect the individual bystander's behaviors. Given the limited channels of communication which generally exist among strangers, Latane and Darley have proposed that the greater the number of people witnessing an emergency, the lower the likelihood that anyone of these bystanders will intervene.

At the first stage of the decision process Latane and Darley argued that the presence of other people would inhibit the extent to which each bystander carefully inspects and monitors the behavior of others, including, of course, the behavior of any potential victim. Because the presence of others increases the possibility of embarrassment and negative evaluations, persons in crowds are likely to observe the norms or social conventions which prevail in public places: One minds one's own business, respects the privacy of others, and so on. If, in the presence of greater numbers of people, a bystander's attention is less likely to be focused on people, he may be less likely to even notice the initial signs of an emergency.

Emergencies are often confusing and ambiguous events in which it is difficult to determine that help is needed. For example, some people may have believed that the Kitty Genovese incident was simply a lovers' quarrel instead of a deadly criminal episode. A person lying in a doorway could be drunk, sleeping, or suffering a heart attack. In the presence of other people, a single bystander may hesitate to take action for fear of placing himself in the embarrassing situation of, for example, getting down on all fours to give mouth-to-mouth resuscitation to a vagrant catching a quick nap. In many such situations the bystander may desire more information about the apparent victim's condition before taking action.

In the presence of others, the intelligent bystander probably looks to these other bystanders for additional information about the situation. If others seem extremely concerned or are themselves preparing to act, he may be convinced that something is wrong and, therefore, interpret the situation as one in which help is needed. Here again, however, the rules of public behavior may result in each bystander's failure to intervene, not because he is unconcerned but because he may be convinced that others believe helping is unnecessary.

In public places people, especially males, are expected to be calm, poised, and unemotional, particularly under stressful conditions. Thus, while a bystander may be seeking information from others about a potential emergency, he may deliberately maintain a calm appearance to avoid public censure and embarrassment resulting from "losing one's cool" in public. The other bystanders, however, may be playing the same game. Unfortunately, "if each member of a group is, at the same time, trying to appear calm and also looking around at other members to gauge their reactions, all members may be led (or misled) by each other to define the situation as less critical than they would if alone" (Latane & Darley, 1969, p. 249).

To test the bearing of such social influence on the acceptance of "no help needed" interpretations, Latane and Darley (1968) staged a laboratory emergency during which the subject was either alone, together with two experimental accomplices posing as naive subjects (who were specifically instructed to remain passive and silent during the "emergency"), or together with two other truly naive subjects. The subjects (who were male students) were in a waiting room completing a questionnaire prior to a discussion of "some of the problems involved in life at an urban university." The experimenters introduced a stream of smoke through a small vent in the wall to the extent that by the end of approximately 7 minutes, vision was obscured by the amount of smoke present. The experimenters, viewing the subjects' behavior through a well-concealed one-way mirror, measured the duration of the period between the time subjects first noticed the smoke (easily detectable by a distinct startle reaction) to the time subjects left the room to report the smoke to a secretary stationed nearby. If the smoke had not been reported within 6 minutes after it was noticed, the experiment was terminated and the postexperimental interview begun.

Witnessing the emergency with other bystanders had powerful effects upon the proportion of subjects reporting the smoke, the speed with which the incident was reported, and the subjects' interpretations of the seriousness of the incident. Seventy-five percent of the subjects witnessing the emergency alone reported the incident before the end of the 6-minute period beginning when the smoke was first noticed. The median elapsed time for subjects in the "alone" condition was 2 minutes. Most subjects reported without panic that, "There's something strange going on in there; there seems to be some sort of smoke coming through the wall."

Only 10% of the subjects witnessing the emergency together with two experimental (calm) accomplices reported the incident within the 6-minute period. The difference in response rate of 75% in the "alone" condition and 10% in the "passive-confederate" condition was statistically significant.

In only 38% of the three-naive-subject groups did even one subject report the incident. Since 75% of the alone subjects reported the smoke, mathematically it would be expected that over 98% of the three-naive-subject groups would contain at least one reporter, assuming the three bystanders failed to influence one another. Evidently, they were influenced greatly by each other's presence. Although 55% of the subjects in the "alone" condition reported the smoke within 2 minutes, only 12% of the three-person groups helped within that time.

Subjects who did not report the incident uniformly said that they had rejected the idea that it was a fire. All the interpretations accepted by these nonreporters suggested that they had been influenced to accept "no help needed," or "nondangerous incident" definitions of the situation. Some of their interpretations of the smoke were that it was air conditioning vapor, steam, smog (pumped in to simulate an urban environment), and truth gas to insure the honesty of the questionnaire responses.

Evidently, the presence of other bystanders had powerful effects upon the subjects' interpretations of the event and their reporting behavior. Yet, when asked, these subjects denied that they were influenced by the presence of others. Furthermore, they claimed that they paid little or no attention to the reactions of the other people in the room. Obviously, subjects were unaware of the subtle influence on their behavior affected by the other bystanders.

Since it is possible that subjects in the "together" condition of the "smoke-filled room" experiment saw themselves as engaged in a game to test their bravery and thus failed to react, a second study (Latane and Rodin, 1969) was designed to test the social-inhibition hypothesis when the emergency represented a danger to someone other than the bystander himself. In the "lady in distress" experiment, male subjects witnessed an emergency (1) alone, (2) together with an experimenter's accomplice instructed to remain passive throughout the "emergency", (3) together with a friend, or (4) together with another naive subject with whom they were previously unacquainted. Latane and Rodin expected the social-inhibition effect to be stronger among strangers than among friends; friends were presumed to be less likely to fear embarrassment in each other's presence and also to be less likely to misinterpret one another's inaction.

Under the pretext of participating in a survey of game and puzzle preferences, each subject was given a preliminary questionnaire to complete. The female experimenter said she would be working next door in her office, accessible through a collapsible curtain which divided the two rooms. After four minutes of shuffling papers and opening drawers, the experimenter activated a stereophonic tape recorder and presented the standardized emergency. If the subject listened carefully, it was apparent that the experimenter was standing on a chair attempting to reach a stack of papers atop a bookcase; a loud crash and a scream followed, the chair apparently collapsing beneath her weight. She screamed, "Oh, my God, my foot. . . . I . . . I . . . can't move it. Oh . . . my ankle. I can't get this thing off me." She continued to cry and moan for an additional minute after which the cries became more subdued. Finally, she was heard to pull herself up, struggle to the door, and leave. The entire emergency took 130 seconds.

The results impressively supported the experimenters' expectations. Seventy percent of the "alone" subjects intervened, but only 7% of the subjects waiting with the experimenter's passive accomplice helped. In the first 60 seconds from the onset of the emergency 64% of "alone" subjects and only 7% of those with the stooge had helped.

When two friends were placed in the emergency situation, at least one of them intervened 70% of the time; strangers offered assistance only 40% of the time. Furthermore, intervention occurred much sooner from friends than from strangers.

Describing the behavior of friends and strangers, Latane and Rodin wrote:

> When strangers overheard the emergency, they seemed noticeably confused and concerned, attempting to interpret what they heard and to decide on a course of action. They often glanced furtively at one another, apparently anxious to discover the others reaction yet unwilling to meet eyes and betray their own concern. Friends on the other hand, seemed better able to convey their concern nonverbally, and often discussed the incident and arrived at a mutual plan of action. (p. 200)

Supporting these impressions, the investigators observed that 85% of the friends and only 60% of the strangers engaged in conversation after the onset of the emergency.

Although both "alone" subjects and friends assisted the victim 70% of the time, the friends did inhibit one another from responding. Using the "alone" subjects to establish a hypothetical base rate, 91% of two-naive-person groups would be expected to intervene in the absence of social influence. Comparing the 70% intervention rate against the 91% expectation yields a difference that statistically is marginally significant. Also, "alone" subjects intervened faster than friends.

In the postexperimental interview subjects who intervened revealed that they did so either because the fall sounded serious or because they were uncertain as to what had happened and felt obliged to investigate. However, many nonintervenors also claimed they were uncertain of what happened (59%) but had decided it was not too serious (46%). Characterizing nonintervenors as callous, selfish, hardhearted people does not explain the fact that these people were obviously concerned. A more logical proposal is that they often failed to intervene because other bystanders subtly influenced them to accept a "no help needed" definition of the situation.

This does not by itself explain the failure of Kitty Genovese's neighbors to intervene. For the most part, Miss Genovese's neighbors were isolated from each other and, therefore, unable to directly influence one another's interpretation of the event. Darley and Latane (1968) pointed out, however, that the mere presence of other bystanders may have been a critical determinant of the failure of each person to intervene. In the third stage of the intervention model presented earlier, a bystander must determine the extent to which he has a responsibility to act once he recognizes an emergency situation. Darley and Latane (1968) suggest that the presence of other bystanders may also affect the outcome at this stage of the decision process. When only one bystander is present, he bears 100% of the responsibility to help or 100% of the guilt and blame for not helping. When other capable bystanders are present, however, this responsibility can be shared or diffused. The individual is no longer the unique focus of all responsibility, and the pressure to act is thereby reduced. Thus, the presence of other bystanders may reduce the likelihood that an individual bystander may intervene and help. As the number of bystanders increases, the less likely any one bystander would be expected to intervene.

To test this "diffusion of responsibility" hypothesis, Darley and Latane (1968) isolated subjects from other bystanders in room-sized cubicles to prevent communication and, thereby, social influence. As part of a group discussion female subjects were led to believe the discussion group consisted of (1) two persons: herself and the "victim;" (2) three persons: the subject, the "victim," and another bystander; and (3) six persons: the subject, the "victim," and four other persons. Since all participants were isolated from one another, discussion was limited to an intercom system which permitted but one person to speak at a time. Early in the discussion, the future victim mentioned that he was prone to epileptic seizures. Actually, all participants were simulated with prerecorded performances for purposes of standardization and convenience. After each participant had the opportunity to speak, the future "victim" began talking again; as the seizure approached, his comments became louder and more incoherent. Then he continued:

> I er um I think I I need er if if could er er somebody er er er er er er er give me a little er give me a little help here because er I er I'm er er h-h-aving a a a a a real problem er right now and I er if somebody could help me out it would it would er er s-s-sure be sure be good . . . because er there er er a cause I er I un I've

got a a one of the er sei . . . er er things coming on and and and I could really er use some help so if somebody would er give me a little h-help uh er-er-er-er-er c-could somebody er er help er uh uh uh (choking sounds) . . . I'm gonna die er er I'm . . . gonna die er help er er seizure er (chokes, then quiet).

After 125 seconds, the victim was cut off by the automatic switching device which controlled which microphone was live during the group discussion. Although the investigators began timing upon the beginning of the victim's speech, judges estimated that a breakdown was not clearly evident until after 70 seconds. If subjects hadn't emerged from their cubicles by the conclusion of a 6-minute period, the experiment was terminated.

Before the end of the seizure episode, 85% of the "alone" subjects, 62% of the subjects with one other bystander, and 31% of the subjects with four other bystanders emerged from their cubicles to report the incident to the experimenter. By the conclusion of the 6-minute period, 100% of the "alone" subjects, 85% of the subjects together with one additional bystander, and 62% of the subjects together with four other bystanders intervened. Interestingly, all interventions occurred within the first 3 minutes after the onset of the emergency. Once again, the results indicated clearly that, the larger the group, the fewer the bystanders who intervene and the longer it takes the interveners to respond.

An important question yet unanswered deals with those subjects who failed to intervene. Were they unconcerned and apathetic or concerned and confused? Darley and Latane suggest the latter. They report that when the experimenter entered the subject's cubicle to terminate the experiment, the subject often asked, "Is he being taken care of?" "He's all right, isn't he?" These noninterveners also appeared extremely nervous, more nervous, in fact, than those who intervened.

Darley and Latane suggested that noninterveners never decided not to respond. Instead they described their subjects as still undecided about whether or not to respond. It appeared that subjects were worried about the guilt and shame they would feel for not helping; while at the same time they were concerned about overreacting and making fools of themselves or ruining the group discussion experiment. When subjects were alone, the victim's distress was more compelling than anxiety over embarrassment and ruining the experiment.

However, for subjects who knew other bystanders were present, the presence of others seemed to slightly reduce the costs for not helping ("Someone else may be helping the victim"), such that the costs for rushing in to help may have been more equivalent to the costs for not helping. In this situation subjects appeared to be constantly vacillating between the two courses of action. At no point did the subject resign himself to inaction, perhaps saying to himself, "Let John do it." These subjects were undecided about action. In the end the victim might have died, yet his death would not appear to have been the result of apathy or callousness. Well-intentioned people were inhibited from acting by the presence of other bystanders.

Bickman (1969, 1971) and Korte (1970) independently tested similar extensions of the "bystander inhibition" hypothesis. Specifically, these investigators asked whether diffusion of responsibility is affected by the perceived ability of the other bystander(s) to help or whether the mere presence of other bystanders is sufficient to produce the effect in full force. Theoretically, bystanders could not diffuse responsibility if they believed other bystanders to be physically incapable or even unwilling to intervene.

In Bickman's research (1969, 1971) subjects believed that the other bystander to the emergency was located either in another building some distance away from themselves and the "victim" (the "not able" condition) or in a third cubicle adjacent to the subject's and the "victim's" cubicle (the "able" condition). The emergency consisted of the subject overhearing a bookcase apparently fall upon the "victim."

Korte's subjects believed that the other bystanders were strapped to their chairs in the "not able" condition and freely mobile in the "able" condition. In Korte's emergency the experimenter was the victim of a severe asthma attack. Both Bickman and Korte reported that subjects whose fellow bystanders were unable to help intervened 13% more frequently than subjects in the "able" condition. In Bickman's study subjects in the "not able" and "able" conditions helped 90% and 77% of the time, respectively, whereas Korte's subjects helped 50% and 37% of the time respectively, in these conditions. Furthermore, Bickman reported that subjects in the "not able" condition helped faster than subjects in the "able" condition, a fact which offers additional support for the assumption that the perceived ability of another bystander to help, not simply his presence, determines the likelihood of intervention. Furthermore, Bickman reported that no differences in helping behavior were apparent between subjects witnessing the emergency alone and those subjects together with the unable bystander. Therefore, diffusion of responsibility seems inoperative when fellow bystanders are unable to help.

Extending the "social influence" hypothesis still further, both Bickman and Korte provided their subjects with a communication from the *Able* and *Not able* bystander which suggested the manner in which these bystanders interpreted the emergency. Because they were more clear-cut, only Bickman's results will be discussed. Just after the emergency Bickman's subjects received the following messages from the "able" or "not able" bystander: " . . . she's not answering—something must've fallen on her—she's hurt" ("crisis" definition), ". . . I hope it's nothing serious, I hope she's OK" ("help may be needed" definition), ". . . something must've fallen on the intercom—well, I guess she'll tell the guy it's not working. We'd better wait for him to tell us what to do next" ("no help needed" definition).

Overall, the definitions provided by the other bystander had powerful effects upon the proportion of the subjects intervening and also upon the latency of their responses. As expected, the more serious the interpretation offered by the additional bystander, the shorter the latency and the greater the proportion of subjects who intervened. More interesting, perhaps, was the expected interaction of the "able" and "not able" conditions with the situational definitions suggested by the other bystanders.

Bickman (1969) reasoned that the diffusion of responsibility effect (i.e., the difference in helping behavior between subjects witnessing the emergency together with an able bystander vs. those together with an unable bystander) would be greatest when the other bystander offered a moderately serious definition of the situation compared to the "crisis" or "no help needed" definitions. On one hand, if a bystander was to receive a "crisis" definition and accept it, the presence of others would probably be irrelevant. For example, consider a child running out into the street and about to be run down by a truck. In this case the seriousness of the event might preclude looking to see if anyone else is around to help or whether others are qualified to help. On the other hand, if a bystander was to receive a "no help needed" definition of the situation and accept it, no diffusion could occur since no responsibility or blame exists to be diffused. However, if the definition were to suggest that help might be needed, the bystander should be in maximum conflict. The situation would not appear so serious that he would ignore others, nor would it seem of such little consequence that he wouldn't worry. Hence, diffusion should be greatest when other bystanders suggest that help *may* be needed.

The results indicated that, as expected, the difference between the "able" and "not able" conditions was greatest when the other bystander suggests that help *may* be needed. However, this difference was marginally significant. Incidently, Korte also obtained the largest difference between the "able" and "not able" conditions when the confederate offered the "help may be needed" definition. His findings also, however, failed to reach traditionally acceptable levels of statistical significance. Nevertheless, the fact that two investigators obtained the identical interaction effect, albeit a statistically nonsignificant one in each case, indicates that the effect is more robust than it would appear on the basis of each study alone. The predicted interaction is intuitively satisfying, given that many emergencies occurring in real life are often rather ambiguous events and, thus, especially susceptible to a diffusion of responsibility effect.

Further, support of the interaction discussed above was given by Russel Clark and Word (1972) demonstrate that the social influence effect provided by the actual presence of others, as in the Latane and Rodin study, was substantially lower when the emergency was unambiguously critical than when the seriousness of the emergency was ambiguous. In the "low ambiguous emergency" condition the subjects overheard a university maintenance man apparently fall from a ladder, groaning with the impact and grunting with each breath and then exclaiming, "Oh, my back, I can't move." For subjects in the "high ambiguous emergency" condition only the crash and thud were heard, the verbal cues from the victim being deleted. An additional finding in this study was that subjects generally helped faster and more frequently when situational ambiguity was low than when the emergency was highly ambiguous.

A subsequent study by Clark and Word (1972) found that subjects given visual and auditory cues about the victim's suffering helped faster and more frequently than subjects permitted auditory cues alone. As in Milgram's obedience research and the work in aggression by Buss and Baron, an increase in available cues about a nonanger-instigating victim's suffering increased the level of "altruistic" response.

Characteristics of the Victim and Helping

Piliavin, Rodin, and Piliavin (1969) performed a field experiment in which a "victim" collapsed aboard the 8th Avenue Subway in New York City. The "victim," either a black or a white male, portrayed two types of victims: (1) a drunk, smelling of liquor and carrying a liquor bottle wrapped in a brown paper bag ("drunk" condition), or (2) a person carrying a cane and obviously ill ("cane" condition). Within the time allotted for spontaneous helping, cane victims were assisted 95% of the time while drunk victims received assistance only 50% of the time from the unsuspecting passengers. Furthermore, help was offered more quickly for the cane than for the drunk victim.

In terms of racial considerations, the black and the white cane victims were as likely to elicit help from a passenger of the same race as from a passenger of a different race. However, in the drunk condition, a nonsignificant trend suggested that the "victim" was more likely to be helped by a bystander of the same race as himself than by one of a different race. In addition, male bystanders were generally more likely to offer assistance than females.

Based on the findings of Darley and Latane and of Latane and Rodin, regarding "diffusion of responsibility" and "social influence," Piliavin, Rodin, and Piliavin expected that help would be less likely and more slowly evoked as the number of bystanders in the immediate area increased. Contrary to expectation, their data offered no support for the bystander inhibition hypothesis (that in the presence of other bystanders persons are inhibited from helping because of diffusion of responsibility and/or social influence). In fact, response times were reliably faster in groups of seven or more than in groups of two or three.

Piliavin et al. (1969) pointed out that the fact that the victims were visually and audibly perceived may have constrained the bystanders' ability to conclude that there was no emergency. The failure here to obtain evidence favoring the bystander inhibition hypothesis is clearly consistent with the findings of Bickman (1969, 1972), Korte (1970), and Clark and Word (1972) in which bystander inhibition effects were more clearly observed when the emergency situation itself or the definitions provided by others were highly ambiguous.

To account for the greater degree of help elicited by the cane victim and the trend toward same-race helping for drunk victims, Piliavin, Rodin, and Piliavin employed the following model of behavior: A person's behavior is determined by the relative costs minus rewards involved for engaging in each alternative response. Thus, when the costs for helping outweigh the costs for not helping, the person should choose not to help.

These investigators proposed that the costs incurred for helping the drunk victim were greater than the costs for helping the cane victim. For example, in helping a drunk victim a bystander might experience greater disgust because of the odor or the situation in general, or he might expect to be subject to rude treatment by a possibly recalcitrant drunk. Furthermore, the costs for not helping a drunk victim may be relatively low. Since the drunk is responsible for his own condition, the bystander may feel less guilt and less censure from his fellow bystanders for not helping, while the costs for not helping the victim of an infirmity would be considerably higher. When the race of the bystander differs from that of the victim, particularly a drunk victim, the costs for helping may be increased by the addition of fear; on the other hand, the costs for not helping may be decreased by a bystander's expectation that members of the same race ought to be responsible for each other.

It is interesting to apply the Piliavin et al. (1969) reward-cost model to the interaction between situational ambiguity and the bystander inhibition effect (i.e., diffusion of responsibility and social influence). Piliavin et al. suggested that diffusion of responsibility is more likely to occur when the costs for helping are relatively high and the costs for not helping relatively low. When the emergency is ambiguous, the cost for helping may be relatively high since the bystander may suffer embarrassment should he intervene when assistance is unnecessary or unwarranted. In addition, the cost for not helping in ambiguous emergency situations may be relatively low since the bystander is less apt to experience guilt or peer censure for not intervening. Therefore, the Piliavin et al. reward-cost model would expect the diffusion of responsibility and social influence effects to be greater when the emergency confronting each bystander is relatively ambiguous. Studies discussed above offer support for this hypothesis.

One difficulty with a reward-cost model is that after the data are collected, the relative costs for each response alternative can be reassessed so easily that the usefulness of the model is bound to be affirmed. A subsequent field experiment by Piliavin and Piliavin (1972), this time aboard subway cars in Philadelphia, tested the predictive utility of the reward-cost model. In this second study the type of victim was varied again. In each case the victim was a neatly dressed, clean-shaven white male carrying a cane. In one condition he simply collapsed aboard the train (as did the cane victim in New York), while in a second condition the collapse was accompanied by the release of a thick red fluid from the corner of the victim's mouth (blood condition). Unlike the drunk and cane victims in the Piliavin et al. (1969) study, both victims in the present study could be expected to elicit a "help needed" interpretation from the bystanders. In the earlier study the drunk may not have presented a real emergency to the bystanders since the cause of his unconsciousness was immediately apparent and could be defined as a nonserious incident.

In Piliavin and Piliavin (1972) it was assumed that the costs to the bystander for helping the blood victim would be greater than the costs for helping the no-blood victim. Therefore, the blood victim should elicit help less frequently and more slowly than his No-blood counterpart. The cost of helping the blood victim was assumed to be greater because it was believed that the sight of blood would cause the typical bystander to feel fear and revulsion.

The results strongly supported the reward-cost model. Within the first 70 seconds following the collapse, help was elicited only 60% of the time in the blood condition and 90% of the time in the no-blood condition. In addition, within this 70-second interval, help was delivered more slowly to the blood victim. As in the Piliavin et al. (1969) study, male bystanders helped more frequently than females.

Although the victims were always white in this second study, the results regarding the bystanders' race are informative. If the victim's race had played no role in the situation, 39% of the help elicited would have come from black helpers since 39% of the passengers in the experiment were black. Apparently, the victim's race was not important for the black bystanders in the no-blood condition since 37% of the helpers in this condition were black. However, the percentage of blacks who helped the bloody victim was only 17%. Although this race effect fell short of traditional levels of statistical significance, it supported the findings in the earlier Piliavin et al. study (1969) regarding the greater likelihood of same-race helping in the drunk condition only (in which the costs for helping were assumed to be highest).

Wispe and Freshley (1971) engaged black and white passers-by in a helping-behavior situation in which a black or white woman, leaving a supermarket, dropped her packages in the path of the oncoming pedestrians. The passers'-by behavior was categorized as: (1) "ignores," in which the subject ignored the victim and walked by; (2) "reacted but without help," in which the subject hesitated and showed surprise but failed to help; (3) "perfunctory help," in which the subject helped the victim with a few of her groceries, and then hurried on; and (4) "positive help," in which the subject helped the victim with all of her groceries, offered to get a new grocery bag, and the like.

With regard to interracial helping, Wispe and Freshley report that there was a suggestion of a racial interaction between helpers and victims, but for white female helpers only. The results were complicated: White females helped the white victim more often than they helped the black victim (category 4), but they also ignored the white victim more often (category 1). The authors concluded that helping behavior was generally nondiscriminatory.

However, a reanalysis of the Wispe and Freshley data which forms a single no-help category by combining category 1 ("ignores") with category 2 ("reacts without help"), but which maintains the integrity of the "perfunctory help" and "positive help" categories reveals a race-of-victim effect for both male and female white subjects which, statistically, is marginally significant. The results of this reanalysis indicated that white passers-by did not discriminate between black and white victims in terms of no-help responses. However, of those white subjects providing at least some assistance, 63% gave "positive help" (complete help) to the white victim while only 30% offered this degree of assistance to the black victims. On the other hand, 70% of the white bystanders offered "perfunctory" help to the black victim while 30% offered this small amount of assistance to the white victim. Evidently, white subjects dealing with white victims are more apt to provide complete help than perfunctory help, but when dealing with black victims they are more apt to provide perfunctory help than complete help. The magnitude of this effect, however, was only marginally significant.

Nevertheless, these results are consistent with this author's view (Gaertner, 1972) that, in situations in which the bystander has relative freedom to define the seriousness of the emergency (as in ambiguous emergency situations), negative attitudes toward the victim may predispose the bystander to accept more readily a "no help needed" or "less help needed" interpretation of the situation, than if the victim was held in high regard.

Gaertner and Bickman (1971) devised a field situation in which 1,109 black and white residents of Brooklyn, New York, received what seemed to be a wrong number telephone call which quickly developed into a request for their assistance. Each wrong number call was made by one of seven black callers or one of seven white callers. Pilot studies indicated that the race of each caller was easily discernable on the basis of the caller's speech characteristics. These pilot studies also indicated that each caller was judged by college students to be over 30 years of age and that the white callers were perceived to be of slightly higher social class than the black callers; both groups of callers, however, were judged to be of lower middle class and as having completed a high school education.

Using grammatically identical messages, the black and white callers contacted subjects between 6:30 P.M. and 9:30 P.M. If the call was received by anyone who was judged to be under 18 years of age on the basis of speech and voice characteristics, the caller apologized for reaching the wrong number and hung up. When an adult answered, the callers repeated the following dialogue:

Caller: Hello . . . Ralph's Garage? This is George Williams. . . . listen, I'm stuck out here on the parkway . . . and I'm wondering if you'd be able to come out here and take a look at my car?

Subject's expected response: This isn't Ralph's Garage . . . you have the wrong number.

Caller: This isn't Ralph's Garage! Listen, I'm terribly sorry to have disturbed you, but listen . . . I'm stuck out here on the highway . . . and that was the last dime I had! I have bills in my pocket, but no more change to make another phone call . . . Now I'm *really* stuck out here. What am I going to do now?

Subject: (. . . Subject might volunteer to call the garage.)

Caller: Listen . . . do you think you could do me the favor of calling the garage and letting them know where I am. . .? I'll give you the number . . . They know me over there.

Prod A: Oh brother . . . listen, I'm stuck out here . . . Couldn't you PLEASE help me out by simply calling the garage for me (pleadingly)?

Prod B Listen . . . If YOU were in my situation. . . wouldn't you want someone to help you?

If after Prod B the subject refused to place the call but did not hang up, he was relieved of any concern he may have had for the stranded motorist when the caller reported: "Oh, one second . . . here comes a police car . . . I think he will be able to give me a hand."

If the subject agreed to help, the victim gave him a telephone number to call. In fact, the subject's call was received by an assistant acting as the garage attendant. The assistant assured the subject that the victim would be helped immediately and graciously thanked him for his helpfulness.

To identify which subjects actually helped, the following procedures were employed. First, black and white callers gave the subjects different telephone numbers to call. Second, each time a subject agreed to call, the caller changed his location on the parkway, rotating eight different locations. At the "garage," the subject was asked for the location of the stranded motorist. Finally, the time at which the call to the subject was completed, along with the time at which the subject's call was received at the garage, was recorded.

Only if the subject actually called the garage was he credited with a helping response. If the subject refused to help after Prod B or hung up after the caller stated "and that was the last dime . . . ," a no-help response was scored. However, if the subject hung up prior to the word "dime," a "premature hang-up" response was recorded and was considered separately from the help, no-help response categories. In the case of a premature hang-up, it was assumed that the subject could not reasonably be expected to realize that the caller needed his assistance.

The results of this study indicated that among white subjects, black victims were helped 53% of the time while white victims were assisted 65% of the time. Black subjects, on the other hand, were not at all anti-white. In fact, among black subjects black victims were accorded assistance 60% of the time while white victims were helped 67% of the time. This 7% difference favoring white victims, however, was not statistically significant.

In terms of premature hang-up responses (i.e., hanging up before the word "dime") white subjects hung up prematurely more frequently than black subjects, but they did not discriminate against black victims on this measure. As in Piliavin et al. (1969) and Piliavin and Piliavin (1972), Gaertner and Bickman observed that male subjects helped more frequently than females.

Using the wrong number situation Russel Clark (1974) found a race-of-victim effect among white citizens of Tallahassee, Florida. Clark observed that 79% of a white sample helped the white male victim while only 54% helped the black male victim. However, when these wrong number calls were made by female victims, a race effect was not apparent. In Clark's study black and white female victims were each assisted approximately 93% of the time.

Although the extent to which white subjects discriminated against black victims (i.e., when the victims were male) was considerably larger within Clark's Tallahassee sample than that obtained within Gaertner and Bickman's New York sample, the magnitude of this regional difference was not different by an amount that is statistically significant.

Gaertner (1973) arranged for black and white, male and female victims to engage New

York City Liberal and Conservative Party members in the wrong-number situation. Earlier studies by Adorno, Frenkel-Brunswik, Levinson, and Sanford (1950), McClosky (1958), Free and Cantril (1967) and others have shown that anti-black sentiment tends to increase as political viewpoints vary from liberalism to conservatism. An examination of the legislative programs and campaign literature of the Liberal and Conservative parties indicated the appropriateness of their labels in terms of the traditional meanings of liberalism and conservatism used by the earlier researchers. Therefore, it was predicted that black victims would elicit help relatively less frequently than white victims from Conservatives than from Liberals.

In terms of the help, no-help response categories the results indicated that Conservatives discriminated against the black victims to a greater extent than Liberals did. In what seemed to be the most appropriate analysis, Liberals helped the black and white victims 76% and 85% of the time, respectively. This 9% difference for Liberals, however, was not statistically significant. Conservatives on the other hand helped the black victims only 65% of the time, while white victims were assisted 92% of the time.

In spite of the nature of the victim's dilemma, the data failed to support a prediction that female victims would elicit greater helpfulness than male victims. In addition, the race-of-victim effect was almost equivalent for male and female victims. However, male subjects helped overall more frequently than females.

Thus, the present study found that in a helping behavior situation, Conservatives discriminated against blacks to a greater extent than Liberals did, supporting previous findings that political and economic conservatism is positively related to more extreme anti-black attitudes. However, the data supported the traditional findings only when subjects obtained reasonably sufficient information to recognize that their personal assistance was required. Actually, a number of subjects hung up prematurely on the stranded motorists (i.e., before the word "dime") before the appeal for help was delivered. In terms of premature hang-up responses, Liberals compared to Conservatives hung up prematurely relatively more frequently on the black than on the white victims. These Liberals discriminated against the black male in particular in that black and white victims received premature hang-ups 27.5% and 9.5% of the time, respectively. However, the percentages of Conservatives hanging up prematurely on the black and white male victims was 8.3% and 4.7%, respectively.

Were members of the Conservative Party, then, less capable of sympathy for, or less willing to give aid to those needing help as suggested by McClosky (1958)? Not at all. Overall, Liberals and Conservatives each helped approximately 80% of the time. Differences in the levels of helping behavior became apparent only when the differential rates of responding to black and to white victims were examined.

It seems that Conservatives have greater social responsibility toward others of their own kind than Liberals. The Liberal's sense of morality may require him to help others regardless of his personal feelings toward the victim. The American Civil Liberties Union, for example, has defended the legal rights of George Lincoln Rockwell and George Wallace. Apparently the Liberal's sense of social responsibility, ability to sympathize, or sense of justice ignores the personal characteristics of who requires assistance and is guided more strictly by the general principle involved. Liberals would thus apply such a principle in an egalitarian manner.

However, the claim that Liberals harbor less

anti-black sentiment than Conservatives cannot be supported entirely in the present research because Liberals, rather than Conservatives, hung up prematurely more frequently on black than on white victims.

Perhaps liberal, anti-black sentiment can be observed more readily in situations in which there are few if any clearly definable standards or norms to guide behavior. In these situations the Liberal need not be concerned with the application of a general principle in an egalitarian manner. For example, is it appropriate or inappropriate to hang up on a person reaching the wrong number after informing him of his error? What further involvement is necessarily prescribed? There is, however, a clearly definable principle, that is, the social responsibility norm, to direct behavior when it is recognized that help is needed. Hence, Liberals who remained on the phone long enough to realize that their help was needed may have behaved in a relatively egalitarian fashion in spite of their possibly less than favorable attitude toward blacks.

In a second phase of the wrong number study (Gaertner, 1973), additional samples of Liberal and Conservative Party members were engaged in a telephone interview during which they were asked whether or not they believed they would call the garage if they received the actual wrong number call from each of the four victims.

On the basis of the extent to which Liberals and Conservatives claimed they would help, the victims would have been helped 97% of the time and without regard for race. Furthermore, no differences were found between Liberals and Conservatives regarding their expected degree of personal helpfulness.

This investigator suspects that most subjects truly believed they would, if called upon, help each of the victims regardless of race. It seems unlikely that even Conservatives perceive themselves as bigoted to the extent that they would deny help to an inconvenienced black person, particularly in a situation in which the cost for helping is relatively small.

Why, then, the disparity between what people claim they would do and the actual level of assistance accorded each of the victims? One possible explanation for this disparity is that in the interview phase the situation was initially defined for the subjects as one in which their help was really needed. In the actual wrong number situation, however, the subjects were free to define the situation as a prank or to reach some other interpretation suggesting that their help was either unnecessary or unwarranted. The hypothesis that if one has negative attitudes toward a victim, he is more inclined to define the situation as one in which help is unnecessary has been partially tested (Gaertner, 1975). In this research the findings suggest that attitudes toward the victim will play increasingly important roles in mediating helping behavior as situational factors more easily permit the bystander to reach "no help needed" interpretations.

Some further research presently in progress by Gaertner permits bystanders to witness various emergency situations involving victims who previously angered them. Perhaps in laboratory studies, helping behavior, and more specifically a failure to help, would be a more sensitive measure of aggression than providing subjects with the opportunity to actively hurt their anger instigators. That is, people may be more willing to diffuse responsibility, accept no-help-needed definitions, or with full awareness passively perpetuate the victim's suffering than they are to actively harm an anger instigator.

This chapter has reviewed a portion of the research literature which argues that situational factors, to some extent, regulate the occurrence of hurting and helping behavior. How then do we evaluate the legal and moral culpability of, for example, the Watergate conspirators, participants in the My Lai massacre, Nazi soldiers, or Kitty Genovese's neighbors? How can we determine in each particular instance the extent to which an act was caused primarily by the dispositional characteristics of the actor(s) or by the situational context in which these actors were embedded?

Objective appraisal of the relative contribution of these alternatives seems difficult, especially in light of the work of Jones and Nisbett (1972). These authors have proposed that actors (those actively involved) and observers often reach different conclusions regarding the causes of the actor's behavior. According to Jones and Nisbett, the actor has a tendency to attribute the causes of his behavior to the environmental context while observers tend to attribute the actor's behavior to dispositional characteristics (i.e., to conclude that he is a brutal, sadistic, or apathetic person). Perhaps thorough exposure to the situational perspective may minimize the observer's dispositional attribution bias. In any event, I hope that now you will consider contextual forces more strongly than before in your attempts to understand or judge the behavior of others.

SUMMARY

The purpose of this chapter was to discuss the research literature bearing on aggression and helping behavior from a perspective emphasizing factors within the immediate situational context which regulate the occurrence of these behaviors. This approach deemphasizes personality or individual differences but does not ignore these factors altogether. For example, Gaertner's study of Liberal and Conservative Party members combines individual differences and situational factors, particularly when explaining the result that Liberals helped the black victim as frequently as the white victim but that they hung up prematurely more frequently on the black callers. Here it was suggested that the expression of liberal anti-black sentiment depends on whether the situation is relatively free of normative prescriptions.

Another purpose of this chapter was to familiarize the reader with the methodology and the reasoning of experimental social psychologists studying the phenomena of hurting and helping behavior. A number of paradigms were explored. A detailed exploration of Milgram's famous obedience study revealed that the degree of obedience varied with a number of factors such as physical distance to the victim and other cues as to the degree of his suffering. Although Milgram maintains that his data are explained in terms of an altered state of consciousness, the presence of various cues and non-obedient confederates seems to weaken the effect. Still in dispute is whether Milgram's subjects truly believed they were hurting the victim or were responding to demand characteristics.

In a survey of the frustration-aggression hypothesis, some clarifications of the original formulation were discussed. Aggression, it seems, is not always a consequence of frustration. In fact, when aggression is not instrumental in reducing the effects of frustration, then only minimal levels of aggression can be expected. In addition, frustration by itself is a much weaker antecedent of aggression than is anger. Thus, subjects made angry will aggress against their anger-instigating victims to a greater degree when the situational context contains aggression-eliciting cues (i.e., cues previously associated with aggression) than in the absence of such cues. It appears, then that it is frustration or anger instigation plus specific cues eliciting aggression that is most likely to produce aggression rather than frustration per se.

A number of other situational factors may increase or decrease the expression of aggression. For example, high ambient temperatures and pain cues from the victim inhibited aggressive responses. However, in the latter case, this was true of unangered subjects only. Angered subjects were not restrained by the pain cues. Finally, aggressive response seems to diminish when the victim consistently maintains eye contact. All of these findings, however, must be viewed in the context of how effectively anger is instigated in the laboratory and whether these findings would apply to higher-intensity real-life situations.

Helping behavior, too, is heavily influenced by situational factors. Contrary to commonsense expectations a victim is more likely to be helped the fewer the bystanders viewing his plight. This effect of the mutual inhibition of helping behavior as the number of bystanders increases is attributed to concepts such as diffusion of responsibility or social influence. The social influence here leads each bystander to accept "no help needed" definitions of the situation. This seems due less to an unwillingness to help or apathy than to confusion. This is supported by the fact that diffusion of responsibility and social influence appear to be more potent effects when the emergency situation itself or the interpretations offered by others are highly ambiguous.

Besides these more general formulations, a number of victim- and situation-specific factors affect helping behavior. For example, whether a victim appears ill or drunk, is black or white, or is or is not bleeding may affect the degree to which he is helped. Many of these results may be consolidated in terms of a reward–cost model which predicts degree of helping as a function of the costs incurred in the helping of different kinds of victims.

Finally, at an additional level of generalization it was proposed that most helping situations are sufficiently ambiguous as to permit the bystander a great deal of leeway in defining whether or not help is really needed. At this point, characteristics of the victim and the reward–cost factors inherent in the situation interact to determine if the situation will be defined as help-needed or no-help-needed.

SUGGESTED READINGS

Latane, B., & Darley, J. M. *The unresponsive bystander: Why doesn't he help?* New York: Appleton Century-Crofts, 1970.

A reasonably complete account of the authors' pioneering research on the social factors which inhibit bystanders from intervening in emergency situations. This volume presents the results of empirical inquiries in a style that is pleasing to both the serious student of the social sciences and to the public at large.

MacAulay, J., & Berkowitz, L. (Eds.). *Altruism and helping behavior: Social psychological studies of some antecedents and consequences.* New York: Academic Press, 1970.

This volume presents the thinking and research of a number of scholars whose work has important implications for the understanding of altruistic or pro-social behavior. This text is highly recommended for the serious student of bystander intervention and/or the development of morality.

Milgram, S. The experience of living in cities. *Science,* 1970, *167,* 1461–1468.

A fascinating analysis of the urban dweller's behavior which is viewed as an attempt to adapt to an environment which "overloads" his system. This analysis is a fine complement to readings in the area of bystander intervention and also has important implications for urban planning, race relations, and environmental psychology.

Zimbardo, P. G. The human choice: individuation, reason, and order versus deindividuation, impulse, and chaos. In W. J. Arnold and D. Levine (Eds.), *Nebraska Symposium on Motivation: 1969.* Lincoln: University of Nebraska Press, 1969.

An interesting, though speculative, account of the process of deindividuation. This article is highly recommended for students in psychology, sociology, and criminal justice.

PART THREE
Attitudes and Attitude Change

6. ATTITUDES AND THE PREDICTION OF BEHAVIOR
Introduction: The Challenge of Attitudes
Attitude Theory
  Definitions / Are attitudes tendencies to respond, or observed responses? / Attitudes and other concepts / Dimensions of attitudes / Comment
Attitude Measurement
  Question form / Attitude scales / Comment
Attitude and Behavior
  Some attitude–behavior studies / A conceptual model of attitude–behavior relationships / What have we learned? A quick look at those early studies / Some recent research
Where Do We Go from Here?
  Individual and group differences in acting on attitudes / Beyond nomothetic psychology: predicting for some of the people some of the time / Some conclusions and implications
Summary
Suggested Readings

7. **THEORIES OF ATTITUDE CHANGE**
   Introduction
   The Inductive Approach: Studies of Source, Message, and Audience Effects
   Communicator effects / Message effects / Audience effects
   The Functions and Structure of Belief Systems
   The functions of belief systems: pleasure and problem solving / The structure of belief systems
   The Dynamics of Change in Belief Systems: Cognitive Consistency Theories
   Affective-cognitive consistency theory / Balance theories / The congruity model / Abelson's model of resolving belief dilemmas / The theory of cognitive dissonance / Consistency versus curiosity / Bem's self-perception theory
   Summary
   Suggested Readings

6

Attitudes and the Prediction of Behavior

Robert Brannon

INTRODUCTION: THE CHALLENGE OF ATTITUDES

Social psychologists don't yet have a good answer to one of those simple questions which usually offer us such nice opportunities to display our wisdom and expertise: *"Is what people say a good indication of what they will do?"*

Questions like this are the sort of thing we normally delight in answering and helpfully pose for ourselves if nobody else will: ("Say, I'll bet you've been wondering whether people will go along with a unanimous majority that disagrees with their private opinion!" "By the way, if you had your choice in a public debate, would it be better to speak first or last?" "When a decision is made by an entire group, won't it just be the average of all the individual opinions?" "What kinds of things make us like other people?") All of these questions are too broad for simple answers, of course; but we fall on them like James Beard on a roast chicken and confidently divide them into manageable units, citing illuminating studies along the way and having a great time in the process.

Occasionally, however, we encounter a "simple" question which proves embarrassingly difficult to answer. Like a high school math teacher who has stumbled onto one of Zeno's paradoxes, we start off confidently but quickly run into trouble, back up and try again with no better results; the blackboard fills with computations, special assumptions, and approximations; and meanwhile everyone else is yawning and wandering away. When this sort of thing happens it often means that we are dealing with a question which disguises deeper issues.

The question of "what people say versus what they do" has received the attention of social psychologists from time to time in the past, but was never answered very well. Recently it has shown alarming signs of deepening and broadening into a virtual San Andreas fault across the social sciences, known as the "attitude-behavior controversy." For many years this issue was regarded as an interesting but minor topic in applied social psychology and sociology; today it has begun to rumble menacingly and is threatening to bring down 50 years of intensive study of attitudes into meaningless rubble.

What's the excitement all about? For most of the brief history of social psychology, the concept of "attitude" has been regarded as "the most distinctive and indispensable concept in American social psychology" (Allport, 1935). In fact, it is today the most widely-used single term in all social science (Berkowitz, 1972b). The brilliant pioneering works on attitude measurement by Thurstone (1928), Likert (1932), Sletto (1937), Guttman (1950), and others gave social psychology its first major methodological achievement and over the next 40 years stimulated thousands of empirical studies on attitudes from "anomie" to "xenophobia." Social psychology was actually once defined as "the scientific study of attitudes" (Thomas & Znaniecki, 1918); although that description has proved much too confining, such familiar topics as prejudice, self-esteem, job-satisfaction, alienation, authoritarianism, political ideology, personal values, religiosity, social desirability, and many others are in effect branches of attitude study, investigated with basic attitude-measurement techniques.

The original and fundamental interest of attitudes was and is that they're believed to have something to do with how people act. The earliest uses of the term were in fact based rather directly on this link; for example, Lange's (1888) report that reactions were more rapid when subjects had an *Aufgabe* or "task-attitude" of readiness-to-respond when a signal appeared. Introductory texts of a decade ago simply asserted a general relation between attitude and behavior, for example, "The actions of the individual are governed to a large extent by his attitudes" (Krech, Crutchfield, & Ballachey, 1962, p. 146). "Words are actions in miniature," stated one explanation of interviewing. "Hence by the use of questions and answers we can obtain information about a vast number of actions in a short space of time, the actual observation and measurement of which would be impractical" (quoted by Hyman, 1954). Guided by such assumptions, implicit and explicit, social scientists have gone about investigating the attitudes of a large part of the western world's population. Attitudes about race, war, work, sex, Communism, religion, politics, money, health, and so forth are reported in articles and books ranging from scholarly treatises to phone-in polls in daily newspapers. Pollsters rush to find out how people feel about new national events. Politicians may shape their views to conform to the mood of the people as revealed by polls. Economists study consumer buying-intentions. Businessmen commission "association studies" before naming a new product. Opinion polling has become a new growth industry, and Presidents carry the latest returns in their pockets.

This is where the tremors from the attitude-behavior issue come in. As early as 1934, one California sociologist had shown in rather dramatic fashion that verbal reports and behavior do not always correspond (LaPiere, 1934). Between 1930 and 1932 Richard LaPiere traveled from coast to coast with a young foreign-born Chinese couple, stopping at over 250 hotels, auto camps, cafes, and restaurants, and receiving normal—sometimes exemplary—service in all but one. Six months after the trip LaPiere mailed to each of these establishments a simple questionnaire which included the question, "Will you accept members of the Chinese race in your establishment?" The answers he received were 92% "No," despite the fact that all of these places had in fact served his Chinese friends not long before.

This study caught the eye of some who were

concerned with attitudes; gradually other studies comparing self-report measures of attitudes with independent observations of behavior began to appear. Corey (1937) measured students' attitudes about cheating on examinations and compared the results with secretly gathered data about actual cheating on exams: The correlation was +.02. There followed a variety of studies (e.g., Bray, 1950; Berg, 1966; Tittle & Hill, 1967; Warner & DeFleur, 1969) of which the results were almost always similar in the most important respect: An attitude measure was unrelated, or only slightly related, to a seemingly relevant behavior which had been independently measured or observed. The investigators usually offered convincing explanations of what had gone wrong—generally that important other variables should have been somehow controlled—but the negative results continued to mount. Each new study seemed to introduce more controls and to account for its disappointing result by hypothesizing still other uncontrolled variables.

In an influential review article, Wicker (1969a) noted that the attitude-behavior correlations had rarely gone above .30 and were often much closer to zero. "Taken as a whole, these studies suggest that it is considerably more likely that attitudes will be unrelated or only slightly related to overt behaviors than that attitudes will be closely related. . . . The present review provides little evidence to support the postulated existence of stable, underlying attitudes within the individual which influence both his verbal expressions and his actions" (Wicker, 1969a, pp. 65, 75).

Meanwhile, researchers in experimental social psychology were uncovering some surprising and exciting facts about human behavior. Asch (1951) had shown that rather easy and obvious visual judgments could be substantially altered by means of group pressures to give a wrong answer. Milgram (1963) found that what seemed to be appallingly inhumane behavior—applying 450 volts to a man with a weak heart—could be successfully commanded by a humorless figure in a white lab coat. Orne (1962) discovered that his subjects would sort messy, smelly garbage into neat piles or add columns of numbers for 5 hours at a stretch, obediently shredding each sheet into bits before going to the next. Latané and Darley (1968) showed that subjects would fill out questionnaires while a room filled with smoke, overhear a dangerous fall without going to help, and listen to a horrifying epileptic fit without intervening. In each of these cases the behavior was startlingly discrepant with how most people, and presumably also the subjects, would have predicted themselves to act, if asked before the experiment. "I am the master of my fate, I am the captain of my soul," the poet had said, . . . but thoughtful psychologists were beginning to wonder to what extent people really do determine their own actions.

Another surprising fact was also noticed: These manipulations of behavior could somehow change verbal reports of "attitudes." When respondents were induced to act in a manner they would normally disapprove and avoid, their attitudes tended to change soon thereafter to approve the behavior that was formerly disapproved (Cohen, 1964; Insko, 1968; Kiesler et al., 1969). Instead of standing up for what they believe, people appeared to believe whatever they happened to stand up for. The behavioral tail was successfully wagging the attitudinal dog, which was especially disturbing since it had proven so difficult to predict behavior from attitude measure. If attitudes don't predict behavior, what good are they? And by the way, what use were all those years of collecting data on attitudes?

By the late 1960s the old common-sense assumption that attitudes influence actions was rapidly disappearing from the technical and professional literature. New articles routinely cited the negative evidence, with a pessimism that seemed if anything to grow stronger with each passing year:

> Verbal measures of attitudes generally have not predicted social behavior toward members of minority groups. (Berg, 1966, p. 215)

> What little evidence there is to support any relationship between attitude and behavior comes from studies showing that a person tends to bring his attitude into line with his behavior, rather than from studies demonstrating that behavior is a function of attitude. (Fishbein, 1967a, p. 477)

> Studies on the relation of attitudes and behavior have almost consistently resulted in the conclusion that attitudes are a poor predictor of behavior. (Ehrlich, 1969, p. 29)

> Attitude research has long indicated that the person's verbal report of his attitude has a rather low correlation with his actual behavior toward the object of the attitude. (McGuire, 1969a, p. 156)

> Attitudes are just another of the many hypothetical and largely unproductive mental states that behavioral scientists have tried to measure and use in prediction of overt behavior. . . . The idea that attitudes are active mental agents that mediate one's responses to social situations leads . . . into the inescapable attitude-action trap. (Tarter, 1970, p. 276)

> Most researchers have had little success in predicting behavior from attitudes toward ethnic groups. (Brigham, 1971, p. 15)

> The stipulation of a direct attitude-behavior relationship . . . has become increasingly untenable. (Ajzen, 1971, p. 263)

> Numerous studies, especially in race relations, have been devoted to this issue, ending almost invariably in negative or ambiguous results. (Weitz, 1972, p. 14)

> There is a growing awareness among investigators that attitudes tend to be unrelated to overt behaviors. (Fishbein & Ajzen, 1972, p. 528)

> Although attitude is frequently considered as a predisposition to behavior, periodic reviews have noted the failure of attitude measures to predict behavior. (Sample & Warland, 1973, p. 292)

> Again and again it has been demonstrated that there is little relationship between attitudes and overt behavior. (Brislin & Olmstead, 1973, p. 1)

Social psychologists continued to do research on attitudes and on attitude change, but a new, "insider's" point of view had begun to develop, which boldly challenged the relevance of attitude research altogether. Attitudes are basically irrelevant to what goes on in life; they're sort of epiphenomenological scum floating on the solid reality of behavior. People do what they must do. Behavior is determined by norms, situational pressures, roles, reference groups, habits, socially mediated rewards, economic realities, and a thousand other realistic pressures. What people think they will do is basically irrelevant, and asking verbal questions is about as futile as asking raindrops in a hurricane where they plan to land. As for all those methodological refinements, such as elaborate scaling models to measure reliability and intensity, "since attitudes . . . play no real role in behavior, an intense nothing contributes no more than a moderate nothing" (Tarter, 1970, p. 277). Psychologists who were still studying attitudes were beginning to feel foolish, and to sound defensive. When Herbert Kelman announced to the American Psychological Association's annual convention in 1971 that "Attitudes are alive and well, and gainfully employed," it had the ominous sound of a final tribute to an old friend.

A Brief Detour Back to Common Sense. If the story could be ended here there would be no postscript: just another useless variable laid to rest by the relentless scrutiny of modern science. But it can't happen, because in our hearts we all know that intentions and attitudes do exist and do influence behavior. Introspection was the original research method of psychology; it has its limitations, but still sometimes comes in handy. As I write these words, for example, I'm aware of being in the mood to eat Chinese food this evening. Since there's a Chinese restaurant nearby, I'm going to translate my attitude into deliciously overt behavior a few hours from now. You may argue that this kind of evidence shouldn't count, and anyway has little social relevance, but it is a true example of behavior following from a personal inclination. Furthermore, I hate liver and I never eat it.

To take a more significant example, I also know whom I'm going to vote for in an election which will take place shortly. In fact most of the other potential voters know who they're going to vote for also, and it is already clear that my candidate will lose by a wide margin. How do I know? Because political polls are remarkably accurate nowadays and can usually predict the outcome of an election within a margin of less than two or three percent. To cite merely one example, in 1962 The New York Times predicted that Nelson A. Rockefeller would get 54.2% of the total gubernatorial votes. When exactly five million, six hundred twenty-one thousand, eight hundred and seventy votes were finally counted, Rockefeller had received 54.6% (Coleman, et al., 1964). What people say does sometimes accurately forecast what they will do later; this much is consistent with common sense, and with our introspective observations of the way we ourselves so often behave.

When we look at the way we behave in everyday life, it is apparent that more often than not we assume that people will keep their word. We go to the place where we agreed to meet a friend, we climb into a taxi and we ask to go to the airport, or we dress up and drive across town to a party. If the friend never appears, we arrive at the city dump, or there's no party, we are both annoyed and surprised. Consistency between words and actions is not an abstract issue in everyday life; it's something we normally depend on and take for granted until we discover otherwise.

Why then did all those published studies find so little relationship between attitude measures and the behaviors they "should" have predicted? One simple answer might be that studies which got the opposite result were not reported for publication. Since for so many years the common-sense connection between attitudes and behavior was taken for granted, only a surprising finding of no relationship might have seemed worth sharing. This is clearly not the whole story however. Whatever their limitations, the series of attitude–behavior studies from LaPiere to the present have effectively shattered the highly naive assumption that behavior is inevitably and primarily an expression of personal attitude. Attitudes may sometimes be irrelevant to actions, but more frequently they appear to interact in some way with a large number of factors which also bear on behavior in the real world. Our task then is to develop a much more detailed understanding of when and how attitudes have a significant influence on behaviors.

What are the circumstances for example which make some kinds of behavior such as voting possible to predict with great precision? When do people act in ways that they never could or would have predicted? What is the practical difference between general attitudes toward an object and a specific intention to act a certain way toward that object at a certain time? These and many other questions will be dealt with in detail later in this chapter. And, we will reveal some new studies that do finally show what most people have believed all along: that attitudes do sometimes determine behavior, even despite strong situational pressures to the contrary. More thoughtful and pragmatic methods are gradually leading us out of the valley of the shadow of invalidity, to the modest comfort of moderate relationships.

What we ultimately hope for is not a series of ad hoc answers to specific problems, but a systematic understanding of how attitudes interact with other personal and environmental variables to jointly influence specific actions; in other words, we'd merely like to know what determines human behavior. This amounts more or less to the fundamental goal of social science, and it's unlikely that it will be accomplished anytime very soon. We can begin to make progress however without expecting to have all the answers immediately, and in the meantime the attitude-behavior controversy is one of the more lively current debates in social psychology. (It's also one of the few areas where sociologists and psychologists are working together profitably.)

Most interesting of all, the attitude–behavior controversy may prove to have been the harsh medicine that saved the attitude concept. When the "Young Turks" declared that attitude theories were irrelevant and that attitude measurement was statistical sound and fury signifying nothing, they were wrong but also right. Attitude theory had gradually become top-heavy with distinctions, debates, and explanations that nobody could understand well enough to test, or care to. Attitude measurement had been receding into the far reaches of scaling models and multivariate analyses, and nobody was listening anymore. The whole attitude area was becoming an academic "saber-tooth curriculum," increasingly out of touch with the interests and concerns of other psychologists. Particularly to those concerned with the real and pressing problems of society, it was an irrelevant parlor game which "dabbles in reality but avoids the real area of action" (Clark, 1965b).

The behaviorist attack on this tradition has been a breath of fresh air, blowing out intellectual cobwebs and exposing some very real problems. Validity is now a crucial concern of most of those working with attitudes; there is concern about the validity of conceptual distinctions, of measurement procedures, and even the validity of attitude-change results (Festinger, 1964). It is premature to judge with much confidence, but the early years of the 1970s seem to reflect a considerable new rigor and sophistication in the area of attitudes.

But we've gotten way ahead of ourselves. In the following pages we will deal more carefully with the definitions of attitudes and related concepts, and review the wild and wonderful theories that have flourished here in the absence of any regular pruning by tests of predictive validity. Next we shall examine attitude measurement: the pride of social psychology, the most highly refined procedure in all social science, a method for measuring something-or-other remarkably well. Finally, after examining the early data in the light of some new concepts and findings, we'll get down to work, to try to show when verbal measures predict behavior and when they don't.

ATTITUDE THEORY

It is almost a truism that among humans as with all organisms, experience modifies behavior. Some residue of experience is retained which is capable of influencing or at least affecting later behaviors. This universal fact is implicitly accepted by all social scientists; it is referred to in many ways and with many terms, of which attitude is but one. Strangely enough we do not have and have never had a widely accepted definition of what is meant by the term *attitude*. It sometimes appears that every writer who has used the term has stated a new definition; this is a small exaggeration, but Nelson

(1939) listed 30 separate definitions in use by 1939, and considerably more have appeared since. We shall not attempt to review all the definitions of attitude proposed in recent years and will even resist the powerful temptation to add yet another to the heap. Gordon Allport's rather vague but elegant definition, stated almost 40 years ago, has probably been more widely used and influential than any other:

> An attitude is a mental and neural state of readiness, organized through experience, exerting a directive or dynamic influence upon the individual's response to all objects and situations with which it is related. (Allport, 1935, p. 810)

It might be added that attitudes are also usually thought of as relatively enduring. That is, they are not necessarily permanent but do tend to be regarded as fairly stable from one day to the next, or until some reason for change occurs.

As with any term which evolved gradually from the natural language, the attitude concept has never been the property of any individual or school of thought. It has been elastic enough to apply to individuals, groups, and whole cultures, to precise preferences and to broad views of life. Psychologists, sociologists, and even anthropologists use it, and it has often provided the common denominator for interdisciplinary efforts. Social psychology in particular has developed closely in concert with attitudes. "This useful, one might almost say peaceful, concept has been so widely adopted that it has virtually established itself as the keystone in the edifice of American social psychology" (Allport, 1935). What observable human behaviors, then, are conveyed by this popular term?

Most theorists agree that the basic evidence for attitudes is a pattern of *consistency* in responses to some social object. Although certain other characteristics (e.g., intensity) are tapped by some measurement techniques, consistency is the preferred and most convincing evidence for attitudes. As an illustration suppose that one day over lunch you observe a businessman angrily snarl at his waiter. Why? Well, perhaps the man's in a terrible mood, perhaps the stock market crashed, perhaps the waiter just delivered cold soup and a warm martini. Now suppose that you eat lunch in this restaurant everyday, and everyday you notice this same irascible character snarling at whomever is serving him. You'd conclude that he feels superior to waiters, or dislikes people, or finds small things irritating, or something of this sort. Rather than attributing his behavior to some aspect of the situation, you'd assume he had an enduring attitude of some sort to explain such consistency across many situations.

The reason that attitude definitions are so diverse is that theorists have so often sought to account for this phenomenon, rather than merely to describe it. The reasons for consistency are variously explained in terms of "perceptual equivalence," "action tendencies," "sets," "central nervous system traces," "symbolic structures," and so forth. Since there is little or no agreement on the psychological mechanisms, attitude definitions have continued to multiply, taking on whatever shapes and forms have suited the theoretical tastes of their authors.

Over the years the realm of attitude theory has thus begun to resemble a peaceable kingdom in which anything grows, everything goes, and old concepts never die! Psychological reality is so complex that almost no formulation is totally wrong, and theorists have not been hesitant to pile plausible new formulations on top of plausible old ones. Ostrom (1968), for example, discusses 34 "major" theoretical formulations offered during one recent span, from 1953 to 1968. Attitude theory has become top-heavy with its venerable controversies, refinements, and distinctions. Three of the more basic areas of theorizing are discussed in the following sections.

Are Attitudes Tendencies to Respond or Observed Responses?

One basic question concerns the most productive way to conceptualize the attitude concept. Allport, Cantril, Bogardus, and many others have viewed attitudes as states of "readiness to respond" which exist in the mind before the response occurs. This fits the evidence of our own introspection; most of us would agree that we have private attitudes towards certain people or events which we have not yet expressed, and may never express, in overt behavior.

Bain (1868), Horowitz (1944), and DeFleur and Westie (1963) have objected to any reliance on unobservable quantities and have argued for a behavioristic definition based solely on some aspect of observable responses: "The attitude, then, is an inferred property of the responses, namely their consistency. Stated in another way, attitude is equated with the probability of recurrence of behavior forms of a given type or direction" (DeFleur & Westie, 1963, p. 21).

These theorists argue that such an approach avoids the need for any mysterious, unseen mechanism in the individual; we simply define attitude as the consistency among responses and don't speculate as to why they are consistent. Although this approach offers the appeal of an operational definition, most social psychologists have been unwilling to accept it. In an insightful response Norman Weissberg (1965) has suggested that it may lead, paradoxically, to theoretical stagnation. The convenience of dealing with precise operational definitions is purchased by giving up reference to most instances of behavior and to a systematic explanatory theory. It is preferable to struggle with a deeper and more explanatory conception of attitudes, he suggests, then to settle for an "engineer's handbook" of conditions under which specific behaviors will occur with such-and-such probability. Besides, reasoned Weissberg (a psychologist), we are all well aware that attitudes do exist in the mind which do not get translated into behavior; Would DeFleur and Westie deny that all men have *sexual* desires, even though we rarely demonstrate most of these desires? DeFleur and Westie—sociologists—were not turned on by Weissberg's argument. "We do indeed deny that all men have sexual desires; a concept as basic as that of attitude should rest upon unequivocally demonstrated empirical evidence" (1965).

More recently McGuire (1969a) has suggested that instead of two positions on this issue there are at least five: the "positivistic," "paradigmatic," "mediationalist," "classinclusionist," and "interactionist" positions. McGuire's contribution has served the useful purpose of halting debate on this question for the last few years while everyone tries to figure out what these terms mean.

Attitudes and Other Concepts

Since theorists cannot agree on precisely what attitudes are, it should not be surprising that they do not agree as to what they are not, or where to draw the line between attitudes and other concepts.

What is the difference between an attitude and a belief? Beliefs are usually considered to be more "neutral"; we would call the statement that "Washington is the U.S. capital" a belief, but not an attitude. But what if one believes that "the President is a scoundrel" (or a great man)? These beliefs begin to sound much like attitudes. Some writers use the terms belief and attitude interchangably, while others carefully distinguish them. Unfortunately, the distinctions are never quite the same (Bem, 1970; Berkowitz, 1972; Fishbein and Ajzen, 1972).

What then is an "opinion"? Harvey et al. (1961) maintain that (1) opinions, (2) beliefs, and (3) attitudes represent increasing degrees of "centrality" in the personality. Bogardus (1933) writes that opinions are a conscious type of beliefs. Osgood, Suci, and Tannenbaum (1957) argue that opinions deal with facts and are verifiable, while attitudes deal with taste and are unverifiable. Thus, a belief about who wrote a poem would be an opinion, while a belief about its merits would be called an attitude. (This seems reasonable enough . . . until one recalls that the authorship of Shakespeare's sonnets is the subject of unending debates, while their quality is generally considered beyond question.)

Other writers have drawn careful distinctions between the preceding terms and others such as convictions, cognitions, assumptions, and preferences. By carefully choosing examples, most of these distinctions can be made to seem logical and useful. From other perspectives, they tend to merge again. (Is the view that "Woodie Guthrie is the greatest American folk-singer" an attitude, a preference, a conviction, an opinion, a belief, or what?)

Certain constructs associated with personality theory (traits, sentiments, and factors) also describe observable consistencies in human behavior. Traits, for example, are said to differ from attitudes in that they have no particular object of reference (e.g., punctuality, shyness, assertiveness), but the difference sometimes appears largely semantic. Authoritarianism is often considered a personality trait; it can also be described as "an attitude toward people." Is patriotism a trait, or an attitude toward one's country? Is optimism a trait, or an attitude about what life will bring?

Then there are motives, interests, and values. Scott (1969) suggests that attitudes are a subclass of motives, while values are, in turn, a subclass of attitudes. Allport (1937) regarded the scope of these terms as progressing in the opposite direction: He saw opinions, attitudes, interests, and values as representing increasingly broader dispositions. Bem (1970) appears to agree with Scott, defining values as a special case of attitudes ("primitive" or basic attitudes toward certain end-states or modes of conduct). Krech, Crutchfield, and Ballachy (1962), however, agree with Allport, seeing values as deeper and more general predispositions than attitudes.

These efforts to define and redefine familiar words sometimes seem to be terms in search of a distinction, rather than distinctions in search of a terminology. Yet in addition to these words borrowed from the natural language, psychologists have coined such new concepts as tinsits, engrams, neurobiotaxes, canalizations, habs, percepts, schemas, life spaces, valences, apperceptive masses, fixations, and a host of others. Campbell (1950) listed over 75 such terms without attempting to exhaust the supply, and then commented dryly: "Today there is a surfeit of such concepts, and each new theoretical effort seems to increase the number. It *might* be possible that the increase in the number of concepts is due solely to the increase in the number of social scientists." (p. 98).

Campbell suggests a radical step toward clarification: All of these concepts can be subsumed under the general term *dispositions* or, more precisely, *acquired behavioral dispositions*. Distinctions among types of dispositions should then be recognized if and only if empirical evidence could be provided showing that such additions were necessary and useful. Response to this suggestion has not been enthusiastic. (Had we titled this chapter "dispositions," few students or teachers would have been sure what we meant.)

Dimensions of Attitudes

Since the term "dispositions" has not caught on with social psychologists, we will continue to speak of attitudes in this chapter, but in the general sense that Campbell had in mind.

Most of the properties of attitudes may be viewed as dimensions along which variation is possible, rather than as categorical or defining properties of the concept. The following are some of the dimensions of attitudes currently mentioned in the theoretical literature.

Intensity or valence (Cantril, 1946; Hartley & Hartley, 1952) refers essentially to the strength with which an attitude is felt.

Extremity or magnitude on the other hand, refers to the nominal content of the attitude. Judges are usually able to consistently rank-order a list of attitude statements in terms of how "favorable" they appear to be toward the attitude object. There *is* evidence that extremity is correlated with intensity, but the relationship is far from uniform. (Suchman, 1950)

Salience (Stern, 1938; Smith et al., 1956) is essentially how "close to the surface" an attitude is. Salient attitudes are those which come most readily to mind.

Centrality (Krech & Crutchfield, 1948) refers to an attitude's position in an "individual's mental universe." The attitude is central if it is an important part of one's way of looking at life or is part of the "self-concept" (Secord & Backman, 1961).

Connectedness or embeddedness (Scott, 1969) or *information support* (Smith et al., 1956) means the number of ties the attitude has with other cognitive elements, particularly logical or functional connections, such that a change in one would tend to exert some influence on the other.

The cognitive, affective, conative trichotomy. Taking their lead from Plato, Western writers and philosophers have commonly distinguished among knowing, feeling, and acting toward an object. So accepted is this conceptualization today among attitude theorists (e.g., Harding et al., 1969; Bem, 1970) that most writers discuss it not as a theory or approach but as a familiar fact.

The cognitive dimension is said to include those elements most like beliefs and opinions: e.g., "women are more emotional than men," "exams test only a small part of what you know." The affective dimension is the feeling or emotional aspect of attitudes: e.g., "I like girls who make me feel smart." "I hate taking exams." The conative dimension is said to consist of "action tendencies": e.g., "I always hold the door for women," "I look for courses that don't have any exams."

Multiplexity or differentiation (Smith et al., 1956) means the degree of "internal differentiation" of an attitude or one of its components. The term usually applies to the cognitive dimension, in which case it has also been called *cognitive complexity* (Scott, 1969), *extensity, degree of structure, permeability,* and *gradient of belief* (Rokeach, 1960).

Affective salience (Scott, 1966) refers to the degree to which an attitude is dominated by its affective content.

Overtness (Krech et al., 1962) refers to the degree of prominence of the conative or action component; the degree to which tendencies to act are inherent in the attitude.

Consistency has been defined as the degree of similarity in intensity, or multiplexity, among the cognitive, affective, and conative dimensions respectively (Krech et al., 1962).

Ambivalence refers to the presence of opposite or antagonistic elements within an attitude (Scott, 1966). Opposing elements may tend to neutralize one another with the result that net intensity is low and ambivalence high.

Consciousness means the degree of awareness of an attitude. French (1947) hypothesizes that attitudes can be conscious, unconscious, or partly conscious.

Stability, tenacity (Chein, 1951), *flexibility* (Scott, 1966) all refer to essentially the same variable: the resistance of an attitude to change. This apparently must be determined empirically, since it is not described as a function of any other dimensions or qualities.

Certainty (Chein, 1951) might be considered an attitude toward other attitudes, but it has also been called a dimension; it refers to the degree of conviction associated with an attitude.

Comment

Say, how about "triadic-interdependence," the degree to which those three dimensions influence one another? Or "solubility," the degree to which an attitude can be incorporated into opposing belief systems? Or "hedonic irony," the degree to which the affective and conative dimensions are inversely related! It's fun, it's easy, and any number can play! The attitude theory literature has become so vast in the last decade that the most industrious reviewers no longer discuss more than a part of it at one time (cf. McGuire, 1969a; Fishbein & Ajzen, 1972; Greenwald, 1968). Distinctions, dimensions, categories, constructs, and terminologies proliferate and disappear over the years, seemingly fueled more by changing fashions than by any fresh data. The most basic problem I believe is a lack of concern with the utility and empirical validity of those abstract concepts.

An excellent example is the continuing popularity of the cognitive-affective-conative model of attitudes. This approach to attitudes is discussed at length in virtually every introductory textbook, usually without question or qualification.[1] Yet on the rare occasions when this scheme has led to the construction of measures tailormade for each of the three components, the data have seldom even vaguely supported the model (Campbell, 1947; Kahn, 1951; MacKenzie, 1948; Ostrom, 1969). More damaging still is the fact that factor-analytic investigations have never isolated anything resembling these three components from a general pool of attitude statements prepared without reference to the theory (Ferguson, 1939; Gardner et al., 1968; Woodmansee & Cook, 1967). Woodmansee and Cook, for example, factor-analyzed several hundred attitude statements reflecting all aspects of racial prejudice and discrimination. Instead of three factors they found eleven: eg., "ease in interracial contact," "acceptance in status-superior positions," "sympathetic identification with the underdog," and so forth. Despite such pointed disconfirmations, and a thirty-year history of lack of any empirical support for the theory, the authoritative *Handbook of Social Psychology*'s recent chapter on Prejudice structured its entire discussion around cognitive, affective, and conative attitudes (Harding et al., 1969, p. 4). Like an intellectual chain-letter that can't be stopped, this model has acquired a life of its own and now proliferates from textbook to textbook unhindered by any need for confirming data.

The realm of attitude theory is now long overdue for a pruning with Occam's razor, the legendary cure for extraneous baggage. This is where the attitude–behavior issue, with its focus on validity and empirical prediction, re-enters the picture. Before expanding on this point however, we must turn to the question of how attitudes are measured.

---

[1] Wrightsman, 1972, p. 259; Middlebrook, 1974, p. 111; Freedman et al., 1974, p. 245, Krech et al., 1962, p. 140; and so on.

ATTITUDE MEASUREMENT

People who are unfamiliar with attitude research are often startled to discover the lack of continuity between theory and measurement techniques. The two areas are almost implausibly separate, even in the professional backgrounds of those identified with one area or the other. (It has been suggested that "those who think don't measure, and those who measure don't think.") How did this come about?

When Thurstone proclaimed that "Attitudes Can Be Measured" in a widely read article in 1928, interest in the attitude concept expanded rapidly. The development of scientific scaling procedures by Thurstone and others seemed to provide a direct and convenient method applicable to almost any social problem. Many researchers who were primarily interested in content areas—prejudice, religion, politics, alienation, conservatism, labor—now enthusiastically began to measure attitudes. While these workers closely followed the development of new methods by Thurstone, Chave, Likert, Sletto, Lazarsfeld, Guttman, Guilford, and many others, they were relatively unconcerned with the complexities of theoretical debates which seemed much less useful to their research interests. A vast empirical literature of methodological and substantive findings thus began to develop rapidly, largely independent of the subtle thinking of Allport, Chein, Droba, and other theorists. Attitude measurement is probably today the most highly researched single topic in all social science. One recent review alone cites over 1,400 references (Summers, 1970); the total number of references in all branches of social science may already have gone beyond counting.

Reviews of attitude measurement techniques (e.g., Rose, 1948; Green, 1954; Nunnally, 1967; Scott, 1969) usually either trace the chronology of measurement developments or compare assumptions of several competing-scaling models. Both approaches emphasize the procedures for combining single questions, or "items," into longer attitude scales. The present discussion focuses on a more basic issue: How is it that a person's responses to a standardized anonymous question can be expected to reveal personal attitudes and feelings? What is the connection between that hypothetical "tendency," somewhere in the mind of a respondent, and the very distinct number (say, 3, or 7, or 25) which will eventually be recorded as his attitude score?

Put yourself in the place of a respondent. You have just agreed to fill out a questionnaire, and now you read question Number One. The question is expressed in a standard fashion (i.e., it's the same for everyone who reads the questionnaire). The actual words you now read were selected months (sometimes years) ago, by a researcher you are unlikely ever to meet. It deals with a topic of interest to its author, but not necessarily to you. It may contain assumptions, or bias, or implicit interpretations of complex events: all those of its author, not your own. At the end of the question there is a list of possible answers from which you must choose the one "closest" to your own point of view—if there is one.

Now the chances are excellent in fact that a typical respondent will choose one of the answers provided. On a typical questionnaire less than 4% of the items are omitted. But how do we know that this choice really tells us anything about the respondent's attitudes? Simply calling it an "attitude question" doesn't insure that this will happen.

By way of contrast, how do we usually know the attitudes of our friends on social issues? More often than not we rely on spontaneous statements we've heard them make. While this method may seem unscientific, it has many methodological advantages. It usually insures that our friends actually have an opinion on the issue and usually, also, that the opinion is sufficiently important to our friend to bother mentioning. It insures that the opinion is expressed in our friends' own *words,* from their own *point of view,* and with their own *selection of facts.* Unfortunately, spontaneous natural statements are far too unpredictable for social scientists to wait for under most circumstances. The only alternative is to provide some standardized stimulus which we hope will elicit attitude-like expressions from all or most of the respondents. A good attitude question, no matter how simple it appears, must thus set in motion a lengthy series of events: The respondent must read and comprehend the words, comprehend the meaning of the question, formulate a reaction of some kind, and express this reaction—as nearly as possible—within the alternatives provided. There are several question formats which aim to facilitate this in various ways—the subject to which we now turn.

Question Form

Open-Ended Questions. A prepared question is posed, but the respondent is allowed to express his views in his own words rather than choose from a set of alternatives. Open-ended questions have the fundamental advantage of letting respondents express themselves naturally. Quite often, answers thus appear which the researchers did not anticipate. When Campbell and Schuman (1968) asked 1,886 whites who had previously blamed "Negroes themselves" for having worse jobs and education: *"What is it about Negroes that makes this happen?"* they expected the answers to be either "genetic" or "environmental." Instead, most white Americans believed in a simple lack of motivation: Negroes could get ahead, if they would just try harder! This striking finding would have been missed had a typical, closed-ended question been used. Yet open-ended questions are so time-consuming to administer and expensive to code and analyze that their use is severely limited by practical considerations. All of the remaining formats discussed here are closed-ended, meaning that the respondent must choose an answer from a set of predetermined alternatives of one kind or another.

Items to Accept or Reject. Apparently first used by Allport and Hartman in 1925, this method requires a respondent to agree or disagree with a specific statement, phrase, or concept. Any statement may be used, but if more than one idea is contained the responses become hard to interpret (What would it mean to disagree that: "Religion once served a useful purpose, but has outlived it, and is now doing more harm than good"?). The choices may be labeled "Agree-Disagree," "Yes-No," "True-False," or some other dichotomy, or the respondent may simply check those items agreed with, on what's called an adjective check-list.

Items with Multi-point Rating Scales. The idea of offering several distinct levels of agreement and disagreement was first introduced by Rensis Likert in 1932; today this basic format is undoubtedly more widely used than any other. The scale may be one of *intensity* ("strongly agree" to "strongly disagree"), *frequency* ("never true" to "always true"), or some other quality, but should define an essentially one-dimensional continuum with as many intermediate points as is practical. Adult respondents not only find it no more difficult than making a simple yes-or-no response, but find it more enjoyable and less frustrating. It's statistically more reliable and takes about the same administration time.

To be used effectively in a Likert format, the statement should take a relatively strong stand. (What would it mean to "strongly agree" with a mild statement, such as "Labor unions have done a few good things"?)

There are normally between four and seven alternatives, each anchored with a verbal label; when a very large number of steps are used, only the end-points are usually labeled. Statistical reliability increases rapidly as the number of steps is increased from 2 to about 7, increases somewhat less up to about 11 steps, and rises very slightly up to at least 20 steps, after which no improvement has been found (Nunnally, 1967, chap. 14).

There is a long-standing controversy over whether a neutral midpoint should be included. Some respondents may use the midpoint to avoid expressing an opinion or even thinking seriously about the statement; on the other hand, respondents often complain about being forced to take sides when they actually have no opinion. Ehrlich (1964) found that as few as 5% or as many as 57% will choose the neutral midpoint when it is offered, depending on the content of the item.

A Forced Choice Between Matched Pairs. Two separate statements, which are not mutually exclusive, are presented, and the respondent chooses the one which is more acceptable. This method is sometimes used to neutralize acquiescence effects and it permits the use of "extreme" items, which if presented alone would be overwhelmingly accepted or rejected. It's especially well suited to issues in which two strongly held positive values are in conflict, since it forces respondents to reveal their priorities.

Forced-choice questions are useful in interviews for dramatizing a controversy: "Do you think movies featuring nudity should be banned for everyone, or do you think adults have a right to see whatever they want?" Interesting combinations may also be built into the two alternatives, as in a provacative study of rationality versus liberalism by Schuman and Harding (1964):

——A. "It is pretty certain that some Jews in this country have been draft-dodgers from the military service that is required of American youth." (true, but sounds prejudiced).

——B. "It may not be widely known, but far more Jewish men have volunteered for the military services than one would expect on the basis of their percentage in the population as a whole." (false, but sounds unprejudiced)

The forced-choice principle may also be extended to more elaborate formats (two out of four choices, etc.) with counterbalanced sets of alternatives (see Scott, 1969).

Multiple-Choice Questions. A choice of just one out of three or more alternatives may appear to be only a slight variation of the forced-choice format, but in practice multiple-choice items have different properties and are used for different reasons. Alternatives may fall along some general dimension (e.g.: "extremely close friends, fairly good friends, casual friends, just acquaintances, don't know each other") or be entirely nominal ("Whom would you prefer for President? Ford, Kennedy, Wallace, or The Incredible Hulk?") Public opinion polls often use this "cafeteria-style" format to provide respondents with a range of alternatives.

The Semantic Differential. A word or short phrase is followed by a series of contrasting adjective pairs, each pair appearing at opposite ends of a segmented line. The respondent must rate the concept wherever it "seems" to belong. The following is an example:

Quotas for minority groups

Fair —— —— —— —— —— —— —— Unfair
     3   2   1   0   1   2   3

Typically each concept is rated between many adjective pairs: good-bad, strong-weak, fast-slow, hard-soft, fair-unfair, and so on. Most of the variance in a large set of such ratings has been found to be contained in the dimensions of "evaluation," "potency," and "activity," represented in the first three types of pairs (Osgood, Suci, & Tannenbaum, 1957).

This method differs from the multi-point rating format in two respects: (1) a single concept is rated on many different dimensions, as opposed to rating many statements or concepts on a single standard dimension; (2) the dimensions are defined by two approximate antonyms (gentle/rough, dependent/independent, active/passive, etc.) rather than by degrees of a single quality. Whether the opposed terms are actually polar opposites is an empirical issue which has received little attention.

Attitude Scales

Why Multi-item Scales? Anyone who has filled out an attitude questionnaire has probably noticed that many items often deal with the same issues. Psychologists seem to have a habit of asking at least 10 to 20 questions about any subject, even when the topic is something quite specific. There is a good technical reason for this, which is not immediately obvious.

The total variance (the variation in responses over many individuals) obtained by any item may be seen as a function of several relatively independent factors (Cronbach, 1951). Any factor which is present in all or most of the items becomes "compounded" in the total score and emerges as a much larger percentage of the total variance than it was in any of the original items. Factors which were present in only one or a few items do not get compounded and become a relatively smaller part of the total variance. The useful result is that even though each individual item may contain only a small percentage of the (common) factor that the scale was designed to measure, the total score may contain a significantly higher proportion of it.

To take a simple numerical example, let's assume that we have a pool of relatively weak individual items: each provides only 9% common factor variance, 9% some irrelevant group factor, 12% specific item factors, and 70% random error. Taken by themselves, these would be almost useless for measuring the common factor. However, in a scale composed of only three such items, the common factor would represent 24%; with 10 items the common factor would represent 47%; and with 20 items, the common factor would represent 60% of the total scale variance. With an infinite number of items such as these, each extremely weak by itself, the total score would be 83% common factor variance. This is the sound basic reason for constructing multi-item scales (for more discussion of this point, see Cronbach, 1951).

Constructing and Scoring Scales. There are obviously many possible ways to combine a group of items into a single numerical score. Item scores may be added, multiplied, averaged, weighted differentially, or scored for adherence to almost any predetermined set of patterns. Common-factor amplification takes place to varying degrees with all these methods, although the proof is different in each case. Of the great number of scoring models which have been used by psychologists at various times, we shall examine only the three most popular and influential models, commonly known as the Thurstone, the Guttman, and the Summative scales. More sophisticated and complicated methods of attitude scaling such as Lazarfeld's Latent Structure Analysis (1950) and Coomb's Unfolding Technique (1964) are available but have not yet found widespread application.

The *Thurstone scale* (also known as the "psychophysical," "consensual-location," or "judgment" method) is directly based on the concept of item extremity: the degree of favorableness or unfavorableness which each item represents. If a group of items range from mild to extreme approval, and different people agree with different items, it is assumed that those who endorse the most extreme items should receive the highest total score. The scale should consist of items placed at approximately equal intervals along the extremity dimension in order to be sensitive to the full range of opinion. Each item is associated with a numerical score representing its degree of extremity. The scores for each item are determined in advance by data from a panel of judges who evaluate a large number of items; those chosen for the scale are selected to have scores at regular intervals along the continuum. The final scale score is the mean (or sometimes the median) of the weights of those items a given respondent has endorsed.

An interesting assumption of the Thurstone method is that each item should elicit agreement from persons who are close to its position (on the extremity dimension) but be rejected by those with both less extreme and more extreme positions. Each item should thus be "sensitive" to only a certain region of the attitude dimension, something like a tuning fork which will resonate only to vibrations near its own frequency.

In practice it has often proven very difficult to find items with one-zone characteristics, especially those at the intermediate values. (Imagine looking for a word which moderately good spellers could spell, but both poor and excellent spellers could not. . . .) Items which do have this property sometimes tend to contain two or more separate statements.

The *Guttman scale* (or "cumulative" or "scalogram" method) is also generally based on item extremity but requires items of a different type, those with "cumulative" characteristics. The scale is constructed along the lines of a series of successively higher hurdles: Anyone who can jump one of the higher ones should naturally be able to jump all the lower ones. Each item is successively more extreme along a preselected attitude dimension, so that anyone who can accept the most extreme item in the scale should also accept all of the preceeding ones.

The score is usually defined as the most extreme item accepted after the smallest possible number of changes is made to make the response pattern fit the model (Guttman, 1944).

The ostensible advantage of Guttman scaling is that obtained scores are always unidimensional; in other words, they measure variations only along the precise dimension depicted by the scale items. Nunnally (1967) has forcefully challenged this contention and showed that apparent unidimensionality can very easily be an artifact of item characteristics. Guttman scales are rather time-consuming to construct and have declined markedly in popularity in recent years.

The *Summative* method of scoring (sometimes called Likert scales) is by far the simplest and most flexible procedure for combining items. Individual item scores are simply added, and the resulting total is the scale score. The only requirement is that items must be at least moderately correlated with one another, a condition which can be checked after the collection of data when deviant items can be dropped from the scale. As variations in scale length and item extremity are relatively unimportant, the scale may be shortened, lengthened, or revised at will. The underlying measurement principle is consistency rather than extremity of responses. Since each item gives the respondent one opportunity to either show the attitude or not, the person receiving the highest score is the one who showed it the most times.

Any scale in which the item scores are summed to provide the total score may be called a summative scale. A Likert scale is the special case in which the items of a summative scale offer a range of agreement–disagreement choices to standard statements. In a lengthy series of comparisons of scaling techniques (e.g., Likert, 1932; Marks, 1943; Barclay & Weaver, 1962; Tittle & Hill, 1967) the Likert-summative method has consistently been found to be both more reliable and less time-consuming to construct than either Thurstone or Guttman scales. The combination of technical superiority, ease of construction, and general flexibility has resulted in an increasing reliance on the summative model by researchers in all areas.

Comment

The literature of attitude measurement has grown inexorably during the last 30 years, the product of a fruitful collaboration of statisticians, methodologists, and problem-oriented activists. While scaling methods and technical issues such as item format have progressed through countless refinements, applications have simultaneously pushed into every substantive area from "alienation" to "xenophobia." Surveying this juggernaut of activity, one is compelled to concede that modern attitude measures must be doing something extremely well.

But what is it that they do? Deutscher (1966) has noted a pervasive "obsession with reliability" in attitude measurement, and we think there is much truth in his observation. As Deutscher wryly comments: "We may have been learning a great deal about how to pursue an incorrect course with a maximum of precision" (1966, p. 241).

In simple terms, *reliability* means how sure you are that a measurement would turn out the same way if taken a second or third time, i.e., to what extent error and other uncontrolled variance has been excluded from the process of measurement. *Validity*, on the other hand, refers to how sure you are that you are measuring what you think, i.e., that the data obtained are in fact related to the psychological quality you intended to measure.[2] The ability to predict in advance some behavior which should follow from such a quality is widely regarded as the most convincing, though not the only, possible evidence of validity. Thus a demonstration that scores on a scale of "racial prejudice" were closely related to "prejudiced behavior" would be the best possible evidence of validity.

Most of the refinements discussed in the preceding pages (the Likert item format, multi-item scales, the summative scoring technique) were based primarily on increasing reliability. There is little if any direct evidence that these innovations increased the relationship of attitude scores to other kinds of behavior.

---

[2]For a full discussion see the APA's "Standards for psychological tests and manuals" (1974). Although the two concepts are often discussed as if they were largely independent, Campbell and Fisk (1959) have made the useful point that in practice they are simply the opposite ends of a long continuum. When agreement is found between two measurements which are methodologically highly similar (the ultimate case being an immediate test–retest correlation), it constitutes evidence of reliability. When agreement is found between two measurements which are extremely dissimilar in form, this constitutes the best evidence of validity.

Thus, while validity is given respectful lip-service in textbooks, it has been largely and increasingly ignored by attitude researchers. Two recent volumes by Robinson and Shaver (1969) and Robinson, Rusk, and Head (1968) summarizing over two hundred current attitude scales illustrate this point quite dramatically: While almost every published scale reports satisfactory evidence of reliability, there is rarely any evidence of validity. Modest correlations with other attitude scales are frequently the only such evidence mentioned; these prove little or nothing when the second scale has not been validated against behavior; and chain-correlations would be very weak evidence in any event.

When evidence of validity is discussed it is frequently the so-called known-group method of validation. Two sets of people (typically social organizations or religious or geographic groups) who are "well-known" to have different views are tested with the attitude scale; if they receive significantly different mean scores, the scale is considered validated. If members of the Sierra Club, for example, have higher scores on an Ecology Attitudes Scale than members of a strip-mining lobby, the scale would be validated. A typical example of this approach is the elaborate Woodmansee and Cook (1967) scale of racial attitudes. The scale was painstakingly developed over several years: There were five stages of factor analysis and item refinement and nearly two thousand subjects in all. Yet the only evidence of validity was that southern college students got higher scores than northern college students and members of "anti-black" organizations (segregated fraternities and right-wing political groups) got higher average scores than members of prointegration campus organizations (CORE and NAACP). Such demonstrations tell us very little about the scale, since it would be ridiculously embarrassing if the results went the other way. Apart from the qualitative, almost-anecdotal nature of such a finding, it is frequently circular in that the groups are chosen mainly on the basis of their verbal pronouncements.

The relationship of attitude scale scores to more socially meaningful kinds of behavior has simply been of little or no interest to most of those who measure attitudes. As McNemar (1946, p. 297) noted, "Some investigators have sidestepped the problem of validity by denying that anything exists beyond the verbal expressions, hence there is no problem of validity. Others have adopted the idea that scales or questions test whatever they test, so why worry."

The attitude-behavior controversy has recently begun to challenge these trends by raising the issue of validity in a dramatic and difficult-to-ignore fashion. In a number of studies sophisticated and highly reliable attitude scales have been shown to have little or no relation to independently observed behaviors which they supposedly should have predicted. The result has been a reassessment and new caution about attitude scales in many places, including some calls for a return to simpler measures of attitudes that might have a more direct bearing on behavior. In the early 1970s the prophesy of LaPiere in 1934 was again winning friends and influencing people:

> The questionnaire is cheap, easy and mechanical. The study of human *behavior* is time consuming, intellectually fatiguing, and depends for its success on the ability of the investigator. . . .
>
> Yet it would seem far more worth while to make a shrewd guess regarding that which is essential than to accurately measure that which is likely to prove quite irrelevant. (p. 237)

ATTITUDES AND BEHAVIOR

Some Attitude–Behavior Studies

Now we've come full cycle to the problem with which we began this chapter: the prediction of behavior by prior measurements of attitudes. As you recall we saw earlier that the original, "common-sense" assumption that attitudes have an obvious influence on behavior was eroded by a long series of studies which seemingly failed to find such a relationship or found it to be extremely weak. When attitude measures were correlated with some index of behavior observed independently at a different point in time, there was typically a low relation between the two. By the early 1970s the remarkable view was being widely expressed that attitudes per se had little or nothing to do with behavior:

> Since attitudes as they are presently conceptualized play no real role in behavior, an intense nothing contributes no more than a moderate nothing. (Tarter, 1970, p. 277)

> Again and again it has been demonstrated that there is little relationship between attitudes and overt behavior. (Brislin & Olmstead, 1973, p. 1)

To see historically how this conclusion was reached, and to enable us to move now into the specific content-issues of this area, we will briefly examine six of these studies in more detail:

LaPiere (1934). The classic article "Attitudes vs. Actions" is ritually cited at the beginning of almost every discussion of this issue. The simplicity of its design, the interesting setting and subject population, and the dramatic results have made it everyone's favorite illustration. Between 1930 and 1932 LaPiere travelled by car in the company of "a young Chinese student and his wife"; they journeyed twice across the United States and up and down the Pacific coast, stopping at 184 restaurants and 67 hotels and auto-camps during this time. "Knowing the general attitude of Americans toward the Chinese," LaPiere wrote, "it was with considerable trepidation that I first approached a hotel clerk in their company." Yet the party was readily accepted in 250 out of 251 establishments, frequently with more than ordinary courtesy and consideration. The Chinese couple are described as personable, charming, confident, well dressed, and speaking perfect English. LaPiere noted that their genial smiles and excellent English tended to quickly evaporate any initial tensions on the parts of clerks or waiters.

Six months after each such visit, LaPiere mailed to the restaurant or hotel a questionnaire containing the question: "Will you accept members of the Chinese race as guests in your establishment?" The responses he received by mail were indeed remarkable. Over 90% replied with an unqualified "No"; the others checked "uncertain, depend upon circumstances", and only one proprietor responded "yes." The results were too dramatic to require statistics: There was an almost perfect contradiction between universal acceptance of the Chinese couple in reality and rejection of "members of the Chinese race" in a standard questionnaire item.

Corey (1937). A few years later Stephen M. Corey reported a comparison of attitudes toward cheating and secretly measured amounts of actual cheating on examinations. The attitudes of a class in educational psychology were measured by a 50-item Likert scale, filled out anonymously but containing hidden identification marks by which scores could later be associated with individuals. The behavioral measure of cheating was obtained over a series of five weekly exams. Test papers were returned to students for grading the day following each exam, at which time the number correct was calculated and reported by each student—a procedure which made cheating extremely easy for those who wished to do so. The true number correct had been secretly recorded in the meantime. Seventy-six percent of the class cheated at least once, with an average of about two points per test. The correlation between attitude scores and amount of cheating, however, was .02—or virtually zero.

Saenger and Gilbert (1950). In 1947 racial desegregation of retail sales workers was being widely debated in New York City. A new state law forbade any discrimination in employment, but department store managers were extremely apprehensive about the reaction of white customers. Saenger and Gilbert unobtrusively observed customers in nine large department stores which had recently and reluctantly hired black sales clerks. Pairs of observers waited near a sales counter where a black clerk was working; white customers who made purchases from the black clerk and other customers who patronized a white clerk nearby were carefully followed until they were outside the store. They were then approached by an interviewer supposedly doing a man-on-the-street survey of public opinion; 114 interviews (success rate not reported) were obtained in this way. The interviews ascertained the shopper's attitudes about black sales personnel, whether he would actually buy from them, and how he felt about them in general. The results indicated that while there was a wide range of individual opinions and much expressed hostility to the idea of black clerks, such attitudes bore no relation to the direct observations of buying which had been made just moments previously. Some customers expressed no prejudice, some moderate prejudice, and some flatly declared they would refuse to buy in stores which hired Negroes; about half of each such category (including the last) had in fact just been observed to make purchases from a black clerk.

DeFleur and Westie (1958). In an apparent effort to maximize the effects of attitude DeFleur and Westie (1958) chose subjects from the extreme upper and extreme lower quartiles on a scale of racial prejudice. Carefully matched pairs of high- and low-prejudice subjects, drawn from an introductory sociology class at Indiana University, in the course of an elaborate laboratory sequence, viewed a series of photographic slides showing black men with white women and white men with black women. The models were attractive, well dressed, and seated in an ambiguous room with a table lamp and window in the background.

The behavioral measure came near the end of this session. The subject was informed that another set of such slides were needed for further research; would he or she consent to be photographed with a black person of the opposite sex? A "photograph authorization form" was handed to the subject which described eight possible uses for which the slides might be authorized, ranging from "laboratory experiments where it will be seen only by professional sociologists" to "a teaching aid in sociology classes, for hundreds of university students," . . . to "a nation-wide publicity campaign advocating racial integration". Each such use required authorization with a signature, and subjects were asked to authorize as many of the eight as they were willing. DeFleur and Westie noted that in American society "the affixing of one's signature to a document is a particularly significant act; the signing of checks, contracts, agreements and the like is clearly understood to indicate a binding obligation." The subjects apparently perceived this request as realistic and often showed discomfort in deciding what to do.

When responses were dichotomized at the median number of uses authorized, 64% of the low-prejudice group and 23% of the high-prejudice group fell above the median. This difference was significant and moderately strong ($r = .40$), though hardly dramatic considering the choice of extreme attitude segments.

Rokeach and Mezei (1966). Common sense would suggest that if an attitude such as prejudice has any influence on behavior, it should be a tendency to avoid casual social interaction with blacks. Rokeach and Mezei (1966) arranged a situation in which subjects had an opportunity to choose whom to accompany them on a coffee break. Students at Michigan State who had scored above or below the mean on a scale of prejudice administered in class were placed in discussion groups with four confederates. Two of the confederates were white and the other two were black.

The experimenter asked that the subjects elect a "chairman," whereupon the four confederates always elected the naive subject. After the discussion had proceeded for a while the experimenter called the chairman into his office for a private interview. At the close of this interview he remarked that the remaining participants would now be interviewed so there'd be enough time to take a coffee break, and asked the subject to choose two of the other participants to accompany him for coffee. The subjects' choice was the behavioral data of the study. Racial attitudes however had no discernable relation to these choices ($r = .04$). High-prejudice subjects were just as likely to choose black confederates as were the low-prejudice subjects.

DeFrieze and Ford (1969). In one of the few studies to use a broader subject population, DeFrieze and Ford interviewed 262 homeowners in a suburban neighborhood near Lexington, Kentucky. The first part of the procedure was a survey interview which included a 14-item scale of racial attitudes (not specifically described). At the end the interviewer explained that the state university was "continually asked to supply information to organizations and the press concerning the climate of opinion surrounding particular social issues. . . ." In order to obtain definite information on one such public issue, open occupancy of residential housing, the University was circulating two documents. Two legal-appearing documents were produced. One stated that: "I, the undersigned, do hereby make public the declaration that I have no objection to having Negro families of social and economic characteristics similar to my own live in my neighborhood." The other document stated in similar language that the undersigned did have such objections, regardless of the social and economic characteristics of the Negro families. Respondents could sign either document or neither one, and no pressure was applied; the interviewer advised however that the documents and signatures might be used in any way, including making them public through the news media.

Not surprisingly, 65% of those interviewed refused to sign either document; of those who did sign, nine out of ten chose the anti-integration document. The index of racial attitudes obtained earlier in the interview was moderately predictive ($r = .40$) of responses to the documents.

The preceding are by no means all of the attitude-behavior studies published over the last 40 years, but they include some of the more widely noted studies and give us an idea of the typical procedures that were employed.[3] Now

---

[3] We refer here only to studies in which independent observations of behavior were recorded. If self-reports of behavior were included this number would be far larger, but there is much evidence to show that self-reports are extremely unreliable (Parry & Crossley, 1950; Hyman, 1945; Dean, 1958).

we're ready for a closer look at the theory of attitude–behavior relationships and the assumptions that underlie research on the problem.

A Conceptual Model of Attitude–Behavior Relationships

As at least one writer has perceptively noted, even after four decades of talk about "attitudes and behavior":

> We still do not know much about the relationship between what people say and what they do . . . attitudes and behaviors, sentiments and acts, verbalizations and interactions, words and deeds. We know so little that I can't even find an adequate vocabulary to make the distinction. (Deutscher, 1966, p. 242)

At least one source of confusion is that responses to attitude scales are themselves technically a form of behavior, so that in practice what we're really interested in is whether one form of behavior can be used to predict another form. Kiesler et al. (1969) thus noted that the attitude–behavior problem should be called "Some Kinds of Behavior and Other Kinds of Behavior" or even more precisely, "The Relationship Between Certain Kinds of Behavior, Arbitrarily Designated by Most Social Scientists as Measures of Attitude, and Other Kinds of Behavior Which, According to Theory Should Be Influenced by the Attitude in Question." But still, they concede: "Ask any social psychologist about the relationship between attitudes and behavior and you are likely to start a lively discussion. Clearly then, the phrase 'behavior and attitudes' must mean something" (Kiesler et al., 1969, p. 23).

In the following sections we'll try to specify more precisely what it means and to suggest a consistent vocabulary to keep these strings untangled. The following is not a model, however, in the sense of a small number of propositions which simplify the issues and attempt to account for the data with just a few parameters. No such model seems realistically possible at present. Our aim here in fact is to complicate things by emphasizing all of the factors which play a role in what we see as a monumentally complex process which has all too often been seen in overly simple terms. At the end, however, it will be clear why the studies in the preceding section obtained the puzzling results they did.

Attitudes and Expressions. We noted earlier a controversy over whether attitudes should be defined as predispositions that exist in the mind and influence behavior or the overt responses which can be actually observed. Though the choice may largely be a matter of semantic preference, we shall use the term *attitude* as do most psychologists to refer to mental predispositions which are not directly observed. We'll also employ a very broad conception of attitudes, analogous to Campbell's (1950) term *dispositions,* which include all such concepts as beliefs, values, opinions, convictions, traits, preferences, and so forth.

For the overt responses which are actually observed and are taken as evidence of attitudes, analogous to Campbell's (1950) term *sions.* In the broadest sense attitude expressions are any overt responses from which attitudes are inferred; most frequently, however, responses to a standard closed-ended attitude question provided the basis for this inference.

While attitude-expressions are our only direct evidence of attitudes, and despite the fact that great efforts are made to avoid or minimize distortion, the two are not the same and can never be safely assumed to be identical. Even in extremely favorable circumstances, such as a personal interview with assurances of anonymity, a variety of factors

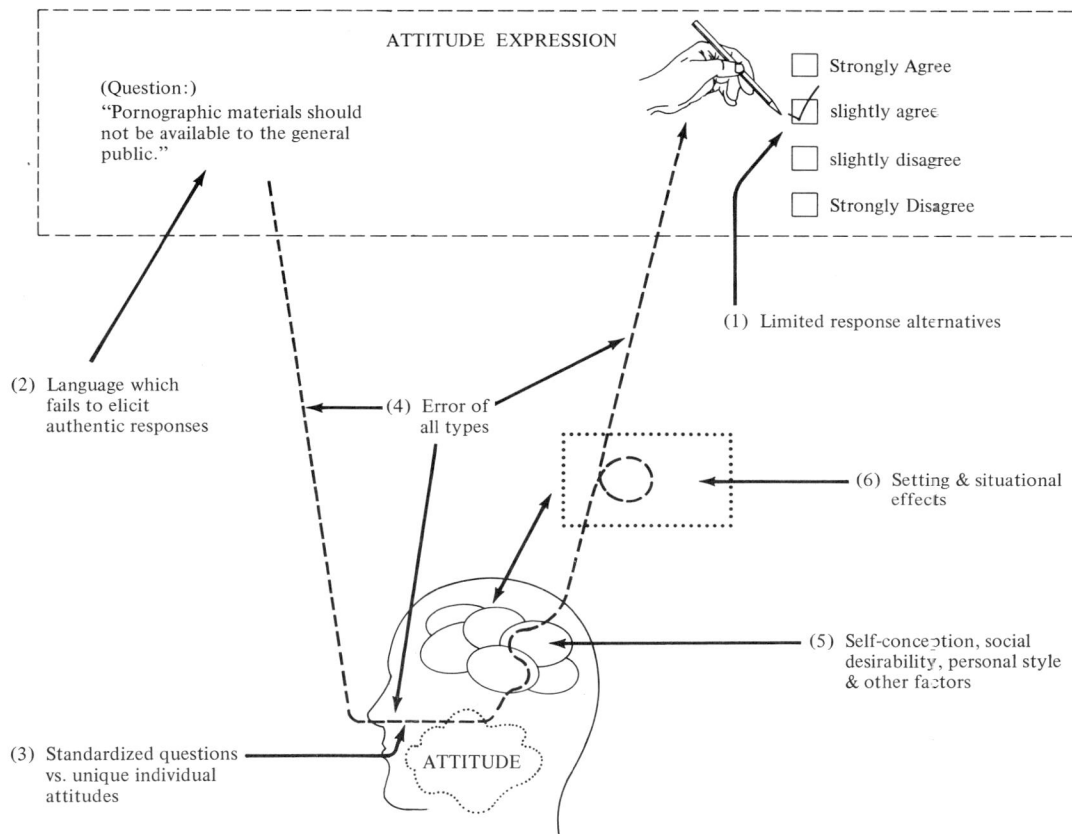

FIGURE 6-1. General factors intervening between attitudes and attitude expressions.

may intervene to prevent or distort the translation of attitudes into expressions. The following factors (summarized in simple graphic form in Figure 6-1) are the most general and basic obstacles to attitude expression in most cases, though a variety of more specific problems are discussed in most texts on questionnaire and interview methodology:

1. Any question with fixed alternatives imposes an obvious limitation on the respondent's ability to communicate his attitude. His real response is probably not one of the listed alternatives; he must choose the closest.

2. The socially acceptable language of standardized questions may fail to elicit typical and authentic reactions. Polite or formal terms such as "premarital sexual activity," "Negroes," and "social background," are often not the terms with which respondents have strong associations. Depending on respondent's imagination or interest, the key terms of the question may fail to engage relevant attitudes.

3. Standardized questions simply cannot tap the complexities, nuances, or exact colorings of the real attitudes people so often hold. On the issue of pornography for example, a real person might think:

I do find pornography distasteful . . . except when I happen to be in the mood for it . . . but then, I prefer that it be a surreptitious, almost Victorian commodity. . . . The sight of those unsmiling middle-aged men elbow to elbow in a "dirty book store" depresses, even frightens me. . . . It's so raffish; so excruciatingly common. . . .

Anyone who introspects will realize that his or her own real attitudes often have at least this degree of complexity and individuality, while standardized questions simply cannot. As even open-ended answers must later be coded into categories, this basic problem is not entirely avoidable.

4. In any large set of human response data there will be some degree of error. In typical attitude-expression data there may be errors in reading, comprehension, interpretation, and response selection on the part of the respondent, and errors in recording, coding, data processing, and data analysis on the part of interviewers and researchers.

5. Respondents are influenced by their own desires for social desirability, consistency, and other individual factors which prevent totally accurate reporting of attitudes even under conditions of anonymity.

6. The interview setting, characteristics of preceding questions, respondent's expectations about the study's purpose, interviewer effects, and countless other aspects of the situation can affect expressions. One example of the effects of situational context will serve to illustrate how powerful such effects can be. Shomer and Centers (1970) discovered remarkably different attitude expressions depending on where respondents filled out the questionnaire. "Male chauvinist" attitudes varied from high to medium to low in three testings of college males. The difference? The group which showed the highest level of male chauvinism had completed the questionnaire in a room with other men; the group which scored medium had filled out the same questionnaire in a room containing half males and half females; the group which reported the least chauvinistic attitudes filled out their questionnaire in a room in which only one female student was present along with 18 males. The authors concluded that males felt chivalrous toward the lone woman, while in an all-male setting a locker-room atmosphere pushed attitudes in the opposite direction. This was despite the fact that the questionnaires were anonymous, the instructions were all the same, and there were no prior differences among the groups.

Expressions and Behavior. Psychology has been called the science of behavior, and yet it is not as easy as one might expect to find a careful definition of the term *behavior*. a review of over 30 articles in the attitude-behavior area turned up only two rather casual efforts to define behavior: "The term overt behavior will be used to refer to nonverbal behavior outside the situation in which attitudes were measured" (Wicker, 1969a); "When we speak of behavior . . . we typically restrict ourselves to a person's overt actions in a situation embodying the attitude object (either physically or symbolically) and calling for a response other than direct affective evaluation" (Leper, 1969).

Yet it's clear that when practitioners and critics ask whether psychologists can predict "overt behavior" they have something more specific in mind. "Most socially significant questions," notes Wicker (1969a), "involve overt behavior, rather than people's feelings." "Our scientific conclusions for the most part are based on analyses of verbal response to questions put by an interviewer; the policy maker is interested in none of these things: as a man of action, he is interested in overt behavior," states Deutscher (1966).

Commonsensical as these remarks may

appear to be they don't actually tell us much. Why, for example, aren't verbal responses overt behavior? Let's briefly consider the possibilities. We might first guess that the important difference is "verbal versus nonverbal." On close examination, this distinction has little significance. Many verbal statements ("Kill this one": "You're fired, Jones") would be universally agreed to be socially significant; one might argue that in a hierarchical and bureaucratic social system, virtually all important acts are initiated verbally or in writing. On the other hand many nonverbal acts are rather trivial: scratching an itch, tapping a foot to music, and so on. Certainly these aren't the things policy makers want to predict.

Physical presence of the attitude object in the situation also fails as a crucial distinction, as illustrated by the act of voting. Voting is one of those significant social behaviors which is quite often mentioned, and one of the few which can be predicted fairly successfully. It may in fact be useful to examine the case of voting more closely. The method which most pollsters use is to show their respondents—a representative sample of all registered voters—a sample ballot similar to the one they will see on election day (Perry, 1960). Responses to the sample ballots are viewed as preferences, or attitudes; yet responses to the real ballots, on election day, are regarded as behavior. What is the difference?

The difference seems to be primarily the consequences of the two acts. One act is merely a favor done for a polling organization; another act elects an important public official. Let's see how this factor consequence applies to other cases. In 1964, Congress was considering a substantial pay raise for itself. A Republican motion to sidetrack the salary increase was defeated by an off-the-record vote of 125 to 37 (*Congressional Record,* March 12, 1964). A few minutes later, however, when a roll call vote on the same issue was ordered, the pay increase was defeated by an overwhelming margin. While one consequence (a fat pay raise) was the same for both votes, the consequence of personal visibility to the voters was unique to the second vote. The first vote was by any reasonable definition "meaningful behavior" (it would cost the taxpayers millions) yet it also probably reflected the legislators' true sentiments on the issue since the negative personal consequences of the anonymous vote would probably have been negligible. In comparison with the second vote the first was more like an attitude expression, since the perceived personal consequences were far less.

The identical act may be viewed as an expression of attitude in one setting and as behavior unrelated to attitude in another setting. When a politician kisses a baby or Communist diplomats kiss each other, no one assumes it was love at first sight or even that any real affection is being expressed. Statements may appear to be either attitude expressions or behaviors, depending mainly on the consequences which might hinge on the act. If a President says to his wife over breakfast, "That guy is a smart cookie," she would probably assume that he meant it. If he made an equally complimentary formal statement on national T.V., she and everyone else would be likely to regard it as a political behavior rather than an indication of his real opinion.

As perceived consequences can take many forms (time, effort, money, votes, social approval) it's clearly an oversimplification to speak merely of high or low personal consequences. However it seems that this is probably the main dimension which differentiates what we see as "overt behavior" from expressions of attitude. In other words, behavior usually means actions which are recognized by the actor as having more-than-negligible consequences for himself or for others he cares about. Since consequences can vary from low to very high, it follows that some acts are more emphatically behaviors than others and that there are intermediate cases.

We might go a little further and attempt to state the general conditions under which any action will be regarded as an expression, a behavior, or neither one (this typology, however, is definitely speculative). Any act with substantial personal consequences will generally be viewed as behavior; there's no clear point at which such judgments will begin, but it becomes more likely as the perceived consequences rise. Not all acts with low personal consequences are regarded as attitude-expressions, however. Saying "hello" when the telephone rings is a social norm which expresses nothing of personal feeling. Paying bills is an unpleasant necessity, we walk up and down stairs because we have no choice, and so forth. None of these is regarded as an expression of attitude. When there are other explanations for behavior—social norms, utilitarian needs, social pressures, economic factors—it is rarely assumed that an act expresses personal attitudes.[4] The usual steps taken when asking attitude questions (anonymity, neutral situation, simple and familiar wording) can indeed be seen as efforts to rule out in advance such external explanations so that the responses may be regarded as expressions of attitude.

Figure 6-2 combines the two dimensions we've discussed, with "perceived consequences" increasing from bottom to top and "external explanations" from left to right.[5] Most actions with high perceived consequences will be seen as behavior, except where an external explanation is very obvious. Only acts for which no reasonable external explanation can be seen are usually viewed as attitude expressions, and most of these also happen to have low consequences to the individual. Yet when a young man burned himself to death to dramatize his horror over U.S. actions in Viet Nam, his action was clearly both behavior and a compelling expression of attitude.

We see then that behavior and attitude expressions are not distinct categories of actions, but more-or-less approximate attributional classes, which sometimes overlap. This gives rise to some interesting comparisons; suppose for example that a verbal question about pornography is compared by one researcher with secretly observed frequency of actually buying pornography. This would clearly be a valid and interesting study of whether verbally expressed attitudes correspond to actual behavior. Another researcher might be interested in businessmen who have made large contributions to the "Clean Up Our City Committee." As an indication of how these men really feel he obtains secretly observed frequency of actually buying pornography. This too, would be a valid and interesting attitude–behavior study.

Let's summarize our model on this point. The main theoretical issues, to which we turn in the following sections, concern the relation between mental processes or attitudes and what we think of as overt behavior. However, attitudes themselves are not directly measurable; in their place we must use attitude expres-

---

[4]Suppose we see a woman shelling peas. We wouldn't normally assume that she was doing this for the fun of it, even though this might be the case. We'd assume they were to be eaten. If she's throwing them on the ground outside, we think: "Those are for the chickens" (Urban readers should tolerate this excursion into Americana). We implicitly favor practical explanations over personal-preference explanations as a rule, when both are possible.

[5]Since consequences are likely to provide plausible external explanations for behavior, these dimensions are not independent and Figure 6-2 might preferably be drawn as a parallelogram.

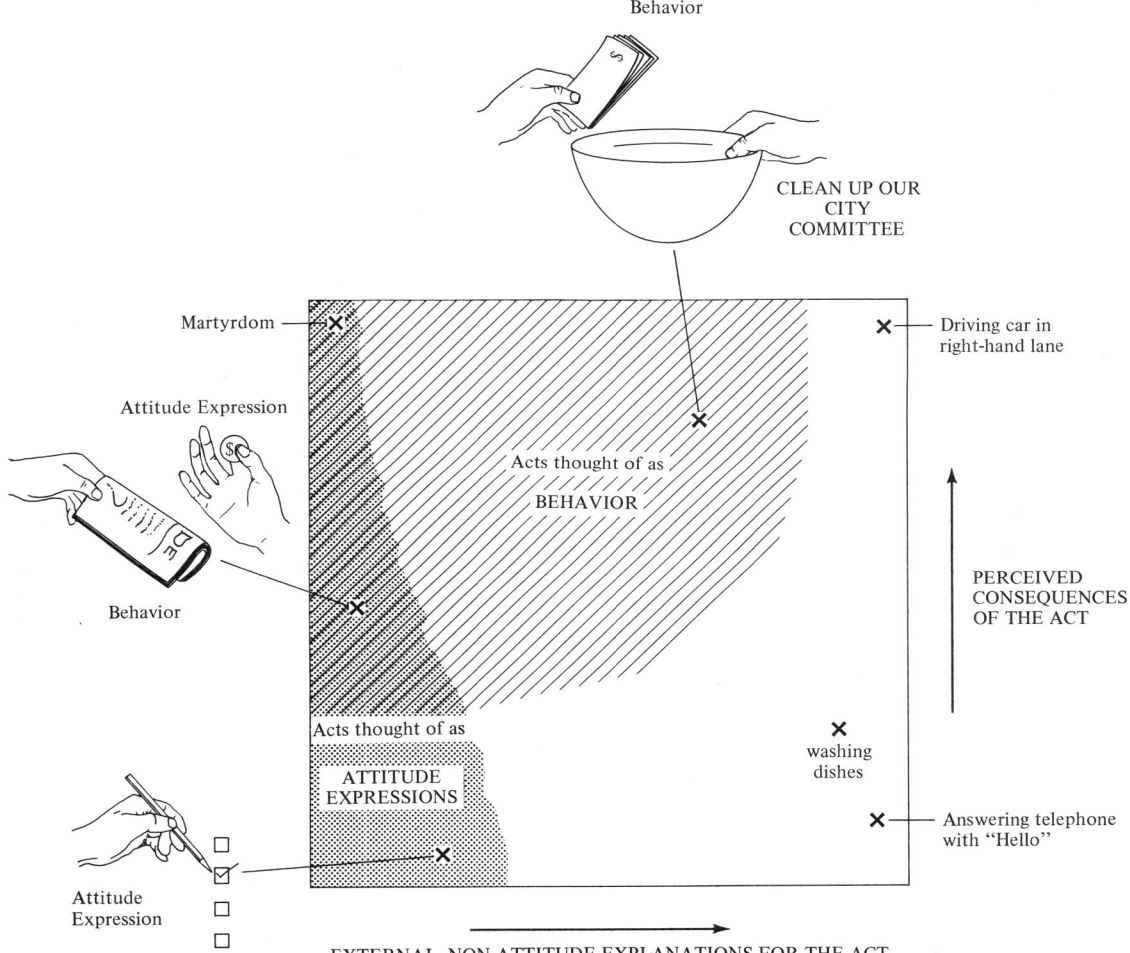

FIGURE 6-2. Approximate charting of acts usually considered "behavior" and those usually considered "attitude-expressions."

sions. Expressions differ only in degree from overt behavior, primarily in having lesser perceived consequences. In practice therefore, attitude–behavior studies are empirical comparisons between measures of two different forms of behavior. This empirical relationship may be the outcome of practical interest, especially if it permits accurate and reliable prediction, but it should not be confused with a true causal relationship. We don't normally believe that Jones discriminates against blacks because he checked "yes" on a questionnaire, but rather that he has racist attitudes which influenced both forms of behavior. While the causal link between attitudes and overt behavior is by no means simple, it can only be studied through the very imperfect evidence provided by expressions. After exploring the theoretical attitude–behavior relationship per se in the next few sections we'll return to the implications of this empirical fact for interpreting research.

Congruence. Suppose I'm delighted with the mechanic who fixes my car. Because he gets the work done fast, holds the bill down, and spots problems before they cause trouble, I have extremely fond feelings about him. Knowing this, would you predict that I will:

A. ask him to redecorate my living room?
B. nominate him for president of the PTA?
C. take my car to him when it needs repairs?
D. invite him on a fishing trip?
E. mention him when I hear friends complain about repairmen?
F. consult him about investing my savings?
G. propose marriage?

The answer of course is "C" (and possibly also "E" though that's not quite as certain). This is an easy task, but it illustrates a point that has sometimes been overlooked in attitude–behavior comparisons. Some behaviors seem to follow quite directly and logically from having a particular attitude. Other behaviors seem possible but a little less likely, and still others might be very slightly influenced by the attitude. This dimension of "apparent fit" between attitudes and behaviors will be referred to as *congruence;* as a general rule, we will hypothesize that an attitude enhances the probability of behaviors to a degree proportionate to the congruence between them. Congruence may technically vary in several ways:

Implicit facts. Suppose we know how much the manager of a baseball team personally likes his players, and we want to predict which player he will choose to bat in the important "clean-up" position. How relevant is the information we have? Although it might permit a slightly better-than-chance prediction (since managers may tend to like their stars), baseball fans would agree that this would not be the most relevant factor. Similarly, a group of politicians engaged in speculating as to whom a presidential candidate would select as his running mate would also not place much weight on whom the candidate liked most. These attitudes would not be totally irrelevant, in either case, but other factors would clearly count somewhat more.

Level of generality. Some attitudes are very specific ("lamb curry is too spicy"), while others are extremely general ("duty must come before pleasure"). Behaviors may also be conceived as very specific (signing a particular petition, stepping on a particular roach) or as cumulative, spanning many times and situations (taking care of one's health, acting fairly toward people).

General attitudes appear to have implications for many kinds of behavior, in many settings. A highly specific attitude, on the other hand, usually is relevant to only a few behaviors. ("Lamb curry is too spicy" is relevant if you're eating out and if lamb curry is on the menu; it's largely irrelevant to the remaining parts of life.)

Most of the behaviors that have been studied in research up to now are quite specific. If behavior were typically measured more generally (e.g., if the researcher measured "eating out regularly" or "taking care of one's health"), the most congruent attitudes should be those at an equally general level. In other words, when other things are equal highly congruent attitudes and behaviors will normally occur at about the same level of generality (cf. Wicker, 1969a, p. 64).

Indices versus single measures. Several previous writers have noted that attitude measures are usually multi-item scales which give us average responses toward classes of people, in a range of hypothetical settings, whereas the behavior measure is usually a single observation of behavior toward a particular person, in only one setting (Fishbein 1967; Hyman, 1969; Chein, 1949; Cook & Selltiz, 1964). This type of difference has been called "inconsistent," "unfortunate," "a blunder," and the like; in the present framework it may be viewed as a diminution of congruence. The reference of measures to different numbers of people and settings tends to reduce congruence, which suggests that multi-item attitude scales should actually be better predictors of multi-act behavioral indices than would single items.[6]

Comment. As described here congruence is clearly more a matter of "psychologic" (Abelson & Rosenberg, 1958) than of true formal logic. One's feelings about the relevance of a given thought for a given action are often strong but they are not precise; they are furthermore based on experiences and observations of life in our own culture. Implicitly we assume a great deal of "standard" background information. The extreme points of congruence are thus easy to identify; i.e., it's usually clear when two things are virtually identical and when they're totally irrelevant, but at intermediate points we must be more cautious. (Note that we can't just find out which attitude predicts a given behavior best and then state that this was the most congruent; this is circular reasoning and would render the concept totally meaningless.) Congruence then has a distinctly limited and special meaning: it's the degree of normally perceived fit between an attitude and a behavior under standard social conditions, the relation which knowledgeable members of the culture would expect without knowing any of the special circumstance of a case.

Constraints. Now we come to the factors which have received by far the most attention in previous discussions of the attitude–behavior issue. There are rather obviously many factors such as time, money, danger, disapproval from others, and the impact of social norms which may simply outweigh the influence attitudes, even attitudes which are perfectly congruent with behavior. Tarter (1970) called these "spoilers"; Ehrlich (1969) called them "intervening-variables." By the late 1960s some theorists seemed convinced there were so many powerful constraints that we should never have expected to have an appreciable effect on behavior. It's a mistake however, to regard constraints as contaminations of the attitude–behavior relationship, maliciously spoiling the data. Behavior is by definition closely related to real-world consequences and would have no meaning in a vacuum.

Certain constraints such as absence of the attitude object may prevent a behavior altogether, but most can be most usefully viewed from an "expectancy-value" standpoint. That is, the value of an outcome to the individual and the perceived probability that it will occur should jointly determine its weight as an influence. In Figure 6-3 the following basic varieties of constraints are indicated:

1. absence of the object toward which the behavior must be directed.
2. physical restraints, e.g., bars and handcuffs.
3. gains and losses directly contingent to performing the behavior itself. Subjects might

---

[6]Fishbein (1973) has stated that multi-item scales will always be poor predictors of single acts. This seems to us an overstatement which confuses the typically assorted contents of scales with the more basic question of congruence. A multi-item scale could probably be constructed to be quite congruent with a single act, while a single irrelevant item can be very low in congruence.

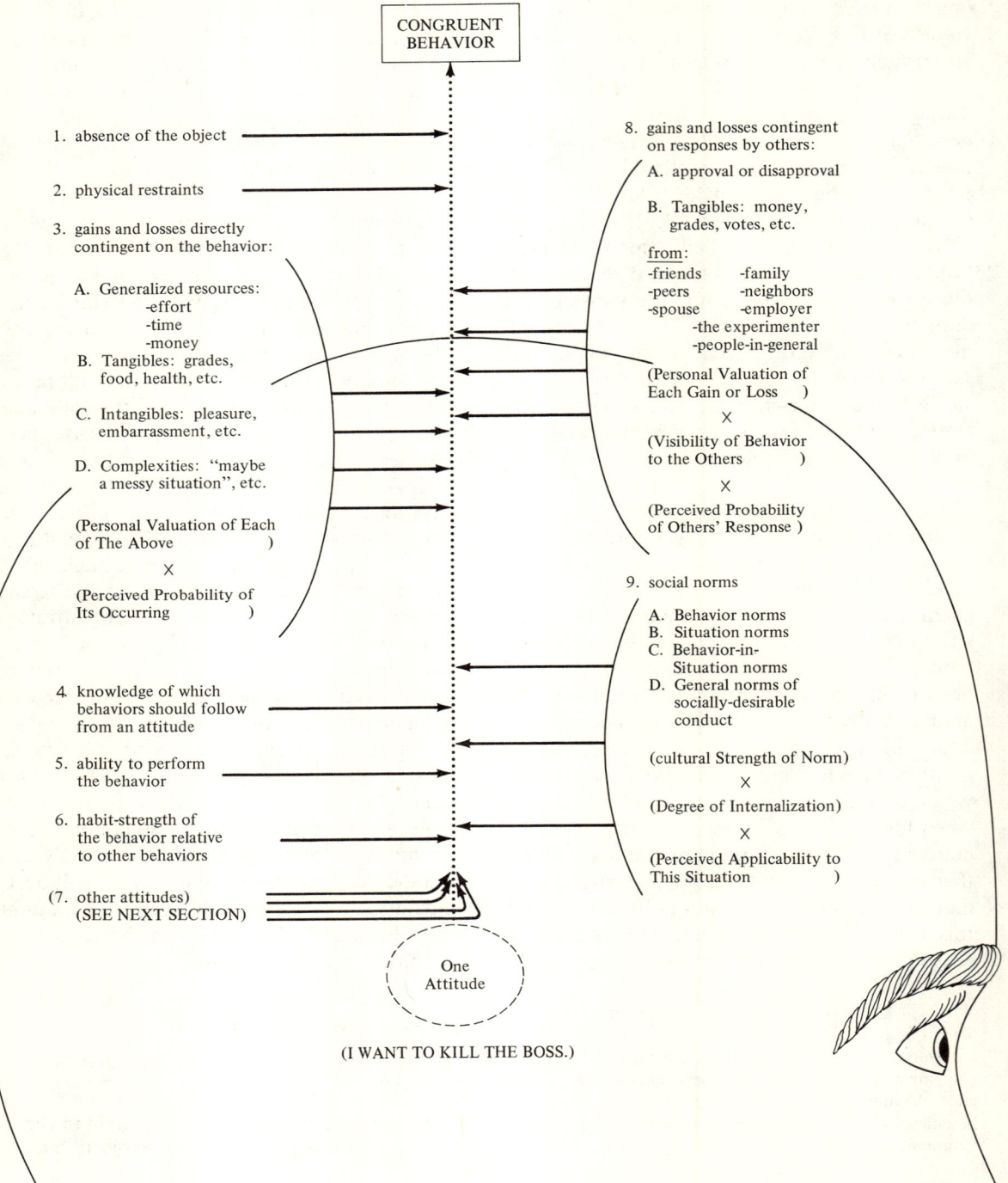

FIGURE 6-3. Nonattitude constraints on the translation of an attitude into congruent behavior.

for example expect a roach to feel repulsive, or to be imprisoned if they killed the boss. Any behavior can of course have many such anticipated outcomes, each with a certain value to the individual and a certain probability of occurring. Their combined influence would be some function of the individual influences.

4. knowledge of which behaviors would normally follow from an attitude. ("He doesn't hate you, Harry, he loves you . . . he just doesn't know how to show it.")

5. ability to perform the behavior. ("Boy, I'd like to say something right now that would sound brilliant.")

6. relative habit-strength of the behavior. Strong habits seem to be an especially potent constraint. There is evidence for example, that medical researchers who have worked for years to link smoking with lung cancer continued to smoke regularly (Lawton & Goldman, 1958); common sense attests to the force of habit in many situations.

7. other attitudes. These factors are so complex and important that the following section is devoted to them.

8. gains and losses contingent on the response of other people.[7] These must be each weighted by their value to the individual, the probability of the other's responding in this way, and the likelihood of the other's observing the behavior (alternately, the latter two might be combined). The process might sound something like: "My family will be furious if they see me in a photo like that, but I doubt if they'll ever see it"; "Henry would hit the ceiling if he heard I signed a thing like that, and heaven knows what the neighbors would think. . . ."

9. social norms. There are norms-about-behavior (don't hit girls); norms-about-situations (funerals are solemn occasions); norms-about-particular-behaviors-in-particular-situations (don't pick your nose in public); and general norms of social desirability (be fair with people). In a given culture some norms are weak, and some very strong (sit up straight in your chair, and don't commit incest). Some individuals internalize social norms more completely than others and finally, the relevance of a particular norm to a particular situation is not always clear ("Gee, is it really cheating if everybody's doing it and the teacher doesn't seem to care?").

Fishbein and his colleagues (1972, 1973; Ajzen and Fishbein, 1970) have cited "behavioral intentions" as the best and virtually only successful way to predict specific behaviors; while we think this is an overstatement, for reasons discussed later, it's true that behavioral intentions are among the most useful verbal predictors of behaviors, in large part because people are able to anticipate many constraints and take them into account. It may be that Henry would like to kill his boss, but since he is well aware of the powerful constraints on that action he probably will not say, "I intend to kill my boss." (If he did say this, we'd perceive the action as far more likely.) A behavioral intention which is also highly congruent with a given behavior is thus apt to be a good predictor. If we hear someone say "I plan to attend the 7:30 showing of *Hud* at the Paramount tonight," there's a reasonably good chance they will do so; better than if they said, "I'd like to see *Hud* tonight," or "I'd like to see a movie."[8]

---

[7]Constraint number eight is not totally separable from number three, but refers to responses by people not immediately involved in the behavior, i.e., to less certain or intrinsic outcomes of behaviors.

[8]Constraints are not perfectly separable from the notion of congruence discussed in the last section. Congruence involves standard constraints which are usually taken for granted, such as that baseball teams and political candidates have opponents and so forth. As a general rule we may ask "would *B* follow from *A*?" and if there is an

During the 1968 presidential campaign large numbers of white unionized auto-workers in Detroit, Michigan, and other industrial cities clearly and firmly stated thier intention to vote for George C. Wallace. Yet on election day most of the professed Wallace vote in Michigan went to Humphrey, whom most rank-and-file union men found far less appealing. To understand why strong pro-Wallace attitudes, the privacy of the voting booth, and even widely announced behavioral intentions did not translate into an avalanche of Wallace votes, we must look to attitude competition.

Attitude Competition. Most of what we've said up to now has purposely focused on single attitudes with respect to single behaviors. In reality of course many attitudes often converge and in some manner jointly influence a behavioral outcome. Words such as "ambivalent," and "conflicted" reflect an implicit cultural recognition of such cross-pressures. The missing Wallace vote was an example of unusually strong conflict, one which left the outcome in doubt until the votes were actually counted. It was clear from the outset that Wallace's flamboyant, populist–racist belligerence held tremendous appeal for these voters, many of whom had family origins in the South. On the other hand they had a deep respect and trust in their union, the United Auto Workers (UAW), which has skillfully played the major auto companies against one another over the years and won for its members one of the highest wage scales for working men in the world. The UAW went down the line for the Democratic Party in 1968 and waged an all-out campaign to convince its members to stick with the Democratic Party. In the end it succeeded with most members and Detroit went heavily for Humphrey, narrowly tipping Michigan's 132 electoral votes to the Democrats. Had Illinois and Ohio had a comparable union Humphrey would have defeated Vice President Nixon and become the thirty-seventh President.

Figure 6-4 portrays some specific attitudes in the minds of many UAW members before this election. To the right of center are four squares representing the individual, the act of voting, and the two potential objects of this action. Triangles connecting these elements are meant to represent the two composite behavior outcomes.[9] We will return to discuss these symbols again shortly, but for the moment let's concentrate on the substantive issues of this example.

Many attitudes, beliefs, values, and so forth converged to produce a positive evaluation of George Wallace and a stated intention to friends and pollsters to vote for him. How can we account for the fact that so few actually did so?

To the extent that a desire to "shake-up" the major parties was contributing to Wallace sentiment, the extensive public concern that was shown over his high standing in the early polls may have diffused some of its urgency; in other words, one good reason for backing Wallace may have disappeared before the election because of the recognition he had already received. The more basic reason, however, was that these voters also had strong attitudinal

---

[9]There are different ways to select and represent relevant elements of such a situation; the choice here is based on clarity and convenience. We have left out the Republican and minor-party candidates entirely, and labeled the main choices "Wallace" and "Democratic candidate" to emphasize the choice as it was probably perceived by most of these voters. It would be plausible to label the bottom box "The Union" and the bottom triangle "voting with the Union." No real change would result from different choices of symbols though the figure would have to be arranged differently.

obvious answer ("sure": "of course not"), this is a judgment of congruence. When the answer is "well, that depends . . .", we are talking about constraints. There is no sharp line between these two terms.

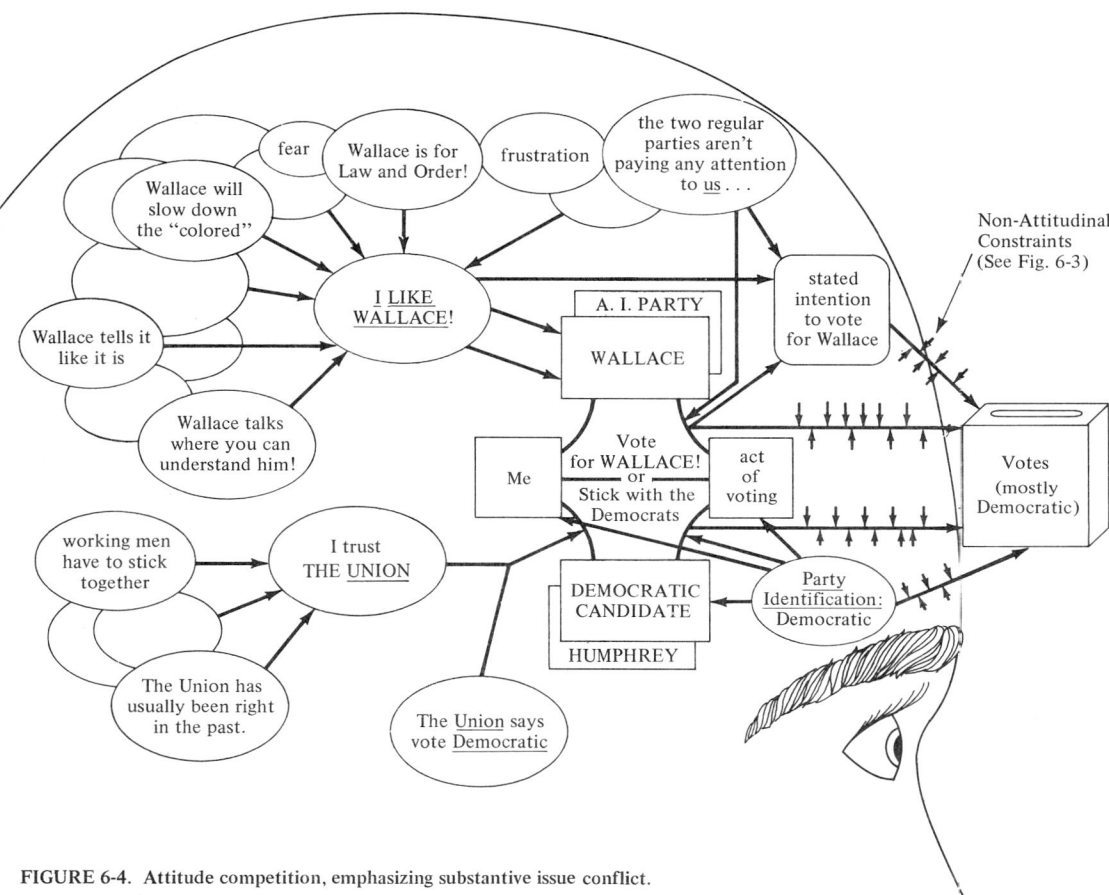

FIGURE 6-4. Attitude competition, emphasizing substantive issue conflict.

pulls toward voting Democratic. They did not by and large admire Humphrey or his supporters, but they had a strong reservoir of trust and affection for the union.[10] Union loyalty was supplemented in most cases by what is usually known as "party identification," revealed by answers to the question: "Generally speaking, do you think of yourself as a Republican, a Democrat, an Independent, or what?"

> This tie can persist without legal recognition or evidence of formal membership, and even without a consistent record of party support. Most Americans have this sense of attachment with one party or the other. (Campbell et al., 1964, p. 67)

Party identification has been shown to have strong and persistent effects on voting decision

---

[10]Previous studies have documented consistently strong effects of union membership on presidential votes. In 1956 union members were 20% more likely to vote for Stevenson than non-members. Highly identified union members furthermore were 28% more likely to vote Democratic than weakly identified members (Campbell et al., 1964, pp. 167 and 169).

across many national elections. Union loyalty and party identification clashed with Wallace enthusiasm and in this instance prevailed.

Combining attitude measures. There is some evidence that better predictions are possible from a battery of measures than from a single scale. In the Presidential election of 1956, the personal popularity of Dwight D. Eisenhower was the best single predictor of votes. A set of six relevant attitudes, including this and five others (attitude toward Stevenson, foreign issues, domestic issues, the Democratic Party, and the Republican Party) permitted substantially better prediction of the final vote:

When prediction was from:	Correlation of Predictor(s) with vote:	Percentage of voters classified correctly:
1. Attitude toward Eisenhower only	.52	75%
2. All six partisan issues	.71	86%

(Campbell et al., 1964, p. 38)

Another example comes from a recent study of how often married couples make love. A social psychologist would probably analyze this question in terms of immediate attitudes and situational constraints (it's too late, it's too early, my toe hurts, I have to feed the goldfish), but DeYoung, Cattell, Gabarit, and Barton (1973) used personality tests and marital-role-concept inventories. Self-reported frequency of lovemaking correlated no better than .27 with each of five separate factors; yet all five together predicted frequency at the .54 level.

What attitudes are relevant? Let's consider in detail a relatively simple example of behavior: "kissing Rita in church." (This was one of the responses to a class assignment to "recall an actual behavior and situation in which you felt conflicting attitudes"; quite in addition to the Deep Moral Issue it raises it has the advantage that all of the words are short enough to fit into a diagram.) Figure 6-5 depicts the three main elements—"me," "kissing," and "Rita." This behavior is completely enclosed by the given situation, "church," but the other elements extend beyond it and hence exist in other situations as well. It's possible to represent most attitudes that have bearing on this behavior as directed toward one or more parts of this system; Figure 6-5 thus illustrates the complexity of any total attitude sphere for even a simple behavior such as this. There may be specific attitudes toward each separate element, and more general attitudes toward larger classes of elements. There are attitudes about combinations of elements, e.g., how I feel about "myself in relation to the act of kissing," which are shown here by branched arrows pointing to both elements. There are attitudes about this situation and about related situations. Furthermore, any other attitude may be specified as applying solely to this particular situation; this is shown by arrows which "loop" through the situation-area of the diagram. One might for example have attitudes about "kissing in church" which are quite different from attitudes about "kissing." The behavior as a whole, "me kissing Rita," is symbolized by the central area and can be the object of specific attitudes.

Broader dispositions such as personality variables and general attitudes are shown in the background of Figure 6-5 and can also have implications for behavior, especially perhaps in the formation of more specific attitudes. There is reason to believe in fact that when fairly deep-seated values are in conflict attitude competition is most fierce and behavior most difficult to predict. Warriner (1958) concluded that

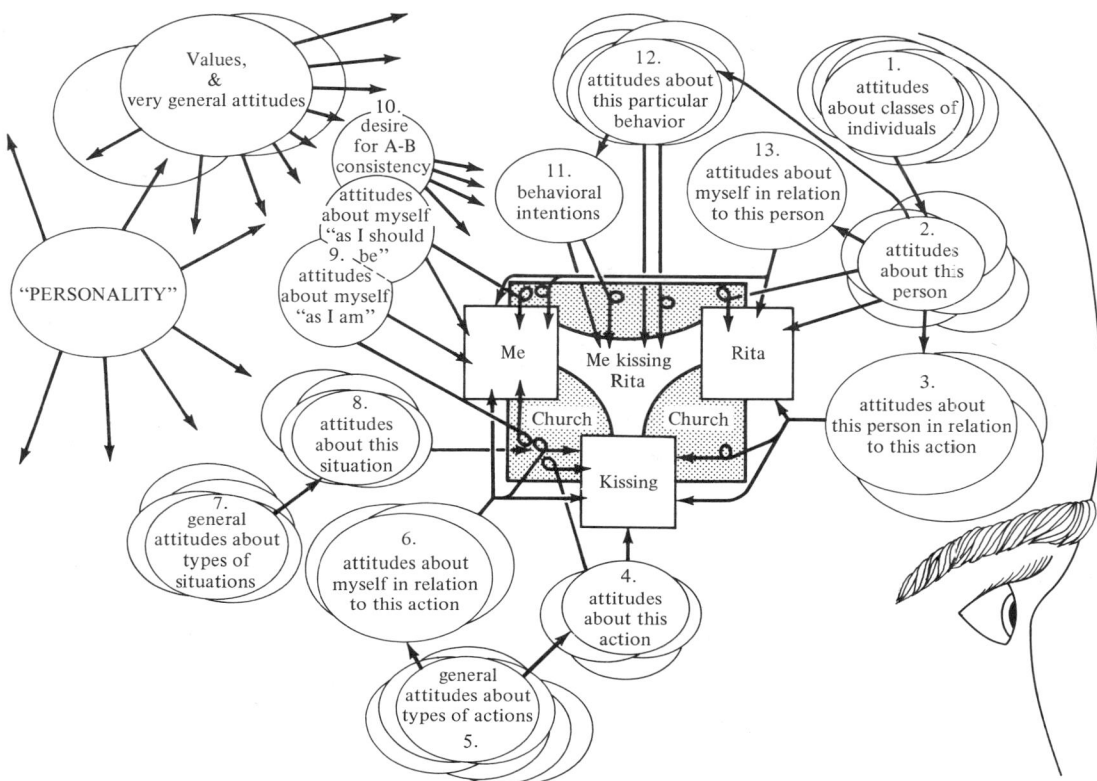

FIGURE 6-5. Attitude competition, emphasizing types of attitudes and the situational context (⚭ means "in this situation").

the remarkably inconsistent and seemingly incongruous behavior of many citizens in a small Kansas community was due to two sets of conflicting values and attitudes which most members of the community held simultaneously: (1) that drinking was morally wrong and (2) that drinking in moderation was normal and acceptable. Race relations in the United States is an almost classic example of deeply held values in chronic conflict. Myrdal's (1944) famous analysis of the American Dilemma was essentially that (1) lofty democratic ideals and (2) ingrained norms of prejudice and group-interest are in long-standing conflict, providing a fundamental tension to race relations in the United States. Schuman (1972) has shown how seemingly conflicting answers to survey questions often reveal the clash of important values. Most white Americans today endorse the idea of equality and believe that racial discrimination is wrong, Schuman acknowledges. However, they also believe in "group harmony," "economic success," "paying attention to the opinions of . . . neighbors," "a good education for their children," "keeping law and order," and many other personal and social values:

> Only to a true believer will any of these values win out in all situations, regardless of other values with which it competes. A few people

will go to the stake for a single value, but history and common sense tell us that most people work out compromises, depending on the exact balance of positions. (Schuman, 1972, p. 352)

Until we stop assuming that every response to an attitude question comes from a true believer who has no other attitudes and values, we will continue to regard these inevitable compromises as evidence of inconsistency.

Which attitudes predict behavior best? Despite the complexity of these issues some theorists have nominated particular forms of attitudes for the role of "best all-round predictor" of behavior. Fishbein (1967) argues that only specific behavioral intentions toward the total act (#11 in Figure 6-5) are able to predict behavior. Rokeach advocates a new, improved combination of attitudes toward the object (#2) and attitudes toward the situation (#8) (Rokeach, 1967). While there is some evidence that behavioral intentions are useful predictors, the record is not conclusive. Brannon et al. (1973) found behavioral intentions no better than an attitude measure, and Sample and Warland (1973) found one condition under which an attitude measure was superior to behavioral intentions. Rokeach and Kliejunas (1972) report some support for Rokeach's theory, i.e., that the combination predicts better than the two elements separately, but this is based on self-reports rather than independent observations of behavior.

We think that efforts to discover a best, all-purpose attitude for predicting behavior are somewhat misguided. Behavioral intentions are often useful because they are usually fairly congruent with the behavior and because they let the respondent help in estimating the impact of constraints and competing attitudes. They become less useful if congruence is lower or when unanticipated constraints and conflicts are likely to arise. One can improve prediction by using two relevant attitudes rather than one, but it remains to be shown that the same two are always best. For the present we should probably try to understand why a given measure works well or poorly in a certain situation, instead of searching for quick and universal solutions.

Situational Cues. To make matters just a bit more complex congruent attitudes and relevant constraints may be minimized or rendered seemingly irrelevant by a psychological process that might best be called "defining the situation." There are certain situations which seem to call for an individual to express himself completely, to say whatever he feels: Encounter groups and unstructured interviews are instances that come to mind. In other situations there is a powerful demand that one set aside personal preferences and biases: jury duty, medical emergencies, professional roles in the helping professions, and military combat, to name a few. Between these clearly defined extremes are many situations—being an experimental subject, standing in a crowded elevator—in which it is much less clear exactly which of one's attitudes are relevant.

In many situations, and perhaps especially in those structured somewhat loosely, human beings seem remarkably sensitive to social and situational "cues" to help define the situation. Such cues seem to have a catalytic effect on behavior far in excess of their reasonable stimulus value. Quite often during a routine group discussion, for example, one value-judgment, complaint, or comment about process will result in a wave of such comments. Even allowing for the stimulus value of the first remark it's often clear that these observations were made some time ago, yet weren't being expressed. An ice-breaking remark may simply lower the "social risk" of speaking out, but it also seems to bring into conscious focus ideas and attitudes which simply weren't previously seen as relevant.

Consider some findings from a variety of studies. Darley and Latane (1968) discovered that the presence of other witnesses to a fire, a robbery, or an accident makes most people less likely to help, quite contrary to what one would expect on the basis of social desirability. It was speculated that the presence of others in these settings may have implicitly defined the situation to most subjects as a non-emergency. The mere presence of a weapon lying on a table can significantly increase the incidence of socially agressive behavior (Berkowitz & LePage, 1967) and viewing agressive behavior by a human model increases the likelihood of many agressive acts, even acts which were never witnessed (Bandura, 1965). The behavior of a stooge in an ambiguous situation can make aroused subjects certain that they feel either wild mirth or boiling rage, depending on cues in the situation (Schachter, 1959). Asking subjects their religious affiliation can dramatically increase their willingness to bear pain (Lambert et al., 1960).

Some of these effects may amount to "monkey see, monkey do," but others are much more complex. A study by Kiesler, Nisbett, and Zanna (1969) suggests that certain situational cues can make subjects feel that their attitudes are more relevant to the situation, whatever those attitudes may be. The cue used in this case was a confederate's statement that he would gladly perform a task (presenting an information issue to passers-by on a city sidewalk), because: "it's something I really believe in; I guess that's the important thing." Subjects who heard this declaration subsequently showed a fairly strong relationship ($r = .69$) between their own attitude toward an issue and the amount of effort they planned to expend in promoting it, while subjects who were not exposed to the cue showed no such relationship ($r = .14$).

The implications of situational cues for predicting future behavior are numerous and complex. In general any factor which increases the contribution of situational variables has to reduce the role of purely individual factors. More importantly, situational cues seem to have a power to change the definition of the situation for individuals, which is probably close to the core of the often-noted difficulty in finding cross-situational consistency (Alker, 1972; Bem, 1972a; Moos, 1969). Without significantly changing attitudes, cues seem able to "move the spotlight" of consciousness or relevance from one set of attitudes to another. This affects attitude–behavior predictions by throwing a wild card into an already-complex network of influences—probably to the detriment of any previous predictions. Behavioral intentions, for example, depend on the subject's ability to anticipate the effects of other attitudes and constraints; yet the powerful effect of situational cues on their own behavior is unknown to most people. Subjects in the experiments mentioned above are usually surprised to learn how the situation affected their actions, and often seem embarrassed at such a sign of "weakness." Attitudes about the substantive issues, which seem highly relevant in advance, can thus get lost in the shuffle of situational dynamics while attitudes about courtesy, authority, or embarrassment suddenly become more relevant.

An Overview, from Attitude Expression to Behavior. The sequence of events from expression to behavior will often involve all the factors discussed up to now, plus in most cases some time interval between the measures. The process is shown in very simplified form in Figure 6-6; let's briefly summarize the points discussed up to now.

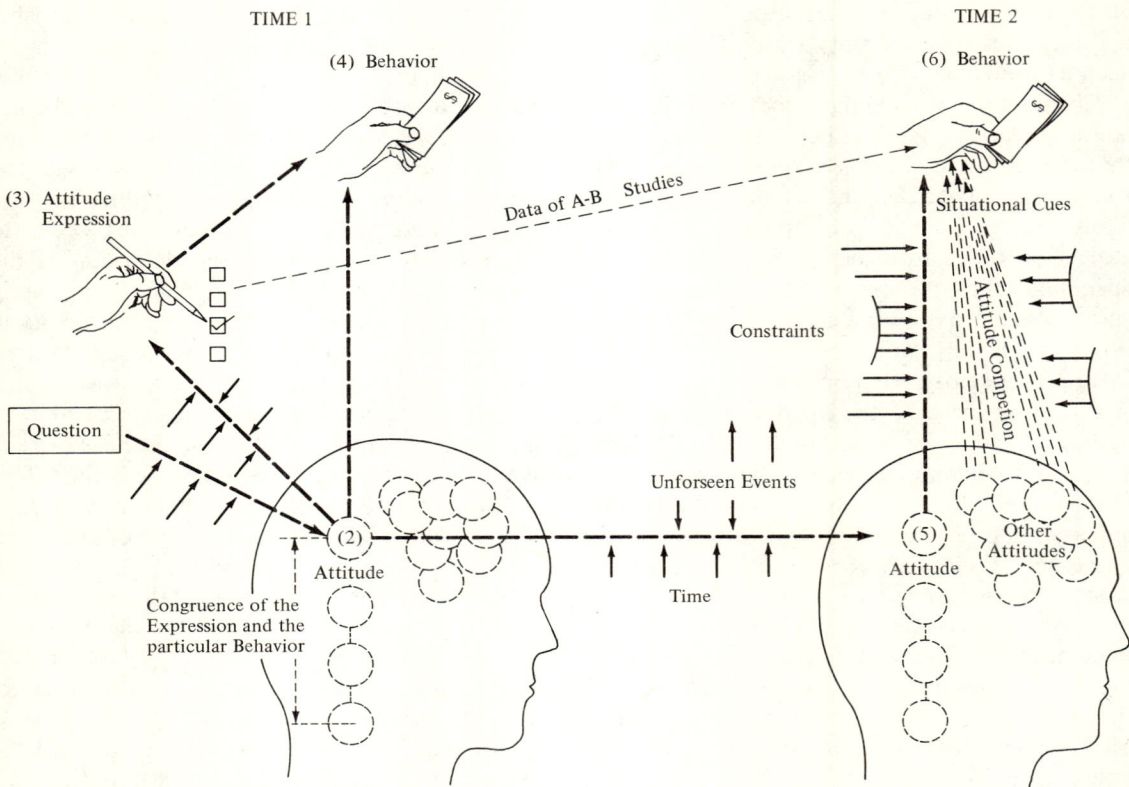

FIGURE 6-6. An overview of expression-behavior predictions.

An attitude [(2) in Figure 6-6] is engaged by a standardized question (1) in an interview or questionnaire, and the response is regarded as an attitude expression (3). This expression does not duplicate the individual's attitude perfectly for reasons examined earlier, but presumably tells us something about it. The attitude measured may be thought of as having some degree of congruence with a particular instance of behavior (4)—in other words, it may be highly relevant, given the standard facts of our culture, or it may have virtually no relevance. The presence of a congruent attitude doesn't mean that a behavior will occur, however. There may be any number of other attitudes with relevance for the behavior and a wide variety of constraints. As one attitude then is only a small part of the picture, from the standpoint of predicting a behavioral outcome, and an expression is at best an imperfect estimate of that small part.

It's quite possible of course to compare expressions with behavior performed at about the same time and in the same situation (4). What we are usually most interested in, however, is behavior at some later date (6): we'd like to be able to predict actions as far into the future as possible, and in situations very different from the one at hand. It is only the attitude as it exists (5) at Time Two therefore, rather than it's predecessor at Time One, which can play any direct role in influencing behavior. Attitudes obviously can and do change with the passage of time, however; scientific data merely confirm common sense (and sad love songs) on this fact of life. Test–retest data on attitudes rarely show correlations above .80 over the span of a year and are often much lower. While some of the apparent instability is due to errors of measurement, attitudes do change in response to maturation, experience, communications with others, and unforeseen events which may influence or modify the attitude. Kurt Lewin (1951) himself expressed considerable pessimism about predictions of future behavior for precisely this reason, the imponderable influences of future events on the individual. In general we must accept the fact that expression–behavior correlations cannot except by chance exceed the attitude's level of stability over the same period.

Notice in Figure 6-6 how the empirical correlation reported in an attitude–behavior study bypasses the various conceptual steps through which a causal relationship must operate. What is usually reported is a statistical comparison of expressions (3) at Time One with behavior (6) at Time Two. These overall correlations (e.g., +.02 in the Corey study, +.11 in the Bray study, +.40 in the DeFleur & Westie study, +.04 in the Rokeach & Mezei study, and so on) tell us only whether prediction was possible under these circumstances, with these materials. As they provide little information about the causal chain, particularly when the obtained relationship is low, we are uncertain as to where the expected relationship went awry.[11]

Intensity and stability. Indications of attitude stability, such as high test–retest correlations, should be favorable for long-range prediction. Common sense tells us also that, when all else is equal, strong attitudes should have greater effects than weak ones. Since in important real-life situations there are usually a variety of competing attitudes, unforeseen events, constraints, and other complicating factors, intensity may be one of the best practical indices of effects on behavior.

While these points seem fairly obvious there are some interesting examples in interview data concerning elections. Of the voters who were most favorable to Eisenhower in 1956, a remarkable 98% reported voting for him; of those least favorable to him, only 6% did so (Campbell et al., 1964, p. 34). Most voters did not feel so intensely, of course, and at intermediate levels the votes were distributed more evenly.

When self-reported stability of the voter's preference is considered together with intensity, the relation to voting becomes somewhat clearer. Some voters reported that they had not made up their minds until the last two weeks before the election; intensity of partisan attitudes in this group correlated only .21 with final voting choice. In a group who said they had made their decision earlier during the campaign, intensity predicted voting choice at the level of .58; and for those that had decided as long ago as the conventions, the correlation was .74 (Campbell et al., 1964, p. 42). Precisely what the time of decision represents is not clear, but the findings suggest that measures of "intensity" may be usefully supplemented by other kinds of data.

---

[11]The reader has probably noted long before now that we speak as if attitudes should always produce behavior unless "something gets in the way." In fact, of course, this is unrealistic. Physicists have found it useful to imagine a fictionless universe; the present model is offered in the same spirit, not as a framework for a general theory of behavior.

What behaviors to predict? On the basis of the principles discussed up to now prediction should be most difficult for behaviors associated with complex constraints, contradictory social norms, fierce group pressures, and sharply conflicting attitudes and values. Perhaps the outstanding example of such an area of course is race relations in the United States. Myrdal's (1944) study is a classic description of these cross-pressures, and countless American writers have discussed the Kafkaesque incongruities of race relations and customs. Since a high percentage of the early attitude–behavior studies for some reason dealt with racial matters, it's not at all surprising that low relationships were so frequently reported.

When researchers more recently turned to predicting low-stakes laboratory game behavior, they met immediately with greater success. Ajzen and Fishbein (1970) chose a prisoner's dilemma procedure (see Chapter 11) in which each player: (1) could respond in only two ways, "x" or "y"; (2) knew all rules and all possible outcomes; and (3) was playing the game solely for experimental credit. After playing for eight moves subjects could "predict" their behavior over the next ten moves quite well. The secret of success, it seems, lies in choosing the right problem to attack.

There is at least one important real-life behavior, however, which social scientists have learned to predict extremely well: voting. Individual votes can't be observed directly for obvious reasons, but the accuracy with which reports of how one voted match official records suggests that reports are highly reliable. It may be instructive to examine the reasons then, in terms of the ideas we've discussed, why this behavior can be so accurately forecast:

1. Votes are cast in guaranteed privacy, so most kinds of external constraints do not apply.

2. There are no surprises or unforeseen pressures in the ballot-booth. The respondent knows in advance exactly what the behavioral situation will be.

3. The concept of an election is simple and well understood. Misunderstanding the meaning of either the question or the behavior alternatives is unlikely.

4. The usual form of the question is maximally congruent with the behavioral situation. Respondents generally check a sample ballot virtually identical to the one they will later see in the voting booth.

5. The decision of whom to vote for is for many an almost-preordained matter. Over 60% of the voters say that they vote "always or mostly" for the same party in every election (Campbell et al., 1964, p. 70). The choice of these voters is thus routinely predictable long before a given election.

6. The consequences of whom one votes for are probably generally perceived as slight from a strictly individual point of view. Many voters doubt that any one officeholder could change things much; still more realize that their one vote will almost certainly never tip an election. Even though the collective action of the electorate may have great consequence, each voter may quite reasonably view his single vote as largely an attitude expression, much like the one he may have made to a pollster a short time ago.

It seems then that voting is almost made to order for successful prediction, but let's consider an interesting complication. While it's not hard to tell whom someone will vote for, if he votes, it is much harder to predict whether people will vote at all. We can easily see now why this should be so. Unlike "whom to vote for," "whether to vote" is not a simple anonymous decision devoid of immediate personal consequences. Furthermore, the respondent cannot totally predict what the constraints and situational pressures will be on Election Day. It may be raining, voting lines may be long, traffic may be bad, one may be feeling sick, friends may exert influence, and so forth. Polling organizations do of course attempt to predict who among their respondents will vote; and the best predictors of this are generally not the same as those which predict whom one will vote for. A belief that it's one's "duty" to vote is surprisingly more influential than interest in a particular campaign or even concern for its outcome. Intensity of liking a candidate influences likelihood of voting, but apparently only when an election is perceived as being "close" (Campbell et al., 1964, chap. 4).

Such facts point to the conclusion that each instance of behavior has a particular system of constraints, contingencies, and congruent attitudinal factors; we should usually expect to find differences in the kinds of factors able to predict different behaviors. This applies both to broad content differences and to seemingly small jumps within the same behavioral sequence. Whom-to-vote for is not the same decision as whether-to-vote, whether-to-attend a meeting is different from how-to-act once there, whether-to-sign a petition is a different decision than which-petition-to-sign, and so forth.

Some Methodological Pitfalls. There are a number of methodological requirements for a valid attitude–behavior study which have rather often been ignored. The most basic is that the people whose behavior is observed must be the same people whose attitudes were measured, since predicting A's behavior from B's statements would seem to be a dubious enterprise. Obvious though this requirement may seem, several studies (including the classic by LaPiere) conspicuously fail to meet it.

It's also important that the behavior measure be an actual observation by the experimenter or some other independent source, not merely a subject's self-reported actions. There is abundant evidence that even the simplest behaviors are often misreported by subjects: e.g., whether one has a telephone, owns a library card, voted in a recent election (Parry & Crossley, 1950; Hyman, 1945). Since errors in self-report on even such simple matters sometimes range up to 40%, to take at face value self-reports of premarital sex (Fishbein, 1966a, 1966b), birth control use (Kothandapani, 1971), church attendance (Poppleton & Pilkington, 1963), and other socially sensitive actions would seem almost to invite errors and artifactual findings. Finally there are two particular methodological problems which are especially problematic for attitude–behavior research, measurement effects and connection effects.

Measurement effects. In the process of measuring attitudes, especially on an unfamiliar issue, one may unknowingly create an attitude where none existed before. Confronted by a question on "pretrial publicity of juvenile offenders," for example, the respondent may think about the issue for a few moments before answering. He had no particular attitude on this subject before; now, though, he has an attitude. If the second part of the study consists of a behavioral measure on this same issue (e.g., contributing money or signing a petition against pretrial publicity) a relationship may be found which wouldn't have existed naturally.

Ajzen and Fishbein (1970) asked the players in their prisoner's dilemma game the question, "I intend to choose ——% X and ——% Y." The behavioral measure was then the percentage of X and Y choices made over the next ten moves. A respondent might have thought something like: "Well, let's see now, I gotta decide . . . O.K., I'll play two X's for every Y;

that'll keep him guessing." While these "predictions" correlated substantially with the actual choices, much of this was probably due to a measurement effect.

We can expect measurement effects to be a problem most often when (1) the topic is one the respondent probably hasn't considered before and (2) when a large number of questions is asked about the same topic, as on a typical attitude scale.

Connection effects. An attitude–behavior study has two parts: a measure of attitude expression and a behavior measure. Human respondents are quick to speculate about the purpose of any study they take part in. If the connection between the two halves is obvious or can easily be guessed, they may conclude that their "consistency" is being studied. Striker et al. (1967) found suspiciousness about experimental procedures correlated with a variety of factors including intelligence, self-esteem, and independence. Among those who do guess there may be a variety of reactions; some will try to behave more consistently while others may resent the "sneaky psychologist" and choose to deliberately act less consistently. It's particularly desirable therefore that attitude–behavior studies conceal the connection between the two steps of the study.

Some researchers have taken excellent precautions to achieve this (remember the department-store "shadows" used by Saenger and Gilbert?), but most have been rather insensitive to it. Lawrence Linn (1965), for example, used as his attitude measure seven items: "I would allow myself to be photographed with a Negro of the opposite sex if the photo were to be seen only by professional sociologists and psychologists," "I would allow myself to be photographed with a Negro of the opposite sex if the photo were to be published in my home-town newspaper," and so forth. Such questions must have certainly created a measurement effect, since these inquiries are unusual to say the least, and they would also seem likely to be remembered for a while. Imagine the suspicions of these students when a few weeks later, a "testing company" representative showed up in class with a request for volunteers for interracial, opposite-sex photos, "to be seen only by professional sociologists and psychologists," "to be published in my home-town newspaper," and so forth.

Main points of the model. The issues discussed in the preceding pages obviously can't be neatly summarized; a simple listing of the main points may be useful, however. In order to successfully predict future behavior on the basis of current verbal expressions:

1. The respondent must have an attitude reasonably congruent to the behavior to be predicted.

2. An attitude-expression must be elicited which fairly represents that attitude.

3. The attitude must not be substantially altered by the process of measurement.

4. The attitudes must not have changed substantially by the time the behavior is performed.

5. The respondent must not be subject to overwhelmingly strong situational constraints at the time the behavior is performed.

6. There must not be conflicting attitudes which are also congruent to the behavior in question, or more realistically if there are such competing attitudes, they must be taken into consideration.

7. There must be no powerful cues in the behavioral situation which render the measured attitude irrelevant.

8. Respondents should not be aware that their attitude expressions and behavior are being compared.

	Lack of Congruence	Strong Constraints	Attitude Competition	Measurement Effect	Connection Effect
LaPiere	✓	✓	✓		
Corey	?	✓	?	?	
Saenger & Gilbert		✓	✓		
DeFleur & Westie	✓	✓	✓	✓	✓
Rokeach & Mezei		✓	✓		
DeFrieze & Ford	✓	✓	✓		✓

FIGURE 6-7. Problems in some representative attitude-behavior studies.

What Have We Learned? A Quick Look at Those Early Studies

How do these requirements compare with the procedures seen in most early research studies, the empirical reports which led social scientists to conclude there was little relation between words and deeds? Let's briefly re-examine the representative studies mentioned earlier in this chapter from the perspective of the issues we've discussed. Figure 6-7 summarizes the incidence in their studies of five of the more important problems we've discussed: Were attitude expressions congruent with the behavior observer? Were there no overwhelmingly strong constraints in the behavioral situation? Were there other important attitudes which could have influenced the behavior and weren't considered? Was there a measurement effect? A connection effect?

The LaPiere Study. The question "Do you accept members of the Chinese race as guests in your establishment?" (arriving by mail from an uncertain source) is not perfectly congruent with the unannounced arrival of one well-mannered, affluent Chinese couple. Had the question asked how this sort of situation would probably be handled rather than assuming there was some set policy on Chinese guests, the answers might have been different. It's not clear that answers to the questionnaire should be seen as attitude expressions at all. Hotel and restaurant managers may have viewed this strange letter as an opportunity to encourage Chinese visitors; and their response, in 1932, was "thanks, but no thanks." In the behavioral situation, however, there were numerous constraints against actually refusing service. Social norms of politeness, the habit of accepting business, the possibility that refusal might be unpleasant, and that a "scene" might draw the attention of other customers, all mitigated against any overt display of prejudice. There were probably also competing attitudinal pressures to welcome these unusual visitors. LaPiere stresses the friendliness, poise, and other social graces of his friends, which probably served as situational cues for activating the usual attitudes of approval toward well-mannered and well-heeled strangers.

The Corey Study. Corey's design is harder to evaluate because of inadequacies in the reporting. As his scale of attitudes toward cheating is not presented, we can't judge its congruence with the behavior measure or whether it incorporated other attitudes that might be relevant. Answering questions about cheating might have influenced attitudes in some cases (a measurement effect), but again we can't be sure. It's clear however that a number of powerful constraints were present in the setting where cheating was measured. There was fear of getting caught and being expelled, social norms against cheating, peer pressures, and so forth; furthermore, in order to cheat one must have the opportunity. If you get all or most of the questions right to begin with there is no opportunity to cheat. Corey states that, while attitudes were not related to cheating, the correlation between cheating and number of questions missed was +.46. Since the average cheating score was less than two points on a 40-item test, it appears likely that many of the subjects had little or no temptation to cheat, whatever their attitude.

The Saenger and Gilbert Study. Statements made by the subjects in follow-up interviews clearly reveal the particular constraints and competing attitudes which prevented prejudiced shoppers from acting out their prejudices. One simple constraint was apparently the need to save time and avoid inconvenience.

One rather prejudiced mailman stated in his interview: " . . . if I want to buy something, and that department store has it, I don't care who sells it to me. I want the article, and especially in a department store the article sells itself" (Saenger & Gilbert, 1950, p. 65).

Several subjects specifically also mentioned that department stores were impersonal public places where any social contact was rather minimal. Furthermore the presence of the black sales clerk was a *fait accompli;* to protest it would probably involve a lot of time and trouble. The fact that other shoppers were buying from these black sales clerks also probably served to define the situation: "Occasionally I go into Chock Full O'Nuts and it's taken for granted there, so you can't object" (p. 65). Many of these shoppers left no doubt, however, that their racial attitudes might have had some influence had the situation been different.

> "To be frank with you, I'd say that perhaps if I went in and there were two people there, one colored and one white, I think I undoubtedly would prefer to deal with the white person." (p. 65)

> "I wouldn't object if they were there, but I would rather not have them there." (p. 67)

The DeFleur and Westie Study. DeFleur and Wastie's famous study of willingness to be in an interracial photograph, hailed as "ingenious" by several commentators (e.g., Hyman, 1969, p. 27), is virtually a textbook illustration of design problems. The prejudice measure with which the study began was Westie's own "summated-differences" scale which requires no less than 500 tedious and repetitive responses. Two hours of puzzling over such stimuli as "Negro ditchdigger—a close personal friend", "Negro bookkeeper—use the same towel as I do" could hardly fail to create some new attitudes (a measurement effect) and the congruence of this ordeal with the request to pose for photographs seems low at best.[12] Many other attitudes probably had an equal or greater effect on this behavior: feelings about receiving publicity, about signing legal forms, posing in photographs, helping researchers of prejudice, and so forth. It was realized that fears of disapproval from the subject's friends or family might be an important constraint on posing for the photographs, but the focus of

---

[12]As Irwin Katz (1970) has pointed out, posing in these photographs was not an act that would help black people. It is logically more a personal favor to the experimenter. Attitudes toward the experimenter and toward the research might have been more relevant than stereotypes about blacks.

subjects' concern was apparently misjudged.[13] The simple constraint that posing would require a new appointment and might be time-consuming is not controlled or mentioned. Finally, there is an obvious connection effect: the request to pose came from the same researchers who had measured racial attitudes, with no effort to conceal the connection. A simple desire on the part of these young subjects to appear consistent to the experimenters may have accounted entirely for the modest reported findings.

The Rokeach and Mezei Study. There is a remarkably obvious constraint in this study which could easily have overpowered any effect of racial attitudes. The discussion group contained only two black confederates and two white confederates; the subject was asked to choose two of the four to accompany him on a coffee break. To choose the two whites and leave both blacks would have been a remarkable gesture, flagrantly violating the implicit norms of racial behavior on a northern campus; choosing the two blacks was hardly a natural and inoffensive alternative. Small wonder that all but a handful judiciously chose one white and one black confederate and that racial attitudes had next-to-no relation to this decision.

The DeFrieze and Ford Study. The authors only state that their attitude measure was a 14-item scale of prejudice toward Negroes. One can't be sure, but it seems unlikely that this measure was highly congruent with a specific request to sign and be publicly identified with an open-housing declaration. The constraints associated with signing a public statement on this controversial issue are obvious, inescapable, and formidable. A variety of other attitudes—about receiving publicity, defying public opinion, relations with neighbors, and relations with family—were probably as relevant to the behavior as racial attitudes. Since behavior measure came immediately after from the same person who administered the attitude measure, a strong connection effect was probably operating.

Should we conclude then that these early studies of the attitude–behavior relationship were invalid and meaningless? On the contrary most of them provide essentially valid and useful information: under X conditions, attitude measure Y is only slightly related to the frequency of behavior Z. They do not justify the conclusion, however, that attitudes are unrelated to behavior, or even that simple paper-and-pencil measures cannot predict actions at a later date.

As we have seen, the attitude measures used in these studies were often remarkably inappropriate. In some cases they are not described except by name; frequently they seem to have been rather casually chosen, as if any scale thought to measure "prejudice" or the like would do just fine. In virtually every case, the particular behavior studied was subject to powerful constraints—economic gains, embarrassment, social norms, reactions of other people, time pressures—and was clearly influenced by many attitudes other than the one measured. Early research on this question was conducted as we've seen against a background of widespread belief that behavior was mainly an expression of personal attitudes. Thoughtful

---

[13]DeFleur and Westie describe the poses they asked subjects to take only vaguely but devote much attention to describing and controlling the amount of public exposure the photographs would receive. They mention in a footnote that female subjects thought that poses looked "romantic," but never refer to this point again; the percentages of males and females in the study are not even reported. A more recent experiment by Green (1968) using similar materials has shown that amount of exposure is of much less concern to subjects than the degree of intimacy portrayed in the photographic poses. There is an independent effect for intimacy of pose, none for degree of exposure.

researchers like LaPiere and Saenger and Gilbert wanted to show that prejudice and discrimination were not one and the same. The situations they constructed made this point extremely well: attitudinal influences could be overpowered by economic, self-interest, and situational factors. In retrospect they seem to have hedged their bets a little with sloppy measures of the attitude variable, but these basically accurate findings were exciting and provocative when reported. For reasons that are open to debate (Deutscher, 1969) they were followed by some increasingly naive research which culminated in pronouncements, in the early 1970s, that "attitudes . . . play no real role in behavior" (Tarter, 1970).

Some Recent Research

In recent years some noticeably more sophisticated work has begun to appear. Attitude measures tailored to a specific behavior are being used, combinations of attitudes are often employed, and some of the attention has shifted to behaviors with less formidable constraint systems than the old favorites. As a result, attitude–behavior correlations have been rising. Some examples:

Goodmonson and Glaudin (1971) chose a timely and unusual behavior to predict: donation of one's body and internal organs for the purpose of medical transplantation after death. Subjects were asked to sign a card leaving their organs to medicine at their death and to carry this card in their billfold or purse at all times. As under Oregon law such a card gave physicians the legal right to transplant organs at the time of death, the request was actually a very real one. A 7-point behavioral scale was used to summarize subjects' willingness to make either this definite legal commitment or a lesser commitment such as reading literature about organ transplants and informing others of the need to donate organs. Attitudes about organ donation, measured 8 weeks previously in a psychology class, correlated .58 with these behaviors. The attitude scale had been designed to be highly congruent with the behavioral measure, which undoubtedly contributed to this encouraging result. Probably still more important was the fact that this "behavior" was largely free of the usual self-interest, normative, and other social constraints. As organ transplantation is a new phenomenon, there are no strong social norms about it or easily predictable expectations of friends and family; it also has no direct personal consequences at all during one's lifetime. The likely sources of reluctance are religious, philosophical, or psychological; these would be expected to show up on a well-constructed attitude measure well before the event and apparently did to a substantial degree.

Wicker (1971) has reported a technique which seems especially promising for predicting highly constrained behaviors. In a study of Protestant church members in one Midwestern community he obtained careful behavioral measures of church attendance over a 10-month period and a record of actual financial contributions to the church. Both behaviors are subject to a variety of external constraints and unplanned events. Of four different types of attitude measures developed for this study, the type he called "judged influence of extraneous events" was the best predictor of both attendance (+.42) and contributions (+.45). On these measures a series of unplanned distractions were described, and subjects were asked to judge how much their behavior would be affected in each case. For example, would they attend if they had weekend guests who did not want to go? Would they contribute if the congregation voted to spend funds on a project they disapprove of?

The advantage of this technique was probably that it gauged the strength of a given attitude relative to competing attitudes and to various constraints which would normally work against it. It probably thus gives a more realistic measure of intensity and resistance to influence than other forms of attitude self-report. In a sense it may capture some of the advantages of a behavioral intention, without the need to describe exactly the behavior to be predicted. Apparently the idea of presenting some potential conflicts to respondents in the process of attitude measurement is a promising one which should be explored in future measurement efforts.

Brannon, Cyphers, Hesse, Hesselbart, Keane, Schuman, Vicarro, and Wright (1973) conducted the largest attitude–behavior study reported to date, and the first performed on a probability sample of an entire city. The topic was also in the area of race relations, where many previous studies have achieved disappointing results. Interviews were conducted in the homes of 640 white adults, selected by a probability sample of the population of Detroit, Michigan, and the three-county surrounding metropolitan area.[14] The 80 or so questions on racial attitudes and beliefs asked during an hour-long interview included one on the sensitive issue of racially open housing:

> Suppose there is a community-wide vote on the general housing issue. There are two possible laws to vote on; which law would you vote for? (The following alternatives were printed on a card; they were read and then handed to the respondent:)
>
> 1. One law says that a homeowner can decide for himself who to sell his house to, even if he prefers not to sell to Negroes.
>
> 2. The second law says that a homeowner cannot refuse to sell to someone because of their race or color.

The elaborate forced-choice format was designed to minimize social desirability factors which often inflate the percentage of "liberal" answers in survey data and to pit the open-housing proposal directly against the "individual freedom" argument which is most frequently cited against it. As expected, the white Detroit population went for the "owner's rights" alternative by about five to one (82% vs. 16%, 2% other responses).

Approximately 3 months later a volunteer citizens' group called on each of these respondents during a door-to-door petition drive and asked them to sign a petition against water pollution. This was an innocuous statement merely supporting the state leaders in their "fight to stop this threat." When the respondent had signed it, as virtually all were quite willing to do, the volunteer said: "Thank you . . . We have also taken a stand on another public issue, and if you agree with us on this, we'd be happy for you to sign it also." The second issue of course was that of open housing. The "volunteers" were in fact members of the research team; no reference was made to the survey three months earlier, and none of the respondents suspected any such connection. The preliminary water pollution petition was a device to determine whether a respondent was willing to sign any petition, so that a refusal to sign the second could be distinguished from any general reluctance to sign one's name to such a document.

There were two separate versions of the second or housing petition: one which clearly supported the enactment of open-housing legislation and another which presented the "owner's-rights" viewpoint that homeowners could refuse to sell to whomever they choose. Respondents who were offered the version

---

[14] The sampled population consisted of all white non-institutionalized adults under 70 years of age residing within the metropolitan borders. The race limitation was due to the survey's topic: white racial attitudes. These interviews were carried out within the context of the 1969 Detroit Area Study at the University of Michigan.

consistent with the position they had stated in the interview signed it 82% of the time on the average. For those offered the version opposed to their previously stated attitude, the rate of signing was only 22%, despite the fact that they had all just signed the first petition. Overall then approximately 80% of Detroit's respondents acted consistently with what they had said in the interviews three months earlier: either signing a housing petition which expressed views they agreed with or rejecting a petition which took a position they had verbally rejected some months earlier.

Merely signing a petition is obviously a relatively mild form of behavior. What would happen if additional constraints and consequences were added to the behavioral situation? In order to partly answer this question, the researchers next asked each petition-signer for permission to print his or her name, along with the names of other supporters, in both local newspapers—supposedly to demonstrate public support for these views. As one might expect, the percentage of respondents willing to take this extra step was fewer, but the general correspondence to attitudes held up. About 59% signed and endorsed newspaper publicity when the petition was consistent with what they had said in the interview; only 12% did so when the alternative petition was offered. Overall, about 73% of the respondents still acted as would be predicted on the basis of their original interview responses.

When other attitude information gained in the interviews was combined with the single question about open-housing, signing of the petitions could be predicted a bit more accurately still. A persistent fear on the part of some white homeowners is that when blacks move into an all-white neighborhood, "problems" may result, ranging from a failure of the new families to keep up the property to an overreaction on the part of whites such as selling out cheaply or engaging in violent protests. Many respondents mentioned some such neighborhood problem in response to an open-ended query, including some of those who said they personally favored open housing. Among respondents who favored open housing and foresaw no problems, or opposed open housing and expected problems, more than 88% responded consistently to the petitions three months later.

Several factors probably contributed to this finding of rather high predictability over a long period even in the area of racial problems: high congruence, an attitude measure based on value conflict and which minimized social desirability, the intensity and stability of white attitudes about open housing, and a "situational cue" which apparently enhanced the effect of attitudes. Respondents were placed in the situation of having already signed a petition just before the critical one was offered. This may have defined the situation as one in which the question was whether one agreed with the second petition or not, with the result that people acted almost entirely on the basis of their attitude.

WHERE DO WE GO FROM HERE?

Individual and Group Differences in Acting on Attitudes

Science searches for general laws, but it's a fundamental fact of nature that people are often different. We know that people's attitudes themselves differ in innumerable ways; why not also the conditions under which attitudes exert an influence on behavior? The usual procedure of finding a correlation between attitude scores and behavior scores for a large number of individuals assumes a general and basically linear relationship. Is this reasonable? We know, for example, that rather simple attitudes such as taste preferences translate into behavior differently for different people.

Cowdry, Keniston, and Cabin (1970) studied the background and personality of a group of seniors at Yale who signed a controversial anti-Viet Nam petition in 1968, possibly thus damaging their job prospects (or so it seemed at the time), and another group of seniors who had similar attitudes but would not sign the petition. The psychologists found that students who acted in concert with their views were no different from the others demographically; they reported however having more respect and affection for their fathers, more time spent with their fathers during childhood, and saw their parents as having more shared values and interests. They also tended to describe their own personalities as significantly more strong-willed, active, optimistic, and open-minded than did those who had not signed.

Personality characteristics in general may have less direct effect on behavior than on the conditions and mechanisms of expressing personal feelings in behavior. Rotter (1967) proposes that internally directed people are more likely to take social action than are externals. Helson, Blake, and Mouton (1958) found that conformity-proneness reduced the effect of personal attitudes, since conformers tended to sign any petition more often.

There is some recent evidence that the general impulse to act consistently with attitudes can be experimentally altered, at least for a short time. McArthur, Kiesler, and Cook (1969) told undergraduates that psychological tests had shown they were "doers": people whose attitudes lead to action, who were good at "figuring out what needs to be done and then doing it," and were "independent enough to do your part no matter what others say." Since the experimenters supposedly "really need people with personality traits like yours," the subjects were paid a bonus—either $1.50 or $10.00—in addition to experimental credit for taking part in the study. Shortly thereafter, in what they thought was a totally unrelated setting, the subjects had an opportunity to volunteer to distribute leaflets against air pollution, an issue they'd all said they cared about.

Subjects in a control condition had volunteered about 50% of the time; the recently-rewarded "doers" volunteered significantly more often: 70% of those who had gotten $1.50 decided to volunteer, and 100% of those who had gotten $10.00 volunteered. This study suggests that the strength of the attitude–behavior linkage may be manipulable by means of reward.

The variable of formal education may also affect this linkage. College undergraduates, the most common subject population for psychological studies, are often concerned with developing a consistent social and political outlook. They may be more concerned about the consistency of their attitudes, beliefs, and actions than are most people and may want especially to avoid seeming inconsistent to an adult experimenter. With greater age and disillusionment one is more likely to conclude, as Walt Whitman: "Do I contradict myself? Very well, then I contradict myself! I am large, I contain multitudes."

Another way of looking at group differences is that attitude–behavior consistency may be a differentially learned goal, a point of pride to intellectuals and moralists but an irrelevant luxury to the average person. Most people never receive much training or practice in doing just what they believe in; unpaid bills, time pressures, arbitrary rules and regulations, and the complexities of coping with a demanding world just don't allow it. The assumption that people should act on their principles may be politically as well as psychologically naive.

Beyond Nomothetic Psychology: Predicting for Some of the People Some of the Time

Although the need to match measuring techniques very closely to the psychological reality of individuals has been a recurrent (if not obsessive) theme of this chapter, our perspective has been almost entirely within the traditional framework of "nomothetic" psychology.

We've assumed, in other words, that it makes sense to measure some predetermined attitude in a member of our subject population and to describe individual variations in terms of the degree, strength, or consistency with which this attitude can be found. We may decide to measure "willingness to discriminate in favor of minorities," for example; then we normally classify people as strongly opposed, strongly in favor, or somewhere in between.

As early as 1937 Gordon Allport pointed out that this practice was theoretically unrealistic and naive. Strictly speaking, he argues, no two people ever have exactly the same attitude, trait, disposition, or tendency. True, certain descriptions are generally meaningful for many people—courteous, dogmatic, aggressive, supercilious—but even then it's a mistake to look for them in all individuals. For some people the preconceived attitude or trait may be irrelevant, simplistic, and inapplicable; to classify them as "medium" on it merely adds error variance and reduces the likelihood of making sense of the data.

The problem with this insight is that it seems at first glance to rule out generalizations about human behavior. One psychologist exclaimed during the 1930s, "of course it is true, but it's one of those truths that can't be accepted." Psychology has devoted itself to the search for nomothetic principles: things that are true of people-in-general, units of explanation that account for as much variance as possible, without trying to capture the exact pattern or essence of any one individual.

This approach has taken us a long way and there's certainly much room for improvement, as we've seen already. Since real people do not really have standardized nomothetic attitudes however, it stands to reason that we could understand their actions better if we could work with the kinds of dispositions they actually have.

A purely individualized (Allport called it "idiographic") attitude–behavior study would allow respondents to describe their own attitudes with all the quirks, peculiarities, and complexities; to say which kinds of behavior in which situations are affected by which attitudes; and to specify the outcome when two or more of these personalized dispositions come into conflict. In other words, we would predict only certain behaviors, in certain situations, for certain people.

It is not necessary to go this far. Suppose that the interests of the investigator require that a particular attitude be the starting point. Recognizing that not all people will have coherent attitudes of just this sort, the investigator can first set out to find those who do. Recognizing that not everyone may see the attitude as applicable to the situation of interest, he can locate those who do. Predictions would then be made for some of the people, some of the time; but as compensation our precision might rise considerably.

After lying neglected for nearly 40 years, Allport's reasoning has been rediscovered and applied to the problem of predicting behavior. A recent paper by Bem and Allen (1975) raises the issues just mentioned with particular reference to the cross-situational validity of personality traits. Like attitude measures, nomethetic measures of personality traits have had their troubles over the years. Mischel (1968) pointed out that they have rarely if ever exceeded a correlation of .30 with behavior, raising serious doubts in the minds of many psychologists that traits exist at all. Bem and Allen measured the traits of friendliness and conscientiousness, using a new self-report measure which—like Wicker's (1971) scale—opposed the trait-tendencies to a variety of situations and constraining factors: "When in a store how likely are you to strike up a conversation with a salesclerk?" "How carefully do you double-check your term papers for typing or spelling errors?" They went further, however, and dichotomized subjects on the basis of transsituational consistency of the trait as reflected in the variability of responses across the various situations in the scale.

Behavior was measured independently and rather objectively. One measure of conscientious behavior was date of returning student course evaluations—seven points for returning the form the same day, one point lost each day thereafter. Friendliness was measured when subjects arrived for a testing session; an experimental confederate tried to engage each subject in conversation while sitting in a waiting room, with responses carefully coded.

The results bore out their suspicion that trait measures could predict behavior well only for those subjects who had general transsituational traits. The verbal measures predicted friendliness ($r = .61$) and conscientiousness ($r = .43$) fairly well for these subjects; the same correlations in the nongeneralized trait group were $-.06$ and $-.12$.

The idea of finding attitude measures that predict behavior for some of the people, some of the time, is not so much a retrenchment as an acceptance of the facts of psychological life. If attitudes aren't present in people in the forms that one is trying to measure, they can't be expected to predict behavior very well. The failure to consider and allow for this may have contributed to much of the frustration and disillusionment of the past.

Some Conclusions and Implications

The most recent research has laid to rest the idea that attitudes never cause behavior, just as earlier studies convincingly shattered the assumption that attitudes always result in behavior. Obviously neither generalization is correct. It seems incontestable today that attitudes are one among many factors which exert influences on the kinds of socially important behavior which planners and social scientists wish to understand. In Kurt Lewin's famous formula $B = f(P, E)$, (read as "behavior is a function of the person and the environment"), attitudes are simply one part of the "P" term. Any one attitude is usually only one of many relevant to an important action. There are attitudes about the object, the situation, the action, oneself-in-such-a-situation, and so forth. There are also habits, abilities, opportunities, internalized social norms. judgments of how others will react, and elaborate (if often implicit) calculations of personal consequences. In a single instance any one of these may prove totally decisive; in the most general case they all must contribute in some manner to the total pool of variance. Add to all this the fact that attitudes are never seen directly but only as they appear through verbal expressions, and it's clear that no simple, routine relationship with behavior should be expected.

If we want to "demonstrate" that attitudes can predict behavior, one route is to choose a behavior largely free of constraints and other influences, such as laboratory game research. This isn't very helpful though, once the overzealous claims of a few radical behaviorists and social reductionists have been blunted. We'd like to predict important behavior in the real world, which means we must live with constraints, competition, and unexpected events. Even in this arena we are now discovering ways to improve predictive power: Use measures as congruent as possible in form, scope, and substantive content (e.g., Weigel et al., 1974). Tailor verbal measures specifically to given behaviors. Measure a variety of attitudes which bear on the behavior and incorporate them all in the prediction equation. Pit representative constraints and competing attitudes against other attitudes in the measurement process, to get realistic estimates of relative intensity. Allow individuals to reveal the dimensions and range of applicability of their own attitudes. If we do all this and more, moderate relationships should be well within our grasp!

If one is interested solely in predicting large-scale behavior as accurately as possible, social science tells us rather clearly today that our best bet is to control the situation. Control the rewards; control the available information; control normative and social pressures. In study after study we see that human beings can be caused to perform the most bizarre, startling, and unlikely of behaviors, frequently without even realizing they are being controlled. In statistical terms, such environmental factors may account for nine tenths of the immediate variance in most people's behavior, despite the curious unwillingness of Western culture to acknowledge the extent of human malleability. We prefer to believe "I am the master of my fate, I am the captain of my soul!" as we march in unison toward the paths of least resistance.

Why then should the relatively modest contribution of individual variations in attitude concern us at all? One inglorious but practical reason is that at the societal level most situations are difficult or impossible to alter to any real degree. The ballot box, the supermarket, the private home are all beyond our practical power to change very much. Attitudes can often make the decisive difference when more powerful factors are in rough equilibrium; price, utility, convenience, and availability may be the critical factors in dictating a purchase, but if these are equal between two brands of a product the consumer will choose on attitudinal grounds. Attitudes can also have some influence on a very wide range of specific behaviors, and in many different situations. Most important of all perhaps, an enormous portion of what social scientists know about people is based on verbal reports; it's vital therefore that there is no magic gap between symbolic verbal expressions and overt behavior. We saw much earlier that there is a theoretical continuum which connects the act of checking a questionnaire with the acts of voting for a president or buying a car. There is every reason to believe that the same general set of principles govern the one as the other and that under the right circumstances, as a consequence, people can tell us how they are going to behave. This does not mean that everything people think today will later come true, or that everything people do can somehow be predicted. It does mean that what we have learned during the last 50 years and are still learning about attitudes is far from irrelevant to the rest of human behavior.

SUMMARY

The concept of attitude is among the most widely used in social science and has long been regarded as close to the core of social psychology. Such diverse substantive topics as prejudice, persuasion, the self, personality characteristics, values, worker satisfaction, and political and religious ideologies are current branches of attitude study and rely on variations of classic attitude measurement techniques. Attitude measurement is perhaps the most highly evolved method in social science, with an enormous literature devoted to questions of format, scaling, refinement, and scoring procedures.

Open-ended questions, closed-ended questions, and questions or statements accompanied by fixed alternatives are among some of the forms used to tap attitudes. These may be presented singly or in concert with other items and most often are to be considered alone or in a forced-choice format with one or more other items. Frequently, because of increased precision of measurement, a number of items tapping aspects of an attitude are presented as a scale. Three common types are the Thurstone, the Guttman and, by far the most flexible and frequently used, the Likert scale.

The original and basic interest of attitudes however is that they have been assumed to be related to how people act. Textbooks until recently blandly asserted this connection, and words were described as "actions in miniature," more convenient to study but otherwise similar to overt actions. Gradually over the last 40 years, however, the implications of a set of studies of empirical attitude–behavior predictions have become recognized. When these investigators compared standard questionnaire and interview measures of attitudes with independently observed behavior in some other context, the relationships were disturbingly low, and not infrequently zero. In conjunction with other recent discoveries which were underscoring the dramatic effects of situational variables on behavior, the inevitable result was a widespread disillusionment—and in some quarters denunciation—of the attitude concept.

It now appears that the burial was somewhat premature. Several recent studies have produced substantial—and in some cases dramatic—predictive relations between attitude expressions and later behavior. The reasons seem to be directly related to the methods and assumptions of the newer studies as compared to the earlier efforts. *Congruence* or the degree of fit between attitude and behavior measures was seldom considered seriously in the early studies, which typically compared a vague measure of "prejudice" with a special instance of racial behavior in an unfamiliar setting. *Constraints* such as economic gains, social pressures, and considerations of time and effort were often solidly arrayed against the performance of consistent behavior. *Other attitudes* which might influence behavior in contrary ways were seldom hypothesized, measured, or controlled. Measures were sometimes used which could change attitudes in the processes of measuring them *(measurement effects)*, and often little care was taken to separate the two parts of the study so that respondents would be unaware their consistency was being measured *(connection effects)*.

In this light, six well-known studies that found a lack of correspondence between attitudes and behavior were described, and the lack of correspondence between attitudes and behavior was viewed in terms of variations of the five factors mentioned. More recent studies designed to minimize such discrepancies yielded much higher predictability of behavior from attitudes.

We conclude that attitude measures will not always tell us how people will act and should not be expected to do so; on the other hand, people sometimes do behave rather closely in accord with their expressed attitudes. We can apparently improve our ability to predict behavior substantially by examining cases of success and failure and by revising older methods; in the process it appears that both theory and measurement developments are benefitting from this new concern with behavior.

SUGGESTED READINGS

Wicker, A. Attitudes vs. actions: the relationship of verbal to overt behavior responses to attitude objects. *Journal of Social Issues.* 1969, 25, 41–78.

A classic review of this area, summarizing over 25 empirical studies and suggesting stern conclusions which have been very influential.

Deutscher, I. *What we say/ What we do: Sentiments and acts.* Glenview, Illinois: Scott Foresman, 1973.

A thoughtful collection of readings interspersed with insightful commentary by one of the pioneers in this area.

Calder, B., & Ross, M. *Attitudes and behavior.* Morristown, N.J.: General Learning Press, 1973.

An excellent learning module which updates previous reviews and attempts a more systematic theoretical treatment of the issues.

Brannon, R., Cyphers, G., Hesse, S., Hesselbart, S., Keane, R., Schuman, H., Vicarro, T., & Wright, D. Attitude and action: A field experiment joined to a general population survey. *American Sociological Review,* 1973, *38,* 625–36.

The largest attitude–behavior study to date and the first to use a probability sample of a natural population.

Thomas, K. (Ed.). *Attitudes and behavior: selected readings.* Baltimore, Maryland: Penguin Books, 1971.

A useful paperback collection of 21 original articles in this area.

7
Theories of Attitude Change

Thomas J. Crawford

INTRODUCTION

American social psychologists have probably devoted more of their time and effort to the study of attitude change than to any other topic. However, the study of attitude change is not conducted in a social vacuum, but is inspired to a great extent by events in the larger society. How can a voter be persuaded to switch candidates or to change his mind about a bond issue? How can a buyer be persuaded to change his preferences among several different brands of a commercial product? How can individuals who hold the "wrong" attitudes—for example, racists or opponents of public health measures—be shown the error of their ways of thinking, feeling, and behaving? Such questions have undoubtedly been behind much of the interest in attitude change, though they are not always explicitly discussed in reports of attitude change experiments published in scientific journals.

In addition to potential practical implications, research on attitude change has served as a testing ground for social psychological theories. The deductive approach to the study of attitude change, in which experiments are conducted to test hypotheses derived from general theories, has characterized most of the attitude change research conducted since the 1960s. Prior to the 1960s, attitude change researchers seemed more interested in gathering information about communication and persuasion than in testing theories of attitude change.

THE INDUCTIVE APPROACH: STUDIES OF SOURCE, MESSAGE, AND AUDIENCE EFFECTS

The beginnings of scientific research on attitudes can be traced at least as far back as the late 1920s, when techniques for constructing attitude scales were developed. A landmark of these early days is L. L. Thurstone's manifesto, "Attitudes Can Be Measured," an article published in the January 1928 issue of the *American Journal of Sociology*. The availability of the attitude measurement techniques developed by Thurstone, Likert, and others, along with the application of sampling theory to the measurement of public opinion by pollsters such as George Gallup, generated a lot of interest in attitude measurement during the 1930s. Along with this interest in measurement, there was a great deal of theoretical speculation about what was being measured.

Although social psychologists of the thirties seemed concerned primarily with defining and measuring attitudes, there was some research during this period on attitude change. However, many of the early attitude change studies lacked the rigor and precision of modern research on communication and persuasion. For that reason, most social psychologists date the beginning of systematic research on the "new scientific rhetoric" with the work of Carl Hovland and his associates during World War II. As a member of the Research Branch of the War Department's Information and Education Division, Hovland studied the impact of a series of "Why We Fight" films upon soldiers' beliefs about and attitudes toward U.S. involvement in the Second World War. There is an interesting historical contrast between the work that Hovland and many other social psychologists did on behalf of the "war effort" of the early 1940s and the work of Hovland's former students and junior colleagues on behalf of the "peace movement" 25 years later. This latter application of principles of attitude change is well illustrated by Robert P. Abelson and Philip G. Zimbardo's (1970) pamphlet, *Canvassing for Peace: A Manual for Volunteers,* and by *Vietnam and the Silent Majority: The Dove's Guide,* a book written by Milton J. Rosenberg and his colleagues (1970).

After the Second World War, Hovland returned to Yale University and launched a large-scale collaborative research program on attitude change that resulted in dozens of journal articles and a series of books by Hovland and his co-workers, including *Communication and Persuasion* (1953), *The Order of Presentation in Persuasion* (1957), and *Personality and Persuasibility* (1959). In most of his research Hovland adopted an empirical and deliberately nontheoretical approach to the study of attitude change. It was his belief that before an adequate theory of attitude change could be constructed, an empirical foundation for the theory should be established in the form of experiments that investigate the effects of variations in communicator, message, and audience characteristics upon attitude change. In adopting this strategy Hovland was adhering to a slightly modified version of political scientist Harold Lasswell's (1948) classic formula for the study of communication: *"Who* says *what* to *whom* with what *effect?"* The first three italicized terms in this formula refer to variations in the characteristics of the communicator, the message, and the audience, respectively. The "effect" most often studied by Hovland and his associates was attitude change, although other message effects, such as comprehension, memory, and subsequent behavior change, were also examined in some studies. Since most of Hovland's research was not based upon deductions from abstract theoretical principles, but was instead an inductive, empirical approach to the relationship between the major communication variables, his numerous experimental findings are not well "tied together" nor interrelated by a general theory of attitude change. Nevertheless, the cumulative result of this inductive, pretheoretical research strategy is a substantial body of information about communication and persuasion.

Communicator Effects

Hovland's contribution to our understanding of communication and persuasion is well illustrated by research on the effects of communicator or *source* credibility. Hovland defined source credibility as the perceived expertise and trustworthiness of a communicator. A well-established "source credibility effect" principle has emerged from numerous experiments. These studies have demonstrated that an identical persuasive message will produce more attitude change if it is attributed to a highly credible source than if it is attributed to a source with less credibility. For example, if two groups of subjects were to read the same argument favoring more lenient treatment for juvenile delinquents, but one group was told that the source of the message is a well-informed juvenile court judge while the other group was told that the source of the message is a former juvenile delinquent currently out on bail on a narcotics peddling charge, the subjects in the high-credibility, "judge" communicator condition could be expected to change their attitudes more in the direction advocated than subjects in the low-credibility, "former delinquent" communicator condition. It is important to note that this differential attitude change effect as a function of communicator credibility occurs even though subjects in the two communicator conditions read exactly the same message.

Source credibility effects are not only important because of their direct effects upon attitude change. The credibility of the source of a communication also has an important *interaction* effect with other communication variables. This is well illustrated by the interaction effect of source credibility upon the relationship between communication distance and opinion change.

A great deal of research has been addressed to the problem of how the amount of induced opinion change varies as a function of the size of the gap between the message receiver's initial opinion and the position taken by a communicator in a discrepant communication. For a long time there was a widely accepted maxim describing the distance–opinion change relationship. For example, Miller, in the first edition of his introductory psychology textbook, stated that:

> The size of the change you will produce in an attitude is usually proportional to the amount of change you try to produce. That is to say, if you are trying to move people in a given direction, you should advocate a position more extreme than the one you actually hold. The bigger the difference between your argument and the listener's initial position, the larger the change you are likely to produce. (Miller, 1962, p. 336)

But more recent statements of the distance–change relationship must be qualified by a reference to source credibility. Thus, for example, in 1966 Bochner and Insko demonstrated that the "proportionality effect" of communication distance upon attitude change occurs only when the communicator is highly credible. With a moderately credible communicator, there is an increase in attitude change with increased communication discrepancy only up to a point; beyond that point, as the discrepancy becomes more extreme, amount of attitude change decreases.

In Bochner and Insko's experiment, subjects who initially believed that 8 hours sleep per night are optimum for good health were exposed to written communications advocating (depending upon the distance condition the subject was in) either 8, 7, 6, 5, 4, 3, 2, 1, or 0 hours sleep per night. Belief change was linearly related to communicator–subject discrepancy for a high-credibility source (a Nobel prize-winning physiologist) and curvilinearly related to communicator–subject discrepancy for a medium-credibility source (a YMCA director). In other words, the more change the highly credible, Nobel prize-winning communicator asked for, the more change he obtained (except for the "ridiculous extreme" of advocating zero hours of sleep per night). On the other hand, the less credible communicator produced the most change when he advocated 3 or 4 hours of sleep. It should be pointed out that even in the condition in which the greatest amount of change occurred—that is, when the physiologist advocated one hour of sleep for optimum good health—few "total conversions" occurred. Most subjects in this high source credibility–high communication distance condition did not end up in complete agreement with the communicator that one hour of sleep was ideal. But, on the average, their final opinion was that slightly less than 6 hours per night was ideal—less sleep than subjects in any other condition of the experiment favored after reading the persuasive message.

This and similar experiments suggest that the positive relationship between communication distance and attitude change is most likely to occur when the communicator is highly credible. With less credible communicators, attitude change may vary as a direct positive function of amount of change advocated only with small or moderate discrepancies. With large communication discrepancies and less credible communicators, amount of induced attitude change may vary inversely with the amount of change advocated. In practical terms, this suggests that a communicator who is perceived by the audience as a trustworthy expert can "get by" with more extreme messages and, in fact, may induce more change in the desired direction if he takes an extreme stand. But a less credible communicator would be well advised to move closer to his audience's initial viewpoint and to advocate a more "moderate" stand. Of course, there are positions so extremely discrepant from the message receiver's initial beliefs that it would be unwise for even a highly credible source to advocate them if he wants to obtain maximum opinion change. For example, even the Nobel prize-winning physiologist in Bochner and Insko's experiment induced more belief change when he advocated one hour of sleep than when he advocated zero hours of sleep. Osgood and Tannenbaum, in the congruity model to be discussed later in this chapter, suggest that under conditions of such extreme discrepancy, an "incredulity" effect occurs; subjects simply refuse to believe that the source made the assertion attributed to him.

The source credibility effect has sometimes been cited as evidence of the irrationality and suggestibility of message receivers. Some have argued that since messages in high and low source credibility conditions are identical, greater attitude change in high source credibility conditions indicates an irrational "source-oriented" response to persuasive communication. This line of argument suggests that the rational message receiver will disregard the source, will be "content-oriented," and will accept or reject an argument on the basis of the logic and evidence presented in the message itself. The charge of irrationality is particularly likely to be levelled in the case of "prestige suggestion" experiments, in which subjects change their attitudes when they are merely informed that a prestigious person holds a view different from theirs, without any accompanying message to support the prestigious source's view.

Asch (1952) disagrees with the view that a message receiver who is influenced by the characteristics of a communicator is somehow more "irrational" than a message receiver who ignores communicator characteristics. Asch argues that it is eminently rational to take the identity of the source into consideration when evaluating a message, since different message sources may use identical words to express different underlying ideas. Asch has conducted research which demonstrates that a message has different meanings to its audience depending upon who delivered it. In Asch's terminology, a persuasive message is an object that a message receiver is asked to judge. Asch concludes that it is not the subject's "judgment of the object" (attitude change) that changes in different communicator conditions, but it is instead the actual "object of judgment" (the message) that is different. For example, Asch argues that it is reasonable to respond differently to the statement, "I hold it that a little rebellion, now and then, is a good thing, and as necessary in the political world as storms are in the physical," when the statement is attributed to Lenin than when it is attributed to its true author, Thomas Jefferson. Lenin and Jefferson would have attached different meanings to these words. Thus, if the reader finds that the extent of his agreement or disagreement with the statement "The average student spends two hundred and fifty dollars a year on soft drinks and tobacco and movies. . . . We need a new Spartan ethic in this country, particularly among the young" varies depending upon whether the statement is attributed to Barry Goldwater or to its real author, Ralph Nader, this differential agreement is not evidence of irrational suggestibility, according to Asch. Instead, it is a reflection of the message receiver's recognition that the "same" message is not really the same message when it is delivered by different communicators.

Another argument in defense of the rationality of a certain amount of source orientation stems from the limitations of human intelligence and memory vis-à-vis the "knowledge explosion." It is unrealistic to expect every message receiver to be a Renaissance Man, up-to-date and fully informed on every subject from literary criticism to the physiology of sleep. Since it is impossible to be well-informed on all topics, we necessarily rely on the experts for many of our beliefs and evaluations.

Credibility is not the only communicator characteristic that may influence attitude change. Hovland's former student, Herbert Kelman, has developed and tested a typology of three communicator types and their bases for producing attitude and behavior change. Kelman distinguishes among *powerful* communicators, who are able to produce overt compliance because they control the fate of the persons being influenced; *attractive* communicators, who influence those who want either to be similar to them or to gain their approval; and *credible* communicators, who may produce genuinely internalized attitude and belief changes because of their expertise and trustworthiness and because their arguments "make sense" to the persons being influenced.

In an article entitled "Beauty Is Talent," Landy and Sigall (1974) report experimental evidence supporting the importance of communicator attractiveness. The male subjects in the different experimental-treatment conditions of this study read identical messages, and all subjects were told that they were reading an essay written by a college freshman co-ed. However, "By means of a photo attached to the essay, one third of the subjects were led to believe that the writer was physically attractive and one third that she was unattractive. The remaining subjects read the essay without any information about the writer's appearance" (Landy & Sigall, 1974, p. 299). When asked to judge the intelligence and ability of the author, subjects in the attractive-author condition gave the most favorable ratings, while subjects in the unattractive-author condition rated the communicator least favorably. While it is logically possible that the male student subjects in the Landy and Sigall experiment had previously found attractive women to be more intelligent, Asch's rational-response interpretation seems less applicable to the results of this source attractiveness experiment than to the results of source credibility experiments.

Message Effects

In addition to studying communicator characteristics, Hovland and his colleagues were interested in the effect of variations in the organization and content of the message itself upon attitude change. For example, in preparing a communication, would-be persuaders might ask themselves questions like: Will an "emotional" appeal be more effective than a "rational" argument? Will "fear appeals" be more powerful than messages without fear-evoking content in persuading people to adopt preventive health practices, such as X-ray examination or vaccinations? Should a communicator explicitly state the conclusion or "moral" of his argument, or will he produce more attitude change if the conclusion is implicit in the message and the audience members draw the "obvious" conclusion of the argument for themselves?

A message organization question that has been the subject of a good deal of research by social psychologists is the question of one-sided versus two-sided arguments. To produce maximum attitude change, should you mention opposing arguments and attempt to refute them, or should you ignore counterarguments and present a one-sided message consisting only of arguments that support your conclusion? In 1934, Knight Dunlap stated that a communicator would be unwise to present the opponent's arguments, as this might suggest new ideas to the audience—ideas that are contrary to the communicator's point of view. However, the results of Hovland's World War II research presenting one-sided and two-sided arguments to U.S. soldiers indicated that Dunlap's rule applies only under certain conditions. If the audience: (1) is already favorably disposed (or at least neutral) toward the communicator's position, (2) is unaware of opposing arguments, and (3) has relatively little formal education, then a one-sided presentation may produce more attitude change. However, with better-educated audience members and with audience members who initially disagree with the communicator or who are already aware of opposing arguments, a two-sided presentation will produce more attitude change.

An additional advantage to a two-sided argument is that it may increase resistance to subsequent counterarguments. Using the analogy of the immunizing effects of vaccinations, McGuire (1964) implied that the listener is "inoculated" against later opposing communications and is better able to discount them if the original persuasive message takes these arguments into account and still reaches a positive conclusion. This seems to suggest that the audience is able to build up intellectual "antibodies," in the form of counterarguments or refutational defenses, when they hear a weakened and "watered-down" version of the other side as part of an initial two-sided communication.

In line with our earlier comments upon the relationship between attitude change research and events in the larger society, it is interesting to note that McGuire's work on increasing resistance to persuasion through two-sided arguments was apparently inspired by the "brainwashing" of U.S. prisoners of war during the Korean War. A Congressional Committee investigating the experiences of U.S. POWs recommended more training in U.S. history and civics as a means of making POWs in subsequent wars more resistant to anti-American and pro-Communist arguments. But McGuire suggested that the U.S. soldiers would have been more resistant to Communist propaganda if they had previously heard pro-Communist arguments along with refutations of such arguments. As it was, without the immunizing effect of two-sided anti-Communist messages, some soldiers apparently changed their attitudes in an anti-U.S., pro-Communist direction when confronted with arguments that they had never heard before and thus had had no practice in refuting. McGuire suggests that cultural truisms that the message receiver has never heard challenged are particularly vulnerable to change through counterargument. Just as an organism raised in a germ-free environment may be particularly susceptible to disease when it is confronted with a virus or bacteria, so beliefs that have never been challenged may be particularly susceptible to change through persuasive argument.

In discussing the possible applicability of principles emerging from research on the effects of one-sided versus two-sided communications to family planning communication programs, Berelson asked, "Now how can we apply the Hovland experiments to family planning? In my opinion we cannot make much use of them. In the first place, on ethical grounds you should present both sides" (Berelson, 1964, p. 104).

If we conclude that two-sided arguments should be presented, for ethical and/or effectiveness reasons, we are then confronted with a new and related question: At what point in the message should the opposing arguments be introduced and refuted? Will their effect be less if they are discussed early or late in the presentation? Or, more generally, if an issue is being debated, is it better to have the first word (primacy effect) or the last word (recency effect)?

The practical implications of this problem of order of presentation for criminal court cases and political debates are readily apparent. In 1925, Floyd Lund formulated a "Law of Primacy in Persuasion" stating that the side of an issue presented first will have greater effectiveness than the side presented subsequently. Later research has not always confirmed this law.

An interesting approach to the problem of the effects of various sequences of information was the study by Luchins on forming impressions of personality, reported in Hovland's book, *The Order of Presentation in Persuasion*. Luchins (1957a, b) presented subjects with one paragraph describing the amiable and outgoing behavior (stopping to chat with friends and the like) of a young man named Jim. This was followed by a second paragraph which described Jim behaving in a somewhat withdrawn manner (sitting in a cafe alone, crossing the street to avoid meeting an attractive female acquaintance, and so on). Another group of subjects heard the two paragraphs in the reverse order. Both groups were then asked to give descriptions of Jim's personality and to predict his behavior in a variety of hypothetical situations. The results showed a clear primacy effect. Those subjects who were given the extroverted paragraph first saw Jim as sociable, outgoing, and popular, while the other groups described him as shy, lonely, and quiet. These results are in accord with common-sense notions about the importance of first impressions. An interesting finding of this experiment was that over a third of the subjects stated that they had not been aware of any inconsistencies or contradictions in Jim's behavior. Luchins interpreted his results as due to "set" or *Einstellung,* contending that the material presented first established a frame of reference into which later information was fitted. With this in mind, he did a follow-up study attempting to minimize the effects of first impressions by techniques which had been shown to reduce the influence of set in problem-solving experiments. Thus, one group was run under conditions similar to those in the first study, another group was forewarned about the dangers of first impressions, and a third group performed an arithmetic task between presentations of the two paragraphs. The primacy effect occurred only in the first group; for the others, the second paragraph exerted the greatest influence on impressions (recency effect).

Research on primacy and recency effects in

persuasion is an ongoing process in social psychology, and as yet no definitive and complete statement of the conditions under which one or the other effect will occur is possible. As Norman Anderson puts it: "The attitude change literature as a whole presents a mixed picture of primacy and recency with no clear pattern" (Anderson & Farkas, 1973, p. 92).

Audience Effects

Is there a general "trait" of persuasibility? Are some individuals generally more easily persuaded than others, regardless of the topic or the characteristics of the communicator and the message? Many psychologists have rejected the notion that persuasibility is a general trait and have argued that persuasibility should be thought of as a trait of the situation rather than of the person.

Hovland and his associates present evidence which indicates that there is a personality factor of general persuasibility. They postulate a trait of general persuasibility in its "barest psychological essence"—the tendency to conform not because of who the communicator is, what he says, or how he says it, but because conformity itself brings satisfaction.

In one set of studies described in *Personality and Persuasibility,* the experimenters systematically varied the topic of communication, the identity of the source, the style of presentation, and other factors in a "persuasibility test" consisting of ten communications. The same subjects participated in all ten of these attitude change experiments. In support of the notion of a general trait of personality, Janis and Field (1959), two of Hovland's collaborators on the personality and persuasibility project, found that subjects who changed their attitudes in one communication experiment were also likely to change in other experiments, whereas subjects who resisted change in one communication experiment also tended to resist change in other experiments.

After establishing (to their satisfaction) the existence of a general trait of persuasibility, the Yale researchers then devote most of the remainder of their volume to discussing individual differences in this trait. In this research, a number of characteristics differentiated the more persuasible from the less persuasible. A greater overall susceptibility to influence on the part of females was a consistent finding, although this difference did not emerge in the case of the younger children in studies by Abelson and Lesser (1959) reported in the same volume. The authors speculate that the cultural sex role for males is less definite in prescribing how to react to persuasive influences. More recent studies of sex differences in persuasibility have not always found females to be more persuasible than males, perhaps because of changes in the role of women during the past few decades.

Related to the overall sex difference in persuasibility was the fact that there were numerous significant relationships between personality factors and persuasibility for males but no significant personality relationships with persuasibility for the female subjects. For example, a significant positive relationship between a self-report of richness of fantasy and persuasibility was obtained for male subjects but not for females. The relationship between hostility and persuasibility was especially interesting. Persons who described themselves as having frequent unpleasant emotional reactions such as anger and irritability were more persuasible. However, when hostility was assessed from observations of overt behavior rather than self-report, there was an inverse relationship with the tendency for opinion conformity. Thus, those who see themselves as hostile were more persuasible, while those who were seen by others as hostile were less persuasible.

One of the clearest findings that the Yale group unearthed was an inverse relationship between persuasibility and self-esteem among male subjects. Perhaps when a male message receiver was confronted with a counterargument, he implicitly asked himself: "Am I correct, or is the communicator correct?" In this internal debate, or contest of credibilities, the message receiver with less credibility (that is, with low self-esteem) was more likely to yield and to defer to the communicator's judgment than a self-assured message receiver with high self-esteem. Thus, there appeared to be a self-credibility effect as well as a source credibility effect in communication and persuasion.

Unfortunately for this line of reasoning, later research has not provided unequivocal support for the notion of an inverse relationship between self-esteem and persuasibility. Indeed, some researchers have found the opposite relationship, with high-self-esteem subjects exhibiting more attitude change. Further muddying the waters, still other researchers have found curvilinear, "nonmonotonic" relationships between self-esteem and persuasibility, with those with intermediate levels of self-esteem being more persuasible than either high- or low-self-esteem subjects. McGuire's (1972) information-processing paradigm may help to integrate these and other apparently contradictory findings in research on the relationship between persuasibility and personality traits. As McGuire points out, thinking of attitude change as a single-step event is an oversimplified characterization of the processing of persuasive messages. For some purposes, it is more fruitful to think of attitude change as occurring in several steps or stages, including attending to, comprehending, and yielding to a message. McGuire hypothesizes that a personal trait such as self-esteem or intelligence might have opposite effects on different stages in the persuasive message processing sequence. For example, if more intelligent people are better informed and better able to refute persuasive arguments, we might expect intelligence to be negatively related to "yielding." But what about the earlier step of "comprehending" the message? A complex argument advocating a particular anti-inflationary fiscal policy might be more readily comprehended by more intelligent audience members. In general, it appears that intelligence (and knowledge) may be positively related to comprehension and negatively related to yielding. Partly because higher intelligence is often associated with higher self-esteem, McGuire suggests that self-esteem may also be positively related to comprehension and negatively related to yielding. In any event, the complexity and rationality of the message itself appears to be a variable that must be considered before precise predictions about the relationship between personality and persuasibility can be made.

THE FUNCTIONS AND STRUCTURE OF BELIEF SYSTEMS

Hovland's inductive and pretheoretical approach to the study of attitude change, and subsequent studies in the tradition he helped establish, have provided us with a wealth of information about the effects of variation in the characteristics of the communicator, the message, and the audience upon attitude change. In giving advice to practitioners, social psychologists have often drawn upon this material. But because the findings are not interrelated by any general theory or principle, they "lack something of intellectual interest," in the words of one influential social psychologist (Brown, 1965, p. 549). This may be one reason why social psychological studies of attitude change took a more theoretical turn during the 1960s. This shift is most clearly illustrated by the cognitive consistency theories of attitude change which we will consider later in this chapter.

The consistency theories attempt to describe the *process* of attitude change. They are primarily concerned with the dynamics of change in belief systems and attempt to answer the question: How does attitude change occur? But before concerning ourselves with the process models which attempt to describe the dynamics of attitude change, we should briefly consider two prior questions, the question of *structure* and the question of *function*. The question of structure, put simply, asks: *What* is an attitude—or, more generally, *What* are the elements of a belief system? How shall we conceptualize and define attitudes? What taxonomy or set of theoretical terms shall we use to describe the elements of a belief system? The question of function, on the other hand, asks: *Why* do we have beliefs and attitudes? Of what use to a man are his attitudes? What needs or functions do attitudes and beliefs serve for the individual personality? Let us first consider this question of functions.

The Functions of Belief Systems: Pleasure and Problem Solving

In order to understand belief systems, it is important to determine what needs attitudes and beliefs serve for the individuals holding them. Katz (1960) has argued that unless we know the psychological needs which are served by an attitude, we are in a poor position to predict the conditions under which the attitude will change. Katz and other social scientists have suggested a number of functions which belief systems may serve for the individual personality. Perhaps a loose interpretation of Freud's distinction between the "pleasure principle" and the "reality principle" may serve as a useful way of organizing our thinking about the functions of attitudes and beliefs.

Explanations of the development and change of attitudes that emphasize the maintenance and enhancement of self-esteem could be included under the general category of pleasure functions. As Bruner pointed out: "If we have learned anything in the last half-century of psychology, it is that man has powerful and exquisite capacities for defending himself against violations of his cherished self-image" (Bruner, 1965, pp. 150–151). An interesting correlational study by Rosenberg (1967) seems in line with Bruner's contention. Rosenberg found that people tend to believe that those traits and abilities in which they excel are more important than traits and abilities on which they consider themselves average or below average.

Another way in which adopting an attitude or belief may serve to bolster self-esteem is through identification with a positive reference group or person. By adopting an attitude held by a group or person he admires, the individual may increase his perceived similarity to the admired group or person and thereby bolster his self-esteem. A classic study of the effects of reference groups upon attitudes was conducted by Newcomb at Bennington College during the 1930s. Most students enrolled at Bennington came from economically privileged families whose social and political attitudes were conservative. By contrast, the faculty at Bennington was predominantly politically liberal and generally shared the conviction that "one of the foremost duties of the college was to acquaint its somewhat oversheltered students with the nature of their contemporary social world." It is not surprising that the college climate of ideas had its impact upon the students. Newcomb reports that:

> The general trend of attitude change for the total group is from freshman conservatism to senior nonconservatism (as the term was commonly applied to the issues toward which attitudes were measured). During the 1936 presidential election, for example, 62 percent of the freshmen and only 14 percent of the juniors and seniors "voted" for the Republican candidate, 29 percent of freshmen and 54 percent of juniors and seniors for Roosevelt, and 9 percent of freshmen as compared with 30 percent of juniors and seniors for the Socialist or Communist candidates. (Newcomb, 1965, p. 216)

Of course, not all Bennington students were equally influenced by the politically liberal college environment, and Newcomb's analyses of individual differences in attitude change are particularly revealing. These analyses indicate that the students who changed most in a liberal direction were those who became most involved in college activities and for whom the college community served as a positive reference group. On the other hand, students whose attitudes were least influenced by the college community looked to their families and home communities as the appropriate groups with whom to check out and validate their political attitudes and beliefs.

While the role of *positive* reference persons and groups in molding social attitudes is well recognized, it is also important to note that an individual may bolster his self-esteem by adopting an attitude that sharply differentiates and contrasts him with the views held by a *negatively* evaluated person or group. Psychologists also have been intrigued by the irrational sources of beliefs and attitudes. However, most would agree that if human beings are to survive, the "pictures in their heads" must bear some correspondence to "the world outside" (Lippmann, 1922). Thus, Katz (1960) has postulated a "knowledge" function of belief systems; and Smith, Bruner, and White (1956) speak of the "object appraisal" or reality-testing function, whereby our beliefs and attitudes reflect our experience and thus enable us to size up and cope with objects and events in the environment.

In the late 1950s and early 1960s, when the influence of the cognitive consistency models became obvious, these theories were generally greeted as illustrations of the knowledge or reality-testing function of belief systems. It is true that in their emphasis upon a need for consistency in our belief systems, these models appear to place a heavy emphasis upon "rationality." However, as several balance theorists have pointed out, their theories deal not with the need for *logical* consistency, but with the need for *psychological* consistency. An internally consistent belief system is not necessarily an accurate and veridical representation of external reality. As we shall see in our discussion of consistency theories, the consistency need is sometimes paid for by bias and distortion.

A rational basis for attitude formation is the development of positive attitudes toward people and situations that give us pleasure and negative attitudes toward those that give us pain. In laboratory experiments, this classical conditioning of attitudes has sometimes been demonstrated with the use of electric shock. For example, Zanna, Kiesler, and Pilkonis (1970) found that words paired with the onset or beginning of shock came to be evaluated more negatively, while those paired with the offset or end of shock were evaluated more positively. Interestingly, the shock-induced attitudes generalized to other words similar in meaning to those that were experimentally paired with shock onset or offset.

Still more rational—or at least cognitive—ways in which beliefs and attitudes may serve reality-testing and coping needs can be best illustrated in conjunction with a description of the *structure* of belief systems. At this point, then, we will take up the structural question: What are the elements of a belief system?

The Structure of Belief Systems

It is useful to think of a human belief system as consisting of three interrelated elements: attitudes, concepts, and beliefs. For our present purposes we will define an *attitude* simply as a favorable or unfavorable evaluation of a concept. The most obvious "knowledge" or coping function of attitudes is to prepare the organism to respond appropriately (favorably or unfavorably) to the attitude object. To operationally define an attitude, social psychologists often ask a respondent to rate a person, a group, or a policy along a good-bad dimension or to indicate approval or disapproval. These measurement techniques are described in Chapter 6.

As the second basic element of a belief system we propose the term *concept* or *cognitive category*. Cognitive theorists define a concept as a set of rules for classifying a stimulus input into a preexisting cognitive category. These decision rules are the defining attributes of the category. This definition is perhaps most easily illustrated in the case of physical objects. When confronted with an object such as a tangerine, we are able to classify or categorize the object as a member of a class of objects that we have learned to conceptualize through experience. This act of categorization is accomplished by comparing the object in question with the defining attributes of a particular category. These defining attributes, such as the shape, color, texture, and taste of the tangerine, serve as a set of "decision rules" that enable us to correctly identify the object as a tangerine. Similarly, we invoke the defining attributes of our concept "police officer" to decide whether a uniformed man should be placed in that category or in some other category such as soldier, chauffeur, or privately employed guard.

The third and final element in the cognitive structure of our minimal person is *beliefs*. Beliefs are perceived relationships between cognitive categories or concepts. Beliefs serve a problem-solving function by enabling us to think in terms of causes and effects, such as "leads to" or "prevents." This definition of beliefs as links between concepts is most easily illustrated in the case of relationships between people, as in Jack loves Jill or Iago envies Othello. Although there are many different kinds of perceived relationships between concepts, in this chapter we will be concerned primarily with positive beliefs such as "likes," "advocates," "helps," and "brings about," and with negative beliefs such as "dislikes," "opposes," "hinders," and "prevents."

THE DYNAMICS OF CHANGE IN BELIEF SYSTEMS: COGNITIVE CONSISTENCY THEORIES

Theories of attitude change dominated the attention of social psychologists during the 1960s. These theories were concerned primarily with the dynamics of change in belief systems. By using a limited number of abstract principles, they attempted to account for the impact of persuasive communication and other events upon beliefs and attitudes. While social psychologists generally agree that belief systems may serve several different functions, most of the models of attitude change that dominated social psychological research during the decade of the 1960s were based upon one hypothesized need: the need for consistency. Heider (1946) is generally given credit for the first systematic statement of the need for consistency in belief systems, but variations of Heider's basic notions are represented in several different consistency models.

While they differ in important respects, each consistency theory has in common the notion that human beings are troubled by the recognition of incongruous, "nonfitting" relationships among their beliefs, attitudes, and behaviors. When such inconsistencies are recognized, the individual is said to experience discomfort, and cognitive processes are set in motion that attempt to restore consistency. A great deal of research has been conducted which purports to demonstrate the existence of a need for cognitive consistency, but relatively little has been said about why human beings should have such a need. However, three possible explanations have been advanced. In the first place, it has been suggested that there may be an inherent need for the "good gestalt"—for balance and symmetry in belief systems as well as in external patterns of stimuli. A second alternative follows from the possibility that imbalance in the mind may inhibit decisive behavior. An individual with equally weighted positive and negative beliefs about the consequences of some action may be unable to act, suspended forever between two alternative choices, as in the fable about the donkey between two bales of hay. Finally, it has been argued that we are socially conditioned to be consistent in our beliefs and behaviors. We are criticized for inconsistencies in our statements and labelled as "hypocrites" when our actions fail to match our stated ideals. It is possible that some combination of these processes accounts for our apparent need for cognitive consistency.

The five consistency models that we will consider in this chapter are affective–cognitive consistency theory, balance theory, the congruity model, Abelson's conception of modes of resolving belief dilemmas, and the theory of cognitive dissonance.

Affective–Cognitive Consistency Theory

Rosenberg's affective–cognitive consistency theory deals with the relationship between an individual's attitude toward a single concept (the attitude object) and the set of beliefs or relationships that the individual perceives between that focal concept and other concepts. In Rosenberg's theory, the attitude object might be any concept, such as a person, a group, an event, or a policy. Rosenberg postulates that our attitude toward a given concept is consistent with our beliefs about that concept. In general, concepts that are seen as leading to positive consequences and preventing negative consequences are valued positively. Conversely, if an individual believes that the attitude object blocks the attainment of positively valued goals and leads to negatively valued consequences, then, according to Rosenberg's theory, the attitude object will be evaluated negatively. Earlier writers expressed hypotheses similar to Rosenberg's, and later theorists (e.g., Ajzen & Fishbein, 1973; Wyer, 1973) have developed quantified extensions of Rosenberg's theory. However, as Rosenberg's work is a straightforward and representative statement of the attitude-belief consistency ideas, we will briefly describe his research in order to illustrate those ideas.

To test his theory that attitude toward a concept is consistent with beliefs about that concept, Rosenberg used a "beliefs × goals" procedure involving three measures. First, he obtained each subject's attitude toward a particular attitude object, in this case: "allowing members of the Communist party to address the public." He next obtained both a measure of goals and a measure of beliefs. The subjects evaluated a number of general goals (such as "having the value of property well protected" and "people having the right to participate in decisions which will affect them") along a continuum ranging from: The goal "Gives me maximum satisfaction" (+10) to "Gives me maximum dissatisfaction" (−10). The final measure in this initial test of Rosenberg's theory was of the subjects' beliefs about the consequences of the attitude object, the policy of "allowing members of the Communist Party to address the public." Subjects indicated what they perceived to be the relationship between allowing Communists to address the public and each of the goals they had previously evaluated. In this belief measurement procedure, subjects judged the efficacy of the attitude object for obtaining or blocking each goal along a continuum ranging from: "The goal (for example, "having the value of property well protected") is completely attained by allowing admitted Communists to address the public" (+5) to (the goal) "is completely blocked by allowing admitted Communists to address the public" (−5). Finally, Rosenberg derived a single summary measure of beliefs about the attitude object by multiplying the strength of belief times the value of the goal for each of the goals perceived to be related to the attitude object. After belief-certainty times goal-importance products for each of the goals were obtained, a single index of beliefs about the consequences of allowing Communists to address the public was computed by algebraically summing all the products.

As Rosenberg predicted, the summary measure of beliefs representing the perceived instrumental consequences of "Communists addressing the public" was closely related to the measure of attitude toward allowing members of the Communist Party to address the public. Those who approved of this policy believed that it led to positive consequences and prevented negative consequences. Those who disapproved believed the opposite. Subsequent research has further supported Rosenberg's hypothesis that our attitudes toward a concept are consistent with our beliefs about what the concept leads to and prevents. For example, Rosenberg replicated the study just described, but using "allowing Negroes to move into white neighborhoods" as the attitude object, with results that parallel those of the study of beliefs about attitude toward allowing Communists to address the public.

Rosenberg's basic notion that beliefs about a concept are consistent with attitudes toward that concept can be tested in a more open-ended way. That is, instead of being presented with a predetermined list of goals, the subjects can be asked to describe the consequences of an attitude object in their own words. A study using an open-ended procedure in which the respondent was asked to express her beliefs in her own words instead of in terms of the researcher's list of possible consequences was conducted by Crawford (1973). In this study,

FIGURE 7-1. **Rosenberg's affective-cognitive consistency theory.**

According to affective-cognitive consistency theory, an individual's attitude toward an activity is closely related to his beliefs about the instrumental relationship of the activity to the attainment or blocking of his valued goals. Rosenberg developed a measure of goals ranging from +10 ("gives me maximum satisfaction") to −10 ("gives me maximum disatisfaction") and a measure of instrumental beliefs ranging from +5 (definitely leads to) to −5 (definitely prevents).

If "birth control" is the attitude object, and Mr. Smith believes that birth control (A) probably leads to (+2) less sexual pleasure (−5),
(B) definitely leads to (+5) smaller families (+3),
(C) almost certainly prevents (−4) unwanted pregnancies (−4),
(D) definitely prevents (−5) a natural and religious life (+5),
the theory would predict that Mr. Smith's attitude toward birth control would be:

____ strongly favorable (algebraic sum of products is higher than +10)
____ mildly favorable (sum between +1 and +10)
____ neutralized at a zero point of ambivalence
____ mildly unfavorable (between −1 and −10)
____ strongly unfavorable (lower than −10)

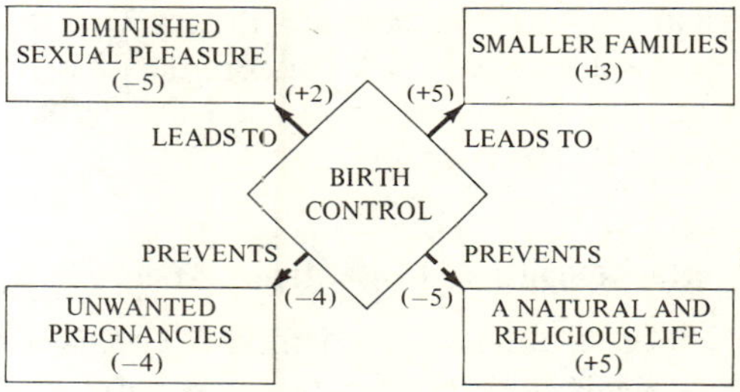

```
   DIMINISHED                    SMALLER FAMILIES
 SEXUAL PLEASURE                      (+3)
      (−5)
            (+2)        (+5)
       LEADS TO         LEADS TO
                BIRTH
               CONTROL
       PREVENTS         PREVENTS
            (−4)        (−5)
    UNWANTED                    A NATURAL AND
   PREGNANCIES                  RELIGIOUS LIFE
      (−4)                          (+5)
```

"birth control" was the attitude object, and the results strongly support Rosenberg's notion that attitude toward a concept is consistent with beliefs about the concept. For illustrative purposes, a hypothetical system of four beliefs about the consequences of birth control is depicted in Figure 7-1. The reader may want to test her or his understanding of the mechanics of Rosenberg's attitude-beliefs consistency model by attempting to answer the question posed in Figure 7-1.

To some extent, the hypotheses and the measurement techniques that Rosenberg has developed appear to represent an empirical demonstration of common-sense notions about the causes of attitudes. "Obviously," people favor persons and policies that they believe will lead to positive consequences and prevent negative consequences and, equally obviously, people will oppose persons and policies that they believe will lead to negative consequences and prevent positive consequences. Persuasive arguments in which attempts are made to change beliefs about the consequences of some activity or policy implicitly assume the affective–cognitive consistency principle. But there is another side to Rosenberg's theory that presents a picture of man as less rational (and therefore, to most psychologists, more interesting) than the "hedonic calculator" we have been depicting.

Rosenberg suggests that since an individual's attitude toward an event or policy tends to be consistent with his beliefs about the event or policy, one way to change his attitude is to change his beliefs about the perceived consequences of the event or policy. But, in addition, Rosenberg has suggested that the reverse causal process may also occur; a direct change in attitude may lead to a change in beliefs. How can attitudes be changed directly? The technique Rosenberg (1960) used for directly manipulating attitudes was post-hypnotic suggestion. Deeply hypnotized subjects were told that their attitude toward "the U.S. policy of giving aid to foreign nations" would be reversed (from positive to negative, or vice versa) and that upon awakening from the hypnotic trance they would have no memory of the affect-reversal suggestion having been made until the presentation of a prearranged amnesia-removing signal. As expected, the subjects changed their attitude in the direction of the hypnotic suggestion. But more interestingly, subjects also changed their beliefs about the consequences of U.S. foreign aid. For example, subjects with originally negative attitudes toward this policy who were hypnotically induced to have positive attitudes changed their minds and decided that they were less certain that foreign aid led to negative consequences or that it prevented the attainment of positive goals. This cognitive realignment was in support of the attitude that was changed directly through hypnotic reversal. Thus, Rosenberg's theory of consistency between beliefs and attitudes suggests that man is both a rational and a rationalizing creature.

Balance Theories

Whereas Rosenberg's affective–cognitive consistency theory addresses itself to the relationship between an attitude toward a single concept and beliefs about what that concept leads to or prevents, most consistency theories have been concerned with inconsistent or imbalanced relationships between two or more concepts or "attitude objects." In this section of the chapter we will illustrate the principles of cognitive balance by considering perceived relationships between a communicator, who will be represented by the letter C, and some person or policy, which will be designated by the letter X. The hypothetical individuals whose belief systems we will depict may have either a positive or a negative attitude toward the communicator and either a positive or a negative attitude toward the issue.

Let us imagine that our hypothetical individual is confronted with a written or verbal communication in which a liked or disliked communicator comes out in favor of or in opposition to some issue toward which the individual receiving the message has an initially positive or negative attitude. There are eight possible communications situations in this simple balance model in which we assume that a communicator, who is positively or negatively evaluated by the message receiver, either favors or

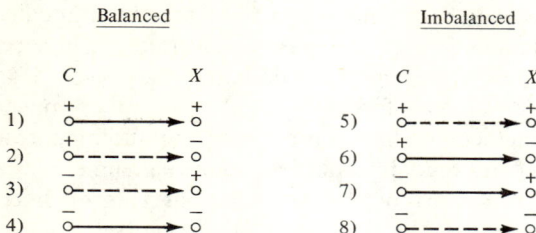

FIGURE 7-2. Representation of cognitive balance and imbalance that occurs when a positively (+) or negatively (−) valued communicator (C) makes a favorable (undotted line) or an unfavorable (dotted line) assertion about some concept (X) toward which the message receiver has an initially favorable (+) or unfavorable (−) attitude.

opposes some person or policy that is positively or negatively evaluated by the message receiver. These eight possible situations are depicted in Figure 7-2.

The four situations (1–4) depicted in the left-hand column in Figure 7-2 represent cognitively balanced configurations. However, the four situations (5–8) depicted in the right-hand column of Figure 7-2 all represent cognitively imbalanced configurations. According to balance theory, the individual is disturbed by the recognition of cognitive inconsistency and is motivated to change his belief system in a direction that will reduce imbalance. Consider, for example, the belief dilemma that is generated by hearing a liked or respected communicator come out in favor of a policy that the message receiver opposes (situation 6). How might this cognitive configuration be altered in the direction of increased balance? The three most obvious modes of resolving this or any of the other belief dilemmas depicted in the right-hand column of Figure 7-2 are: (1) change attitude toward Communicator (C); (2) change attitude toward Issue (X); (3) reverse or deny belief about the "favors" or "opposes" relationship between the communicator and the issue. In the case of situation 6, this would involve either: Derogating the communicator (C changes from + to −), attitude change (X changes from − to +), or belief change (relationship between C and X changes from + to −). This last resolution could be achieved if the message receiver misperceives the stand the communicator has taken on the issue. To the degree that a communicator is very forthright, direct, and unambiguous in his condemnation or support of some policy, it is difficult for the message receiver to misperceive the communicator's stand. Fortunately for those who prefer to see themselves in agreement about election issues with the political candidates they favor, it is not uncommon for candidates to take ambiguous positions on such issues.

This elementary balance model provides a useful conceptual tool for tying together a great many hitherto seemingly unrelated studies of the effects of persuasive communication. The results of hundreds of experiments on attitude change, source derogation, and message misperception that might otherwise be viewed as fragmented and unrelated empirical findings can be viewed from the perspective of balance theory as manifestations of a single need, the need to perceive ourselves in agreement with those we like and in disagreement with those we dislike. Furthermore, many of the situations depicted in Figure 7-2 have "phenomenological validity" for those of us who have experienced the discomfort involved in disagreements with a friend or a respected public figure. Balance theory may help to make past instances in which we have changed our attitude toward an issue or a communicator (or have observed others make such changes) more understandable. I urge the reader to apply this model to his own experience, not only for a possible gain in self-insight, but also because this mental exercise of "application to personal experience" may result in a better understanding of both the value and the limitations of balance theory.

Two limitations of the version of balance theory we have presented are particularly troublesome. In the first place, there is a lack of precision in the model. Assuming that a message receiver hears someone he likes and respects express a favorable view of a policy that the message receiver initially opposes, how will the message receiver respond to this imbalance-generating situation? Will he derogate the communicator, misperceive the message, or change his attitude? Nothing said so far gives us a basis for predicting which of the three responses will be the preferred mode for restoring balance. If, as seems likely, two or more of the responses will be used in conjunction, to what extent will each of the several responses be employed?

A second major difficulty with the version of balance theory that we have presented so far, and one that the reader who has attempted to apply the theory to his own experience may have noted, is that there are other possible responses to communication-produced imbalance in addition to source derogation, message misperception, and attitude change.

Attitude theorists have recognized these and other problems with the various formulations of the consistency idea. In the next two sections we will consider two consistency models which attempt to cope with the problem of imprecision and the problem of the many possible ways of restoring cognitive balance. First, we will consider the most precise of the cognitive consistency theories.

The Congruity Model

Osgood and Tannenbaum's (1955) congruity model is the formulation of the consistency idea that best deserves the label "scientific theory," in the sense that its theoretical terms are defined by empirical operations and in the sense that the theory makes precise and testable predictions. Congruity theory deals with the same situation described in our account of the basic balance model. A message receiver is confronted with a situation in which a communicator whom the message receiver likes or dislikes delivers a message either in favor of or against some person or policy toward which the message receiver has an initially favorable or unfavorable attitude. Thus, the basic situation dealt with by congruity theory is that previously depicted in Figure 7-2.

However, congruity theory differs from the version of balance theory depicted in Figure 7-2 in several important respects. In the first place, the *degree* of positive or negative affect that the message receiver feels toward both the communicator and the issue is specified in congruity theory. This assignment of a specific positive or negative numerical value to both the communicator and the issue is achieved by a precommunication measurement of the message receiver's evaluation of the communicator and the issue. The *semantic differential* attitude scale is used for this purpose. Before being confronted with a communication linking the communicator and the issue, the message receiver rates both along a scale of evaluative antonyms, such as "good-bad," "fair-unfair," or "clean-dirty." Each pair of evaluative antonyms is separated by seven underlined steps or spaces. Numerical values ranging from $+3$ to -3 are assigned to each of these seven steps. Thus, for example, if a subject asked to evaluate Henry Kissinger checked the space three steps away from the "good" end of the good-bad antonym scale, his attitude toward Kissinger would be said to be $+1$. An illustration of such an evaluation is given below:
HENRY KISSINGER:

Good ___ ___ X ___ ___ ___ ___ Bad

(Actually, this is an oversimplification of the measurement procedure, since the subject's rating of Kissinger along several other 7-point evaluative antonym scales would also be taken into consideration in computing his attitude toward Kissinger.) A similar method would be employed to arrive at a measure of the subject's attitude toward the issue—for example, "Soviet-American detente" or "the pardon of Richard Nixon."

Once his attitudes toward both the communicator and the issue have been obtained, the subject in a congruity experiment is told that the communicator opposes or favors the issue. If the message indicates a positive association between a communicator and an issue that are evaluated by the message receiver as identical both in sign (+ or −) and degree of polarity (0, 1, 2, or 3), there is no incongruity. This would be the case, for example, if both the communicator and the policy were initially evaluated by the message receiver at +1 and the communicator delivered a message in support of the policy. Similarly, if the message indicates a negative association between a communicator and an issue that are opposite in sign but identical in degree of polarity (e.g., communicator at +2 opposes issue evaluated at −2), the subject presumably experiences no incongruity and, consequently, no need to change his attitude toward either the source or the issue. However, all other combinations of evaluated sources and concepts are, by definition, "incongruous." It is important to note that a message could be balanced but not congruous. For example, if the communicator is evaluated at +2 and a particular policy at +1, an assertion positively linking the communicator and the policy would be balanced, but not congruous.

The most important distinguishing feature of the congruity model is its precise prediction of the outcome of situations operationally defined as incongruous. Basically, this prediction is that the message receiver will change his attitude toward both the communicator and the issue, and the amount of change will be inversely proportional to the polarization or extremity of the initial attitude. The latter prediction is a formal statement of a principle that is supported by both common sense and empir-

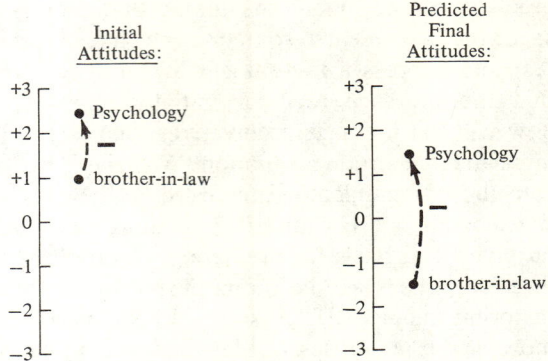

FIGURE 7-3. Depiction of hypothetical situation of incongruity generated by hearing brother-in-law (initially evaluated at +1) criticize the student message receiver's major, Psychology (initially evaluated by the student at +2.5). Congruity theory predicts that attitudes toward both concepts will change, and that attitude change will be inversely related to initial polarization. In this instance, congruity theory predicts that the student's evaluation of "Psychology" will move one step to +1.5 and his evaluation of his "brother-in-law" will drop two and one half steps to −1.5.

ical research: Extremely favorable and extremely unfavorable attitudes are more resistant to change than less extreme attitudes.

An example may help to illustrate both the precise outcomes predicted by the theory and the "more polarized concepts change less" principle. Suppose that a college student who is majoring in psychology hears his brother-in-law strongly condemn psychologists and their activities. Let us further suppose that the student's attitude toward the field of psychology is quite positive, say +2.5 on the semantic differential scale, while his attitude toward his brother-in-law is only a mildly favorable +1. This situation is depicted in Figure 7-3. What will happen to the student's attitude toward the field of psychology and to his attitude toward his brother-in-law according to the congruity model?

To answer these questions, we first look at either of the two concepts *separately* and ask ourselves where the person's attitude toward that concept should be in order to achieve congruity. The *difference* in scale steps between the present position of either concept and the scale location that would be in perfect congruity with the other concept is equal to the total amount of attitude change that will occur. Stated more formally:

1. The total amount of attitude change that will occur toward both the communicator and the issue is equal to the distance between the present attitude position of either concept and the hypothetical "congruent position" for that concept.

But how are we to determine the "hypothetical congruent position" for either of the two concepts, the communicator or the issue? Consider only the student's attitude toward the field of psychology. Assume for the moment that attitude toward brother-in-law is immutable and permanently stuck at +1. Where along the 7-point evaluative continuum should the student's attitude toward psychology be if it is to be in perfect congruity with attitude toward this in-law who has expressed negative views about psychology? Osgood and Tannenbaum's rule for answering this question is:

2. Whenever one concept is associated with another by an assertion, its (hypothetical) congruent position along the evaluative dimension is always equal in degree of polarization to the other concept and in either the same (positive assertion) or opposite (negative assertion) evaluative direction.

Since in this example we are dealing with a negative assertion, the scale position for "psychology" that would be congruent with the +1 evaluation of brother-in-law is −1. Minus one is the position along the evaluative dimension that is equal in degree of polarization to, and in the opposite evaluative direction from, the attitude toward the brother-in-law critic of psychology.

The field of psychology is presently evaluated at +2.5; but, as we have seen, it would have to be at −1 to be perfectly congruent with the in-law message source now at +1. Looking at Figure 7-3 and counting the number of steps separating the concept "psychology" at +2.5 from its position of hypothetical congruity of −1, we can see that "psychology" is three and one-half scale steps away from what would be its congruent position if the attitude toward the brother-in-law could not be changed. Three and one-half scale steps represents the total amount of attitude change that both the communicator and the concept will undergo. In other words, attitude change toward psychology plus attitude change toward the brother-in-law will add up to three and one-half scale steps.

We could have arrived at this same "total attitude change" value of three and one-half scale steps by computing the difference between the present attitude toward the brother-in-law and his hypothetical position of maximum congruence. This time we would ask where the brother-in-law concept should be placed along the 7-point evaluative continuum to be in perfect congruity with psychology. Again assuming for the moment that the other concept ("psychology") cannot be moved from its attitudinal position of +2.5, rule number two tells us that brother-in-law should be evaluated at −2.5 to be in perfect congruity with the field of psychology, which he has criticized. There are three and one-half scale steps between −2.5 and brother-in-law's initial evaluative position of +1. Again, we would have arrived at the same "total attitude change" answer, three and one-half scale steps. As the number of steps between the present position and the hypothetical position of maximum congruence is always the same for both the communicator and the topic, it is only necessary to compute this value for one of the two concepts.

Having determined that the amount of change toward the communicator plus the amount of change toward the topic will add up to three and one-half steps, we must next ask how this total amount of attitude change will be distributed between the two concepts:

3. When a communicator and a topic are associated incongruously, the message receiver will change his attitude toward both the communicator and the topic. Both concepts will move in the direction of their hypothetical "congruent position," but the amount of movement each concept will exhibit will be inversely proportional to its degree of polarization.

The mechanics of applying the third rule are slightly more complex than those of the previous two principles. In this case we predict that the message receiver's attitude toward psychology will move in the direction of its hypothetical congruent position (-1), but it will change only one step—a proportion that is equivalent to the degree of polarization of the other concept, the brother-in-law. Thus, "psychology" will end up at $+1.5$ according to the theory. Conversely, the message receiver's attitude toward the brother-in-law will also move in the direction of its hypothetical congruent position, but this will be a change of two and one-half steps, again a value that is equivalent to the degree of polarization of the other concept, psychology. Thus, we move brother-in-law two and one-half steps in the direction of his hypothetical congruent position, and he lands at -1.5. Notice that "psychology" at $+1.5$ and "brother-in-law" at -1.5 are now in a relationship of congruity. Notice also that the total amount of scale movement or attitude change that the two concepts have undergone is three and one-half scale steps, the amount initially separating either of the two concepts from its hypothetical congruent position. Finally, we can see that the concept toward which the message receiver had the more intense initial attitude ("psychology") underwent less attitude change.

In actual application, two correction factors must be added to the congruity model predictions. The first is termed the *assertion constant* and represents the empirical finding that, in general, attitudes toward issues (X) change more than attitudes toward communicators (C). In their research, Osgood and Tannenbaum found that for more precise prediction, a certain amount of movement (in their experiment, .17 of a scale step) should be added to the amount of attitude change otherwise predicted toward the issue X.

In our earlier discussion of the interaction between the effects of source credibility and the effects of communication distance, we pointed out that one possible reaction to a highly incongruous message, in which, for example, the message receiver is told that a highly respected source advocates a policy that the message receiver despises, is denial that the communicator ever made such an assertion. The congruity model formally embodies a specific and quantitative correction for incredulity to take account of this reaction. The incredulity reaction of denying the asserted link between the source and the issue is strongest in instances when highly polarized, similarly valued concepts (e.g., both at $+3$ on the scale) are associated negatively, and when highly polarized but oppositely valued concepts ($+3$ and -3) are associated positively. Presumably, a reaction of incredulity, in which the message receiver denies that the communicator made the assertion attributed to him, is most likely to occur when the report of the communication is relayed secondhand. This mode of resolving incongruity would be less available to the message receiver when he directly hears the communicator deliver the message and has no reasonable grounds for deciding that the communicator "really doesn't believe that."

Abelson's Modes of Resolving Belief Dilemmas

So far we have discussed four possible reactions to persuasive communication: attitude change toward the issue; attitude change toward the communicator; misperception or misrecall of the communicator's message; and incredulity or denial that the communicator actually holds the belief attributed to him. But if we reflect upon instances in which we ourselves have been confronted with cognitive inconsistency, we see that these four reactions do not exhaust the possible responses.

In a discussion of alternative modes of reducing cognitive inconsistency, Abelson (1959) has depicted three responses to imbalance that we have not discussed so far: *bolstering, differentiation,* and *transcendence.* Bolstering refers to a process in which the attitude toward one of two concepts in an imbalanced relationship is strengthened by increasing the salience of affect-consistent beliefs which link the bolstered concept with other concepts. A familiar example, and one that Abelson uses to illustrate the cognitive process of bolstering, is the smoker's reaction to the evidence linking smoking with lung cancer. One possible balance-restoring response to this dilemma is attitude change and behavior change, i.e., quit smoking and change attitude toward cigarettes from positive to negative. For many people this turns out to be a very difficult solution. An alternative, and one that was frequently employed when the evidence linking cancer and smoking was first presented to the public, is to deny the association between the two concepts by criticizing and undermining the scientific value of the research presuming to show such an association, e.g., it was based primarily on "correlational" and not experimental evidence, and some other factor might be responsible for the apparent relationship. But as the scientific evidence accumulated and as more and more respected scientists asserted that there is a causal relationship between smoking and cancer, this response became less available to smokers. In such a situation, bolstering may provide a partial solution. The smoker may remind himself that smoking is enjoyable, relaxing, and an activity that increases sociability in some groups. Bolstering can be thought of as an attempt to increase the valence and intensity of attitude toward a particular concept by remembering or developing beliefs that are consistent with that concept. Although this technique does not completely eliminate imbalance, it may reduce it by reinforcing and strengthening the attitude toward one of the two concepts in an imbalanced relationship. The technique of bolstering is depicted in Figure 7-4.

A second interesting mode of resolving an imbalanced belief dilemma that Abelson describes is differentiation. It is likely that almost everyone has solved a cognitive inconsistency problem with this technique at one time or another. Essentially, differentiation

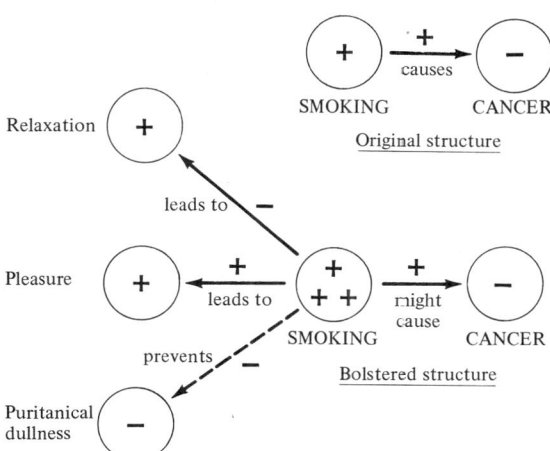

FIGURE 7-4. Illustration of the mechanism of bolstering as a means for partially reducing cognitive imbalance (adapted from Abelson, 1959).

involves splitting or subdividing a concept into two new concepts that are either not associated or are negatively associated with one another. For example, a devout white Christian who also happens to be a racist or an anti-Semite may hear his respected and positively valued minister deliver a sermon condemning racism or anti-Semitism. In several studies it has been demonstrated that racial attitudes are relatively stable and resistant to change. But suppose that this particular devout Christian's positive attitude toward his priest or minister is also resistant to change. While he may be able to tune out or misperceive some parts of the sermon, misperception would be less likely to occur if the sermon is clearly delivered and strongly worded. One possible out for the parishioner is to differentiate or subdivide his conception of his minister, and perhaps of the clergy generally, into two separate categories: (1) clergy as spiritual authorities, toward whom he has a positive attitude, and (2) clergy as spokesmen on social and political issues, a category he evaluates negatively as naive, unworldly, and inadequately informed. Differentiation of the communicator may be especially likely to occur when attitude toward the communicator is highly resistant to change, as would often be the case, for example, with communicators who are close friends or relatives. The mechanism of differentiation is depicted in Figure 7-5.

Perhaps the most intriguing and ingenious of the partial solutions to imbalanced belief dilemmas that Robert Abelson described is that of *transcendence*. Abelson illustrates this solution by presenting the not uncommon discomfort that is experienced by religious persons who simultaneously believe that (1) God created all men and (2) some men perform evil actions. This dilemma, in which the most positively valued concept is associated with a negative concept, can be partially resolved by the use of a superordinate category. It is true that some men perform evil deeds, but most Christians believe that men freely choose their actions, that God has given men the choice between good and evil. The superordinate category of "free will" is so positively valued that it at least partially resolves the dilemma created by the association between the Creator and the evil, but freely chosen, actions of his creations. This example of transcendence is depicted in Figure 7-6. In a way, the process of transcendence, in which a concept is combined with another concept into a superordinate category, is the opposite of the process of differentiation, in which a single concept is subdivided into two oppositely valued concepts.

In addition to describing cognitive mechanisms for reducing inconsistency that are alternatives to source derogation, attitude change, message misperception, or incredulity, Abelson has speculated about the order of preference or sequential hierarchy among the various potential modes of resolving a belief dilemma. We noted in the congruity model that people tend to change their attitude less toward initial-

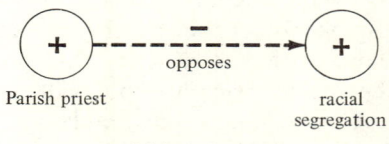

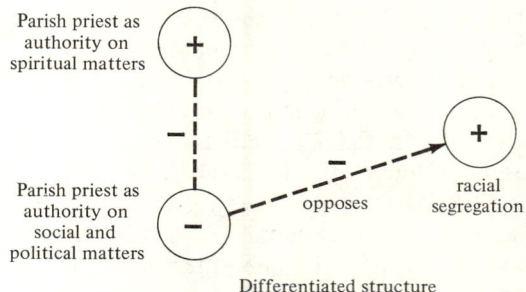

FIGURE 7-5. Illustration of the mechanism of differentiation as a means for reducing cognitive imbalance (adapted from Abelson, 1959).

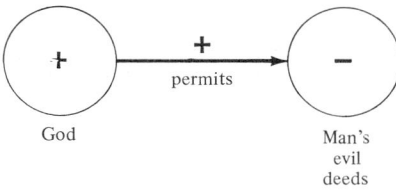

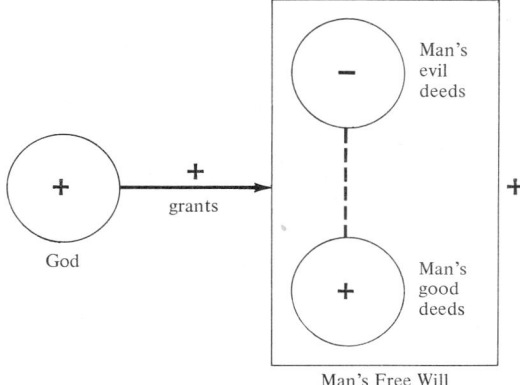

FIGURE 7-6. Illustration of the mechanism of transcendence as a means for reducing cognitive imbalance (adapted from Abelson, 1959).

ly more polarized and intensely valued concepts. Abelson and Rosenberg (Abelson & Rosenberg, 1958; Rosenberg & Abelson, 1960) add an additional principle that is helpful for specifying which of several potentially available modes of resolving imbalanced belief dilemmas will actually be employed, the principle of minimum effort. This principle suggests that changes in beliefs and attitudes that involve more cognitive "work" will be less likely to occur than changes that require less effort. With regard to the three modes of resolution we have just considered, Abelson makes the reasonable suggestion that bolstering requires less effort and is therefore more likely to occur than differentiation. On the other hand, Abelson

Theories of Attitude Change **221**

suggests that transcendence requires even more thought than differentiation and thus will be resorted to only when other and less effortful means for restoring cognitive balance have failed. Another implication of the least effort principle suggests that in a complex belief system with a large number of interconnected concepts, attitude changes which seem to call for or imply numerous other changes in related attitudes and beliefs will be less likely to occur than attitude changes that necessitate less extensive realignments of related beliefs and attitudes.

Unfortunately for those of us who are attracted to parsimonious and elegant models of cognitive consistency, there are still other reactions to message-produced imbalance, in addition to the seven responses we have discussed so far. For example, in a face-to-face confrontation with a brother-in-law who criticizes our chosen profession, we might argue back and attempt—perhaps successfully—to change the brother-in-law's point of view. Or we might get up, go to a movie, and "stop thinking" about the imbalanced relationship. Since imbalance is aversive only when it is consciously recognized, this would represent a solution of sorts. Finally, we may find that we simply have to live with and tolerate a certain amount of evaluative inconsistency. As the list of possible responses to cognitive inconsistency grows, the possibility of keeping track of the multiple modes and the relationships among them becomes very difficult indeed. This is especially true if, as is undoubtedly the case, several responses to imbalance occur simultaneously.

One research strategy for coping with the troublesome fact that multiple modes of responding to persuasive arguments are available to message receivers in the real world is to experimentally block off or at least reduce the likelihood of all but one or two responses that are of interest to the experimenter. Thus, for example, most attitude change experiments are one-way communications in which the message receiver is not given the opportunity to talk back to try to change the communicator's opinion. Furthermore, subjects in such experiments are usually asked to respond immediately to a persuasive message, so there is little time for employing complex mechanisms like differentiation or transcendence. An experiment which neatly illustrates the "blocking off of other alternatives" strategy was performed by Zimbardo (1960). Zimbardo led pairs of close friends to believe that they disagreed either slightly or a great deal with regard to the locus of responsibility for a case of juvenile delinquency. The subjects were not allowed to communicate with one another, thus eliminating one possible reaction to the imbalance generated by the perceived disagreement. Zimbardo reduced the likelihood that communicator derogation would occur in several ways. In the first place, the subjects believed that the person disagreeing with them was a close friend. Furthermore, the friend was said to be certain of her opinion and to believe that the issue was an important one. Zimbardo attempted to increase the friendship bond between pairs of subjects by informing them that they had performed significantly better than strangers perform on a cooperative "alternate in naming as many social problems as you can in sixty seconds" task. Finally, in another rigged preexperimental task, in which the subjects were asked to select the photograph of the delinquent from among three photographs, the best friend was made to appear much better at this delinquent-identification task than the message-receiver subject. This presumably increased the friend-communicator's perceived expertise in the realm of juvenile delinquency, the issue over which the two friends later disagreed. Zimbardo's finding in this experiment that attitude change increased with communication distance can apparently be attributed to (1) the greater imbalance created by extreme as opposed to slight disagreement and (2) the blocking off or removal of responses to disagreement other than attitude change.

Another strategy for dealing with the "multiple possible modes of responding" problem, and one that has not yet been fully developed by social psychologists, is to represent the multiple message response modes and the relationships among them in a more formal, quantitative manner. Obviously, verbal formulations of the relationships among all of the consistency-restoring reactions that we have described would be cumbersome and unwieldy and, given the limits of human information-processing capacity, would be subject to the problem of the attitude theorists overlooking or neglecting some of the responses to belief dilemmas or the relationships among such responses. What is needed for depicting this state of affairs is a language capable of representing organized complexity. Some promising beginnings in this direction have been made by representing the dynamics of complex belief systems in terms of linear graph theory or matrix algebra and in computer simulation of cognitive processes. The interested and quantitatively oriented reader may enjoy pursuing these attempts in the writings of Abelson (1963), Abelson and Rosenberg (1968), Anderson (1971), Cartwright and Harary (1956), and Feather (1964).

A third strategy for coping with the multiple modes problem is to narrow the theoretical focus to a subset of all the possible kinds of cognitive inconsistency that might be generated. Cognitive dissonance researchers have employed this strategy, and dissonance experiments will be described in the next section. In anticipation of this discussion, it can be noted that dissonance research appears to have added, at least by implication, an additional principle that may help us predict which of several modes of responding to a belief dilemma will be employed. The dissonance studies seem to suggest that changes in beliefs and attitudes that result in loss of self-esteem will be less likely to occur than changes that do not result in self-esteem reduction.

The Theory of Cognitive Dissonance

In the opening paragraph of his textbook discussion of dissonance theory, Roger Brown commented that: "At this writing, early 1964, the principles of cognitive dissonance are probably the most influential ideas in social psychology" (Brown, 1965, p. 584). In retrospect, it seems clear that Brown's impression was correct. During the decade of the 1960s, the theory of cognitive dissonance generated more research and more controversy than any other theory in social psychology. Furthermore, a significant proportion of a generation of social psychology graduate students in the early 1960s became fascinated by dissonance theory and found themselves using the theory not only in laboratory research, but also in interpretations of events in their own lives. I am one of many who tried to adopt a dissonance theory perspective and who, in the process, experienced the excitement of apparently understanding instances of attitude change that would not have been understood prior to exposure to the dissonance ideas. It is my impression that relatively few psychological theories are actively and frequently used, even by the professional psychologist, to make sense out of everyday experiences. Therefore, while the reader should be critical in evaluating dissonance theory, it might be interesting to become immersed in the theory and to try to see the world through the dissonance theorist's glasses.

Toward the end of social psychologist Roger Brown's discussion of dissonance theory, from which the quote about the extensive impact of the theory was taken, Brown concludes that: "Dissonance theory itself is a mixed bag of ad hoc ideas. There is nothing common to all the derivations but a notion of inconsistency and a certain vocabulary" (Brown, 1965, p. 603). For those, like your author, who (1) respect Brown's judgment and (2) have found the dissonance ideas intriguing, Brown's statements generate some cognitive inconsistency. We might depict this dilemma as a negative relationship (criticizes) between a positively valued critic (Brown) and a positively valued theory (dissonance theory). It doesn't help the admirer of dissonance theory to find that dissonance theorists themselves seem to agree with Brown! Several years after Brown's review, Elliot Aronson, one of the major contributors to dissonance theory and research and one of the theory's strongest proponents, tells us that the theory has generated more research than any other in social psychology. But Aronson also states that: "As a formal statement, Festinger's theory of cognitive dissonance (1957) is quite primitive; it lacks the elegance and precision commonly associated with scientific theorizing" (Aronson, 1968, p. 5).

The mode of resolving this belief dilemma that I have employed is *differentiation*. I have concluded that there are really two dissonance theories. One theory, represented by the statements in Festinger's 1957 book, *A Theory of Cognitive Dissonance,* really is not much more than a relatively imprecise statement of the general notion that human beings dislike cognitive inconsistency and will try to avoid or reduce it. We can find that much in the passing comments of earlier writers. For example, Alexander Bain, the Scottish philosopher, postulated in *The Emotions and The Will,* a book published in 1880, that "Contrary statements, opinions or appearances, operate on the mind as a painful jar, and stimulate a corresponding desire for a reconciliation." But the differentiation suggested here is between the original general statement of dissonance theory and the narrower range of ideas tested in a series of ingenious experiments conducted by Festinger and his followers. I will attempt to derive some relatively precise implications of this second and positively valued theory of cognitive dissonance. In a book published five years after *A Theory of Cognitive Dissonance,* two revisionists, Brehm and Cohen, suggested that the theory be limited to instances in which a feeling of voluntary *commitment* has been evoked. Brehm and Cohen argued that:

> Commitment is a condition under which: (1) the specification of dissonance and the manner in which it is likely to be reduced are relatively unequivocal; and (2) the implications are relatively unique in comparison with other theoretical approaches and frequently nonobvious in terms of common sense. (Brehm & Cohen, 1962, p. 10)

While specifying the essential role of voluntary commitment helps to distinguish the range of phenomena to which dissonance theory is relevant from phenomena to which the theory is not applicable, something is still missing from Brehm and Cohen's theoretical explanation. Aronson supplies part of the missing explanation of the dynamics of dissonance theory when he comments that:

> At the very heart of dissonance theory, where it makes its clearest and neatest prediction, we are not dealing with just any two cognitions; rather, we are usually dealing with the self concept and cognitions about some behavior. If dissonance exists it is because the individual's behavior is inconsistent with his self concept. (Aronson, 1968, p. 23)

In a later publication, Aronson elaborates upon the "self-justification" interpretation of dissonance theory when he tells us that "Dissonance-reducing behavior is ego-defensive behavior; by reducing dissonance, we maintain a positive image of ourselves—an image that depicts us as good, or smart, or worthwhile" (Aronson, 1972, p. 98).

By combining the Brehm and Cohen emphasis on voluntary commitment with Aronson's emphasis on the self-concept, we can gain a better understanding of what dissonance theory deals with, that is, the voluntary commitments that have negative implications for the individual's self-concept. We might depict the dissonance-arousing experience as in the diagram.

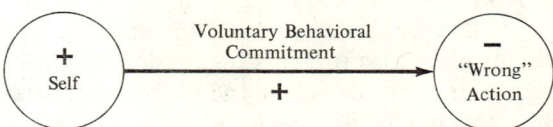

One way in which to reduce the inconsistency depicted in the diagram is to change the evaluation of the self from positive to negative. But the power of the dissonance ideas stems from the characteristically human resistance to information that would lead to a reduction of self-esteem. As the positive self-attitude is resistant to change, and as the voluntary behavioral commitment link is difficult or impossible to undo or deny, dissonance theory predicts that such inconsistencies will be resolved by changing one's negative attitude toward the immoral or incompetent behavior linked with the self. Stated differently, dissonance theory suggests that voluntary behavioral commitments which have negative implications for the individual's self-esteem will result in defensive distortion of information. Thus, dissonance theory involves a combination of the cognitive consistency ideas developed by Fritz Heider and others with Freudian insights about ego-defense mechanisms. Perhaps the best way to see this principle in operation is to consider some representative experiments conducted by dissonance theorists. We will review three experimental paradigms investigated by dissonance researchers: forced compliance, severity of initiation, and post-decision conflict resolutions.

The forced compliance paradigm refers to experimental investigations of situations in which individuals are induced to engage in behavior that is counter to their initial attitudes. Typically, the counterattitudinal behavior involves a form of role-playing in which the individual says something that he does not believe is true or argues in favor of a position that he initially opposes. Prior to the advent of dissonance theory on the social psychological scene, a number of experiments had demonstrated that role playing can have an effect upon attitudes. Under some conditions, when individuals advocate a position they initially disagree with, they may find themselves moving in the direction of the initially counterattitudinal position they are advocating. In a sense, their faces may grow to fit their masks. The special contribution of dissonance theory to understanding this phenomenon has to do with variations in the amount of reward or threat that are employed to induce compliance with the experimenter's request that the subject engage in counterattitudinal advocacy. The basic dissonance theory prediction is that the *smaller* the amount of force used to induce counterattitudinal advocacy, the *greater* the amount of subsequent attitude change in the direction of the position advocated. This idea, which seemingly contradicts an elementary reinforcement theory principle, is neatly illustrated in the classic but controversial, "one dollar, twenty dollars" study published by Festinger and Carlsmith in 1959.

In this study, subjects performed boring and tedious tasks, such as packing and unpacking a box full of spools of thread or repeatedly winding pegs a quarter turn. After the subjects had completed the boring tasks, the experimenter explained to them that they had just taken part in an experiment on the effect of set or expectancy upon motor performance. Subjects were told that they were in the control group and that other subjects who were in the experimental group were told before the experiment that the tasks would be interesting and enjoyable. At this point the experimenter, who appeared to be flustered and uncomfortable, explained that the next subject, a coed, had arrived and was waiting out in the hall. (In reality, this waiting subject was a paid accomplice of the experimenter.) The waiting subject was to be assigned to the positive set condition, in which she would anticipate participating in an interesting experiment. The experimenter went on to say that this positive expectancy was induced by a research assistant who played the role of someone who had just taken part in the experiment and casually but convincingly told the waiting subject that the experience of participating in the experiment had been interesting and enjoyable. Today, however (the experimenter nervously explained), the research assistant had not showed up, and so the waiting subject would be lost to the experiment—lost, that is, unless the subject would be willing to perform the research assistant's task of role playing a satisfied subject by telling the student waiting in the hall that the experiment was an interesting one. The experimenter offered to pay the subject for helping out in the study. At this point, the key experimental manipulation was introduced. Some subjects were offered 20 dollars to tell the waiting coed that the experiment was interesting, while other subjects were offered one dollar to perform this same task.

Festinger and Carlsmith predicted (and found) that those who were paid one dollar for counterattitudinal advocacy would change their attitudes to coincide with their behaviors more than those paid 20 dollars. On a rating form administered after the entire experiment was concluded, those subjects who had been paid one dollar for saying that a boring task was interesting rated the task as more enjoyable than did subjects paid 20 dollars. On the other hand, subjects paid 20 dollars did not differ significantly in their rating of the experiment from a third group of subjects, who performed the boring task but had not been asked to tell a waiting student that the boring task was interesting.

How does the less force/more change prediction derive from the general principle of defensiveness previously cited? The prediction derives from a hypothesized process of "self-justification." Having performed the counterattitudinal behavior, the subject must explain to himself why he did so. Being paid 20 dollars apparently provides a reasonably adequate explanation for and justification of the counterattitudinal act. But in the other experimental condition, subjects were faced with the realization that they had told a lie to a fellow student for the paltry sum of one dollar. How can this behavior be explained? One possible explanation for an individual in this predicament is the conclusion that "I am an easily bribed liar." Whatever the logical merits of this explanation, it is evidently not a popular solution to the dilemma, since it would normally entail a loss in self-esteem, assuming that the individual values the trait of honesty and thinks of himself as an honest person. The preferred resolution to the dilemma created by the low-incentive and, therefore, presumably highly voluntary commitment between the self-concept and the negative behavior of lying is to lessen the negativity of the behavior. In the case of the Festinger and Carlsmith experiment, if a subject could convince himself that the boring task was really not so boring after all, then the statement that he made to the waiting subject would be a less blatant falsehood. That is evidently what the subjects in the one-dollar condition, who presumably had the strongest need to justify their behavior, were able to do.

The Festinger and Carlsmith experiment has inspired a great deal of research by both opponents and supporters of dissonance theory. Arrayed against the dissonance theorists are the "incentive" theorists, who believe that greater attitude change should result from greater incentives for counterattitudinal role playing. Although the results of several relevant experiments are contradictory, this research literature seems to me to suggest that variables which increase a feeling of personal responsibility and voluntary commitment will increase the likelihood of the "less reward, more change" dissonance effect.

A second paradigm used in investigations by dissonance researchers involves the relationship between severity of initiation and liking for a group. Following the self-justification line of reasoning, dissonance researchers have predicted that those who go through stressful or painful initiations in order to become members of a group will value the group more highly than those who gain membership with less difficulty. Again, the underlying supposition is that individuals must justify or explain to themselves why they have voluntarily undergone the stress of an initiation experience. If the stress is relatively mild, or if the group turns out to be fascinating and worthwhile, the question is answered. But what about the person who voluntarily goes through a severe initiation to join what turns out to be a worthless group? As in the case of the forced compliance paradigm, there is a logically possible and consistency-restoring change that will resolve the inconsistency. But it is a solution that is seldom employed because of its negative implications for one's self-esteem. The individual could simply decide: "I am the sort of person who typically does foolish things such as voluntarily going through a stressful initiation in order to join a worthless group." The preferred alternative (as in the case of counterattitudinal role playing for small incentives) is to lessen the negative valence of the concept that has been linked to the self by voluntary commitment. In severity-of-initiation studies, this takes the form of deciding that the group is not all that bad and that, consequently, going through a severe initiation to get into the group was really not all that foolish.

The initial experiment purporting to demonstrate this phenomenon was carried out by Aronson and Mills (1959). These researchers advertised for female volunteers to take part in a sex-discussion group. When the volunteers arrived at the designated time and place, the male experimenter explained that he had previously had difficulty with some participants in the group discussion who were too shy to discuss issues related to sex in a frank and open manner. To avoid further difficulties of this sort, he had therefore devised an embarrassment test which all prospective participants had to take and pass to gain admission to the discussion group. The embarrassment tests for these female subjects consisted of reading some sex-related materials aloud to the male experimenter, who purportedly noted the subject's degree of apparent embarrassment. "Severity of initiation" was manipulated by asking some of the female subjects to read a list of relatively mild and innocuous sex-related words to the male experimenter (mild initiation condition), while other female subjects were asked to read a list of obscene words and lurid passages from pornographic novels to the male experimenter (severe initiation condition).

All subjects in both conditions were told that they had passed the initiation test and were then led into the "group discussion" room. The experimenter explained that all the discussion participants were seated within walled-off cubicles, as previous experience had demonstrated that this arrangement produced a more frank and open discussion than face-to-face seating arrangements. The experimenter went on to show the subject both a microphone and a receiver through which the subject could listen to the discussion. The experimenter then explained that because this was the subject's first meeting and the subject had not done the assigned reading for this discussion, she would be at a disadvantage. Therefore, it would be better if she only listened to but did not take part in today's discussion. Next time, when she had done the assigned reading, she would be able to take part in the discussion. At this point, the experimenter unplugged the microphone and turned on the receiver.

The subjects in this experiment assumed that they were listening to a discussion currently taking place among other young women seated in walled-off cubicles like the one in which the subject was seated. In actuality, however, all subjects, whether in the severe or the mild initiation condition, heard an identical prerecorded group discussion. (This ruse would have become obvious to the subjects if their microphones had not been disconnected, since the prerecorded discussants would naturally not have responded to any comments made by the real subjects.) The prerecorded discussion, which all subjects listened to, was deliberately designed to be extremely boring. The discussion topic involved the secondary sex characteristics of rodents, the comments were confused, banal, and uninsightful, there were long periods of silence during the discussion, and so forth. As Aronson and Mills had predicted from their dissonance theory perspective, those who went through a severe initiation to join this boring discussion group rated the group discussion more favorably than did those who had only gone through a mild initiation.

The third dissonance paradigm we will consider is that of post-decisional conflict reduction. After you have freely made a choice between two closely related alternatives, there are two kinds of information that are consonant with the choice and two kinds of information that are dissonant with the choice. The information that is consonant with the choice consists of (1) positive aspects of the chosen alternative and (2) negative aspects of the rejected alternative. On the other hand, (3) negative aspects of the chosen alternative and (4) positive aspects of the rejected alternative are dissonant with the decision. Information of the last two kinds is dissonant because such information implies that you made the wrong decision. By contrast, good things about what you chose and bad things about what you rejected are "consonant" with your choice in the sense that they imply that you made the correct decision. Thus, the involvement of self-esteem through commitment is again the basic dissonance-arousing dilemma. If we concentrate upon information consonant with our decision and avoid dissonant information, we can upgrade the value of the chosen alternative vis-à-vis the rejected alternative and therefore look back upon our freely made choice as a wise decision.

In dissonance experiments on the effects of post-decision conflict reduction, the usual procedure has been to ask subjects to rate a number of objects in terms of their desirability or value to the subject. For example, children might indicate their preferences by rating toys, or adults might evaluate a number of household utensils. The experimenter then offers to give the subject one of the articles he has evaluated. The subject is presented with a choice between two objects he had previously rated as similar in value. For example, an adult might be given a choice between the two utensils he had ranked as second and third most valuable to him from among an array of eight utensils. At some time after the choice between two approximately equally valued objects has been made, the subject is asked to reevaluate the objects. As dissonance theorists assume that people like to think of themselves as wise decision makers, the theory predicts that after a choice is made, the chosen object will be rated more favorably and the rejected object less favorably. This reevaluation in effect implies to the subject that "I made the correct choice." Once again, as in the case of both the forced compliance and the severity of initiation studies, evaluations are made in a way that defends or enhances the subject's self-esteem.

Dissonance theory presents us with an image of man that is not very flattering. According to dissonance theory, people distort and misrepresent information that, if evaluated objectively, would suggest that they are immoral or incompetent. This view of man has led one reviewer to characterize dissonance as "a good theory about poor thinking." But people are at times able to overcome defensiveness, to examine their behavior objectively, and to admit to their mistakes. As dissonance theorist Aronson puts it:

> Man cannot live by consonance alone.... people do frequently grow—people do frequently profit from their mistakes. How? Under what conditions? Ideally, it would be useful for a person to be able to bring himself to say, in effect, "O.K., I blew it. What can I learn from the experience so that I will not end up in this position again?" (Aronson, 1972, p. 139)

Boden, the critic who described dissonance as a good theory about poor thinking, apparently had the limitation Aronson refers to in mind when she paraphrased a statement attributed to Abraham Lincoln. As Boden expressed it:

> Dissonance theory describes how all of the people think some of the time, and (cynically) perhaps it describes how some of the people think all of the time. But it remains to be modified and extended before it can give us a reasonably adequate account of how all of the people think all of the time. (Boden, 1963)

Consistency versus Curiosity

One motive which appears to be almost diametrically opposed to the need for consistency is the need for variety and surprise. The basic postulate of the consistency theories—that the mind loathes inconsistency—appears to be a "one-sided" homeostatic principle (Kohn, 1962). Calling attention to evidence which is inconsistent with this principle, Hovland and Rosenberg (1960) commented: "There are certain settings in which, and certain persons in whom, motives favoring the *arousal and maintenance* of inconsistency are sometimes dominant." As an example of such behavior, Zajonc (1960) cited the fact that people seek out and enjoy watching a magician create cognitive inconsistency for them by showing them what they know to be impossible on the basis of previous knowledge. Beswick (1964) aptly characterized the incompatibility between these two motives as "the need to order experience vs. the need to experience disorder."

Several possible integrative solutions to the simultaneous existence of the apparently conflicting needs for consistency and for variety might be suggested. Berlyne attempts to explain some incongruity-seeking behaviors as an "arousal jag." As Berlyne sees it, we do not seek out puzzles and paradoxes because we enjoy the experience of cognitive inconsistency. We are willing to endure and even seek out incongruity not because we enjoy incongruity per se, but because the anticipated pleasure of resolving the incongruity is greater than the pain we undergo on the way to the resolution. Working with a puzzle, riddle, or problem consisting of inconsistent information may be difficult and not intrinsically pleasant work. The same can be said for carrying a sled up to the top of a hill. But the consistency-restoring solution to the problem, like the ride down the hill, makes it worth the effort. As Berlyne expresses it, "Resolution of conflict is evidently so gratifying that we deliberately seek out conditions in which mystifications and clarification, disconcertions and reassurances, aggravations and alleviations of conflict, are suitably apportioned" (Berlyne, 1963, p. 352).

Human beings and other higher animals appear to have a need for an optimum, intermediate amount of novelty and incongruity. The perfectly predictable series of events can be very dull indeed. But as Berlyne and many other observers of playful, incongruity-seeking exploratory behavior have observed, such behavior is most likely to occur in the absence of other needs. The starving or terrified animal shows little of the playful curiosity that characterizes the content organism. The need for intermediate levels of incongruity evidently emerges only when more "prepotent" (Maslow, 1943) needs are satisfied. In the case of the cognitive consistency theories, this principle suggests that we may seek out certain kinds of cognitive imbalance and incongruity—either for their own sake or, if we accept Berlyne's "arousal jag" idea, because restoration of balance is so pleasant. The need for mild amounts of cognitive incongruity might exhibit itself, for example, in the enjoyment that some people derive from debates with their acquaintances about relatively uninvolving topics. But the form of inconsistency that is generated in cognitive dissonance experiments activates a need that may be more important than the need for consistency: The need to maintain and enhance a positive self-image. In dissonance-arousing situations, therefore, we might expect that the hypothesized need for even small amounts of inconsistency would not be activated. Few of us enjoy getting ego-deflating information that suggests that we are incompetent or immoral—even if the information comes in small doses. As Aronson suggested, we might cope with and learn from such information once we are confronted with it. But most of us don't have much appetite for data that damages our self-image.

In sum, it appears that we may seek out mild amounts of cognitively inconsistent information if the information is not too threatening to us. Such behavior cannot be easily explained by the current one-sided versions of models of cognitive inconsistency. This suggests that these models should be extended to take inconsistency-seeking as well as inconsistency-reducing behaviors into account.

Bem's Self-Perception Theory

The number of articles criticizing consistency theories and presenting alternative explanations of the findings of consistency theory studies is probably as numerous as the articles published by the consistency theorists themselves. Perhaps because it has been the most influential of the consistency theories, dissonance theory has been the prime target for the bulk of this criticism. Many authors have found fault, at both a conceptual and a methodological level, with dissonance experiments. But Bem's self-perception theory has been by far the most influential of the many challenges to the theory of cognitive dissonance.

Dissonance theory has been described by its proponents as nonobvious and counterintuitive. At first glance, Bem's ideas seem to run counter to common sense—or at least counter to the common sense of those cognitive theorists who assume that people know what their own attitudes are. Because Bem challenges what many of us take for granted, it may be useful to say a few words about the background of self-perception theory before presenting the theory itself.

Many of Bem's self-perception ideas are derived from the writings of B. F. Skinner. Skinner (1953) has argued that parents and other socializing agents have a very difficult task when they attempt to teach a child to label his own emotions. This is because the child's own feelings and beliefs are "invisible" to everyone but the child himself. The parent must infer the child's feelings from the child's facial expressions, from what he says and does, and from situational factors that the parent has observed or knows about. Thus, a child with what a parent takes to be an unhappy expression on his face might be told "You feel sad because you can't find your ball," or "Don't be afraid of the baby sitter, she is a nice lady and Mommy will be home early," or "Remember that you will get a lot of toys on your birthday"—depending upon the parent's interpretation of the situation. In the case of external objects and events, both the parent and the child have access to the same stimuli. Consequently, after considerable practice, a consensus develops about what is or is not a kitty or a flower or a tricycle. But, according to Skinner and Bem, no such reliable taxonomy can be achieved by the individual for describing his own emotions. Subtle variations in mood or unexpressed beliefs do not lend themselves to the kind of consensual validation that we can achieve with variations in color and shape. Because of necessarily inadequate socialization in the realm of emotions and beliefs, in many instances we do not know exactly how we feel or what we believe about a particular object, event, or policy.

Thus, Bem and Skinner reject the widely held assumption that the individual himself has privileged access to and knowledge of his own true internal beliefs and feelings. What can we do, then, in those instances when we are asked to express an attitude—for example, when a social psychologist asks us to fill out a questionnaire? According to Bem, we do pretty much what parents and other outside observers must do: We note both the situational context and our own behaviors, and on the basis of these observations we attribute an attitude to ourselves. Bem concludes that if an individual is asked to express his attitude, he will generally attribute the same attitude to himself that an outside observer would attribute to him. Furthermore, the attribution of an attitude to oneself and the attribution of an attitude to another person result from essentially the same processes, observation of behavior (one's own behavior or that of another person) and observation of the situational context in which the behavior occurs. Bem is fond of expressing this idea with the suggestion that if asked whether or not he likes brown bread, a person might reply, "I guess I do—I'm always eating it." A related example of self-perception is the frequently heard statement, "I guess I was hungrier than I thought I was," made by individuals who observe that they have just consumed a large meal.

With this background we can state the basic position of self-perception theory more formally:

> Individuals come to "know" their own attitudes, emotions, and other internal states partially by inferring them from observations of their own overt behavior and/or the circumstances in which this behavior occurs. Thus, to the extent that internal cues are weak, ambiguous, or uninterpretable, the individual is functionally in the same position as an outside observer, an observer who must necessarily rely upon those same external cues to infer the individual's inner states. (Bem, 1972b, p. 2)

The controversial and interesting application of this idea derives from Bem's view that in most of the cases that attitude researchers deal with, internal cues are "weak, ambiguous, or uninterpretable." Let us now reconsider some of the dissonance experiments from the perspective of self-perception theory. At the outset it is important to note that, unlike some critics of dissonance research, Bem generally accepts the results of dissonance experiments as valid—and not due to methodological problems or artifacts. However, Bem believes that dissonance theorists have been right for the wrong reasons.

Bem's reinterpretation is perhaps most easily illustrated in the case of forced-compliance experiments. If we accept Bem's premise that the individual asked to attribute an attitude to himself is "functionally in the same position as an outside observer," then the reverse incentive effect of forced compliance can be explained as the result of self-observation. In those instances in which an outside observer hears a "stimulus person" express a belief or a felling about some issue, several factors influence the extent to which the outside observer believes the stimulus person. Evidently, one of the important determinants of the outside observer's conclusion that the stimulus person's statements correspond to his true internal feelings and beliefs is the amount of apparent incentive that the stimulus person has for expressing a particular feeling or belief. For example, a television viewer who hears a famous athlete or actress praise a commercial product is unlikely to conclude that the performer actually has a strongly favorable attitude toward the product. The viewer knows that the athlete and the actress are giving paid testimonials. This monetary incentive is sufficient explanation for making favorable statements about a particular brand of detergent or deodorant. Consequently, if the viewer were asked what the famous athlete really thinks about the deodorant, the viewer would find the athlete's favorable public statements to be of little help in determining the athlete's true internal feelings. On the other hand, if you are at the laundromat and a friend or acquaintance makes apparently spontaneous favorable statements about a detergent, you are in a better position to use his verbal statements as clues to his true feelings. In the absence of any obvious external incentive for expressing a particular attitude, we tend to assume that the individual actually holds the attitude he is expressing.

Bem has applied this line of reasoning to the forced-compliance situation in which the individual is asked to attribute an opinion to himself. As Bem expresses it:

> Self-perception theory asserts that subjects in the Festinger-Carlsmith experiment (and other experiments utilizing this paradigm) are themselves behaving just like these hypothetical observers. They survey their own behavior of making favorable statements about the task and then essentially ask themselves (implicitly): "What must my attitude be if I am willing to behave in this fashion in this situation?" (Bem, 1972b, p. 7)

In low-compensation forced-compliance situations, such as the one-dollar condition in the Festinger and Carlsmith experiment, subjects conclude that they must agree with the statements they have made. However, in high-compensation situations, such as the 20-dollar condition of the Festinger and Carlsmith experiment, the subjects cannot reliably infer their attitudes from their statements. The statements can be explained as caused not by true internal attitudes but by the payment of 20 dollars. Consequently, the statements are of little help in determining what one's own true attitude about the task must be.

The research method Bem has employed to support his alternative interpretation of dissonance experiments is that of *interpersonal simulation*. In this technique Bem asks subjects either to read about or to actually observe a "subject in a psychological experiment" who is performing the same actions subjects in dissonance experiments perform. The observers in Bem's interpersonal simulation experiments are then asked to attribute an attitude to the dissonance experiment subject they read about or observe. Bem argues that if, as self-perception theory hypothesizes, the original subjects in dissonance experiments are essentially in the same position as outside observers with regard to deciding what their own attitudes are, then outside observers should be able to replicate the original dissonance theory experimental findings.

In a series of interpersonal simulation experiments, Bem has shown that observers are able to produce essentially the same results as the participants in the original dissonance experiments produced. For example, in an interpersonal simulation replication of the Festinger and Carlsmith "one dollar, twenty dollars" study, Bem asked subjects to listen to a tape recording of a brief conversation in which "Bob Downing," who had just participated in an hour-long experiment winding pegs and packing and unpacking spools of thread, argued "rather imaginatively that the tasks were fun and enjoyable" to a girl who was waiting to take part in the same experiment. Some of Bem's observer subjects were told that the experimenter paid Bob Downing 20 dollars to tell the waiting subject that the experiment was interesting. Other observers in Bem's experiment heard an identical recording of Downing's conversation with the waiting subject, but they were told that Downing was paid one dollar to make favorable statements about the experimental task. In line with the original experiment, the observers who listened to Bob Downing's conversation and who were told that Downing was paid one dollar for making the argument that the experimental task was interesting judged Downing's attitude toward the task to be significantly more favorable than did observers who listened to the same recorded conversation but were told that Downing was paid 20 dollars for making the argument.

Bem performed a similarly successful interpersonal simulation replication of one of the dissonance theory "post-decision conflict resolution" studies (Bem, 1967). Bem's observer-subjects were told that an 11-year-old boy in a psychology experiment was given a choice among several toys. The toys were described to the observers, and they were told which toy the boy had decided to keep for himself. Bem's observer-subjects were then asked to indicate how the 11-year-old boy would evaluate the chosen and the rejected toys. As in the free-choice experiments originally conducted by dissonance researchers, the displacement effect occurred. The chosen toy was inflated in value, and rejected toys were downgraded in value in the observer's judgments of the boy's evaluation of the toys. This effect did not occur in a control condition in Bem's experiment in which subjects were simply asked to indicate how a typical 11-year-old boy would evaluate the toys.

Several critics have taken issue with Bem's interpersonal simulation studies of dissonance effects. The seemingly most telling criticism of Bem's studies is that he left out one vitally important piece of information: He neglected to inform his observer-subjects about the initial pre-decision opinions of the subjects in dissonance experiments. Thus, the critics argue, Bem's observer-subjects mistakenly infer that no attitude change has occurred. They assume that the one-dollar subjects in a forced-compliance experiment are simply reporting what they thought about the experiment all along or that the 11-year-old boy made his choice in the first place because of his pre-decision evaluation of the toys. To bolster this criticism, Bem's critics demonstrated that when observer-subjects in a simulation experiment are informed about the dissonance experiment subject's pre-decision opinions, they do not replicate the findings of the original dissonance studies (Jones et al., 1968).

Bem's reply to his critics is quite consistent with the general position of self-perception theory with regard to the ambiguity of internal cues about our own attitudes. Bem argues that the subjects' own "pre" attitudes were not salient for them in the original dissonance experiments. Consequently, making "pre" attitudes known to an observer departs from the true situation of the original experiment. To try to prove this point, Bem and McConnell (1970) conducted a role-playing attitude change experiment and asked subjects who had changed their attitudes to try to recall what their initial attitude before role playing had been. There was a strong tendency for attitude changers to misrecall their "pre" attitudes as close to or identical with their final attitudes. In other words, subjects in attitude change experiments often do not see themselves as having changed. From their point of view, their final attitudes are simply "what I believed all along."

Although this demonstration of the lack of salience of "pre" attitudes after they have been changed appears to rebut the most serious criticism of Bem's interpersonal simulation methodology, Bem acknowledges that there are other explanations for errors in recalling "pre" opinions. An explanation that would be consistent with the dissonance theory emphasis on defensiveness is the possibility that subjects who have changed their attitudes do not want to correctly recall their earlier attitudes. To correctly recall an attitude that has been changed by an experimenter's manipulations might lead to the ego-deflating realizations that "I was wrong in my initial attitude" and "I have been persuaded to change my attitude." Bem and McConnell state that a "crucial" experiment for discriminating between dissonance theory and self-perception theory is unlikely to be conducted. While subsequent researchers (e.g., Ross & Shulman, 1973; Green, 1974) have gathered data that they interpret as supporting dissonance theory and refuting self-perception theory, it appears to be true that, as Bem and McConnell put it, the choice between the dissonance and the self-perception explanations is largely "a matter of loyalty or aesthetics."

SUMMARY

American social psychologists have probably devoted more of their time and effort to the study of attitude change than to any other subject. Although attitude researchers have learned a great deal about the effects of variations in message organization and content, no simple or final answers are available to message-effect questions such as "Are one-sided or two-sided arguments more effective?" or "In a persuasive communication do arguments presented first have more impact than arguments presented later?" During the 1950s researchers found some interesting relationships between susceptibility to persuasive arguments and personality traits. Subsequently, attitude theorists have hypothesized that a personality characteristic like self-esteem or intelligence may have opposite effects upon comprehension and yielding—the sequential steps in processing messages.

Belief systems provide a basic conceptual tool for viewing the attitude change process. In answer to the structural question "What are the elements of a belief system?" three basic elements emerge: concepts, attitudes, and beliefs. Concepts or cognitive categories consist of the defining characteristics of classes of objects or events. They enable the perceiver to classify what are really unique and "one-time-only" objects or events as, for some purposes, equivalent. Although attitudes have been viewed in many different ways, in this chapter they were defined as positive or negative evaluations of cognitive concepts. Beliefs, on the other hand, were defined as perceived relationships between concepts.

The needs or functions which belief systems may fulfill for people might be thought of in terms of a "pleasure principle" and a "reality principle." The former includes belief systems that maintain and enhance self-esteem, sometimes by distortion of information. The latter includes conceptions of, attitudes toward, and beliefs about objects and events that result from direct or vicarious experience, from logical deduction, and from a curiosity drive or need to know.

Social psychologists generally agree that belief systems may serve several different functions, but most of the models of attitude change that dominated social psychological research during the decade of the 1960s were based upon one hypothesized need: the need for cognitive consistency. A number of cognitive consistency theories reflect this dominant interest. While Rosenberg's affective-cognitive consistency theory deals with the relationship between an individual's attitude toward a single concept and beliefs about that concept, balance theory and congruity theory are concerned with inconsistent relationships between two (or more) concepts. Elementary cognitive balance theory provides a useful conceptual tool for tying together and making sense out of a great many seemingly unrelated studies of attitude change, source derogation, and message misperception. But one of the limitations of the elementary balance theories is a lack of precision in predicting to what extent each of several possible imbalance-reducing responses such as attitude change or derogation of the message source will actually occur in a given situation. The congruity model attempts to cope with this problem by making precise quantitative predictions about the amount of attitude change and the amount of source derogation that will occur in response to an imbalance-producing communication.

In addition to attitude change, source derogation, and message misperception, other possible responses to cognitive inconsistency include bolstering, differentiation, and transcendence. Keeping track of the multiple potentially available responses to inconsistency and of the relationships among these multiple responses presents a formidable and as yet unsolved problem for cognitive consistency theories. One way of partially avoiding the multiple modes problem is to narrow the theoretical focus to a subset of all the possible kinds of cognitive inconsistency that might be generated. Cognitive dissonance researchers have employed this strategy.

During the decade of the 1960s, the theory of cognitive dissonance generated more research and more controversy than any other theory in social psychology. The basic assumption underlying dissonance theory is that voluntary behavioral commitments which have negative implications for one's self-esteem will result in defensive distortion of information. This "dissonance leads to choice-produced defensiveness" perspective was applied to a review of research on: (1) forced compliance (less reward may lead to more attitude change), (2) severity of initiation (we may come to love those things we suffer for), and (3) post-decision conflict resolution (sour grapes and sweet lemons).

Dissonance theory and research has many critics, but Daryl Bem's self-perception theory has been by far the most influential of the many challenges to the theory of cognitive dissonance. Bem doubts that people are usually able to simply introspect, or look inward, to clearly know their own attitudes and beliefs. Instead, Bem argues, individuals come to know their own attitudes by making an inference from observations of their own actions and the circumstances surrounding these actions.

SUGGESTED READINGS

Fishbein, M. (Ed.). *Readings in attitude theory and measurement.* New York: Wiley & Sons, 1967.

In addition to reprints of the classic attitude measurement articles, this collection contains the original statements of most of the theories reviewed in this chapter.

Himmelfarb, S., & Eagly, A. H. *Readings in attitude change.* New York: Wiley & Sons, 1974.

Many of the most important studies of source, message, and receiver effects are reprinted here. This reader also contains the most important studies in the forced-compliance (less reward = more attitude change) controversy.

Insko, C. I. *Theories of attitude change.* New York: Appleton-Century-Crofts, 1967.

This is one of the two standard textbooks for courses in attitude change. It is a clearly written and well-organized summary of the field.

Kiesler, C. A., Collins, B. E., & Miller, N. *Attitude change.* New York: Wiley & Sons, 1969.

This is a widely used textbook for attitude change classes. These authors are somewhat more critical than Insko in their treatment of models of attitude change.

McGuire, W. J. The nature of attitudes and attitude change. In G. Lindzey & E. Aronson (Eds.), *The handbook of social psychology* (Vol. 3, 2nd ed.). Reading, Massachusetts: Addison-Wesley, 1969.

McGuire's chapter is a highly respected and exceptionally comprehensive overview of the field.

PART FOUR

Interpersonal and Group Processes

8. PERSON PERCEPTION
Introduction
Perception: Objects and Persons
   Perceptions as veridical / The role of language / The tendency toward stability and invariance in perceptions / The perception of persons
The Judgment of Nonverbal Behavior
   The recognition of emotion / Other expressive behaviors / Accuracy in the judgment of nonverbal behaviors
Impression Formation
   Processes of impression formation / Implicit personality theories / Accuracy in the judgment of personality
Attribution Theory
   Theoretical formulations / Attribution studies / Attributional errors and biases / Self-attribution / Misattribution therapy
Future Trends in Person Perception Research
Summary
Suggested Readings

9. INTERPERSONAL ATTRACTION
Introduction
Interpersonal Attraction: A Definition
A conceptual definition / Operational definitions
The Reinforcement Model of Interpersonal Attraction
The impact of specific reinforcements on liking / Do we like those who are merely associated with reward? / The reinforcement model: problems and limitations
Equity Theory
The heart of equity theory / Applications of equity theory
Current Status of Interpersonal Attraction
Theoretical Applications and Future Research Directions
The impact of power on justice / Equity and the law / The participants in inequity—the exploiter and the victim
Summary
Suggested Readings

10. INTERPERSONAL INFLUENCE AND CONFORMITY
Introduction
Definitions and basic issues / Historical review
What Is Conformity?
Two ways to measure conformity / Description and explanation
What Are the Alternatives to Conformity?
The diamond model / Mapping models / Other alternatives to conformity
Why Conformity and Why Deviation?
Independence of influence versus independence of change
When Conformity and When Deviation
Group unanimity / Stimulus characteristics / Obedience to authority
Conformity—Good or Bad?
How rational? / The conforming personality / The conforming society
Summary
Suggested Readings

11. POWER AND BARGAINING
Introduction
Forms of Personal Power
Legitimate influence / Informational influence / Expert and co-oriented influence / Referent influence / Reciprocal influence / Coercive and reward influence
Threats and Promises
Research on compliance with threats and promises / Resistance to the use of threats and promises / Conflict spirals / Evaluation of threats and conflict spirals / Advice to prospective leaders
Influence Through Allies
The Power of the Group
Bargaining
Motivation in bargaining / Other determinants of the process and outcome of bargaining / Integrative bargaining / A perspective on bargaining
Summary
Suggested Readings

12. GROUP DEVELOPMENT AND STRUCTURE
Introduction
What is a group? / Three kinds of groups / Encounter groups / Task groups
Group Formation and Development
Group formation / Stages in group development / The development of group norms
Group Structure
Physical space / Communication / Composition / Attraction / Perception of structure
Summary
Suggested Readings

13. GROUP PROCESSES, PRODUCTIVITY, AND LEADERSHIP
Introduction
Group Processes
The "risky shift" / Deindividuation
Group Performance
Social facilitation / Individual versus group productivity / Together versus alone / Group size / Group composition and performance / Cohesiveness and performance / Group think
Leadership
Leadership in encounter groups / Leadership in task groups / The trait approach / The leadership style approach / The situational approach / The style-situational approach
Summary
Suggested Readings

8

Person Perception

*Teresa Amabile and
Albert H. Hastorf*

INTRODUCTION

Imagine a class of about 20 students enrolled in a psychology course at MIT. One day a faculty member announces to the class that the regular instructor is out of town, and, since the department is interested in how different classes react to different teachers, he will introduce a new instructor to take over for the day. The guest instructor then leads the class in a 20-minute discussion, after which the students are asked to complete a short questionnaire on their impressions of him. This scenario describes an altogether commonplace occurrence in college classrooms everywhere; what is unusual is the pattern of results obtained when Harold Kelley had a guest instructor introduced into an MIT classroom in 1950. In this particular instance, about half of the students saw the newcomer as significantly more considerate of others, more informal, more sociable, more popular, better-natured, more humorous, and more humane than did the rest of the students. One short and extremely simple experimental manipulation induced half these college students to differ widely from their peers in their impressions of the same man, in the same classroom, leading the same discussion.

Before introducing the "guest instructor," the faculty member (who was actually the experimenter) distributed one-paragraph biographical notes about the guest instructor in order to give the class "some idea of what he's like." Two different types of notes were randomly distributed to the class; the two differed in only one small detail, a single word. The first set of notes read as follows:

> Mr. ——— is a graduate student in the Department of Economics and Social Sciences here at MIT. He has had three semesters of teaching experience in psychology at another college. This is his first semester teaching Ec. 70. He is 26 years old, a veteran, and married.

People who know him consider him to be a rather cold person, industrious, critical, practical, and determined. (Kelley, 1950, p. 433)

The second note was identical to this, except that the last sentence read: "People who know him consider him to be a very warm person, industrious, critical, practical, and determined." Those students who had received the "cold" information before the discussion consistently rated the instructor more unfavorably than did those given the "warm" information. Beyond this, the "cold" information students interacted less with him during the discussion. The fact that people who are told that a newcomer is cold will describe him as cold is obvious and probably uninteresting. It is of interest, however, that one detail of description could cause such widely different perceptions of the same behavior and that these different perceptions could lead not only to widely divergent ratings of the newcomer on dimensions such as consideration, formality, popularity, humor, and humaneness, but to quite different behavior as well.

The relevance of such a phenomenon to our everyday lives is quite extensive. Consider, for example, these instances: a student enrolled in a course asks a graduate for information on the professor's personality; a young man seeks out a character description of his prospective blind date; an employer contacts a job applicant's character reference and requests a recommendation. In each of these cases, if Kelley's results generally apply, the information given to the individual may shape not only his first impression of, but his future interaction with, the person in question. A great many other such "real world" examples, some trivial, some of considerable impact, could be generated to point up the potential importance of preinformation in our interpersonal relationships.

Because this phenomenon and others similar to it have such impact on personal interactions, they are of much interest to psychologists engaged in the study of social behavior. Such study demands attention to a wide variety of variables (ranging from preinformation to personal appearance to facial expression) and effects (for instance, the formation of total impressions, and behavior resulting from impressions). The Kelley experiment raised several issues of interest; we will use it as a starting point for discussing some of the concepts that will be examined throughout the course of this chapter.

The first such issue represents the major concern of Kelley's study. It is the influence of *set,* or expectation based upon prior information, on perceptions and interpersonal behavior. Set is what Kelley calls an "inner-observer variable"; it does not depend upon circumstances or the actual behavior of the stimulus person. As will be discussed later, certain personal qualities are thought to be more important than others in determining an overall impression of a person. The "warm-cold" dimension is one such central quality. As a result of this, the set that each student had been given regarding the newcomer on this particular dimension was found to cause differential shifts in ratings on several other personality dimensions.

There is a second phenomenon which may also provide a partial explanation of these results. This is the "halo effect." It is said to occur when a favorable impression of an individual on one characteristic spreads to other characteristics; virtually everything the individual does is judged in a favorable light. To give a familiar example, the halo effect could also be called the "teacher's pet" phenomenon; if Johnny is an A student as regards classroom conduct, the teacher may tend to assume that Johnny is also an A student in reading and math, that he is kind to animals and helpful to old ladies, and that the latest classroom prank could not have been Johnny's work. Of course, negative halo effects of unfavorable characteristics are also possible. This phenomenon does seem to be evidenced in the Kelley experiment. Students told that the stimulus person had one very favorable trait described him as having others; a negative halo seemed to apply for those students told that he had one very unfavorable trait. However, Kelley asserts that his "warm-cold" findings cannot be totally explained by a simple halo effect, since the halo effect is defined as a rather indiscriminate spreading of "favorableness" to all other characteristics, more or less equally. In Kelley's study, ratings of traits such as intelligence were affected to a much smaller degree than were traits "related" to warmth or coldness, such as considerateness and good-naturedness. The phenomenon of the halo effect raises a number of questions about exactly how we proceed to convert various isolated items of information into a more cohesive and organized impression of another person.

A third issue, one of great current interest to social psychologists, concerns attributions about a person's *dispositions,* or underlying personality characteristics, from his behavior. We are referring to the powerful tendency of perceivers to infer the existence of enduring dispositions in another person, and to attribute that person's behavior to those dispositions. Perceivers appear eager to make such inferences and attributions, even when the behavioral information is quite minimal. The "warm-cold" study demonstrates that quite different attributions about a person may be derived from exactly the same behavior. Kelley requested his subjects to write free descriptions of the "guest instructor" as well as complete the questionnaire on characteristics. He found that "warm" subjects interpreted the stimulus person's behavior very differently than did "cold" subjects. For example, "warm" subjects saw the rather shy newcomer as someone who makes friends slowly but forms lasting friendships, while "cold" subjects saw him as intolerant and easily angered. The behavior was the same but, because of differing precognitions, the attributions made of underlying personality dispositions were quite divergent.

Finally, once it has been established that perception of a person can depend upon prior set, the question of interest becomes this: Does actual behavior toward a person depend upon one's perception of him? Kelley obtained data to answer this question by stationing an experimenter in the classroom to keep count of the number of times each student participated in the discussion. He found that 56% of the students who had been given the "warm" biographical note participated, while only 32% of the "cold" students did so. This, of course, raises the possibility of a vicious circle being set up between perceptions and behavior, something that Theodore Newcomb (1947) termed "autistic hostility." This means that an initially unfavorable impression of an individual leads to restricted communication and interaction with that individual, which in turn makes it quite unlikely that that unfavorable impression will ever be disconfirmed. For example, if a new neighbor ignores the greeting you call to her because she is slightly hard of hearing, you may assume that she is hostile and aloof. On the basis of this impression, you would probably avoid her company in the future, and you might be suspicious of any friendly gestures on her part. Consequently, you would have very little chance of ever discovering that your first impression had been mistaken.

This chapter will consider the issues raised above as well as several others which have been important in the study of man's perceptions of those around him. The major topics of discussion will be these: (1) person perception as contrasted to object perception; (2) the judgment of a person's feelings from his nonverbal behavior; (3) the formation of first impressions;

and (4) attributions about ourselves and others judging from circumstances, behavior, and prior information. The discussion throughout will focus on both the traditional and contemporary study of man as a creature actively attempting to make sense out of and achieve stability in his social world.

PERCEPTION: OBJECTS AND PERSONS

Before beginning a discussion of the problems unique to person perception, it seems appropriate to examine some of the more general issues in the study of perception. In this section, we will consider four such issues and attempt to answer some questions related to each: (1) The "realness" of perceptions. Most of our perceptions seem clear and veridical; does this mean that in fact they are determined directly by the stimulus we perceive? (2) The role of abstractions and stereotypes in person perception. Can these abstractions distort perceptions? (3) Tendencies toward stability and invariance in perceptions. There is evidence that people simplify complex social perceptions, leading to stable and organized views of others. This pervasive tendency to simplify perception raises the question as to whether all individuals simplify a given stimulus in the same way. (4) Unique aspects of person perception. What are the similarities and differences between object- and person-perceptions?

Perceptions as Veridical

There is a feeling of "realness" about most everyday sensory experiences; our perceptions feel as though they are directly "given" to us by the action of the stimulus on our senses. If we experience a chocolate mousse as fluffy-looking, pleasantly aromatic, and delicious, we tend to assume that it is fluffy, aromatic, and delicious and that other human beings perceive it as such. This seems to be true not only for object perception, but often for person perception as well. If we see a neighbor as loud, boorish, and ignorant, we commonly expect that others in the neighborhood will regard him in the same light. This problem has been of perennial interest to psychologists: Is perception determined directly by the stimulus and the sense organs, or do intervening cognitive processes work to construct perception? Since our perceptions do feel "direct," and we are not aware of any intermediate cognitions that may play a role, simple introspection would not yield the necessary evidence to indicate the operation of these cognitions. If intermediate cognitive processes do act to construct perceptions, however, their effects should produce different perceptions of the same stimulus in persons from different cultures or learning histories.

It appears that people from different cultures and, thus, with different learning histories do see the world differently. It is well known that the favorite food of one culture may taste terrible to a person from a different culture. Before turning to studies exploring those sorts of differences, we will discuss one study that indicates some cross-cultural uniformities. It is an early study, one that investigated such cultural universals through use of the metaphor. Asch (1958) studied such metaphors as "a sweet smile" and "bitter tears." Investigating usages in seven different languages besides English, he attempted to discover whether metaphors are universal. If people of different cultures used different metaphors, it would suggest that cognitive processes heavily influenced by language were playing a role. If, on the other hand, metaphors had similar usages in different languages, it would suggest that there was something intrinsic in the perceptions of objects and persons which determines common descriptions across different cultures and languages.

Asch's findings were quite supportive of the latter proposition; he found many terms which describe both the same physical and psychological qualities in all eight languages. Here are examples of usages of the word "bitter": Hebrew—"I will complain in the bitterness of my soul"; Greek—"bitter pain," "bitter tears"; Chinese—"bitter fate" = hard lot in life; Thai—"bitterly disappointed"; Hausa—"bitterness of character" = an unpleasant disposition; Burmese—"to speak bitterly" = to speak in an unfriendly manner. In each of these languages, the equivalent of "bitter" also described the physical sensation that quinine produces in the mouth. Moreover, the metaphor "bitter," when applied to persons, did not simply connote something unpleasant. The meaning was more specific; it did not refer to something depressing or boring or frustrating. It seemed to describe only those experiences which we would, in English, call "bitter." The implication that Asch wishes us to draw from this data is that perceivers are willing to make certain perceptual "leaps" from qualities of things to qualities of persons and that these leaps do not seem to be bound by culture or language.

Although perceptions may seem veridical, and there is some evidence that certain perceptions may be "given" by the stimulus, there is also substantial evidence of the role that values, expectations, and needs can play in determining both object and person perception. This evidence strongly suggests that constructive cognitive processes influence perceptions. An example of the effect of expectation upon visual perception is provided in a study by Engel (1956). Subjects in this experiment were asked to look into a stereoscope and describe what they saw. The picture projected to one eye was that of an upright human face; the other eye received the image of the same face, upside-down. Both images "competed" in the same visual field. The overwhelming majority of subjects saw only the human face in its familiar right-side-up orientation.

Similar influences of needs, values, and expectations can be demonstrated in the perception of social events. One such demonstration was provided in a study of Dartmouth and Princeton students whose football teams had recently met in a particularly rough game:

> On a brisk Saturday afternoon, November 23, 1951, the Dartmouth football team played Princeton in Princeton's Palmer Stadium. It was the last game of the season for both teams and of rather special significance because the Princeton team had won all its games so far and one of its players, Kazmaier, was receiving All-American mention and had just appeared as the cover man on *Time* magazine, and was playing his last game.
>
> A few minutes after the opening kick-off, it became apparent that the game was going to be a rough one. The referees were kept busy blowing their whistles and penalizing both sides. In the second quarter, Princeton's star left the game with a broken nose. In the third quarter, a Dartmouth player was taken off the field with a broken leg. Tempers flared both during and after the game. The official statistics of the game, which Princeton won, showed that Dartmouth was penalized 70 yards, Princeton 25, not counting more than a few plays in which both sides were penalized. (Hastorf & Cantril, 1954, p. 129)

When interviewed after the game, only 36% of the Dartmouth students said they thought Dartmouth had started the rough play; 86% of the Princeton students blamed the trouble on Dartmouth. While viewing a film of the game, Princeton students saw twice as many Dartmouth infractions as did Dartmouth students. Many other examples of the influence of predisposition upon perception can be generated from common experience. These instances point up the importance of realizing that, while there is some "veridical" element to perceptions, perception is also a constructive, selective process influenced by inner-observer variables.

The Role of Language

It is clear that perceptions involve cognitive work beyond the simple nerve impulse arising from impingement of the stimulus upon sensory nerves. The process therefore includes conceptualizing and abstracting. Language plays a vital role in this process; it is a device for simplifying, for categorizing the varied stimuli impinging upon us. Through language, cognitions of persons and things are represented and communicated. We will explore some of the implications of the abstract categorization process as manifested through language.

When we first meet another person, we are prone to categorize her on certain dimensions. Is she likeable? Is she smart? In recent years, researchers have begun to wonder how these categories are selected. Do they derive from the characteristics of the stimulus person, or do they derive from the category system of the observer?

This was the question investigated by Dornbusch and his co-workers (1965): in *unconstrained* descriptions of persons, what determines the particular categories used—very salient characteristics of the person who is being described, or the idiosyncratic cognitive organization of the perceiver? In order to study this problem, Dornbusch et al. interviewed dozens of children in summer camps. Each child was interviewed twice, and during each interview he was asked to describe two (randomly chosen) other children in the camp. Responses were completely free; the interviewer requested "Tell me about —————," and gave no hints as to what the child was supposed to say. The researchers analyzed the content of each description by identifying the categories of remarks made and counting the number of times each category appeared in a given description. Some such categories were: "Religion," "Physical attractiveness," "Generosity," "Cooperation," "Humor," "School ability," and "Honesty." The experimenters then compared the various descriptions to discover whether the categories used were more similar when two children were describing the same child or when one child was describing two different children. These two possibilities can be schematized as follows:

Child A — describes — Child B and Child C   1. "Common Perceiver"

Child D and Child E — both describe — Child F   2. "Common Perceived"

Dornbusch et al. found that there were more reappearing categories in two descriptions given by the same perceiver of two different persons than in two descriptions given by different perceivers of the same person. This research suggests that the most important influence on interpersonal description is the way in which the perceiver structures his interpersonal environment. There are certain categories which are salient to any given perceiver; these are the traits or personality dimensions which that perceiver tends to notice in others. His linguistic expression of these categories reveals what may be called his cognitive or perceptual "organization."

A great deal of work has been done recently on the way in which each person engages in his somewhat unique manner of perceiving others. What categories does a given person use to describe others? Which traits does he see as "going together"? How does he make predictions about the behavior of other people? These issues define the *implicit personality theory* which each individual uses in perceiving and categorizing others. Such theories will be discussed in more detail in the section on impression formation.

One end-product of the person-categorization process can be the formation of stereotypes. If ethnic background is a particularly important dimension for an individual along which to categorize others, it is in a sense more economical, cognitively, for that individual to apply traditional ethnic stereotypes of people than to devise an entirely new conceptualization each time he meets someone. It should be noted that the word "stereotype" has a generally negative connotation, because of the dangerous overgeneralizations stereotypes often represent. However, they can provide useful simplifications of the world; as we mentioned earlier, they save much cognitive work. On some occasions, stereotypes may actually aid an individual in arriving at reasonably effective interpersonal judgments. If you were about to meet a graduate student, you would have a fairly high probability of being correct if you expected him to be intelligent, hold rather liberal political views, and have a high need for achievement. You would be safe with this assumption simply because, in this instance, the stereotype accurately describes a high percentage of the individuals in question. These statements are not meant, however, to deny that there are numerous tragic instances in which inaccurate and unfair stereotypes are perpetuated, elaborated, and acted upon.

Very often, stereotypes are widely accepted within a given group and are particularly resistant to disconfirmation. However, it is possible for stereotypes to fade (Karlins et al., 1969). White Princeton undergraduates in 1933, 1951, and 1967 were asked to name traits characteristic of various groups. A general decline in ethnic stereotypes seemed to be evidenced over this time (see Table 8-1). In 1933, 45% of the undergraduates said the Irish are pugnacious, 53% said Italians are artistic, and 84% said Negroes are superstitious. By 1967, the percentages had dropped to 13, 30, and 13 respectively. In addition, there was an overall drop in the percentage of undergraduates agreeing on any of the stereotypes that had been strongest in 1933. It may well be that the amount of stereotyped thinking has actually declined among college undergraduates, or it may be that a new set of stereotypes have developed to replace the ethnic labels: "hippie," "jock," "straight," and so on.

A stereotype of a group of people may be formulated in the following way: an individual "samples" some number of people belonging to the group and generates some concept which he believes characterizes all members of that group. Just as this process is applied to a group, it may also be applied to one individual. A perceiver may sample the behavior of one person and arrive at some conceptualization (a set of traits) which he believes accurately summarizes that person's behaviors. Just as an individual may form stereotypes of the British, Irish, and Italians if ethnic background is an important dimension for him, he may tend to develop a stereotype of the conscientious and nonconscientious person if conscientiousness is an important category for him. In this way,

TABLE 8-1
Stereotypes of Five Ethnic Groups

		Percentage reporting		
		1933	1951	1967
Americans	Industrious	48	30	23
	Intelligent	47	32	20
	Materialistic	33	37	67
	Ambitious	33	21	42
	Progressive	27	5	17
Irish	Pugnacious	45	24	13
	Quick-tempered	39	35	43
	Witty	38	16	7
	Honest	32	11	17
	Very religious	29	30	27
Italians	Artistic	53	28	30
	Impulsive	44	19	28
	Passionate	37	25	44
	Quick-tempered	35	15	28
	Musical	32	22	9
Jews	Shrewd	79	47	30
	Mercenary	49	28	15
	Industrious	48	29	33
	Grasping	34	17	17
	Intelligent	29	37	37
Negroes	Superstitious	84	41	13
	Lazy	75	31	26
	Happy-go-lucky	38	17	27
	Ignorant	38	24	11
	Musical	26	33	47

SOURCE: Adapted with permission from M. Karlins, T. L. Coffman, and G. Walters, "On the Fading of Social Stereotypes: Studies of Three Generations of College Students," *J. personal. Soc. Psychol.* vol. 13 (1969).

NOTE: These values represent the percentages of white Princeton undergraduates in 1933, 1951, and 1967 who checked each trait as a typical characteristic of the group being rated.

personality traits can be conceived of as stereotypes that we apply in the perception of a single person.

Stereotypes not only act as cognitive shortcuts, but they may also produce selective biasing in information processing and storing. They may cause us to see only that evidence which fits our stereotype, or even to ignore evidence which disconfirms it. A study by Loren and Jean Chapman (1969) demonstrated rather dramatically that even a sophisticated group of clinical psychologists can be biased by popular stereotypes in their perception of diagnostic signs. The Chapmans circulated a questionnaire among clinical psychologists asking which responses to Rorschach inkblots most often indicate that the patient has homosexual tendencies. Most of the clinicians failed to report the few responses which have actually been found to indicate homosexuality; they instead reported several clinically invalid responses. Their mistakes, moreover, were not at all random. The signs which these psychologists incorrectly believed to indicate homosexuality were responses which are highly associated with homosexuality in the common language; in other words, these responses fit the usual stereotype of homosexuality. Some examples of these are "part man–part woman creatures" or "feminine clothing." On the other hand, Rorschach responses which have been found to indicate homosexuality but were not reported by the clinicians surveyed are those which are not associated with homosexuality in popular usage: "part animal-part human creatures" and "monsters." These clinicians believed what the popular stereotype dictates, that a patient who "sees" feminine clothing in an inkblot is homosexual, even though rigorous tests have shown this conclusion to be unfounded. In addition, these psychologists ignored the accurate indicators of homosexuality, indicators which do not happen to fit the stereotype.

This research suggests that, while abstraction and categorization may be necessary components of person perception, it is very possible for us to become "locked into" our categorization schemes to a point where we selectively code new information so that it fits into these schemes. This may in turn lead us to make incorrect judgments and form unfounded inferences.

The Tendency Toward Stability and Invariance in Perceptions

Our physical and social environments present an array of constantly varying stimuli. Man attempts to identify invariant and stable features of these variable and often confusing surroundings in order to achieve some measure of predictability and, therefore, control over them.

In the realm of object perception, there are a number of *constancies,* or pervasive tendencies toward stability. In visual perception, for example, some of these phenomena are: (1) size constancy, or the perception that an object remains constant in size regardless of its distance. Obviously, even though the retinal image of a person changes drastically in size as he walks toward us, we always perceive his height as constant; (2) shape constancy, or the tendency to perceive an object as constant in shape even though the shape of the image on the retina may change due to orientation of the object. For instance, as a door opens, the shape of its retinal image becomes trapezoidal; in spite of this, we continue to perceive the door as rectangular; (3) closure, or the perception that a familiar form, though it may be incompletely drawn, is still a whole. An example of this is the perception that a partially drawn circle is still a circle, even though it may be drawn through only 320 instead of 360 degrees.

The tendencies towards stability in person perception are analogous to the constancies in physical perception, and they seem to serve the same purpose: to provide the perceiver with a relatively predictable world in which to operate. There are certain persistent and seemingly universal invariance phenomena in person perception. One of these is the *halo effect,* which has already been discussed in connection with Kelley's "warm-cold" study; this effect is said to occur when a perceiver, believing that a particular person has one favorable quality, assumes that he possesses a myriad of other favorable qualities as well. For example, the belief that a person is generous may spread and lead us to assume that he is also honest and patient.

The halo effect may be thought of as a special case of the phenomena which result from the *logical error*—the tendency to see different traits as "belonging together" when they logically do not (Bruner, Shapiro, & Tagiuri, 1958). When the halo effect occurs, the error consists of assuming the presence of many positive traits from the existence of one favorable characteristic. Other types of logical errors are possible, however, which do not involve strict favorableness or unfavorableness. One such error might be to assume that a shy person is also intelligent, well-read, and polite. There is nothing in the dictionary meaning of "shyness" which implies intelligence, accomplishment, or politeness. Such implications, however, are often drawn. These logical errors provide clues about the perceiver's *implicit personality theory,* his individual "master scheme" of assumptions about which traits and behaviors go together.

Another consistent finding is that the most basic dimension in our perceptions of others is *evaluation.* This means that we tend to categorize the traits we use to describe others as generally good or bad (Osgood, Suci, & Tannenbaum, 1957). It also means that most of us, in most situations, will draw more inferences about a person if we know that he is good or bad than if we know how he is categorized on any other personality dimension. A third implication is that we are most prone to make logical errors in the evaluative dimension; that is, we tend most often to infer the existence of many good qualities from the presence of one good trait.

Despite a great deal of evidence which suggests the importance of the evaluative dimension (Rosenberg & Olshan, 1970), it seems that, in some situations, other dimensions can become crucial. For example, if I am overcome by a wave in the ocean, I do not care whether the person leaping into the water is good or bad, but only whether he can swim. It is clear that sometimes purely descriptive terms can be just as important as evaluative terms in person perception.

The halo effect, the logical error, and the centrality of evaluation and description are three manifestations of the attempts perceivers make to impose structure and stability upon their interpersonal world. A fourth tendency, one of great current interest to psychologists, is that of perceiving the behavior of other persons as more consistent across different situations than it actually is. Although it seems to us that a person should be fairly predictable in different situations, the experimental evidence for consistency is very weak (Mischel, 1968). For example, it is quite possible that a young woman may believe her boyfriend is consistently jovial, well-mannered, and relaxed when in fact his behavior varies considerably. There are a number of possible reasons for this (Bem & Allen, 1974). First, we are prone to see someone else's behavior as caused by his own unchanging personality traits and not by external circumstances (Jones & Nisbett, 1972); hence, we assume that his behavior is fairly predictable in a wide variety of situations. To continue our example, the young woman may not realize that her boyfriend is consistently jovial only when he is in her company; with other, more sober individuals, he may be quite subdued. Second, as we mentioned above, we all hold implicit personality theories. If we observe a person behaving in a certain manner, we use our preconceived notions of personality to infer a trait from that behavior and to assume other traits as though we had evidence for those, too. The boyfriend in our example may indeed be well-mannered. If, according to his young lady's implicit personality theory, politeness and generosity always go together, she may feel confident in assuming that he is a very generous man as well. Of course, this assumption may be completely incorrect. Third, we observe most people in only a very limited set of situations, so the behaviors we observe may not properly reflect the variability that really exists. If she sees him on week-end dates only, the young woman has no way of knowing that her boyfriend may be ill-tempered, rude, and anxious in the presence of his parents. Fourth, there is evidence (Mischel, 1968) that people are fairly consistent across time in a particular situation: we may observe this consistency and assume that it means behavior is consistent across different situations as well. It is quite possible that the young man in question always behaves in the same way when he picks up his date at her apartment. However, this is consistent behavior in the same situation; it says nothing about his cross-situational behavior.

We have presented several manifestations of the striving for invariance and stability in interpersonal perceptions. Such invariance may or may not reflect the "true" state of the social world, but whatever the case, a structured and orderly social world is undoubtedly of great importance to us. It may be misleading, however, to assume that this tendency towards invariance means that, given a particular set of stimuli, all persons will have the same perception of those stimuli. In other words, people all strive for invariance, but they may achieve it in different ways.

One factor which can cause different individuals to perceive an event in different ways is the influence of set. Set was defined earlier as preinformation or a predisposition to respond which causes an individual to see an ambiguous stimulus in one particular way. A familiar example of the influence of set upon visual

FIGURE 8-1. The young woman and the old hag (adapted from Leeper, 1935).

(a)   (b)   (c)

perception is the "Young Woman and the Old Hag" drawing (Leeper, 1935). It presents an ambiguous figure which can alternately be seen as a beautiful young woman or an ugly old hag (Fig. 8-1a).

Persons who are given a set for seeing the young woman by first being shown the drawing with the young-woman features accentuated (Fig. 8-1b), almost universally later perceive the ambiguous figure as a young woman and have great difficulty seeing the hag. Similarly, those who are first shown the old hag (Fig. 8-1c) persist in seeing the hag in the ambiguous figure. Some examples of the operation of set upon person perception have already been mentioned in accounts of the "warm-cold" study and the football study.

In summary, then, it can be said that, while there are forces which influence individuals to perceive social situations in different ways, each particular individual exhibits a striving towards structure, stability, and invariance in his interpersonal perceptions.

The Perception of Persons

We have listed a number of similarities between object- and person-perception. Both often "feel given" by the stimuli; both involve abstract cognitions and language; both are influenced by tendencies toward stability and invariance, as well as by perceptual sets. There are, however, several important differences (Heider, 1958). Objects are used by us, they are manipulated, they are judged in terms of their functional properties. There are some special properties, however, which are unique to persons: "they are action centers, they can do something to us, they can benefit or harm us intentionally, and we can benefit or harm them. Persons are perceived as having abilities, as acting purposefully, as having wishes or sentiments, as perceiving or watching us" (p. 22). These are the most salient aspects of persons which set them apart perceptually from objects in the environment. It is another individual's ability or power, his intentions, and his emotions which we must accurately recognize and appropriately deal with in order to successfully navigate our interpersonal worlds.

THE JUDGMENT OF NONVERBAL BEHAVIOR

Consider the following scenario: Having won a scholarship for study abroad, you arrive at the University of Hamburg and are introduced to your German roommate for the coming academic year. During the first few moments following your introduction, you begin to form impressions of one another. In doing so, you pay attention not only to what is said but to each other's nonverbal behavior as well. Imagine the kinds of nonverbal cues you would be concerned about. What does the expression on his face mean: Is he pleased, or shy, or indifferent? How should you interpret his intent gaze and his use of gestures as he speaks? You wish to appear friendly. Does your face express this? Does he believe you are sincere? Are you standing at a "friendly" distance? Does his culture interpret facial expression in the same way yours does? This imaginary scene describes aspects of nonverbal behavior which play an important role in all types of interpersonal perception. In this section we will describe some of the research on nonverbal communication, and discuss issues of traditional and contemporary interest to psychologists working in the area: the expression and perception of emotion in the human face, the effects of such expressive behaviors as eye contact and body placement on our perception of others, and the accuracy with which people judge internal states from nonverbal behaviors.

The Recognition of Emotion

There are three separate issues related to the role of emotion in interpersonal encounters. The first of these concerns the "emotion-to-expression link": does a given emotion always produce the same facial expression, for all humans? The second central question involves the "expression-to-perception link": once a given expression of emotion is present, is that expression correctly and universally interpreted by other humans? The third issue, one which only indirectly relates to interpersonal perception, concerns the subjective experience of emotion: By what mechanism does a given individual experience a particular emotion? This last question can be important to a theory of the perception of emotion because, as will be elaborated below, some theorists consider the mechanisms of self-perception and other-perception of emotion to be identical.

The work of Charles Darwin (1872) served as the starting point for the systematic study of emotions. His major interest was with the emotion-to-expression link, and he conducted a number of informal experiments to explore the universality of emotional expression. For example, he sent standard questionnaires to friends in various parts of the world asking how the various emotions are expressed by natives of the area. One question, for instance, was "When in low spirits, are the corners of the mouth depressed, and the inner corners of the eyebrows raised?" Although his method had obvious flaws, he received remarkably consistent results. The cultural similarities far outweighted differences.

Darwin believed that the expression of emotion was innate (inherited) and therefore the same the world over. He formulated three propositions (discussed in Izard, 1971) to explain the seeming innateness of emotion, drawing upon his evolutionary theory. His first two are the only ones of central interest to our discussion here: (1) The Principle of Serviceable Associated Habits states that an expression is originally part of some functional behavior; gradually the expression becomes associated with a state of mind present during that behavior, and the emotion can be produced by the state of mind alone. An example might be the "startle" expression. Originally, Darwin argued, this expression was part of the behavior of leaping away from danger. Gradually an association was formed, so that the feeling of surprise by itself could elicit the expression. Darwin assumed that these learned associations would be passed on genetically from one generation to the next. Note that it is possible to accept Darwin's hypothesis of an emotion-to-expression link (as some contemporary theories of emotion do) without having to accept Darwin's demonstrably incorrect notion that a parent's acquired habits can be genetically passed on to the children. (2) The Principle of Antithesis states that once an association is formed between a state of mind and an expression, the opposite state of mind can elicit the opposite expression. Darwin contended, for example, that the expression of helplessness (shoulders shrugged, head moved to one side, hands opened) was the antithesis of the expression of indignation (head erect, fists clenched).

Darwin's major hypothesis, then, is that there is a direct linkage between an emotional state and its expression and that this linkage is inborn. Obviously, the counter-theory to this is that there are no innate linkages: that the expression of emotion is learned, and emotional expression will vary from culture to culture and from individual to individual. It is this opposite theory, stressing the role of learning, that was most popular for a long while; recently, Darwin's original notion has again received both theoretical and empirical support.

Landis (1929) was one of the early proponents of the learning viewpoint. He requested a number of people to engage in a variety of activities ranging from viewing pictures of nudes, to plunging their hands into buckets of frogs, to decapitating rats. He took photographs of these individuals while they were engaging in these activities and later asked different subjects to identify the emotions expressed in the various photographs. His major concern, then, was with both the emotion-to-expression and the expression-to-perception links. Landis found very little consistency in his data. First, there seemed to be no single expression that all people exhibited when performing a particular activity: second, different subjects viewing photographs of different people engaged in the same activity seemed to see very different emotions. Landis regarded these results as evidence that expressions are learned and interpretations are different for different individuals. Moreover, he believed that the correct identification of an emotion also depended on information about the situational context in which the emotion is elicited.

Landis' study is flawed because it was conducted under the assumption that all people will experience and express the same emotion when, for example, they touch live frogs. Therefore, Landis's sweeping conclusions must be considered as premature. However, it is important to stress his point that context can play an important role in determining our perception of emotion in others. A face indicating considerable strain may be perceived as expressing pain in one circumstance and ecstasy in another.

During the past few years there has been a dramatic growth of interest in a theory of emotional expression that strongly resembles Darwin's original ideas. Izard (1971), heavily influenced by Tomkins (1962), has made the most complete statement of this position. Izard's major proposal is identical to that of Darwin: the "basic" emotions are innate and universal: all humans are born with the same basic "expressive pathways" and, therefore, can identify the emotional expressions of other humans. Although Izard's theory addresses itself to all three issues in emotion (subjective experience, the emotion-to-expression link, and the expression-to-perception link), the mechanism he proposes for the normal emotional experience focuses most centrally on the expression-to-perception link. His model of the emotion process has three components: (1) The process is initiated by some emotion-specific neural message received in the cortex. This message may be generated by external stimulation upon the receptors or by activity in the cortex itself (e.g., thoughts which are emotion-laden). (2) The neural message is then transmitted through subcortical centers to the facial muscles, causing the facial expression. (3) The configuration of the face then provides information to the cortex, which leads to the subjective experience of a particular emotion. In other words, Izard proposes that facial expression is the cause, not the effect, of emotional experience. For both outsiders and the person experiencing the emotion, the expression itself is the source of information about what that particular emotion is. Since, in Izard's system, the neural "loops" from emotion-producing stimulation to facial expression to emotional experiences are built in (at least for certain basic emotions), then all humans should be able to readily interpret one another's expressions.

Some research evidence has been produced recently in support of Izard's hypothesis that expression itself leads to the subjective experience of emotion. In a series of experiments (Laird, 1974), subjects were induced to form a "smile" or a "frown" with their facial muscles. They were told that these facial contortions were a necessary part of the perceptual experiment they were involved in. In fact, this cover story was presented so that the subjects would not be aware of the exact nature of the expression they were forming and would not realize that the experimenters were primarily interested in the effect of their facial expressions. Following this, each subject's mood was assessed either through a self-rating questionnaire or through reactions to cartoons. It was found that, while smiling, subjects felt more happy and rated cartoons as being more humorous; when frowning, they felt more angry and saw cartoons as less humorous.

A recent cross-cultural study has also supported the more general Darwinian notion of the universality of emotions. Ekman and Friesen (1971) worked with preliterate observers in New Guinea who were considered "visually isolated": they had never observed Caucasians, had never seen movies or magazines, and did not understand English. The researchers showed each observer three photographs depicting different emotions. The photographs they used had been reliably judged by Western literates as depicting specific emotions, such as happiness or sadness. As the preliterate observer was shown the three photographs, he was told a story which involved a single emotion; following this, he was asked to point to the picture which he thought best fit the story. For example, one set of stimuli included pictures depicting sadness, anger, and surprise. In this case, the observer might have been told to indicate the expression a man would show "if his child died and he felt sad." The results were very convincing; remarkable agreement was found between these preliterate observers and members of more advanced literate cultures.

Several tentative conclusions about facial expression and the recognition of emotions can now be formulated, drawing upon the research evidence collected since Darwin's pioneering work 100 years ago. First, the experience and perception of emotion appear to be important in the social life of highly complex organisms. Second, the actual expression of emotion seems to be closely linked with the subjective experience of emotion, and may even play a causal role (Laird, 1974). There appears to be an innate association between specific emotions and specific facial configurations; humans from different cultures can reliably identify expressions of certain emotions. This holds true for the basic emotions of anger, sadness, happiness, disgust, surprise, and fear (Ekman & Friesen, 1971). Third, learning and cognitive factors also play a role in our perception of emotions in ourselves (Schachter & Singer, 1962) and others (Frijda, 1969). Fourth, learning may cause differences between cultures concerning the set of situations which will evoke certain emotions and the rules of self-control in displays of emotion (Ekman & Friesen, 1968).

Other Expressive Behaviors

One of the most important expressive behaviors which have been found to influence person perception is eye contact; the most central components of this nonverbal behavior appear to be frequency and duration of gaze. During conversations, you may occasionally be conscious of your own eye behavior and that of your conversation partner. There seem to be unspoken rules governing the appropriate times to engage in eye contact and the times to look away. Even without verbal communication, staring or averting one's eyes can do much to produce feelings of tension or ease. A number of studies have shown that two individuals are more likely to engage in mutual glances if there is a feeling of warmth and attraction between them (Exline, 1971). In our culture, it is generally accepted that prolonged eye contact can be one sign of flirtation.

It is obvious, however, that under some circumstances eye contact can both signal and produce feelings that are far from warmth and attraction. Consider the normative eye behavior in elevators: It consists of staring at walls or floors. The discomfort you feel can be considerable if some stranger breaks this rule by persistently staring at you. In fact, a wealth of recent research on eye contact has discerned certain definite rules which seem to govern this nonverbal behavior. For example, there is evidence that eye contact can be a determining factor in the amount of punishment an aggressor delivers to a victim. Ellsworth and Carlsmith (1973) found that subjects who had been angered delivered significantly fewer shocks to a confederate who consistently established eye contact with them than to a confederate who constantly looked away. The researchers concluded that eye contact was aversive for the aggressors and served to inhibit their aggression against the victim. Further evidence that steady eye contact can, under some circumstances, be aversive comes from a series of studies by Ellsworth and her co-workers (1972). In one of these experiments, an experimenter on a motorcycle pulled up alongside automobile drivers stopped at a traffic light. The experimenter turned and stared at half of these drivers during the time they were stopped; he did not stare at the other half. Apparently, being stared at was aversive for drivers in the first condition: the time in which they crossed the intersection after the light changed was significantly shorter than the time taken by drivers who had not been stared at.

A variety of factors appear to influence eye behavior in normal social interactions. A study by Exline, Gray, and Schuette (1965) investigated the effect of the topic of conversation and the sexes of the persons involved in conversation upon visual behavior. In this experiment, a number of male and female subjects were each interviewed twice, once by a male graduate student and once by a female graduate student. The content of the interviews was either very innocuous or unpleasantly personal. Their first general finding was that all subjects tended to look at the interviewer more while listening to than while speaking to him or her. It is possible that this effect occurred because there is an unwritten law, at least in our culture, that people should show attentiveness when being spoken to. In addition, it is thought that people may look away while speaking in order to avoid distraction. A second finding was that, while speaking, subjects looked significantly more at the interviewer when the content of the interview was innocuous than when it was unpleasant. Finally, female subjects looked at the interviewer more than male subjects overall, regardless of the sex of the interviewer.

Most everyday social interaction suggests that there is a trade-off between eye contact and physical distance, such that it is more acceptable for two individuals to stand closer if they are not engaged in eye contact. This interaction between visual behavior and personal space was documented in a study by Argyle and Dean (1965). Their results suggest that there is an "equilibrium distance" at which any two individuals will place themselves, depending upon the amount of eye contact involved in the interaction. The closer two subjects sat to one another, the less eye contact they engaged in. Similarly, a subject would stand closer to his partner if that partner had his eyes closed. In discussing their results, Argyle and Dean proposed that eye contact is not the only factor which influences the equilibrium distance. They suggest that intimacy of topic, sex of interactants, and amount of smiling may also serve to determine the limits of personal space.

The use of interpersonal distance, or personal space, has also been found to figure significantly in the total matrix of expressive behaviors occurring during interpersonal interaction. The rules which appear to govern the use of interpersonal distance are evident in typical encounters between persons. For example, when two acquaintances approach one another on the street, there seems to be an appropriate distance at which they engage in eye contact and greet one another. When two strangers are introduced at a party, they generally position themselves so as to appear neither overly familiar nor stand-offish.

Although much research on personal space has been conducted in the past decade, consistent findings have been lacking due to the many variables involved. A few conclusions, however, can be drawn with reasonable certainty (Evans & Howard, 1973, p. 337): (1) Personal space is influenced by sex. Male-female pairs require less personal space than female-female pairs who in turn require less than male-male pairs. (2) Individuals from North America seem to require more personal space than those from the Mediterranean. (3) As might be expected, people who wish to be friendly interact at smaller personal distances than those who are hostile.

Accuracy in the Judgment of Nonverbal Behaviors

We have mentioned several nonverbal behaviors, and have discussed the effects that facial expression, visual contact, and personal distance can have upon interpersonal perception and behavior. It is clear that certain internal states can be accurately judged from expressive behavior by people of various cultures and backgrounds. Although this evidence is convincing, however, it was collected using a very limited set of stimuli, photographs which unambiguously portray the basic emotions. It seems possible, therefore, that some people are more adept than others at judging subtleties in nonverbal behavior. These were the questions addressed in a 1970 study conducted by Lanzetta and Kleck: Are there certain people who are "good judges" of the expressive behavior of others? If so, are these same people "good stimuli," that is, are their expressive behaviors clear and easily judged by others? Lanzetta and Kleck had each of their subjects observe a series of red and green lights: the red light signalled the onset of electric shock. During these trials, measures of the subject's physiological reactions were taken, and videotape records were kept of the subject's nonverbal reactions. In the second part of the study, each subject viewed the videotapes of the other subjects, and was asked to indicate when the person on the tape was about to receive shock. Analysis of the errors made by each subject showed that those subjects who exhibited the greatest physiological reactions to shock were the most difficult for others to accurately judge. This may mean that those who seem the most placid and unemotional may be those whose physiological reactions are the most intense. The most surprising and intriguing result of this study, however, was that those subjects who were the best judges of others were themselves the most difficult for others to correctly judge, and vice versa.

In summary, nonverbal behaviors add much to the overall impressions of persons. There are at least some emotions which seem to be basic; their expression appears to be innate, and these expressions can be accurately discriminated by humans everywhere. Nonverbal behaviors are, to some extent, affected by learning and context. In addition to facial configuration, nonverbal responses such as eye gaze and physical distance can provide information about internal states and influence interpersonal behavior. There is evidence that individual differences do exist in the ability to accurately judge internal states from more subtle expressive behaviors. In particular, it appears that some individuals are good judges and that some are good stimuli (easy for others to judge), but that few individuals are both. We shall return to this question of individual differences in the accuracy of interpersonal judgments in the next section.

IMPRESSION FORMATION

Most common social experience suggests that, in order to arrive at an overall impression of an individual, we must process a wealth of information about him. Although it is true that people are often willing to characterize others on the basis of only one or two pieces of evidence, we typically have a great deal of information to evaluate and integrate. Consider the wealth of clues provided in this description of Tom Buchanan from *The Great Gatsby:*[1]

> . . . he was a sturdy straw-haired man of thirty with a rather hard mouth and a supercilious manner. Two shining arrogant eyes had established dominance over his face and gave him the appearance of always leaning aggressively forward. Not even the effeminate swank of his riding clothes could hide the enormous power of that body—he seemed to fill those glistening boots until he strained the top lacing, and you could see a great pack of muscle shifting when his shoulder moved under this thin coat. It was a body capable of enormous leverage—a cruel body.
>
> His speaking voice, a gruff husky tenor, added to the impression of fractiousness he conveyed. There was a touch of paternal contempt in it, even toward people he liked.

There are several aspects of the character which the author draws upon in creating this sketch: physical appearance and clothing, eye behavior, body movements, and speaking voice. In addition, the author does not merely

[1]F. Scott Fitzgerald, *The Great Gatsby,* (New York: Scribner's Sons, 1953), p. 7.

mention these features impassively but draws inferences from them: Buchanan was arrogant, dominant, and aggressive.

The descriptive tools used in this passage seem so rich and compelling because they are often the same ones that we draw upon in forming impressions of others. In this section we will consider some of the important issues in impression formation: (1) the major theories of the process involved and research evidence relevant to these theories; (2) the overall schemes that people use in drawing inferences about others from limited bits of information; and (3) the accuracy of personality judgement.

Processes of Impression Formation

Solomon Asch (1946) produced one of the earliest theories of impression formation. His work was heavily influenced by the tradition of Gestalt psychology, which included the thesis that the whole of any perceptual experience is greater than the sum of its parts. This basic assumption implied, for example, that the visual perception of a human face had an entirely different character from the separate perceptions of eyes, nose, and mouth. For Asch, this meant that the total impression of another person is the product of a dynamic integration of all available information. One's perception of a kind, generous, intelligent person, for instance, would have a very different quality from the "kind + generous + intelligent" sum that a computer might calculate. The Gestalt psychologists saw the human organism as an active data processor which acts upon information, counting some bits of input more than others and organizing the transformed information into a complete and structured whole.

Asch conducted a number of experiments to test out these hypotheses, using a methodology which has since become a standard procedure in person perception research. In one of his most well-known studies, Asch presented two groups of subjects with lists of traits that supposedly described a particular person. Group *A* heard the stimulus person described as intelligent, skillful, industrious, *warm,* determined, practical, and cautious. Group *B,* on the other hand, was told that the stimulus person was intelligent, skillful, industrious, *cold,* practical, and cautious. After hearing this information, all subjects were asked to rate the supposed stimulus person on a variety of personality dimensions.

Asch found that his two groups of subjects had formed very different impressions of the stimulus person, even though both groups had heard identical descriptions, except for the terms "warm" or "cold." Group *A* (the "warm" group) rated the stimulus person as significantly more generous, wise, happy, and good-natured than did Group *B* (the "cold" group). Asch viewed this as support for his Gestalt theory of impression formation. First, it appeared that, indeed, certain bits of information carried more weight than others. Second, the rather dramatic effects obtained by varying only one adjective out of seven seem to be more than a strict summation model would predict.

In order to compare these results with the "baseline" impression created by the other six stimulus terms, a third group of subjects was also run in Asch's experiment. These subjects were given descriptions which consisted of only six adjectives; the terms "warm" and "cold" were not included. The data from this group, when compared with responses of subjects in the other two groups, indicated that inclusion of "warm" or "cold" had a very powerful effect. For example, 55% of this third group rated the stimulus person as "generous." By contrast, however, only 8% of the "cold" group, and a full 91% of the "warm" group saw him as "generous." Apparently, the presence of "warm" or "cold" in the description list had a strong attenuating effect upon the total impression. For this reason, Asch postulated that these terms represent *central traits,* traits which are more important than others in the determination of an impression. He strengthened this assumption by running the same experiment again, substituting "polite" and "blunt" for "warm" and "cold." Responses for these two groups were not nearly so divergent as the responses for the "warm" and "cold" groups had been. For instance, 56% of the "polite" subjects rated the stimulus person as "generous"; 58% of the "blunt" subjects did so. Asch's conclusion: "warm" and "cold" are central traits which play an important role in the organization of overall impressions. Other descriptive terms, such as "polite" and blunt," are of only secondary significance in molding such impressions.

In addition to emphasizing the totality of impressions and the importance of central traits, Gestalt psychologists also argue that the perception of any given stimulus depends to a large extent on its *context.* Perhaps you have experienced the effect of context upon color perception; a gray square seems very light when placed next to a black square, and very dark when placed next to a white one. This phenomenon suggested to Asch that the trait "warm," for example, might produce different impressions when presented with other traits than when presented alone.

Later careful investigation along these lines supported the notion that the centrality of traits depends upon context (Wishner, 1960), but it appears that the determining context is not made up of other stimulus traits presented in a description, as Asch had assumed. Wishner's research indicates that the important context consists of the *response* traits on which the subject is asked to rate the person in question. That is, if a certain stimulus trait is closely associated with one or more of the response dimensions, then its inclusion in a description is likely to make a great difference in the subject's answers on those response dimensions.

That stimulus term is likely to become a central trait in that context. For example, it has been found that most people consider warmth to be closely associated with imaginativeness, but not associated with strength at all. Consequently, warmth is a central trait of description if imaginativeness is one of the items to be rated; on the other hand, the inclusion of "warm" in a list of descriptive traits will not make much difference if subjects are asked to rate the stimulus person on his strength.

Central traits, then, are those which seem to carry the most weight in the formation of impressions. Different descriptive traits can become central, depending upon the specific dimensions along which the stimulus person is judged. In addition, since the perception of all traits seems to depend upon their context, the impact of central traits can be dampened by the other stimulus terms with which they appear.

Much research conducted since Asch's early work has applied more strict mathematical models to re-examine the possibility that a "whole" impression might really be just a "sum" of its parts. Two general types of models have been investigated. One has proposed that the effect of all stimulus traits are added together to arrive at a total; the other has proposed that all traits are averaged. This research has used only the evaluative meanings of traits, since it would be impossible to mathematically describe all the other subtle meanings of traits. Such a limitation, however, does seem reasonable. You may recall that evaluation is one of the most important and indeed the most persistent tendencies in person perception.

Before the adding and averaging models could be tested against one another, preliminary testing was necessary to determine just how positive or negative different personality traits are judged to be. The general methodology for this determination involves asking a number of people to rate how "likeable" each trait is, using a numerical scale. A great many such ratings have been obtained, and it has been found, for example, that warmth is considered an extremely favorable quality, persistance moderately favorable, and dishonesty extremely unfavorable (e.g., Anderson, 1968b). In studies comparing the two models, each subject is presented with a list of trait descriptions and asked to rate how much he would like a person possessing such traits. Using this information, the researchers can determine whether the subject added or averaged the evaluative meanings of the various traits to arrive at his overall rating of the stimulus person.

The following lists provide an example of the different predictions that the two models would produce, assuming that each of the traits has the positive value assigned to it in parentheses. According to the adding model, the inclusion of any additional positively evaluated trait will improve the total "likeableness" of the person being described. The averaging model, however, predicts that the inclusion of a trait which is only moderately positive can actually lower the overall evaluation of the stimulus person. It suggests that in order to increase the likeable-

	List 1		List 2		List 3	
	Sincere	(10)	Sincere	(10)	Sincere	(10)
	Happy	(8)	Happy	(8)	Moral	(10)
	Bold	(6)	Bold	(6)	Happy	(8)
	Cautious	(2)	Cautious	(2)	Bold	(6)
			Persistent	(2)	Cautious	(2)
Adding Model	26		28		36	
Averaging Model	6.50		5.60		7.20	

ness of the stimulus person, any additional information must be more positive than the average of the traits already given.

A great many experiments have been conducted comparing these models (e.g., Anderson, 1965, 1966) and it appears that the averaging model most often seems to hold. The most consistently correct model is a weighted-average model developed by Anderson (1968a). According to his formula, certain traits figure more heavily into the average; that is, they are more salient. One factor which may affect salience is the serial position of a trait on the description list. For example, if "sincere" is presented first on List 1, it may "count for" more than 10 towards the average: if it is last, it may count for less. Order of presentation of stimulus traits can have important real-life analogues; if initial information is most salient, it may mean that first impressions of persons may be difficult to erase. Presumably, other factors besides serial position, such as context and previous learning experience, can influence the weight given to any particular stimulus trait. Of all the mathematical models, this weighted average scheme seems to best handle the data. It is also reminiscent of Asch's original ideas on impression formation: the total impression is more than a simple sum of stimulus traits, and certain traits are more important than others in organizing the overall perception of the stimulus person.

Implicit Personality Theories

Another approach to impression formation which has become increasingly more popular includes the work on *implicit* or *naive personality theories* (Schneider, 1973). The research in this area suggests that each of us has his own theory of personality, his own ideas about which traits go together and what "types" of people there are in the world. Because of this interest, implicit personality theory research attempts a complete statement on how each individual perceiver structures his interpersonal perceptions.

This research assumes that, in forming impressions of others, people will draw inferences from the bits of information they are provided. Of course, Asch's work was concerned with the response traits subjects would infer from the stimulus traits they were given; however, a more detailed study of inference was carried out by Bruner, Shapiro, and Tagiuri (1958). Their method is frequently used to determine a given subject's implicit personality theory. Basically, the technique involves asking the subject, "Given that a person has Trait X, how likely is it that he has Trait Y?" The subject's responses are indicated on a numerical scale. Bruner, Shapiro, and Tagiuri analyzed these responses in order to study the inferences subjects made from stimulus traits presented alone and in combination with each other. They found that, using the inferences subjects made from single traits, they could predict fairly reliably the inferences subjects would make from those traits in combination. This suggests that the underlying structure from which subjects form their inferences must be relatively stable and permanent. A long history of research since this study argues that examination of this inference process is essential to an understanding of the personality theories people apply to one another (e.g., Hays, 1958; Lay & Jackson, 1969; Warr & Sims, 1965).

Research on implicit personality theory, then, relies heavily on the inferences and implications that people draw from limited pieces of information and on the ways in which these inferences are organized. The inferences reflect on the structure of an implicit personality theory. There have been three major emphases in this research: (1) Individual differences in implicit personality theories. Is there a "general" theory used by all members of a given culture, or do individuals have different theories, depending upon their own particular learning experiences? (2) The role of language. Do our "cognitive maps" of personalities show the influence of our language? Do our assumed relationships between traits closely parallel linguistic associations between trait names? (3) The issue of realism. Do implicit personality theories accurately reflect the *true* patterns of traits actually exhibited by people?

In his *Psychology of Personal Constructs* (1955), George Kelly postulated individual differences in naive personality theories as a basic assumption. Kelly stated that each person employs *constructs,* or ways of categorizing similarities and differences between people. It is within the structure of these constructs that inferences about other people are drawn. For example, one person may use "kind-indifferent" as a construct; this would mean that he tends to categorize individuals as either kind or indifferent. Another perceiver may not use this construct, but use "kind-cruel" instead. Kelly proposed that a person's system of constructs is idiosyncratic to his own expectations and perceptual experiences. Research evidence regarding such individual differences, however, has been conflicting. One study (Kuusinen, 1969) reportedly found few such differences, although the interpretation of this data has since been challenged. Nevertheless, it does seem probable that we share at least some of the same constructs; for example, certain stereotypes are fairly prevalent in our culture. And, as we discussed earlier, a stereotype is technically nothing more than an assumed pattern of traits and characteristics. Many people in our culture, for instance, seem to have implicit personality theories from which they infer that muscular truck drivers are aggressive, nonintellectual, and uninterested in the culinary arts. However, the bulk of evidence (e.g., Walters & Jackson, 1966; Messick & Kogan, 1966) suggests that, although certain uniformities may obtain, there are many differences between individuals in the implicit personality theories they hold. The ultimate key to this puzzle, of course, is to identify the type of individual who holds a particular type of naive personality theory about others. Could one say, for example, that authoritarian people tend to be more extreme in their impressions of others? Or that introverted persons have more finely discriminated ways of categorizing those they perceive? Research endeavors on this question, however, have not yielded firm findings.

The question of the influence of language upon implicit personality theories is closely related to that of individual differences. If these theories are predominantly determined by language (i.e., if actual perceptual experience is restricted by the linguistic labels available), then all those who share a language should also apply the same theory of personality to their interpersonal perceptions. It has been found that implicit personality theories do seem to have a mental structure that closely resembles the mental structure of the perceiver's language (Rosenberg & Olshan, 1970). That is, the similarities and differences which are inferred between traits are very close to the ways trait terms are associated in our language.

Perhaps the most difficult question put to researchers studying implicit personality theories is that of *realism:* Do these theories arise from an unbiased appraisal of the actual correlation of personality traits in real people? Do people actually fit these naive theories of personality into which we try to fit them? The best evidence suggests that the answer to both questions is "no." Several researchers (e.g., Passini & Norman, 1966) have found that the inferences people make about those they hardly know are strikingly similar to inferences made about those with whom they have had much contact. Actual experience seems to have very little influence upon the naive personality theory that is applied. However, this evidence, though it may be the best available, is only suggestive. A satisfactory answer to the realism question would have to indicate whether the judgments people make of each other's personalities are accurate or not, no matter how much information is available. This, of course, would require a solid assessment of the stimulus person's real personality against which to compare the subject's estimate of that person's personality. As we shall see in the following section, such assessment is a monumental problem in its own right, and has made the question of realism a very difficult one indeed.

Accuracy in the Judgment of Personality

Social psychologists have long been interested in assessing the accuracy with which people judge the personalities of those they meet. Aside from any theoretical relevance such investigations might have, there are many purely practical reasons for identifying the characteristics of people who are especially good interpersonal judges. Consider the variety of situations in which such an ability is invaluable: choosing a friend or a marriage partner; deciding whether the patrolman who stopped your car will yield to arguments; determining which candidate to vote for in an election; deciding whether to fear or befriend the stranger who approaches you on the street. If, indeed, certain people are better than others in accurately judging those they meet, then perhaps these people have abilities which may be identified and taught to those who do not have the native skill. On the other hand, if such abilities can not be learned, it would still be important to identify good interpersonal judges, so that they may utilize their talent where it is most needed. There are dozens of professions and occupations where correct assessment of others is not only desirable but often essential: clinical psychologists, personnel managers, prison supervisors, college admissions officers, and courtroom judges, to name only a few. It is for these reasons that the study of accuracy in the judgment of personality (sometimes called "empathic ability") has been considered so interesting and important.

In previous sections of this chapter, we have already introduced a number of factors which can cause bias and may lead to inaccurate judgment. Despite these several tendencies which bias person perception, it still seems possible that some perceivers might be better than others at overcoming these tendencies or at using information in such a way that these biases become less important. This is the question psychologists have sought to answer: Just as there appear to be "good" and "bad" judges of emotional state from nonverbal behavior, might there also be "good" and "bad" judges of personality? If so, what qualities characterize accurate and inaccurate judges?

One of the early studies on accuracy in judgment was carried out by Vernon (1933). He obtained a number of personality, skill, and intelligence measures on one group of college students, his judges, and similar (though more intensive) measures on a second group, the subjects of judgment. He then had the judges rate themselves, each other, and the subjects on a variety of personality traits, with the judges' ratings of the "subjects" being by far the most extensive. Although the judges never met the subjects, they made various judgments using photographs, handwriting samples, artwork samples, and character sketches of the subjects. Vernon then compared the judges' assessments of these people with the assessments he had independently obtained. Using this analysis, he could find no evidence that there was a general "trait" of accuracy on which some judges were high and some were low. In other words, he had a great deal of difficulty in discerning any consistent pattern in the data. There was some suggestive evidence, however, that some types of people were good judges in some types of circumstances. "Good judges of self are more intelligent and possess more sense of humor than the average. Good judges of friends and associates are less socially inclined and less intelligent, but more artistic than good self-judges. Good judges of strangers are distinctly more artistic and intelligent than the average, and, under certain conditions, more asocial" (p. 57). Vernon concluded that accuracy depends not only on the judge and the person being judged but also on the nature of the judgement task and the conditions under which it is undertaken.

Another early study, carried out by Estes (1938), utilized different stimuli but yielded a similar pattern of results. He also obtained extensive personality assessments on both judges and subjects before the experiment was conducted; instead of photographs, however, he had his judges make ratings on the basis of silent films of the subjects performing certain behaviors (such as removing a coat and holding a lighted match). This study also failed to find a general trait of "intuitive ability" but again concluded that accuracy depends on the judge, the subject of judgment, and the particular judgment task. In general, it seemed that judges whose interests were mainly in the graphic and dramatic arts were more accurate than judges interested in science or philosophy. Introverted, contemplative subjects appeared to be the most difficult to judge. Finally, certain traits seemed easier for all judges to pick out in subjects: "inhibition-impulsion," "apathy-intensity," "placidity-emotionality," and "ascendance-submission."

There was a flaw in these early studies which might be termed the validity problem. The criteria that the early researchers relied upon to determine accuracy consisted mainly of personality tests on the stimulus person. A judge was considered accurate if his judgments of that person corresponded to the personality profile obtained from those tests. However, doubt had been growing for some time as to just how accurate personality tests are as valid indicators of a person's actual behavior. This doubt implied that these tests may not be the best criteria to use in determining whether a judge could accurately assess what another person was like. Dymond (1950) proposed that the test validity problem be solved by simply asking judges to predict the actual behavior of the stimulus person (or, at least, the stimulus person's rating of his own behavior). For example, the judge might be asked to predict the stimulus person's answer on this question: "I become nervous and forget my question when called upon in class (1) always (2) often (3) sometimes (4) rarely (5) never." The judge's prediction is then compared with the answer the stimulus person actually gave to that question. It was thought that accurate judges must be more knowledgeable, sensitive, and empathic than inaccurate judges. Although investigations using this improved methodology seemed to be making some headway into the problem on accuracy, subsequent criticism of the interpretation of these studies left much doubt as to their utility. In a 1955 article, Gage and Cronbach explicated several reasons for discounting these earlier results. First, they pointed to evidence that a large part of a judge's ratings are determined by *assumed similarity,* or the tendency to rate others as similar to oneself. Because of this, the accuracy of a judge's rating would depend not only upon his intuitive ability, but also upon the degree to which the subject happened to be similar to him. For instance, if I exhibit a tendency towards assumed similarity, I will be very accurate in assessing people who happen to be similar to me, such as friends and colleagues, but I may still be very inaccurate in judging people who are dissimilar. My accuracy in the first case need have nothing to do with my ability to judge other people in general. Since the early studies did not separate out the effects of assumed similarity, it is impossible to distinguish real from coincidental accuracy in their results. Gage and Cronbach suggested methods of handling data which could overcome this artifact.

The second issue which Gage and Cronbach discussed concerns the definition of accuracy. Unlike the early researchers, they distinguished two different components which seem to play a part in determining an overall accuracy score. The first of these is *stereotype accuracy,* or the ability to accurately estimate the population average on a given personality trait. The second is *differential accuracy,* the ability to estimate the difference between a particular subject's score on a trait and the population average on that trait. Presumably, a given judge could have high or low stereotype accuracy, and either high or low differential accuracy. Imagine, for example, that you were given a brief biography of a particular college student and asked to predict how friendly she would be in a certain situation. Suppose that you rated her as moderately friendly, but in fact she was very shy and withdrawn. In this case, you would have displayed high sterotype accuracy in knowing that most college students are moderately friendly, but poor differential accuracy because in fact she deviated from the average. It seems important to be able to distinguish these different types of accuracy, and Gage and Cronbach proposed methods for doing so.

Parenthetically, it should be noted that Cronbach (1955) also raised a third issue which had not previously been uncovered in this research. He described the tendency towards *overdifferentiation* as a major source of judgmental error. This means that the judge is too sensitive to individual differences in the persons he judges. In most cases, a judge will be more accurate in his assessments of personality if he makes most of his ratings close to the average on each particular trait, because that is where most individuals actually score. A judge may be correct if he reacts to differences in the persons he judges, and rates them as above or below the average on particular traits. Cronbach's point, however, is that judges tend to overestimate differences between persons and make their ratings too far from the average, even if their error is in the right direction. This, then, is another biasing tendency which must be added to the list of factors which can lead to inaccuracy in judgment.

After the publication of the criticisms by Cronbach (1955) and Gage and Cronbach (1955) of the early accuracy studies, research on accuracy in personality judgment attempted to incorporate the suggestions made in those two articles: compensation for assumed similarity and a distinction between stereotype and differential accuracy. One apparently successful attempt was made in 1960 by Cline and Richards. Their methodology was quite similar to that used by earlier researchers, but their analysis and interpretation of results utilized the precautions outlined by Gage and Cronbach. The subjects of judgment in this experiment represented a cross-section of adults in Salt Lake City. A sound-and-color film interview was made of each subject; the interview consisted of questions on personal values, personality strengths and weaknesses, reaction to the interview, hobbies and activities, self-concept, and temper. Subsequent to the filming of these interviews, a great deal of information was obtained on each of the subjects: (1) interviews with the subject on life history and personal habits, (2) nine pencil-and-paper personality tests, and (3) interviews with five close associates of the subject on their knowledge of his behavior and history. Judges were college students who viewed the films and rated the personalities of the subjects in a variety of ways. Unlike the earlier studies of Vernon and Estes, this experiment did not obtain personality information on the judges. Cline and Richards were interested in distinguishing people who had a general ability to judge personalities accurately, and not in determining characteristics of good and bad judges.

The judges rated each subject by: (1) predicting the subject's behavior in a number of situations, (2) rating the subject's personality traits, (3) predicting the subject's opinions, (4) attempting to complete sentences in the way the subject had completed them, and (5) describing the subject using a variety of adjectives. It is important to note that in this study the criterion of accuracy of the judges' ratings was the pattern of responses given by the subject and his close associates describing the behavior of the subject. Cline and Richards did discern a general ability to perceive others accurately; some of their judges appeared to score high on this ability, others scored low. The researchers also distinguished the two components of stereotype and differential accuracy and concluded that "a good judge may be accurate because he has an accurate stereotype or because he is able to predict specific differences between individuals (or both)" (p. 5). Apparently, however, a large part of the general ability is accounted for by stereotype accuracy alone. For the most part, then, a good judge is one who can accurately estimate the personality traits of the average adult. This substantiates the point made by Cronbach on overdifferentiation: The good judge does not overestimate individual differences.

The Cline and Richards results seem encouraging. It appears that the methods of data analysis suggested by Gage and Cronbach do much to clarify the definition of an accurate judgment of personality. Recently, however, another and possibly more basic problem for this line of research has become apparent. Previously, we discussed the validity problem, which was recognized long ago in studies on accuracy. Steps were taken to correct this problem: Since it appeared that typical personality tests did not accurately describe a person's behavior, researchers had stimulus persons describe their behavior in a fixed set of situations. Judges were then asked to predict how the stimulus persons had rated themselves; there was usually one standard set of behavior items on which all judges predicted all stimulus persons. These predictions were later compared with the stimulus person's responses for a measure of judgmental accuracy. It was assumed that these criteria were valid. If a stimulus person described himself as behaving in a friendly manner in a certain situation, it was assumed, first, that this was an accurate self-description and, second, that this behavior meant the stimulus person was indeed friendly. Lately, however, much doubt has been cast upon these assumptions. There may be a new validity problem: it appears that a person's friendly behavior in a given situation may indicate nothing about his behavior in another situation, much less signal that he is truly a "friendly" person.

In his 1968 book, *Personality and Assessment,* Walter Mischel reviewed the research on cross-situational consistency in behavior. He concluded that there is very little evidence that any particular person will behave consistently in different situations. In fact, in many instances, the behavior of all persons seems to be determined by the specific situation and not by personality characteristics of each particular person. This means that, perhaps, researchers may find greater accuracy if they ask their judges to describe the "average" behavior of a number of persons in one specific situation than if they continue to request their judges to predict consistencies in the behavior of one stimulus person across a variety of situations. Another implication is this: perhaps the "accurate" judges discovered by researchers such as Cline and Richards are those people who are somehow skilled at predicting the consistent test and interview responses of stimulus persons, rather than being able to judge what those stimulus persons are really like. This would mean that traditional accuracy research has not really been looking at true accuracy of personality judgment. Mischel's work seemed to raise the counter-intuitive possibility that there is no such thing as "personality," that individuals do not really have unique, consistent, predictable ways of behaving.

Although this general problem of personality assessment has not yet been overcome, a solution may be in sight. Just as Gage and Cronbach suggested answers to the "assumed similarity" and "stereotype or differential accuracy" problems, Bem and Allen (1974) have suggested a method for assessing personality which may be more valid than any used before. They propose that any given personality trait may simply not apply to all persons in the same way. The trait of altruism, for example, may be very pertinent for a description of a person who devotes all her spare time to volunteer organizations and contributes one fifth of her annual income to charities. Similarly, the term altruism would (in a negative sense) be quite central for describing a person who staunchly refuses any requests for help from volunteer groups and makes it a point to harrass any persons collecting money for charitable causes. On the other hand, altruism, either in a positive or negative sense, would just not be an important descriptive trait on which to rate someone who occasionally donates money to charity, but sometimes fails to do so, without any apparent consistency. Rather than applying the same set of traits to all persons, it appears necessary to first determine which personality traits are appropriate for a particular stimulus person. When this is done, as Bem and Allen demonstrate, the trait-rating thus obtained can be quite valid, in the sense that a stimulus person's real behavior can be accurately predicted from them.

We have attempted to illuminate the problem that researchers have in deciding just what a stimulus person's real personality is, before they can attempt to assess the accuracy of a judge's rating of that person's personality. We have described one possible solution: tailoring the application of personality traits to each particular stimulus person; in this way, researchers may feel reasonably confident that they have a valid criterion against which to compare any assessments made by naive judges. This method of tailoring may seem somewhat familiar to you. In our earlier discussion of the perceptual process and the role that abstraction plays in that process, we examined the tendency perceivers have to categorize persons. You may recall that we described a study conducted by Dornbusch and his co-workers (1965) in which children were asked to give free-response descriptions of their acquaintances in a summer camp. It was found that each child seemed to have a particular limited set of categories which he relied upon to describe others. These researchers were following an earlier suggestion (Hastorf et al., 1958) that perhaps experiments on person perception should allow the perceivers to choose their own terms for describing stimulus persons, rather than constraining all perceivers to use the same experimenter-determined categories. Just as Dornbusch et al. suggested a "tailoring" of response items to each particular judge, Bem and Allen suggest a "tailoring" of criteria for accuracy to each particular stimulus person.

ATTRIBUTION THEORY

Until February 4, 1974, Patricia Hearst was the quiet and rather apolitical young heiress to a famed publishing fortune. She was studying art history at Berkeley and devoting much of her spare time to preparing for her wedding the following August. On February 4 these plans were abruptly ended when she was apparently kidnapped by three terrorists of the so-called Symbionese Liberation Army (SLA). For two months Patricia's family attempted to comply with her captor's demands to feed the needy of California. On tape recordings made by the SLA, Patty's kidnappers recited their radical philosophy and answered the bargaining offers made by the Hearsts. On these same tapes, Patty assured her family that she was well. It was expected that she would be released sometime in early April.

Then came a tape recording of Patty denouncing her family, saying that she had decided to stay with the SLA and fight "for the people." She announced that her previous identity was dead and that she was now called by the revolutionary name "Tania." Soon afterwards, a gang of SLA members stormed a San Francisco bank and took more than $10,000. During the hold-up, one of the gang gestured to a young woman who stood holding a carbine on the bank customers and employees, and shouted, "This is Tania Hearst!" Bank photos later revealed that, in fact, that woman was the same person who had been dragged, screaming, from her apartment only two months before.

This episode gave rise to a host of questions concerning the kidnapping and the events which followed. Why did Patty say that she had joined her captors? Under what circumstances had the tape been made? Did the bank robbery mean that she had in fact embraced the radical cause? Could more terrorist activities be expected of her in the future?

Several different explanations for Patty's actions were offered (*Time,* April 29, 1974): (1) She had been killed, and the bank robber was an imposter. (2) She had been an SLA member before the kidnapping and had actually helped to plan an abduction, not knowing that she had been targeted as the victim. (3) Fearing that she might be killed, Patty pretended to be converted, in the hopes of finding some opportune time to escape. (4) During her two months of captivity, Patty had undergone extensive brainwashing and had, in fact, willingly joined the SLA and participated in the hold-up.

The fact that such directly opposing explanations could be generated for Patty's behavior supports a conclusion we can draw from most everyday social experience: our perceptions and evaluations of other people take account of much more than just the behavior we see them perform. It seems that we have a tendency to make inferences about causality. Rather than being satisfied with objectively noting and remembering a behavior, we are almost impelled to first decide why it occurred. This tendency to see events as being caused and to generate explanations about the causes seems to extend even beyond person perception. Heider and Simmel (1944) prepared a film in which three geometric shapes moved around and inside a rectangle. In one "scene" (see Figure 8-2) the large triangle and the circle were moving about inside the rectangle, and the small triangle was outside.

Subjects were shown the film, then asked to describe it. They most often related the scene

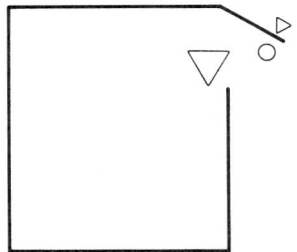

FIGURE 8-2. "Scene" from Heider and Simmel film.

pictured in Figure 8-2 as follows: The small triangle and the circle are a woman and man in love. The large triangle is a villain who lured the woman into a house and chased her around. Her lover, in desperation, threw open the door to the house, allowing the woman to escape. It is clear that these subjects were quick to infer intentionality and causality, even in the movement of geometric shapes.

The inference process seems immediate and essentially unconscious. Apparently, this process helps us develop and maintain an orderly and understandable world. An individual's behavior may change dramatically, but the attribution process can serve to keep the events sensible. In the kidnapping case, the Hearst family was painfully aware of the drastic changes in Patty's behavior. We can guess that they could maintain stability by seeing her new, "radical" behavior as having been caused by forces external to her; in this way, the behavior was not her own "fault." It is commonly accepted that "good people do good things and bad people do bad things." We can maintain this rule by, first, seeing as much "good" behavior in a "good person" as we can, and second, by seeing any "bad" behavior by that person as being caused by external forces beyond his control. Thus we maintain an orderly and sensible perceptual world by shifting the causal attributions we make about behavior.

More generally, attribution problems include three different types of processes: (1) The judgment of causality. Why did a particular event occur? What particular person or object or set of circumstances caused it? (2) The formation of inferences. What did I learn from this event about that person or object or set of circumstances? (3) The generation of predictions. What can I expect of this person or object or set of circumstances in the future?

The investigation of attribution processes has recently become of central interest to social psychologists. Current research in attribution theory represents a shift of interest from the accuracy of interpersonal judgment to the processes involved in such judgments and the factors which can influence those processes. Essentially, research in attribution attempts to explain and expand upon the common-sense way in which people judge causality, draw inferences, and make predictions. It is obvious that, informally, the man on the street does understand how people make attributions and uses this understanding to control the impressions others have of him. For example, a traditional ploy of ambitious students is termed "sneaky booking." This tactic consists of telling your fellow students, on the night before a big exam, that you just don't feel like studying and are going out to the movies. Following this, you sneak off with your books and notes and proceed to study far into the night. When you achieve an A on the exam, your colleagues decide that you must be truly brilliant. You realize that, if they can not attribute your success to effort, they will be forced to attribute it to ability. In this section, we will explore the reasons why tricks such as "sneaky booking" work, and we will examine some of the strengths and weaknesses of common attribution processes.

Theoretical Formulations

Many of the ideas on attribution which have been investigated recently were first discussed by Fritz Heider (1944, 1958). He stated that man seeks to make sense out of his world, in order to understand, predict, and if possible, control his physical and social environments. In these attempts to discover the invariances which underlie his everchanging surroundings, Heider argued, man seeks to know the causes of events. Some of the ideas which Heider introduced and which have been investigated by attribution theorists are: (1) Behavior may be attributed to either an internal cause (something about the person himself) or an external cause (something in the situation or circumstances). Heider suggested that possible internal causes are ability and effort. He termed external causes environmental difficulty; these presumably include the difficulty of the behavior the person is trying to perform as well as factors of luck and external helps or hindrances. (2) There is a tendency to perceive persons as causes of events, unless very strong situational forces are immediately apparent. This tendency can lead to an underestimation of other causal factors such as environmental influences and to an overestimation of the role played by permanent personality characteristics of the person in question. (3) If we see strong external forces operating, we attribute behavior to those forces. On the other hand, if we see the person involved as having the ability and the intention to perform that behavior, we will perceive that person as a cause. The effort expended by the person is often used as a basis for inferring his intention. (4) There is a tendency to "assimilate" persons and acts. For example, if a person causes an unpleasant event, people will assume that he is an unpleasant person. Similarly, we tend to be more impressed by a work of art, if we know the artist is considered to be a master by art critics.

Some consequences of the internal attributions of ability and effort were explored by Jones and deCharms (1957). These researchers had their subjects work on intellectual tasks in groups. It had been prearranged that one person (a confederate of the experimenters) would fail at the task. In some cases, the subjects were led to believe that success on the task depended upon effort; the task was something "anybody could do." In other conditions, however, they were told that success depended upon ability; the task was very like a standard IQ test. The researchers found that the failing confederate was seen as less dependable, less likeable, and less competent when subjects believed his failure was due to lack of effort than when they thought he lacked ability. More recent evidence (Weiner et al., 1972) supports the notion that people are more prone to condemn and punish low effort than low ability.

The more cognitive approach to person perception outlined by Heider (1958) was not taken up again in a formal manner until the publication of "From Acts to Dispositions: The Attribution Process in Person Perception" by Jones and Davis (1965). Heider had stressed the fact that behavior can be explained either in terms of environmental forces or in terms of certain personality characteristics (dispositions) of the person engaged in that behavior. The model proposed by Jones and Davis is concerned primarily with understanding the conditions that lead to the attributions of internal causality and the confidence (or strength) with which those attributions are made. According to this model, a perceiver observes the behavior of a given individual, draws inferences from the behavior about that individual's intentions, and, finally, infers that individual's dispositions from those intentions. For example, if you receive a gift from a new acquaintance, you may infer that she intended it as a gesture of friendship and, on that basis, may decide that she is a friendly person. Under a different set of circumstances, however, you may infer that she intended to ingratiate herself and, therefore, that she is a selfishly ambitious person. Jones and Davis discuss four variables which can be important in determining the nature and strength of the inferences made from a person's behavior: social desirability, common effects, hedonic relevance, and personalism.

If a person performs a socially desirable act, we can usually make very few inferences about him, because such acts are expected and even demanded by society (an external force). However, if an action has low social desirability, then we feel more confident in drawing inferences about that person's dispositions. For example, if you are standing in line at a movie theater, and someone takes his place behind you, you would probably not draw any conclusions as to the type of person he is. You have learned nothing about him, other than the fact that he is like most people. In contrast, if he pushes you aside and steps in front of you, you would feel confident in deciding that he is rude and boorish.

The inspection of the common and noncommon effects of a person's behaviors can lead to increased certainty about that person's intentions and dispositions. Suppose an individual engages in the following behaviors: (1) She subscribes only to the Sunday newspaper (from which we may infer either that she has no time to read during the week or that she wants to save money). (2) She turns away the Boy Scout selling a baseball ticket (leading to the inference that either she dislikes baseball or wants to save money). (3) She grows her own vegetables (from which we may infer either that she likes gardening or wants to save money). On the basis of the one common effect of these three behaviors, we would probably decide that she is a thrifty person. In the same way, we examine the common effects between chosen and rejected courses of action in order to judge the reason for the particular choice that was made. For example, suppose that a person has a choice between two apartments which are identical in every way including price, except that one is on an isolated corner of the apartment complex and the other is in the center of activity. If she chooses the former, we could infer from the one noncommon effect that she values quiet and solitude.

Hedonic relevance refers to the importance of the stimulus person's behavior for the perceiver. If an event is important to the perceiver, he is more likely to make internal causal attributions about the person involved in that event. For example, if I feel very strongly about environmental protection, a litterbug's behavior has hedonic relevance for me. Because of this, I will be more likely to infer dispositions about that litterbug (such as inconsiderateness or ignorance) than would a perceiver for whom such behavior is not hedonically relevant. Recall the Jones and DeCharms (1957) experiment where subjects were more prone to blame the confederate who apparently failed because of lack of trying rather than lack of ability. They also reported that this attribution tendency was stronger when the consequences of the failure were greater for the subject.

Personalism refers to the effects of the stimulus person's behavior upon the perceiver. Jones and Davis suggest that the more direct the effects of a person's behavior upon the perceiver, the more confidence the perceiver will have in making dispositional attributions about that person. For instance, you would feel more strongly that a stranger is a friendly person if he stops and talks with you than if you observe him talking to someone else. The behavior may be the same, but when it is directed towards you, you are more likely to infer internal dispositions about the person involved.

Harold Kelley (1967, 1973) has made significant additions to the attribution models set down by Heider and by Jones and Davis. The Kelley model is similar to Heider's, in that it deals mainly with the judgment of causality. However, it is a more formal theory which draws upon mathematical analogues. Kelley proposes that, in everyday problems of attribution, people act as rational information processors and automatically analyze the available "data" about an event in much the same way that a statistician analyzes data. There are two different types of attribution problems, which Kelley distinguishes in terms of the amount of information available to the attributor: Case 1, in which the attributor has information from multiple observations, and Case 2, in which the attributor has information from only a single observation.

The covariation principle applies to Case 1, where the perceiver has information about a particular behavior ("effect") from a number of different instances. This principle can be stated as follows: "An effect is attributed to the one of its possible causes with which, over time, it covaries" (1973, p. 108). That is, if one of the possible causes is present every time the effect occurs, the effect is then attributed to that particular cause because the two covary. Kelley lists three classes of possible causes for any effect: persons, entities, and times (unique sets of circumstances). Consider an example in which the "person" is a student named Carol, the "entity" is a new jazz recording, and the "times" consist of Carol listening to the recording in a music store, by herself, and at a party with friends. Suppose that the effect here is that Carol says the recording is "fantastic." If we note that (1) Carol does not say this of all recordings, but only of this one, (2) she has this same reaction to the recording under different sets of circumstances, and (3) her friends also say it is fantastic, then we would attribute this effect to the recording itself. The effect ("It's fantastic!") covaries with the entity (the recording) over time and over persons. The effect does not covary with one particular person (Carol and her friends all have the same reaction), or one particular set of circumstances (it doesn't matter if the listener is in a music store or at a party). Therefore, we would not attribute the effect to either of these two potential causes. This set of factors fits the criteria Kelley describes for an "entity attribution": the effect is distinctive to this particular entity, there is consensus with other persons, and the response is consistent over time.

When a perceiver has only one observation on which to base his attribution (Case 2), the

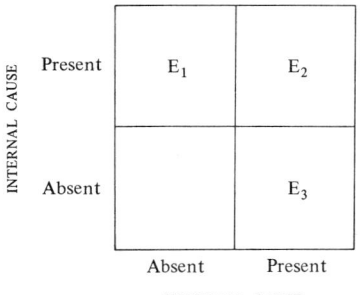

FIGURE 8-3. Causal schema for multiple sufficient causes.

discounting principle applies: "The role of a given cause in producing a given effect is discounted if other plausible causes are also present" (1973, p. 113). Application of this principle can be illustrated using the following example: Suppose that we are trying to decide whether someone made a charitable donation because he is altruistic (an internal, or dispositional, cause) or because the solicitor made it impossible to refuse (an external cause). This dilemma is represented diagrammatically in Figure 8-3 (from Kelley, 1973, p. 114), where "E" represents the effect (the donating of money).

If the effect occurs without external pressure being exerted (E_1), we attribute that effect to something about the donator himself. In contrast, if he donates money when it is clear he does not want to (E_3), we know that his action was caused by the pressure of the solicitor. However, when he donates money after being asked, and we have no way of knowing whether he really wanted to (E_2), the discounting principle implies that we will discount the internal cause as an explanation of the effect.

Kelley's formulation, then, consists of a series of statements describing the way in which people may go about making attributions under various circumstances. He assumes that, for each set of circumstances and information, a particular mental model (a "causal schema") is used by the attributor to "analyze" that information and arrive at an attribution of causality.

Attribution Studies

Although formal statements on attribution theory were not formulated until fairly recently, studies concerned with the same issues had been conducted long before. Thibaut and Riecken (1955), for example, carried out an experiment which investigated external and internal causal attributions of behavior. Subjects were asked to participate in a three-person experiment, believing that the other two persons were also subjects. In fact, they were confederates of the experimenter. One confederate was of "high status"; neatly and formally dressed, he was introduced as a Ph.D. currently on the faculty of the university. The second, "low-status" confederate, unkempt and sloppily dressed, was introduced as a member of the freshman class at the university. The real subject was told that it was his job to try to persuade the other two persons to donate blood for a Red Cross blood drive. Following this persuasive communication given by the subject, both confederates agreed to donate blood.

The subject was then asked his opinion as to why the confederates complied. Nearly all subjects said they thought that the low-status person was pressured into it by the talk, but that the high-status person had "wanted to anyway."

Thibaut and Riecken suggest that their subjects assumed that the high-status person was powerful enough to resist their sales pitch if he had wanted to; therefore, he must have had his own, internal reasons for complying. On the other hand, an external force (the pressure of persuasion) was seen as the cause of the low-status person's compliance. It is clear that, in both cases, both an internal and an external force could have caused the behavior in question. In the case of the high-status individual, the external force was discounted; in the case of the low-status person, the internal cause was discounted.

A later attribution study (Strickland, 1958) investigated not only the effects of a given variable upon causal attributions, but also the influence of these judgments upon the attributor's subsequent behavior. In this experiment, the subject was set up as "supervisor" over two "workers" (A and B) performing a boring task for a period of 10 trials. The subject was told to monitor worker A on 9 out of 10 trials and to monitor B on 2 out of the 10; furthermore, the subject was given the power to punish the workers if they failed to meet high performance standards. The experimenter had prearranged the overall performance records of A and B so that they were virtually identical. In spite of this, however, subjects stated that they trusted A less than B and that they saw A's behavior as more externally controlled than B's. Apparently, where the external force was strong (surveillance, and the possibility of punishment, on 9 out of 10 trials), internal causality was discounted. In addition, these causal attributions affected the behavior of the subjects. During a second set of trials in which subjects were free to monitor A and B as often as they chose, they spent more time checking up on A.

Strickland's study demonstrates that attributions may be manipulated by changing the apparent external force upon the person whose behavior is being judged. In a later experiment (1967), Jones and Harris obtained results that were similar, with one important additional finding. Jones and Harris presented their subjects with essays that had been written by other students. The essays either supported Fidel Castro or opposed him. (At the time this experiment was run, anti-Castro sentiment was by far the most popular.) Subjects were told that certain essays in each group had been freely written and that others had been assigned. As expected, when subjects read the "free-choice" essays (low external pressure), they inferred that the writer was expressing his true attitudes. However, an interesting and unexpected result occurred when subjects read the unpopular pro-Castro "no-choice" essays. Logically, subjects should have guessed that the students who wrote these essays were, like most students, opposed to Castro. However, subjects felt confident that a pro-Castro "no-choice" essay represented the attitude of the writer, even though they knew he had been forced to write it. These subjects were making a common attribution error: They underestimated the situational causes of a person's behavior and overestimated the influence of that particular person's traits or attitudes. In other words, we often tend to attribute a person's actions to something about his underlying personality, and we tend to ignore the external pressures which may have forced him to act as he did.

Attributional Errors and Biases

The results of the Jones and Harris study suggest that attribution processes may not always be rational and logical. It is clear from everyday experiences that the judgments, inferences, and predictions we make about others are often mistaken or, at least, do not agree with the judgments and predictions made by other people. Apparently, there is more to attribution than simple, unbiased information processing. Indeed, some of the most interesting and provocative attribution research has investigated the factors which distort judgments and cause "misattributions."

We mentioned above that Harold Kelley's attribution model depicts man as a "naive psychologist" who analyzes the data from social observation in much the same way that a statistician analyzes scientific data. However, Kelley does admit that this naive scientific method is not infallible; it is " . . . incomplete, subject to bias, ready to proceed on incomplete evidence, and so on" (1973, p. 109). Kelley (1973) lists several "illusions" which cause people to make inaccurate causal attributions. One of these is the "illusion of external constraint," whereby a person does not realize that his own behavior caused a certain effect; instead, he believes that circumstances or other persons were the cause. For example, it is quite common for a person who is playing a game to ignore the fact that other people become increasingly competitive in response to his competitive moves. He is under the illusion that forces external to him, such as the other players' personalities, lead them to become competitive.

These illusions influence the judgment of causation; similar factors, such as hedonic relevance and personalism, can influence the formation of inferences about stimulus persons. Until recently, little work was done on the biases which affect the generation of predictions. However, a series of experiments by Ross and Amabile (1974) suggest that there may be a general tendency towards "riskiness" in prediction. In these experiments, subjects are given information on the behavior of a stimulus person in one situation and asked to predict his behavior in a different situation. Subjects realize that there is a very poor correlation between behaviors in the two particular situations. Therefore, it seems they should know that their safest strategy would simply be to make predictions close to the average behavior in the second situation. However, subjects fail to do this. They overuse the unreliable information they were given and make extreme predictions. Subjects make the error of assigning too much dispositional meaning to the first piece of information. It seems that they use that information to generate images of what the stimulus person is like and, on the basis of that logically flimsy image, make risky predictions. This research is closely related to Cronbach's (1955) ideas on overdifferentiation, which were discussed earlier. He suggested that people would be much more accurate in their trait assessments of one another if they would simply make those assessments closer to the average on each particular trait.

Perhaps the most well-documented and persistent attribution error is that demonstrated in the Jones and Harris study: the error of underestimating the situational causes of a person's behavior and overestimating the influence of that particular person's traits or dispositions. This error, though it does seem pervasive, does not apply to all attribution problems. It appears that almost the opposite error occurs when we make attributions of our own behavior; we tend to emphasize the situational forces which we are responding to and underestimate the role of our own personality characteristics. Jones and Nisbett (1972) formalize this supposition in terms of the "actor" (the person whose behavior is in question) and the "observer" (another individual who perceives that behavior): " . . . there is a pervasive tendency for actors to attribute their actions to situational requirements, whereas observers tend to attribute the same actions to stable personality dispositions" (p. 80). They suggest several reasons for these divergent attributions of the same behavior. First, the actor and the observer have different information available to them. The actor knows his own intentions, feeling states, and personal history; he is aware of the differences in his behavior from one situation to another. The observer does not have this information. As a result, it is easy for him to see the actor's behavior as representative of stable personality characteristics; there is little to stop the observer from assuming that the actor's behavior is the same in other situations. Second, actors and observers may process the available information in different ways. Simply because of their different physical perspectives, different pieces of information are salient. The actor's movements, words, and facial expressions are salient to the observer. On the other hand, the actor does not see himself, but he does see the many environmental factors to which he is responding. A study by Storms (1973) has shown that reversing the visual perspectives of two persons involved in a conversation can actually reverse the usual actor-observer effect. An actor who sees himself attributes more of his behavior to his own disposition, and an observer who sees himself attributes more of the actor's behavior to situational forces.

Third, Jones and Nisbett suggest that we all feel that "personality traits are things other people have" (p. 92); we believe that we ourselves are complex and flexible, too responsive to changes in situations to be characterized by a small list of traits. Because of this, we describe our own behavior in terms of situations, and the behavior of others in terms of personality traits.

Self-attribution

Jones and Nisbett have shown that we are likely to attribute our own behavior to external, situational forces. What happens, though, when our behavior is apparently not caused by situational constraints? When we seem to be acting in response to our own emotions, attitudes, and beliefs, how do we decide just what these emotions, attitudes, and beliefs are? These are problems in self-attribution: if no external force appears to be controlling us, we must find an appropriate explanation for our own behavior.

Daryl Bem (1972b) has proposed a theory of self-perception, or self-attribution. He suggests that the processes of self-perception and interpersonal perception are very similar. This is especially true if, in a particular situation, our own internal cues are weak or difficult to interpret. In these situations, we look at our own behavior and the circumstances in which it occurs to decide what our internal states must be, just as people observing us must do. Unlike the more loosely defined attribution theory, self-perception theory has been set down in a single formal statement:

> Individuals come to "know" their own attitudes, emotions, and other internal states partially by inferring them from observations of their own overt behavior and/or the circumstances in which this behavior occurs. Thus, to the extent that internal cues are weak, ambiguous, or uninterpretable, the individual is functionally in the same position as an outside observer, an observer who must necessarily rely upon those same external cues to infer the individual's inner states. (Bem, 1972b, p. 2)

A number of experimental results can be adequately explained by self-perception theory. One of these is the Schachter and Singer study (1962) on the self-perception of emotion, which also was discussed in Chapter 3. Subjects in that experiment were given injections of epinephrine, which later caused them to feel emotionally aroused. Some of these subjects were told that the injection was a vitamin whose effects would be studied during some tests of vision; these subjects (the "ignorant" group) were not informed of the feelings of arousal which were to come. Other subjects (the "informed" group) were told exactly what symptoms to expect. Subjects in both groups were then asked to wait with another person before they took their "vision test." This other person was a confederate of the experimenters, who had been instructed to act either very euphoric or very angry. Each subject's behavior was observed during this session; in addition, each subject filled out a mood questionnaire immediately afterward.

Schachter and Singer found that their "ignorant" group seemed to catch the mood of the confederate, while the "informed" group did not. That is, "ignorant" subjects acted euphoric and rated themselves as feeling euphoric if they were in the presence of a euphoric confederate; they appeared to act and feel more angry if they were with the angry confederate. The mood of the "informed" subjects, however, seemed stable, no matter which confederate they were paired with. Bem suggests that the "informed" subjects had clear internal information about what was happening: they knew they felt emotionally aroused because of the injection. On the other hand, the "ignorant" subjects felt physiological arousal, but their internal cues as to what that arousal meant were not clear. So, Bem argues, they looked to external circumstances in order to arrive at a definition of the emotion they were feeling. They observed the confederate's emotional behavior and decided that their own arousal must have meant they were feeling the same emotions as that confederate. This decision is not postulated as a necessarily conscious one.

Misattribution Therapy

It is apparent that self-attribution as well as other-attribution processes are subject to errors and illusions. Several investigators have suggested that the errors in self-attribution processes might be exploited to effect therapeutic results, such as anxiety reduction or improvement of a patient's self-concept. One such investigation of "misattribution therapy" was conducted by Ross, Rodin, and Zimbardo (1969). A subject was presented with two puzzles and told that he could work on either one (or both) during the experiment. He was not told that the puzzles were actually insoluble. One was the "shock" puzzle; if the subject solved that puzzle, he was told, he would avoid receiving shock later on in the experiment. If he solved the "reward" puzzle, on the other hand, he would later receive a sum of money. During the puzzle-solving trial, a loud noise was piped into the headphones worn by the subjects. Some of the subjects (the "misattribution" group) had been told in advance that this noise would cause physiological arousal. These subjects consequently spent significantly less time trying to solve the "shock" puzzle than did subjects who had not been led to believe their arousal would be caused by the noise. The first group of subjects, incorrectly attributing their fear symptoms to noise, actually acted as if they were less afraid. Their behavior showed that they were less concerned than the other subjects about the possibility of receiving shock.

Ross, Rodin, and Zimbardo suggest that this same sort of "therapy" might be applied to reduce fear in real-life situations. For example, someone who is afraid of heights might be told that physiological arousal is a common reaction to the optical effects of viewing convergent lines. In this way, the acrophobic may attribute his fear symptoms to a normal biological reaction and not to actual fear of heights. He should, therefore, act less afraid and eventually believe he is less afraid.

Misattributions may also be effectively induced by the preinformation provided to a patient when he is given a placebo. It is generally assumed that if a patient is given a placebo and told that it is actually a powerful drug, the effect of the suggestion can cause the patient to improve. However, work by Storms and Nisbett (1970) suggests that, under some circumstances, this usual "placebo" procedure may boomerang and cause negative effects. They gave placebos to their subjects, all of whom were insomniacs. They told some of their subjects (the "arousal" group) that the drug would cause arousal symptoms—alertness, heart-rate increase, and high temperature. The rest of the subjects (the "relaxation" group) were told that the drug would cause them to feel relaxed and drowsy. Contrary to what might be expected by the placebo effect, Storms and Nisbett found that arousal subjects got to sleep in less time than usual, but the relaxation subjects took more time than usual to get to sleep. The authors hypothesize that insomniacs are typically victims of a vicious circle. They go to bed in a state of physiological arousal, have trouble going to sleep, begin to worry about the fact that they can not go to sleep, and then have even more trouble relaxing. Storms and Nisbett reason that their "arousal" subjects felt aroused, as they usually do, when they went to bed. However, these subjects had been led to attribute this arousal to the drug they had taken, and consequently did not worry about these arousal symptoms. Their "relaxation" subjects also went to bed in a state of arousal. However, these patients had been told that the drug would relax them. Consequently, they reasoned that they must have been more emotionally upset than ever if they could not even feel the effects of a powerful relaxant. This conclusion caused them increased worry about their insomnia, and it took them longer to fall asleep.

FUTURE TRENDS IN PERSON PERCEPTION RESEARCH

Having presented the major questions of historical and contemporary interest to psychologists studying person perception, we would like to briefly speculate on the future course of this line of inquiry. Although there are many possibilities for new ways to investigate social perception, and similarly a great number of particular phenomena which now lack adequate explanation, we wish to point out four areas which seem particularly "ripe" for investigation.

1. Errors and biases in attribution. It appears likely that, far from being only troublesome deviations in an otherwise logical, ra-

tional attribution process, errors and biases may be important parts of the process itself. Perhaps at least some of these biases are necessary in order to achieve clarity, consistency, and simplicity of causal explanation. It is also possible that overcoming certain biases might require sophisticated understanding which can be gained only through training and insight. In addition, although some work on the question has been conducted (Storms, 1973), it seems important to study the ways in which these attributional biases may be overcome. For example, it is possible that many difficulties in interpersonal relationships arise through errors in attribution, and that these may be alleviated by some form of attribution training. Finally, misattribution therapy appears to hold much promise for clinical application.

2. The process of understanding consistency in individuals. We have noted that perceivers generally assume much more cross-situational consistency in behavior than actually exists. As we pointed out, however, it has recently been suggested (Bem & Allen, 1974) that different people are consistent along different dimensions. If this is true, does the "ordinary" perceiver ever discern the particular dimensions on which a given person is consistent? How might the perceiver go about doing so?

3. The process of developing a conceptualization of another person. Person perception research has typically studied only single encounters between individuals. Often these individuals are strangers. Sometimes they are well-acquainted. In both cases, the dependent measures by which perceptions are measured have been quite limited: listing personality traits, predicting behavior in a variety of situations, rating overall "likeableness." One worthwhile line of research may be to examine interactions of more extended duration, enabling us to investigate the process by which people come to feel they know one another over a period of time. In addition, this sort of research might provide insight into the errors people make in judging others and the changes they make in their judgments once these errors are realized.

4. The categorization of situations. It appears that person perception researchers, like the man on the street, pay too much attention to personality traits and not enough attention to situations. It is becoming clear that situational variables play a much more important role in determining behavior than people (including psychologists) previously realized. Therefore, it would be worthwhile to complement our rich store of information on the ways in which people conceptualize personality traits with some research on the ways in which people categorize situations.

SUMMARY

Although there is evidence that at least some perceptions may be stimulus- and nerve-determined, research strongly suggests that perception is also a constructive, selective process which can be influenced by inner-observer variables. Social perception in particular appears to involve abstractions and categorizations. Each individual perceiver has a certain limited number of categories which he tends to use in describing other people.

One end product of the person-categorization process can be the formation of cultural and ethnic stereotypes. A perceiver's trait description of a single person can also be conceived of as a stereotype of that person. Although their use permits simplicity of cognitive functioning, stereotypes can also produce selective biasing in information processing and storage, so that perceivers tend to see only that evidence which fits their stereotypes or trait attributions.

Man attempts to identify invariant and stable features of his variable and confusing surroundings in order to achieve some measure of predictability and control over them. There are several manifestations of the striving for invariance and stability in interpersonal perceptions: (1) Logical errors, or tendencies to see different traits as "belonging together" when they logically do not. The halo effect can be thought of as a special type of logical error. (2) The centrality of evaluation and description. Evaluation and description of a stimulus person appear to be of central importance in a perceiver's impression of that person. (3) Assumed consistency, or the tendency to perceive the behavior of others as more consistent across different situations than it actually is. The tendency towards invariance in perceptions, however, does not necessitate that all individuals share the same perception of a given stimulus or event. A number of variables (such as perceptual set) may lead to divergent perceptual experiences.

There are several similarities between object- and person-perception: both feel given by the stimuli; both involve abstract cognitions and language; both are influenced by tendencies toward stability and invariance, as well as by perceptual sets. However, there are salient aspects of persons which set them apart perceptually from objects in the environment: ability or power, intentions, and emotions.

There are three separate issues related to the role of emotion in interpersonal encounters: (1) the emotion-to-expression link, (2) the expression-to-perception link, and (3) the subjective experience of emotion. Darwin assumed that there are innate emotion-to-expression links in all humans; he believed that facial expression and the interpretation of facial expression are universally the same for each particular emotion. This position was later attacked by psychologists who proposed that all emotional expression is learned and is therefore dependent upon an individual's learning history and upon situational context. Recently, Carroll Izard has formulated a theory of emotion which closely resembles many of Darwin's original ideas. Although Izard does not deny that learning can play a role in the expression and perception of emotion, he hypothesizes that the facial expressions of certain basic emotions are innate. There is cross-cultural evidence to support the proposition that certain emotions are expressed and interpreted in the same way by all human beings.

In the Gestalt tradition, Asch argued that a total impression of another person represents a dynamic integration of all available information, that is, an overall impression is something more than a simple addition of the separate perceptions that make up that impression. He also postulated that there are certain central traits which are of particular importance in the determination of an impression. Finally, Asch argued that the perception of any given stimulus trait depends to a large extent upon its context.

Of the mathematical models which attempt to formally analyze the way in which interpersonal evaluations are generated, the weighted-average model of Anderson provides the best fit in most instances.

A perceiver's implicit personality theory is his conception of which personality traits are related to one another and what types of people there are in the world. Each perceiver uses his implicit personality theory to structure his interpersonal perceptions and to draw inferences about other people from the information he has about them. Although these naive theories appear to be influenced by cultural factors such as language, there is evidence that each individual has an implicit personality theory which is unique in some ways. Research data is conflicting, but the best evidence indicates that people are not accurately described by the naive theories which we use to describe them.

The question of accuracy in person perception is a difficult and largely unanswered one. Some of the factors which can lead to inaccuracy are: perceptual sets (preinformation), logical errors, primacy and recency effects, and overdifferentiation. Accuracy research originally consisted of judges rating stimulus persons on various personality traits. Because it became clear that personality trait descriptions are difficult to validate, researchers began to obtain predictions of the stimulus person's actual behavior from the judges. Gage and Cronbach illuminated two problems with this research: (1) it did not compensate for assumed similarity and (2) it did not differentiate between stereotype and differential accuracy. Appropriate corrective measures for these problems were suggested by Gage and Cronbach. Later, Mischel pointed out that, since cross-situational consistency in behavior appears to be a rarity, the criterion against which to check a judge's behavior predictions becomes unclear. However, this problem might be solved if researchers attempt to discover beforehand the behaviors in which a stimulus person is consistent (Bem & Allen, 1974).

Research in attribution theory has represented a shift of interest from the accuracy of interpersonal judgment to the processes involved in such judgments and the factors which can influence them. Three attribution processes can be distinguished: (1) the judgment of causation, (2) the formation of inferences, and (3) the generation of predictions. Many of the modern ideas on attribution were first discussed by Heider; he emphasized that behavior may be attributed either to external, environmental causes or to internal personality dispositions. Jones and Davis, concerned only with person-attributions, listed four factors which may influence the inferences made about a stimulus person: (1) social desirability of the person's behavior; (2) common and noncommon effects of different behaviors; (3) hedonic relevance, or the importance of the behavior for the perceiver; and (4) personalism, or the directness of effects of the behavior upon the perceiver.

Kelley proposes a model for the judgment of causation which depicts man as a rational information-processor. He states that when an attributor has several observations on which to base his attribution, the covariation principle applies. When he has information from only one observation, the attributor is thought to apply the discounting principle.

Bem suggests that the processes of self-perception (or self-attribution) are very similar to the processes of other-attribution, especially when a person's own internal cues are weak or confusing. There is a great deal of evidence to support this hypothesis.

It is clear that attribution questions are not always answered in a rational, logical, accurate manner. Several biases in attribution processes have been discussed: (1) There is a tendency to overestimate dispositional causes of behavior and underestimate situational causes. (2) Actors tend to see their own behavior as being caused by environmental forces. Observers tend to see this same behavior as caused by the actor's personality dispositions. (3) There are several illusions which attributors may experience.

Although such attributional errors can cause inaccurate judgments, recent investigation has examined the possibility of exploiting errors in self-attribution to effect therapeutic results.

SUGGESTED READINGS

Ekman, P., Friesen, W. V., & Ellsworth, P. *Emotion in the human face.* New York: Pergamon, 1972.

A well-integrated account of the major conceptual problems, research methods, and empirical findings on the expression and recognition of emotions.

Goffman, E. *Stigma: Notes on the management of spoiled identity.* Englewood Cliffs, N.J.: Prentice-Hall, 1963.

An interesting exploration of the way individuals form impressions of and interact with handicapped others.

Hastorf, A. H., Schneider, D. J., and Polefka, J. *Person perception.* Reading, Mass.: Addison–Wesley, 1970.

A complete but concise discussion of major areas of interest in person perception.

Heider, F. *The psychology of interpersonal relations.* New York: Wiley, 1958.

A classic discussion of the nature of interpersonal perception and the role of causal inference in social life.

Jones, E. E., Kanouse, D. E., Kelley, H. H., Nisbett, R. E., Valins, S., & Weiner, B. *Attribution: Perceiving the causes of behavior.* Morristown, New Jersey: General Learning Press, 1972.

The major theory and research in attribution, in a series of monographs by contemporary leaders in the field. This higher-level collection is suggested for the more advanced student.

Tagiuri, R., & Petrullo, L. (Eds). *Person perception and interpersonal behavior.* Stanford: Stanford University Press, 1958.

An important collection of articles by 27 of the early theorists and researchers in person perception.

9
Interpersonal Attraction

Elaine Walster and G. William Walster

INTRODUCTION

Emperor Constantius II was in a quandary: Should he execute his cousin Julian—a potential rival? He summoned Julian to the Court of Milan, so he could decide. The Empress Eusebia was charmed by the personable Julian and interceded on his behalf. Julian was spared. In 361 A.D. Julian challenged Constantius II and became Julian the Apostate, Emperor of Rome.

* * *

Piliavin and Scott (1964) accompanied Berkeley police on their rounds for three weeks. They found that polite, deferential youths were rarely arrested for minor crimes, while arrogant, sassy youths very frequently were.

* * *

Peter Abelard (1079–1142) was a brilliant . . . and much despised . . . theologian and philosopher. His views were unpopular and he was unpopular. After violent intellectual disputes with his masters, he was forced to leave Paris and Lyon. He didn't get on very well at St. Denis either. Then Abelard made a fatal mistake. He fell in love with one of his students, Heloise. They had a child and were then secretly married. Such affairs were not unusual in that period, but the vindictiveness of Abelard's colleagues was. Accomplices of Heloise's uncle castrated Abelard. The Council of Soissons ordered his theological work burned. The Pope and the Council of Sens condemned him. Monks from St. Gildas de Ruys in Brittany tried to murder him.

The moral of these stories is simple: A person who is liked by his comrades will amass enormous benefits; a person who is hated is in trouble.

INTERPERSONAL ATTRACTION: A DEFINITION

A Conceptual Definition

Scientists, by training and by inclination, tend to be compulsive and stubborn. When eminent authorities and common sense both dictate that the sun must revolve around the earth, young Keplers are always around to point out that the ancients have made a few calculation errors. To make matters worse, they insist on explaining their half-baked hypotheses in precise, minute, and agonizingly lengthy detail.

Many social scientists have speculated about interpersonal attraction. Given what we know about scientists, we should not be surprised to discover that they could not even agree on what they were studying. Almost all felt compelled to modify the "slightly inaccurate" definitions of interpersonal attraction which their predecessors had proposed. Thus, by now, an extravagant number of definitions of attraction exist.

Most of the definitions share a core of meaning, however. Almost all theorists agree that interpersonal attraction is an attitude toward another. Interpersonal attraction (or interpersonal hostility), then, can be defined as an individual's tendency or predisposition to evaluate another person or the symbol of the person in a positive (or negative) way. Our *conceptual definition* of interpersonal attraction states in general terms what we mean by attraction. This conceptual definition allows us to quickly delineate the general area we plan to discuss.

Operational Definitions

Scientists, however, need both a general conceptual definition of interpersonal attraction and an accompanying precise operational definition of their concept. They need a definition that will allow them to state unequivocally how Person A's attraction to Person B should be assessed. They need an *operational definition* of attraction, i.e., a definition which consists of the operations or procedures employed in distinguishing the object referred to from others.

Potentially, attraction could be operationally defined in an infinite number of ways. Attraction could be defined as subjects' scores on the Interpersonal Judgment Scale of liking (IJS), or the frequency with which they have lunch with others, or how wildly the pupils of their eyes dilate when they gaze at others. When a scientist chooses an operational definition, he is not arbitrarily deciding what attraction really means. He is simply settling on a standard operational procedure for defining the term. How has interpersonal attraction been operationally defined? Have social scientists settled on a single operational measure of attraction—or several?

Most social scientists insist that interpersonal attraction must be operationally defined in a single way. An eloquent spokesman for this position, Donn Byrne (1971), states:

> A necessary, though hardly sufficient, condition for progress in research is consistency of operations across experiments. . . . A meaningful and cumulative increase in knowledge is possible only if identical or equivalent operations serve as connecting links across experiments. (pp. 44-47)

Byrne's philosophy of science has guided his research. He has consistently (and profitably) utilized the Interpersonal Judgment Scale as his operational definition of attraction.

Other eminent social scientists staunchly oppose Byrne's point of view. For example, Webb et al. (1966) insist that scientists should settle on several equivalent operational definitions of interpersonal attraction. They argue that one should be less convinced by three experiments demonstrating that "similarity breeds attraction" as measured by the IJS than by three experiments demonstrating that similarity breeds attraction as measured by (1) respondent's reaction to the other on the IJS, (2) his willingness to loan the other money, and (3) his pupil size when looking at the other. They argue that any single measure of attraction is bound to be inadequate in some ways. For example, the three operational measures we cited are likely to reflect both the subject's interpersonal attraction and such irrelevant variables as (1) how the respondent thinks he should answer the IJS in order to make a good impression on the experimenter, (2) how much money he has, and (3) whether he has just come from a dark movie or a bright beach.

Webb et al. say:

> The most persuasive evidence comes through a triangulation of measurement processes. If a proposition can survive the onslaught of a series of imperfect measures, with all their irrelevant error, confidence should be placed in it. (p. 3)

Whether for good or ill, interpersonal attraction has been operationalized in a variety of ways. If social scientists have found it difficult to agree on a conceptual definition of attraction, they have found it impossible to agree on an operational one. Let us examine some of the measures that have been used by researchers as indicants of attraction:

Self-report Questionnaires. The easiest way to find out whether an individual likes another person is to ask him. Usually people are not only able to tell you how they feel about others, but they are eager to describe, at length, the kindnesses of their friends and the despicable acts of their enemies. Thus, the self-report questionnaire is a popular technique for assessing liking.

Three popular self-report scales (the Thurstone Scale, the summative or Likert Scale, and the Guttman Scale) have already been described in Chapter 6. Here we will give a detailed description of the Bogardus Social Distance Scale, one of the earliest and most widely used measures, and Byrne's Interpersonal Judgment Scale, one of the most recently developed.

The Bogardus Social Distance Scale. The Bogardus Scale measures Social Distance, i.e., how close the respondent is willing to permit members of various social groups to get to him.

Individuals are shown the following scale:

1. Would exclude from my country.
2. As visitors only to my country.
3. To citizenship in my country.
4. To employment in my occupation and my country.
5. To my street of neighbors.
6. To my club as personal chums.
7. To close kinship by marriage.

Then, they are asked to indicate to which groups they are willing to admit members of diverse ethnic groups. Bogardus makes the reasonable assumption that items in this scale are ordered along a continuum. For example, he assumes that if someone is willing to have Swedes as neighbors (i.e., item 5), he will be willing to allow them to visit the U.S. (item 2), to become U.S. citizens (item 3), and to be employed in his occupation (item 4). Presumably, from a knowledge of a respondent's total score, one can guess how he responded to each of the items in the scale. (A scale possessing this property is often labeled a *Guttman Scale,* in honor of Louis Guttman, a pioneer in the development of scaling techniques.)

In 1925, Bogardus asked young American businessmen and public school teachers to indicate "in how many groupings may the members of any race, as a class, be admitted?" It is startling to discover how restrictive American society was perceived to be in 1925.

Americans thought that most of their fellow Americans would grant only rights to citizenship to Bulgarians, Chinese, Japanese, Negroes, and Turks. They would be willing to allow Czechoslovakians and Armenians to work in their occupations. Danes, French, and Germans could be accepted as close personal chums, but only the English and Canadians were "good enough" to be admitted to kinship by marriage.

The Interpersonal Judgment Scale. The Interpersonal Judgment Scale (IJS) was developed and tested by Byrne (1971). The IJS is comprised of six items. Respondents are asked to estimate another's (1) intelligence, (2) knowledge of current events, (3) morality, and (4) adjustment. They are also asked to indicate (5) their personal feelings toward the other, and (6) their feelings about working with him in an experiment.

(5) *Personal Feelings (check one):*

___ I feel that I would probably like this person very much.

___ I feel that I would probably like this person.

___ I feel that I would probably like this person to a slight degree.

___ I feel that I would probably neither particularly like nor particularly dislike this person.

___ I feel that I would probably dislike this person to a slight degree.

___ I feel that I would probably dislike this person.

___ I feel that I would probably dislike this person very much.

(6) *Working Together on an Experiment (check one):*

___ I believe that I would very much dislike working with this person in an experiment.

___ I believe that I would dislike working with this person in an experiment.

___ I believe that I would dislike working with this person in an experiment to a slight degree.

___ I believe that I would neither particularly dislike nor particularly enjoy working with this person in an experiment.

___ I believe that I would enjoy working with this person in an experiment to a slight degree.

___ I believe that I would enjoy working with this person in an experiment.

___ I believe that I would very much enjoy working with this person in an experiment.

These last two items (items 5 and 6) constitute Byrne's measure of attraction.

Byrne has also developed a version of the IJS which measures romantic attraction. On this extended scale, questions 7 through 10 ask respondents to estimate: (7) how much they would like to date the other person; (8) how much they think they would like the other person as a spouse; (9) how sexually attractive the other person seems to them; and (10) how physically attractive the person is.

Unobtrusive Measures. Although most researchers have assessed interpersonal attraction via self-report questionnaires, other nonconforming researchers have utilized a variety of other indicants.

In their delightful book, Webb et al. (1966) describe a plethora of ways the wily researcher can quickly and unobtrusively assess a person's liking for another. Some of these measures have been used—and some could be used—as indicants of attraction.

Proximity. By systematically analyzing how much time people spend in close contact, we can get a rough gauge of their liking for one another.

Clustering. Campbell, Kruskal, and Wallace (1966) used the "clustering" of blacks and whites in various classrooms as an index of interracial attitude. They argued that if blacks and whites randomly mix together in a classroom, it is reasonable to conclude that friendship preferences are only minimally influenced by race. If, on the other hand, blacks always sit with blacks and whites always sit with whites, one suspects that race is a potent determinant of friendship choices. The authors found significant racial clustering in all the schools they studied. Aggregation by age, sex, and race has also been observed on elevated trains and at lunch counters (Sechrest, 1965).

A photographic record of clustering. A profoundly simple measure for assessing children's interactions was devised by Clore and Johnson (1971). A council for interracial projects invited 48 children (from 8 to 12 years of age) to a one-week summer camp. At the beginning of the week, directors gave half of the children cameras and rolls of film to use as they pleased. At the end of the week, the remaining children were given cameras and film. As the director developed the children's film, he recorded the race of each child appearing in a camper's pictures. He found that during the first half of the camp, 32% of the children's pictures were of children of a different race. By the end of the week, 45% were of children of a different race.

Other Measures of Associations. Webb et al. (1966) remind investigators that archive information also yields some clues as to who associates with whom. They note: "So humble a document as a desk calendar might be checked. This record might provide information on who lunched with whom, with what degree of frequency, and across which departments" (p. 94). Some analysts have systematically observed how much time politicians, U.N. delegates, and student radicals spend socially with people of various political persuasions in order to get some clues as to who is in secret sympathy with whom.

Physical propinquity as a measure of attraction. People habitually stand a set distance from others when conversing. A child soon learns how far away from others it is "correct" to stand; he learns to adjust his standing distance smoothly as he and his partner gesture and move about.

If you want to get a profound impression of how important maintaining a correct speaking distance is in social interaction, try a quick experiment. Try standing extremely close to or extremely far away from your partner the next time you're engaged in a discussion. As you move your nose to within inches of your friend's, he will quickly and instinctively back up. If you persist in speaking "eyeball to eyeball" he will become acutely uncomfortable and/or irritated. The same thing will happen (in reverse) if you persist in carrying on a long-distance conversation. At first your partner will relentlessly pursue you. If you persist in moving away, he will probably abandon you to seek out a better socialized conversationalist.

The norms about how close one should stand to others vary for acquaintances and friends. People stand slightly closer to those they like than to those they abhor. Byrne, Ervin, and Lamberth (1970) demonstrated that propinquity can serve as a useful index of interpersonal attraction. They introduced 44 student couples to one another and sent them out on a 30-minute "blind" coke date. Eventually, the couples wandered back to the experimental office to report on their date. As the two students stood together in front of the psychologist's desk, he unobtrusively recorded how close to one another they were standing. He rated their closeness on an ordinal scale ranging from 0 (touching one another) to 5 (standing at opposite extremes of the desk). Byrne found that the couple's expressed liking for one another, as measured by the Interpersonal Judgment Scale, correlated $-.36$ (females) and $-.48$ (males) with the physical distance measure. The more the couple liked one another, the closer they stood.

One's "inclination" toward another. Galton (1884) was intrigued by the idea that one could assess another's character and personality without the other ever realizing that he was being scrutinized. Galton conceived of an amazing array of schemes for invading privacy. Fortunately for his hapless potential victims, he never had time to carry out his luxuriant schemes. He states:

> The poetical metaphors of ordinary language suggest many possibilities of measurement. Thus when two persons have an "inclination" to one another, they visibly incline or slope together when sitting side by side, as at a dinner table, and they then throw the stress of their weights on the near legs of their chairs. It does not require much ingenuity to arrange a pressure gauge with an index and dial to indicate changes in stress, but it is difficult to devise an arrangement that shall fulfill the three-fold condition of being effective, not attracting notice, and being applicable to ordinary furniture. I made some rude experiments, but being busy with other matters, have not carried them on, as I had hoped. (p. 184)

Eye contact as a measure of liking. When two people are engaged in conversation, they intermittently look one another in the eye. Argyle (1967) found that the amount of time individuals gaze at one another as they talk is influenced by interpersonal attraction. Individuals have been found to glance at those they like (or love) more than at those they feel cooler toward (see Exline, 1963; Argyle, 1967; Efran, 1968; and Rubin, 1970).

Sociometric measures. Moreno and Jennings developed the Sociometric Measure, a technique for assessing individuals' preferences in associates.

In a classic study, Jennings (1943) recorded the friendship choices of girls, who were committed to the New York State Training School for Girls. Jennings asked the girls who ranged in age from 12 to 15 to "write the name of whatever girls there are, anywhere on the campus or in your own house, whom you would prefer to live with." She also asked them to record their preferences in work partners, recreation partners, and study partners. On the basis of this information, she drew a sociogram —a visual depiction of who likes whom. (See Fig. 9-1).

The sociogram shown in Figure 9-1 enables one to see at a glance how girls feel about one another. One can see that Louise, Hazel, and Betty are social isolates; no one is willing to room with them. Ellie, on the other hand, seems to be the first choice of a number of girls.

During the post-depression and World War II era, sociometric measures thrived. Researchers doggedly charted the sociometric choices of grade school, high school, and college students; of orphans, delinquents, and prison inmates; of Air Force bomber crews; of the inhabitants of El Cerreto, New Mexico, of small farm and *hacienda* communities in Latin America, of woodcutters in Sofia, Bulgaria; and of Nazis, Communists, and Social Democrats in Hanover, Germany.

The sociometric measures had one flaw which led to their decline, however. As the

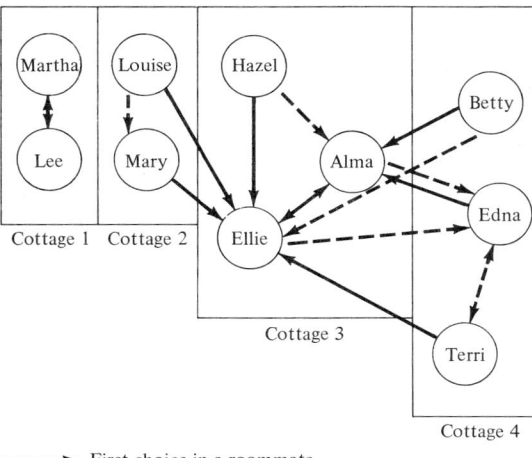

FIGURE 9-1. A sociogram of girls' preferences in roommates.

→ First choice in a roommate
--→ Second choice in a roommate

group under study gets larger and larger, a sociogram becomes more and more complicated. For example, Loomis' (1960) sociogram of visiting relationships in Dyess Colony, Arkansas, a New Deal resettlement community which then consisted of only 484 families, is almost unintelligible.

From the preceding discussion, it is obvious that a wide variety of measures have been conceived and utilized as operational definitions of an individual's attraction toward another. However, whether the experimenter uses the Interpersonal Judgment Scale, physical proximity, or eye contact as his operational definition of attraction, he intends to assess the same hypothetical construct, interpersonal attraction.

THE REINFORCEMENT MODEL OF INTERPERSONAL ATTRACTION

The reinforcement paradigm is the theory which is most often invoked to explain interpersonal attraction. Essentially, reinforcement theory states that:

A person who rewards us (or who is merely present when we are rewarded) comes to be associated with pleasure; thus, we like him. A person who punishes us (or who is merely present when we are punished) comes to be associated with pain; thus, we dislike him.

The reinforcement theory of interpersonal attraction has a long and venerable history. Aristotle (1932) observed:

Men love anyone who has done good to them . . . men like those who are able and inclined to benefit them in a pecuniary way, or to promote their personal safety . . . those who are pleasant to live with, and to spend the day with. . . . we like those who praise our good qualities, and especially if we are afraid we do not possess them . . . we like those who take us seriously—who admire us, who show us respect, who take pleasure in our society. . . . (pp. 103–106)

An impressive array of social psychologists have accepted the reinforcement paradigm. Such luminaries as Doob (1947), Staats and Staats (1958), Thibaut and Kelley (1959), Homans (1961), Albert and Bernice Lott (1965), and Byrne (1971) have used reinforcement theory to derive predictions as to who will be attracted to whom.

Based on the reinforcement paradigm, Byrne and Clore (1970) articulated a precise model of liking. According to these authors, "any stimulus with reinforcement properties functions as an unconditioned stimulus (UCS) for an implicit affective response." (That is, when a person receives a reward or is denied a reward, he has an emotional reaction. This affective reaction may be "pleasure" or "pain.") "Any discriminable stimulus, including a person, which is temporally associated with the unconditioned stimulus can become a conditioned stimulus (CS) which evokes the implicit affective response. The implicit affec-

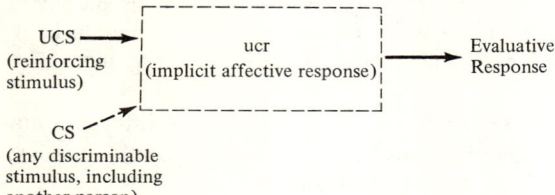

FIGURE 9-2. Evaluative responses as a function of reinforcing stimuli associated with a conditioned stimulus. CS, conditioned stimulus; UCS, unconditioned stimulus; UCR, unconditioned response (after Byrne & Clore, 1970, p. 107).

tive response is conceptualized as mediating the relationship between the CS and subsequent evaluative responses." (That is, if a person is present when you are denied reward, you associate him with pain, and you dislike him.) The Byrne-Clore formulation is graphically depicted in Figure 9-2.

The Impact of Specific Reinforcements on Liking

Presumably, a computer could calculate all the rewards a stimulus person provides us and all the punishments he inflicts and compute an Index of the Total Outcomes he provides for us (i.e., Rewards minus Costs). Psychologists could test the reinforcement model by assessing whether this Index of Outcomes was linearly related to Liking. Such an experiment is not practical, however. A multitude of things may be rewarding or punishing to any individual at a given time.

Researchers have chosen to test reinforcement theory in a simpler way. They have specified stimuli that most people, in most situations, most of the time, find rewarding. They then test whether or not people who provide such "transituational reinforcers" are better liked than people who do not.

Similarity: A Transituational Reinforcer. The idea that people tend to like those similar to themselves did not originate with social psychologists. "Birds of a feather flock together," was a tired truism in Aristotle's time. An impressive amount of research demonstrates that attitudinal similarity is a transituational reinforcer; the discovery that someone has ideas similar to our own does generate pleasure, and does generate interpersonal attraction.

Byrne (1961) agreed that similarity should be a transituational reinforcer:

> Any time that another person offers us validation by indicating that his percepts and concepts are congruent with ours, it constitutes a rewarding interaction.... Any time that another person indicates dissimilarity between our two notions, it constitutes a punishing interaction.... Disagreement raises the unpleasant possibility that we are to some degree stupid, uninformed, immoral, or insane. (p. 713)

Similarity and affect. Several experiments have demonstrated that when we discover others have similar attitudes, we feel pleasure; when we discover others disagree with us, we feel distress. In one study, Clore and Gormly (1969) asked two students to give their opinions on a variety of subjects. One student was a plant; one was a real subject. Half of the time, the imposter pretended to share most of his partner's convictions. Half of the time, he pretended to share few of them. The experimenter continuously recorded the student's autonomic activity during the interview. As predicted, the student showed a lower arousal (as measured by skin conductance) when his partner shared his beliefs than when he did not. Other research has demonstrated that a person who purports to share our attitudes generates more pleasure than does a person who does not. Similar attitudes induced "comfortable, high, happy, pleasant, and positive" feelings, while dissimilar attitudes generated "uncomfortable, low, sad, unpleasant, and negative" feelings.

Similarity and liking. A multitude of well-controlled laboratory studies demonstrate that attitudinal similarity produces interpersonal attraction. For example, in the Clore and Gormly study already described, subjects liked the confederate who pretended to share their convictions far more than they liked the confederate who "marched to a different drummer."

A staggering number of correlational studies demonstrate that in daily life people select friends, lovers, and spouses on the basis of similarity. For example, Newcomb (1961) found that if he assessed the attitudes of new college students he could accurately predict which students would become chums after long acquaintances. Birds of a feather did come to flock together.

Burgess and Wallin (1943) discovered that individuals tend to become seriously involved with dates who are similar to themselves. Young adults generally chose fiancés who were born and raised in similar localities and who had childhoods similar to their own. They tended to pick partners who had siblings of the same sex, were equally gregarious, preferred the same leisure-time activities, drank equally heavily, had comparable numbers of friends, had been previously engaged the same number of times, dated comparable numbers of people, and so on. Engaged couples even had parents who were similar; generally, they had comparable educations and comparable incomes, and their marriages were similar in happiness (or unhappiness).

Individuals have been found to prefer spouses who are similar to them in height (Pearson and Lee, 1903), mental health (Murstein, 1967), physical health (Harris, 1912), intelligence (Reed and Reed, 1965), and education (Garrison, Anderson and Reed, 1968).

It appears that, like Narcissus, most of us do tend to fall in love with our own reflections.

Interpersonal Attraction: A Transituational Reinforcer. An observer from another planet would have little trouble discovering a second transituational reinforcer. A glance at a few television commercials, newspaper advertisements, and advice-to-the-lovelorn columns would make it evident that people are willing to spend appalling amounts of time, effort, and money to obtain the esteem of others. Advertisers assume they can sell cough drops, tanks, eyewash, and cake mixes, if they can convince the desperate consumer that the product will help him win admiration and affection—or, at the very least, allow him to avoid offending others and reaping their scorn. If it is true that we tend to like those who reward us and if esteem is indeed a reward, it follows that we should like people who like us.

To test the hypothesis that one will come to like those he discovers like him, Backman and Secord (1959) asked groups of students to come to a meeting. Before the first meetings of the groups, they informed each student that personality test analyses revealed that certain members of his group would probably like him very much. Each group then met for informal discussion. After the initial meeting, the experimenter informed the group members that the group might eventually be subdivided into two-person teams. Members were asked to indicate their first, second, and third choices in a team partner. As would be expected, members preferred to work with the person they had been told would probably like them. These, and other data, provide support for the notion of reciprocal liking.

As Hecate (2nd century B.C.) stated, "I will show you a love potion without drug or herb or any witch's spell; if you wish to be loved, love." . . . or pretend that you do.

Deprivation and satiation. Learning theory would advise us that, if we deprive a person of social approval, when he finally receives approval from another person, he will experience unusually strong positive affect. Similarly, if we satiate a person with approval, he should experience only weak positive affect when he receives yet another helping of social approval. These and similar hypotheses have been tested by a number of investigators. Gewitz and Baer (1958a, 1958b), for example, demonstrate that if a teacher socially isolates a child before asking him to perform a task, the child's performance will be unusually shaped by his teacher's approval or disapproval. They interpret their results as indicating that the effectiveness of a social reinforcer is increased by its own deprivation.

Romantic liking. Jacobs et al. (1971) tested the impact of deprivation versus satiation on an individual's liking for a romantic partner. The authors hypothesized that if a date finally expressed love and affection for a suitor who had recently suffered intense social rejection, he would experience unusually intense pleasure and feel unusual liking for her. (Of course, if the recently rejected suitor was rejected by the date, he should experience unusually intense pain and feel unusual hatred for her.) Thus, the authors proposed that deprived individuals should have more volatile social relations than their satiated counterparts.

Jacobs et al. tested their hypothesis in the following way: The authors invited college men to participate in a computer dating project. The men took a battery of personality tests. A few weeks later they were given a psychiatrist's analysis of their personality. This analysis was bogus. One half of the time the men were given a very approving analysis. The psychiatrist seemed to like everything about them. One half of the time the analysis was very negative.

The men then were given a chance to become acquainted with a coed. The coed was an actress. Half of the time she was warm and affectionate. Half of the time she was cold and rejecting. The men were then asked about their reactions to her.

As predicted, if the college man had been rejected before entering the dating situation, he was unusually appreciative of and unusually attracted to the warm, affectionate girl and unusually resentful of the rejecting girl. If the man had been laden with praise before entering the dating situation, he was only moderately appreciative of the affectionate girl and moderately resentful of the rejecting girl.

Other Transituational Reinforcers. Other researchers have documented the wide variety of ways in which human beings can reward one another. Those people who reassure us when we are frightened, entertain us when we are bored, keep us company when we are lonesome, make love to us when we are passionate, all provide valuable rewards, and cause us to like or love them for the favors they provide.

Do We Like Those Who Are Merely Associated with Reward?

There appears to be compelling evidence that we like people who provide us with reward. But, the student with a long memory will recall that reinforcement theory made a more startling prediction: Lott and Lott (1961) point out that according to Hullian reinforcement theory, a person should come to like not merely those who provide him with rewards but also those who are merely physically present when he is rewarded. Is there any evidence that people like those who happen to be present at the time they are rewarded? Yes.

Lott and Lott divided grade-school children up into three-member groups. Each group then played a game called "Rocket Ship." The object of the game was to move past four "danger zones" and to successfully land a cardboard rocket ship on a planet. Half of the children reached the planet safely and returned to class with their prize, a small auto model. Half failed to reach the planet.

At the end of the school day, the teacher administered a sociometric test. She asked, "Suppose your family suddenly got the chance to spend your next vacation on a nearby star out in space.... Which two children in this class would you choose to take with you?" Children who won a reward in the "Rocket Ship" game chose members of their three-person group (who were present at the time of reward) significantly more often than did unrewarded children. Children came to like those who had been present when they won and to dislike those who had been present when they lost, even though the other children had in no way promoted their reward or loss.

The Reinforcement Model: Problems and Limitations

The reinforcement paradigm is the most comprehensive and most compelling paradigm for organizing what scientists know about interpersonal attraction. And yet, this paradigm is not totally satisfying. Major problems perplex researchers who try to use this paradigm to derive predictions about interpersonal attraction. For example:

What Is "Rewarding?" What Is Not? While we can readily accept that "people will like those who reward them and dislike those who punish them," we must admit that this statement does not, to any great extent, increase one's ability to predict precisely to whom a given person will be attracted.

We have no equation which will permit us to add up all the rewards Person *A* provides, subtract all the punishments he inflicts, and thus arrive at a Total Outcome index that will tell us how much Person *A* will be liked. A multitude of things may be rewarding or punishing to any individual at a given time. In addition, it is often the case that "one man's meat is another man's poison"; individuals disagree about what is rewarding or punishing at a given time.

If it were to be maximally useful, the reinforcement paradigm would include a set of rules which would tell us (1) which, if any, stimuli are transitational reinforcers for all human beings and (2) which stimuli are rewarding to individuals in a given culture under given conditions. Then we could predict which stimuli will lead to interpersonal attraction and which will lead to interpersonal hostility.

Of course, such specifications do not yet exist, but they might not be so impossible to develop as it appears on the surface. When clusters of individuals—all competing to maximize their rewards—congregate, certain social structures must evolve. From an examination of these inevitable core structures, it might be possible to discover certain behavioral patterns that every society will reward or punish. But, at present, such analyses do not exist.

Are Rewarding People Always Liked? Even when researchers think they can specify the major rewards operating in a situation, reinforcement theory sometimes falters in predicting human behavior.

Simple reinforcement theory is embarrassed by two facts:

1. Individuals do not inevitably strive to maximize their immediate material rewards.
2. They do not always prefer people who provide large material rewards to people who provide small rewards.

Individuals do not always strive to maximize immediate reward. Sometimes individuals voluntarily perform altruistic acts, which bring them little reward and great personal suffering (Rubin, 1973). In fact, altruistic behavior is generally defined as behavior that benefits another more than oneself. But such a definition flies in the face of reinforcement theory, which states that that behavior will be performed which enables one to maximize his rewards and minimize his costs. It is, of course, possible to postulate that an altruistic person gains some intense inner satisfaction from helping others and thus argue that his behavior is reward motivated. But this sort of analysis smacks of circular reasoning such that prediction is no longer possible. It is reasoning like "Rats work for reinforcement" and "A reinforcement is what rats will work for." If one wishes to understand "altruism," "compromise," "sharing," and other "unselfish" behaviors as being under the control of rewards and punishment, one needs to find some independent way of specifying when these rewards will be greater and lesser and of predicting when such "unselfish" behavior will or will not occur.

Nor do individuals always prefer people who provide maximum material reward at minimum cost. Simple reinforcement theory is also embarrassed by the unnerving discovery that individuals do not always seem to prefer to associate with individuals who provide them with the maximum reward at minimum cost.

Some people are attracted to friends who allow them to monopolize almost all available rewards. The fact that they are luxuriously benefited while their friends are destitute does not disturb these "natural" men. However, most people feel distinctly uncomfortable when they are granted an inordinate share of the resources. They are less comfortable in monopolistic, unequal relations than in equitable, egalitarian ones.

In the next section we will describe a theory—equity theory—that attempts to transcend some of the limitations of the simple reinforcement theory just described.

EQUITY THEORY

The Heart of Equity Theory

Equity theory is a strikingly simple theory. The theory formulated by Walster et al. (1973) is comprised of four simple, interlocking propositions:

Proposition I: Individuals will try to maximize their outcomes (where outcomes equal rewards minus costs).

Proposition IIA: Groups can maximize collective reward by evolving accepted systems for equitably apportioning resources among members. Thus, groups will evolve such systems of equity, and will attempt to induce members to accept and adhere to these systems.

Proposition IIB: Groups will generally reward members who treat others equitably, and generally punish (increase the costs of) members who treat others inequitably.

Proposition III: When individuals find themselves participating in inequitable relationships, they will become distressed. The more inequitable the relationship, the more distress individuals will feel.

Proposition IV: Individuals who discover they are in an inequitable relationship will attempt to eliminate their distress by restoring equity. The greater the inequity that exists, the more distress they will feel, and the harder they will try to restore equity.

Let us now attempt to understand these crucial propositions. Proposition I is an old friend by now. It simply reminds us of the most fundamental assumption of reinforcement theory, that all men are motivated by self-interest. We can summarize all the research reported in the previous section in a few terse sentences: "Individuals try to maximize their outcomes. When they succeed in doing so, they experience pleasure and like their associates. When they fail to maximize their outcomes, they experience frustration and dislike their associates." So far equity theory and reinforcement theory are in accord.

In Proposition II, however, equity theory pushes into new territory. Reinforcement theory treats individuals as if they were in isolation. They are not. A society is comprised of many individuals, all eager to attain the same goal, to possess all the good things in life. If these individuals were unrestrained in their pursuit of pleasure, life would be frightening, violent, and unstable. As soon as a man captured community resources, a coalition of ruthless rivals would try to wrench back these resources. The only way a group can avoid continual warfare and maximize collective outcomes is by working out a compromise. Thus, as Proposition IIA states, societies eventually must hammer out a set of rules for allocating community resources.

How can the group entice its citizens to accept its equity rules? There is only one way to control human behavior. As is acknowledged in Proposition IIB, the only way a group can induce its members to accept and to adhere to equity norms is to reward members who treat others equitably and to punish those who do not.

What Constitutes an Equitable Relationship? Although all societies develop some system for equitably apportioning resources among members, they differ startlingly in what they think is equitable. Some societies assume a good family name entitles one to large rewards; thus, "He who has, gets." Others assert, "To each according to his needs." Still other societies contend that "all men are created equal" and thus are entitled to identical outcomes.

A principle to be presented shortly portrays the widely diverse conceptions of equity that societies have evolved. However, to understand this principle, the student will have to input a little work; but it will be repaid by the forthcoming outcomes.

Definition of terms

Inputs (I_A or I_B) are defined as "the participant's contributions to the exchange, which are seen (by a scrutineer) as entitling him to reward *or* cost." In different settings, people assume that different inputs entitle one to reward or punishment. In industrial settings, they assume that assets such as capital or manual labor entitle one to reward. In social settings, they assume that assets such as beauty or kindness entitle one to reward, while liabilities such as boorishness or cruelty entitle one to punishment (costs).

Outcomes (O_A or O_B) are defined as "the positive *and* negative consequences that a scrutineer perceives a participant has received in the course of his relationship with another." The participant's total outcomes, then, are equal to the rewards he obtains from the relationship minus the costs that he incurs.

Now, you should be able to understand the statement that: "An equitable relation exists if a person scrutinizing the relationship concludes that all participants are receiving equal relative outcomes from the relationship; i.e., when $\frac{O_A - I_A}{|I_A|^{k_A}} = \frac{O_B - I_B}{|I_B|^{k_B}}$; where I_A and I_B designate a scrutineer's perception of Person A and Person B's Inputs.

O_A and O_B designate the scrutineer's perception of Person A and Person B's Outcomes. $|I_A|$ and $|I_B|$ designate the absolute value of their Inputs (i.e., the perceived value of their inputs,[1] *disregarding sign*).

The exponents k_A and k_B take on the value $+1$ or -1, depending on the sign of A and B's inputs and A and B's gains (Outcomes − Inputs). [k_A = sign (I_A) × sign ($O_A - I_A$) and k_B = sign (I_B) × sign ($O_B - I_B$).] The exponent's effect is simply to change the way relative outcomes are computed: If $k = +1$ then we have $\frac{O - I}{|I|}$, but if $k = -1$, then we have $|I| \cdot (O - I)$. Without the exponent k, the formula would yield meaningless results when I < O and (O − I) > O, or I > O and (O − I) < O.

A participant's relative outcomes will be zero if his outcomes equal his inputs. His rela-

---

[1] There is one restriction on inputs: The smallest absolute input must be ≥ 1, i.e., $|I_A|$ and $|I_B|$ must both be ≥ 1.

tive outcomes will be positive if his outcomes exceed his inputs (O > I) and negative if his outcomes are less than his inputs (O < I). Thus, the sign and the magnitude of this measure indicate how "profitable" the relationship has been to each of the participants.

Mathematically sophisticated students may find the detailed description of the logic underlying the formula for relative outcomes, which is presented in Walster (1975) helpful.

Let us practice using this formula. Consider this example: Al and Bob agree to make dinner for two very special dates. They agree to spend two hours apiece preparing steak, Sauce Bearnaise, and a Caesar salad. Al arrives on time, completely drunk; he contributes less than nothing to the dinner. Bob puts Al to bed and prepares dinner from scratch. In the end, Bob contributes +5 units to the dinner; Al contributes −2 units.

If, at the party, both Al and Bob had an equally good time (say, 20 units worth of fun), Bob might justifiably feel exploited:

$$\frac{O_{Bob} - I_{Bob}}{|I_{Bob}|^{k_{Bob}}} = \frac{20 - (5)}{|5|^{+1}} = \frac{15}{5} = 3.00$$

[$k_{Bob} = +1$ since $I_{Bob} > 0$ and $(O - I)_{Bob} > 0$]

$$\frac{O_{Al} - I_{Al}}{|I_{Al}|^{k_{Al}}} = \frac{20 - (-2)}{|-2|^{-1}} = \frac{22}{\frac{1}{2}} = 44.00$$

[$k_{Al} = -1$ since $I_{Al} < 0$ and $(O - I)_{Al} > 0$]

Thus, $RO_{Bob} < RO_{Al}$.

Only if Bob enjoyed the party 225 units would he feel equitably treated;

$$\frac{O_{Bob} - I_{Bob}}{|I_{Bob}|^{k_{Bob}}} = \frac{225 - (5)}{|5|^{+1}} = \frac{220}{5} = 44.00$$

Thus, $RO_{Bob} = RO_{Al}$.

Alternatively, Bob would also feel equitably treated if Al had only a miserable −.5 units of fun at the party;

$$\frac{O_{Al} - I_{Al}}{|I_{Al}|^{k_{Al}}} = \frac{(-.5) - (-2)}{|-2|^{-1}} = \frac{1.5}{\frac{1}{2}} = 3.00$$

Thus, $RO_{Bob} = RO_{Al}$.

Who Decides Whether a Relationship Is Equitable? Proposition II points out that societies develop systems of equity and insure that their members adhere to them. In simple societies there may be a consensus as to what really constitutes equitable relationships. Even in these societies, however, there will always be slight disagreements in detail as to what is fair. A scrutineer's assessment of how equitable a relationship is depends upon his assessment of the value of the participants' inputs and outcomes. If observers assess participants' relative outcomes differently, and it is likely that they will, it is inevitable that they will show slight disagreements as to whether or not various relationships are equitable.

Do People Generally Behave Equitably? Some critics of equity theory have scoffed at the proposal that people will voluntarily behave equitably; they deny that people will voluntarily cede material benefits to their deprived companions. These critics insist that people will monopolize everything they can get. We agree. We acknowledge (Proposition I) that man is motivated by self-interest. We agree that we would all monopolize resources if we knew we would not be caught and punished. The point is that all of us have learned, albeit painfully, that if we always take without ever giving, we will get caught and punished. We soon learn that the most profitable way to be selfish is to be "unselfish."

There is some evidence that individuals do generally behave equitably. Individuals who secure more reward than they feel they deserve voluntarily share their unearned benefits. Individuals who secure less reward than they deserve quickly demand additional benefits

(Leventhal, Allen, & Kemelgor, 1969; or Schmitt & Marwell, 1970).

Occasionally, individuals realize that in a particular situation they can maximize their outcomes by exploiting their partners. In such cases, equity theorists would expect them to behave exploitatively but to feel badly about it.

Proposition II points out that society punishes those who are caught behaving inequitably. Children and adults learn, again and again, that the man who dares to take too much and gets caught can expect venomous retaliation; the man who accepts too little is not only deprived of material benefit, but he may reap derision as well. Proposition III points out that as a consecuence of inevitable and repeated socialization experiences, individuals who find themselves in inequitable relationships come to experience distress.

Experimental evidence (Austin & Walster, 1974) provides compelling support for the contention that both the beneficiary and the victim in an inequitable relationship experience intense distress. Those who are unjustly benefited feel guilty. Those who are unjustly deprived are angry. Both are distressed.

In Proposition IV the authors propose that individuals who are distressed by their inequitable relations will try to eliminate their distress by restoring equity. There are two ways that a participant can restore equity to an inequitable relationship: He can restore either actual equity or psychological equity to the relationship.

A participant can restore actual equity by appropriately altering his own or his partner's relative outcomes. For example, a laborer who discovers that his boss has been paying him less than the minimum wage can reestablish actual equity in four ways: He can become a slacker (thus lowering his inputs), steal from the company (thus raising his own outcomes), make so many mistakes that his employer must work far into the night rectifying them (thus raising his employer's inputs), or sabotage company equipment (thus lowering his employer's outcomes). The ingenious ways individuals contrive to bring equity to inequitable relationships are documented by Adams (1963).

A participant can restore psychological equity to a relationship by appropriately distorting reality. He can try to convince himself that an inequitable relationship is, in fact, equitable. For example, an exploitative employer may convince himself that his relationship with his underpaid and overworked laborer is in fact equitable in four ways. He can restore psychological equity to their relationship by minimizing his inputs ("You wouldn't believe how stupid he is"), exaggerating his outcomes ("Work gives him a chance to see his friends"), exaggerating his own inputs ("Without my creative genius the company would fall apart"), or minimizing his outcomes ("The tension on this job is giving me an ulcer").

Applications of Equity Theory

Researchers have applied equity theory to four major types of human relationships: business relationships, exploitative relationships, helping relationships, and intimate relationships. The research in these last three areas is of special interest to students of interpersonal attraction.

Equity Theory and Exploitative Relationships. Relationships between exploiters and their victims are easily analyzed within the equity framework. An exploiter (or harm-doer) can be defined as "a participant who seizes more relative outcomes than he deserves." A victim is "the participant who is deprived of some of the relative outcomes he deserves."

Is there any evidence that when exploiters and their victims find themselves enmeshed in exploitative relationships, they feel distress? Yes. Numerous theorists support the contention that exploiters feel distinctly uncomfortable after exploiting others. Theorists have labeled this distress as "guilt," "conditioned anxiety," "fear of retaliation," "dissonance," or "empathy"—but all theorists agree that harm-doers experience acute distress. Common sense suggests that if inequity is distressing to harm-doers, it should be even more distressing to their victims. There is compelling evidence that exploitation causes victims to become acutely distressed.

Theoretically, participants in an inequitable relationship can reduce their distress in one of two alternative ways: They can restore actual equity or they can restore psychological equity to their relationship.

The harm-doer's response to inequity

RESTORATION OF ACTUAL EQUITY: When a harm-doer is caught up in an injustice he will often try to reestablish a truly equitable relationship. Numerous studies verify the fact that harm-doers do often try to "do the right thing" and compensate their victims (Berscheid & Walster, 1967; Berscheid, Walster, & Barclay 1969).

RESTORATION OF PSYCHOLOGICAL EQUITY: As we noted earlier, a harm-doer can restore psychological equity to his relationship with the victim by appropriately distorting reality. Instead of actively working to make things right, the exploiter merely needs to convince himself that things are right. Exploiters, disturbed by guilt, have been detected using a variety of comforting rationalizations. The most soothing self-deceptions seem to be minimization of the victim's suffering, denial that one was responsible for the victim's suffering, or derogation of the victim.

MINIMIZATION OF THE VICTIM'S SUFFERING: An exploiter can sometimes soothe his balky conscience by protesting to himself that the victim suffered little harm or, his delusions escalating, that the victim even reaped sizable benefits from their association. Sykes and Matza (1957) and Brock and Buss (1962) demonstrate that harm-doers will consistently underestimate how much harm they have done to another. Brock and Buss, for example, found that college students who administer electric shock to other students soon start to markedly underestimate the painfulness of the shock they are delivering.

DENIAL OF RESPONSIBILITY FOR THE ACT: If the harm-doer can convince himself that it was not his cruelty but some other malignant influence that caused the victim's suffering, then his relationship with the victim becomes an equitable one. That harm-doers will often deny their responsibility for harm-doing has been documented by Sykes and Matza (1957), Brock and Buss (1962; 1964), and Katz et al. (1973). In daily life, denial of responsibility seems to be a favorite strategy of those who feel pangs of guilt about exploiting others. I was "only following orders" is the stereotyped excuse of all war criminals.

DEROGATION OF THE VICTIM: An exploiter can mollify his conscience by righteously insisting that the victim deserves his deprived state. That harm-doers often derogate their victims has been demonstrated by Berkowitz (1962), Glass (1964), and Walster and Prestholdt (1966). In a typical experiment, Davis and Jones (1960) found that students who were hired to humiliate other students (as part of a research project) ended up by convincing themselves that the students deserved to be ridiculed. Sykes and Matza (1957) found that juvenile delinquents often defend their brutalization of others by arguing that their victims are really homosexuals, bums, or possessors of other traits that make them deserving of punishment. In tormenting others, then, the delinquents can claim to be the restorers of justice rather than harm-doers.

Some harm-doers get to be so skilled at self-deception that they can rationalize injustice in advance. Genesirac, an ally of Attila the Hun, trusted "that the winds would bear him to a land the inhabitants of which had provoked the divine vengeance." Thus, his Vandals could murder, burn, and rape—confident that they were serving as God's avengers.

The preceding findings both startled and fascinated students of interpersonal attraction. The reinforcement paradigm led us to believe that liking for another is simply determined by the extent to which the other rewards or punishes us. The preceding equity research adds a startling amendment to that conclusion. Equity research demonstrates that how we treat another person is as important in determining our liking for him as how he treats us. Equity research demonstrates that we often come to dislike people we exploit and come to like people we benefit as well as the other way around.

The victim's response to inequity. If he can, a victim will induce the exploiter to restore actual equity and to make restitution to him. Sometimes, however, the impotent victim is not able to elicit restitution. In such cases, the hapless victim is left with only two options: He can acknowledge that he is exploited but that he is too weak to do anything about it, or he can justify his exploitation. Often, victimized individuals find it less upsetting to distort reality and justify their victimization than to acknowledge that the world is unjust and that they are too impotent to elicit fair treatment (Austin & Walster, 1974; Lerner & Matthews, 1967).

Startlingly, in such cases, victimized individuals have been found to restore psychological equity in exactly the same ways exploiters favor! Victims sometimes console themselves by imagining that their exploitation has brought compensating benefits. ("Suffering brings wisdom and purity" . . . or at the very least "natural rhythm.") They may console themselves that in the long run, the exploiter will be punished as he deserves. ("The mill of the Lord grinds slowly, but it grinds exceeding fine.") Victims may also convince themselves that their exploiter actually deserves the enormous benefits he has seized, because he possesses previously unrecognized inputs. Recent data demonstrate that the exploited will justify the excessive benefits of others. Jecker and Landy (1969), Walster and Prestholdt (1966), and Hastorf and Regan (personal communication) pressured individuals into doing a difficult favor for an unworthy recipient. They found that the abashed favor-doer tried to justify the inequity by convincing himself that the recipient was especially needy or worthy.

Long before equity theory existed, Benjamin Franklin (published in 1916) was well aware of the fact that people come to like those they are induced to benefit, and he cunningly used this fact to political advantage. For example, once Franklin became disturbed by the enmity of a member of the General Assembly of Pennsylvania. He decided to make his opponent like him.

> I did not . . . aim at gaining his favour by paying any servile respect to him but . . . took this other method. Having heard that he had in his library a certain very scarce and curious book I wrote a note to him expressing my desire of perusing that book and requesting he would do me the favour of lending it to me for a few days. He sent it immediately and I return'd it in about a week with another note expressing strongly my sense of the favour. When we next met in the House he spoke to me (which he had never done before), and with great civility; and he ever after manifested a readiness to serve me on all occasions, so that we became great friends and our friendship continued to his death. This is another instance of the truth of an old maxim I had learned, which says, *"He that has once done you a kindness will be more ready to do you another than he whom you yourself have obliged."* (pp. 216–217)

Franklin knew that when a person is led to help an "undeserving" recipient, he is likely to end up concluding that the recipient deserved his help after all.

Reformers who have worked, at great personal sacrifice, to alleviate social injustices are often enraged when they hear the exploited themselves vehemently defend the status quo. Black militants encounter "Uncle Toms" who defend white supremacy. Women's liberation groups must face angry housewives who threaten to defend to the death the traditional status of women. Reformers might have more sympathy for such "Uncle Toms" and "Doris Days" if they understood the psychological underpinnings of such reactions. When one is treated inequitably but has no hope of altering one's situation, it may be less degrading to deny reality than to face up to one's humiliating position.

What Determines Whether Individuals Restore Actual or Psychological Equity to Their Relationships?

We pointed out that individuals can respond to injustice in two startlingly different ways, with demands for justice or with justification. The student's next question is, obviously, "What factors determine how individuals respond?" When he asks this question, the student bumps up against the frontier of equity research. Walster et al. (1973) suggest that two variables will determine how an individual responds to inequity. They suggest that a harm-doer will be especially likely to compensate his victim if adequate and noncostly compensation is available. However, few studies have been conducted to test these hypotheses.

Here is a place where students' insights may well surpass those of established researchers. Give it a try. Take out a piece of paper. Imagine that you are living in the Middle Ages, and are dedicated to promoting social reform. The local lord is piqued by guilt. How would you pressure him to free his serfs and make restitution to them? What factors do you think would induce this "exploiter" to behave with justice rather than with justification?

Equity Theory and Altruistic Relationships

"A certain man . . . fell among thieves . . . which . . . wounded him . . . leaving him half dead. . . . there came down a certain priest. . . . when he saw him he passed by on the other side. And likewise a Levite. . . . passed by on the other side. But a certain Samaritan . . . came where he was: and when he saw him, he had compassion on him, and went to him . . . and set him on his own beast, and brought him to an inn, and took care of him. And on the morrow when he departed, he took out two pence, and gave them to the host, and said unto him, ''Take care of him: and whatsoever thou spendest more . . . I will repay thee.'' (Luke 10:30–35)

People routinely volunteer to help one another. Parents care for their children, Boy Scouts help elderly ladies across the street, Congress aids underdeveloped nations, and eager suitors urge gifts on overdeveloped maidens.

Can equity theory give us any insight into philanthropic relations? Theorists have thought so. Equity theorists categorized three different kinds of "helping relationships." Although all three are ordinarily labeled "helping relationships," they are, in fact, strikingly different types of relationships.

Exploitive relationships. Sometimes a philanthropist is not really a philanthropist; he helps another merely to help himself. In fact, philanthropist/recipient relationships of this type are best labeled "exploitive relationships."

$$\frac{(O_A - I_A)}{|I_A|^{k_A}} > \frac{(O_B - I_B)}{|I_B|^{k_B}}$$

where
A = The philanthropist
B = The recipient

Reciprocal relationships. Sometimes, participants alternate between being the "philanthropist" and the "recipient." Philanthropist/recipient relationships of this type are best labeled "reciprocal relationships."

$$\frac{(O_A - I_A)}{|I_A|^{k_A}} = \frac{(O_B - I_B)}{|I_B|^{k_B}}$$

Altruistic relationships. Sometimes the philanthropist is truly a philanthropist. He offers the recipient greater benefits than the recipient could ever hope to return. For the moment, we will label relationships of this type "altruistic relationships."

$$\frac{(O_A - I_A)}{|I_A|^{k_A}} < \frac{(O_B - I_B)}{|I_B|^{k_B}}$$

This relationship has fascinated generations of social psychologists.

To the man in the street, altruistic relationships evidence man at his best. The social workers who help their clients, the Schweitzers who give up a luxurious life to live among the lepers, the church members who donate turkeys to poor families at Thanksgiving are assumed to be good people. Their needy recipients are expected to be grateful. Equity theory, however, suggests that we must be slightly more skeptical of altruistic associations.

Equity theorists have pointed out that "noble" altruism should produce mixed feelings in both the benefactor and the recipient. After all, the benefactor who gives and gives and gives and gets little in return is a participant in an inequitable and unprofitable relationship. Equity theory leads us to expect that benefactor and recipient should experience at least some discomfort when they discover they are participating in an inequitable relationship. The only way they can alleviate their distress is by restoring actual equity, or psychological equity, to their relationship.

The potential for alienation: the altruist's response. One of society's most perplexing problems is to decide how the needy should be treated. People feel that if their fellow is so young, so disabled, so sick, or so old that he is unable to care for himself, society should care for him. On one hand, then, people define "need" as a legitimate input which entitles a citizen to the minimum outcomes he needs. And, people do help the needy to a remarkable extent. People give the "time of day" to passers-by, dole out change at bus-stops, return lost wallets to their owners, and fix flat tires for stranded motorists.

On the other hand, people do not consider "need" to be an entirely legitimate input. They often resent the obligation to help (Berkowitz, 1972a). Often people begrudge the help they accord others and feel that the help should be considered a loan rather than a gift. They feel the recipient is obligated to repay them in whatever ways he can.

The potential for alienation: the recipient's response. It is easy to see why the altruist has mixed feelings about being forced to contribute benefits to another with no hope of return. A little thought, however makes it clear that help is a mixed blessing for the "lucky" recipient as well. The altruistic relationship is an unpleasant relationship for the recipient for three different reasons:

1. *The altruistic relationship is an inequitable relationship.* When the benefactor bestows undeserved benefits on a recipient, he places the recipient in an inequitable relationship. As we indicated in Proposition III, inequitable relationships are unpleasant relationships.

2. *The altruistic relationship is a potentially exploitative relationship.* When a philanthropist grants benefits which his recipient cannot repay in kind, the recipient may well feel that he has become obligated to repay his benefactor in unspecified ways for an indefinite period.

The recipient might reasonably fear that his benefactor may attempt to extract a greater repayment than the recipient would have been willing to give, had he been warned of the conditions of the exchange ahead of time.

3. *The altruistic relationship is a potentially humiliating relationship.* The recipient may be hesitant to accept "charity" for still another reason. He may fear that the benefactor's gift will establish the benefactor's moral and social superiority to the recipient. The recipient may be unwilling to accept such a menial status.

Observational evidence suggests that recipients fear that by accepting help they risk being assigned to a menial status; fears which are probably well founded. Social observers have noted that in a variety of cultures gift-giving and humiliation are linked. Small wonder then that men have learned to "look a gift horse in the mouth" (Joffe, 1953; Oliver, 1967; Homans, 1961).

When we contrast equitable helping relationships (relationships in which altruist and recipient periodically trade favors) with totally altruistic relationships, it becomes clear that a single factor seems to have a critical impact on the benefactor/recipient relationship, i.e., the beneficiary's ability to make restitution.

Researchers who have investigated the interactions of Christmas-gift givers and kindness between neighbors have dealt with donors and recipients who know that eventually their helpful acts will be reciprocated in kind. Researchers who have investigated the interactions of welfare workers versus their clients, developed versus underdeveloped nations, and the medical staff versus the physically handicapped have dealt with recipients who know they will never be able to repay their benefactors. The differing reactions of participants in reciprocal and nonreciprocal relations underscores the importance of the recipient's ability to repay in determining how help affects a relationship. Ability to repay seems to determine whether favor-doing generates pleasant social interactions or resentment and suffering.

An abundance of research supports a single conclusion: Undeserved gifts produce inequity in a relationship. If the participants know the recipient can and will reciprocate, the inequity is viewed as temporary, and thus it produces little distress. If the participants know the recipient cannot or will not reciprocate, however, a real inequity is produced; the participants will experience distress and will therefore need to restore actual or psychological equity to the relationship.

Evidence in support of this conclusion comes from four diverse sources:

1. On the basis of ethnographic data, Mauss (1954) concludes that three types of obligations are widely distributed in human societies in both time and space, (1) the obligation to give, (2) the obligation to receive, and (3) the obligation to repay. Mauss (1954) and Dillon (1968) agree that while reciprocal exchanges breed cooperation and good feelings, gifts that cannot be reciprocated breed discomfort, distress, and dislike.

2. There is evidence that individuals prefer gifts that can be reciprocated to gifts that cannot be repaid (Gergen and Gergen, 1971).

3. There is evidence that individuals are more eager to accept gifts that can be reciprocated than gifts that cannot (Krebs and Baldwin, 1972).

4. Most importantly, there is evidence that a benefactor is liked more when his beneficiary can reciprocate than when he cannot.

Gergen and his associates (Gergen, 1969) investigated American, Swedish, and Japanese citizens' reactions to reciprocal and nonreciprocal exchanges. Students were recruited to participate in an experiment on group competition. Things were arranged so that during the course of the game, the subject discovered that he was losing badly. At a critical stage (when the student was just about to be eliminated from the game) one of the "luckier" players in the game sent him an envelope. The envelope contained a supply of chips and a note. For a third of the subjects (low-obligation condition subjects), the note explained that the chips were theirs to keep, that the giver did not need them and that they need not be returned. One third of the subjects (equal-obligation condition subjects), received a similar note, except that the giver of the chips asked the subject to return an equal number of chips later in the proceedings. The remaining subjects (high-obligation condition subjects), received a note from the giver in which he asked for the chips to be returned with interest and for the subject to help him out later in the game.

At the end of the game, subjects were queried about their attraction toward various partners. The results support our conclusion: Those partners who provided benefits without ostensible obligation or who asked for excessive benefits were both judged to be less attractive than were partners who proposed that the student make exact restitution later in the game.

Gergen et al. (in preparation) conducted a variation of the preceding study. Just as subjects were about to be eliminated from a game because of their consistent losses, another player in the game loaned the subject some resources. The donor loaned the chips with the expectation that they would be paid back. However, in subsequent play, only half of the subjects managed to retain their chips. Thus, half of the subjects were unable to return the gift; half were able to do so. In subsequent evaluations of the donor, recipients that were unable to repay the donor evaluated him less positively than did recipients that were able to repay. These results were replicated in both Sweden and the United States.

Equity Theory and Intimate Relations. When equity theorists argue that business or casual social relationships will endure only so long as they are profitable to both participants, few demur. Yet, if one argues that intimate relations—relations between husband and wife, parent and child, or best friends—might be similarly dependent on the exchange of rewards, objections are quickly voiced. People insist their intimate relations are "special" relations, relations untainted by crass considerations of social exchange.

For example, Simmel (1950), an esteemed sociologist, states:

> The fact is that whatever the participants in the gathering may possess in terms of objective attributes—attributes that are centered outside the particular gathering in question—must not enter it. Wealth, social position, erudition, fame, exceptional capabilities and merits, may not play any part in sociability. (pp. 45-46)

More poetic writers insist that the beauty of familial and romantic relationships is that in their intimate relations individuals transcend selfish concerns. For example, Liebow (1967) points out that cynical ghetto blacks have very romantic ideas about the nature of friendship:

> The pursuit of security and self-esteem push him to romanticize his perception of his friends and friendships. . . . He prefers to see the movement of money, goods, services, and emotional support between friends and according to need, rather than a mutual exchange resting securely on a *quid pro quo* basis. (pp. 176-177)

Anticipating inevitable opposition, then, equity theorists contend that even in the most intimate of relations, equity considerations determine both how viable and how pleasant a relationship will be.

One equity hypothesis which has received thorough investigation is the "matching hypothesis.'' Equity theorists contend that when each partner contributes approximately equal inputs to an intimate exchange, both participants should be maximally satisfied, and their relationship should be maximally enduring. When marked inequalities in inputs exist, the short-changed partner should be frustrated and unhappy and tempted to look for a better bargain on the marriage market. The over-benefited partner should be nervously apprehensive that his partner will desert him and may be tempted to look for a more secure relationship himself.

On the basis of such reasoning, Homans (1961), Backman and Secord (1966), Walster et al. (1966), and Blau (1967) proposed the matching hypothesis. They proposed that partners of similar "value" will be most compatible and will tend to pair up and to stay paired up.

It is in this area that equity theory receives the weakest support. Several studies find no support for the matching hypothesis; a very few find compelling support for this hypothesis. In an early experiment, Walster, Aronson, Abrahams, and Rottman (1966) proposed three hypotheses: (1) The more "socially desirable" a suitor is (i.e., the more physically attractive, personable, famous, or rich he is), the more socially desirable a romantic partner he will feel he deserves; (2) Couples who are similar in social desirability will like one another better than will markedly mismatched couples; and (3) Couples who are similar in social desirability will be more likely to continue to date one another. Figure 9-3 depicts graphically the prediction that participants will prefer dates of approximately their own attractiveness.

These hypotheses were later tested in the field. Entering college freshmen were invited to attend a get-acquainted dance. They were told that dates would be assigned by computer. Physical attractiveness was chosen as the indicant of participants' social desirability. (Data indicate that physical attractiveness is strongly

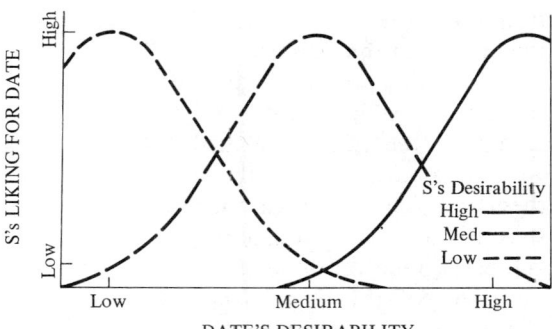

FIGURE 9-3. Amount of liking unattractive, average, and attractive subjects are predicted to feel for dates of various attractiveness.

correlated with popularity, self-esteem, and other indices which comprise "social desirability.") The freshmen's physical attractiveness was evaluated by four college sophomores who "happened" to be present while they were purchasing a ticket.

Whether or not students expected and preferred partners of approximately their own social desirability was assessed in several ways: First, when freshmen signed up for the dance, they were asked how socially desirable they expected their date to be. (They were asked how physically attractive, how personally attractive, and how considerate they expected him or her to be.) Equity theory predicts that the more attractive the freshman, the more desirable he should expect his date to be. This prediction was confirmed.

Second, freshmen were randomly assigned to a date. Then they met for the first time at the dance. Equity theory predicts that the more similar the dates are in attractiveness, the more viable their relationship will be. The viability of the dates' relationships was assessed in three ways: During intermission, students were asked (1) how much they liked their partner and (2) how eager they were to continue the dating relationship. (3) Whether or not couples actually continued to date was determined by interviewing all participants six months after the dance.

Once partners had met one another, equity theory predictions were not supported. Everyone, regardless of his or her own social desirability, best liked and most often attempted to continue to date the most desirable dates available. Equity considerations seemed not to limit the participants' aspirations in any way. To make things even worse for the theory, these nonfindings were replicated by Brislin and Lewis (1968).

Kiesler and Baral (1970) did find support for the equity theory predictions. The authors recruited Yale students for a study on intelligence tests. The experimenter told the men that he was perfecting a new intelligence test that had already been successfully used on hundreds of students. Men were then given a difficult test. Men in the high self-esteem condition were led to believe that they were doing extremely well on the test. (The experimenter nodded and smiled at their answers and mentioned that other men had much more trouble with the questions.) Men in the low self-esteem condition were led to believe that they were doing badly on the test. (The experimenter made it apparent that he was displeased with their performance. He frowned, looked away, and mentioned that other subjects had performed better.)

During a break in testing, the experimenter and the subject visited a nearby canteen. When they entered the canteen, the experimenter recognized a woman (actually an experimental confederate). In one condition (the attractive condition), the confederate was made up to be very physically attractive. She wore becoming make-up and fashionable clothing. In the unattractive condition, she was far less attractive. She wore no make-up, heavy glasses, and had her hair pulled back with a rubber band. Her skirt and blouse clashed and were arranged sloppily.

The woman sat down and chatted with the experimenter and the subject. After a minute, the experimenter excused himself to make a phone call. While he was gone, the woman continued to engage the Yale student in conversation for half an hour.

The dependent variable was the extent to which the male indicated to the female confederate that he was romantically interested in her and the effort which he expended to prolong their relationship. The confederate kept track of whether the man asked her for a date, asked for her phone number, offered to buy her a snack or coffee, offered her a cigarette, complimented her, or finally, ignored her when at the end of the prescribed time she said that she should get back to work.

Kiesler and Baral found strong support for the matching hypothesis. When the man's self-esteem had been lowered, he behaved most romantically toward the unattractive confederate. When the man's self-esteem had been raised, he behaved in a far more romantic way with the attractive confederate than with the unattractive one. Berscheid et al. (1971) provide additional support for the matching hypothesis.

At the present time, then, data do not consistently support either equity theory or the notion that individuals' intimate social choices are unchecked by reality. The best summary of results would seem to be as follows:

> Individuals' romantic choices are somewhat influenced by equity considerations.

> Individuals tend to choose and prefer partners of approximately their own "social worth." However, there is a constant upward bias in one's choices.

> Individuals persist in trying to form relations with partners who are somewhat more desirable than themselves.

> One's romantic choices thus seem to be a delicate compromise between the insistent

demands for an ideal partner and one's realization that one must accept what he deserves.

The conclusion that one's social choices are a compromise between fantasy and reality seems to be consistent with our own observations in the daily world.

Sometimes individuals talk and act as if they have unlimited social inputs and thus are deserving of perfection. They talk as if the fact that they had to compromise in selecting a marriage partner is an inequity. For example, we can all think of prestigious but aging professors who leave their wives and marry beautiful young graduate students. Often, within a short time, our professor begins to lament his protegée's shortcomings. "If only she were more intelligent and more considerate," he complains. Observers sometimes smile, because they are more attuned to the operation of exchange processes in determining social pairings than is the participant in the relationship. They are smugly aware that if his lady were smarter, she would not have to settle for the company of the aging professor.

Sometimes, however, individuals are aware of equity considerations. The man with the undeservedly beautiful wife often manifests vague unease. Whether the unease is generated by his own recognition that he has married a better woman than he deserves, or whether his unease is generated by the fact that she constantly reminds him that he has married too well, we do not know. Intimate relations, then, seem to be influenced in part by equity considerations and in part by fantasy.

CURRENT STATUS OF INTERPERSONAL ATTRACTION

The interpersonal attraction area is in the midst of a lively Renaissance. One cluster of researchers is wholly engaged in deriving and testing predictions from the reinforcement paradigm. They argue compellingly that only by establishing a mini-Manhattan Project[2] and painstakingly testing all aspects of the reinforcement paradigm will interpersonal-attraction research flower. Donn Byrne (1971) and his associates are typical of these researchers.

First, the Byrne group set out to painstakingly prove that the similarity-attraction relationship was a general one. They found it was. They discovered that attitudinal similarity breeds friendship, racial tolerance, romantic attraction, and marital happiness. Then they set out to discover exactly how the similarity-attraction link works. For example, they attempted to ascertain whether it is the number of attitudes that people share that determines liking or whether it is the proportion of similar attitudes to dissimilar ones that is important. After clever and lengthy research, they concluded that: "Subjects respond not simply to the number of similar or dissimilar attitudes expressed by the stranger but to the relative number of the two types of attitudes, regardless of the total number of topics involved." They even became convinced that the base relationship between attitude similarity–dissimilarity and attraction was so regular that it could be expressed in mathematical form [i.e., $Y = 5.44X + 6.62$ (where Y = attraction and X = proportion of similar attitudes)].

Other enclaves of researchers are roughly pushing forward the frontiers of interpersonal-attraction research. For many years researchers contented themselves with studying only the mildest forms of interpersonal attraction. They limited their curiosity to the genesis of tepid friendships, since to study more intense and fascinating feelings was taboo. Government granting agencies, sensitive to the feelings of the public, were nervous about awarding money to projects concerned with such trifling

---

[2]The mammoth World War II project which developed the atomic bomb.

matters as passionate love, sex, or hatred. Psychologists, with their blinders on, rationalized that to study these taboo topics was not only impossible but undesirable. A scientist wishing to cultivate information in these exotic areas must be softheaded, unscientific, and obsessed with the trivial. Suddenly a revolution occurred. The humanists invaded psychology and forced psychologists to acknowledge that tender and brutal emotions are important human concerns. Masters and Johnson's pioneering research made it obvious that a daring researcher could even study *Human Sexual Response*. In the last five years more psychologists have begun to study and investigate love, sex, and hatred than explored these phenomena in the history of psychology.

The work of Driscoll et al. is representative of the fascinating research into the nature of love that has begun. Driscoll et al. attempted to determine what effect parental interference has on the intensity of a heterosexual love affair. The authors observed how frequently parental opposition and intense love are pitted against one another in literature. (For example, Romeo and Juliet's short but intense love affair took place against the background of total opposition from the two feuding families. The difficulties and separations which the family conflict created appear to have intensified the lovers' feelings for each other.)

The authors tested the hypothesis that parental opposition would deepen romantic love in the following way. Ninety-one married couples and 49 dating couples (18 of whom were living together) were recruited to participate in a Marital Relations Project. During an initial interview, all the couples filled out two scales, (1) an assessment of parental interference scale which measured the extent to which the couple's parents interfered and caused difficulties in their relationship, and (2) a romantic love scale which measured the extent to which participants loved, felt they cared about and needed their partner, and felt that the relationship was more important than anything else.

The authors found that parental interference and passion were related. Parental interference and romantic love were correlated .50 for the unmarried sample and .24 for the married sample.

Next, the authors investigated whether increasing parental interference would provoke increased passion. Six to ten months after the initial interview, the authors invited all of the couples back for a second interview. During this second interview, the participants once again completed parental interference and romantic love scales. By comparing participants' initial interview responses with their later ones, the authors could calculate whether the participants' parents had become more or less interfering in the relationship and how these changes in parental interference had affected the couples' affair. The authors found that as parents began to interfere more in a relationship, the couple appeared to fall more deeply in love. If the parents had become resigned to the relationship and had begun to interfere less, the couples began to feel less intensely about one another. (Changes in parental interference correlated .30 with changes in romantic love and also .34 with changes in conjugal love.)

Data indicating that parental interference breeds passion are fascinating. When parents interfere in an "unsuitable" match, they interfere with the intent of destroying the relationship, not of strengthening it. Yet, these data warn that parental interference is likely to boomerang if the relationship survives. It may foster desire rather than division.

Other clusters of researchers have begun to apply theories of interpersonal attraction to social problems. They are confident that, by propagating existing theoretical knowledge, psychologists can insure that the world will become a more fulfilling, pleasant, exciting, or relaxing place. These activists have applied attraction (and equity) theory to improve dating and marital relations, helping relations to the development of "social indicators" (i.e., indicants of human happiness), to the reformation of homes for delinquent children and prisoners, to reducing international tension, and the like.

A fourth cluster of researchers have begun chopping away at the tidy borders which have conventionally existed between social psychology (and interpersonal attraction) and other disciplines, such as political science, economics, law, anthropology, and history. For example, one team of psychologists and lawyers merged forces in an effort to determine whether the legal structures existing in the United States do in fact push harm-doers to make voluntary restitution to those they injure. Other teams of psychologist-lawyers have tried to determine whether judges and jurors' "curious" reluctance to adhere to prescribed procedures and "the letter of the law" in assigning sentences may, in fact, reflect the fact that they are more concerned about restoring equitable relations between defendant and plaintiff than with following legal prescriptions.

THEORETICAL APPLICATIONS AND FUTURE RESEARCH DIRECTIONS

Only recently have psychologists fully assimilated the profound truth of Lewin's contention that: "There is nothing so practical as a good theory." Many young activists—always the first to be swept forward by social change—are now scrutinizing theory, in order to uncover the best way to promote profound social changes. Other activists are busily engrossed in applied research.

Equity theory was developed to explain interpersonal attraction. Yet, activists soon found that the equity approach was useful in understanding a variety of diverse human problems. Let us review a potpourri of these recent developments.

The Impact of Power on Justice

Philosophers, who contemplate the evolution of social justice, seem eventually to come to the unsettling conclusion that Man's social philosophy is inevitably a mere rationalization of the status quo. For example, Sampson (1968) notes: ". . . it is a truism that political philosophy has traditionally concerned itself with the search for some kind of moral justification for the power and coercion of governments." Powerful groups survey their inputs and unfailingly come to the conclusion that it is just these resources which entitle one to monopolize community resources. Deprived groups have little choice but to accept their reasoning (see Walster, 1975).

Theories of social justice have an unvarying history. The current generation becomes aware of the pressure of emerging groups for "fairer" treatment. The current generation concludes that it is the first generation blessed with clear vision. They correctly perceive the "fair thing" to do and work toward amending the social order.

Then a new generation comes along. They too become sensitive to the fact that the power balance has shifted. The masses of serfs, merchants, second sons, migrant workers, middle Americans, youths, or elderly now assert their claims, and the new generation again realizes that the principles of justice that their fathers found so compelling were, in fact, merely a response to the prevailing power balance.

It is easy for us to feel appalled at the way nobles "exploited" their serfs, slaveowners "exploited" their slaves, or men "exploited" their women. But these landowners, slaveowners, and male chauvinists were not fundamentally different people than we are. They were simply responding to different pressures, and to a different status quo.

The message, then, is clear. There is little chance that the majority will recognize the claims of exploited minorities unless these minorities can amass sufficient power to press for equal treatment. Minority members can and have used a variety of techniques to make majority members realize that sharing with them will be a more profitable strategy than hording. The exploited can use praise, passive resistance, sabotage, or moral opprobrium or approbation. But unless they have some real power to affect the outcomes of the majority, their case is hopeless. The powerful can always generate a satisfying, justifying philosophy.

Kipnis (1972) has been fascinated by the impact that power has on men's social relations. He argues that as soon as men acquire power, they are tempted to use that power to enrich themselves. Inevitably they succumb to temptation. Power thus leads to corruption, of several sorts. According to Kipnis, the powerful (1) monopolize resources, (2) are tempted to develop an exploitative morality (and soon conclude that they are exempt from ordinary morality), (3) develop an exalted and vain view of their own worth, (4) become alienated from their fellow man, and (5) come to despise him. In a series of laboratory experiments, Kipnis (1972) amasses evidence in support of the sequence he proposes.

Kipnis, too, would surely agree that minority members have no hope of wrenching equal rights from the majority unless they gain sufficient political, economic, or physical power to enforce their claims.

Equity and the Law

Legal philosophers have insisted that a wise society would structure its institutions so that its citizens find it profitable to be good. In Bolt's *A Man for All Seasons,* Thomas More rightly observes: "If we lived in a State where virtue was profitable, common sense would make us good, and greed would make us saintly." But society has not yet arranged its institutions so neatly. In our time, as in More's, humility, chastity, fortitude, justice, and thought are often less profitable than avarice, anger, envy, pride, sloth, lust, and stupidity. Yet, the goal of a sensible society is clear. Goodness should be profitable.

This principle would suggest that social institutions should be designed to promote justice and discourage derogation and justification. When human relationships become alarmingly inequitable, society should intervene and attempt to persuade harm-doers to voluntarily compensate their victims. Everyone benefits when harm-doers volunteer to compensate those they have injured. The harm-doer becomes more profoundly committed to the equity norm (see Mills, 1958) and serves as a good behavioral model for others (see Bandura and Walters, 1963).

If it becomes evident that state agencies are not going to be able to prod the harm-doer into restoring equity, legal and religious agencies might escalate their activities and insist that the harm-doer make restitution. Such agencies can pressure a harm-doer to make restitution in a variety of ways. For example, in the Hungarian and Norwegian legal systems, the harm-doer's willingness to make restitution is taken into account when determining his sentence. When a prisoner's sentence is contingent on whether or not he "chooses" to make restitution, restitution is clearly not voluntary. However, the Hungarians consider it better, from a rehabilitative point of view, to elicit semivoluntary restitution than none at all. Macaulay (in Macaulay and Walster, 1971) points out that in the United States, formal and informal techniques are used to pressure individuals to make restitution:

> On its face, American law is consistent with the goal of supporting compensation. . . . the common-law of torts consists of rules which say a wrong-doer must compensate his victim. In addition, the legal system in operation provides more avenues to restitution than are available in its formal rules. A wide variety of informal procedures encourage compensation. For example, criminal sanctions are sometimes used as leverage to induce restitution. A police officer may decide not to arrest a shoplifter if the wrongdoer is not a professional thief and if the stolen items are returned; a district attorney may decide not to prosecute if the amount embezzled is returned. (p. 179)

The psychological literature (Brehm & Cohen, 1962) and the anecdotal evidence of penal theorists (Spencer, 1874; Del Vecchio, 1959; Schafer, 1960) provide some support for the contention that if society induces "fair" behavior, "fair" attitudes will follow.

Sometimes social agencies cannot elicit restitution. (For example, harm-doers are often unknown or indigent.) In such cases it may be wise for society to acknowledge that an injustice has been perpetrated and for welfare agencies and insurance agencies to intervene to alleviate the victim's suffering. Such intervention is consistent with our notion of fairness (as the innocent victim is recompensed) and is expedient (as the legitimacy of equity norms is affirmed by society). For a lengthy and fascinating discussion of this point, see Fry (1956).

The student who is interested in the way legal rules and processes encourage or discourage harm-doers from making restitution should see Macaulay in Macaulay and Walster (1971) or Austin and Walster (1974).

The Participants in Inequity—the Exploiter and the Victim

When one examines the current status of interpersonal attraction, a curious anomaly appears. Equity theory presumably deals with the reactions of two participants to a relationship—the exploiter and his victim, the innocent bystander and the innocent victim. Yet, virtually all of the equity research focuses on the reactions of only one participant, the one who has managed to amass excessive relative outcomes. We know a great deal about exploiters and bystanders to an emergency; we know very little about the exploited and innocent victims. Theoretically, we would predict that the exploiter's and the exploited's reactions should echo one another, but evidence to document this prediction is virtually nonexistent.

Why have psychologists been so fascinated by harm-doers and so disinterested in victims? Perhaps psychologists, like everyone else, prefer speculating about the lives of the powerful and rich to those of the weak and poor. We do not know. In any case, the advancing era of humanism has generated a sudden curiosity about the feelings of victims. Research is now underway to test whether or not our theories about how victims feel are valid. Let us describe just one of these numerous research enterprises.

The Making of an Uncle Tom. According to equity theory, when a victim perceives that he is being exploited, he has two options: (1) He can become angry and demand justice. (2) He can suppress his anger and justify his own deprivation, becoming an apathetic "Uncle Tom."

One team of researchers (Austin and Pate) has proposed three variables that they predict will determine whether individuals caught up in the wake of injustice will insist on justice or accept justification.

1. *Previous Expectations.* Austin (1972) proposed that individuals will be more enraged when they encounter unexpected, startling injustices than when they finally encounter a long expected injustice. Austin argued that when one knows he faces eventual exploitation, he is tempted to gain tranquility by minimizing the seriousness of the injustice. Thus, he hypothesized that unexpected injustice should provoke a far more emotional response (and more vigorous demands for restitution) than should long-awaited and thus well-rationalized injustice. Austin and Walster (1974) found compelling support for Austin's contentions.

2. *Hope.* If a citizen who is victimized is confident that if he makes a fuss his fellow citizens will see to it that equity is restored, he should be likely to allow his righteous anger full expression. He should demand compensation. However, a victim who has learned through crushing experience that "you can't fight city hall" should try to dampen his sense of outrage and to justify his exploitation.

3. *Previous Commitments.* If an individual repeatedly suffers discrimination, he eventually develops some strategy for coping with his pain. Some deprived blacks declare themselves to be black militants; others become Uncle Toms. Some women who encounter discrimination become unwavering women's liberationists; others join "MOM" ("Men Our Masters"). Once a person becomes committed to a specific strategy for coping with inequality, he should find it embarrassing and difficult to adopt a new strategy, should the world change.

The data that will tell us whether or not these researchers' hunches about "the making of an Uncle Tom" are correct are not yet in. If they are correct, their discoveries may have a revolutionary impact on the relations between militants and reactionaries. It may be easier for militants to understand Uncle Toms, and for Uncle Toms to understand militants, once they become aware that they are simply coping with the same pain in different ways.

SUMMARY

This chapter has progressed from a *Remembrance of Things Past* to an *Intimations of the Future.*

First we explored the reasons why men have always been eager to uncover the antecedents of interpersonal attraction. The reason why people are so unfailingly eager to be liked soon became clear: A person who is liked by his comrades can amass enormous benefits; a person who is hated is in trouble.

We then sketched the ingenious techniques observers have used to gain information about who likes whom. We discovered that social scientists are not limited to blatant devices such as self-report questionnaires if they want to find out how people feel about one another. Social psychologists have used such unobtrusive indicants as how close one stands to another, how often he gazes at another, or how much his pupils dilate when he looks at another, in order to detect how people really feel about one another.

Next, we described the reinforcement theory of attraction. Numerous studies lead to the conclusion that people come to like those who reward them (or who are merely present when they are rewarded) and come to hate those who frustrate them (or who are merely present when they are punished). For example, if a person claims to share our convictions or reveals that he finds us fascinating, we will like him. If he frustrates our desires, we will dislike him.

The reinforcement paradigm raises problems that have long plagued psychologists and students. It sometimes falters in predicting human behavior and is embarrassed by two facts: (1) Individuals do not inevitably strive to maximize their immediate material rewards. (2) They do not always prefer people who provide large material rewards to people who provide small rewards.

The most recent reinforcement theory, equity theory, is a general theory designed to integrate the numerous existing theories of interpersonal attraction. Equity theory, a strikingly simple theory, consists of four basic propositions: Men try to maximize their outcomes (Proposition I). A group of individuals can maximize their total outcomes by agreeing on some equitable system for sharing resources. A relationship is defined as equitable when a scrutineer perceives that all participants are securing equal relative outcomes from the relationship.

Groups try to insure that members can maximize their outcomes by behaving equitably; they reward members who behave equitably and punish members who behave inequitably (Proposition II). When individuals socialized by this system participate in inequitable relationships, they experience distress (Proposition III). Participants reduce their distress either by restoring actual equity or by restoring psychological equity to the relationship (Proposition IV).

Researchers have applied equity theory to various types of human relationships such as business relationships, exploitative relationships, helping relationships, and intimate relationships. The research in these last three areas was discussed in terms of its relevance for interpersonal attraction.

Finally, the direction of future research in attraction was surveyed. Interest in interpersonal attraction has burgeoned and some of the most intriguing equity research may still be forthcoming.

SUGGESTED READINGS

Berscheid, E., & Walster, E. *Interpersonal attraction*. New York: Addison-Wesley, 1969.

This volume provides a broad overview of recent theorizing and research on love, interpersonal attraction, interpersonal hostility, and hatred.

Homans, G. C. *Social behavior: Its elementary forms*. New York: Harcourt, Brace and World, 1961.

Homans succinctly reviews the Skinnerian learning paradigm and then details the effect that rewards and punishments should have on an animal's behavior, including man's. Homans then proposes the original exchange model. He observes that animals' activities reciprocally influence one another. Thus, social relations inevitably become exchange relations. Homans demonstrates the truth of his contentions with persuasive anecdotes and research data.

Walster, E., Berscheid, E., & Walster, G. W. New directions in equity research. *Journal of Personality and Social Psychology,* 1973, *25,* 151–176.

This article presents an up-to-date summary of equity theory and existing equity research. It describes the equity research advances in four major areas of human interaction: business relationships, exploitative relationships, helping relationships, and intimate relationships. The authors point out the relevance of equity theory for various social problems.

10
Interpersonal Influence and Conformity

Richard H. Willis and John M. Levine

INTRODUCTION

Consider the following miscellaneous collection of episodes, some actual and some not:

In 1938, on the evening before Halloween, a radio program based on H. G. Wells' *War of the Worlds* described with vivid realism the invasion of earth by technologically superior Martians. Many listeners missed the opening announcement and concluded that they were listening to a news broadcast. Mass panic occurred in several localities in the U.S., and it was later estimated that at least a million people were frightened or disturbed by the program (Cantril, Gaudet, & Hertzog, 1940).

Two neighbors, Kelly and Cohen, are discussing politics again. The arguments and counterarguments fly back and forth for almost an hour. In the past, each has sometimes succeeded in getting his view on a particular issue accepted by the other, but not today. In fact, the two neighbors actually move further apart as the discussion goes on.

A college sophomore appears to participate as a subject in a psychological experiment. The experimenter hands him a list of nonsense syllables and asks him to memorize them in order in five minutes. He does so. Down the hall another subject in a different experiment is requested to administer, repeatedly, electric shocks of several hundred volts to someone with a weak heart. He does so.

In a stage show once seen by one of the authors, the performer first put several volunteers—three or four young men and one young woman—into a hypnotic state. He then produced a pair of "magic glasses" which he asserted allowed one to see through any kind of fabric or clothing and invited his volunteers to try them. All the young men willingly accepted the invitation, each in turn taking a look around and apparently enjoying the experience. The young woman, however, could not be persuaded to try the magic glasses.

In George Orwell's prophetic novel *1984,* by means of excruciating electric shocks the protagonist, Winston, is made to assert that his tormentor is holding up five fingers when in fact he is holding up four fingers. Later, Winston actually comes to believe his assertion.

In a classic investigation of conformity, Solomon Asch (1956) confronted a single naive subject with a unanimous majority of other "subjects" who were actually confederates of the experimenter. On certain trials all members of this majority gave responses to simple discrimination items which normally would have been about as believable as the assertion that four fingers actually equals five fingers. The typical subject went along with the erroneous majority about a third of the time.

Examples could easily be multiplied, but these are sufficient to illustrate certain points. First, in each case the behavior of someone changes as a result of the behavior of someone else. Second, the changes can be brought about in many different ways and for various reasons. Sometimes the actor seems to be acting of his own free will, and sometimes he does not. Finally, the changes themselves can be of many different kinds. Some, for example, involve actual changes in beliefs or attitudes while others are confined to changes in overt behavior. Several kinds of changes can take place at one time. Although not all of the changes constitute conformity, all of our examples are instances of social influence. A broad interpretation of our chapter title would carry an obligation to discuss all of these kinds of situations, and many more. We will not be this ambitious, however.

In this chapter, we shall concentrate on how an actor is affected by the behavior of a relatively small number of others who are in contact or communication with the actor. (The impact on individuals of broad societal norms and of mass behavior and social movements are treated elsewhere in this book.) In addition, we shall be especially interested in changes in behavior, for it is only through observed or inferred change that social influence can be gauged.

Definitions and Basic Issues

Definitions

Influence. The most basic concept in this chapter is influence, which in its general meaning refers to the power (or potential) to produce an effect or to the actual production of an effect. Influence is the capacity to cause things to be different than they otherwise would have been, or a concrete instance of this. By social influence we mean influence between or among individuals or groups. Although interpersonal influence can be defined quite broadly (e.g., Wheeler, 1970), in this paper the term will be taken to mean social influence between or among a relatively small number of individuals.

Conformity. The other basic concept in our chapter title, conformity, implies an intention on the part of the actor to behave in the desired or prescribed manner. He may not succeed completely, but from a motivational point of view his behavior consists of conformity. Formally, we may define social conformity as behavior intended to fulfill normative group expectations as these expectations are perceived by the individual (Willis, 1965a). It is important to distinguish between such intended conformity and incidental conformity, in which the actor behaves in a conforming way but without intention or perhaps even awareness of the fact. It is also important not to confuse unsuccessful efforts to conform with intentional nonconformity, for these are quite different indeed even when leading to the same pattern of overt responding.

As for *nonconformity,* it can be defined as behavior intended to facilitate the attainment of any goal other than that of fulfilling perceived normative expectations (Willis, 1965a).

Although this global definition-by-exclusion is not erroneous, neither is it by itself especially revealing. Later we shall delve more deeply into the process of conceptualizing nonconformity and deviance. For the moment we shall only point out that research on conformity has typically failed to deal adequately with nonconformity and, indeed, has largely neglected it. Hollander and Willis (1967) comment that this is especially curious, for conformity, being the modal response, tells us the least about individual differences.

Especially in the sociological literature, the terms *deviancy* and *deviant behavior* typically connote socially undesirable patterns of behavior. In this chapter these terms and the term *deviation* will be used interchangeably with nonconformity and will carry no value connotation.

Some related concepts. In an edited volume appearing a few years ago (Berkowitz, 1965a) two literature reviews appeared one right after the other. The first (Allen, 1965) dealt with conformity, the second (Schopler, 1965) with social power. Although the two literatures are somewhat separate, as suggested by these adjacent reviews, there is no advantage to maintaining a distinction here. *Power* will be defined as potential influence—that is, the capacity to influence—and in practice the terms power and influence will usually be used interchangeably.

The term *imitation* refers to behavior often quite difficult to distinguish from conformity. One person exhibits behavior identical or similar to that shown by another. Normative expectations may or may not be clearly involved. If they are, imitation amounts to conformity. Non-imitation is frequently called *opposition behavior*, especially in the case of only two response alternatives, for then non-imitation is in fact in direct opposition to imitation. *Contagion* is sometimes defined as imitation produced unintentionally by the initiator and is often used in contexts in which the particular type of behavior can spread throughout a group, crowd, or social sector. *Obedience* refers to compliance or conformity to normative expectations as these are communicated on particular occasions by an authority agent. The behavior of a person under *hypnosis* might be considered to be a special kind of obedience. It has been defined by English and English (1958) as an artificially induced state characterized by greatly heightened suggestibility to the hypnotist. Sarbin and Coe (1972) have recently offered a role-theory analysis of hypnosis which also emphasizes compliance with the hypnotist's demands.

A central topic in social psychology, closely related in principle to conformity, is *attitude change*. As with social power, the literature on attitude change has developed somewhat separately from that on conformity and social influence. In general, attitude change research is more concerned with inferred changes in beliefs and feelings, while conformity research tends to be oriented more towards observable behavioral changes (see Chapter 7).

Conformity, attitude change, imitation, contagion, and obedience all refer to reactions to intentional or unintentional influence. This multiplicity of concepts and variations in research procedures, like the diversity in our introductory collection of examples, serves to underscore the protean nature of interpersonal influence phenomena. Rather than attempting a systematic survey of the entire area, which would necessarily be superficial, we shall instead concentrate on a few selected issues. Each of the basic issues enumerated below is taken up in a subsequent section of the chapter.

Basic Issues

1. What is conformity? Although conformity has already been defined and distinguished from related concepts, this is by no means the end of the matter. Terms must be defined oper-

ationally as well as conceptually. In other words, we must not only say what conformity is in the abstract, but we must also outline concrete operations for measuring it.

2. What are the alternatives to conformity? The traditional view, as we shall see, is a unidimensional view. Only a solitary alternative to conformity is considered. Sometimes this is called nonconformity and sometimes independence. But if we take nonconformity to be our generic term, then independence is just one of several kinds of nonconformity. Another kind of nonconformity is negativism, in which the actor is influenced (and thus not independent) but moves away from the conformity position. Our task in connection with this second issue is to delineate a number of basic modes of nonconformity and to show how they are related to conformity and to one another.

3. Why does the actor conform or deviate? What are the actor's personal goals and motives? What are his interpersonal objectives? How does he see the situation? Why are public responses sometimes different from privately given reactions? When the actor deliberately deviates from normative expectations, what is he trying to accomplish?

4. When does the actor conform, and when deviate? In other words, what are the conditions under which various modes of social response occur? Whereas the third issue will be discussed primarily in terms of various conceptual analyses that have been proposed for improving our understanding of the psychological processes underlying reactions to influence, this fourth question will be answered by citing illustrative research findings, mostly experimental. We have chosen three topics out of a large number of possibilities for particular attention. The first is social support. In the context of Asch-type conformity, what effects are observed when the single naive subject is provided with one or more allies, and how are these effects modified by the attributes of the allies and the circumstances under which they agree with the naive subject or differ with the majority? The second topic concerns the characteristics of the stimulus items or issues about which judgments are being made. Judgments may involve sensory discriminations, opinions about various issues, personal preferences, or other kinds of responses. In some cases a right answer obviously exists (although it may not be obvious which answer is the right one), while in others it is equally obvious that there is no right or wrong answer. Judgments may differ in difficulty, or put another way, stimuli may differ in ambiguity. We shall examine the effects of these stimulus and issue characteristics on conformity and nonconformity. Finally, we shall deal with the timely topic of obedience to authority. Although social philosophers, religious authorities, jurists, and editorial writers have not hesitated to deal with this intriguing phenomenon, it was neglected by experimental social psychologists until about 15 years ago. We shall review the research conducted and inspired by Stanley Milgram in an effort to understand the conditions which produce obedience (and disobedience) to authority.

5. Conformity—good or bad? Is the conformist, the yes-man, yielding blindly and without reason? Is this also true for the anticonforming no-man? Is it only the independent thinking man who rises above the level of conditioned responses, or is even his behavior explainable in S-R terms? More generally put, how rational is conformity relative to its alternatives? In addition, the quality of the underlying thought processes aside, what are the consequences of conformity behavior? Is conformity an effective strategy from the standpoint of the individual? From the standpoint of the group? What about the concepts of "the conforming personality" and "the conforming society"? Do these terms have any meaning and, if so, can value judgments legitimately be made about them?

Historical Review

The very first experiment in social psychology was one on interpersonal influence, conducted by Norman Triplett in 1885. Triplett was not only a psychologist but also a bicycle-racing enthusiast. From an inspection of official records he determined that bicycle racers did best in simultaneous competition, somewhat less well in paced races against time, and least well when racing alone against time. He theorized that the presence of another rider is a stimulus arousing the competitive spirit that releases more energy than the racer could by himself release. In order to test this idea, he did an experiment in which the performance of children winding fishing reels when working alone was compared with their performance when working in the presence of one another. Again he found a *social facilitation* effect similar to the one he had noted in the bicycle racing records (Triplett, 1897). This early lead was not followed up immediately.

F. H. Allport selected social facilitation as the topic of his early experimental work (Allport, 1920, 1924). Social facilitation, as studied earlier by Triplett, refers to the impact on task performance of the presence of others working on the same task. Allport also looked at the effect of observers. He found that the most usual effect of either co-workers or observers is an increase in speed but a decrease in accuracy. Allport and others continued work on social facilitation through the 1930s, but then the topic went out of fashion. Recently, however, interest in social facilitation has revived (Henchy & Glass, 1968; Zajonc, 1965; Zentall & Levine, 1972).

It was surely no accident that Allport chose to work on social facilitation. Not only had Triplett and a very few others (e.g., Moede, 1920) led the way, but the topic lent itself quite naturally to Allport's predilection for working with individual variables. His groups were not really very "groupy," as each person worked on a similar but separate task, or one worked and the others merely observed. There were no group goals and no group norms. No cooperation was required, and even the competitive aspects were somewhat implicit. In short, experimental social psychology had not yet become very social.

Later Allport moved out of the laboratory. When he did he continued to make important contributions. In his monographic article on the J-curve hypothesis of conformity (Allport, 1934), he reported a series of pioneering field studies. These studies demonstrated that, when measured along a dimension of purpose (a "telic" continuum, as Allport called it) and in the presence of a well-defined norm, deviations from full conformity decrease in frequency so rapidly with increasing amounts of deviation that the highly skewed distribution is reminiscent of the letter J. Most drivers, for example, were observed to come to a full stop at a stop sign, while almost all others slowed down to a near stop. Such a distribution is shown in Figure 10-1, although the "J" is reversed because of the convention of placing the zero point of the horizontal scale on the left.

Although Allport had now incorporated social norms and "conformity-producing agencies" (such as leaders, social approval and disapproval, education, punishment, and institutional controls) into his theoretical analysis, he was still focusing on individual responses of a kind that are not highly interdependent. Another feature of the J-curve research, also shared by the social facilitation work and indeed by most early social psychology research, was a preoccupation with social *products,* such as levels of task performance or distributions of conformity responses, and a relative disregard of *process*. The J-curve, however, attracts very little attention today, and no research relating to it has been done for a long time. This may be, as McDavid and Harari (1968) believe,

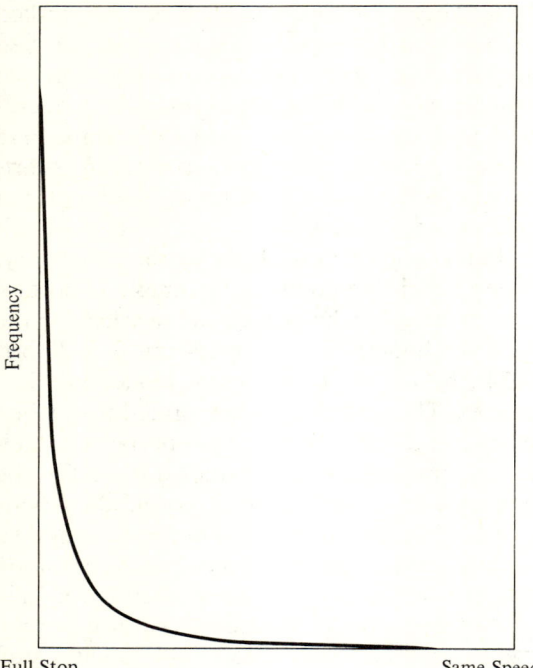

FIGURE 10-1. The J-curve of conformity. The majority of drivers conform completely by coming to a full stop at a stop sign. More generally, the frequency of cases decreases very rapidly as deviation from a full stop increases.

because of certain defects in Allport's analysis and techniques of measurement; he regarded overconformity as conformity, for example, rather than deviant behavior.

At about the same time that Allport published his J-curve findings, some ingenious experiments were reported by a young Turk (literally), Muzafer Sherif. Starting with an interest in the formation of social norms, Sherif moved into the laboratory in order to investigate interpersonal influence under controlled conditions (Sherif, 1935, 1936). He made innovative use of the *autokinetic phenomenon,* already well known to experimental psychologists and astronomers. If a person is placed in a completely dark room and exposed to a stationary pinpoint of light, it will appear to move.

The illusion of movement is created because the individual lacks any frame of reference, any sensory anchor.

Such a highly ambiguous situation is ideal for studying interpersonal influence without interference from actual sensory or judgmental capacities. Sherif found that a given subject responding alone tends to establish his own characteristic range of apparent movement over a series of trials. In other words, *individual norms* are established. When groups of two or three subjects confront the autokinetic phenomenon together, either with or without prior experience alone, *group norms* are established. These group norms are not just a mere averaging of individual norms, but have a coherence, a "life" of their own, so to speak. Evidence for this comes, for example, from the fact that shifts in group norms in a given group from session to session are truly group shifts. Norms of the individual members rise and fall towards a common norm in each series and, in general, interdependencies among responses are pronounced. Furthermore, there is considerable transfer of an established group norm from the group situation to a subsequent individual situation.

Certain aspects of Sherif's work are noteworthy. First, to a greater extent than in the studies on social facilitation or the J-curve, in Sherif's experiments the groups were really groups in the sense that a *group product* (a norm) emerged from interdependent individual responses. Second, although Sherif was interested in the product, the norm, he was even more interested in the process whereby this product is formed out of the interaction among group members. Possibly for these reasons, or perhaps because Sherif had introduced a clever methodology, the autokinetic experiments have had a more lasting impact on the study of conformity than has the J-curve.

Another important tributary into the mainstream of research on interpersonal influence originated with Kurt Lewin, who is usually credited with founding the group dynamics movement. As an illustration of Lewin's work on interpersonal influence, consider the experiments (conducted during World War II) on group discussion followed by public decision as a technique for producing changes in attitudes and behavior of group members (Lewin, 1952). In two experiments, the effectiveness of lecture was compared with group decision in increasing the use of certain kinds of foods by housewives, while a third study compared individual instruction with group decision in getting new mothers to give their babies proper amounts of cod liver oil and orange juice. In all three comparisons, group discussion followed by public decision (a show of hands) was substantially more effective than either the group lecture or the individual instruction.

We note in passing that subsequent work (Bennett, 1955) demonstrated that a positive decision, and the perception that others had also made a positive decision, are more important than group discussion per se.

Lewin's theoretical analysis stressed certain system concepts. He postulated both driving forces and restraining forces and hypothesized that the group tends towards a state in which the resultant force is zero, that is, an *equilibrium* state. Because the group can be moved to another equilibrium state, either by changes in the driving forces or the restraining forces, Lewin referred to this state as a quasi-stationary equilibrium. One of the implications of this analysis is that it is generally preferable to bring about a group change by the reduction of restraining forces than by an increase in driving forces, for the latter produces a higher level of tension. For example, one would be wise to persuade a group to try something new by reducing the causes of hesitation rather than by increasing the threat of punishment if the new course of action is not tried.

The "post-Lewinians" (Lewin's students) have usually dealt with situations of intermediate levels of ambiguity—less ambiguous than Sherif's autokinetic situation but less highly structured than the conflict confronting Asch's lone real subject when pitted against a unanimous majority in judging the relative length of clearly perceived lines. In addition, they have been much concerned with the "groupiness" variable, usually referred to as group cohesiveness and sometimes defined as the resultant of all forces acting on members to remain in the group (Festinger, 1950). In a study of two university housing projects, Festinger, Schachter, and Back (1950) found that residents in the more cohesive units showed more attitudinal and behavioral conformity than those in less cohesive units. An experiment by Kurt Back (1951) demonstrated that members of highly cohesive dyads influenced one another to a greater extent than did members of low cohesive dyads. This finding was obtained regardless of whether cohesiveness was based on (1) interpersonal attraction, (2) perceptions of group competence, or (3) perceptions of group prestige.

Stanley Schachter (1951) conducted an experiment to test some theoretical notions about group pressure generated, in part, by the housing project study just mentioned and further developed by Festinger (1950). Simply stated, Schachter found that consistent opinion deviates tend to be rejected by the other group members and that, depending on the measure of rejection used, rejection is greater if the group is highly cohesive or if the issue is highly relevant to the purpose of the group. In the early stages of group discussion most communications were directed towards deviates, as opposed to conformers. If the deviate moved to a position of conformity, he was fully accepted by the group and communications directed towards him decreased. If the deviate persisted in his nonconformity, communication to him increased over time in all conditions except the

High-Cohesive-Relevant condition, where a final decrease occurred among a subset of subjects, perhaps indicating that these people had given up on trying to change the deviate.

Without a doubt the conformity research that has most captured the attention of social psychologists and others is that of Solomon Asch (1951, 1952, 1955, 1956, 1961). In what has come to be known widely as the "Asch-type situation," already briefly described, Asch placed a single naive subject face-to-face with a group of confederates who, on certain critical trials, unanimously reported answers to simple visual discrimination items that were obviously wrong. Each item required the selection, from three lines, of the one equal in length to a fourth. The line selected by the majority on critical trials was off by 20% to 40%. As the lone real subject always gave his report last, and as reports were given aloud, he had to choose between publicly going against the group or giving an obviously incorrect answer. Subjects understandably experienced strong conflict and often continued to feel discomfiture after making their choices.

Asch varied the size of the unanimous majority from zero (when control subjects were run alone) up to 16. For the range of majority size from zero to 3, the amount of conformity progressively increased, the mean number of errors on the 12 critical trials being .08, .33, 1.53, and 4.00. Beyond this, however, increases in majority size had no consistent effect, the mean number of errors for 4, 8, and 16 confederates being 4.20, 3.84, and 3.75, respectively.

Asch interviewed his subjects at length after the experiment. Independent subjects fell into three categories: (1) those who were confident in their continued disagreement with the group, (2) those who withdrew—not physically, but emotionally—basing their independence on explicit principles of being an individual, and (3) those who experienced considerable doubt and tension. Conforming subjects, those yielding on at least half the critical trials, could be classified into three groups according to the type of distortion involved: (1) distortion of perception, (2) distortion of judgment, and (3) distortion of action. Subjects whose actual perceptions were distorted were rare, and perhaps no subject can be so classified without any doubt. A majority of the yielding subjects fell into the second category. They continued to see the stimuli in the same way but became convinced that, for some reason, they were seeing incorrectly and that the majority was right. Those yielding subjects in the last category were the expedient conformers. They complied publicly but privately they remained convinced that they were right and the majority wrong.

Asch investigated a number of other experimental variations, some of which we shall look at later, and many other researchers have been inspired to use some form of the Asch-type situation in later studies. Crutchfield (1955) "automated" the procedure, isolating subjects from one another and giving each one false feedback about the responses of the others. In this way he was able to dispense with confederates and run five real subjects per session, each believing that he responded last on all trials.

WHAT IS CONFORMITY?

Although conformity has already been defined, this is by no means the end of the matter. As we said before, terms must be given operational definitions as well as general conceptual ones. It often turns out that a conceptual definition will suggest more than one operational definition and, if so, it does not necessarily follow that only one is correct and the rest wrong. Several operational definitions may each tap some valid part of the whole concept.

Two Ways to Measure Conformity

Two distinct criteria have been used for measuring conformity, *congruence* and *movement*

(Willis, 1963, 1965a,c,d). Congruence refers to the degree of matching between the observed behavior and perfect conformity behavior. This was the criterion used by Allport in his field studies of the J-curve. In the stop-sign study, for example, a driver who brought the speed of his car down to zero at the intersection thereby executed an act perfectly congruent with conformity. Another driver who slowed down to 5 miles an hour before crossing the intersection would be nonconforming to some extent, and the difference between his minimum speed and zero is a convenient index of his level of nonconformity.

The other criterion, movement, refers to changes in behavior from one time to another. In particular, it refers to changes in congruence following exposure to some source of social pressure. If a driver habitually slows down to 5 miles an hour at a stop sign when no policeman is present, but comes to a full stop whenever there is a policeman around, the change in congruence from the first occasion to the second provides an index of his movement conformity.

Each of these criteria applies more naturally to one of two kinds of situations. In the first kind of situation there is an ongoing normative expectation—a social norm, for example—which is constant or nearly so over the time interval considered. The norm or ongoing expectation may apply only to the members of a particular group or subgroup, or it may extend to just about all members of an entire society. Because the definition of conformity remains constant, the congruence criterion can be applied by observing the amount or level of behavior directly.

The movement criterion applies more naturally to the second kind of situation. Here it is a source rather than a norm that provides the continuity. The actual expectation will vary from occasion to occasion as explicitly communicated by the source or merely implied by his behavior. The source need not be another individual. It may be a group or even an impersonal source of information. On each occasion a different stimulus or object of judgment is presented, and the individual is exposed to information about the source-reaction to that stimulus before giving his own response. The actor's pre-exposure level of congruence is either observed directly or inferred (as in the Asch paradigm). Because the conformity response is redefined on each occasion, there is no constant baseline against which the individual's behavior can be compared. This is why changes from pre-exposure to post-exposure levels of congruence must be noted.

When the congruence criterion is used, conformity is usually contrasted with nonconformity. When the movement criterion is used, the contrast is almost always with independence. In addition, most experimental work on conformity relies on the movement criterion while most nonexperimental work employs congruence. Thus, field studies such as Allport's use a conformity-nonconformity model of social response while experimental studies such as Asch's use a conformity-independence model. In almost all cases these models are assumed rather implicitly; that is, it is not made very clear which is used and why the other is not.

Some experimental social psychologists, such as Kiesler and Kiesler (1969), admit only the movement criterion, on the grounds that inferences about the effects of influence pressures are very tenuous if based solely on levels of congruence rather than changes in levels. Rather than disallowing either criterion, it seems preferable to differentiate between them consistently, for they do indeed tap different aspects of social response. The movement criterion best gets at immediate reactions to immediate pressures, while the congruence criterion is better designed to pick up longer-term, cumulative effects, including the net results of socialization processes.

Perhaps distinctive labels should be conscientiously used, such as those suggested by

Beloff (1958). In her terminology, congruence conformity is called *conventionality,* while movement conformity is called *acquiescence.* Even a person who yields much less than average to immediate pressures may be socialized into a very conventional mold if he is a well-accepted and thus well-rewarded member of a stable society. Beloff found acquiescence to be more highly correlated with political conventionality for her male subjects but more highly correlated with aesthetic conventionality for female subjects. This finding appears to lend some indirect empirical support to the theoretical distinction.

To recapitulate, conformity is operationally defined either by congruence or movement, each criterion applying more naturally to a different kind of situation and each presumably tapping different aspects of social response. It should be noted, in fact, that congruence conformity and the potential for movement conformity are inversely related, for the better the initial match the less room for change.

Description and Explanation

It is important to realize that both criteria are purely descriptive. That is, they describe observable events and provide a basis for measurement, but these measures do not by themselves eliminate alternative explanations. A given overt pattern of response, such as movement conformity, can be produced by a variety of underlying psychological processes and conditions—the conformer may seek social approval, fear punishment, aspire to improve his accuracy, wish to avoid hurting the other's feelings, and so on.

In fact, overt "conformity" may not be conformity at all. This is the problem of *incidental conformity,* which leads some authors to use the noncommittal term "uniformity" to refer to overt similarities of behavior. If one were to stand by the door of an office building and observe employees leaving work on a rainy afternoon, one might see each one in turn put up an umbrella, but this would most probably be attributed to a nonsocial cause, the rain, and not called conformity.

Another measurement pitfall is posed by *anticipatory conformity.* Suppose Kelly thinks that his boss will probably ask him to stay overtime on Friday afternoon in order to meet an impending deadline on a report. He stays late on Thursday and finishes the job. On Friday, sure enough, his boss asks him to stay late, at which time Kelly is able to hand him the completed report. An observer would surely conclude that the boss had successfully exerted influence over Kelly, for he complied with the anticipated request before it was made. Here the situation is clear, but in general the problem of anticipatory reactions poses some challenging methodological and conceptual problems. A person who is completely successful in anticipating and complying to a given source of influence is probably best considered a perfect conformist, yet he would never actually respond to pressures immediately present in the situation. The anticipatory socialization observed by Kinsey, Pomeroy, and Martin (1948) is a type of anticipatory congruence conformity. They found that socially mobile males tended to adopt in advance the patterns of sexual behavior prevailing in the social class into which they are moving.

Yet another kind of pitfall stems from *delayed conformity.* A person could be highly responsive to a source of social pressure, but this would be difficult to determine if his responses were much delayed. If these delays were of variable intervals, his acceptance or rejection of influence could be almost impossible to detect.

These three pitfalls, as well as others, must be taken into account when devising explanations for observed behavior. Incidental conformity looks like true intentional conformity, but is not. Anticipatory and delayed conformity do not look like true conformity, but are. One strategy for avoiding false inferences is to use the experimental method, whenever feasible, for this often allows the elimination of at least some of the possible explanations for a given observed result. Another very useful strategy is to use more than one kind of measure. Beyond this, one might wish to administer a post-experimental questionnaire to one's subjects. If a subject answers that he conformed during the experiment only because he wished to avoid social disapproval, this may not necessarily be the whole truth, but his answer at any rate gives us additional information that may be useful in explaining his behavior.

WHAT ARE THE ALTERNATIVES TO CONFORMITY?

As already noted, the traditional view is a unidimensional one, with conformity and its solitary alternative located at opposite ends of a single response dimension. Researchers using the congruence criterion generally adopt a conformity-nonconformity model, while those working with the movement criterion most often adopt a conformity-independence model.

In order to see the limitations of such unidimensional views, consider a person who invariably responds to social pressure by moving even farther away from the position advocated by the influence source. Where could we locate him along the usual conformity-independence scale? It will not do to put him at the independence end, for a completely independent person will not respond at all to the attempted influence, and of course our contrary friend cannot be put at the conformity end. Intermediate positions will not do either, for any intermediate point corresponds to some compromise between no reaction and full compliance, and our friend is no compromiser.

The simplest solution is to make room for movement away from conformity by extending the scale beyond independence. This solution is often adopted in attitude change research, where the design usually calls for the observation of just a single change. A change in attitude away from the advocated position is called a boomerang effect. In the conformity literature such a negative change is called anticonformity, or sometimes counterconformity or negativism.

The Diamond Model

The diamond model (Willis, 1965a,c,d) was devised to help conceptualize various possible reactions to social pressure. As Figure 10-2 shows, the diamond model has a horizontal and a vertical axis. The horizontal axis can be thought of in two related ways. First, this dimension can be seen as representing an individual's total amount of movement when

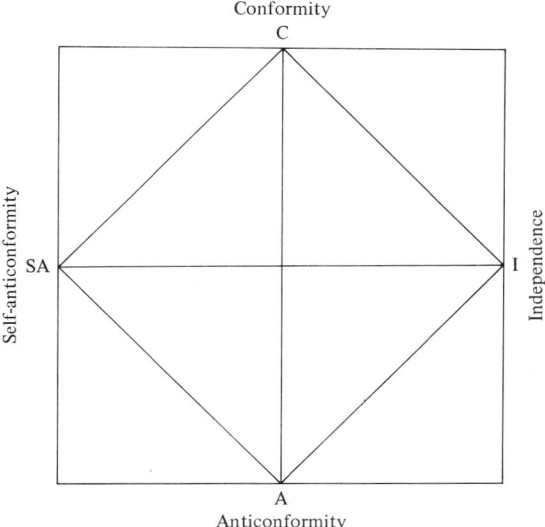

FIGURE 10-2. The diamond model. The horizontal axis is total movement, and the vertical axis is direction of movement. Possible combinations fall inside the diamond or along its perimeter.

exposed to social pressure. Seen in this light, the horizontal axis runs (from right to left) from (1) no movement at all (Independence) to (2) maximum movement (Self-anticonformity). Thus, an Independent person never changes his position, while a Self-anticonformer always changes his position as much as he can (i.e., he always anticonforms to his own previous position). A second way to think about the horizontal axis is in terms of an individual's degree of dependence on social pressure. Seen in this light, both Independents and Self-anticonformers are quite "independent," since neither is influenced at all by social pressure. On the other hand, someone who falls in the middle of the horizontal axis is quite "dependent" on social pressure. This second interpretation of the horizontal axis makes it easy to understand the vertical axis. The vertical axis merely represents an individual's direction of movement. Thus, a person who is "dependent" on social pressure may move either (1) toward the source of pressure (Conformity) or (2) away from the source of pressure (Anticonformity). In short, the diamond model diagrams Conformity and three modes of movement nonconformity in their interrelations to one another. In addition to the usual Independence, two other varieties of nonconformity are included. Of these two, Anticonformity is the more important insofar as Self-anticonformity is apparently quite rare.

If the diamond model is on the right track, it should be possible to bring its various modes of social response under experimental control. Willis and Hollander (1964a,b) were able to do so with Conformity, Anticonformity, and Independence (the only response modes they sought to manipulate). In addition, in an unpublished experiment by the authors in collaboration with Ross Buck, Self-anticonformity was brought under some degree of experimental control, but with less success than the other response modes.

Mapping Models

A source of possible misunderstanding regarding the diamond model should be cleared up. The diamond model is based on the descriptive criterion of movement, and is a descriptive or mapping model (Willis, 1972). It differs in its purpose from the more frequently encountered scientific models or theories which aim to predict which of various outcomes will occur, or at least which are most probable. A mapping model, just like a map, lays out the possibilities within some domain, and it leaves the matter of probabilities to predictive models or theories. Ideally, perhaps, one should first devise an appropriate mapping model and only then formulate a predictive model, for one naturally wants to be sure that no important possibility has been overlooked.

Because the diamond model is a mapping model, it has nothing to say about the relative probabilities of outcomes within the total response space, nor, given different locations for two individuals, does it attempt to explain the reason for the difference. It could be due to a difference in personalities, or a difference in the situations, or some combination of both. The two locations might even correspond to the same person in the same situation on two different occasions. On the second occasion he may have learned something he didn't know before, or he may have decided on a different goal, or he may even have become so fatigued that he is responding carelessly. In brief, the diamond model is neither predictive nor explanatory; it was designed to give an improved description of conformity and some of its basic alternatives. To the extent that it is successful in doing this, however, it contributes to better prediction and explanation by laying a groundwork.

One does not always need the full diamond. If anticonformity and self-anticonformity tendencies are negligible, the simpler conformity-independence model is appropriate. The assumption of negligible self-anticonformity appears to be quite safe, except in special circumstances. The assumption of negligible anticonformity tendencies requires more caution, however.

In the absence of anticonformity tendencies, all subjects or groups will be located someplace along the right-hand upper edge of the diamond, that is, between conformity and independence (see Figure 10-2). No doubt the results obtained by Asch and others using similar techniques are not invalidated in most cases by the diamond-model analysis, for with such techniques the assumption of negligible anticonformity usually appears warranted. Still, even in an Asch-type situation, one-dimensional thinking can lead to unwarranted conclusions. This will be explained later, in connection with an experimental comparison of nationality differences in conformity (Milgram, 1961).

Other Alternatives to Conformity

The diamond model does not include all possible reactions to social pressures, of course. There are, for example, *withdrawal, overconformity,* and *innovation,* among other possibilities. In withdrawal, the individual rejects the situation or the source itself, rather than specific responses over a series of occasions. Although this can be thought of as a kind of anticonformity, its implications are different. Rather than continuing to interact, the individual says, in effect, "I won't play." An experimental subject showing this kind of nonconformity would just get up and leave before the end of the experiment. A person who shows this "won't play" reaction to society at large, or at any rate to the Establishment sector of society, might be described as alienated.

Overconformity can be defined as movement in the direction of conformity which overshoots the mark. If it is the norm in a particular community for shopkeepers to stay open a few minutes after 5:00 in order to accommodate customers who arrive a little late, the shopkeeper who can never bring himself to close before 6:30 might be considered an overconformer. Here the overconformity might be due to a stronger-than-usual motive to be helpful. It would then truly be overconformity. In other cases, overconformity is a disguised form of anticonformity. Observing the letter of a rule with unreasonable strictness is one way of defeating its spirit.

Innovation is often conformity and nonconformity at the same time. The scientist who devises a new theory may be said to be conforming to the norm of his scientific community which rewards contributions to his discipline, but his new theory may be seen as highly deviant at first, even if it is later accepted.

WHY CONFORMITY AND WHY DEVIATION?

The question of Why? can be answered at different levels. At the societal level, conformity to normative expectations often makes things function more smoothly and efficiently. A certain degree of conformity exists in all societies and social institutions, for any group in which there is no conformity (if, indeed, it can be said to be a group) would not be able to function well enough to perpetuate itself. Either the members of the group would fail to survive, or they would desert the group for others better capable of meeting their individual needs. Groups which demand too much conformity may also fail to compete if matched against those with a superior capacity for innovation and adaptation.

However, it is not the societal but the interpersonal level which interests us most. Here too, norms and roles make things easier, as they provide "canned" solutions to many common problems of social life. If a husband and wife are both comfortable with the parts assigned them in marriage by society's traditional role definitions, this solves many practical problems. One needn't deliberate and negotiate about every little thing. Many couples, of course, work out their own role definitions that meet their needs better than the traditional ones. She may be the handy one with tools, while he may prefer and excel in cooking, for instance. To make the arrangements work, there must be consensus about what is to be expected of each, and each must in fact conform reasonably well to these expectations. This is equally true whether the expectations are taken over from society or emerge from interaction within the dyad.

Except for such exceptional cases as reflex behavior, an individual's actions—whether or not conformity—will be in the service of attaining some goal or set of goals. Most behavior, that is, is directed by one or more motives. For this reason we have chosen to approach our task in this section by reviewing some of the attempts that have been made to analyze and categorize broad motive bases underlying reactions to interpersonal influence.

According to Festinger (1950), there are two main sources of pressures toward group conformity—or uniformity, as he terms it—*group locomotion* and *social reality*. Group locomotion just means making progress towards group goals. The group generally exerts pressures on the individual to behave cooperatively so that group goals can be more fully attained, and cooperation, or conformity, is rewarded, while nonconformity is punished. In the case of social reality, the group defines "correct" beliefs for the individual, and the individual is motivated to go along with these definitions of reality in order to reduce cognitive ambiguity. Social reality stands in contrast to physical reality, defined not by the group, but by the objective or physical environment.

In a related distinction, Kelley (1952) pointed out two functions of reference groups, the *normative* and the *comparative*. When a reference group serves a normative function, it provides rewards and punishments for conformity and nonconformity. If it serves a comparative function, it provides a standard against which to evaluate ourselves or others. In this way it helps to define reality. The normative function is motivational in nature, while the comparative function is "perceptual" (in Kelley's word) or cognitive.

Shortly after Kelley made this distinction, Deutsch and Gerard (1955) suggested a related two-fold typology of social influence. They speak of *normative* and *informational* influence. Normative influence is wielded by a group serving a normative reference function, while informational influence is exerted by a group serving a comparative function. The first kind of influence is especially effective in determining our actions and statements, if group approval is important to us, while the second kind of influence more directly affects our private beliefs and attitudes. Similar dichotomies have been proposed by Thibaut and Strickland (1956) and Jones and Gerard (1967).

It is interesting that several investigators have offered similar *dichotomous* models of the motives underlying interpersonal influence. It appears that these analyses were attempting to cope with the dual nature of human nature. Man has both a rational and a social side. He seeks both to be right and to be accepted. Sometimes, however, these two goals are incompatible and, if so, the question arises as to how the individual resolves this conflict. In particular, how will public behavior and statements be related to private beliefs and attitudes?

One way to look at the matter is to assume a straightforward one-to-one correspondence between the social and the normative, on the one hand, and the rational and the informational, on the other. According to this view, a person's public behavior will be determined by social rewards and punishments while his private views will be determined by the sources of information that define social and physical reality for him. Although one could do worse than this, this view is not entirely satisfactory. Don't people sometimes express unpopular opinions deliberately? Doesn't Man have an irrational, or at any rate a nonrational, side to him? Must rewards and punishments be lumped together on one side? Must physical and social reality be lumped together on the other? What about Man's image of himself?

These and other questions led to more elaborate attempts to delineate the motive bases of influence, power, and attitude change. In addition to public *compliance* and private acceptance (or *internalization*), Kelman (1958, 1961) found the need for a third category, *identification*. Identification occurs when the individual adopts behavior or an attitude derived from a group or a person because doing so is associated with a satisfying *self-defining relationship* to this group or person. The fraternity pledge who attempts to model his behavior and attitudes after an admired senior member of the chapter provides an illustration. Kelman advanced the interesting hypothesis that the process of internalization is least dependent upon external circumstances, while compliance is the most dependent. Thus, for compliance to occur it is necessary that the influence source be able to monitor the person's behavior, while this is not necessary for either identification or internalization. At the same time, salience of the source-recipient relation to the recipient is necessary for identification, but not for internalization.

Raven and his collaborators (Raven, 1965; see also Collins & Raven, 1969, pp. 166–184; French & Raven, 1959; Raven & Kruglanski, 1970) have developed the following outline of the bases of social power. (The formulation given here is treated with a different emphasis in Chapter 11, "Power and Bargaining.")

Independent influence, also called informational influence, is based on the content of the message and is independent of its source. For influence to be truly independent of the source, the information must be of a kind the recipient can verify himself. If one attended a lecture advancing the thesis that there is life on Mars, it would not be possible to verify this thesis directly, and one would certainly consider the source in assessing its probable validity. If, by contrast, the lecture consisted of a clear, easily followed demonstration of the theorem that there is an unlimited number of primes, one could perhaps verify the conclusion by following through the proof step by step. If so, it would really make no difference whether the source were a highly trained mathematician or a jazz musician.

The effects of independent or informational influence are not confined to public compliance but include private acceptance. Sometimes the effects are confined to private acceptance and do not include public compliance. A prejudiced college student might come to believe firmly in the equality of all races on the basis of information brought to his attention, but he still might not date interracially because of peer group pressure not to do so.

Notice that independent influence is socially independent but still depends upon the initial knowledge, beliefs, and attitudes of the recipient. In the example of the prime number theorem, if one had no mathematical background at all or suffered from "symbol shock," one would have to fall back on judgments of the expertise and the motives of the source.

Public-dependent influence depends both on the perceived ability of the source to mediate sanctions (rewards and punishments) and on conditions allowing the source to monitor the behavior of the actor. *Coercive* or *punishment power* is distinguished from *reward power* because it has different consequences. First, the use of coercive power is more costly, for the agent must maintain surveillance of the actor in the face of attempts by the latter to prevent it. With reward power, the actor will cooperate actively in the monitoring. Second, coercive power may cause the actor to abandon the relationship with the agent entirely, whereas reward power often tends to strengthen the relationship. Finally, even if the relationship continues, the use of coercion which is perceived as unfair will cause the actor's attitude toward the agent to change negatively.

The boundary separating reward and coercive power is not always distinct in practice, for the withholding of a reward can be experienced as a punishment, just as the withholding of a punishment can be experienced as a reward. That is, the expectations of the actor, as well as the behavior of the agent, determine what is reward and what is punishment. Beyond this, the beliefs and feelings of the actor about the agent play a role. A gift from someone we like may be rewarding but the same gift from someone we detest may not.

Private-dependent influence depends critically on the perceived nature of the source, but not on the ability of the source to check up on the actor or on the ability of the actor to check up on the content. With *expert power,* the recipient is willing to take the expert's word for it, provided that the issue is seen as falling within the source's domain of expertise.

In the case of *referent power,* the source serves to define correct beliefs, feelings, and behavior because the recipient identifies or wishes to identify with the source. The source is used as a frame of reference. Social comparison processes (Festinger, 1954; Latane, 1966) and comparative reference group phenomena, to some extent, involve influence of this kind.

Referent power becomes especially important when the recipient has strong feelings about the source and when the criteria of correctness are not provided by physical reality. If the source is attractive, the actor is likely to accept the influence and conform. If the source is highly unattractive, arousing strong negative feelings, an anticonformity reaction is probable. Both conformity and anticonformity reactions will be more pronounced in the absence of other guides to action, for the actor must then depend upon the source. Similar effects can be observed with expert power (Willis, 1965d; Willis & Willis, 1970).

Legitimate power is perhaps the most complex of all. It is based on very general norms about attitudes and conduct deemed appropriate in certain kinds of situations. These in turn depend upon the individual's position within a social structure and his role relations to others. In the case of legitimate power, the recipient has accepted, either on a specific occasion or over the course of time, a relationship to the source such that the source is permitted or even obliged to prescribe behaviors and perhaps even attitudes for him, and the recipient is obligated to accept such influence. When a driver pulls off the highway after being signaled by a state patrolman, he does so (in part at least) because he is accepting the legitimacy of the influence. According to some theories of hypnosis, a person in a hypnotic state accepts specific suggestions from the hypnotist because he has already accepted a role relationship which legitimizes these suggestions (cf. Sarbin & Coe, 1972). One of the things that makes legitimate power so complex is the fact that it almost always involves a combination of several of the more elemental bases.

In summary, we have seen that independent influence is based on *content,* public-dependent influence is based on *sanctions,* and private-dependent influence is based on the *source*—either source attributes as such, or the nature of the relationship between the source and the recipient.

Independence of influence versus independence of change

Raven speaks of *secondary effects* of influence. Because of secondary effects, dependent influence can produce independent change. The immediate effects of public-dependent influence is public-dependent change, but if the influence is maintained over a period of time the changes may become independent and surveillance will no longer be necessary. Similarly, the changes produced by private-dependent influence can also become independent, and indeed one would expect the transition here to take less time than in the case of public-dependent influence. *Negative influence* as well as positive can be accompanied by secondary effects. For example, when anticonformity is initially motivated by the actor's desire to flaunt his disagreement with the source, the actor's private beliefs may be brought into alignment with his anticonformist public assertions over time.

The operation of secondary effects, which often are delayed effects, means that one cannot assume a simple matching between the level of independence of the influence and the level of independence of the change it ultimately produces. What probably can be safely assumed, however, is that the more dependent the influence, the more time and effort will be required to achieve independent change, and the less reliably will it be achieved. Of the two types of public-dependent influence, the coercive is the more dependent, making it the most dependent of all the six. In order to illustrate the variety and pervasiveness of secondary effects, let us consider some of the exceptions to the generalization that coercive influence produces only public compliance.

First, if an individual is coerced into behaving a certain way, this behavior may have unanticipated consequences that, in turn, produce real attitude change. A mother may coerce her children into trying a new breakfast cereal by threatening to withhold allowances for the week, but the reluctant children may discover, much to their surprise, that they really like the new food.

A second class of exceptions is the one called to our attention by dissonance theory and discussed in detail in an earlier chapter in connection with the $1–$20 experiment (Festinger & Carlsmith, 1959), among others. It will be recalled that under certain conditions an individual who is "gently forced" into behaving in a way incompatible with his true beliefs will subsequently change these beliefs, and change them more than another person on whom stronger-than-necessary sanctions have been used. Force just barely sufficient to bring about a decision to engage in the discrepant behavior is hypothesized to produce more post-decision dissonance, making a greater change in private attitude necessary to reduce the dissonance to a tolerable level.

Yet a third class of exceptions probably occurs only over an extended period of time. In one of our introductory examples, George Orwell has the protagonist of his novel *1984* change one of his most firmly held beliefs in order to avoid further unbearable pain. Whether physical pain alone can induce fundamental belief change is not a question that has been systematically researched, because of the obvious ethical problems. However, the question of psychological pain—ego-threat, in particular—has received a great deal of attention, especially from psychoanalytically oriented theorists. Although much of the evidence is indirect, coming from clinical observation, there is also experimental evidence for the process of repression (e.g., Zeller, 1950a, b, 1951), and a rather large body of correlational research relating ego-threat to attitudes, especially prejudice (e.g., G. W. Allport, 1954; Harding, Proshansky, Kutner, & Chein, 1969). The implication of this work which is relevant for us is the following. Social sanctions brought to bear on an individual in a way that threatens the favorability of his self-concept are likely to produce a more immediate behavioral effect and a less immediate effect on internal beliefs and feelings. If the coerced behavior is one that goes against the individual's moral code, the resulting guilt will be ego-threatening and internal cognitive and affective changes will occur over time in order to reduce the guilt and protect the ego.

Very much the same argument can be put into the language of dissonance theory. Kelman and Baron (1968) and Baron (1968) distinguish between *moral* and *hedonic* dissonance. Moral dissonance is experienced when the individual perceives that he is overrewarded or underpunished, while hedonic dissonance follows from perceptions of underreward or overpunishment. Moral dissonance produces guilt, while the result of hedonic dissonance is a feeling of resentment. While moral dissonance leads to ego-defensive changes, hedonic dissonance leads to what might be called "alter-offensive" changes. In the former, the individual strives to think well of himself, while in the latter he goes out of his way to see the other in a bad light.

The remaining class of exceptions to be mentioned also involves changes in attitudes towards the source, but is not so directly related as the previous one to underreward or overpunishment. If the individual feels that he is being coerced, he is likely to feel also that his freedom to act in a particular way is being threatened, quite aside from the question of ego-threat. If he does, psychological *reactance* is aroused, that is, a motive is aroused to restore the lost freedom (Brehm, 1966, 1972). Reactance is often the motive underlying anti-conformity. Pressure to take a premature stand on an issue tends to produce a motive to avoid taking any stand, and pressure to take a particular stand tends to increase receptivity to information supporting the opposing position.

An interesting aspect of the reactance motive is its capacity to produce public and private change in opposite directions. If the coercion to adopt a given position is both powerful and lacking in legitimacy, the recipient may agree outwardly but disagree even more strongly in private. What is even more likely to happen is that the recipient will make a show of liking the powerful source but will in fact dislike him because of his unfair use of power.

WHEN CONFORMITY AND WHEN DEVIATION?

In the previous section, we dealt with the question of "why" conformity occurs in terms of internal, underlying motives. We turn now to the related question of "when" conformity occurs, i.e., the external situational factors which affect what kind and how much reaction to social pressure occurs. Probably the bulk of the research done on conformity has been directed toward clarifying how these situational factors, alone and in combination, operate. Since an extended discussion of all such factors is beyond the scope of this chapter (see Allen, 1965 and Kiesler, 1969), we shall instead take a look at three representative topics: group unanimity, stimulus characteristics, and obedience to authority.

Group Unanimity

We have already looked at Asch's findings on the effect of the *size* of the unanimous majority on conformity. Another interesting variable originally investigated by Asch is the *degree of group unanimity.* Essentially, Asch wanted to find out how much of the conformity obtained when one person was confronted by several disagreeing others was due to the complete unanimity of the group, i.e., the fact that all group members gave the same (wrong) response. To test the importance of unanimity, Asch (1951) had a confederate, who answered before the naive subject, break group unanimity by giving the correct answer. In this social support condition, conformity was reduced dramatically, to about 6%, compared to 33% when group members all gave the same response.

In trying to explain why social support reduced conformity, Asch pointed out two characteristics of the social support condition: (1) the partner breaks group unanimity, and (2) the partner gives an answer which agrees with the subject's private answer. If merely breaking group unanimity is what causes conformity reduction, it should not matter whether the dissenter agrees or disagrees with the subject, as long as he clearly disagrees with the majority. On the other hand, if agreement with the subject is crucial, a dissenter would have to give a response that the subject thought was correct in order to reduce conformity.

Asch (1955) tested the importance of these two alternatives by having a confederate respond even more incorrectly than the erroneous majority. He found that this extreme dissenter reduced conformity almost as much as a social supporter who agreed with the subject. That is, as long as one group member disagreed with the majority, regardless of the "validity" of this person's answer, conformity was reduced dramatically. Asch therefore concluded that merely breaking group consensus, rather than agreeing with the subject, was the crucial factor underlying the social supporter's ability to reduce conformity.

Recently, however, Asch's explanation has been challenged by studies which indicate that extreme dissent is not always sufficient to reduce conformity. Allen and Levine (1968, 1969), using a Crutchfield-type apparatus, had a simulated subject dissent in one of two ways from the unpopular responses of three other simulated subjects on both visual perception and opinion items (e.g., "Most young people get too much education"). In the social support condition, the dissenter gave popular answers; in the extreme dissent condition, the dissenter gave even more unpopular answers than the erroneous majority. Finally, in a unanimous condition, all four simulated subjects gave the same unpopular answers.

In both studies, subjects conformed significantly less in the social support than in the unanimous condition on both visual and opinion items. Consistent with Asch's earlier findings, on visual items the extreme dissenter also significantly reduced conformity. However, on opinion items the extreme dissenter did not significantly reduce conformity. It seems, then, that while Asch was correct in asserting that "mere dissent" is enough to reduce conformity on visual perception items, on opinion items a partner who agrees with the subject is necessary for conformity reduction.

Although the results of Allen and Levine's studies take us beyond Asch's original explanation of how a dissenter affects conformity, our knowledge is still far from complete. For example, we do not know if extreme dissent and social support work the way Allen and Levine's data suggest in all kinds of social pressure situations. One useful way of differentiating social pressure situations is in terms of the dominant motive underlying the subject's susceptibility to influence. Recall that earlier we discussed two basic motives that can produce acceptance of social influence—desire to obtain valid information and desire to gain group reward and avoid group punishment. Influence based on the first motive was termed "informational" and influenced based on the second was termed "normative" (Deutsch & Gerard, 1955).

A study was recently conducted to find out how extreme dissent and social support operate on visual and opinion items under *both* informational and normative pressure (Levine, Saxe, & Ranelli, 1974). The normative pressure condition was designed to maximize subjects' motivation to avoid group punishment. To accomplish this, subjects were led to believe that agreement among group members was essential for obtaining reward and that, after the experimental session, group members would have the opportunity to punish individuals who failed to go along with the group. In the informational pressure condition, an attempt was made to minimize motivation to avoid punishment and to maximize motivation to give "correct" answers. Here, subjects were told they were working for rewards based on individual accuracy on the experimental stimuli. In addition, no mention was made of punishment for not going along with group consensus.

Subjects were exposed to (1) a social supporter who dissented from the erroneous majority by giving popular answers, (2) an extreme dissenter who gave even more unpopular answers than the majority, or (3) a unanimous group. Results showed that under both normative and informational pressure, both social support and extreme dissent significantly reduced conformity on visual items, but on opinion items only social support was effective. These findings demonstrate the robustness of Allen and Levine's (1968, 1969) results. That is, regardless of the type of social pressure operating, a social supporter effectively reduces conformity on both visual and opinion items, but an extreme dissenter produces substantial conformity reduction only on visual items.

Although the above studies indicate that (at least on visual items) social support and extreme dissent are about equally effective in reducing conformity, the question arises whether all social supporters produce equivalent resistance to group pressure. That is, do the characteristics of an individual who "correctly" dissents from erroneous group consensus affect how much subjects conform to the group? Research evidence indicates that the answer to this question is "yes," and that two basic factors underlie social supporter effectiveness: (1) the supporter's ability to increase the subject's confidence in his own position (assessor utility) and (2) the supporter's ability to reduce the subject's fear of group retaliation for deviating from group consensus (ally utility).

Rather convincing evidence for the "assessor utility" explanation of social support was recently obtained by Allen and Levine (1971c). In this study, two social supporters were created who gave identical responses to the experimental stimuli but who differed in terms of how adequate they were as sources of information. In the invalid condition the confederate wore extremely thick eyeglasses which distorted his eyes and gave the impression that he had very poor vision. In addition, the confederate expressed concern about his ability to see the experimental stimuli and then failed an easy "vision test" administered by the experimenter. In the valid social support condition, the same confederate neither wore eyeglasses nor voiced concern about his ability to perform the experimental task. Both the valid and invalid social supporters reduced conformity significantly, compared to a unanimous condition. In addition, the valid social supporter reduced conformity significantly more than the invalid supporter. These results suggest, consistent with the "assessor utility" interpretation mentioned above, that the supporter's ability to judge the experimental stimuli may be one crucial determinant of how effective he is in reducing conformity.

In another study (Allen & Levine, 1971b) the

answering position of the social supporter was varied because it seemed plausible that this factor might affect the supporter's "assessor utility." In the social support first condition, the supporter answered in response position one; in the social support fourth condition, the supporter answered in position four. Both these conditions were compared to a unanimous condition. Results showed that while conformity was significantly lower in both social support conditions than in the unanimous condition, the supporter responding first was significantly more effective than the supporter answering fourth. Allen and Levine suggested that, compared to the supporter responding fourth, the supporter answering first may be seen as quite independent in his response, since no one answered before he did and therefore his response could not have been influenced by other group members. On the other hand, the supporter answering fourth responded after three other group members and therefore his nonconformity may be seen as anticonformity. That is, the supporter answering fourth may be seen as an individual who, rather than giving an independent assessment of the stimuli, is in fact just reacting against the responses of the first three persons. If the supporter's perceived ability to provide information is important, it would follow that a supporter answering first would be more effective than a supporter answering fourth.

Let us now turn to studies relevant to the second mechanism suggested as important in explaining supporter effectiveness, i.e., the supporter's ability to reduce the subject's fear of group punishment. Two studies provide evidence consistent with this explanation. First, Allen (1966) conducted an experiment in which subjects were led to believe that their opinion on a particular topic disagreed with the unanimous opinion of several other group members. In addition, some subjects were told that they dissented alone, while others were informed that one group member (i.e., a social supporter) agreed with them. When asked after the experiment, "Whom do you think the majority will vote to eliminate from the group?", significantly fewer subjects anticipated rejection when they dissented with a partner than when they dissented alone. This finding appears quite consistent with the notion that the presence of a social supporter can reduce a dissenting subject's anticipation of group punishment.

Additional evidence bearing on the fear-reduction explanation was obtained by Boyanowsky in a series of interesting studies which investigated the relationship between the social supporter's race and his ability to reduce conformity (Boyanowsky, 1970; Boyanowsky & Allen, 1973). These studies were inspired, in part, by a well-known experiment by Malof and Lott (1962) which found that black and white supporters were equally effective in reducing conformity on visual stimuli for highly prejudiced white subjects. Boyanowsky replicated this finding on visual perception items, but found that on personally relevant opinion items (i.e., opinion items dealing with personal values) a black supporter was much less effective than a white supporter in reducing conformity for highly prejudiced white subjects.

In seeking to explain the discrepancy between the effectiveness of a black supporter on visual and personally relevant opinion stimuli, Boyanowsky created two conditions in which highly prejudiced whites were led to believe that a black person agreed with their answers. In a surveillance condition, each subject was told that his responses were observed and evaluated by three persons (all white), none of whose answers were available to the subject. In a nonsurveillance condition, each subject was told that his responses were private, i.e., not observed by a group of whites. Results indicated that in the nonsurveillance condition subjects agreed with the black on both visual perception items and personally relevant opinion items. However, in the surveillance condition (where subjects ostensibly were observed by three white persons), subjects failed to agree with the black partner on personally relevant opinion items though they did agree with him on visual items. That reluctance to agree with the black person on opinion items was due to his race, rather than the type of item, was demonstrated by the fact that in another surveillance condition highly prejudiced subjects did agree with a white person on these items.

Boyanowsky's findings have bearing on why prejudiced subjects failed to accept support from a black partner on personally relevant opinion items in the standard social support situation. It seems likely that subjects' movement away from the black (i.e., anticonformity) in Boyanowsky's surveillance condition and in his original group pressure situation was caused by fear of group rejection. That is, subjects may have expected agreement with a black to elicit punishment from the group of whites, since the subject would be seen by the group as allied with an outgroup member on important personal values. Therefore, rather than serving as a useful ally in decreasing group punishment, the black supporter may have actually caused the subject to anticipate *increased* group punishment. On the other hand, alliance with a white in-group member on personally relevant opinion items, or alliance with a black on less personal issues (e.g., the visual stimuli used by Malof & Lott and Boyanowsky), probably was not expected to elicit group punishment and, therefore, the partner freed the subject from group pressure.

This reasoning, of course, is based on the assumption that highly prejudiced white subjects in the surveillance condition perceived the white onlookers as also highly prejudiced and, hence, prone to punish agreement with a black person. It would be interesting to vary both the subject's own prejudice and the subject's perception of onlooker prejudice in a single study. It may be that subjects' own prejudice is relatively unimportant in this situation and, regardless of their own prejudice, subjects who perceive onlookers as prejudiced will avoid agreement with a black person, while subjects who perceive onlookers as unprejudiced will seek agreement with a black person.

Research on group unanimity provides us with important information about how people react to group pressure. This research is particularly interesting because it focuses on factors which reduce susceptibility to social influence, an emphasis which Hollander and Willis (1967) argue has been underrepresented in conformity research. It might be noted, in concluding our discussion of the impact of unanimity on conformity, that the resistance to group pressure conferred by the presence of a social supporter is not restricted to adults. Recent data indicate that social support also reduces conformity for children as young as six years old (Allen & Newtson, 1972).

Stimulus Characteristics

In our discussion of group unanimity, we presented data concerning the differential effectiveness of social support and extreme dissent on visual and opinion items. These findings highlight the importance of stimulus characteristics in determining interpersonal influence. In this section we shall focus our attention directly on some of the general relationships social psychologists have discovered between stimulus characteristics and conformity.

It can be argued that conformity, at least that based on informational influence, will increase as group consensus becomes a more important factor in establishing the validity of a particular response. If so, it seems likely that conformity will increase as a function of the ambiguity and difficulty of the stimuli under consideration, since high ambiguity and difficulty will reduce subjects' confidence in the validity of their own responses, which, in turn, will lead to reliance on responses of others (Festinger, 1950).

Consistent with these hypotheses, several studies suggest that as stimulus ambiguity and difficulty increase, conformity also increases. For example, Crutchfield (1955) presented stimuli of two types: items for which one alternative was obviously correct and items for which no alternative was correct. Results indicated higher conformity on the latter than on the former items. Deutsch and Gerard (1955) had subjects respond to stimuli which were either physically present during responding or had been removed several seconds prior to the subject's response. Conformity was higher when subjects answered after, rather than during, stimulus presentation. In a study employing factual questions of varying difficulty, Coleman, Blake, and Mouton (1958) obtained a positive correlation between stimulus difficulty and conformity. Finally, one of the simplest and most direct manipulations of task difficulty was employed by Luchins and Luchins (1963). In this experiment, subjects were asked to judge the length of lines drawn on notecards; confederates of the experimenter made incorrect judgments on the stimuli before the subject answered. In one condition subjects were given rulers to use during the experiment, while in another condition subjects had to rely on visual acuity alone. As might be predicted, subjects who had rulers conformed less than subjects forced to rely on unaided visual perception.

As mentioned above, it seems likely that the positive relationship between stimulus ambiguity/difficulty and conformity is mediated by subjects' confidence in the validity of their responses. Consistent with this notion, Krech, Crutchfield, and Ballachey (1962) reported a negative correlation between subjects' initial certainty on stimuli and yielding to group pressure on these items. Moreover, results from a number of studies consistently indicated that manipulations which increase subjects' confidence in their own task-relevant ability, relative to the ability of a potential influence source, decrease conformity (e.g., Croner & Willis, 1961; Ettinger, et al., 1971; Geller, Endler, & Wiesenthal, 1973).

In spite of the well-established relationship between stimulus ambiguity/difficulty and conformity, it has been argued that on one type of particularly "ambiguous" stimulus (i.e., personal preference judgments) people are virtually immune to social influence. It has been suggested that, although these judgments are ambiguous in the sense that no single "correct" answer exists, this very fact frees subjects from constraints imposed by others' answers and thus allows subjects to respond according to their own personal preferences. This hypothesis gained support from some of Crutchfield's (1955) data which indicated that, contrary to results on other types of stimuli, subjects did not conform to majority consensus when asked to state preferences between two simple line drawings.

Because Crutchfield's data were inconsistent with the well-documented relationship between stimulus ambiguity and conformity and because Crutchfield's subjects were Air Force officers, rather than college students who typically are tested in conformity studies, Allen and Levine (1971a) decided to replicate Crutchfield's experiment using a wider range of preference stimuli and a different subject population (introductory psychology students). Results indicated, contrary to Crutchfield's data, that subjects did conform to group consensus on items dealing with personal preferences.

In speculating about the basis for the difference between their own and Crutchfield's findings, Allen and Levine (1971a) noted that on Crutchfield's line drawings group pressure was applied to the more asymmetrical, or abstract, alternative. If Air Force officers perceived this alternative as artistic, or feminine, and if these men were concerned with appearing highly masculine, perhaps they chose the symmetrical alternative to avoid appearing effeminate. Although no data are available regarding the officers' perception of the masculinity-femininity of the alternatives, available data do indicate that Crutchfield's subjects scored significantly higher on several paper-and-pencil masculinity tests than did samples of male college students. Regardless of the validity of this interpretation of Crutchfield's findings, however, Allen and Levine's study, using college students as subjects and a wider range of stimuli, indicated that preference judgments are indeed susceptible to social pressure.

It might be useful at this point to suggest a more complex typology of stimuli than has been presented above. This endeavor, while speculative, may be helpful in clarifying our ideas about how social influence operates. We suggest there are three main categories of stimuli. First are questions, the answers to which are defined as "verifiable at present." Here, the subject feels that he has the stored information, perceptual acuity, or problem-solving ability to give an immediate answer which is "true" according to some universally-shared criterion. It is suggested that this class of issues is relatively immune to informational social influence because the subject perceives that he himself has enough information to answer the question. These issues are defined as "verifiable at present," not because social consensus is unnecessary to validate the subject's perception, but because the subject has learned through past experience that social consensus can be taken for granted on such issues (Moscovici & Faucheux, 1972). Moreover, if the subject should suddenly discover that other individuals disagree with his judgment, he is likely to assume that the disagreers are in reality deviating from a wider social consensus which agrees with the subject's judgment.

The second class of stimuli are questions the answers to which are perceived as unverifiable at present but "verifiable in principle." On these issues the subject feels that an answer definable as "true" according to some universally shared criterion exists, but that he does not know this answer. Therefore, he does not feel confident in the validity of his current response tendency, but feels that he could give the "true" answer if allowed sufficient time to acquire more information, sharpen perceptual acuity, or increase problem-solving capability. It is suggested that this class of items is amenable to social influence to the extent that the subject perceives (1) that the information source has greater issue-relevant expertise than he and, in addition, (2) that the source's expertise exceeds some absolute minimal level.

The third class of stimuli are questions the answers to which are seen as "unverifiable in principle." This category encompasses issues which are perceived as unknowable according to any universally defined criterion (e.g., the relative tastiness of chocolate vs. vanilla ice cream, the probability that the Vietnamese war would have ended sooner if John Kennedy had lived, or the relative importance of science vs. art). It is suggested that this class of issues is relatively immune to social influence, since the perceived absence of a single "correct" answer frees the subject to believe that his own response is as good as any other.

It might be useful to label category 2 stimuli ("verifiable in principle") as *difficult* and category 3 stimuli ("univerifiable in principle") as *ambiguous*. Both types of stimuli are unverifiable at present according to a universal criterion of validity, but only category 2 stimuli are expected to produce feelings of uncertainty about the validity of one's own position. Therefore, according to present definitions, conformity should vary positively with stimulus difficulty and negatively with stimulus ambiguity. That is, conformity should increase as the stimulus becomes more difficult and decrease as the stimulus becomes more ambiguous. Considering all three stimulus categories, conformity should vary in a curvilinear fashion with stimulus verifiability. That is, conformity should be low on "verifiable at present" and "unverifiable in principle" items and high on "verifiable in principle" items (when the criteria discussed above are met).

Clearly, it is often very difficult, if not impossible, to predict into which category a given stimulus will be placed by a given individual. For example, a visual perception item may be labeled as "verifiable at present" by a man with good vision but only "verifiable in principle" by a man with poor vision. In the same vein, the statement "There is a God" may be "unverifiable in principle" to one man (because he believes no universally shared criterion of God's existence can ever be established) but "verifiable at present" to another man (because he believes the existence of an ordered universe is "undeniable" evidence for the existence of God).

The potential variability in categorizing almost any stimulus has two important implications. First, it suggests that great caution must be exercised by experimenters in assuming that their own categorization scheme accurately reflects a particular subject's categorization scheme. What to the experimenter is "unverifiable in principle" and hence not susceptible to informational influence (e.g., the relative attractiveness of two line drawings) to the subject may be "verifiable in principle" and hence quite amenable to influence (Allen & Levine, 1971a). Second, the notion that people can disagree about what category a given question belongs in, as well as the "correct" answer to the question, suggests some interesting possibilities regarding the origin and resolution of interpersonal disagreements. It may be, for example, that categorization disagreements commonly occur but often are unrecognized. Rather than establishing a common categorization for a given question, each participant in any interaction may simply assume that the others agree with his own categorization. Therefore, what is actually a disagreement between categories may be erroneously perceived and treated as a disagreement within a single shared category. This hypothesis, if correct, may prove useful in analyzing at least some types of interpersonal conflict.

Obedience to Authority

As we said earlier, obedience refers to compliance or conformity to normative expectations as these are communicated on particular occasions by an authority agent. As reported at length in Chapter 5, this phenomenon has been investigated in a series of ingenious experiments conducted by Stanley Milgram (1974). In this series of studies subjects were told they were teachers in a learning experiment and that by applying electric shock to the learner when he erred they could teach him to perform a task better. To Milgram's surprise many subjects, even while protesting the orders of the experimenter, administered large doses of shock to the learner over a wide variety of conditions and despite apparent evidence that the shocks were painful and even seriously harmful.

What do these results imply about Americans' propensity to obey orders which involve inflicting pain on others? Some may derive comfort from the fact that at least we are no more obedient than several other nationalities. Recent studies indicate that Germans, Italians, South Africans, and Australians all manifest higher obedience levels than do Americans (Milgram, 1974). In this context it is interesting to learn that, in a cross-sectional sample of almost 1000 adult Americans interviewed in 1971, 51% said that, if ordered to do so, they would shoot all inhabitants of a Vietnamese village suspected of aiding the enemy, including old men, women, and children (Kelman & Lawrence, 1972).

In attempting to explain why obedience to authority occurs, Milgram (1974) contrasts two psychological states: (1) the "autonomous" state, in which a person feels that he is directing his own actions and (2) the "agentic" state, in which a person feels that his actions are directed by someone else. This latter state seems closely akin to the concept of legitimate power, discussed earlier. According to Milgram, there are several antecedents to the "agentic" state, which presumably underlie obedience in the studies just discussed. These include prior experience (and reward for) submitting to authority in the family and school settings, perception of the experimenter as a legitimate authority in the experimental situation, and perception of the scientific enterprise as itself legitimate. Milgram goes on to argue that, once the "agentic" state has been induced, certain consequences follow. Among these are acute sensitivity to the experimenter's wishes, acceptance of the experimenter's definition of the situation, and decreased feeling of responsibility for the content of one's own actions. Finally, Milgram identifies several factors which operate to restrain a subject from leaving the "agentic" state during the experiment (e.g., the sequential and interdependent nature of the subject's task, hesitation to disrupt the situation and embarrass the experimenter, and anxiety about defying authority).

It is obvious, in light of Milgram's findings and theoretical analysis, that obedience to authority is a complex phenomenon which cannot be explained glibly in terms of "aggressive instinct," "sadism," "identification with the aggressor," or any of the other unverified (and often unverifiable) explanations of why people sometimes inflict pain on one another. In spite of disagreements about how to explain obedience, however, there is probably a high degree of consensus that obedience in the real world (and, some would argue, in Milgram's laboratory) raises serious ethical questions. In the next section we turn to a consideration of the pros and cons, for the individual and the group, of compliance to social pressure.

CONFORMITY—GOOD OR BAD?

Is conformity, by and large, a good thing or not? This question can be asked in different ways. One interpretation leads directly into the question of value judgments, and from that on to the difficult issue of the relationship between values and science. One view on this issue holds that science should not and cannot say anything about values. We shall not adopt this view. Rather, we begin by acknowledging that science cannot dictate ultimate values or final ends, but note at the same time that science is largely a matter of specifying effective means for attaining given ends or goals. Because means are subgoals and goals are usually means to further goals, the means-ends distinction is often blurred in practice. Nevertheless, we shall observe this distinction, for it permits a consideration of the goodness or badness of conformity as a means of achieving specified objectives. In particular, we will ask about the objectives of personal adjustment, and of group or societal functioning.

Asked in another way, the question of the goodness of conformity is addressed to the nature of the processes, not of the products. This interpretation concerns the quality of the mental processes underlying conformity behavior. Is the conformist "blind," an automaton, or is he actually engaging in relatively high-level thought processes based on premises appropriate to his circumstances? Let us postpone a consideration of the first interpretation and turn directly to this second way of asking about the nature of conformity.

How Rational?

Different theoretical orientations give different answers, or at any rate put the emphasis in different places. Freudian psychology and psychoanalysis can be said to view man as an *irrational* creature, controlled by his animal impulses. Strict stimulus-response learning theory is only a little less uncomplimentary, seeing man as a *nonrational* organism whose behavior is determined by S-R connections that have been built up over the span of his reinforcement history. In contrast to these positions, we prefer the more generous portrait of man painted by the cognitive theorists. Most cognitive (or perceptual-cognitive) theorists hold that—within the limits imposed by prevailing conditions—man is *rational*. If a person is confronted with an insoluble problem or has been denied information required for a solution, it cannot be held against him that he fails to come up with a solution. Beyond this, behavior that appears clearly irrational might appear quite reasonable if the observer could correctly ascertain the assumptions, the available information, and the objectives of the actor. Consider a subject in an Asch-type experiment. Assume that this particular subject invariably goes along with the unanimous majority on critical trials and, furthermore, does so with alacrity. Is he indulging in "blind" conformity? Apparently, but what if we interview him afterwards and find out that yesterday he broke his glasses, without which he is very nearsighted, and anyway his main goal during the experiment was to get it over with in time to meet his girlfriend before class? In the light of these facts, his behavior appears highly reasonable, albeit not well designed to yield the best data from the experimenter's point of view.

Asch himself is an excellent example of a cognitive theorist who stresses man's potential for rationality, a fact closely associated with his affiliation with Gestalt psychology. Asch did in fact interview his subjects after his experiment (Asch, 1956). He does not report cases in which broken glasses or appointments with girlfriends influenced conformity behavior, but he does show that his subjects, both conforming and independent, had their reasons for behaving as they did and that these various reasons might well be considered good ones in light of the assumptions and objectives of individual subjects. These findings cast strong doubt on the notion that some kind of automatic suggestion is operating.

At an earlier time, Asch had attacked the doctrine of prestige suggestion (i.e., automatic or conditioned suggestion) as a way to explain the impact of an assertion attributed to a particular source (Asch, 1948, 1952). The doctrine of prestige suggestion (e.g., Lorge, 1936), a simple version of S-R theory, held that the prestige of the source became automatically associated with the assertion and in this way caused the recipient to be more accepting in the case of a high prestige source or less accepting in the case of a low prestige source. Asch argued that the effect of a source upon an assertion was not at all automatic. Rather, the assertion itself was changed in its meaning by a change in the attributed source. Thus, for example, if Thomas Jefferson is quoted as saying "I hold that a little rebellion, now and then, is a good thing," he is presumed by the recipient to mean something quite different from that intended by Lenin if he were to make precisely the same assertion. As Asch so aphoristically put it, it is not a change in the judgment of the object, but a change in the object of judgment. In other words, the individual is cognitively reorganizing the stimulus pattern so as to make it more likely and more meaningful, a better Gestalt. This is certainly a "rational" thing to do.

Thus, although man is probably a mixture of irrationality, nonrationality, and rationality insofar as his conformity behavior is concerned, we, along with Asch and the cognitive theorists as a group, prefer to stress man's potential for rationality. Our preference stems, not from faith that people are necessarily reasonable most of the time, but rather from the fact that adopting such a position forces or at any rate encourages the observer to put himself in the actor's shoes before interpreting his actions. The current popularity of "attribution theory" in social psychology (Bem, 1972; Jones et al., 1972) suggests that taking into account an actor's interpretation of his own situation can be quite useful in helping us to understand his behavior.

Let us now turn our attention to the other way of asking our question. How effective is conformity as a means of attaining good personal adjustment, on the one hand, and harmonious group or societal functioning, on the other? The question of personal adjustment can be approached through a critical consideration of the idea of "the conforming personality," while that of collective functioning leads naturally into the analogous concept of "the conforming society."

The Conforming Personality

Crutchfield (1955), in a frequently cited study, found amount of conformity in his automated situation to be negatively correlated with ratings of intellectual competence ($-.63$) and ego strength on the Barron scale ($-.33$), and positively correlated with the California F scale (.39), a measure of authoritarianism. There were also systematic differences between amounts of conformity and responses to personality items. In very general terms, and with some exceptions, the more independent subjects appeared to be more confident and effective in their personal functioning than the conformists.

In a field study by Stouffer (1955) it was found that community leaders were more tolerant than the rank and file toward attitudinal nonconformity (e.g., communistic and atheistic attitudes). As this tolerance of socially disapproved views is itself one kind of nonconformity, and if one is willing to assume, in this Watergate age, that community leaders are healthier in some ways than average, then high levels of conformity are in fact associated with lesser levels of personal effectiveness of some kinds.

These results seem to say that conformity is, by and large, bad, and probably a majority of experimental social psychologists adopt this view, at least implicitly. Conformity is taken as indicative of intellectual or temperamental weakness, while independence is seen as strength.

The opposite opinion is sometimes held by those interested in clinical assessment. According to this position, conformity implies a "fitting in," a good adjustment to one's social environment, while nonconformity (here thought of as deviation rather than independence) implies poor social adjustment. As an example, consider the T method of scoring developed by McQuitty (1954), where T stands for typicality. A multiple-alternative test of almost any kind is administered to a "normal" group, and each alternative of each item is scored for its popularity. The individual whose mental health is to be evaluated is assigned a score based on the sum of the popularity scores of the alternatives he checks. The more typical his responses, the higher this score and the better his mental health is assumed to be. The *deviation hypothesis* (e.g., Berg, 1961) also represents the "conformity is good" view. According to Berg's hypothesis, an individual deviating from a "normal" group in his responses in noncritical areas (those having no apparent connection with adjustment) will also deviate in critical or diagnostically significant areas. In other words, deviation in any area is taken as indicative of deviation of an undesirable kind. In practice, Berg has relied primarily on an inventory requiring the individual to indicate his preferences among sets of abstract designs.

Who is right? The first thing to notice is that the term "conforming personality" has no meaning if differences in conformity are entirely determined by differences in situations. Only to the extent that some persons tend to show more conformity than others across situations does the concept have any significance. However, a review of the literature on generality of conformity shows only a rather low level of consistency (McGuire, 1968), suggesting that the concept of a conforming personality has very limited utility. Furthermore, there is another complication. Even if general tendencies are lacking, that is, even if one cannot speak of a conforming personality type, individual differences may be important in a somewhat less obvious way. Individual differences—either personality traits or those of other kinds—may interact with situational differences. In other words, one person may conform more than another in one kind of situation but the difference may be in the reverse direction in another kind of situation. Kelly may conform more than Cohen when the issue relates to science, while Cohen may conform more than Kelly when the issue concerns music. In fact, one would expect this if Kelly were a musician and Cohen a scientist.

Data are available demonstrating that such interactions between individual differences and situational differences can sometimes be more important than either individual differences per se or situational differences per se. In the terminology of analysis of variance, the interactions are more important than the main effects in such cases. Hunt (1965) and Endler and Hunt (1966) looked at levels of anxiety aroused in individuals in each of a number of situations. Some people were generally more anxious than others, and some situations were generally more anxiety-arousing than others, but the interactions were the most important of all, accounting for from four to eleven times the proportion of variance due to differences among persons!

Because of the modest degree of consistency in conformity behavior from situation to situation and because of liklihood of strong interactions between personality traits and situations, we feel that there is no simple relationship between conformity as a personality trait and personal adjustment or effectiveness. Within fairly wide limits, it is not so much a matter of how much conformity or nonconformity one shows, but rather what specific reactions one shows in which specific situations, and for what reasons. Even "thinking men" sometimes act as if they are "yes men" or "no men" (Willis, 1964, 1965b).

An experiment reported by McDavid and Sistrunk (1964) illustrates how conformity might be "good" in some situations but "bad" in others. They found that with unambiguous stimuli, to which there were correct answers, conformity to an unreasonable majority was associated with timidity, deference to others, tendency to avoid arguments, reluctance to speak out, and strong needs for acceptance and approval. With ambiguous stimuli, on the other hand, conformity was related to trust and faith in others, respect for others, respect for traditional sex-role differentiations, and a desire for closure and successful completion of tasks.

The Conforming Society

The thesis is presented, from time to time, that some societies require more conformity from their members than others, and at least one experimental study (Milgram, 1961) has demonstrated consistent differences in amount of movement conformity between subjects of different nationalities. Norwegian university students were observed to be consistently more conforming than French university students across five variations of the Crutchfield procedures. Concerning these results, Milgram wrote, "no matter how the data are examined they point to greater independence among the French than among the Norwegians (p. 50)." He went on to relate this difference in "independence" to differences in the two national cultures.

Our discussion of the conforming personality led to the conclusion that the concept is of very limited utility, and we may well be suspicious also about blanket assertions regarding conforming societies. Although it may be true that the French are more independent than the Norwegians, Milgram's data do not actually allow this sweeping generalization. There exists at least one other equally tenable interpretation. If it is recalled that anticonformity, like conformity, is a variety of dependence, it becomes apparent that one very real possibility is that the French group was exhibiting substantially stronger anticonformity tendencies than the Norwegians. If so, it could well be that the French subjects were at the same time less conforming but more dependent. While the Norwegians felt less free to nonconform, the French may have felt less free to conform. Or, if one may put it this way, the French may have been in some degree conforming to a norm of anticonformity. In fact, some of the anecdotal evidence presented by Milgram regarding stylistic differences between the groups suggests that this was indeed the case.

Whether or nor Norway does in fact constitute a conforming society, a whole school of social criticism sprang up in the 1950s devoted to the thesis that American culture can be so described. David Riesman (1950), in *The Lonely Crowd,* informed us that we are becoming excessively other-directed, while Whyte (1956), in *The Organization Man,* told us in no uncertain terms that our Protestant Ethic is being replaced by a Social Ethic, as he terms it, which dictates that being a good team player is the highest value. In *The Status Seekers* Vance Packard (1959) has documented the attempts of each social stratum of our society to imitate the manners, actions, and even thoughts of those perched on higher rungs of the status ladder.

As Hollander and Willis (1967) point out, a characteristic tack of many such critiques is to describe conventional behavior, label it conformity, invoke the "self-evident" premise that conformity is in opposition to individuality or independence, and therefore conclude that modern American society hampers constructive initiative and is accordingly bad.

This literature often neglects and even hides the instrumental value of conformity to the individual. Under many circumstances an objective analysis of possible courses of action leads to the conclusion that conformity will most effectively serve the individual's goals, whether these are social (e.g., need for approval) or nonsocial (e.g., need for food). The distinction, made earlier, between conventionality and acquiescence (Beloff, 1958), or more generally between congruence and movement conformity, is useful for liberating conventional behavior from the blanket stigma of acquiescent conformity. Thus, the convention of wearing clothes in public cannot be treated as slavish conformity in the same sense as accommodating to any and all fads indiscriminately. In addition, it hardly seems reasonable to conclude that a mathematician lacks creativity just because he adopts the conventional notation of mathematics, for this is obviously a necessary precondition for the demonstration of whatever professional skills he may have.

Clearly, much of the social criticism regarding conformity is misplaced in that it ignores the fact that an individual's culture severely limits alternatives that are socially and psychologically economical. Beyond this, apparent differences between societies can be misleading, as demonstrated by Milgram's (1961) discussion of his French-Norwegian comparison.

Like the idea of a conforming personality, the conforming society concept appears to be of limited utility.

At the same time, certain interesting differences have been noted between various segments of society-at-large. For example, Kohn (1969) has observed consistent differences in values relating to conformity between the middle class and the working class in the United States, and also in Italy. According to Kohn, the essence of the middle-class orientation is the expectation that one's decisions and actions can be consequential, while the essence of the working-class position is the belief that one is at the mercy of forces and people beyond one's control, and often beyond one's understanding. Thus, in the language of the personality psychologist, the middle-class member perceives the locus of control to be internal, while the member of the working class perceives the locus of control to be external.

This difference in perception of locus of control leads to a middle-class orientation emphasizing *self-direction,* while that of the working class emphasizes *conformity.* Self-direction, which is a kind of active independence, means among other things, acting on the basis on one's own judgment, attending to internal dynamics as well as to external consequences, and holding personal moral standards. Conformity as Kohn uses the term, means following the dictates of authority, focusing on external consequences to the exclusion of internal processes, and having moral standards stressing obedience to the letter of the law. Kohn argues that independence or self-direction requires opportunities and experiences that are available to people favorably situated in the hierarchal order of society, whereas conformity is the natural consequence of inadequate opportunities to be self-directed.

Very much the same kind of differences can be seen, according to some observers, when society is segmented by sex rather than by class. Thus, the argument goes, women are accorded less status and opportunity in our society than are men, and the natural result is that the feminine value orientation places much more emphasis on conformity and less on self-direction than does the masculine orientation.

There are a number of experimental studies supporting this point of view insofar as they show female subjects to conform more than male subjects. For example, Tuddenham (1958) found that females yielded more than males in mixed-sex groups, especially when there were more males than females. In another study, Tuddenham (1961) found more conformity for females than males both among college students and among boys and girls between 9 and 13. In a fairly recent review of the experimental literature, Nord (1969) concluded that, in our culture at least, females conform more than males under almost all conditions.

On the other hand, there is evidence that this view of greater female conformity is overly simplistic. In one study, McDavid (1965) used items based on issues that had previously been identified as masculine, neutral, or feminine with regard to the interests and judgmental accuracy of the sexes. He found that females did in fact conform more on the masculine issues, but not on the neutral or feminine issues.

More recently, Sistrunk and McDavid (1971) reported a series of four experiments, using the same three types of issues, that challenges the doctrine of female conformity even more strongly. On masculine issues, females conformed more than males three out of four times, with no difference in the fourth case. On feminine issues, males conformed more than females two out of four times, with no differences in the remaining two cases. On neutral issues, there was no difference three out of four times, with males conforming more in one case. Thus, of the twelve comparisons, eight were in the direction predicted by the hypothesis of an inverse relationship between conformity and task sophistication and interest, and there were no significant reversals.

With regard to sex differences and conformity, it cannot be said that women generally conform more than men. In fact, for feminine tasks the difference seems to run in the other direction. It should be noted also that, even in instances in which women do conform more, it does not necessarily follow that they are more dependent. The same reasoning applied earlier to the Norwegians and the French also applies here. Men may show less conformity but also more anticonformity over a given set of tasks or situations, relative to women. If so, they may exhibit no more, and maybe even less, true independence. As with the nationality differences, this argument applied to the sexes is speculative.

SUMMARY

Influence can be defined very generally as the power to cause things to be different than they otherwise would have been, while conformity, attitude change, imitation, contagion, and obedience all refer to various reactions to intentional influence. In particular, conformity is behavior intended to fulfill normative expectations.

What is conformity? In operational or measurement terms, we distinguished between congruence and movement conformity. Congruence refers to the degree of matching between observed behavior and perfect conformity, while movement refers to changes in the level of congruence from one time to another. The congruence criterion is more applicable in cases of more-or-less constant ongoing normative expectations, such as a social *norm,* whereas the movement criterion is more applicable to situations in which a *source* of social pressure provides the continuity. When congruence is used, conformity is usually contrasted with nonconformity or deviation, while independence is the most common contrast when the movement criterion is used.

What are the alternatives to conformity? The diamond model was developed for interrelating movement conformity and its alternatives. The model incorporates the two dimensions of independence and of conformity. Three alternatives are delineated, the most important being independence and anticonformity. The third mode of nonconformity, self-anticonformity, is relatively rare. The diamond model is a descriptive or "mapping" model which maps out possibilities rather than making predictions. It facilitates accurate prediction, however, by providing an improved "map" of the response patterns to be predicted. An important implication of the diamond model is that greater conformity does not necessarily imply less independence, for both conformity and anticonformity contribute to dependent behavior.

Why conformity and why deviation? At the interpersonal level, the answer to "why?" involves motives. Among several simpler typologies, the bases of social power stand out. This formulation distinguishes, first of all, between independent or informational influence, based on the content of the message independently of its source, and dependent influence, which is dependent in its effects on the perceived nature of the source. Dependent influence is subdivided into public-dependent and private-dependent, based upon whether or not the source must be able to monitor the responses of the recipient to make the influence effective. Public-dependent influence can be further subdivided into reward and coercive power, while private-dependent influence subsumes expert, referent, and legitimate power.

When conformity and when deviation? On simple perceptual stimuli almost any type of dissenter is likely to reduce the power of a majority over an individual, even one who is more incorrect than the majority. On opinion items a person agreeing with the individual is effective if he is perceived either as a competent judge or as sharing the responsibility for deviating from the group, or both.

The experimental results concerning the effects of stimulus characteristics suggest that difficult stimuli produce more conformity than do either easy or ambiguous stimuli. The work of Milgram on obedience demonstrates that many people are willing to administer dangerous electric shocks to another person, even when the subject has no fear of punishment for noncompliance. It is sufficient that he perceive the responsibility for his actions as resting on the shoulders of a high-status authority.

Is conformity good or bad? Although there are undoubtedly individual differences in general tendencies to yield to social pressure, the interactions between personality and situation are often more important. In addition, modern societies probably differ more importantly in kinds of normative expectations than in overall demands, although some internation and intrasocietal differences were noted. Any individual in any society must conform in many ways before he can become a functioning member of that society. Reasonable conformity is thus necessary to—but certainly not sufficient for—rational nonconformity. Conformity can reflect either positive adjustment or an unhealthy passivity, while nonconformity can take such forms as healthy independence, plain "pigheadedness," immature anticonformity, neurotic self-anticonformity, or creative innovation, among others. Clearly, one cannot assert that conformity is either good or bad in an absolute sense.

SUGGESTED READINGS

Allen, V. L. Situational factors in conformity. In L. Berkowitz (Ed.), *Advances in experimental social psychology* (Vol. 2). New York: Academic Press, 1965.

A comprehensive and well-organized review of research on reaction to group pressure.

Hollander, E. P., & Willis, R. H. Some current issues in the psychology of conformity and nonconformity. *Psychological Bulletin*, 1967, *68*, 62–76.

A critique of much past and current conformity research, with suggestions for future investigations.

Kiesler, C. A., & Kiesler, S. B. *Conformity*. Reading, Mass.: Addison-Wesley, 1969.

A clearly written introduction to conformity research, with special emphasis on the distinction between compliance and private acceptance. For a more advanced review by the first author, containing additional material on the diamond model, see: Group pressure and conformity. In J. Mills (Ed.), *Experimental social psychology*. New York: Macmillan, 1969.

Tedeschi, J. T. (Ed.). *The social influence processes*. Chicago: Aldine-Atherton, 1972.

An edited volume of papers, at a somewhat advanced level, seeking to stimulate new approaches to the investigation of social influence.

Wheeler, L. *Interpersonal influence*. Boston: Allyn & Bacon, 1970.

A very readable historical review of theoretical ideas which have guided inquiry on interpersonal influence.

11
Power and Bargaining

Dean G. Pruitt

INTRODUCTION

Power can be defined as one party's capacity to influence another party's behavior in a direction desired by the first. The parties involved in this definition can be individuals, groups, or organizations.

Power is not a new topic in this volume. Earlier sections on attitude change and conformity to group pressures have dealt with it in part, either directly or indirectly. But a full discussion has been reserved to this chapter, which also covers the closely related topic of bargaining.

Some readers may find themselves depressed or even shocked by theoretical discussions of influence and power. Such discussions may seem too oriented toward interpersonal manipulation, too crass and inhuman. Yet influence and power are omnipresent in human affairs. Indeed, groups cannot possibly function unless their members can influence one another. Power can of course be used for the wrong purposes. But if so, it must be understood in order to protect oneself and others. Furthermore the principles described in this chapter are intended to be value free. Hence the strategies they imply can be adopted in the pursuit of any goals, from the most reactionary to the most progressive, from least to most benevolent.

Consider the case of Mr. X, a hypothetical 29-year-old lawyer who has just been elected chairman of the Democratic Party in a small midwestern city. The party has been successful in the past, but in recent years has become rather shaky. Its candidates are not getting the votes they formerly had, and several offices in the city government that were previously occupied by Democrats have been lost. Perhaps as cause and perhaps as effect of these developments, the "party faithful," those men and women who previously worked hard to raise money and get out the vote, have become a dispirited and inactive lot. As so often happens in a group that is failing (Ziller & Behringer, 1960), those few of the faithful who still take an interest in the party's welfare have decided to turn to new leadership. They are hoping that Mr. X, with his youthful vigor, can rekindle a spark in their tired organization and persuade the faithful once again to throw their energies into the pursuit of victory.

This case poses a problem of influencing behavior and hence of power. It will be used to illustrate many of the points in this chapter, though it cannot by any means bear the full weight of all of them. The crucial issue in this example is how Mr. X can achieve the power that is needed to return the party faithful to their historic task.

The answer to this question is highly complex. There are many kinds of power and hence many possible strategies for Mr. X. He will certainly want to develop and employ various forms of *personal power*. He will also need to rely on others—governing in part through *allies* and in part by enhancing, and guiding the use of, the *power of the group,* i.e., the capacity of the faithful, as a social group, to influence its membership.

FORMS OF PERSONAL POWER

Raven and Kruglanski (1970) have identified six ways in which one party can affect another's behavior, i.e., six types of influence: Legitimate, informational, expert, referent, coercive, and reward influence. To this list can be added two others, co-oriented and reciprocal influence. Underlying these eight types of influence are eight classes of power.

In discussing these varieties of influence and power, the term *source* will be used to refer to the party who originates an influence attempt and the term *target* to refer to the party at whom such an attempt is directed.

An explanation will be given for the target's decision to comply in the case of each of the eight types of influence and power. Three quite distinct *models of decision making* will be employed in these explanations: norm following out of a sense of obligation, the rational calculation of self-interest, and imitation of an identification figure.

Legitimate Influence

The target of an influence attempt sometimes conforms because he feels that the source of the attempt has the *right* to prescribe behavior for him in the matter at hand. In such cases, the source's influence derives from a social norm (i.e., a rule) that has been internalized (accepted as correct) by the target. We are dealing, in such cases, with legitimate influence.

The norm in question is often one that obliges the target to comply to certain types of request from anyone occupying the source's position in society. If so, the source achieves his power by virtue of his position and the norms associated with this position. Legitimate power of this kind is usually called authority.

Mr. X is likely to have some authority by virtue of his chairmanship of the party. He may, for example, have the right to call meetings of the faithful and expect their attendance. Authority, being based on group norms, is always limited in scope. For example, the customs of the party may not give Mr. X an element of authority which he deems crucial, such as the right to name the candidates for City Council.

Legitimate influence rests on the target's sense of how he *should* behave—his sense of obligation, his moral or ethical impulses. Such impulses are amazingly potent in all human societies, but they are by no means totally effective in governing behavior. Hence most societies and groups have a second line of defense for their norms, in the form of rewards and penalties. Members who conform are smiled at, thanked, accorded prestige, or given tangible benefit. Those who fail to conform are rebuked, fined, imprisoned, or executed. Influence that is based on the capacity to provide rewards and penalties will be discussed later in this chapter.

What can Mr. X do to enhance his legitimate power?

Authority rests, in part, on the target's recognition that the source is the legitimate holder of the position in question. Hence Mr. X can request a formal inauguration ceremony in which other members of the party hail him as their new leader in front of the assembled faithful. Or he may attempt influence in settings that remind people of his high position, such as seated in a chair behind the desk in his office or standing at the center of a stage. Whether these or other tactics will have their intended effect will depend on the culture of the group involved. In some groups, for example, leaders who take an overly formal approach are viewed with disfavor.

Authority also rests, in part, on group approval of the specific rights involved. If Mr. X wants to name candidates for City Council, he must get the party to agree that he has this right. He may pursue such a dispensation formally, e.g., through a vote of his party's executive committee. (Every society and group has its own way of making legitimate formal decisions. In our society, majority rule of the whole group or some democratically elected representative body is a common approach.) Or he may proceed informally, by attempting to convince as many powerful members of the party as possible that they should listen to him when the candidates are being chosen.

Mr. X may conceivably have the legitimate right to request such an extension in the scope of his authority. This is especially likely to be true under two circumstances: (1) at the beginning of his tenure in office, when many (though by no means all) groups grant their leaders something of a "honeymoon," and (2) at times when the faithful see their party as in a crisis, because decision making often becomes more centralized in crises (Hamblin, 1958). But, most of the time, Mr. X will have to rely on other forms of influence in order to extend his authority.

Even if Mr. X is able to keep his position salient in people's thinking and gain formal endorsement of his right to make the decisions he wishes to make, he is likely to find legitimate power a thin staff to lean upon, particularly when he tries to persuade the faithful to make sacrifices for the cause. He may, for example, be accorded the right to call meetings as frequently as once a week. But will people come? Or if they come to the first few meetings, will they stay in the organization or drop out because "it takes too much time"? Mr. X must face the two problems that vex most leaders of voluntary organizations: (1) members do not feel their obligations so keenly because they are donating their time and (2) there is little to hold them in the organization when their responsibilities entail costs.

The problems associated with legitimate power can sometimes be remedied. People conform more fully to group norms, and are more likely to maintain their membership in the face of heavy costs, to the extent that they are attracted to the group and value their membership (Festinger, 1950). Hence, in order to strengthen his legitimate power, Mr. X might begin a campaign designed to make the party seem more vital and important to the faithful. Suggestions for such a campaign are presented later, in the section on the power of the group. But such campaigns often take a long time and do not always work. In the meantime, Mr. X may have to rely on other forms of power to supplement his legitimate power.

In formal organizations, as opposed to informal groups, leaders are often tempted to lean too heavily on their authority. When they look at formal power charts, of the kind distributed by many organizations to their members, they see that they are the "boss" and others are the "subordinates." Hence they expect obedience, and wonder why they do not get it. This mistake can be called the *formalistic error*, because it results from placing too much emphasis on the formal structure of the organization.

People on the outside looking at an organization often make the same error. They assume that the top man can make decisions that will stick, and they are often surprised when this assumption fails. According to legend, President John F. Kennedy often felt that he had to combat this error by telling people about how little real influence he had over the Executive branch of the Government.

In actual fact, authority is a relatively weak form of power, even in organizations that pay their members. It must be continually supplemented by other types of influence, despite the formal power charts. And it appears to be diminishing in importance in the United States, as the spirit of decentralization and democratic decision making gains greater currency (Parsons & Platt, 1973).

Authority is not the only form of legitimate power. For example, Berkowitz (1972) describes a *norm of social responsibility* that requires people to provide a modicum of help to anyone in need. The power that this norm gives to a person in need derives not from his titles or status but from his needy condition. Other writers (Adams, 1965; Pruitt, 1972) describe *equity* and *fairness* norms that provide support to an individual when his claims can be construed as equitable or fair. These norms will be discussed more fully in the part of this chapter that deals with bargaining.

Informational Influence

Sometimes the target of a persuasive communication conforms because the source of the communication has provided information that makes conformity seem rational. For example, Mr. X might attempt to launch a campaign to register new voters by presenting poll data to the party faithful showing that new voters are partial to the Democratic Party. This approach will work to the extent that the faithful value a victory by the Democrats and believe the poll.

Informational influence is successful because of the target's sense of self-interest. He decides to comply because the information provided makes this course of action look like the most rational way to satisfy his needs and values.

A two-step process is sometimes found in informational influence, with an initial effort to change values so that information can have an effect on behavior (Michener & Suchner, 1972). For example, Mr. X may first have to persuade some of his faithful that a Democratic victory is desirable before his poll will have the desired effect. Information may be used to change values as well, building one value upon another. If those who doubt the desirability of a Democratic victory value the welfare of Israel, he may be able to prove to them that the Democratic Party favors close relations with Israel and hence that they should value a victory by the Democrats.

Knowledge is power (Mulder & Wilke, 1970); and the more unique is a man's knowledge in areas that are important to others, the more powerful will he be.

The importance of informational power appears to be steadily increasing in our society as authority loses its luster. People want to know why it is rational for them to conform rather than what they are obliged to do. Furthermore we are in an *information explosion*, in which knowledge is expanding so rapidly that only a few people can know any particular fact. Hence the educated man, and especially the man who continues his education by keeping up with current trends, is sought after and may well be the effective leader in areas where he has special knowledge, regardless of the organizational charts (Katz, 1957).

What can Mr. X do to achieve informational power? He can, of course, seek knowledge that will help him sell his policies. At a minimum, he should keep up with local and national news. He should also read material put out by the national Democratic Party and talk to other party leaders, to tap into pools of information relevant to the campaign. In addition, he may need to develop specialized knowledge about his particular situation. For example, he might run a poll in his own city to identify those groups that are most likely to vote for the Democrats if they can be persuaded to register.

Informational power also requires an understanding of the values and assumptions of the potential target, because persuasive information must link the desired behavior to the target's values (Peak, 1955), and information that is consonant with the target's view of the world is more likely to be believed than information that is alien to this view (Sherif & Hovland, 1961). Hence, if he hopes to enhance his information power, Mr. X should make a careful study of the party faithful.

Finally, if he is somewhat unethical, Mr. X can try to prevent certain information from reaching the faithful—information that might subvert his influence attempts. For instance, he might decline to reveal to them poll data indicating that the party has little chance of winning an election, because of fear that they would become discouraged in their efforts. If he did so, he would be acting in the capacity of a *gate-keeper,* allowing certain information to reach his group and barring other information. All groups, organizations and societies have gate-keepers who control the flow of information—and they are often inordinately powerful. Examples in our society are governmental press secretaries, newspaper editors, and (at least according to some people) college professors.

Expert and Co-oriented Influence

People sometimes comply for rational reasons without full information about the link between their values and the behavior in question. For example, most people will take the pills prescribed by a physician without his providing a detailed rationale. This is because they regard him as an expert on medicine and as oriented toward their health. They assume that he can and will use valid information to determine how they ought to behave in order to return to health. There is no need for him to transmit this information, since he is trusted to use it properly.

Expert power derives from a reputation for being knowledgeable. Such a reputation is usually limited in scope. One person in a group is known as the local expert on recipes, another as the expert on shrubs, a third as the expert on new drugs (Katz, 1957). A man's reputation may derive from his formal credentials (as in the case of a physician), his experience, or the success of his past predictions and decisions (Hollander & Julian, 1969). Formal credentials mean relatively little in politics, but Mr. X might to able to develop a reputation for expertise about the psychology of the voter by means of a series of adroit predictions about the outcomes of elections. It ordinarily takes time to build such a reputation.

Co-orientation is a source's reputation with the target for having values similar to those of the target (Jones & Gerard, 1967). If Mr. X can gain such a reputation with the party faithful, he will be able to make successful recommendations without fully spelling out the details of the rationale behind them. They will trust him to act on their behalf. Similar background is one basis for co-orientation. Hence, if most of the faithful are teachers, Mr. X's power will be greater if he is also a teacher. A man's values are also deduced from his statements and actions. Hence, if he wishes to gain co-oriented power, Mr. X will have to study the values and norms of the faithful and attempt to ally himself with those that are most deeply felt (Hollander & Julian, 1969). Again we see the need for careful study of the target.

When the members of a group view a leader as an expert in his field and as sharing their values, they can be said to "trust" him, in one sense of the term. In larger organizations or nations, an entire administration or government may be the object of greater or lesser trust. Trust increases if the leader or government takes actions that satisfy the values of constituents and diminishes if these actions are ineffective or costly to the constituents. The greater the trust, the greater the willingness to be influenced by the leadership and to support the leadership when questions arise about its continued tenure.

Gamson (1968) has pointed out the *self-reinforcing quality* of greater or lesser trust in a government. When trust is great, the government can gain the cooperation of many people and hence launch major programs that benefit the country and thus further enhance trust. But when trust is small, few people cooperate willingly and the government is likely to be ineffective, further diminishing trust. In less democratic countries, governments that are not trusted frequently come to rely on coercive power in order to persuade people to cooperate. While coercion may help maintain the efficiency of the government, it also tends to erode trust, making coercion all the more necessary.

Referent Influence

According to Raven and Kruglanski (1970), "Referent influence stems from (the target's) identification with (the source), or from a desire for such identification—a desire for 'oneness.'" Such identification leads to imitation of the source's behavior, beliefs, attitudes, and values. In the imitation of an identification figure, we have a third model of human decision making, to be placed alongside the following of internalized norms and rational efforts to achieve self-interest.

Literary writers often employ the notion of a "charismatic" leader, a man who achieves a following by virtue of his personal characteristics. The notion of charisma has much in common with the notion of referent power.

Identification comes about in many ways. On the basis of experimental evidence, Bandura (1962) lists the following characteristics of people who are imitated: they are attractive, rewarding, prestigeful, competent, high-status, or powerful, or a combination of these traits. Raven and Kruglanski also emphasize the importance of perceived similarity in producing identification. People tend to identify with those who are similar to them in background, values, attitudes, beliefs, and the like. (As was mentioned earlier, perceived similarity is also a basis for co-orientation.)

If Mr. X wishes to be the target of identification and hence to gain referent power over the faithful, he should probably take seriously the old adage that a successful political leader must be "one of us, the most of us and the best of us." He must be "one of us," in the sense of sharing significant background characteristics with his constituents. Hence, Mr. X should stress the ways in which his background is similar to those of the faithful. He must be the "most of us," in the sense of conforming to as many elements of the culture of his constituents as possible. Thus if the faithful are bowlers, Mr. X should go bowling; if they like classical music, he would do well to develop and exhibit such a taste; if they believe passionately in the negative income tax, he would be well advised to voice a similar conviction. He must be the "best of us" in the sense of exhibiting skills that are respected by his constituents and leading a life that accords with their moral convictions. Of course, it is possible to overdo anything, and Mr. X must be careful not to conform to the expectations of his constituents so completely that he seems to be doing it for the effect.

If he is successful in these tasks, Mr. X will

be liked and respected and hence become the object of identification. The ideas he articulates will begin to be accepted because members of the faithful will model themselves after him.

Many of the theories that were encountered in the chapter on attraction are also relevant here, including the notion that Mr. X can make himself more attractive and thereby increase the extent of identification with him by providing rewards to the faithful and interacting a fair amount with them.

Reciprocal Influence

Reciprocity, the returning of benefit for benefit, appears to be one of the major moving forces in politics. Political leaders often gain influence at critical points in their careers by what is popularly called "collecting on political debts." Similar exchanges of favor for favor have often been observed in ordinary interpersonal interaction (Berkowitz, 1972). The influence which an individual is able to exert by virtue of having helped another person in the past can be called "reciprocal influence."

By no means all favors are reciprocated. Experimental research suggests that the *motives* attributed to a favor-giver determine the extent to which his favors will be reciprocated. Thus Goranson and Berkowitz (1966) have shown that help which appears to have been given voluntarily is more likely to be reciprocated than that which appears to have been elicited by coercion. Nemeth (1972) and Schopler (1965) have suggested, on the basis of other research, that benefits which are attributed to the generosity of the giver are more likely to be reciprocated than those which are interpreted as rational efforts to maximize his own gain. Pruitt (1968) has shown that reciprocity is an inverse function of the extent of the giver's apparent resources at the time of giving. The less money the confederate in Pruitt's experiment had at the time he made a donation to the subject, the more money the subject subsequently gave him. In an effort to explain Pruitt's findings, Kelley (1971) has suggested that a gift from a person with small resources is seen as more costly to the giver than one from a person with large resources. Hence it is less likely to be viewed as an effort to gain some tangible benefit (e.g., to impress the recipient) and more likely to be viewed as the product of some selfless motive, such as generosity or the desire to cooperate.

Reciprocity has been explained in terms of all three models of decision making: Some writers see it as rational behavior, designed to gain further benefits from the favor-giver (Nemeth, 1972). Others see it as the product of attraction felt by the receiver toward the giver and hence of identification (Berkowitz, 1972). Still others postulate a "norm of reciprocity," that requires repaying favors (Gouldner, 1960). One suspects that all of these positions have part of the truth.

The assumption of a norm of reciprocity is supported by evidence that cultural differences exist in the extent of reciprocity. Berkowitz and Friedman (1967) worked with middle-class adolescent boys from Wisconsin between the ages of 13 and 16. They divided their subjects into those from "bureaucratic" families, where the father drew wages from a firm or government bureau, and those from "entrepreneurial" families, where the father was self-employed or worked for a commission. The latter kind of occupation was assumed to require more favor-giving and receiving, and hence to entail more reciprocity, than the former. It was assumed that parents who practiced reciprocity in their work would pass the pattern on as a recommendation (i.e., a norm) to their sons. The data supported this prediction, in that boys from entrepreneurial families showed more reciprocity in a laboratory task than boys from bureaucratic families. In a similar study run in Oxford, England, Berkowitz

(1968) found that working-class boys reciprocated favors more reliably than middle-class boys.

The norm of reciprocity appears to be particularly strong in the political subculture, an entrepreneurial realm if there ever was one. Hence Mr. X should probably rely heavily on the performance of selected favors for members of the faithful. To do so, he must, of course, have access to resources needed by the faithful, such as jobs, influence over government decision making, and the like. By performing favors, Mr. X will also probably enhance his attraction to the faithful and hence his referent power. In addition, the faithful are likely to come to see him as understanding their needs, which should augment his co-oriented power.

Coercive and Reward Influence

Coercive influence occurs when the target complies because he expects the source to punish him for noncompliance; reward influence, when he expects to be rewarded for compliance. In both cases, the target expects the source's actions to be contingent on his compliance. As we saw earlier, rewards can be used to gain influence in another way as well. The source can provide them to the target at time one in an effort to achieve referent and reciprocal influence at time two. But the term "reward influence" will be reserved for the case in which the target complies in the hope of achieving some sort of reward.

Clearly the notions of coercive and reward influence assume a rational, self-interest-oriented model of human decision making.

The number of possible rewards and penalties is practically endless. Some are physical. Others involve increased or diminished opportunity. Still others are purely psychological, including "approval, love, affection, disapproval, hatred and dislike" (Raven & Kruglanski, 1970). Whether an item or event is rewarding, neutral, or punishing depends on the target's needs and values. The most potent rewards and penalties are those that intersect with strong needs and values of the target. It follows again that a person who wishes to acquire coercive or reward power must study his potential targets, to discover what they most like and dislike. In some cases, he may be able to change their needs and values before attempting reward or coercive influence (Michener & Suchner, 1972).

There are two basic ways in which the source can establish a relationship in the target's thinking between compliance and the provision of reward: (1) By reinforcement, rewarding the target when he complies and/or punishing him when he fails to comply. (2) By explicit or implicit threats or promises, e.g., the message, "If you fail to comply, I shall punish you." A good deal of research has been performed on social reinforcement (see McGinnies & Ferster, 1971), but it is covered elsewhere in this volume and hence will not be discussed here. Instead attention will be focussed on the small but growing research literature on threats and promises.

The key to successful reward and coercive influence is *credibility* (Schelling, 1960), which can be roughly translated as "believability."

For a threat to be credible, the target must believe that he is likely to be punished if he does not comply and not to be punished if he does comply. This means that he must see the source as having (1) the probable capacity to punish him and (2) the probable intent of punishing him for noncompliance and withholding punishment for compliance. The terms "likely" and "profitable" are appropriate here, because 100% credibility is often not essential for the success of a threat (or promise). Indeed, less credibility is needed the more potent the penalty (or reward) involved.

An example of an effort to establish the

credibility of a threat comes from the February–March 1970 student crisis on the author's campus. The Administration tried to enhance the credibility of its threat to discipline disruptive students by suspending 20 students who were allegedly involved in blocking the entrances to the Administration Building. This effort failed because members of the Administration were unable to identify the students who were engaged in the blockade and therefore suspended the wrong students. Hence the suspensions gave the actual demonstrators no reason to believe that they would be punished if they continued their disruption and not punished if they desisted.

Successful promises have similar credibility requirements: The target must believe that he is likely to be rewarded if he complies and not rewarded if he fails to comply. Often promises and threats are used simultaneously in a "carrot-and-stick" approach, where an effort is made to persuade the target that he will be rewarded for compliance and punished for noncompliance.

A critical requirement for the credibility of threats and promises is the source's apparent capacity for surveillance of the target's behavior. Surveillance is not an element of the kinds of influence mentioned earlier, since in all the earlier cases, the target complies because he wants to or feels that he should.

Mr. X would be utilizing reward and coercive influence if he established an incentive system, in which benefits and penalties were contingent on the performance or nonperformance of such activities as raising money, advertising the party, or getting out the vote. Rewards to which he might have access include advancement to higher office in the party, the opportunity to meet visiting dignitaries, praise, and various political plums. Penalties might include stripping a member of his party position or excluding him from decision making. Surveillance might be accomplished by arranging for people to report their activities at meetings and, if necessary, making spot checks to be sure that they are telling the truth. Another approach to surveillance would be to reward or punish people for their products rather than their activities. This is often a better approach, since products are often easier to monitor than activities. Thus Mr. X might keep track of the number of votes cast for the party's candidate in each district and reward or penalize the district chairman accordingly.

A good deal of experimental research has been performed on threats and a certain amount on promises. Some of this research will now be reviewed.

THREATS AND PROMISES

Research on Compliance with Threats and Promises

Several studies have used variations on a method developed by Horai and Tedeschi (1969). The subjects, always college students, believe that they are interacting at a distance with another subject, though in actual fact their partner is simulated by the experimenter. As the task is presented to them, they and their partner will make a series of simultaneous choices in the matrix shown in Figure 11-1. On each trial, they must choose between the two columns of the matrix and their partner will choose between the two rows. The cell of the matrix defined by these two choices contains the number of points that are credited to each party on that trial, the first number referring to the partner and the second to the subject. Thus, if the subject chooses column 2 and his partner row 1, the subject will gain 5 points and the partner will lose 5 points. The reader will note that, on any trial, a choice of column 1 is better for the partner but worse for the self than a choice of column 2.

The subject is also told that his partner can,

if he wishes, send a standard message to him on any trial. In the studies of threats, this message reads, "If you do not push the 'Choice 1' switch on the next trial, I will take *n* points from you," the number of points (*n*) being a function of the experimental condition. Concerning this message, the subject is instructed, "If you do not do what the message says to do, the other participant can, if he (she) wants to, take away the number of indicated points." The subject is also told that his goal should be "to obtain as many points as possible."

This method is an example of what has been called "experimental gaming." The matrix shown in Figure 11-1 is a version of the famous Prisoner's Dilemma game, which was originally devised and analyzed by mathematicians specializing in game theory (see Rapoport, 1966).[1] The entries in the matrix are technically called "payoffs," and the association between choices and payoffs can be called "payoff structure." The term *game* in this connection is very misleading. Game theorists and experimental gamers regard structures such as that shown in Figure 11-1 not as competitive parlor games but as models that capture the essential features of many real-life situations. The payoffs in real life are usually in currency other than points, of course. In experiments of this kind, the subjects are told not that they are playing a game but rather that they are engaged in interaction with another person.

In the original study employing the method just described, Horai and Tedeschi (1969) manipulated two independent variables: the

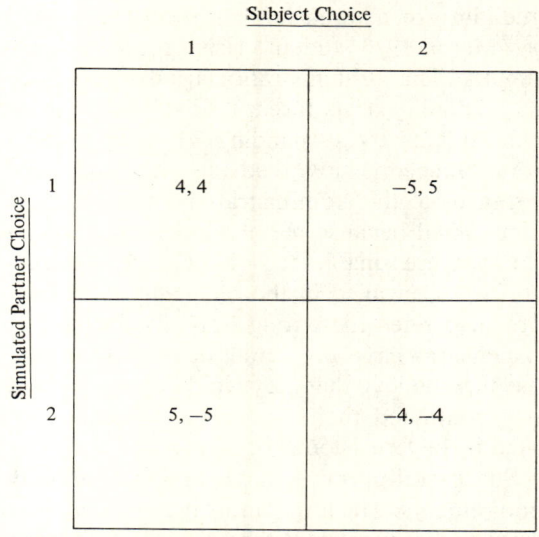

FIGURE 11-1. Prisoner's Dilemma game matrix used by Horai and Tedeschi (1969). The first payoff in each cell goes to the simulated partner and the second to the subject.

magnitude of punishment threatened (5, 10, or 20 points) and one element of threat credibility, the percentage of times the threat was actually carried out on trials in which the subject failed to comply with the threat (10%, 50%, and 90%). The results provided support for two conclusions: People comply to threats more readily (1) the greater the punishment threatened and (2) the more often the threatener has enforced his threats in the past. On the basis of subsequent studies, Tedeschi (1970) has modified these conclusions and now holds that they apply only when the magnitude of the punishment threatened is discriminably greater than the loss that will be incurred if the target complies.

In a parallel study that employed a similar method, Lindskold, Cullen, Gahagan, and Tedeschi (1970) found support for the assumption that people comply to promises more readily (1) the greater the reward promised and (2) the more often the promiser has followed

---

[1]The Prisoner's Dilemma has an interesting feature that is not relevant to the present context but has been the subject of much research (Vinacke, 1969; Wrightsman, O'Connor, & Baker, 1972). On any trial, both parties are tempted to choose option 2 because it provides greater immediate payoffs. Yet, paradoxically, they are both better off if both choose option 1 than if both choose option 2. Many real-life situations have this structure, including some with moral implications.

through on his promises in the past. Again it appears that these conclusions are valid only when the magnitude of the reward promised is discriminably greater than the gains that accrue from failure to comply (Tedeschi, 1970).

Other research in the Tedeschi tradition (Tedeschi, Bonoma, & Schlenker, 1972) indicates that threats are more credible when delivered by a disliked, as opposed to a liked, source.

Mogy and Pruitt (1974) have investigated the impact on the target's behavior of the costs incurred by the threatener if he enforces his threat. Their method was quite similar to that employed by Horai and Tedeschi, except that a different Prisoner's Dilemma matrix was used (the payoffs were 11, 11; −10, 20; 20, −10; 9, 9) and points were allegedly taken away from the threatener whenever he enforced a threat. The target (the subject) always lost 25 points when a threat was enforced, while the threatener (the simulated partner) purportedly lost 5, 15, 25, 35, or 45 points, depending on the experimental condition. Credibility was measured by means of a question about the partner's likelihood of enforcing his threat. The results from the first trial involving a threat are presented in Figure 11-2. They clearly suggest that the credibility of a threat and compliance to it are an inverse function of the cost of enforcement. The more painful it is for the threatener to carry out his threat, the less credible and effective it will be.

No research has been done on the impact of surveillance on conformity to threats and promises, but two studies by Kelley and Ring (Kelley & Ring, 1961; Ring & Kelley, 1963) are related to this issue. These authors point out that people are often motivated to conceal their noncompliance from a source of influence. This can be a particular problem when compliance is being sought in the realm of ideas, as in teaching spelling or arithmetic to a child, because ideas are so easy to conceal. The solution suggested by these authors is to motivate the target

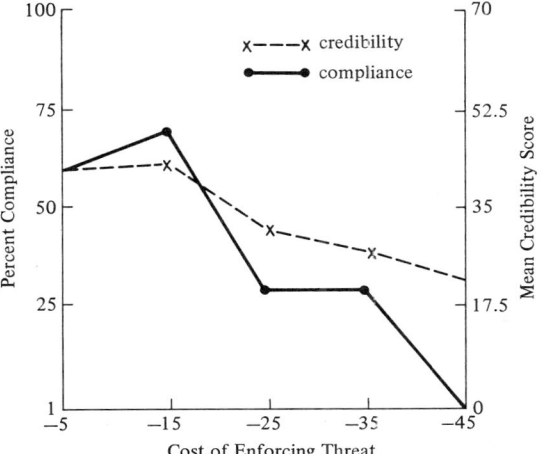

FIGURE 11-2. Credibility and compliance on the first trial involving a threat (from Mogy & Pruitt, 1974).

to submit to surveillance. One can proceed directly, by rewarding him for submitting such evidence and/or punishing him for failing to submit it. Or if such an approach is not feasible, the same result can often be achieved indirectly by providing him a great deal of reward when he presents evidence of compliance (e.g., correct answers in homework problems) and very little if any penalty when he presents evidence of noncompliance (e.g., wrong answers in homework problems).

The results reviewed so far in this section are concerned with compliance at the time of a threat or promise, when the target is more or less under the source's surveillance. Research in the dissonance tradition suggests that threats and promises can also have a longer-range effect which is due to attitude change and hence does not require surveillance. Ironically, if the target initially complies, long-range effects are pretty much the reverse of those obtained in Tedeschi's laboratory. The *smaller* the punishment threatened, the more likely is the target to tell himself that he did the right thing and hence to continue to comply when surveillance is lifted (Aronson & Carlsmith, 1963; Freedman, 1965). Similarly, he is more likely to develop attitudes that rationalize his behavior when he complies to the promise of a small reward than when he complies to the promise of a large one (Festinger & Carlsmith, 1959; Linder, Cooper & Jones, 1967).

The implications of these research findings for Mr. X are fairly clear. The incentives he uses to reward the faithful for hard work or punish them for doing nothing should be sufficiently large to outweigh the cost of the work itself, so as to ensure compliance; but they should be sufficiently small that the faithful experience dissonance concerning their compliance, which can be resolved by developing positive attitudes toward the work. To obtain compliance, he must also be fairly consistent in his enforcement of threats and punishments and should choose penalties that are not so costly to himself as to lack credibility. Incentives should be arranged in such a way that the faithful are motivated to submit evidence of their efforts and accomplishments so that surveillance will be reliable. This is likely to require that Mr. X place more emphasis on rewarding compliance than on punishing noncompliance.

Resistance to the Use of Threats and Promises

Threats are often abrasive because they tend to impose *psychological costs* on the target. For example, the target may find surveillance distasteful, or he may resent the implication inherent in being threatened that his status is lower than that of the source (Kelley, 1965). The cost to the target is obvious if he fails to comply and penalties are actually imposed. On the other hand, if he complies, he may have the uncomfortable feeling that his freedom is being restricted without compensation, in other words, that he is being exploited.

Threats impose heavier psychological costs under some circumstances than under others. When the threatener's status is already higher than that of the target, the latter is not so likely to be offended by the status implications of a threat (Deutsch, 1973). The more legitimate a threat, the less likely it is to give offense (French & Raven, 1959). (We are surrounded at all times by legitimate threats that give us little concern, for example, the threat of arrest for not stopping at a red light. But nonlegitimate, and especially illegitimate, threats often give offense.) In addition, Kelley (1965) has suggested that people are less offended by threats that serve strong needs than those that serve weak needs, because the former are "more in the nature of a frantic plea for help than an attempt at intimidation." Likewise, threats whose rationale is carefully explained are probably more palatable, on the whole, than those that are imposed without comment, because the latter are more likely to seem arbitrary. Threats that are aimed at stopping an ongoing activity are probably more enraging than those intended to deter an activity that has not begun. Threats that are directed toward the target as an individual rather than toward a group of which he is a member are particularly unpleasant, as are threats that are delivered in front of an audience he hopes to impress (Johnson, 1971). It also seems reasonable to suppose that threats which are accompanied by promises are not so likely to be resented as are threats alone.

Because of the costs often associated with threats, the targets toward whom they are directed frequently adopt *countermeasures* that are designed to undermine the influence of the threatener, either in the present or at a later point in time. These include: (1) Making a counterthreat: "If you punish me, I shall punish you in return." Threats are often followed by counterthreats (Hornstein, 1965). (2) Avoiding receipt of the threat (Schelling, 1960). It will be hard for Mr. X to justify punishing a constituent if the latter can convincingly claim that he never heard of the new incentive system. (3) Avoiding surveillance. (4) Calling on other people (e.g., other members of the party) to persuade the threatener to withdraw or not enforce his threat. (5) Developing a credible counterthreat capacity, e.g., seeking information about the threatener that can be used to embarrass him if he employs threats again or, in international relations, building retaliatory missiles.

Emerson (1962) has described five additional countermeasures, which he calls "power balancing operations." These are designed to combat the source's long-run power by diminishing the target's dependence on the source or increasing the source's dependence on the target. These measures are: (6) Developing relations with other people who can be called on for future protection from the threatener. In international relations, this would entail building defensive alliances. (7) Withdrawing from association with the threatener, e.g., dropping out of the party. This strategy, which is particularly likely to be employed in a voluntary organization, was encountered earlier in the discussion of legitimate influence. (8) Seeking viable substitutes for association with the threatener (e.g., for party membership) that satisfy the needs currently satisfied by this association, so as to be able to threaten to withdraw if he employs threats in the future. For example, some of the faithful could join or form a rival political organization and hence credibly threaten to leave the Democratic Party if Mr. X continues to employ his incentive system. (Such a threat need not be explicitly voiced to be communicated.) (9) Losing interest in the needs or values upon which the penalty is based. For example, some of the faithful who are threatened with loss of status in the party for not working hard enough could decide that this status is not worth having. (10) According so much status, attention, love, and affection to the threatener that he feels guilty about making further threats or enforcing penalties.

Emerson argues that, when power is balanced, it is usually not completely cancelled out. Rather, each party comes to have power over the other. Each can take the role of source at one time and target at another. Such an outcome can be visualized for operations 6, 8, 9 and 10. But the case of operation 7 seems to be different, in that withdrawing from association with the source completely cancels the source's power.

Emerson argues that his power balancing operations can account for the emergence of some elements of group structure. Status hierarchies are, at least in part, due to operation 10, in which the group neutralizes some of the power of its strongest members by according them status and thus making them emotionally dependent on the group. Group norms that regulate the use of power are produced by operation 6, in which subgroups coalesce to divert the behavior of the more powerful group members into acceptable channels.

Promises and rewards do not usually pose the same costs as threats and penalties. But they can be distasteful if a costly type of compliance is required in exchange for meager compensation, or if they are seen as illegitimate (e.g., as "bribes"). A comparable set of countermeasures is available for protection against the power of promises or to force the source to increase the level of reward that is promised in exchange for a given degree of compliance. But such countermeasures are not so likely to be employed as in the case of threats.

Conflict Spirals

Threats also sometimes have the effect of creating a *conflict spiral* (Deutsch, 1973), in which the target responds with counterthreats and retaliatory measures that provoke further threats and other coercive measures from the source. Such spirals, which have other sources as well, can go on and on. When they do, conflict is progressively intensified. Anger and hostility materialize, communication between the parties deteriorates, a "devil" image of the adversary may develop, short-range and impoverished thinking ensues, and tactics and bargaining positions become more rigid. Such dynamics are the basis of ghetto riots, arms races, and sometimes, as in 1914, wars. Such events leave community scars that may encourage the development of future conflict (Coleman, 1957).

Conflict spirals are not an inevitable outcome of the use of threats. The likelihood of their development depends on the extent to which the target resents the threat and the extent to which the source resents any retaliation that is initiated by the target. In addition, their development is inhibited by such factors as a sense of membership in the same community, a perception that the other party's cooperation is needed in other situations, conflict-limiting norms, and the activities of third parties who attempt to resolve or suppress the conflict in the interest of peace in the broader community (Deutsch, 1973).

In a study where both parties had the capacity to threaten one another, Hornstein (1965) found more conflict spirals when the parties were able to hurt each other moderately than when they had small or large coercive capability. Presumably counterthreats and retaliation are relatively unlikely when both parties have low coercive capacity because they seem so ineffective, and they are relatively unlikely when both have high coercive capacity because of fear of a ruinous conflict spiral. This leaves intermediate levels, where conflict spirals are most likely to occur.

Hornstein also found that a slight inequality of coercive potential was more likely to lead to a conflict spiral than equal potential or a large inequality. Both the weaker and the stronger party issued more counter-threats, and fewer agreements were reached when the disparity in threat potential was small than when it was large or nonexistent.

Evaluation of Threats and Conflict Spirals

The use of threats as a mode of influence is often ill-advised, because they so frequently elicit resentment, countermeasures, and conflict spirals. Indeed, threat use may be quite self-defeating in that it damages or destroys other existing forms of power. This is obvious if the target of a threat withdraws from association with the threatener, because all forms of power require some sort of contact between source and target. In addition, the target of a threat or penalty often begins to dislike the source (Kipnis, 1958; Raven & French, 1958; Zipf, 1960), thus endangering the latter's referent power. The use of threats may also reduce reciprocal power. To the extent that other forms of power are destroyed, the leader will have to rely further on coercive power, and the use of coercive power may become self-reinforcing.

In contrast, it can be argued that the use of reward power enhances referent power by heightening attraction and hence identification (French & Raven, 1959). Hence one is tempted to advise the use of promises rather than threats where other forms of power are unavailable or too weak.

While such advice is often quite appropriate, one must be careful not to overgeneralize about the relative value of threats as compared with promises. In one sense, promises are more costly than threats, because something must be given in exchange for conformity and there are always limits to how much one can give. Imagine the misallocation of resources in a family with small children if the parents had to provide a tangible reward (e.g., money or candy) every time a child conformed to a rule of good conduct! Praise and warmth are, of course, alternative media of exchange in the family and can also be used to reward children. But beyond a certain level, where the child becomes satiated, neither they nor any other form of reward can be effective.

The solution to this problem in most families is to mix rewards and punishments, promises and threats. Conformity is rewarded within a range of more-or-less acceptable behavior. But outside limits on the child's behavior are set by threats, which include as a major component, but are usually not limited to, the withdrawal of accustomed rewards. Such a strategy is usually reciprocal, in that the child also exercises some coercive influence over the parent. In relations between adults, threats are ordinarily less explicit than between children or between parents and children but are nevertheless always present to guard the limits of acceptable behavior on both sides.

Conflict spirals have the capacity, at times, to create tragedies, such as the involvement of the United States and North Vietnam in the Vietnamese War. Yet it is also necessary to be careful not to overgeneralize about their harmfulness. Short conflict spirals (lovers' quarrels, childrens' fights) are a common feature of many dyadic relationships. They are typically arrested by a variety of mechanisms before they go too far. Such spirals are usually benign and may, at times, have benevolent effects on the relationship in the form of (1) clarifying one's own and the other party's needs so that more rewarding patterns of interaction can be negotiated and (2) generating enough concern about the future of the relationship to motivate problem solving about how to improve it. In addition, some relationships deserve to be broken up, and conflict spirals do so. Furthermore conflict spirals are an inevitable, and often essential, part of social change—including change for the better.

Advice to Prospective Leaders

Because his party is a voluntary organization whose members can easily withdraw, Mr. X should keep his use of threats to a minimum, though he cannot avoid them altogether. Promises are less problematical, but also pose some difficulties. Hence a more effective approach to using the rewards Mr. X controls might well be to dispense them on a noncontingent basis at first, providing them to those of the faithful who seem most likely to devote time to the party, in the hope of generating reciprocity. Later those constituents who have provided the greatest benefit to the party could be further rewarded.

If Mr. X finds that he must use threats or promises, he should strive to gain the legitimate right to do so. This might mean persuading the executive committee or a gathering of the faithful as a whole of the merit of his proposed incentive scheme.

As in the case of legitimate influence, Mr. X would be well advised to try to strengthen the bonds that attach the faithful to the party, by making the party seem more important to them. If he can do so, he will run less risk of driving people out of the party by threatening or penalizing them, and coercive tactics will become more viable. Indeed loss of membership in that august group, the party faithful, can become a potent threat if such membership becomes attractive.

INFLUENCE THROUGH ALLIES

So far, we have pictured the man who is trying to influence another as dealing directly with his target, but this is not a necessary element of influence. He can deal indirectly, by means of an intermediary or chain of intermediaries. Indeed this is essential in large organizations, because one man at the top cannot have access to everybody. For example, Mr. X may deal with some of his constituents through political allies or lieutenants. The types of influence used at different points in this chain may vary. Thus, Mr. X's power over a particular lieutenant might result from the favors he has performed in the past and can perform in the future (reciprocal and reward influence), while his lieutenant's power could be due to the fact that some of the faithful like and admire him (referent power).

Having allies in a group tends to strengthen an individual in another way: It makes him more likely to try to exert influence on behalf of his ideas or interests, in other words, to use his power. There are rational reasons for this effect, in that an alliance usually combines the power of its members and hence is more likely to be successful than an individual. But there are irrational reasons as well. One person acting alone may begin to doubt the validity of a position that is challenged by others and not press his point. But this is much less likely to happen if he has the support of even a single other group member (Asch, 1956). Furthermore the support of one or a few other group members can cushion the ego against the embarrassment of being rejected by the group and hence increase the likelihood of taking the kinds of psychological risk that may be needed to launch a persuasive campaign. To summarize, having allies makes it psychologically possible to be assertive. Because of this, efforts to create change in groups, organizations, and nations often begin with the mutual identification of one another by a set of like-thinking individuals (Dahrendorf, 1959).

THE POWER OF THE GROUP

The discussion so far has been one-sided in stressing what Mr. X, or any group leader, can do as an individual to increase the productivity of his group. But Mr. X cannot be a one-man show. If the Democratic Party which he heads is to be successful, the party faithful as a group must also take a great deal of responsibility for its success (Katz & Kahn, 1966). To be effective, the group as a whole, or subgroups thereof, must (1) adopt a set of goals and plans that are relevant to winning the next election and (2) influence its members to work toward these goals and on these plans. Mr. X might well put the bulk of his time into facilitating these group activities rather than into efforts to influence individual workers.

The capacity of a group to influence its members can be called the "power of the group," a concept that sounds more mystical than it really is. Group power is identical with the capacity of group members to influence one another on behalf of group goals, group tasks, and group norms.

The power that a group has over one of its members depends, in large part, on the extent to which that member finds the group attractive and sees his membership as important (Cartwright, 1968). Hence, once again, we see the need for Mr. X to devote his energies to the task of enhancing the attractiveness and importance of the party to the erstwhile "faithful."

The attractiveness and importance of a group to its members is sometimes called "group cohesiveness." Cohesive groups are not only more capable of influencing their members but also more likely to try to influence them (Festinger, 1950).

Cohesiveness has a number of roots. Research by Back (1951) suggests that it is a function of the extent to which members (1) can find one another attractive, (2) view the goals of the group as worthwhile, or (3) perceive the group as having prestige in the outer community. Raven and Rietsema (1957) have supplemented Back's second point with the observation that cohesiveness is a function of the extent to which group goals are viewed as clearly formulated and likely to be achieved. Groups whose members must work together to achieve their ends tend to be more cohesive than those whose members compete with one another (Deutsch, 1973). On the other hand, competition with an outgroup, or another threat from the outside world, can enhance attraction to one's group (Mulder & Sterding, 1963). In our society, groups that are democratically organized, with broad participation in decision making, tend to be more cohesive than those in which decision making is narrowly concentrated at the top (Cartwright, 1968).

A number of the points just made may be useful to Mr. X. We realize he could try to strengthen ties between the faithful as individuals by bringing them into more frequent contact with each other, for example, in a series of meetings or parties. He might make an effort to build the prestige of the party by recruiting already-prestigeful members of the community. An endorsement of the local party by a national leader might also help in this connection. In addition, he should try to get the faithful as deeply involved in party decision making as is practical.

The power of a group is also a function of the clarity of its goals and norms and the unanimity with which they are supported. Furthermore, for groups to be effective in their mission, it is necessary that they have goals and norms that are appropriate to that mission.

In our society, group goals and norms are frequently determined by the group as a whole or by elected representatives. Decisions made in this fashion tend to be more motivating than those made more narrowly (Coch & French, 1948). Hence, in addition to, or instead of, spending his time trying to persuade individual group members to work harder, Mr. X might make an effort to organize meetings and discussions about the party's goals and activities. What power he has will often be better devoted to persuading people to come to planning meetings, pushing task-relevant ideas, and trying to build consensus in these meetings than to pressuring individuals to do more work.

Democratic decision making, involving all group members either directly or through their representatives, has been recommended several times in the last few paragraphs. It appears to have four functions: (1) strengthening cohesiveness, (2) increasing the chances that a decision will be consonant with the needs and values of the people who must implement it, (3) increasing the likelihood that a decision will be seen as a legitimate group norm or goal, and (4) heightening the sense of identification with a decision by the individuals who feel that they have participated in making it. All of these functions can contribute to group effectiveness in a situation such as that facing Mr. X. However, it must be borne in mind that democratic decision making can be carried too far, by involving so many people in so many decisions that they have little time left for effective pursuit of group goals. People can also feel overburdened by "too many meetings." Hence some sort of balance must be struck between the need to consult group members and the need to move ahead.

BARGAINING

There has been one major oversimplification in our discussion of power. The source of an influence attempt has been pictured as either successful or unsuccessful at altering his target's behavior. In reality, even when he is quite successful, he must often settle for less than he initially requested. A compromise, which lies somewhere between total compliance and absolute failure to comply, emerges from his interaction with the target. For example, Mr. X might propose that each of the faithful be required to register 50 new voters. Even if he were in a powerful position, his board of directors might ratify a quota of only 35, meeting his request only part-way because they are reluctant to overburden the membership.

When the source employs information, expert, co-oriented, referent, or reciprocal power, the nature of the compromise is totally in the hands of the target. But in the case of reward, coercive, and legitimate power, it often emerges as a tacit or explicit agreement between target and source. The target agrees to comply partially in exchange for the source's willingness to provide rewards, withhold penalties, or agree that the target has fulfilled his obligations. The sequence of events that lead to such an agreement can be called "bargaining."

Paraphrasing Nemeth (1972), bargaining can be defined as the process by which at least two parties with initially different preferences make a series of concessions in search of a solution which is mutually satisfactory. This definition has five main parts:

1. The *process* of bargaining always consists of an interaction between the parties. This interaction may be verbal, with each party stating its proposals and the arguments favoring them, in which case we speak of "negotiation." Or the interaction may be nonverbal, consisting only of moves and countermoves, which is called "tacit bargaining." The distinction between these two kinds of bargaining can be illustrated by the case of two travelers sitting next to each other with a common armrest between them. They might discuss the use of the armrest and negotiate a verbal agreement about its use. Alternatively they might both put up their elbows and work out a tacit agreement by means of a series of shoves and retreats. Some agreements are worked out by a combination between negotiation and tacit bargaining.

Most research on bargaining deals with negotiation. Hence, this topic will be of central concern in the rest of this chapter. The research on this topic is more difficult to grasp than that on power. But careful attention will reward the reader.

2. Bargaining often involves more than two *parties*. However, this discussion will be devoted exclusively to the two-party case, which has been the focus of most of the research in this area.

3. Several alternative solutions are always available in bargaining; and at the beginning of interaction, the parties always have *different preferences* among them.

4. We can speak of a "proposal" when one bargainer suggests an alternative to the other. Thus Mr. X might initially propose a quota of 50 new registrations, and his board a quota of 25. When a new proposal is worth less to a bargainer than his just previous proposal, we say that a *concession* has been made—for example, if Mr. X comes down from 50 to 45. Bargaining, and especially negotiation, often proceeds by both parties making a series of concessions.

5. If bargaining is successful, a *mutually satisfactory solution* will be found—not one about which the bargainers are necessarily ecstatic, but one with which they can both live and which will end the controversy.

Bargaining is not always successful. Sometimes no agreement is reached, and the bargainers try other ways to satisfy their needs or alter these needs.

Bargaining was introduced as a process that often follows an influence attempt. But this is not the only place where bargaining is found. When two parties are in conflict or competition, they will sometimes jointly decide that they must negotiate their differences. In such cases, entry into bargaining is often a very difficult and yet crucial first step toward conflict resolution. There are also circumstances that require a joint decision before either party can proceed—e.g., the division of profits in a partnership, the division of labor between two workers assigned to repair a single piece of machinery, or legally prescribed negotiation over the terms of a new labor-management contract when an old one is expiring. Here bargaining is mandated by the situation.

Four basic research questions can be asked about bargaining: (1) What determines the likelihood of reaching agreement in bargaining? (2) If agreement is reached, what determines the speed at which it will be reached? (3) Under what circumstances will one party do substantially better than the other in the final agreement? (4) Under what circumstances will the parties be able to find nonobvious alternatives that are highly beneficial to both sides? Most of the rest of this chapter will be devoted to answering these questions.

Motivation in Bargaining

Two sets of motivational concepts have been particularly useful for understanding the behavior of bargainers and hence the outcome of bargaining. One characterizes the bargainers' ultimate goals, the other their perceptions of what is needed to achieve these goals.

Ultimate goals can be described in terms of two concepts: level of aspiration (LOA) and limit. A bargainer's LOA is the level of benefit toward which he is currently working. It is also sometimes called his "target point." For example, at the beginning of bargaining, Mr. X might be working toward a goal of 45 new registrants (his proposal of 50 being a tactic aimed at achieving this goal), while his board might have a goal of 30. A bargainer's limit is the smallest level of value acceptable to him in the foreseeable future. Operationally it is that level below which he would rather break off negotiation than reach agreement. Thus Mr. X might be unwilling to concede below 30 and his board of directors unwilling to move above 40.[2] The limit is also sometimes called the "fall-back position" or "resistance point." LOA is always equal to or greater than limit.

Four concerns or orientations can also be described that represent the bargainers' perceptions of how to achieve their goals:

1. The *distributive orientation,* which is the desire to gain concessions from the other party and which leads to the use of "distributive tactics" such as making extreme proposals, committing oneself to one's current position, making threats, and attacking the rationale underlying the other party's position. This orientation is ordinarily adopted on the assumption that gains in the negotiation must be achieved at the expense of the other party. This assumption is sometimes correct but tends to rule out the possibility of discovering new alternatives that benefit both parties more fully than those currently under consideration.

2. *Defensiveness,* the desire to avoid exploitation by the other party. This concern develops when bargainers suspect their adversary of being distributively oriented. It leads them to adopt distributive tactics in return.

3. The *problem-solving orientation,* which is the desire to find a point of agreement that satisfies both parties. This orientation is often instrumental to the discovery of new and better alternatives.

4. The *desire to reach agreement,* which leads to a reduced level of aspiration, concession making, and efforts to coordinate the exchange of concessions.

Research on Level of Aspiration. The earliest experimental research on negotiation was performed by Siegel and Fouraker (1960). In their experiments, two subjects were used at a time, one acting as seller and the other as buyer of a commodity whose identity was not revealed. The task was to reach agreement on both the price of the commodity and the quantity to be exchanged. Each party had a payoff schedule that showed the value to him of each combination of quantity and price. No information was available on the other party's payoff schedule. An individualistic orientation was used, the subjects being told that they should attempt to "get the largest possible profit" and being led to believe that they would actually be paid their profit at the end of the experiment. The sub-

---

[2] In this example the two parties' limits are compatible. But this does not guarantee that they will reach agreement, because their LOA's may be so far apart that one or both of them despairs of reaching agreement and breaks off negotiation.

jects sat apart from each other and negotiated by sending notes, on which only a quantity and price could be written. Negotiation was continued until agreement was reached. Level of aspiration (LOA) was manipulated by telling the subjects that they would have a chance, in a second part of the study, "to double the amount of money you take home, at no cost to you." High aspiration subjects were told that they could get into this second part by making a profit of at least $6.10. For low aspiration subjects, the required minimal profit was $2.10. A high-aspiration subject always negotiated with a low-aspiration subject. The payoff schedules provided five alternatives that satisfied both parties' LOA's, whether the buyer or the seller had the higher LOA.

The results from this experiment were very simple: While not every subject achieved his aspiration, the bargainer with the higher LOA achieved a higher profit in 10 of the 11 dyads run.

Using a different experimental task, Kahan (1968) manipulated LOA while keeping it equal for the two bargainers. He found that more time was required to reach agreement the higher the joint LOA (sum of the individual LOA's). Had he not required all dyads to reach agreement, it seems reasonable to suppose that he would have found more dyads breaking off negotiation the higher the joint LOA.

The results from these two studies can be summarized as follows: The higher a bargainer's aspirations, the less likely are he and his partner to reach agreement and the longer it will take them if they are successful. But if and when agreement is reached, a bargainer's profits will be greater the higher his aspirations.

Process information from other studies (Holmes, Throop, & Strickland, 1971; Yukl, 1972) provides a simple, plausible explanation for the results just cited. The higher a bargainer's LOA, the more extreme (in the direction of his own interests) will be his initial proposal and, often, the slower will be his concession rate. Hence his demand level will be more extreme at any given time. Assuming that this is true at the point of agreement, the bargainer with the higher LOA will achieve an agreement that is more in his interest. But the higher is one party's LOA, the farther apart will the two parties be at any given time; hence it will take them longer to reach agreement, and one or both of them will be more likely to despair of reaching agreement and break off negotiation.

The results of these studies permit us to link the process and outcome of negotiation to existing theories about the determinants of LOA. For example, LOA has been found to be a positive function of an individual's own degree of past success in similar endeavors and a positive function of the past successes of people with whom he identifies (Lewin, Dembo, Festinger, & Sears, 1944). Later in this section, evidence will be provided that LOA also responds to perceptions of where the other party's limit is located.

Research on Limit. Bargainers do not always have clear notions about the location of their limits (their fall-back or resistance points). But when they do, these limits influence their behavior.

In a study performed by Kelley, Beckman, and Fischer (1967), pairs of subjects played a card game in which they held up black cards simultaneously. Play continued until the sum of the cards held up equaled nine. Each subject was then paid in points the amount to which his black card exceeded a red limit card which had earlier been dealt to him. This limit card thus represented the minimum level to which he could go with his black card and still break even. If one of the bargainers did not feel that he would be able to reach his limit, he could break off negotiation and receive zero points.

Some of the results were very similar to those already found for LOA: The greater the joint limit (sum of the two individual limits), the fewer agreements were reached and the longer it took to reach agreement. When the two bargainers had unequal limits, the one with the higher limit usually held up a higher card in the final agreement.

Another finding was that bargainers easily made concessions when they were far from their limit but reduced their demands more slowly as they approached it. Perhaps, as a bargainer approaches his limit, he becomes afraid that further concessions will reveal the exact location of this limit, or perhaps he wishes to retain room to maneuver. This finding is probably related to the common observation that larger concessions are ordinarily made in the earlier, as opposed to the later, parts of negotiation (Komorita & Barnes, 1969; Pruitt & Drews, 1969; Pruitt & Johnson, 1970), since at a later stage one is ordinarily closer to one's limit.

In a partial replication of the Kelley, Beckman, and Fischer study, Schoeninger and Wood (1969) found similar results for subjects who were strangers to each other, but not for married couples. As joint limit increased, the strangers took longer to reach agreement and more often broke off negotiation, as in the earlier study. But married couples showed neither effect, and they usually reached agreement. These results were apparently due to a difference in the approach to negotiation. Strangers usually displayed a distributive orientation, starting with high demands, conceding slowly, exaggerating their limits and trying to persuade the adversary to make concessions. Married couples more often showed a problem-solving orientation, in which they exchanged truthful information about limits and developed a joint strategy for gaining as much as possible for the dyad as a whole.

Time Pressure. Negotiation tends to fill up all available time (Kelley, 1966). One possible reason for this is that negotiators typically wait for a long time, hoping that the other party will make the next concession. The more time is available, the longer they wait.

When one or both parties feel time pressure, negotiation tends to speed up (Komorita & Barnes, 1969). Time pressure may be imposed by such factors as the cost of maintaining a negotiation team in the field, the need to get started on implementing the agreement, or the perceived possibility that the other party will drop out of the negotiation or rescind recent concessions if there is no progress. Time pressure apparently has its effect by heightening the desire to reach agreement and thus inducing a lower LOA, which shows up in less extreme proposals (Pruitt & Drews, 1969; Yukl, 1972).

The party who feels greater time pressure in negotiation is at a disadvantage, because he must make a less extreme initial proposal and/or concede more rapidly than his adversary. For this reason, negotiators often try to manipulate time pressure for strategic reasons, increasing the time pressure on the adversary and decreasing it on themselves.

Other Determinants of the Process and Outcome of Bargaining

Reactions to the Other Party's Behavior. In the material presented so far, bargainers have been treated as if they were alone in the situation, making occasional concessions as a function of their LOA and limit, but not reacting to the other party until the point of agreement. Such an approach, which is explicitly taken by Kelley, Beckman, and Fischer (1967), can account for numerous findings. But there are some results that can only be explained by assuming that bargainers react to the other party's situation and behavior.

The most significant study on this topic has been performed by Liebert, Smith, Hill, and

TABLE 11-1
Results from Study by Liebert, Smith, Hill, and Keiffer (1968)

	Favorable first bid		Unfavorable first bid	
	Complete information	Incomplete information	Complete information	Incomplete information
Value of initial proposal	3220	3570	3394	3210
Value of final agreement	646.5	765.5	628.0	525.7
Number of bids to contract	3.8	10.4	10.2	8.3

Kieffer (1968). The task involved negotiation in the laboratory between buyer and seller in a hypothetical used car market. The seller's profit was the difference between the cost of the car to him ($2500) and what the buyer would pay for it. The buyer's profit was the difference between what he paid for the car and the price for which he could sell it ($3500). Thus to the extent they were logical, the seller's limit was $2500 and the buyer's, $3500. The buyer always made the first proposal. In actual fact, all subjects played the role of seller, and the buyer was a programmed input from the experimenter. Two variables were manipulated: (1) the buyer's initial proposal ("first bid"), which was either favorable ($3050) or unfavorable ($2615) to the subject, and (2) the information available to the subject about the buyer's limit, the subject being either informed (he knew the other's limit) or uninformed (he did not know it).

The results from this study are shown in Table 11-1. Uninformed bargainers made more extreme initial proposals when the other party's first bid was favorable than when it was unfavorable. Their final profit from the sale of the car was also greater when they had received a more favorable first bid. Informed bargainers, on the other hand, reacted to an unfavorable first bid with a more extreme counterproposal and took longer to reach agreement.

These results can be easily interpreted if we assume that a bargainer's LOA will be higher, and his proposals therefore more extreme, to the extent that the other party's limit seems favorable to him. (In terms of the task used in this experiment, this assumption is that the seller will aspire to achieving a higher price, and will consequently ask for more, to the extent that he thinks the buyer's maximal price is high.) The interpretation is in two parts: (1) When the other's limit is unknown, it must be inferred from available information, such as the other party's initial proposal. The more extreme this proposal, the less favorable the other's limit is assumed to be. Hence the lower will be the bargainer's LOA and the less extreme his proposals, as was found for the uninformed bargainers. (2) When bargainers believe that they know the other's limit, another dynamic comes into play. The other is seen as *bluffing* when he makes an extreme initial proposal. Hence his intentions are seen as distributive, and the bargainer becomes defensive. He counters with distributive behavior of his own, taking an extreme initial proposal and conceding from this position only when the other party concedes, as was found for the informed bargainers.

Liebert's results suggest the following advice for a bargainer who wishes to achieve a settlement that is favorable to himself: If the other knows little about one's limit, one should start with an extreme demand and concede slowly. One should also try to conceal and, if possible, exaggerate one's limit, to make the other party think that settlement is possible only on one's terms. The better informed the other party is about one's limit, the less demanding one should be, unless the other party is very demanding. The reason is that if one's proposals are too extreme, the other party will see one as bluffing and become defensive and rigid.

These findings also suggest that one should try to find out as much as possible about the other party's limit so as to set a realistic LOA and to detect when the other is bluffing. The detailed defense of their own positions which bargainers customarily make at the beginning of negotiation provides an opportunity for each party to gain some information about the other's limit. This defense is ordinarily conducted in logical and factual terms, so that it is harder to conceal or exaggerate one's limit than it would be if there were no such defense.

Liebert's finding that people behave more distributively when they perceive their opponent's behavior as distributive has considerable generality. This phenomenon was encountered earlier, in the finding that threats tend to elicit counterthreats (Hornstein, 1965).

Other research suggests that bargainers tend to match the other party's *concession rate* (Chertkoff & Conley, 1967; Pruitt & Johnson, 1970). When he concedes, they often concede; when he fails to concede, they often fail to concede. There is one exception to this generalization, in the case where the other party concedes at every opportunity, regardless of the bargainer's behavior. Some bargainers match his concessions, while others stop conceding altogether and thus exploit him (Maciejko, 1972). The tendency to match the other party's concession rate may be due to a desire to reward him for conceding, a sense that one is obliged to reciprocate his concessions, or to a tendency to behave distributively when the other party's actions seem to indicate that he has a distributive orientation.

Findings with respect to the impact of the other party's *concession size* are fairly consistent under conditions of high time pressure, where reaching agreement is important and there is a real danger that negotiation will end in the near future without agreement. Under such conditions, small concessions from the other party lead most bargainers to make large concessions (Komorita & Barnes, 1969; Druckman, Zechmeister, & Solomon, 1972; Yukl, 1972). No clearcut generalizations have emerged from studies under low time pressure.

Prominent Solutions and Fairness. Except for the material on married couples, the theory presented so far has pictured the results of negotiation as emerging exclusively from the extremity of the two parties' demands. Only variables that affect initial demand and the speed of concession-making have been reviewed. While this approach has considerable value, it would appear to be incomplete, in that certain alternatives may have an inherent attractiveness that makes them candidates for the final solution. If one party reaches such an alternative before the other, he may simply stop conceding and wait for the other to meet him. If the other party also finds this particular alternative acceptable, the negotiation will be easily settled. If not, it may be hard to settle; but the settlement is likely to be fairly close to the alternative that is inherently attractive.

Schelling (1960) has referred to alternatives that have special appeal to both parties as *prominent solutions*. Some solutions are prominent because they stand out perceptually, e.g., a river in a dispute over the location of a national boundary or the middle item in a list of options (Joseph & Willis, 1963). Others are prominent because of historical precedent, e.g., an old political border in a boundary dispute or a prior quota in Mr. X's dispute with his board of directors. Still others are prominent because they satisfy an ideal of "fairness" that is shared by both parties.

An example of an ideal of fairness would be the norm that recommends *equality* in the payoffs received by two similar parties. This norm was apparently operating in a study by Morgan and Sawyer (1967), where the payoffs for both parties were out in the open. When nonfriends bargained with each other, most dyads ended up with a solution that involved the same payoff, despite the fact that one party had to make much larger concessions than the other to reach this point.

Interestingly, even though they were only able to send messages about their proposals, bargainers who were friends more often agreed to a solution that provided unequal payoffs to the two parties but a greater joint payoff for the dyad as a whole. Again, as in the study of married couples, we find evidence that bargainers who value one another's welfare are more willing to accept a situation in which one party does substantially better than the other.

From the viewpoint of equity theory (Adams, 1965), the norm of equality applies only where the two parties are perceived to have equal inputs (age, status, or other indices of merit). This was true of Morgan and Sawyer's study, where the subjects were all 5th- and 6th-grade boys. Where inputs are unequal, the prominent solution may be more favorable to the party with greater inputs.

There are many different standards of fairness and equity, and wishful thinking is fully capable of determining the standard chosen by an individual. Hence bargainers do not always agree about which alternatives are fair and equitable and may spend considerable time and energy debating this matter without settling it (Pruitt, 1972). In such cases, ordinary concession dynamics are likely to determine the outcome.

When there is disagreement about the nature of a fair solution, bargainers are often tempted to employ distributive tactics in order to force the other party to accept an alternative that he considers unfair. However such a goal should not be adopted lightly, because it is likely to affect future relations between the two parties. A bargainer who has been forced to accept what he considers to be an unfair solution in the present may adopt countermeasures that make him harder to deal with in the future or may leave the relationship altogether. Hence it is not always wise to press one's maximal advantage in bargaining.

Intimacy of Communication and Machiavellianism. Bargaining is not always conducted on a face-to-face basis. Other possibilities are by telephone, message, or intermediary. The channels just mentioned can be ordered in degree of *intimacy*, from face-to-face (most intimate) to intermediary (least intimate). There is some evidence (Bavelas, et al., 1963; Morley & Stephenson, 1969, 1970; Vitz & Kite, 1970) that bargainers behave less distributively to the extent that the channels of communication are more intimate—taking more flexible positions and conceding more rapidly when they are face-to-face than when they are at a distance. This may tie in with the finding in other research that it is easier to impose costs on another party when he is at a greater physical distance (Gahagan, 1970; Milgram, 1963).

There is some evidence (Christie & Geis, 1970) that difficulty in holding firm in an intimate setting is more characteristic of low than of high machiavellians. Machiavellianism (mach) is a personality trait that is usually measured by means of a questionnaire. High machs have a less complimentary view of humanity and are less trusting, less bound by conventional morality, and more manipulative than low machs. In face-to-face settings, high machs are apparently more capable of maintaining an impersonal orientation toward self-interest, while low machs are more likely to become emotionally involved with the other bargainer and lose sight of their own personal interest as they respond to his feelings and needs. Hence high machs tend to do better than low machs when they bargain face-to-face with one another. This difference disappears when they interact at a distance, where it is easier for the low mach to retain an impersonal orientation toward self-interest. The difference also tends to diminish in face-to-face settings if the low mach bargainer has so much reason to be sure of the correctness of his position that he can ignore the entreaties of the high mach bargainer.

Third-Party Intervention. Third parties often intervene in bargaining, either as a result of being called in by the bargainers or on their own initiative. They frequently facilitate reaching agreement and can have a major impact on the nature of the agreement. There are dozens of ways in which a third party can be facilitative, including the following: providing a neutral location for negotiation, pointing out the dangers of no agreement or the benefits of agreement, educating the parties about the tradeoffs entailed in adopting too distributive an approach, locating new alternatives that are better for both parties than those currently under consideration, reassuring each party about the other's intentions, and coordinating concession making.

The functions just described are loosely called *mediation*. Another category of third-party intervention, where the third party decides on the final agreement, is called *binding arbitration*.

Mediators sometimes provide a simple suggestion for the final agreement. Research by Pruitt and Johnson (1970) indicates that such a suggestion is effective in precipitating a decision because it helps the bargainer save face with himself. If he concedes on his own, he tends to feel weak. But if he concedes on the basis of a mediator's suggestion, he can rationalize the concession to himself as following the advice of an expert counsellor, and he does not feel so weak.

In other research by the same authors (Johnson & Pruitt, 1972; Johnson & Tullar, 1972), bargainers were found to concede more rapidly when they anticipated that binding arbitration would be imposed on them in the future than when they anticipated mediation. This suggests that binding arbitration is distasteful to many bargainers, who prefer to make rapid concessions toward agreement rather than submit to such intervention. However, a cautionary note must be sounded with respect to this generalization: The prospect of binding arbitration can slow negotiation down rather than speed it up if one party believes that the arbitrator will side with him or be convinced by his arguments. Why compromise with the adversary if you think you can win at the hands of the arbitrator?

Negotiators Who Are Representatives. All of the research reviewed up to this point has dealt with the individual negotiator bargaining on his own behalf. However, in real life we very often find groups or organizations dealing with each other. In such cases, the actual negotiation is typically performed by an individual or small team that represents the group or organization. If one party does not have such a representative, the other will often insist that one be found, to simplify the communication channels and ensure that there is somebody on the other side who can be held responsible for executing the agreement. Other terms used for the representative are "agent" and "delegate."

The representative can be thought of as a middleman, whose job is to reconcile the interests of his own and the opposing team in consultation with the other team's representative. He negotiates not only with his opposite number but also with his constituents. Informed observers (Walton & McKersie, 1965) have alleged that, in intraparty negotiation, representatives tend to be more favorably inclined toward making concessions than are their constituents. This tendency probably arises in three ways: (1) Representatives often see their role as one of achieving agreement, which of course usually requires some concession making. (2) Representatives are typically better acquainted than are their constituents with the other party's priorities and hence are more realistic about the difficulty of achieving substantial concession from the other party that would obviate the necessity for their own party to make concessions. (3) Representatives have a more intimate relationship with the other party; hence, at least if they are low machs, they are less likely to take a harsh stance toward the other party's needs.

There are several ways in which a representative can relate to his constituents, and some of these affect his likelihood of making concessions. Benton (1972) has shown that a representative's willingness to make concessions depends, in part, on the extent of his *accountability*, in other words, the extent to which his constituents are able to reward or penalize him for his actions. He has found that representatives who are more accountable concede more slowly, take longer to reach agreement, and achieve more favorable settlements for their side. In a related study of the extent to which a representative is trusted, Frey and Adams (1972) found that a representative who knew he was not trusted was particularly unwilling to make concessions when the other bargainer was conciliatory and particularly willing to make concessions when the other was exploitative. This study shows that the behavior of a representative is a joint function of the behavior of his constituents and the behavior of the other negotiator.

Bargaining About Norms. The outcome of negotiation may be settlement of a single or a recurring issue. In the latter case, the outcome is a *norm* or rule which applies to various instances. Norm bargaining typically arises from circumstances in which two parties have reward or coercive power over one another on a continuing basis. One party's willingness to use his power benevolently is exchanged for the other's willingness to do the same.

Thibaut and his associates have found that norm bargaining is more likely to occur (1) the greater each party's capacity to affect the welfare of the other (Thibaut and Faucheux, 1965), (2) the larger each party's reputation for willingness to impose unfavorable outcomes on the other (Murdoch, 1967; Thibaut, 1968), and (3) when there has been prior experience with power use in the dyad (Murdoch & Rosen, 1970; Thibaut & Gruber, 1969).

Integrative Bargaining

We turn now to the question of how bargainers can locate and agree on the alternatives that are most beneficial to both of them. Such alternatives can be called "integrative solutions," because they reconcile or integrate the needs of the two parties. The process by which they are reached can be called "integrative bargaining" (Walton & McKersie, 1965).

An integrative solution to our hypothetical problem of registration quotas might be to set a quota of 25 new registrants per party member while hiring people to register additional voters. This would be a creative approach to reconciling Mr. X's need for a vigorous recruiting program with his board's fear of overburdening the faithful—better for the two sides taken collectively than a simple compromise on a quota of say 35.

The desirability of finding alternatives that provide high joint benefit to the bargainers can be defended per se. In addition, integrative bargaining is important to the extent that (1) limits are so high that agreement can be reached only if an alternative is found that is highly beneficial to both parties or (2) there is danger that the agreement will later become "unstuck" unless both parties are quite satisfied with it.

Integrative solutions are sometimes suggested by third parties, who often have greater perspective than the bargainers. But they can also be located by the bargainers themselves. Bargainers often have difficulty finding integrative solutions, for either or both of two reasons: (1) They may not know all of the possible alternatives. For example, it may be necessary for someone to have a flash of creative inspiration before Mr. X and his board of directors become aware of the possibility of hiring outside workers to supplement the work of the faithful. (2) They may not understand each other's profit structure well enough to be able to tell which of the known alternatives is best for both of them. (By "profit structure" is meant the other's values and how they relate to the elements of the negotiation problem at hand.)

Regardless of which of these two reasons is at work, one route to finding an integrative solution is for the bargainers to exchange valid information about their profit structures—i.e., to communicate about their needs and values and how these relate to the issues at hand. For example, Mr. X should explain in detail why he favors a high quota and his board should provide a similar explanation for its preference for a low one. With all this information out in the open, either (1) somebody may gain insight into a new approach that reconciles both party's needs or (2) it may be possible to identify a known alternative that is quite beneficial to both sides.

For bargainers to exchange such information, they need to have a problem-solving rather than a distributive orientation. They also need to trust each other, in the sense of believing that the other bargainer also has a problem-solving orientation and will not use the information divulged for distributive purposes. (For example, they have to believe that he will not simply use the information to ascertain the probable location of their limit and then demand that they concede to this limit.) Such trust sometimes derives from a sense that the other bargainer's interests are consonant with one's own in situations outside the issue under question. Such trust can also be derived from a belief that the other party is anxious to reach agreement and hence not likely to expend the time and effort needed to gain an advantage through distributive behavior (Pruitt, 1971b). Positive attitudes toward the other and a sense that he shares one's beliefs and values can also contribute to such trust (Deutsch, 1973).

When full information exchange is not possible because of the lack of trust, another approach to integrative bargaining can be taken. This involves what Pruitt and Lewis (1975) have called *heuristic trial and error*. The action is totally within the realm of proposal making and does not require communication about such sensitive matters as needs and values. The bargainers must frequently vary their proposals and seek one another's reactions to each proposal as a guide to developing new ones (e.g., Q: "What do you think of this one?" A: "It's better than the last one but still not good enough," or "It's not as good as the last one."). In addition, they must concede in a systematic fashion, exploring as many alternatives as possible at one level of profit to them-

TABLE 11-2
Buyer and Seller Payoff Schedules Used by Pruitt and Lewis (1975)

	Buyer						Seller					
	Iron		Sulphur		Coal		Iron		Sulphur		Coal	
	Price	Profit	Price	Profit	Price	Profit	Price	Profit	Price	Profit	Price	Profit
	A	$2000	A	$1200	A	$800	A	$000	A	$ 000	A	$ 000
	B	$1750	B	$1050	B	$700	B	$100	B	$ 150	B	$ 250
	C	$1500	C	$ 900	C	$600	C	$200	C	$ 300	C	$ 500
	D	$1250	D	$ 750	D	$500	D	$300	D	$ 450	D	$ 750
	E	$1000	E	$ 600	E	$400	E	$400	E	$ 600	E	$1000
	F	$ 750	F	$ 450	F	$300	F	$500	F	$ 750	F	$1250
	G	$ 500	G	$ 300	G	$200	G	$600	G	$ 900	G	$1500
	H	$ 250	H	$ 150	H	$100	H	$700	H	$1050	H	$1750
	I	$ 000	I	$ 000	I	$000	I	$800	I	$1200	I	$2000

NOTE Prices were referred to by letters. The number under each commodity represents profits to be made on the commodity at the particular price.

selves before descending to a lower profit level. This approach to proposal making essentially maximizes the likelihood that the bargainers will "stumble onto" an integrative solution.

Pruitt and Lewis have shown that heuristic trial and error leads to the adoption of integrative solutions when the problem is one of discovering which of a set of known alternatives is best for both parties.[3] However, the exchange of valid information about profit structures would appear to be essential where the problem is one of finding a totally new alternative, because there must be some basis for creative thinking about how to integrate the two parties' needs and values.

The Pruitt-Lewis study employed the payoff schedules shown in Table 11-2. In their task, the subjects play the roles of buyer and seller in a wholesale market for basic minerals. An agreement has to be reached on the prices of three minerals: iron, sulphur, and coal. (The quantities to be exchanged are irrelevant to the task.) The prices are given only by letters. Each subject has access only to his own payoff schedule. The reader can see that the payoffs (profits) increase with price for the seller and decrease with price for the buyer.

The structure of this task requires tradeoffs to achieve an integrative solution, in the sense that each party must be willing to accept a bad price on the commodity that is least important to him in exchange for a good price on the most important commodity. For the buyer, the most important commodity is iron, because his profits advance by a factor of $250 for each change in price, and the least important is coal, because his profits advance by a factor of only $100. For the seller, the order of importance for these two commodities is reversed. Hence the most integrative alternatives, in the sense of providing the highest joint profit (profit for buyer plus profit for seller), involve a low price on

---

[3] The value of one component of heuristic trial and error, systematic concession making, has also been demonstrated by Kelley and Schenitzki (1972).

iron and a high price on coal. The reader can verify that all combinations that include price *A* for iron and price *I* for coal yield a joint profit of $5200, which is the largest available.

In this situation all of the possible alternatives are known, at least in principle, from the first. The difficulty of locating the more integrative alternatives is due to the fact that the bargainers do not know enough about one another's payoff schedules to locate these alternatives analytically.

These authors manipulated two variables: limit level and orientation. In the high-limit condition, each bargainer was told that his firm required him to make a profit of at least $2300. In the low-limit condition, the firm required only $2000. Under an individualistic orientation, the subjects were told that their firm wanted them "to maximize your company's profits without considering the needs of the other participant." Under a problem-solving orientation, they were told to consider the needs of both parties and treat the negotiation task as a jointly solvable problem. The results are shown in Table 11-3.

It will be seen that by far the greatest joint profit was achieved under a combination of the problem-solving orientation and high limits. It is interesting that both elements of this combination were essential for integrative bargaining. High limits presumably block the bargainers from settling for easy solutions (such as EEE, which is pretty obvious since it involves a simple compromise on all three commodities). But a problem-solving orientation is also necessary to encourage heuristic trial and error, which was the method by which integrative agreements were usually reached.

The condition involving high limits and an individualistic orientation is also interesting. Only 55% of the dyads reached agreement in this condition, in sharp contrast to the other conditions. Analysis of the verbalizations during bargaining indicated that members of the dyads that failed to reach agreement had taken on a distributive orientation. They made frequent use of threats and positional commitments, belittled each other on occasion, and put a great deal of energy into trying to persuade each other to concede. This orientation was inappropriate to the problem, since solution could not be achieved simply by eliciting concessions from the other party. So these dyads failed to reach agreement. Members of the dyads that reached agreement appear to have adopted, on their own, the kind of problem-solving orientation that had been induced by instructions in the other condition. They engaged in heuristic trial and error: throwing out many proposals, seeking feedback on each proposal, and conceding systematically by trying out various combinations of prices at one

TABLE 11-3
Results from Study by Pruitt and Lewis (1975)

	Individualistic orientation		Problem-solving orientation	
	High limit	Low limit	High limit	Low limit
Joint profit*	4420	4312	5011	4525
Percent of dyads reaching agreement	55%	100%	100%	100%

*Buyer profit plus seller profit. Scores never go below 4000 (the score assigned to no agreement) or above 5200.

level of profit to themselves (e.g., $2550) before descending to a lower level (e.g., $2400).

In summary, these results suggest that integrative solutions are most likely to emerge from a situation in which limits (or, by extension, levels of aspiration) are high and bargainers take a problem-solving orientation. In the absence of high limits (or LOA's), bargainers will not be motivated to seek solutions that are highly beneficial for both parties and will settle for obvious, and hence often nonintegrative, solutions. In the absence of a problem-solving orientation, bargainers are likely to take a distributive approach, which will lead to failure to reach agreement if limits are high.

A Perspective on Bargaining

Most of the theories presented so far assume that the parties understand the issues that divide them and know which alternatives are available and how they stand on them. A partial exception can be seen in the theories of integrative bargaining, and yet even there the bargainers are assumed to have a fairly clear notion of the situation confronting them. In reality, many bargaining situations are not so well defined at their inception. The participants may not even be aware at first that their interests are opposed. When this awareness initially develops, they may not be at all clear about the issues upon which they disagree or the alternatives that are available for resolving their disagreement. A great deal of time and effort must go into defining the situation before any of the processes described in this chapter can go forward. As theories and research on this preliminary phase of bargaining are not available, the author can provide little guidance on this topic other than to point it out.

When people become aware that their interests are opposed, several approaches can be taken, of which bargaining is only one. Another approach is *norm following,* in which the conflict is resolved by following a pre-existing rule. As was mentioned earlier, norms are often developed through bargaining. But once developed, they become substitutes for bargaining. For example, two people who travel together a lot may have developed a pattern of alternating use of the armrest that obviates the need for bargaining about its use in each new situation.

Equality and equity norms often have this function. These were mentioned earlier as one basis for solution in bargaining. But they are so salient at times that bargaining is omitted altogether. Neither side makes a demand or calls for concessions. They simply adopt the obviously equitable solution. For example, if two hungry men are given one apple, they will ordinarily divide it equally without bargaining over the division.

Another nonbargaining procedure for settling differences of interest involves what can be called a *need discussion,* in which the parties exchange valid information about their needs, and preference goes to the one whose needs (weighted by some coefficient of importance) are stronger. For example, two travelers might compare the extent of their need for the armrest between them. If one revealed that he had recently had an operation which required that his arm be kept propped up, the other would very likely yield the armrest to him for the entire trip. Need discussions can be distinguished from the exchange of information in integrative bargaining, in that they do not originate in the context of bargaining and are resolved by a process other than the exchange of concessions. However, it may be difficult to make this distinction in some cases.

Need discussions are employed by a dyad to the extent that *mutual responsiveness* exists, such that each party values the other's welfare to some extent (Pruitt, 1972). It is also necessary for each party to believe that the other values his welfare. Without this form of trust, each party would fear that the other is really engaged in bargaining and would be reluctant to provide accurate information about his needs for fear of being exploited by the other side.

Need discussions may well have been the method by which married couples so rapidly and reliably reached agreement in the study by Schoeniger and Wood (1969) mentioned earlier. However this method is not confined to close interpersonal relationships. Indeed such discussions have even been found in relations between friendly nations, where they substitute for bargaining on some issues (Pruitt, 1965). In international relations, responsiveness is primarily a strategic orientation: we yield to your needs in the present situation because we are confident that you will yield to ours in the future, at a time when we feel more strongly than we do at present. Such strategic considerations are also present in interpersonal relations, but responsiveness there is also presumably an outcome of interpersonal attraction.

Need discussions are superior to bargaining in several ways (Pruitt, 1972). They ordinarily take less time and do not pose the same danger of failure to reach agreement. Furthermore, there is less likelihood of interparty friction, with its potential for engendering conflict spirals and poisoning future relations between the parties. In addition, because both parties exhibit their needs in such debates, information is available upon which insights into integrative solutions can be based.

One more advantage is that need discussions provide flexibility in resolving differences of interest. It is not necessary to find a solution that seems completely fair to both sides in the present situation, because the party that yields can be confident that the other will capitulate at a later time when the balance of needs falls in the other direction.

Despite these advantages, bargaining rather than need discussion is often the dominant mode of relationship between two parties, because mutual responsiveness and trust have not developed.

Mutual responsiveness ordinarily breaks down during periods in which changes are occurring in one or both parties' reward and coercive capability or willingness to use such capability. During such periods, need discussions are replaced by ordinary bargaining. But after a while, if a ruinous conflict spiral has not taken place, mutual responsiveness is likely to reassert itself with new and different weights on the needs of the two parties and need discussions return to the relationship.

Relations between blacks and whites in the United States appear to be going through such a transition. Previously, white needs were weighted substantially more heavily than black needs in most need discussion. We are now going through a period of extensive bargaining, in which a variety of distributive tactics are being used by both sides. Out of this struggle will presumably emerge a new tradition of need discussions, in which black and white needs will be equally weighted.

SUMMARY

Power, one party's capacity to influence another in a direction desired by the first, should not be viewed as a unitary phenomenon. At least eight types of influence can be distinguished, each based on a different class of personal power. These are: (1) Legitimate influence, which results from the target's feeling that he has an obligation to comply to certain requests from the source. This sense of obligation ordinarily derives from an internalized social norm. (2) Informational influence, in which the source provides information which persuades the target that conformity is rational. (3) Expert influence, where the target complies because he regards the source as an expert on the matter at hand. (4) Co-oriented influence, which stems from the target's belief that the source shares certain of his values. (5) Referent influence, where the target imitates the source because of an identification with the source. (6) Reciprocal influence, in which the target complies because he is obligated to the source for a past favor. (7) Coercive influence, where compliance results from fear of punishment at the hands of the source. (8) Reward influence, where compliance derives from the target's belief that he will be rewarded by the source.

In addition to the forms of personal power just listed, power can be derived from having allies or from group processes. A group has more power over its members the greater its cohesiveness, the clearer its norms and goals, and the more unanimously these norms and goals are supported by the membership.

Coercive and reward power are often implemented by communicating threats and promises to the target. Research suggests that people are more likely to conform to a threat the greater the punishment threatened, the less cost the source must bear when he enforces his threat, and the more often the source has enforced threats in the past. All of these variables can be said to affect the *credibility* of the threat. Roughly similar results obtain for promises. Efforts to exert influence by means of threats (and to a lesser extent promises) are often distasteful to the target, especially where these measures lack legitimacy, seem arbitrary, aim to deter ongoing activity, or are delivered before an audience or in a situation where other means of communication are available. As a result, resistance may develop. Countermeasures may be adopted by the target, in an effort to blunt the source's power, or a conflict spiral may ensue. The use of coercive power also tends to damage or destroy other forms of power.

Bargaining can be defined as the process by which at least two parties with initially different preferences make a series of concessions in search of a mutually satisfactory solution. Bargaining between source and target is frequently found in the exercise of coercive, reward, and legitimate power. Many other settings also entail bargaining. Bargaining may be either tacit, consisting of moves and counter-moves, or verbal, in which case it is called "negotiation." Most experimental research on bargaining has dealt with negotiation in laboratory settings that simulate the relations between buyer and seller, representatives of management and labor, and so on.

The theoretical approach underlying most of this research assumes that the outcome of bargaining depends on the bargainers' initial demands and rates of concession. If agreement is reached, it will favor that party who began with the more extreme demand and conceded more slowly. However, to the extent that both parties start with extreme demands and concede slowly, agreement will be harder to reach. Proponents of this approach have found that the extremity of a bargainer's initial demand and the slowness of his concessions are (1) a positive function of his level of aspiration and the extremity of his limit and (2) an inverse function of time pressure, the perceived extremity of the other bargainer's limit, and the intimacy of contact with the other bargainer.

Another theoretical approach, which has received little attention from experimenters but seems to have merit for some situations assumes that the outcome of bargaining is dependent on the existence and location of prominent solutions that stand out perceptually or recommend themselves for historical or normative reasons.

A third theoretical approach takes the position that agreement is more likely to be reached if the bargainers are able to discover new alternatives that are more beneficial to both parties than those initially envisioned. The processes underlying such discovery are called "integrative bargaining." Where bargainers can communicate freely, such alternatives are more likely to be identified if both parties maintain a high level of aspiration and take a problem-solving approach to their task.

Mediation by third parties often makes it easier for bargainers to reach agreement. There are various reasons for this, including the fact that a mediator's suggestions allow the bargainers to make concessions while saving face.

Bargaining is but one means of reconciling opposing interests. Others entail norm following and need discussions between parties who are, and recognize that they are, responsive to one another's needs.

SUGGESTED READINGS

Deutsch, M. *The resolution of conflict*. New Haven, Conn.: Yale University Press, 1973.

Summary of the results from a long and fruitful research program on the psychology of bargaining and social conflict.

Pruitt, D. G. Indirect communication and the search for agreement in negotiation. *Journal of Applied Social Psychology*, 1971, *1*, 205–239.

Describes and analyzes six methods for resolving the fundamental dilemma over whether or not to make a concession in negotiation.

Raven, B. H., & Kruglanski, A. W. Conflict and power, Chapter 3 in P. Swingle (Ed.), *The structure of conflict*. New York: Academic Press, 1970.

Describes six forms of personal power and examines the question of which will be selected by the aspirant source of influence. Analyzes the impact of various combinations of these forms of power.

Rubin, J. Z., & Brown, B. R. *The social psychology of bargaining and negotiation*. New York: Academic Press, 1975.

Summary and integration of experimental evidence on bargaining.

Walton, R. E., & McKersie, R. B. *A behavioral theory of labor negotiations*. New York: McGraw-Hill, 1965.

Comprehensive and creative integration of theoretical knowledge about industrial negotiation.

12

Group Development and Structure

Dalmas A. Taylor and Bruce Kleinhans

INTRODUCTION

Human beings spend a significant portion of their lives in interaction with others in the pursuit of some common purpose—in other words, in groups. As the groups in which we live, work, and play are major determinants of our feelings and self-concepts, the study of groups is essential to understanding human behavior.

We shall begin our analysis by distinguishing three different kinds of groups—task groups, growth groups, and social-friendship groups. We shall then focus on two specific examples of groups, pointing out various characteristics of them which will be discussed in greater detail in later sections of this chapter or in the next chapter. Our concern will first be with how groups begin, grow, develop, and establish guidelines of appropriate behavior. We shall then examine some aspects of group structure—ways in which members are related to each other along various dimensions. The relationships of physical space, communication, attraction, and composition to group interaction will be considered. Finally, we shall offer a few comments on how members perceive the structure of their own groups.

What Is a Group?

Our first task, however, is to define just what we mean by a group. Most social psychologists would probably agree that a group consists of *a collection of two or more persons who interact in the context of shared norms and goals.* Although most groups consist of persons in physical proximity to each other, we will not consider proximity or face-to-face contact as a necessary condition for defining a group. For example, a team of police officers tracking a suspect from their respective cars and maintaining radio contact constitutes a group even though the individual officers may be miles apart from each other. On the other hand, six persons standing at a bus stop would not ordinarily be considered a group. However, if two cars collided in their presence, creating an emergency situation, and the six people began to respond to this situation by interacting in pursuit of a common goal—rescuing the passengers—then the six individuals would become a group. Once the passengers were rescued and the six persons returned to the bus stop, they would no longer constitute a group.

It should be emphasized that the interaction among the members of a group is not limited to spoken or written words. Mutual communication and influence may occur through overt behavior, facial expressions, or body positions. Members of athletic teams and musical groups communicate primarily by such nonverbal means while performing. In most groups, both verbal and nonverbal communication occur simultaneously.

Most of the time when psychologists talk of groups they mean small groups. How small is small? We usually refer to groups of fewer than 20 members as small groups. A useful definition of a small group which does not set any arbitrary number of members is given by Bales. He suggests that in a small group:

> Each member receives some impression or perception of each other member distinct enough so that he can, either at the time or in later questioning, give some reaction to each of the others as an individual person, even though it be only to recall that the other person was present. (1950, p. 33)

Three Kinds of Groups

We can distinguish different categories of groups by looking at the major purpose or goal of their activity. Some groups, such as our bus-stop rescue team, have certain *tasks* to accomplish, sometimes cast upon them by chance, as in our example. However, tasks are usually assigned to the group by some external agency or chosen by the group members themselves. Groups working on some common task usually produce (or attempt to produce) a readily observable single group product, something which serves as evidence of the group's activity. This group product may take the form of a physical object, a written report, or the rearrangement of existing objects. In any case, a task group tries to produce some change in the external environment. Task groups work with objects, ideas, or situations which are separate from the group members themselves.

Other groups are also interested in change, but in change of the members themselves rather than the outside world. Since this individual change is intended to be in a positive direction, we can call such individually oriented groups *growth groups*. Groups aiming at some kind of self-improvement and personal change have been with us throughout history in the form of educational or religious groups. In recent years, however, we have witnessed an increasing popularity of self-improvement groups which are neither educational nor religious in the traditional senses of these terms. Psychotherapy groups, encounter groups, consciousness-raising groups and discussion groups of all kinds are some of these newer types of growth groups. Whether such a group is successful or not can be judged only by evaluating the knowledge, beliefs, and feelings of the members themselves; there is no common group product to which one can point as an indication of what the group has done.

Many groups have as a common purpose neither task accomplishment nor individual growth, but rather the personal satisfaction of the members—that is, having a good time. Cliques, gangs, and sets of people getting together to play cards, shoot baskets, or just "socialize" can all be considered as examples of such informal social or *friendship groups*.

Since, almost by definition, friendship groups cannot simply be created by some outside agency but rather develop over time by the purely voluntary choices of the participants, friendship groups have proved difficult to study in the laboratory. Most research on groups has investigated growth groups or task groups. Here the investigator can recruit individuals and then assemble sets of them with a designated objective and study what happens. Much social psychological research has investigated interpersonal attraction, but usually from the standpoint of individuals rather than groups. Little work has focused on groups of persons assembling purely for the purposes of pleasurable interaction. The few studies of friendship groups which have been conducted (e.g. Whyte, 1943) are descriptive rather than experimental in nature.

Of course, it is not always possible to place any particular group in one of our three rather arbitrary categories of task, growth, or social-friendship. In most groups, changes in the environment, changes in the individual members, and pleasurable interaction are all produced in varying degrees, although one usually predominates. One of these goals may be pursued as a means of fulfilling another purpose. For example, individuals often play basketball simply as a means of having fun.

Perhaps the most influential group in which we hold membership is the family. Families are unique kinds of groups in many ways, not the least of which is the mixture of all three purposes. Families provide opportunities for pleasurable interaction, they usually have as a "task" the producing and rearing of children, and they often result in personal growth, at least among the children.

Encounter Groups

Let us take an example of a kind of growth group, namely an encounter group, and see how it exemplifies some of the characteristics of groups to be analyzed in later sections of this chapter. The encounter group movement began in the years following World War II, and in the last 10 years it has mushroomed into a widespread phenomenon. King (1973) estimates that over five million persons have taken part in some form of encounter group. Until recently, however, little research has been directed toward either evaluating the effectiveness of encounter groups or investigating the interpersonal processes occuring within them.

Encounter groups are known by many other labels—sensitivity groups, T groups, and human relations workshops, to name a few. Although the various names may indicate some differences in orientation, we shall use the term "encounter group" to designate all growth groups composed of normal individuals which aim at general improvement in psychological functioning.

The specific goals of encounter groups can be described as enhanced self-esteem, more accurate self-knowledge, and improved ability to relate effectively to others. The focus is typically on the "here and now"—the interactions and feelings that emerge within the group setting itself. An effort is made to create an atmosphere of openness, honesty, emotional sensitivity, and freedom of expression. Participants are encouraged to give prompt and honest feedback to each other. These groups often provide unique opportunities for intimacy with others as well as an opportunity for social comparison of oneself with others.

Most of the aspects of groups to be discussed later can be observed in the typical encounter group. We may start by considering why people join encounter groups. Most encounter group members undoubtedly join because they share the basic goals of the group, personal insight and growth. However, other reasons also play a part. Although most encounter groups begin as sets of strangers, some persons may be attracted to individual members of the group. The immediate satisfaction of a need to be with others may be another motive. For some people, encounter groups provide an antidote to loneliness and alienation. Growth groups also offer opportunity for intimacy which may be unobtainable in everyday relationships. Individuals may be especially interested in using encounter groups to compare themselves with others or to gain social support. Still other motives may include making friends or participating in a popular activity.

Once an encounter group is formed, it undergoes certain changes over time. The particular developmental phases may vary from group to group, but both the nature and the level of a group's activities change. In some groups changes in group functioning may be initiated by a highly directive leader. More commonly, the formal leader takes a relatively passive role. In the beginning, a group may spend hours trying to determine its goals and ways to accomplish them. Some members may express frustration because there is no formal group structure or clearly identifiable leader. Eventually, someone will usually assume a leadership role by suggesting a specific activity, such as having each member express why he joined the group or how he feels about the group at the present time. Or someone may "break the ice" by disclosing intimate information about himself. In any case, the group typically moves from a more superficial to a more intimate level of interaction, from generalities to specifics, and from a concern with the past to a focus on the immediate present. There is often a feeling of progress and growth, alternating with periods of "leveling off" or regressing to earlier levels of interacting. If the group meets on several different occasions, each session may have to begin with a new period of "warming up."

All groups have various structural aspects, their patterns of relationships among the members. Some structural relations in encounter groups tend to be ignored or de-emphasized by the participants, while others are dealt with openly. Participants are not usually aware of the arrangement of physical space among themselves; however, this issue may be brought to the group's attention when one member moves toward or away from another member or when interpersonal touching occurs. Intentional changes in the total physical arrangement of the members usually occur only within the context of a directed exercise initiated by the leader or a group member.

Patterns of communication also develop in groups. In any group, some members will talk far more than others. In encounter groups, conscious efforts are often made to equalize the amount of communication per person by directly encouraging the quiet persons and discouraging the overly talkative ones. Who speaks to whom about what may also be discussed by the group.

The composition of the group in terms of the individual qualities of the members is another aspect of structure. Members enter any group having pre-existing individual differences; their behavior in the group and their satisfaction with it are influenced by the characteristics of the other members. A particular "mix" of persons may result in an unproductive encounter group. The same individuals, however, may have very worthwhile experiences as members of other encounter groups.

By their nature, encounter groups attract a highly selected portion of the population. Encounter participants are usually better-educated and more liberal and open-minded than the population as a whole. Few lower-class individuals have the time, money, or desire to join encounter groups. There are few, if any, encounter groups in rural and small-town communities. Perhaps there is less need for them since family and friendship ties may be closer than is the case for urban residents. Therefore, members of encounter groups tend to be fairly similar to each other in that they are mostly well-educated urbanites. However, personalities and experiences may vary widely among members.

Since two of the primary purposes of encounter groups are to enable the participants to compare themselves to others and to discover how they are perceived by others, having a variety of different viewpoints available may foster growth. Also, groups composed of a diverse assortment of people may help the members realize that many of the differences among them are fairly superficial and unimportant. These perceptions may also help decrease prejudice and stereotype thinking.

Perhaps the most obvious and explicit kind of relationship among encounter group members is their attraction to each other. A great deal of the time in encounter groups is spent dealing with expressions of liking and disliking among members. Attraction of members to the group as a whole is another favorite topic, fostered by such practices as eliminating distractions by physically separating the group from other people and meeting for extended periods of time.

It should be emphasized that the structural relationships we have been discussing are being observed from the outside. Each member of the group also has his own view of the group's structural characteristics. While there may be high agreement among various members and among members and outside observers regarding some structural features of the group, there is bound to be much disagreement about other characteristics. Furthermore, different persons will be aware of and sensitive to different aspects of structure. Thus, for one person, the most important pattern of relationships among members of a particular group may involve communication, for another, attraction, and so on.

One characteristic of encounter groups is the intense emotion aroused. The open and direct expression of intense feelings, both positive and negative, which occurs in encounter groups represents a lowering of the normal social inhibitions concerning appropriate behavior. Our internal controls based on shame, guilt, and fear (what Freud termed the "superego") are weakened. Behavior may be charged with emotion and be irrational, impulsive, and childlike. Some group leaders encourage such "regressive" behavior and may initiate exercises designed to release it. Participants may be asked to fantasize or to act out imaginary situations. Persons may become so involved in their immediate acts that past and present are forgotten, and evaluations from self or others are pushed out of mind. Thus, while the ultimate goal of an encounter group is to help the person become more of a unique individual, the activities of the group often promote a loss of individuality, especially during nonverbal activities in which everyone does the same thing. Encounter group participants often report a loss of separateness, a submergence in the group, a feeling of unity and loss of self. The problem here is whether surrendering oneself to the group in such a manner promotes a greater or a lessened sense of self-identity.

The release of socially inhibited behavior in encounter groups represents an increased acceptance among the participants to accept the risks of such behavior. Opening up to others always involves the possibility of misunderstanding, rejection, hostility, or regret. The encounter group encourages people to accept the risks inherent in authentic encounter and to realize that the possible dangers of self-disclosure are not as great as members fear.

The role of the encounter group leader is a critical one. The outcome of the group may depend to a significant degree on the leader's skill, sensitivity, and experience. The leader may attempt on the one hand to be a regular member of the group, not inhibiting his or her own expression of feelings. On the other hand the leader is the expert, the professional, and must know when to intervene in the ongoing interaction, when to guide, suggest, and confront, and when to refrain from doing so. The leader must help establish group norms without imposing standards and biases on the group. Aronson notes " . . . the leader must come to terms with his own power; for him to ignore it, or to pretend that it isn't there, could be malfunctional for the group" (1972, p. 256).

Do encounter groups work, that is, do they accomplish their goals? Probably the most extensive and well-designed study of encounter-group effectiveness to date is the investigation conducted by Lieberman, Yalom, and Miles (1973a). This study had several laudable features: (1) A number of different groups and leaders, representing a variety of different theoretical orientations, were studied. (2) Participants were randomly assigned to groups. (3) Two control groups were employed. Instead of a live leader, the control groups played a tape-recording which periodically suggested exercises and activities. (4) Both short-term and long-term effects were measured. (5) A number of different measures of effectiveness were used, including self-reports of the participants and ratings by their fellow group members, the group trainers, and their families and friends.

Most participants felt that the experience had been worthwhile and had resulted in positive changes in themselves. They tended to feel more honest, spontaneous, confident, accepting of others, and more insightful about both themselves and others. It was also found that the particular leader made a major difference in the participants' outcomes as measured by the relative benefit or harm they received. However, after six months, the participants' enthusiasm and positive evaluation of the group experience had declined considerably.

One problem which illustrates the difficulties in outcome-evaluation research of this kind was that there was little agreement among the different sets of judges—self, co-participants, trainers, family and friends—regarding how a person had changed. Therefore, the authors combined measures from all four sources, as well as objective test measures, to yield an overall index of change. The overall measure showed that, immediately after the group experience, about one third of the participants exhibited positive changes, one third negative changes, and one third remained essentially unchanged. The results were substantially the same 6 to 8 months later. Most of the control group participants showed little change at either time. Compared to the control group, the encounter-group participants tended to have more positive self-images but changed little in their views of others or their interpersonal behavior.

Task Groups

In contrast to growth groups, where the goal is change in the individual members, in task groups the goal consists of some kind of change in the environment. One is able to evaluate what a task group has accomplished without evaluating the group members individually. Group tasks include such activities as playing football games, deciding upon the guilt or innocence of a criminal defendant, conducting a surgical operation, recommending policy changes in an organization, and creating advertising slogans.

Let us take a concrete example of a task group. In a social psychology course, students are given the chance to plan and conduct an experiment. Again, we will use this example to exemplify some of the different aspects of groups which we will examine later in more detail.

Why will a particular individual join our group? Perhaps he is personally attracted to the other members. Or perhaps he considers the others to have high ability on the task. On the other hand, an individual may be attracted more by the particular group goal—in this case, the kind of experiment contemplated—than by any qualities of the individual group members. If more than one group is available to join, he will probably compare the probable rewards and costs of working in each of the alternative groups. Furthermore, if the only alternative available consists of working on an experiment alone, an individual may be motivated to join a group simply to be with others. Being with others may serve to reduce fear of failure. Also, one may wish to compare one's abilities and feelings with similar others. On the other hand, the anticipation of being evaluated by the other members of the group may be a reason for working alone.

Once a group is formed, it goes through definite stages of functioning. Here the stages are much more dictated by the requirements of the task than in an encounter group. To conduct an experiment, various subtasks must be performed in the proper order—generating ideas, selecting an idea for investigation, devising a procedure, preparing materials, practicing and rehearsing, conducting the experiment, analyzing the data, and preparing the final written report.

Certain aspects of being in a group situation will affect all the members. First, they are apt to feel some degree of apprehension about the others evaluating them. Second, they may find themselves supporting decisions and policies quite different from those which they would endorse as individuals. During the existence of the group, the members may wonder to themselves, or even aloud, about how effective the group is. Could each member have done a better job alone than the group did? Given that the group was formed, would more be accomplished by the members working alone or together? Finally, are there specific techniques or methods which might encourage better group functioning? How is the members' attraction to the group affecting its productivity?

The question of leadership is also likely to be important to members. Whether or not a leader is formally chosen, sooner or later someone emerges as the person with the most influence. Why this person? Because of his personal characteristics? Or because he just happened to be in the right place at the right time? Or perhaps because his particular style of exercising leadership was satisfying to the members and effective in getting the job done? We will try to answer some of these questions later.

GROUP FORMATION AND DEVELOPMENT

Group Formation

Why do individuals choose to form groups or to join already existing groups? We can identify three possible sources of a person's attraction to a group. These three sources of attraction are mentioned in our definition of a group: Two or more *individuals* who *interact* in the pursuit of common *goals*.

The basis of attraction to a group sometimes lies in the other members, sometimes in the group goals, and sometimes in the interaction itself. A person's attraction to a group is often based on his attraction to the group's members. Thus, all the factors discussed in the chapter on interpersonal attraction, such as similarity, physical attractiveness, and physical proximity, may influence group formation. Researchers usually assume that attraction to a group is best measured by the personal attraction among the individual members.

A second basis for group membership is identification with and attraction to the group's activities and goals. One may sometimes be attracted to the group's activities without being attracted to its goals, or vice versa. Undoubtedly most members of the Boy Scouts join not so much to further the ideals of scouting, but rather to engage in camping and other enjoyable group activities. On the other hand, people sometimes tolerate very tedious and unexciting work, such as stuffing envelopes, because they believe in the goal their group is working towards, such as electing a particular political candidate. In most cases, however, an individual is attracted to both the group's activities and its goals.

In addition to having attractive members, activities, and goals, a group may be attractive simply because it provides an opportunity to be with others. People appear to have a need for affiliation, for human interaction, which can be satisfied by group activities. Perhaps the best demonstration that a need for affiliation exists and acts in ways similar to physiological needs comes from a study by Gewirtz and Baer (1958a). These investigators engaged young children in a game involving dropping marbles into different holes. After a few minutes, the experimenter began to offer approving comments, such as "good" or "fine," every time the child dropped a marble into his least-preferred hole. Just before the game, some of the children had either spent 20 minutes alone in a room (social deprivation condition) or had engaged in conversation with the experimenter (social satiation condition). Other subjects began the game as soon as they arrived at the laboratory (control condition).

It was found that the effectiveness of the experimenter's approving comments (social reinforcement) varied according to how well the child's need for human interaction had been satisfied. The subjects showed the most change in marble-dropping behavior in response to the experimenter in the deprivation condition, and the least change in the satiation condition. Of course, it is likely that a much longer period in isolation would be required in order to demonstrate similar effects with adult subjects.

Stages in Group Development

It is readily apparent that groups are not static; they develop and change over time. A number of different writers have attempted to identify various stages of development which groups pass through. Tuckman (1965) has reviewed various theories of group development and concludes that four stages can account for the changes occuring in task and growth groups.

The first stage, labeled *forming,* consists of orientation and testing of the boundaries of appropriate behavior. Members at this stage are dependent on the leader, other members, or pre-existing standards for guidance and support. Members attempt to identify the group's goal as well as the "ground rules" which will enable them to realize their goal.

Once the group has successfully passed through the forming stage, a period of conflict ensues. During this *storming* stage, interpersonal hostility and resistance to structure are expressed. The group becomes divided, and members resist the group's influence and the requirements of the task.

Tuckman terms the third stage *norming.* During this developmental phase members come to accept the group and the individual characteristics of other members. Opinions are openly exchanged without the occurence of infighting. Group norms are established and accepted.

During the final stage, *performing,* interpersonal problems are resolved, and the group's energy can be directed toward accomplishing its goals. Members' roles are flexible and serve to further the common group purposes.

Tuckman draws a parallel between his four stages of group development and stages of individual development. Children can be viewed as passing through successive stages of dependence, rebellion, group identification, and realistic interdependence. Although Tuckman found most of the research on group development to be consistent with his model, he notes that little work has investigated the development of groups other than encounter groups or laboratory task groups. Whether the forming-storming-norming-performing model is applicable to long-term task groups or to social-friendship groups remains to be seen.

The Development of Group Norms

Groups have certain standards of conduct for their members. These rules of what members are expected to do and not to do insure that behavior in the group is to some degree predictable. Uncertainty is reduced by having general guidelines for behavior.

Norms are more than just expectations, however. They have an evaluative nature, expressing what actions are correct or appropriate. A person who violates a social norm is judged to be acting "abnormally." Furthermore, standards of conduct must be shared by most of the members to be considered as norms.

Some group norms may be established by an external authority—either a powerful individual, a larger organization, or society as a whole. Other norms may be determined by the group's leader. Still other standards develop during the group interaction. These group-developed norms may change over time.

Violations of important norms may be punished by the other group members in various ways, ranging from raised eyebrows and stares to verbal ridicule or exclusion of the deviating member from the interaction. Unimportant norm-deviations, on the other hand, such as arriving at class barefoot, are often ignored. A group may encounter problems if members hold differing views of the importance of various norms.

Encounter groups usually create their own special set of norms which differ from those of ordinary groups. These rules may be explicitly stated at the outset by the trainer or the sponsoring organization, or they may remain unverbalized and implicit, although still enforced, throughout the life of the group. In general, any kind of honesty, especially the open expression of immediate feelings, is highly valued by an encounter group and receives positive reinforcement in terms of praise. On the other hand, excessive quietness, evasiveness, phoniness, superficiality, or irrelevancy is disapproved and subject to criticism. In well-conducted encounter groups, however, norms of personal privacy and noncoerciveness are developed which prevent members from being pressured into saying or doing anything which they do not freely choose to say or do.

Some specific encounter-group norms concern the role of the leader, the value of touching and other nonverbal interaction, and the place of games and exercises. In an encounter group, one is usually expected to speak to another person rather than about him, and to avoid labeling or judging others. Finally, an encounter group may be headed for serious trouble unless it develops norms about the limits of hostile feelings which will be expressed.

GROUP STRUCTURE

Many of the characteristics of groups which we will be dealing with can be considered as structural qualities, or general patterns of relationships among the members of a group. There are several things we should note initially about these patterns of relationships in groups. First, there are many different group "structures." Patterns involving physical space, communication, composition (i.e., the "mix" of individual member characteristics), and attraction can all be viewed separately, although each of these patterns does influence each of the others.

Dimensions of groups can be analyzed as a number of subdimensions. Communication, for example, can be looked at from the standpoint of how much each member talks, or to whom talking is directed, or the different topics talked about. Also, most structural relationships do not remain static but change over time. Depending on which particular aspect of group structure we examine, we may find certain structural characteristics which vary from minute to minute, and others that are constant throughout the life of the group.

We are used to thinking about structures of objects in terms of readily observable relationships of parts. But structural characteristics of groups may be of a highly abstract or unobservable nature. Different structural characteristics vary in terms of how apparent they are to the group members. Some structural features may be formal and explicit, imposed on the group by an outside agency or decided upon by the group or its leader. Others may be informal and implicit, arising spontaneously from the interaction.

Finally, we may note that in addition to structural relationships which an outside observer may identify, each member of the group has his own conception of the group's structure. Different members may not agree on the relationships along any given structural dimension. For example, member *A* may believe that members *B* and *C* like each other, while *B* and *C* actually do not like each other. If we asked each of six members who likes whom in the group, we may obtain six different perceptions of the group's attraction structure. Different members also may vary in which dimensions of structure they consider important and which dimensions they are aware of at all. One member may be primarily concerned with communication patterns within the group, another member with attraction, and still another with status.

We have chosen the structural dimensions of physical space, communication, composition, and attraction to discuss in detail. These four dimensions have important influences on group functioning and have also been subjected to considerable research. Roles, status, and power are other important dimensions of group structure, but we will not deal with these topics here.

Physical Space

One of the more subtle and easily ignored structural dimensions of groups involves the members' relationships to each other and to the group as a whole in terms of physical space. People in groups develop feelings about geographical areas (territoriality), about their physical distance from other members (personal space), and about how members are oriented in relation to each other (space arrangement). These feelings in turn affect the group interaction in complex ways which are still not well understood. The next time you are in a group, try noticing where you meet, how close people sit to each other, and who sits next to whom, and how these factors seem to affect the group process.

Territory. Whenever people interact in groups or public situations they are likely to develop feelings of ownership toward geographical areas. Even when the occupation of a certain location is only temporary, and no legal right of ownership exists, feelings that "This is *my* place" often occur. Both individuals and groups establish territories which they regard as their own property and which they defend against intruders. Three important effects make the concept of territoriality relevent to the study of groups. First, individuals within groups defend their own territories against other group members. Second, groups establish territories which are defended against other groups or individual outsiders. Finally, whether or not one is occupying his "home territory" affects his functioning in a group.

Ethologists, who study the social behavior of animals, have investigated territorial possession and defense in subhuman species since the seventeenth century. One writer (Ardrey, 1966) has even used the animal studies to develop a theory of human behavior built around the idea of territorial defense. However, the study of territoriality in humans is still in its infancy.

Individual territorial behavior is exemplified by a student quickly establishing a particular classroom seat as his own. He regards his usual seat as belonging to him and feels uncomfortable when prevented from occupying it. He may even ask an intruder to move.

Changing patterns of individual territoriality were found by Altman and Haythorn (1967), in studies of isolated dyads. Sailors who were initially strangers were assigned to work in small rooms without outside contact for 10 days. Over time, territorial behavior increased. For the completely isolated pairs, territoriality first was expressed in relation to beds, later to tables, and finally to chairs. These findings illustrate how norms of territorial possession develop over time, as well as how some objects and areas may be more strongly claimed (e.g., beds) than others (e.g., chairs).

Individual territorial behavior has been studied in families by Scheflin (1971). Families appear to develop their own characteristic set of norms concerning who may use particular areas, including which members are entitled to exclusive use of a given room. The norms which develop will be influenced by the home's size and layout, the size of the family, and the ages of the children. The older the children are, the more they are likely to assert their territorial rights and to have such claims respected and observed by other family members. In general, the greater status and power an individual possesses within a family, the stronger will be his power of territorial exclusion.

Territoriality may serve a number of functions. First, it may be necessary for efficient operating of a group. Certain activities, such as watching TV and studying, may conflict with each other when they occur in the same room. Having areas assigned to persons also increases the predictability of life; one doesn't have to waste time deciding where to position oneself or decide anew in every encounter who sits where. Territoriality is also related to needs for privacy. Finally, the possession of particular objects and locations may help define one's sense of personal identity. In all these ways, territorial behavior, if not carried to extremes, helps the group members maintain interaction with a minimum of conflict. Altman, Taylor, and Wheeler (1971) suggest that territoriality serves "to set boundaries among group members, to facilitate and establish bases of interaction, and to smooth out functioning in a way analogous to social norms and conventions" (p. 95).

In public places, territories may be claimed and defended on a temporary basis. In a study of territorial behavior in college libraries, Sommer and Becker (1969) found that seating choice was influenced by whether the person wanted to avoid territorial invasion or to defend his territory. Those wishing to avoid intrusions on their territories tended to select chairs in the rear of the room, facing away from the door, next to a wall, and at a small table. Territory-defending subjects tended to choose more centrally located seats, facing the door.

Temporary territories can be defended against intruders by means of "markers," objects which signify that the space is occupied. In a library, books and jackets inform others that the space is taken. Territorial markers thus serve to reduce conflict over space by acting as warning devices. Becker (1973) found that markers are not as effective as the actual presence of their owners in protecting territory, however. For example, students in a library spent an average of 77 minutes at an unoccupied table, 53 minutes at a marked table, and only 32 minutes at an occupied table.

Groups as well as individuals can establish territories and defend them against invaders. Group territories are often much larger than individual territories and have less definite boundaries. As with individual territories, group territories serve the functions both of establishing and maintaining group identity and of reducing conflict with outsiders.

In cities, various ethnic groups stake out their own areas of interaction and residence. On a college campus, various hang-outs or particular tables in cafeterias may become associated with various types of students, such as blacks, graduate students, fraternity men, sorority women, or athletes. The territoriality of smaller face-to-face groups can sometimes assume great importance. As dramatized in *West Side Story,* city youths often form gangs and will defend their own "turf" to the death against rival gangs.

Being on one's own home ground appears to have advantages for both individuals and groups during conflict or competition with others. A recent study (Martindale, 1971) provides evidence that people are in fact more aggressive and influential when at home. Pairs of undergraduate men argued a criminal case and attempted to reach agreement on how severe the sentence should be. One member of each pair was assigned the role of prosecuting attorney, the other of defense attorney. In each case, the debate took place in the dormitory room of one of the subjects. Regardless of whether a subject was defense or prosecuting attorney, being in his own room gave him an advantage. A "home" subject tended to talk longer and to be more persuasive than his opponent. When the "home" debater was defending the suspect, the average sentence was only 22 months; however, when the home participant was prosecuting, the average sentence was 60 months. Furthermore, territory proved to be a much stronger determinant of talking time and persuasiveness than scores on the dominance scale of a widely-used personality inventory. These results have far-reaching practical implications. Among other things, they suggest that the tradition of conducting international negotiations on neutral territory is well founded.

Personal and Group Space. Human interaction is strongly affected by the physical distance between the participants. Most interaction takes place within a particular zone of distance between persons. Violating spacing norms, by being either too close or too far away from the other person, interferes with smooth, harmonious social functioning. In a group, members who are too far apart may have difficulty communicating. Too close a distance to another person, on the other hand, may create feelings of discomfort and efforts to move back to a more comfortable distance.

The area around oneself into which others are expected not to intrude is usually termed "personal space." The concept of personal space is somewhat similar to that of personal territory. Both cases involve a sense of exclusive possession and reluctance to allow others to use what belongs to oneself. There are two important distinctions between personal space and territory, however. First, personal space is relative to the individual and is carried around with him as he moves from place to place; it is not tied to any particular physical location. Second, territories usually have boundaries which are relatively identifiable and stable, while zones of personal space are less sharply defined and also vary in size over persons, relationships, and situations.

Groups in which the personal spaces of other members are violated are likely to encounter difficulties in interpersonal relations. Too great an intermember spacing, on the other hand, may result in feelings of aloofness and impersonality. Although most of the personal space research has been conducted from the standpoint of individuals rather than groups, the findings apply fairly directly to group behavior.

Responses to the invasion of one's personal space typically involve feelings of discomfort, stress, and hostility. These negative feelings may result in efforts to move away from the intruder, to have the invading person move away, or to depersonalize the situation. Often neither the invader nor the person whose space is invaded is aware of the reasons for his responses. We sometimes retreat from those who get too close without directing our negative emotions toward the invaders (McDowell, 1972).

One study (Felipe & Sommer, 1966) investigated responses to personal-space invasion at library tables. Experimenters sat down only inches away from subjects. The most common reaction was departure. Most subjects whose space was invaded left, while few non-invaded control subjects departed during a comparable time period. Other responses to invasion, such as turning away from the experimenter, were also noted. In public areas such as libraries, individuals may attempt to protect themselves against personal-space violation by choosing isolated locations.

Groups as well as individuals feel a sense of possession of the area around them. There is no agreed-upon term to designate the group equivalent of an individual's personal space, but "group space" may be the most appropriate. The ease with which group space can be violated is influenced by a number of factors. The smaller the size of the group (Knowles, 1973) and the farther apart the members are standing (Efran & Cheyne, 1973), the more willing outsiders are to penetrate the group's space. Groups with high-status members are less likely to be invaded than those with low-status members (Knowles, 1973). Additional evidence suggests that the greater the interpersonal attraction (cohesiveness) within the group, the less likely the members are to tolerate invasion. In one study (Knowles, 1972), a stationary experimenter stood in the middle of a sidewalk and noted whether pairs of approaching individuals moved around him or allowed him to pass through their space. Mixed-sex pairs were more likely to move around the stationary experimenter than were same-sex pairs. Perhaps this difference was due not so much to the sex composition of the group as to the closeness of the pair's relationship. The more a group of people are attracted to each other and think of themselves as a unit, the less willing they should be to tolerate invasion of their space. Another study (Cheyne & Efran, 1972) found that if a dyad is stationary, it is less likely to be invaded when it consists of a male and a female than when it is composed of two males or two females. Perhaps a mixed-sex couple is perceived as having a closer relationship than a same-sex pair and is thus considered less invadeable.

It is not difficult to think of other factors which probably affect the ease of penetration of group space. In general, we would expect that the more an invasion is likely to disrupt a group's activities, the more hesitant outsiders would be to intrude into its space. We would expect a relatively permanent group to have stronger spacial boundaries than a more temporary one. Thus, the space of a seated group should be less invadeable than that of a standing group. A formal group meeting probably creates a stronger barrier to penetration than an informal gathering. Likewise, it may be easier to pass through a group engaged in friendly interaction than through one having a heated argument.

While individuals, either alone or in groups, feel uncomfortable having their space violated, intruders also feel uneasy. The intruding person is not only violating the space of others but is also causing his own space to be violated. In a study of reactions to being an invader, Efran and Cheyne (1974) had subjects walk down a hallway. In some cases two conversing confederates were positioned in the hall so that the subject was forced to pass between them. In a mild intrusion condition the confederates' positions required the subject to pass beside them.

Immediately following the passage down the hall, subjects were asked to rate their moods. Subjects in the intrusion conditions felt more negative than those in a control condition who walked down an empty corridor. During the walk, the intrusion subjects also displayed more behavioral expressions of discomfort, such as closing the eyes, looking downward, and holding the mouth in a tight, tense manner. Walking between the confederates produced more evidence of discomfort than did walking around them. In subsequent description of their feelings about intruding, subjects used words such as "awkward," "embarrassed," "unpleasant," and "uncomfortable."

In those situations where people are forced to violate each other's personal space for extended periods of time, as in a crowded subway or elevator, the typical response is to depersonalize the situation by treating the other people as if they were objects (e.g., by ignoring their presence). One can also reduce the discomfort of inescapable physical closeness by avoiding eye contact and face-to-face confrontation (Sommer, 1969).

Personal space is affected by differences in the type of relationship between the people involved. The general finding is that the more positive the emotional tone of the relationship, the smaller the interaction distance. Friends interact at smaller distances than acquaintances, who in turn are physically closer than strangers (Little, 1965). Similarly, persons attempting to be friendly to another individual place themselves closer than those not trying to be friendly (Evans & Howard, 1973). Among persons who know each other well, liking is associated with small personal space (Aiello & Cooper, 1972). Personal space is also smaller in groups which are either engaging in or have previously engaged in cooperative interaction than in those which are noncooperative (Batchalor & Goethals, 1972; Tedesco & Fromme, 1974).

The status relationship of the interacting persons is also related to their spacial distancing. Lott and Sommer (1967) found that unequal status relationships elicited greater spacing than peer relationships. Here again, we find similarity associated with closer interpersonal distance. The distance between interacting individuals can also serve as a clue to their relative statuses. In a study by Hutte and Cohen (cited in Sommer, 1969), persons interacting at closer distances were judged more equal in status by observers.

Personal space is also affected by the nature of the situation. Intimate conversation draws people closer together physically. When females expect to discuss personal matters, they tend to sit closer together than when expecting a casual conversation (Harford, 1971). Stress originating from some external source has been found to increase interpersonal distance (Dosey & Meisels, 1969). The structure of the physical environment surrounding the interaction can also affect personal space requirements. A person in a corner of a room feels "cornered" and requires more personal space than if he were standing in the center of the room (Dabbs, Fuller, & Carr, 1973).

As is the case with the other physical space variables of territoriality and spacial arrangement, the study of personal space in humans is still in its infancy. As Evans and Howard (1973) point out in their review of the literature, "We do not as yet thoroughly understand all the variables which are relevant to personal space behavior, and we are even further away from being able to explain why and how personal space operates for human beings" (p. 341).

Arrangement of Individuals in Space. In any face-to-face group, some people are directly facing each other, others are facing at an angle, and still others are side-by-side. Also, the group as a whole may assume various spatial patterns—circle, half-circle, straight line, and so on. Differences in spatial structure have important influences on the patterns of communication among members and, in turn, on the influence, status, and leadership structures which develop. Before exploring some of the consequences of spatial arrangement on other structural characteristics of the group, let us examine how group members arrange themselves initially.

The spatial arrangements that are possible or preferred are affected by various aspects of the group's physical environment, such as the size and shape of the room and whether the group is standing, sitting in chairs, sitting on the floor, or some combination of these. Other environmental influences include whether the group meets around a table and, if so, the size and shape of the table. Little research has systematically explored these and other environmental effects. Typically, investigations of how members arrange themselves have used only one standard group setting. For example, most studies have used a rectangular table surrounded by four chairs. Experimental subjects have been allowed to choose seats or arrange chairs within the limits of that given setting.

Given the constraints imposed by the environmental setting, seating preferences are influenced by individual differences in status and personality, as well as by the particular kind of group activity anticipated. Persons who are accustomed to being influential in groups tend to choose the seating positions which are associated with power. For example, Strodtbeck and Hook (1961) found that, in simulated juries, jurors from professional and managerial classes sat at the head of the table more often than did persons from other occupational backgrounds. Similarly, Hare and Bales (1963) found that subjects who received high scores on a questionnaire assessment of dominance tended to choose centrally located seats. That certain seating positions are associated with leadership is universally recognized. Felipe (1966) found that if two people are observed facing each other at both ends or both sides of a rectangular table, the persons are judged as much more equal than if one person is located at the end and the other person at the side.

The spatial structure of the group also depends on the nature of the group's activities. Sommer (1969) presented subjects with a number of different seating plans for two people around a rectangular table and asked which arrangement was preferred for various types of interactions. For casual conversation, subjects preferred either corner-to-corner or face-to-face seating. Face-to-face was the arrangement most often chosen for competition, while side-by-side was preferred for cooperation. For co-acting persons (working independently with no interaction), the most preferred position was diagonal (i.e., on opposite sides of the table, but not facing). Further studies by Sommer (1969) of actual dyads confirmed that side-by-side positions were preferred for cooperation and face-to-face positions were preferred for competition. Activity also affects the spatial structures chosen by larger sets of people. In one experiment (Batchelor & Goethals, 1972) sets of subjects were taken to a room to work on a decision-making task and allowed to arrange their chairs any way they wished. Half the time, the decisions were made individually. Since these sets of subjects were not interacting in pursuit of a common goal, they did not constitute groups by our definition. In these nongroups, the chairs were not placed in any definite patterns, and the average interpersonal distance varied widely both within each set of persons and also from one set to another. In other words, since there was no true group activity, there was no need for the persons to structure themselves in space in any particular way. The other half of the subjects, however, were required to make collective rather than individual decisions. In these true groups, a somewhat circular arrangement of chairs resulted. The average distance between members was highly consistent both within any particular group and also from one group to another. Thus, unless a true group exists, with interaction directed toward a common purpose, we would not expect a set of people to arrange themselves in space in any particular fashion.

The reasons why certain seating arrangements are preferred over others is not always clear. Sommer's (1969) subjects explained their seating preferences at tables in terms of efficiency. For example, they suggested that conversation is made easier if the participants are in close physical proximity and can maintain eye contact. It seems unlikely, however, that people consciously evaluate possible arrangements according to such criteria. Rather, positions are probably chosen because of either cultural standards about the socially "correct" seating for the situation or because pleasant or unpleasant past experiences are associated with particular positions.

Spatial arrangements affect group interaction in a number of ways. For example, the more difficult it is to look at another person, the less nonverbal communication (gestures, facial expressions, and so on) one will receive from that person.

One everyday situation in which spatial arrangements influence group interaction is the classroom. Maximum student participation is probably not obtained by the almost universal practice of arranging student seats in straight rows, all facing in the same direction. To investigate whether altered seating would result in increased student participation, Becker and his colleagues (Becker, Sommer, Bee, & Oxley, 1973) rearranged the straight-row seatings in a number of college classrooms into circular arrangements. Unfortunately, the original hypothesis could not be tested, because the new arrangements were seldom accepted by the classes. The power of established norms and traditions compelled students and professors to rearrange the seats back to straight rows in 20 out of 25 classes. Students often initiated the rearrangement on their own; in other cases, the instructor requested it. Yet when asked what seating arrangement they preferred for a small class, only 6% of the instructors interviewed desired a straight-row pattern.

Communication

In most groups there is a continuous flow of communication among members. Much of this communication is at the nonverbal level—facial expressions, positions of the body, and the like. In this section we shall focus on the structural characteristics of verbal communication in groups. Much more research is needed before we can make confident generalizations about nonverbal communication patterns in groups.

Amount of Communication. One fact which appears to be true of virtually any group is that the amount of communication is not uniformly distributed. Some of the members talk much more than others. Stephan and Mishler (1952) studied discussion groups composed of college students and found that, regardless of the size of the group, most of the talking was done by the two most talkative members. In an eight person group, for example, the most talkative person was responsible for 40% of the talking, the next most talkative person for 20%, the next for 15%, and so on, with the quietest people saying very little.

A similar pattern was observed for the receipt of communication: Some members received far more than their share of other members' comments, and some far less than their share. As might be expected, the amount of communication given was highly related to the amount received—talkative people were talked to and quiet people were ignored.

Those who talk the most in a group are likely to become leaders (Bales, 1970). Positive relationships have also been found between talking and being liked by the other members (Borgatta & Bales, 1956). However, some evidence (Bales, 1970) indicates that it is not the most talkative person who is best liked, but rather the second and third most talkative persons. Since all these data are correlational in nature, however, we cannot be certain that the talkativeness itself is the cause of the attractiveness and influence. Perhaps people who are attractive and influential for other reasons also happen to be the most talkative. To clarify the role of communication rate, an experiment is required in which the amount of talking is manipulated, but all other characteristics of the members are held constant.

In just such an experiment Stang (1973) required subjects to listen to tapes of group discussions, which were arranged so that one member spoke 50% of the time, another 33%, and the third 17% of the time. Subjects liked the moderately talkative member better than either the quiet member or the very talkative one. Ratings of leadership, on the other hand, increased steadily with talkativeness—the more a member talked, the more she was seen as a leader.

That some people are seen as too quiet and others as too talkative is not surprising. We have all been in social, growth, and task groups where one or two individuals "hog" the conversation, repetitiously elaborating their own ideas and experiences, while other members never seem to have anything to contribute. A greater variety of ideas could result from a more equal distribution of input. Often group leaders or other members attempt to discourage the overtalkative and encourage quiet members to talk more. Can such efforts be effective?

An experiment by Bavelas, Hastorf, Gross, and Kite (1965) suggests that talking time can indeed be changed if feedback is given. During an initial discussion period, a quiet member of a four-member group was chosen as the "target person." During a second discussion period, the quiet person was positively reinforced by the experimenters every time he spoke, while the other members were negatively reinforced each time they spoke. A third discussion session was then held, without any reinforcement. As might be expected, the target person talked less than his share (16%, on the average) during the initial session, much more than his share (37%) during the second (reinforcement) session, and about his share (27%) during the third (no reinforcement) session. Furthermore, the target person's leadership potential, as judged by the other members, varied according to his verbal output.

Bavelas and his colleagues showed that the effects of reinforcement on speaking rate persist to some extent even after reinforcement ceases. But the change does not seem to be permanent. David (1972) found that reinforcing quiet members did not change their amount of speaking in new groups. We might conclude on the basis of these results that in order to be effective in equalizing verbal input among members, reinforcement must be maintained for a long period. We should also note that in the Bavelas study the quiet person was positively reinforced for talking. In most groups in which comments about peoples' quietness are made to them, negative reinforcement for being quiet is given instead (e.g., "You're too quiet, Joe. Why don't you talk more?"). Rewards are probably more effective than punishments in encouraging quiet individuals to talk. Finally, merely encouraging the quiet person to talk is not sufficient. Bavelas et al. (1965) found no effect of positive reinforcement unless the other members were negatively reinforced for talking. Apparently the less talkative member needs "room" within which he can increase his participation rate.

Type of Communication. Of course the meaning of the communication is important as well as the sheer amount. A number of systems have been devised to enable observers to code small-group communications into categories. The most widely used system of this type is Robert Bales' Interaction Process Analysis (IPA). Using the IPA system, observers of a group can classify any communicative act into one of 12 categories (see Table 12-1). Only the observable, overt behavior is classified; no attempt is made to guess the speaker's underlying feelings.

Studies using the IPA system have shown marked differences in the types of communications made by the two most talkative members (Bales, 1958). One of these two members tends to be warm, friendly, and emotionally supportive. He helps to maintain smooth interpersonal relations. His comments show tension release, agreement, and solidarity or ask for information, opinions, or suggestions.

The other highly talkative member is more oriented toward getting the task accomplished than insuring that the members get along with each other. The communications of the task specialist give information, opinions, and suggestions, as well as express disagreement.

One of the IPA categories is "seeks information." Some recent research (Crawford & Haaland, 1972; Crawford, 1974) has focused on the specific determinants of information-seeking behavior in groups. The results indicate that group members are most likely to ask for information when: (1) the group atmosphere is cooperative rather than competitive, (2) the members are uncertain about the correct decisions, (3) the decision for which information is required is important, (4) previous information has tended to be correct, and (5) correct decisions have been highly rewarded.

Another aspect of communication structure in groups concerns the relationships between various types of communications (stimuli) made by one member and the types of communications (responses) given in reply by other members. Shannon and Guerney (1973) coded communications in discussion groups into eight categories based on Leary's (1957) interpersonal theory of personality (a different classification scheme from IPA). The data indicated that certain communicative stimuli do tend to elicit certain communicative responses in groups. In particular, comments which express dependency or cooperativeness tend to be answered with responses expressing advice and leadership, and vice-versa. Self-enhancing, competitive, aggressive, or rejecting comments, on the other hand, are followed by self-enhancing or competitive comments in reply.

Communication Networks. The most commonly used approach to studying communication patterns in groups has been for the experimenter to impose a communication structure on the group. Communication is restricted to certain member-to-member channels. For example, members A and B may be able to communicate with member C, but not with each other. This type of "centralized" communication structure, with one person acting as a focal point, receiving and giving information to each of the other members, often occurs when a high degree of coordination of individual members is required, as in our example of a team of policemen tracking a suspect by radio. Rather than

TABLE 12-1
Bales Category System: Interaction Process Analysis

	Category	Examples
Social-emotional area: Positive reactions.	1 Shows solidarity, raises others status, gives help, reward.	"That's fine." "I can see how you feel."
	2 Shows tension release, jokes, laughs, shows satisfaction.	Any type of humorous remark.
	3 Agrees, shows passive acceptance, understands, concurs, complies.	"Yes." "I see." "I think you're right."
Task area: Attempted answers.	4 Gives suggestion, direction, implying autonomy for others.	"There are two points I'd like to make." "Go right ahead." "Then I guess we're all agreed on that."
	5 Gives opinion, evaluation, analysis; expresses feeling, wish.	"I think it might be . . ." "It seems right to me that . . ." "Perhaps this situation is like the one you told me about yesterday."
	6 Gives orientation, information, repeats, clarifies, confirms.	"The number is 868-7600." "We only have two days left." "I have a headache."
Task area: Questions.	7 Asks for orientation, information, repetition, confirmation.	"When did he . . . ?" "Who is in charge of arrangements for the next meeting?" "What did you say?"
	8 Asks for opinion, evaluation, analysis, expression of feeling.	"What do you think?" "I wonder what that would involve?" "How is it going?"
	9 Asks for suggestion, direction, possible ways of action.	"What shall we do?" "What do you think we ought to aim at?"
Social-emotional area: Negative reactions.	10 Disagrees, shows passive rejection, formality, withholds help.	"I don't think so." "I can't accept that." "What!"
	11 Shows tension, asks for help, withdraws out of the field.	Hesitations; embarrassment, stammering, nervous laughter.
	12 Shows antagonism, deflates other's status, defends or asserts self.	"Hurry up!" "You can't be serious!" "It's your fault!"

having everyone listening to everyone else, it may prove more efficient for all communications to flow into and out of one central coordinator. Some communication networks grow out of the voluntary choices of the members rather than the orders of an external authority. For example, in a student research team, members *A* and *B* may decide to contact each other when either encounters difficulties, but to communicate with member *C* only during formal meetings of the whole group. In this way, the communication structure during regular sessions is open and unrestricted, while between sessions the structure is limited, and only certain member-to-member channels of communication are open.

Dozens of laboratory experiments have investigated imposed communication networks in task groups. Virtually all the studies have shared the following characteristics: (1) Each group member had information essential to the solution of the group's problem. (2) Every member had to know and agree with the correct answer in order for the group to be successful. (3) A channel between one member and another was either completely open or completely closed, that is, *A* could either communicate with *B* at any time, or he could never communicate with him. (4) All channels were reciprocal or 2-sided, so that if *A* could communicate with *B*, *B* could also communicate with *A*. (5) A group's communication network did not change during the experiment. (6) The communication network was imposed by the experimenter, rather than arising spontaneously or by members' deliberate decisions.

Five of the commonly used communication networks, illustrated for the case of five-member groups, are shown in Figure 12-1. The major differences are between the centralized networks (Wheel, Chain, and Y), in which one person is best able to collect and distribute information, and the decentralized networks (Circle and All-Channel), in which no member

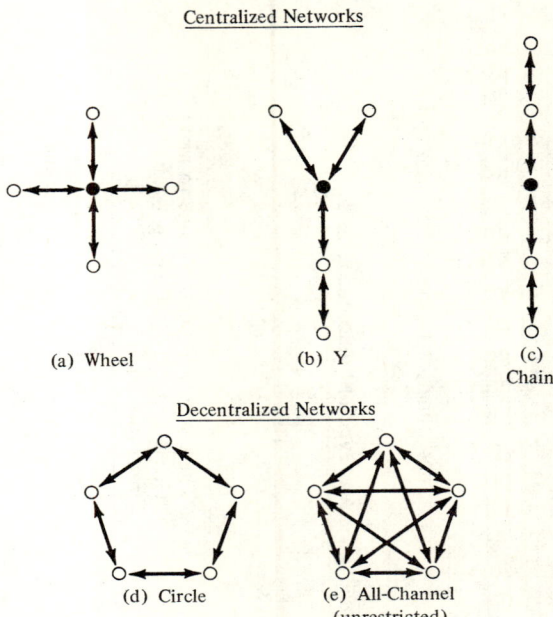

FIGURE 12-1. Communication networks used in laboratory studies (five-member groups). The darkened circle indicates the central position in diagrams (a), (b), and (c).

occupies a more central position than any other. In the centralized structures, the "key person" generally collects information from the other members, makes a decision by himself, and then relays his decision to the others. In the decentralized structures, on the other hand, all members can share in the decision-making.

The relative efficiency of the centralized versus the decentralized networks depends on the complexity of the group task (Shaw, 1964). On simple tasks, involving only the collection and distribution of information, centralized networks are considered more efficient. On more complex tasks, however, where the information must be processed or operated upon, decentralized structures are superior. Shaw (1971) points out that "Since most of the problems that groups are faced with are more complex than the most complex task used in laboratory experiments, it is evident that a decentralized communication network is most likely to be effective in natural group situations" (p. 144). Regardless of the level of task complexity, decentralized networks result in greater member satisfaction (Shaw, 1964), probably due to the greater sharing of decision making.

Whether the results of the communication network studies can be safely applied to established natural groups is doubtful. Studies by Burgess (1968) indicate that differences in performance between centralized and decentralized structures disappear over time. Thus, a group may be able to devise an efficient operating procedure in spite of initially awkward communication patterns. Similarly, Snadowsky (1974), using groups that were given a chance to develop stable work procedures and had formal leaders, found that communication network structure had relatively little effect on member satisfaction. Style of leadership (democratic vs. authoritarian), Snadowsky found, was much more influential than communication structure in determining satisfaction: "Although the communication network *per se* may define the limits within which the group must work, the leadership has considerable leeway in maximizing or minimizing the positive and negative aspects of a given communication structure" (Snadowsky, 1974, p. 52).

In addition to having formal leaders, most natural task groups differ in a number of ways from groups used in communication network experiments. First, most tasks do not require participation from all members. Although involvement of all members may be desirable, it is seldom necessary for successful completion of the task. As Steiner (1972) points out,

> Outside the laboratory, it is sometimes possible to circumvent a participant who performs his phase of the job poorly, or to have several persons work collaboratively on critical parts of the task. Furthermore, in many situations it is unimportant whether every member of a group receives and accepts the correct solution to a problem; acceptance by the majority, or even by a minority, is sometimes sufficient. (p. 55)

Second, in few cases is a communication channel completely closed. In natural groups it is sometimes more difficult to communicate with one member than with another, but communication is seldom impossible. Openness of communication should thus be considered a continuous, rather than a dichotomous (either open or closed) variable.

In naturally functioning groups, the openness of A's channel to B is often different from that of B's channel to A. A low-status member may refrain from initiating communication with a high-status member, while the high-status member may feel free to communicate to the low-status member whenever he wishes.

We might also note that naturally occurring communication structures change over time. In the few studies of laboratory groups in which the groups were permitted to change their communication structures, they took advantage of the opportunity to do so.

Most of the work on communication networks is directly relevant only at those times when the group is not having a regular face-to-face meeting. Members may communicate in a variety of different network patterns between formal group meetings.

Composition

One of the structural dimensions of a group that involves the relationships which exist before group members ever come in contact with each other is composition. The composition of the group refers to relationships among pre-existing characteristics or qualities of the individual members. The concern here is how particular combinations of member characteristics affect group functioning.

Relatively little research has been concerned with member characteristics. What work has been done has generally not dealt with qualities of members in structural terms. Rather, the tendency has been to measure the average level of some individual characteristic. This approach ignores the pattern of relationships of the individual characteristics. Two groups may have equal average levels of a particular quality, yet in one group all members possess the quality to a moderate degree, while in the other group half the members are very high on the quality and the other half are very low. One of the basic assumptions underlying the study of groups rather than individuals is that certain phenomena occur only on the group level as a result of the relationships among members. In other words, group activity is seldom either a simple adding or averaging of individual activity. In their survey of group research, McGrath and Altman (1966) make the same point:

> We suspect . . . that it would not be wholly profitable to pursue research in this area from the point of view of *individual* personality characteristics. Rather, such properties should be studied with respect to the composition of the group. It is probably not the presence or absence of member anxiety per se, for example, but rather the *pattern* of anxiety among group members that makes a difference for groups. (p. 57)

Similarity of Members. The most common approach to composition has compared groups with similar members (homogeneous groups) to groups with dissimilar members (heterogeneous groups). The results of different studies are seldom directly comparable because different characteristics or combinations of characteristics have been used to establish the similarity–dissimilarity.

The effects of similarity of biographical characteristics, such as age, occupation, or education, depend on the particular characteristics and groups involved. In one study (Gross, 1956), friendship groups among Air Force personnel were investigated. Among dyads, attraction (group cohesiveness) was associated with similarity of some qualities, such as length of time in service, but with dissimilarity for other qualities, such as marital status. Similarily of other characteristics, such as age, showed no relationship to attraction. Similar results were found for larger groups.

Perhaps the most obvious characteristic for which groups can be heterogeneous or homogeneous is sex. There appears to be general agreement among both psychologists and laymen that mixed-sex (heterogeneous) groups differ from same-sex (homogeneous) groups, yet little research has investigated the effects of sex composition. Typically, psychologists studying groups have dealt with sex-composition effects by controlling them, that is, by studying only all-male or all-female groups.

Nevertheless, some work has been done. One early study (South, 1927) found that mixed-sex groups spent more time on social-emotional activity than same-sex groups. Because of the greater concern with interpersonal relations in mixed-sex groups, we might expect more conformity in such groups than in same-sex groups. Reitan and Shaw (1964) did in fact find that for both men and women, greater conformity to the incorrect majority occurred in mixed groups. Members of mixed-sex groups also expressed more concern about disagreements and less confidence in their judgments.

Do people prefer mixed-sex to same-sex groups? One recent study (Marshall & Heslin, in press) indicates that men generally prefer groups which include both men and women. Women also like mixed-sex groups, as long as the groups are large. For small groups, however, females would rather have all female members.

The trend in recent years to integrate women

into previously all-male work groups demonstrates the need for further research on sex composition. Marshall and Heslin point out that their mixed-sex groups included equal numbers of men and women. It seems likely that having only one man or only one woman in a group may yield quite different results.

The relationship between heterogenity and group cohesiveness or satisfaction is not a simple one. Some studies (Hoffman, 1959; Hoffman & Maier, 1961) show no difference in satisfaction between groups of persons with similar and dissimilar personality profiles. On the other hand, Levy (1964) showed his subjects sets of pictures of similar and dissimilar faces, asked them which they would most "prefer meeting and getting to know," and found a decided preference for dissimilarity.

Some order was introduced to these conflicting findings by Reckman and Goethals (1973), who found that the group's goal affects preferences for heterogeneity versus homogeneity. When the group's purpose was described as accuracy of judgment, dissimilar others were preferred as fellow members. However, when the goal of the group was simply to be congenial and friendly, similar others were chosen. Thus, the relative preference for variety versus uniformity in group membership may depend on the relative emphasis of the group on task functions versus social functions.

Heterogeneity-homogeneity has been researched in the context of encounter groups. As regards background characteristics of a biographical nature, such as age, sex, and occupation, some group leaders favor as great a variety as possible, providing a wide range of viewpoints. Others believe that homogeneity of members will tend to make communication and mutual understanding easier.

Complementarity of Members. A different approach to group composition focuses on complementarity of needs rather than similarity-dissimilarity. Winch (1955) has proposed a rather controversial theory of mate selection based on this approach. His basic hypothesis is that we choose marital partners who satisfy our needs. For example, a dominant person would not be expected to marry another dominant person, but rather a submissive person. Similarly, a person needing much affection will most probably marry someone who gives him affection. The research testing Winch's theory has sometimes supported it and sometimes not. The results seem to depend on precisely what "needs" are measured and just how they are measured. Unfortunately, Winch does not specify which needs are the most important. Also, the concept of complementarity seems to make sense only when applied to those personal characteristics that are distinctly interpersonal in nature, such as dominance-submission. Other opposing personality traits are not necessarily complementary, nor are they necessarily needs. Consider anxiety, for example. An anxious person may be attracted to nonanxious people because they help to calm him. But why should nonanxious people be attracted to anxious people? It certainly seems plausible that anxious and nonanxious people will have greater difficulty understanding and empathizing with each other than would those similar in anxiety level.

A much more sophisticated approach to the question of complementarity of needs was proposed by Schutz (1958). First, Schutz identified the three general needs which he believed were most important in determining interpersonal behavior: control, affection, and inclusion. Schutz further differentiated two dimensions of each need: first, the amount of control, affection, and inclusion behavior that a person wished to see expressed in his relationships, and second, whom he wanted to initiate the behavior, himself or the other person. Within each of the three needed areas, the two people must agree on both dimensions in order to be compatible. For example, if *A* and *B* both desire a great deal of affection in relationships,

		AMOUNT OF AFFECTION WANTED TO GIVE	
		High	Low
AMOUNT OF AFFECTION WANTED TO RECEIVE	High	"Spouse"	"Infant"
	Low	"Parent of infant"	"Drill instructor"

FIGURE 12-2. Four need types in the affection area, according to Schutz, 1958, p. 166.

but each expects the other to give affection and himself to receive affection, they would be incompatible. On the other hand, both *A* and *B* may agree that *B* should be the primary source of affection in their relationship, yet disagree over just how much affection *B* should express, again producing incompatibility. A slightly different way of looking at this same problem is to think of each person having both a need to give and a need to receive each of the three types of behavior. Thus, for each of the three needs there are four different need types. Schutz's terms for the four need types for affection are show in Figure 12-2. We can see that two persons who each want to give affection as well as receive affection ("spouses") would be compatible, as would two persons each with low needs for receiving and giving affection ("drill instructors"). Another complementary combination would be "parent"-"infant," where one party (the "parent") desires to give what the other wants to receive, yet does not need to receive what the other cannot give. Similar analyses can be performed for each of the other two need areas. For instance, in the example presented earlier of a dominant person and a submissive person being compatible, the dominant person would be high in need to control others and low in need to be controlled by others, while the submissive person would have just the opposite pattern of needs.

Schutz has performed a number of studies testing his theory of compatibility, with generally supportive results. In one study, fraternity members were measured for needs in the three areas and also asked to nominate other members for roommate, traveling companion, and house officers. Compatibility was found to predict choice for each of the three types of relationship. As Schutz's theory predicts, inclusion compatibility was most important for sporadic, superficial relationships (officer), control compatibility was most important for short-term relationships (traveling companion), and affection compatibility was most important for long-term (roommate) relationships.

By adding together the compatibility scores of each pair of persons in a group, Schutz was able to measure the total compatibility of a group. He found a strong relationship between cohesiveness and total compatibility of nine experimental groups. Smith and Haythorn (1972) formed compatible and incompatible groups by means of scores on Schutz' affection and control dimensions. During 21 days of isolation, the members of compatible groups felt less hostility toward their partners.

Similarity in Encounter Groups. As we pointed out earlier, encounter groups have a natural tendency to be fairly homogeneous in some respects. Given this "natural" homogeneity, however, members may vary considerably in personality, values, and interests. The primary argument in favor of composing encounter groups of similar people is that communication and empathy will be facilitated, and unnecessary conflict reduced. On the other hand, some investigators (e.g., Bennis & Shepard, 1956; Harrison & Lubin, 1965) argue that heterogeneous groups present the participants with a wider variety of learning opportunities and behavior models. Furthermore, it is claimed that change in heterogeneous groups will generalize more to the outside social environment, which is heterogeneous.

Research has not revealed a clear-cut superiority for either homogeneous or heterogeneous encounter groups. In one study (Harrison & Lubin, 1965), participants were dividied into heterogeneous or homogeneous groups according to their preferences for formal structure in the group. The homogeneous groups were harmonious, and ran smoothly. On the other hand, the heterogeneous groups encountered much more conflict and frustration. However, the members of the heterogeneous groups felt that they gained more understanding of both themselves and others. Harrison and Lubin suggest that a certain amount of conflict is necessary to force members out of their usual habits of thought and behavior.

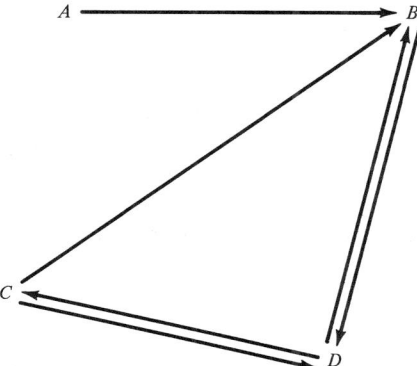

FIGURE 12-3. Diagram of the affect structure of a four-person group. Arrows indicate liking and the absence of lines indicate the absence of liking.

Attraction

Perhaps the most noticeable characteristic of a group is the pattern of attraction. The pattern of who likes whom determines to a major extent whether a voluntary group continues or breaks into two or more independent subgroups.

The attraction structure of a group can be discovered by asking each member about his liking for other members. The resulting pattern of relationships can then be pictured as in Figure 12-3. Here we can readily see that person B is the most popular, being liked by all the other members. Person A, on the other hand, is an "isolate," not being liked by anyone in the group. Some of the liking relationships between members are reciprocal (e.g., B and D both like each other; A and C both do not like each other); others are one-way (e.g., A likes B, but B does not like A).

Social psychologists have tended to focus their attention not on specific patterns of liking among individual members, but rather on the liking for the group as a whole. This liking for the group, averaged over all the members, is usually termed the group's *cohesiveness*.

Group cohesiveness can be measured in several different ways. One indirect method is to count the relative frequency of the words "I" vs. "we" in group discussion. One could also ask the members directly about their identification with the group or their sense of belongingness to it. Most often, however, a method which compares liking for other members with liking for nonmembers is employed. This procedure, called the sociometric technique (described in Chapter 9), involves asking each member to name the person or persons he would most like to join him in various activities. The degree of the group's cohesiveness is then measured by the relative frequency with which members and nonmembers are chosen. Thus, a group can be considered cohesive to the extent that the people whom the members like best are other members.

Measurement of Cohesiveness. One problem with cohesiveness research is that different measures of cohesiveness often give different results (Eisman, 1959). In particular, sociometric measures based on personal attraction may not agree very well with the results of direct questions about attraction to the whole group. To some extent this reflects the fact that cohesiveness is determined by many factors in addition to attraction to members. As we pointed out in the section on group formation, a person may be attracted to a group primarily because he likes its activities or goals rather than its members.

Another problem with the usual sociometric technique is that it is not sensitive to a lack of liking between some of the members. A group may consist of two or more subgroups, each made up of people who like each other but do not like members of the other subgroups. The usual sociometric procedure can give a misleading picture of the group's cohesiveness in this case. Members may prefer the people in their subgroup to any nonmembers, which would give the group a high cohesiveness score. However, the sociometric method will not pick up the absence of liking between members of different subgroups.

Another reason why it may be misleading to measure group cohesiveness on the basis of personal attraction is that we usually assume with such a method that all members are equally important to each other. Of course, this is not true. The attractiveness of the more important members of the group may be more critical than the attractiveness of the less important members. For example, Anderson, Linder, and Lopes (1973) found that leaders of groups, whether liked or disliked, were given more weight than were nonleaders in determining the liking for the whole group. These findings suggest that a group may be moderately cohesive if everyone likes the leader, even though the other members do not like each other.

Determinants of Cohesiveness. A number of variables have been found to influence the level of cohesiveness of a group. First, how a new member joins a group may have an impact on his eventual liking for the group. The theory of cognitive dissonance predicts that we come to like those things for which we have chosen to suffer. Thus, the more harsh and unpleasant the initiation into a group, the more attractive it should eventually be. This effect may explain the intentionally harsh basic training period in military organizations, as well as the puberty rites of many primitive cultures in which boys must endure isolation, torture, and even bodily mutilation in order to be accepted into the tribe. Two studies support the proposition that painful initiations lead to cohesive groups. Walker (1968) found a strong relationship between the cohesiveness of fraternities and the degree of suffering which their pledges underwent. However, we cannot be sure from these results that the severe initiation was the cause of the liking for the group. Perhaps fraternities which are attractive for other reasons also just happen to have harsh initiations. However, a laboratory experiment by Aronson and Mills (1969) showed that it is indeed the severe initiation itself which is responsible for a member's greater attraction to the group.

In addition to personal attraction and initiation, a number of other factors may influence liking for the group. A group's style of leadership may be preferred to another group's. There is also evidence that cohesiveness decreases with increasing group size (Porter & Lawler, 1965; Gibb, 1951). As a group gets larger, either it will break up into several independently functioning subgroups or, if a single focus of interaction is maintained, the time that each person has available for participation will decrease.

In general, the more successful the group is in attaining its goals, the more cohesive it is (Lott & Lott, 1965). This relationship has been found in growth groups as well as task groups. Lieberman et al. (1973a) found a fairly strong relationship between overall success of the group (in terms of individual growth) and cohesiveness during its later phase.

The idea that a common threat to the group from outside forces draws the group closer together has been proposed by many writers. For example, Karl Marx argued that individuals form a unified class only when faced with a common struggle against another class. Similarly, feelings of patriotism and national unity have been noted to increase during wartime.

The threat-cohesiveness relationship has been investigated in a number of studies, with generally supportive results. Mulder and Stemerding (1963) called meetings of small grocers in Dutch towns and informed them there was a possibility of a large supermarket chain opening a branch in their town. The grocers were also told that the probability of such a threat to their livelihood was either high (80%) or low (10%). The high-threat grocers expressed a greater desire for future meetings than did the low-threat grocers.

In another study (Sherif et al., 1961), boys in summer camps were assigned randomly to one of two groups. The two groups were isolated from each other for a time and were then set in competition to each other. Increased cohesiveness within each group and hostility toward the other group soon followed.

Bramel (1969) has proposed a number of possible reasons why external threat should facilitate internal solidarity in groups. For one thing, the existence of disliked others affords opportunities for the displacement of aggression. Hostility that would normally be directed toward other group members may instead be directed toward the external target. Another reason is that sharing a common danger increases the similarity of members to each other, which should increase attraction to them. Distraction of attention away from minor internal conflicts may be another result of threat to the group. Some support for this proposition comes from a study (Rabbie et al., 1974) which found decreased attention to interpersonal emotional relations in groups faced with competition from another group. The increased cooperative interaction among the group members necessitated by the external threat may also lead to increased attraction. Finally, the expending of effort to meet a common challenge may lead to increased cohesiveness through the process of dissonance reduction.

Cognitive dissonance theory predicts that we come to like what we work or suffer for—in this case, the group. Another possibility, not mentioned by Bramel, is that the heightened relevance of outsiders who are different from the group members may serve to accentuate the perceived similarity of the members by contrast. One common reaction of Americans traveling abroad is an increased attraction to fellow countrymen. In a foreign country, Americans may find themselves drawn to other Americans with whom they would never associate at home. Because of the contrast with the very different foreigners surrounding them, the other Americans seem more similar than they would normally.

Another basis for threat leading to greater cohesiveness involves social comparison. In a threatening situation, we desire to compare our feelings with those of similar others, to help us interpret our feelings and decide whether or not they are justified and appropriate to the situation. Schachter (1959) threatened subjects by telling them they would be receiving painful electric shocks. The threatened subjects preferred to wait with similar others more than did nonthreatened subjects. No differences in preferences for being alone or with others were found when the others were dissimilar (not expecting shocks) and thus could not be used as a source of social comparison.

Threat does not always lead to greater cohesiveness, however. With a low expectation of success, threat may lead to lowered cohesiveness (Rabbie et al., 1974). This may be what happened in the United States during the Vietnam war. As the conflict dragged on without any American victory in sight, the country became increasingly divided rather than more united.

The Schachter threat-affiliation effect has also been shown to apply only under limited circumstances. When the threat produces anxiety or anticipation of embarrassment, rather than fear, threatened subjects prefer to be alone rather than with similar others (Sarnoff & Zimbardo, 1961). Furthermore, subjects who feel threatened by anxiety prefer dissimilar (nonthreatened) to similar (threatened) others as associates (Firestone, Kaplan, & Russell, 1973).

Effects of Cohesiveness. Attraction to a group, we have just seen, is influenced by many factors—attraction to individual members, initiation, group success, and threat. In turn, the cohesiveness of a group influences many aspects of the group interaction. We will now consider the effects of cohesiveness on communication, influence, and reaction to other groups. We should keep in mind that in natural groups cohesiveness both affects communication and influence and is at the same time affected by these factors (Collins & Raven, 1969).

The cohesiveness of a group is related to both the quantity and the quality of verbal interaction. Members of cohesive groups talk more. Lott and Lott (1961) found a correlation of .42 between cohesiveness and communication activity in groups of students. Differences in quality of communication as a function of cohesiveness in dyads have been noted by Back (1951). Here cohesiveness was manipulated by the experimenter in three different ways: attraction to the partner, attraction to the task, and attraction to the prestige of the group. For all three kinds of highly cohesive groups, partners influenced each other more than in low-cohesive groups. Differences in the bases of cohesiveness also led to differences in communication and influence patterns. When the cohesiveness was due to personal attraction, members wanted to turn their discussion into a long pleasant conversation. A member's resistance to persuasion was resented. Task-based cohesiveness resulted in desires for speedy and efficient performance. Cohesiveness based on group prestige brought about cautiousness and conformity, with one partner assuming a dominant role and the other submitting to his direction.

Additional studies have provided support for the proposition that in cohesive groups, members both attempt to influence other members more and also are themselves more influenced (Lott & Lott, 1965). In perhaps the best known of these studies, Schachter (1951) manipulated group cohesiveness and the relevance of the discussion topic to the group's goals. In each group cohesiveness and the relevance of the rest of the group on the assigned topic. In the high-relevant, high-cohesive group, communication to the deviate tended to drop off toward the end of the discussion.

Cohesiveness in Encounter Groups. In encounter groups, attraction to the group appears to be a necessary prerequisite for personal growth; however, merely liking the group is not enough to insure lasting benefits. Apparently many people enjoy encounter-group experiences without being changed by them. Lieberman et al. (1973a) found that members with little liking for their group tended to change in a negative direction. High attraction to the group, however, was exhibited both by those who changed positively and those who did not change at all. Thus Lieberman et al. conclude, "Achieving a sense of belonging . . . does not itself guarantee success; it is the lack of it that guarantees failure. . . . the psychosocial relationship an individual has to the encounter group provides the floor upon which productive work can take place. Without this base, the learning opportunities of the group are less available" (1973a, pp. 345–346).

Perception of Structure

So far, we have been discussing group structure from the "outside," that is, from an external observer's point of view. The view of the group's structure that an individual member has may be quite different from that of the outsider. The outside observer is usually less involved in the group. The actions of the members seldom have personal relevance to him. He may therefore be less sensitive to some aspects of the group but more sensitive to other aspects. Being "caught up in the action" gives one a different perspective from that of the detached nonparticipant. This difference was demonstrated by Welkowitz and Kuc (1973), who found no relationship between the ratings participants in a conversation made of their partners' empathy, warmth, and genuineness and the ratings of observers.

In addition to being less involved in the group, the outside observer is able to view every member of the group as an "other." The group member, on the other hand, must view one of the members, namely himself, from the "inside." Jones and Nisbett (1972) have developed a theory stating that people interpret their own behavior in distinctly different ways than they interpret other people's behavior. Thus, while the participant in the group sees his own and other members' behavior in different terms, the outside observer tends much more to view every member's behavior in the same way.

Just as an observer's viewpoint is different from a participant's, so each participant's perspective is different from those of the others. Different individuals may be aware of different structural dimensions. One member may be conscious of the communication pattern, another of the attraction pattern, and so on. Members also vary regarding which dimensions they think are important and how the members are related along the dimensions.

The perceptions that members of a psychological laboratory had of the structure of their group were studied by Jones and Young (1972). The most important dimensions of group structure for the members were status, political persuasion, and professional interests. The member's own status affected how important he considered each of these dimensions. The faculty members placed relatively more weight on the status dimension, while the graduate students were more concerned with the dimensions of political persuasion and professional interests.

Jones and Young repeated their study a year later and found both change and stability in members' perceptions of the group's structure. For both graduate students and faculty, political persuasion had become more important. However, the longer a member had been in the group the less change there was in his judgment of the relative importance of the dimension. This finding suggests that the longer we are in a group, the more stable our perceptions of its structure become.

SUMMARY

We have defined a group as a collection of two or more persons who interact in the context of shared norms and goals. Types of groups can be distinguished according to their primary goal. Task groups attempt to change their external environment. Growth groups attempt to change their individual members. Social-friendship groups attempt to provide pleasurable interaction for their members.

An encounter group represents one popular form of growth group. The effectiveness of encounter groups is not easy to evaluate, but one study indicates that they may produce moderate positive change in some members. However, other members may be unaffected by the experience, while still others may be harmed.

Groups may form because of attraction to the other people, attraction to common goals and activities, or simply a desire to associate with others. Groups often encounter conflict until stable "rules" of behavior develop. These rules, or norms, help reduce uncertainty and anxiety over what behavior is appropriate.

Groups can be analyzed along a number of structural dimensions. Territory, personal and group space, and the arrangement of members in space affect the group's interaction and its relations with nonmembers. Member comfort and influence are often affected by how members position themselves in relation to each other and to their environment.

The communication structure also is related to member influence. Members who talk the most and engage in particular kinds of communication are likely to emerge as leaders. Studies of communication networks have found that for most situations, both satisfaction and performance are highest when communication is unrestricted.

Group composition has been investigated in regard to both the similarity of members and the compatibility of their needs. While similarity may or may not lead to greater satisfaction, depending on other factors, having members who are able to fulfill each others' needs does appear to be an advantage.

Members may remain attracted to their group for many reasons, such as a severe initiation, the successful attainment of group goals, or an external threat. The more cohesive a group, the more influence it exerts on members to conform to group norms and majority opinions.

Finally, the perception of a group's structure depends on whether it is viewed from the "outside" or the "inside." Members may differ in their conceptions of which aspects of their group's structure are most important.

SUGGESTED READINGS

Back, K. W. *Beyond words: The story of sensitivity training and the encounter movement.* Baltimore: Penguin, 1973.

Beyond Words critically assesses the encounter-group phenomenon as a social movement. Back examines the historical roots of the movement and its development over the last three decades. He argues that encounter groups have conflicting goals of self-expression and of personal growth and shows how these contradictions have affected the movement. Finally, he analyzes the movement's overall impact and its meaning as a symptom of the state of society.

Howard, J. *Please touch: A guided tour of the human potential movement.* New York: Dell, 1971.

Howard, a journalist, presents a lively account of her personal experiences as a participant in a variety of types of encounter groups. She creates vivid portraits of the leaders, members, and experiences which she discovered, and concludes with an analysis of how she has changed as a result of her experiences.

Lieberman, M. A., Yalom, I. D., & Miles, M. B. *Encounter groups: First facts.* New York: Basic Books, 1973.

This is the account of the study which we have referred to so often. The authors present a wide array of data on the effects of the 17 groups investigated. Each group is described in considerable detail, with many excerpts from the actual sessions included. Hazards, group norms, and the characteristics and styles of the group leaders are among the topics discussed.

Shaw, M. E. *Group dynamics: The psychology of small group behavior.* New York: McGraw-Hill, 1971.

This excellent textbook provides an in-depth analysis of all aspects of groups. Shaw provides an integrated account of what research has established about group development and interaction, using a generally structural approach. He ends each chapter with a list of plausible hypotheses about group phenomena.

13
Group Processes, Productivity, and Leadership

Bruce Kleinhans and Dalmas A. Taylor

INTRODUCTION

In the previous chapter our primary concern was group structure. In this chapter we shall begin by focusing on group process—how the group as a whole or its individual members change over time. Two group processes which have attracted great interest among social psychologists in recent years will be analyzed in detail: (1) how group discussion results in more extreme decisions and judgments and (2) how antisocial behavior may become released in a group setting.

Group productivity will be our second major topic. Beginning with a consideration of the influence of the presence of others on individual performance, we will discuss how groups compare with individuals and how working separately compares with working together. The advantages and disadvantages of different-sized groups will be probed next. The effects of composition and interpersonal attraction on group performance will also be examined. Finally, we will look at some of the dangers of making important decisions in groups, and at how to minimize these dangers.

Finally, we will discuss the topic of leadership. Here our primary attention will be on the strengths and weaknesses of various theoretical approaches to leadership which psychologists have employed over the years.

GROUP PROCESSES

The "Risky Shift"

Groups must often choose between a safe course of action and a more risky one. Consider our earlier example of the students planning and conducting a psychology experiment. They might be faced with the following choice: Either test a hypothesis that has been tested and supported many times before, or test an entirely new hypothesis. The cautious course would be the first choice. The attempt to find the same results as have been found previously is safe in the sense of having a high probability of success. The "payoff," however, would not be very great; such a study would be relatively unexciting and the results would not be especially impressive. The second course, performing a totally original study, is more risky. There is a smaller chance of success (i.e., of obtaining statistically significant results). The rewards of success, on the other hand, would be great. A study which discovers something new constitutes a contribution to the field and can be published in a scientific journal.

Suppose most of the members of the research team decide on their own to follow the safe course. After a group discussion, however, the group finally decides to take the risky course. Is such a process of cautious individual decisions becoming a risky group decision typical, and if so, why does such a shift occur?

The change in decisions involving risk from the initial, individual decisions, to the later group decisions has come to be known as the "risky shift." As the name implies, the most frequent finding has been that group decisions are riskier than the average of the initial individual decisions. However, "risky shift" is a rather misleading term, since "cautious shifts" (as well as no shifts) can occur under certain circumstances. For this reason, many psychologists prefer a more neutral term such as "choice shifts."

A finding that groups make riskier decisions than individuals was first reported in a master's thesis in 1961 (Stoner, 1961). Since then, literally hundreds of experiments have investigated the phenomenon. It is the clear impression of the present authors that in recent years more group research has focused on group versus individual choices involving risk than on any other topic. Why has this particular problem generated such enormous scientific interest?

Cartwright (1971) suggests a number of different bases for the popularity of risky shift research. First, the risky shift contradicted previous research findings. That groups are riskier than individuals was also contrary to popular belief and folklore. The group has traditionally been seen as a conservative force, rejecting the new, unusual, or risky. Furthermore, if groups really are riskier than individuals, there would be important practical implications. The amount of collective versus individual decision making in business, government, and the military might best be changed. As more studies were performed, a number of different explanations of the risky shift arose; this theoretical controversy, perhaps more than any other factor, helped to maintain the interest of researchers in the area.

Most risky shift research has employed the Choice Dilemmas Questionnaire (CDQ). This instrument consists of 12 items, each presenting a hypothetical situation involving a cautious course of action which would bring moderate but secure benefits and a risky alternative which would bring high rewards if successful, but high losses if unsuccessful. For example, in one item a man must choose between staying in his present job at a modest salary or accepting a better-paying position at a company with an uncertain future. Other items involve realistic choices between conservative versus speculative financial investment, changing one's habits of life versus attempting a delicate operation, settling for a tie versus going all out for a win in a football game, and staying single versus marrying a less-than-ideal mate. Subjects indicate in each case how good the chances of success would have to be in order for them to recommend the risky alternative.

The usual experimental procedure has been for subjects first to complete the CDQ individually. Riskiness scores are averaged over the 12 items to yield an index of general riskiness. Then subjects are assembled into groups to discuss the items one at a time, coming to a group consensus on each of the 12 choices. Again, riskiness scores are averaged across items. Then the average of the initial individual scores is compared to the final group score. When this standard procedure is followed, the results almost invariably show that the group decisions are riskier than the individual decisions. Risky shifts of comparable size have been obtained using subjects of both sexes, of various occupational backgrounds, and of different nationalities (Cartwright, 1971).

Questions regarding the generality of the risky shift effect have not been concerned with the types of subjects, but rather with the types of items used. In other words, as in so many comparisons of individuals versus groups (as well as comparisons among different kinds of groups), the particular *task* is critical. The typical practice of averaging scores over different items obscures the fact that different items produce different shifts. Some items result in reliable moderate shifts in the risky direction, others in much smaller shifts toward risk, and still others in small but reliable shifts toward caution.

This observation led several investigators to try to construct sets of items which would produce strong cautious shifts. These efforts (e.g., Stoner, 1968) have been successful. Thus, groups are sometimes more risky than individuals, but sometimes less risky, depending on the particular choices.

Another criticism relating to the generality of the risky shift has been that the CDQ items are all imaginary situations. A person's or a group's decisions on the CDQ have no actual consequences. Therefore, some investigations have used a gambling task in place of the CDQ. In this way, the decisions have meaningful consequences, gains or losses of money, for the persons making them. Here again, however, the results have been mixed. Sometimes groups are riskier gamblers than individuals, sometimes they are more cautious gamblers, and sometimes there is no difference.

Four major theories have been proposed to account for choice shifts in group decision making. Most theorists have assumed that, in general, groups are riskier than individuals. However, to be considered as a fully adequate explanation, a theory should also be able to explain why groups sometimes are more cautious than individuals.

The Diffusion-of-Responsibility Explanation. Perhaps the theoretical account which accords most closely with common sense is that in a group, concerns over possible negative consequences of the risky alternative are reduced (Wallach & Kogan, 1965). This is due to the shifting or diffusion of responsibility for the decision from oneself onto the other group members. A person can be blamed for bad decisions that he alone makes, but in a group no one person is required to assume the blame for a poor choice.

No direct evidence and only weak indirect evidence in favor of the responsibility-diffusion theory has been generated. Assuming that diffusion of responsibility does in fact reduce anxiety, then anxious people might be more affected by the opportunity to diffuse responsibility in a group. Therefore, it could be predicted that anxious people should show a greater shift toward risk. This has been found to be true (Kogan & Wallach, 1967).

There are a number of arguments against the responsibility diffusion explanation, on the other hand. For example, why should anyone be concerned about responsibility for imaginary choices having no real outcomes? Furthermore, individuals who simply observe a group discussing the CDQ problems shift toward risk (Lamm, 1967). Here it is difficult to explain how a person can place the responsibility for his own decisions on persons with whom he has had no interaction. Finally, diffusion-of-responsibility theory cannot explain shifts toward caution.

The Familiarization Explanation. Another theory of the risky shift proposes that underlying mechanism is familiarization with the decision items (Bateson, 1966). The more a person thinks about one of the CDQ situations, the better he is able to reduce his uncertainty, and the more willing he should be to accept the risky alternative. Thus, according to this explanation, the risky shift is not a group phenomenon at all; the group discussion simply serves as one means of gaining familiarity with the choice dilemmas.

A direct test of the familiarization explanation is possible. Compare the usual group shift with that produced in individuals who make initial choices, study the items and list arguments pro and con, and then make the same choices a second time. Two studies using this method (Bateson, 1966; Flanders & Thistlethwaite, 1967) have obtained individual risky shifts of the same size as group risky shifts. However, at least 7 later attempts to demonstrate the familiarization effect have failed (Pruitt, 1971a).

In addition to a lack of solid empirical support, the familiarization theory suffers from other deficiencies. In the first place, it does not do an adequate job of explaining the supposed familiarization effect. Why should people necessarily become more certain the more they think about a choice? And assuming that uncertainty is reduced through familiarization, why should a person therefore necessarily become more risky? Familiarization does not seem to agree with our common-sense experience of individual decision making. Thinking over a choice sometimes results in a more risky decision, sometimes a less risky decision, and sometimes no change. Finally, the familiarization theory cannot explain either individual or group shifts toward caution.

The Leadership Explanation. Leadership theory proposes that risky people are more pursuasive than cautious people in group discussions that produce risky shifts (Collins & Guetzkow, 1964). Leadership theory can handle the case of cautious shifts by assuming that cautious people are more influential in group discussions which produce cautious shifts. Support for this theory comes from studies indicating that, for risky shifts, risky group members are perceived by comembers as having been more influential during the group discussion (Wallach, Kogan, & Burt, 1965), while with cautious shifts, cautious members are seen as more persuasive (Brown, 1965). However, a plausible alternative explanation of these results is that the high risk taker (or low risk taker, in the cautious case) is viewed as more influential only because the other members have shifted towards his position (for other reasons). Members observe themselves becoming riskier and infer from this shift that they must have been influenced, and were probably influenced most by the member who was initially riskiest. So the risky members may be perceived as more influential without actually having been so.

The Value Explanation. The most widely accepted theory of choice shifts regards risk and caution as general cultural values (Brown, 1965). The cultural value theory makes two basic assumptions. First, in certain situations society values risky actions while in other situations it values cautious actions. Second, in group discussions each member compares his initial level of riskiness with those of the other members. This social comparison process enables the person to judge just how risky he actually is and to change his position toward either more risk (when risk is culturally valued) or more caution (when caution is culturally valued) in order to appear at least as good as other members. Thus, if a particular choice involves a cultural value of risk, people will make initial private decisions which they believe are risky, at least as risky as those of similar others. However, during the actual discussion, some persons discover that they are not as risky as the other group members. These persons will then move in a risky direction in order to express better the dominant cultural value of risk and to appear at least as risky as everybody else. A similar process occurs for choices in which a cultural value of caution is aroused.

Considerable evidence supports the assumption that risk is culturally valued for items which show a risky shift ("risk-oriented items") and that caution is culturally valued for items that show a cautious shift ("caution-oriented items"). When asked what level of riskiness they would most admire, subjects choose levels more risky than their own on items producing a group risky shift (Levinger & Schneider, 1969). Similarly, subjects give more favorable evaluations to fictitious persons who make risky choices on risk-oriented items. Furthermore, on caution-oriented items, the most admired decisions are more cautious than the subject's own choices (Fraser, 1970).

Another implication of the value theory is that the arguments involved in the discussion are less important in producing risky shifts than is the simple knowledge of the other member's risk levels. Thus, mere exchange of information about initial choices, without actual group discussion, should be sufficient to produce a risky shift on risk-oriented items. This prediction was confirmed in a study by Teger and Pruitt (1967).

When Are Groups Cautious Rather Than Risky?
Let us return to the question of when we can expect a risky shift and when a cautious shift. Clark and Willems (1969) found that greater risky shifts occur on CDQ items which subjects perceive to have less serious consequences. Similarly, Marquis and Reitz (1969), using a gambling task, found risky shifts on bets in which the odds favored winning and cautious shifts when the odds favored losing. Similar results were obtained by Johnson and Andrews (1971), using a unique type of choice situation. Female subjects made hypothetical choices between their usual brand (cautious) and a new, unknown brand (risky) of a variety of consumer products. Some of the choices (high risk) involved products having both a high probability of failure and relatively severe negative consequences if they failed, such as deodorants, hair conditioners, and cold remedies. Other products (low risk) had both a low probability of failure and only very mild negative consequences if they failed, such as bobby pins, facial tissues, and chewing gum. A third group of products (medium risk) were intermediate in terms of probability of failure and severity of negative consequences. As the other studies would suggest, the greater the risk of negative outcomes associated with the risky alternative, the more cautious the groups became. In particular, high-risk product choices, showed a cautious shift, medium-risk choices no shift, and low-risk choices a risky shift. These results agree well with the value theory of choice shifts. Risk is a cultural value as long as one is not risking too much. But if the stakes are high, we admire cautious decisions. We may admire the athlete who risks losing a game or the businessman who risks losing money, but we probably feel quite differently about a surgeon or an airline pilot who needlessly risks others' lives.

Deindividuation

Why do people in groups sometimes engage in behavior which they would otherwise condemn? The many riots and violent crowds in recent years have led to increased interest in a process known as deindividuation. People who lose their sense of personal identity through being caught up in the activities of an emotional crowd may engage in aggressive, destructive, and antisocial behavior which they would never consider performing when alone. Internalized norms of morality and appropriateness are weakened or completely absent.

Deindividuated behavior was described during the last century by LeBon in a highly influential book, *The Crowd* (1896). LeBon argued that people in crowds change radically, losing their normal self-control and letting irrational and savage impulses emerge. Extreme emotions are aroused, and violent and destructive acts are performed without thinking. According to LeBon, people in agitated crowds are highly suggestible, as if hypnotized, and feel little or no sense of personal responsibility for what may occur. Furthermore, he wrote, the person in a crowd loses his sense of individuality, submerging himself in the homogeneous "group mind." *The Crowd* had a major impact on Freud (1922), who described crowds in similar terms, emphasizing the individual's loss of conscience, or superego, in a crowd.

Zimbardo's Theory of Deindividuation. Recent research in deindividuated behavior has been stimulated by a theoretical analysis proposed by Zimbardo (1969). According to Zimbardo, deindividuated behavior is facilitated by the presence of a number of situational factors. Anonymity, the feeling of being unidentifiable to authority figures, victims, or fellow group members, means that one cannot be singled out for punishment or blame. In addition to being simply one of a number of people, feelings of anonymity may be fostered by wearing identical uniforms or masks, or by darkness. Weakening of feelings of personal responsibility for antisocial actions may occur through sharing the responsibility with others, ignoring the relationship between the action and its effects or displacing responsibility onto a leader. The presence of a group tends to increase anonymity and shared responsibility. It can also serve to provide models for behavior and to increase arousal. A present-time orientation leads to a diminished importance of past learning experience and decisions, as well as of future consequences of one's actions. The deindividuated person feels he is living for the immediate moment. Emotional arousal is another aid to deindividuation. The arousal occurring in crowds is often increased by vigourous physical activity, such as chanting, marching, singing, and dancing. The deindividuated person tends to become absorbed in the action itself, without rational assessment of the meaning or consequences of the action. A novel or unstructured situation decreases the inhibitions associated with familiar circumstances. Finally, altered states of consciousness, such as those produced by drugs, can weaken normal standards of conduct.

Facilitating conditions may result in certain subjective changes in the individual. The deindividuated person becomes less concerned with self-evaluation and evaluation by others. Internal controls based on guilt, shame, fear, and commitment are weakened. Individuals feel free "to act, to be spontaneous, to shed the strait jacket of cogitation, rumination, and excessive concern with 'ought' and 'should'" (Zimbardo, 1969, p. 248). Thus, the threshold for expressing normally inhibited behaviors is lowered.

The behavior which emerges during a process of deindividuation is intense, emotional, impulsive, irrational, regressive, and atypical. It is distinguished from other similar-appearing behavior by not being under the usual influence of external stimuli. Events lose their normal meanings. Thus, the victim's cries of suffering do not stop the deindividuated aggressor's attacks. Deindividuated behavior is self-reinforcing, and is intensified and amplified the more it is repeated. Deindividuated actions are difficult to terminate and may be difficult for the actor to remember once they do stop. In a deindividuated group, what happens is not simply conformity to a new norm of what is acceptable. Deindividuated persons are not reacting to any experienced group pressures for uniformity. Rather, the mere awareness of others stimulates or triggers the deindividuated behavior. Finally, since deindividuated behavior is pleasureable in itself, stimuli associated with it, such as the group in which it takes place, should become more attractive.

Research on Deindividuation. Zimbardo (1969) tested his model of deindividuation by assigning groups of college women to either anonymous or non-anonymous conditions. Anonymous subjects were dressed in large lab coats and hoods which covered their heads as soon as they arrived at the laboratory, and their names were never used. By contrast, non-anonymous subjects wore large name tags. The experimental task involved shocking another subject (actually a confederate) as part of a study of learning. Unlike most studies involving aggressive responding, the subjects were never frustrated or angered. Unlike the famous studies by Milgram (1963; 1964) on obedience to authority, there was no coercive agent present to urge the subject to deliver the shock. The results strongly supported the hypothesized effects of anonymity in groups. Anonymous subjects gave shocks lasting over twice as long as those of the non-anonymous subjects. Zimbardo's proposal that deindividuated responding is insensitive to the stimulus characteristics of the victim was also supported. Non-anonymous subjects shocked the victim longer when they didn't like her. Among the anonymous subjects, however, shock duration was unrelated to what subjects thought of the victim.

Contrary to his original predictions, Zimbardo found that when he ran his subjects individually, rather than in groups, anonymous subjects delivered less rather than more shock.

Zimbardo suggested that when alone, "the individual has no group support and is made to feel self-conscious by obvious cues of difference from those observing him" (1969, p. 279). That anonymity has different effects on aggression depending on whether the individual is alone or in a group was confirmed by Diener, Westford, Dineen, and Fraser (1973). These investigators created a more realistic situation than Zimbardo's. The group members directly interacted with the victim as well as with each other, and the aggression was delivered directly by the subject's own overt behavior, rather than indirectly by pressing a button. The victim in this experiment was described as a pacifist, who would have his nonviolent convictions tested by the subjects. The victim played the role of an antiwar sit-in demonstrator, and the subjects assumed the roles of hecklers. They were free to harass the pacifist either verbally or by use of the materials provided. These materials included balls of paper, rubber bands, sponge rubber bricks, picket signs, pistols that shot plastic pellets, and foam swords. Hidden observers rated the total aggressiveness of each subject. The results were rather complex, but they confirmed Zimbardo's findings that anonymity increases aggression in a group situation, but decreases aggression when the subject is alone.

It could be argued that Zimbardo's experiment did not really involve antisocial behavior, since the subjects were always aware that they were in a psychology experiment and that their actions were not causing any permanent harm or involuntary suffering to the victim. It could even be argued that by acting "aggressively," subjects were showing greater, not less, adherence to established social norms (in this case, obedience to an authority figure, the experimenter). Fortunately, deindividuation hypotheses have been tested in two field studies in which the subjects were unaware that they were participating in a psychological study, and in which the behavior involved the clear and direct violation of social norms.

Fraser and his colleagues (Fraser et al., in press) found that children stole more candy on Halloween when in groups than when alone. However, as with most correlational studies, it is not clear that one variable (presence of a group) necessarily *caused* the other (more stealing). It may be that children who are more likely to steal for other reasons (e.g., because they are older) also go trick-or-treating in groups. A second study (Diener, Westford, Diener & Beaman, 1973) also used the Halloween situation but experimentally manipulated group presence. Children who arrived in groups were sent to another room to get their candy either alone or as a group. All children were instructed to take only one piece of candy. A hidden observer recorded the amount of candy actually taken. Each time a child took more than one piece of candy, the extra pieces were considered "stolen." The results lend strong support to the Zimbardo model. Children in groups stole four times as much candy per person as they did when alone.

In addition to manipulating the alone versus group variable, the experimenters manipulated the subjects' emotional arousal. One third of the subjects in both the alone and the group conditions were aroused by playing a game of "Simon says." Another one third were aroused by hearing recordings of spooky noises. A final third were not aroused. As Zimbardo's model predicts, arousal increased norm-violating behavior. Children stole two to three times as much candy in the two arousal conditions as in the control condition. Furthermore, the amount of stealing was extremely high when subjects experienced both arousal and presence of a group at the same time. When the children were both emotionally aroused by the game and in a group, they stole 23 times as much candy as when they were not aroused and alone. This finding suggests that a number of the situational conditions must be present at the same time in order for fully deindividuated behavior, such as observed in mobs, to occur.

We have emphasized the negative consequences of deindividuation. However, under some conditions, a lessened sense of personal identity can "allow a range of 'positive' behaviors which we normally do not express overtly, such as intense feelings of happiness or sorrow, and open love for others" (Zimbardo, 1969, p. 251).

Some of the positive forms of deviance from social norms resulting from deindividuation were demonstrated in a study by Gergen, Gergen, and Barton (1973). Mixed-sex groups of college students were placed in a room for an hour under conditions of either normal lighting or total darkness. Since they were strangers to begin with, as each student entered the room separately and had been told that he would never meet the others, participants in the dark room were assured of total anonymity. Compared to the subjects in the normally lighted room, subjects in the dark room spent little time talking. However, nonverbal intimacy was widespread. Almost 90% of those in the dark room touched another person intentionally, and almost half hugged another person. Almost none of the lighted-room participants touched each other. Dark-room persons reported feelings of joy, freedom, and wantonness. When subjects were placed in the dark room after being told that they would be introduced to each other after the session, however, they were less likely to touch or feel close to each other. The authors conclude that " . . . the state of anonymity seems to encourage whatever potentials are most prominant at the moment—whether for good or for ill. When we are anonymous we are free to be aggressive or to give affection, whichever expresses more fully our feelings at the time." (Gergen, Gergen, & Barton, 1973, p. 129).

Deindividuation in Encounter Groups. The process of deindividuation occurring in violent mobs has many parallels in encounter groups. Relative anonymity is fostered by using only first names and ignoring one's background outside the group. Also, having the group composed of strangers who will never meet again creates a sense of anonymity. Whatever one does in the group will not be punished, disapproved of, or even known, by one's family, friends, or work associates. A strong present-time (here and now) orientation in most encounter groups encourages members to discard (at least temporarily) old inhibitions and ways of behaving. Emotional arousal is strongly encouraged by many leaders. The encounter group itself is not structured in usual ways. The fatigue occuring in long marathon group sessions may alter some members' states of consciousness.

GROUP PERFORMANCE

Social Facilitation

Since all groups are composed of individuals, and group products are the consequences of individual contributions, a logical first step in the study of group performance is to consider the influence the presence of others may have on individual performance. Studies of *social facilitation* (enhancement) provide evidence that the presence of others does affect individual performance.

Social facilitation represents one of the first areas of social psychology to be studied experimentally in the laboratory. In 1897 Triplett noted that bicycle racers consistently rode faster when competing with others than when riding along. Intrigued by this finding, Triplett had children operate a fishing reel apparatus both alone and in competing pairs. Again, as with the bicyclists, the presence of others improved performance.

The problem with Triplett's situation, however, was that the effects of others' presence was combined with the effects of competition. Since Triplett's work, numerous studies have investigated the simple audience situation. Performance alone versus in front of others has been compared on tasks as varied as finger weight-lifting (Meumann, 1919), multiplication (Dashiell, 1930), nonsense-syllable learning (Pessin, 1933), maze learning (Pessin & Husband, 1933), and light monitering (Begum & Lehr, 1963). The results across different experiments have not been consistent. Sometimes audiences improved performance; sometimes they harmed performance.

Zajonc's Arousal Theory. The problem remained unresolved until Zajonc, in 1965, reviewed the social facilitation literature and proposed a theory to reconcile the conflicting findings. Zajonc noted that all the studies showing a performance increase with an audience employed well-learned tasks in which the subject's most probable response would be the correct response. On the other hand, experiments finding a harmful effect of an audience used tasks in which a new response had to be learned, and thus the subject's most likely response would be incorrect.

If we think of a person at any time as having a set of competing response tendencies, then some of these tendencies will be strong or "dominant," and will be the most likely to be emitted. Therefore, on a well-learned task, correct responses are dominant, while on a new or poorly-learned task, incorrect responses will be dominant.

Studies of learning have established that increasing an individual's arousal level will increase his emission of dominant responses. Zajonc proposed that the presence of others is arousing, and that this arousal in turn facilitates the emission of dominant responses. Whether an audience helps or hinders performance, then, depends on how well the task has been learned. On well-learned tasks, performance will improve in the presence of others. However, on new or difficult tasks, a person will do better alone. According to Zajonc's theory, therefore, a student would be advised to study new material alone but to review and take tests with others present.

Several studies have sought to test Zajonc's propositions. In all of them, the audience members have remained as passive as possible, in order to rule out an explanation of the results in terms of cues or reinforcement provided by the spectators. Zajonc and Sales (1966) first experimentally established responses of varying strengths. Subjects pronounced various nonsense words either one, two, five, ten, or twenty-five times, depending on the particular word. These responses were then set in competition with each other by means of a false recognition test. Subjects were required to identify which of the words was flashed on a screen on each of a number of trials. In reality, the words themselves were not exposed, but rather an ambiguous wordlike stimulus. Compared to the alone condition, when observers were present subjects were much more likely to identify the stimulus as one of the well-practiced words (dominant responses) and less likely to identify it as one of the poorly-practiced words (nondominant or subordinate responses). Thus, Zajonc's predictions regarding the social facilitation of dominant responses were supported.

Another study (Hunt & Hillary, 1973) found that, as Zajonc would predict, the presence of others resulted in poorer performance during the early learning trials of a task. Later, as the response became better learned, the performance of the audience subjects moved up to the level of the solitary subjects.

Neither of these studies provided direct evidence that the presence of others is arousing. However, other investigations have found increases in such symptoms of arousal as sweating on the palms of hands (Martens, 1969) and muscle tenstion (Chapman, 1974) in the presence of an audience.

Cottrell (Cottrell et al., 1968) has challenged the Zajonc position that the mere presence of others is sufficient to produce the social facilitation effect. Cottrell suggested that the results Zajonc and others found were due to the subject's awareness of being observed and possibly evaluated by the audience members. Unless the performer experienced evaluation apprehension, Cottrell argued, the presence of another person would have no effect. To test this proposition, Cottrell and his colleagues (Cottrell et al., 1968) repeated the Zajonc and Sales experiment, with the addition of a mere presence condition to the alone and audience conditions. The mere presence subjects performed in front of a blindfolded person who was thus unable to moniter their performance. As predicted, the social facilitation effect did not occur in the mere presence condition, only in the audience condition. Other studies (Henchy & Glass, 1968; Gore & Taylor 1973; Paulus & Murdock, 1971; Martens & Landers, 1972) have supported the conclusion that social facilitation is principally due to the person's concern about others' evaluations of his performance.

Some studies, however, have provided support for Zajonc's original position. Chapman (1973) had children listen to humorous stories over earphones, either alone or with nonlistening companions. More dominant responses of laughter and smiling were exhibited by children in the presence condition. Here it was unlikely that the listening children were concerned about their companions evaluating their level of amusement. A further study by the same investigator (Chapman, 1974) found an increase in subjects' muscle tension when observed. However, the subjects made no overt responses which could be evaluated. Also, postexperimental interviews revealed few feelings of evaluation apprehension among either the alone or the observed subjects.

Any explanation of social facilitation employing cognitive concepts such as "evaluation apprehension" would encounter difficulty dealing with social facilitation in cockroaches. Yet an ingenious experiment has demonstrated just such an effect. Zajonc, Heingartner, and Herman (1969) constructed two special tasks for their six-legged subjects to perform. In both tasks, the insects could escape an aversive light by running into a dark bottle. One task consisted of a runway. Here the correct response was running in a straight line—a well-learned (dominant) response for cockroaches. The second task was a maze, requiring the roach to make a right-angle turn—a poorly learned response. As Zajonc's theory predicts, runway performance was better in the presence of "observer" roaches, while maze performance was worse.

Despite differences over details, the evidence strongly supports Zajonc's basic proposition that dominant responses, whether correct or incorrect, are facilitated in the presence of others. Evaluation apprehension undoubtedly plays a part in this effect, but perhaps a more basic tendency to become aroused in the mere presence of others also exists. Such a "pure" social facilitation effect may be innate, as Zajonc argues, or may be based on some conditioning process, whereby the presence of others becomes associated with positive or negative reinforcement.

The presence of others has been found to raise concerns regarding evaluation, competition, and comparison with others. These concerns, in turn, tend to make us more anxious and may prevent the kind of concentration on difficult tasks which is possible when we are alone. There appears to be a general tendency to interpret most social situations as competitive. When two or more people are working in the same situation, they each may feel that somehow their performances will be compared or that they are competing with each other even though there is no logical reason for the feelings.

Individual Versus Group Productivity

Is a group more productive than an individual member of the group working independently? Are "two heads better than one?" This problem of individual versus group productivity can be dealt with more easily by breaking it down into two separate questions: (1) Do groups outperform their average individual member? and (2) Do groups outperform their best individual member?

Are Groups More Productive Than Their Average Members? To answer the first question it will be helpful to consider different types of tasks separately. If we disregard motor (physical) tasks and limit the discussion to intellectual tasks, one meaningful way to classify tasks is in relation to information-processing (Davis, 1969). Some tasks primarily require the reception, organization, and storage of information; we can call these learning tasks. Other tasks require the use of already-stored information to formulate various response alternatives; they are problem-solving tasks. Still other tasks require some decision, choice, or judgment among various alternatives; they are decision-making tasks. Although any one task contains a mixture of these three intellectual functions, one of the three usually predominates, especially when we consider specific subtasks. For example, our student research team must collect and store information about previous research in their area of interest (learning); they must devise various alternative methods of testing their hypotheses (problem-solving); and they must agree on a particular experimental procedure to use (decision-making).

On decision-making tasks, more often than not, group judgments are more accurate than the average individual judgment of the group members. But sometimes there are no significant differences between group and individual judgments. For example, Burtt (1920) found that groups could not tell whether a confederate was lying or telling the truth any better than individuals. Similarly, Marston (1924) found no difference between groups and individuals in accurately remembering staged classroom incidents; and Walker (1974) discovered that judicial decisions made by multijudge panels were reversed just as often by higher courts as were decisions of individual judges. On the other hand, several other investigators (Bruce, 1935; Knight, 1921; Eysenck, 1939) have found a decided superiority of group judgment. The nature of the decision task may be responsible for these contrasting results. Groups are more accurate for some types of judgments because: (1) The average of a number of different judgments, whether made by interacting groups or simply sets of independent judges, will usually be more accurate than will be any single judgments. (2) Groups have available a variety of different perspectives and ways of processing information. For example, in trying to judge an experimental subject's emotional state, some observers may focus on his tone of voice, others on his facial expressions, and still others on his overt body movements. In a group this variety of information can be combined. (3) Finally, those persons with the most accurate judgments may also be the most confident and persuasive in a group discussion.

Studies of learning tasks have been much more consistent in demonstrating the superiority of groups. Groups have been found to outperform individuals in learning algebra (Barton, 1926), mazes (Gurnee, 1939), nonsense syllables (Perlmutter & de Montomollin, 1952), prose (Yuker, 1955), and many other kinds of material.

Groups are also generally superior on problem-solving tasks. More and better solutions are typically produced by groups for various types of problems, including constructing different words from a given set of letters (Watson, 1928), solving puzzles (Shaw, 1932; Davis & Restle, 1963), deciphering codes (Husband, 1940), constructing jigsaw puzzles (Husband, 1940), identifying objects by asking questions (Taylor & Faust, 1952), and solving logical syllogisms (Barnlund, 1958).

Thus, groups are consistently superior to their average members in learning or problem solving but not in decision-making tasks. These conclusions concern the quality or "goodness" of products of individuals and groups. Although groups usually produce a better product than average individuals, groups are slower (Kelley & Thibaut, 1969). Even in the few cases where groups have been found to complete their tasks more quickly than individuals, they are still inefficient in terms of the total number of person-hours required. Thus, although a group of three will probably complete a task in less time than will a single person, it seldom will complete the task in one third the time.

Why are groups superior to individuals on learning and problem-solving tasks, and often on decision-making tasks as well? To some degree the superiority of groups is due to the fact that the best member is superior to the average member. For many tasks, once the best or the correct solution is produced, it is soon accepted by all members of the group. Other times, the best member is more confident of his solution than the other members and is thus more influential. On the other hand, the interaction in a group may result in superior performance above and beyond the contribution of the best member. In order to see the effects of the group interaction itself, the performance of the group should be compared with the individual performance of the best member of the group.

Are Groups More Productive Than Their Best Members? A "best member" effect, in which the group performs at the level of the most skilled member, is most likely to occur for those tasks in which (1) there is one correct or best answer; (2) the task is relatively simple, with few steps required for its solution; (3) all the group members start with the same information about the task; and (4) the solution is easily proved to be correct (Kelley & Thibaut, 1969). If the task is too complex, the distraction of the other members will interfere with the efforts of the best member, and he will not perform as well in the group as alone. Furthermore, if the best member is not recognized as competent by the other members, he may not be able to convince them of the correctness of his solution. Preestablished status may influence a member's perceived task competence, often to the detriment of group effectiveness. For example, Torrance (1955) had aircraft crews solve problems together. When the correct solution was offered by the pilot of the crew (high status), the other members accepted the solution 100% of the time. However, when the correct answer was given by the gunner (low status), the group agreed with him only 40% of the time.

When these conditions are not met, the group may perform below the level of its best member. If the task is complex and multistage, such that a number of interrelated steps must be thought through and conclusions reached at earlier points must be kept in mind, then the potential of the best member may not be realized in the group (Faucheux & Moscovici, 1958; Davis & Restle, 1963; Lorge & Soloman, 1959). This decline in performance for complex problems is due partially to less-skilled members interfering with the individual thought processes of the most-skilled member. It is also probable that the more complex the problem, the greater difficulty the best member will encounter in demonstrating to his co-members that his solution is correct. If the task is extremely difficult, a group may not be superior even to an average individual. Moore and Anderson (1954) tested Navy enlisted men on problems from the calculus of symbolic logic and found no difference between groups and individuals. Thus, if all members of a group have great difficulty solving a problem individually, they are not likely to do better in a group.

On some type of tasks, however, what we might call a "true" group-interaction effect occurs, with the group product being superior to the individual product of the best member. This most often occurs when the task consists of a number of relatively independent parts or subtasks. Although no one member may be able to complete all of the subtasks successfully, the group may still be able to combine the successful performances of different members on each part to produce a successful whole product. This is the old "division of labor" or complementary skill idea. For our student research team, it is not necessary that each member be skilled on all phases of the task. For example, one member may specialize in analyzing the data, another in writing the final report, and a third in typing up the final copy of the report.

Is there any effect of groups which may facilitate performance other than this simple pooling of information or abilities? The evidence is not clear, but it is likely that individuals are often more motivated in groups than when working alone. As we saw in the section on social facilitation, the mere presence of others is a source of arousal. In a group, moreover, effective performance is likely to be rewarded by praise from the other group members. (However, as we also observed earlier, too high a level of motivation or arousal may interfere with effective performance on difficult or poorly learned tasks.) Also, the exchange of ideas may stimulate new or different thought processes in individuals which they would not have alone. Another advantage of working in groups is that members can check each other's work, spot errors, and reject incorrect solutions. Finally, members may be able to learn better techniques of problem-solving from each other during the group interaction.

Whether any of these resource-pooling, stimulation, checking, or learning effects will occur depends on the difficulty of the task. Groups are most likely to outperform their best members on tasks of moderate difficulty (Goldman, 1965; Laughlin & Johnson, 1966). If the task is so easy that each member can solve it on his own without difficulty, little will be gained by working in a group. If the task is very difficult, members may interfere with each other or may have little to contribute to each other. Tasks of intermediate difficulty, which are challanging yet not impossible to solve, should enable members to stimulate and teach each other as well as allow for the combining of different members' information and skills and the checking of each others' responses.

Together versus Alone

Given the general superiority of groups over individuals in terms of quality of results, if not in time, we can ask the further question of whether groups can be even more effective if the members first work individually and then combine their products. If the task can be broken down into a number of relatively independent subtasks, then individual work may indeed produce a superior product. However, some tasks cannot be easily subdivided. For example, our student research team must produce a discussion section for their final report. They could assign the responsibility entirely to one of the members, but the group may not be sure which members are the best writers and furthermore, they want the section to include the ideas of each member. The group could attempt to write the section as a group. Anyone who has tried this procedure knows how extremely time-consuming it is. Another possibility is for each member to write a version of the section independently, and then the best parts of the different versions can be combined. However, the attempt to combine different people's written products may prove to take just as much time as would the group doing the writing together. Because of these and other complexities of the situation, we cannot say with any certainty whether the group members would be more effective working together or alone.

Brainstorming. There is one type of task in which the combining of the independently-produced products is not a problem, namely the simple production of ideas. A classic example would be advertising men thinking up names or slogans for a new product. Separately produced lists of ideas can simply be added together, with duplications eliminated. There have been a number of comparisons of the effectiveness of people working alone versus separately to generate ideas. Most of these studies have been concerned with the technique of "brainstorming."

Brainstorming was first described by Osborn (1957), an advertising executive, who claimed that more ideas could be produced by a group than by the same number of independently-working individuals, as long as certain principles were followed: (1) Ideas are freely expressed, without regard to quality; (2) Criticism of the ideas produced is not permitted; and (3) Ideas which are variations of previously expressed ideas are encouraged.

Research on Brainstorming. Contrary to Osborn's contention, in 9 of 12 experiments comparing sets of individuals working independently (under brainstorming instructions) with actual brainstorming groups, the individuals produced more ideas (Lamm & Trommsdorff, 1973). In the other three experiments, no differences were found. The notion that groups sacrifice quantity of ideas by producing ideas of higher quality was not supported by the evidence.

In their review of the brainstorming literature, Lamm and Trommsdorff (1973) consider several possible explanations why people produce fewer ideas together than separately. The most common explanation is that in groups people suffer from social inhibition, a fear of negative evaluations of the other members. Although the brainstorming instructions rule out explicit criticism, a member may still hold back ideas for fear that the others will consider them bizarre or worthless. However, postexperimental self-reports of subjects (Bouchard, 1969; Collaros & Anderson, 1969) indicate little if any inhibition due to fear of other members' evaluations. Furthermore, when subjects in groups were later asked individually to list any ideas which they had not expressed in the group, very few inhibited ideas were produced (Collaros & Anderson, 1969). Thus, we can safely reject social inhibition as an explanation for the inferiority of idea-generation in groups.

Another possible reason why groups produce fewer ideas than individuals working alone is simply that in a group everyone cannot talk at the same time. Listening to others' ideas, even without attempting to evaluate them, takes up time which could otherwise be devoted exclusively to thinking up one's own ideas.

Finally, we can note that two of the prime sources of group effectiveness on other types of tasks, namely the combination of skills and the division of labor, are not possible in the simple idea-generation task. Indeed, in this type of task it is likely that a group situation may interfere with the maximum use of member's different skills. Taylor, Berry, and Block (1958) suggest that brainstorming groups may develop "one-track thinking." An idea produced by one member may stimulate other members to devise other ideas of the same type, but in the process they may neglect other possible types of ideas.

Group Size

If two heads are generally better than one, then are three better than two? Is a larger group more effective than a smaller one? Steiner (1972) concludes that for most tasks group productivity increases with group size up to a certain point, after which it levels off and then declines. A large task group has certain advantages over a small group. Large groups generally have greater member resources. On the other hand, large groups have difficulties in the areas of organization and motivation. Beyond a certain size, the disadvantages outweigh the advantages, and group performance declines.

Advantages of Large Groups. The *potential* productivity of a group goes up when more members are added. The more members, the greater the total pool of group resources (information, skills, etc.). For tasks that can be divided into a number of subtasks, the more members are available, the less work any one person must perform. However, there are limits to the potential advantages of dividing a task into parts, since the more parts there are, the more difficult it will be to assemble them into a satisfactory whole. For those tasks in which a division of labor is not possible, very often the effectiveness of the group will depend on the most competent person.

Disadvantages of Large Groups. One major disadvantage of large groups is the increased problem of organization and coordination of the members. These organizational problems, moreover, increase more and more rapidly as group size increases. The larger the membership, the more time must be spent deciding who does what (assuming that a division of labor is possible). If we consider a task which can be easily broken into two subtasks, then if the group has two members, there are only two possible ways to match subtasks with members. However, with three members, there are six possible assignments of members to two subtasks, and for 4 members, 20 different arrangements. Furthermore, the more complex the division of labor, the greater the chance that some members will be assigned duties for which they have little ability. Also, the larger the group the more difficult it will be to monitor how well each member is performing his job.

Besides problems of organization, the large group tends to suffer from a loss of member motivation. One source of the lack of involvement in large groups lies in the idea of diffusion of responsibility, which we have previously discussed in relation to the risky shift and deindividuation. The less an individual feels that his performance will affect the total group product, the less incentive he will have to work hard. Furthermore, poor performance is less visible and less likely to be punished in a large group than a small group. One study (Wicker, 1969b) found that the larger a church, the less active was the typical member, and the less critical he was of nonactive members.

Another reason for the lower involvement in large groups is that whatever rewards the group may receive for successful task performance must be distributed among more people. The larger the group, the smaller the "slice of the pie" each member receives. Finally, the larger the group, the less opportunity each member has to participate and influence the group's decisions.

Optimum Sizes of Groups. Determining the optimum size of a task group is not easy. Both the nature of the task and the abilities of the members must be taken into account. Slater (1958) measured the satisfaction of members of discussion groups varying in size from two to seven. The members of five-person groups expressed the greatest satisfaction with their group size. Dissatisfaction with larger groups centered on organizational problems and lack of opportunity to participate. The members of smaller groups may have felt that they lacked a sufficiently wide range of viewpoints to analyze the discussion topic satisfactorily.

Figure 13-1 summarizes the effects of group size on productivity. Potential productivity increases steeply as new members are added to the group, but eventually levels off. Problems of organization and motivation, on the other hand, become progressively greater as the group becomes larger (Figure 13-1a). Subtracting the organizational and motivational losses from the potential productivity gives the actual group productivity (Figure 13-1b). At a certain point these losses begin to offset the gains of increased potential, and the resulting actual productivity peaks and declines. Finally, if we divide the actual group productivity by the number of members, we find that the average actual productivity per member (Figure 13-1c) decreases with increased size.

Group Composition and Performance

How do the individual qualities of the members of a task group affect the group's performance? As before, when we considered group composition in relation to satisfaction and cohesiveness, we shall not be concerned with the average individual level of a particular characteristic, but rather with the relationships among member qualities. How do various combinations of qualities affect task performance?

Problems with Research on Group Composition. Steiner (1972) points out certain inherent difficulties in research on composition. The most common research strategy has been to construct some similar (homogeneous) groups and some dissimilar (heterogeneous) groups and to

FIGURE 13-1. Effects of group size on productivity (adapted from Steiner, 1972, p. 96).

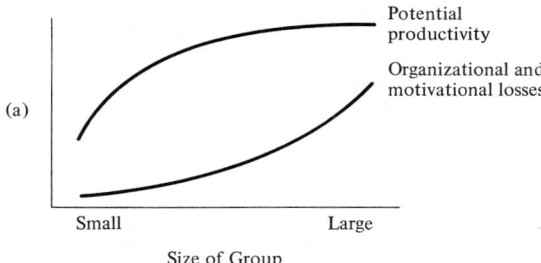

(a)

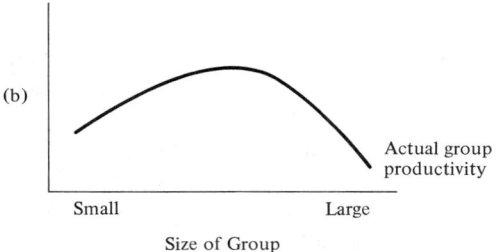

(b)

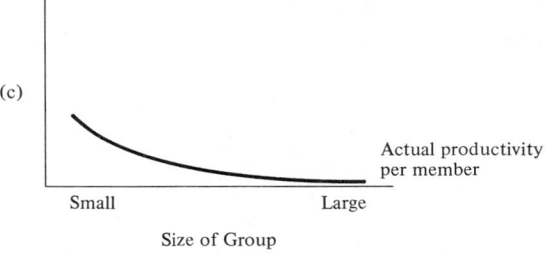

(c)

compare the performance of the two types. However, by manipulating homogeneity on one dimension, we may at the same time be manipulating homogeneity on other dimensions. For example, groups whose members are similar on level of anxiety may also be similar on extroversion-introversion and dissimilar on intelligence. At the present time, we still have a very incomplete idea of what individual qualities tend to "go together" in people. Since we cannot measure or manipulate all variables which might be relevant, we can seldom be sure that the variables we have used to compose heterogeneous and homogeneous groups are the true causes of any observed effects. In spite of these methodological problems, some conclusions can be drawn from the research evidence. We will first consider heterogeneity of ability; and then heterogeneity of personality.

Heterogeneity of Abilities. Although two groups may have the same average level of ability, they may still differ greatly in the heterogeneity of ability levels of their members. According to Steiner's (1972) theoretical analysis, the particular task determines the effect of heterogeneity of abilities on group performance. The more heterogeneous the group's abilities, the more competent will be the best member and the less competent will be the worst member. Thus, for those tasks which can be performed alone by one competent member, such as the statistical analysis for our research team, heterogeneity of abilities is an advantage. On the other hand, some tasks depend for success on an adequate performance from all the members; one low-ability performer can spoil the total product, as in the performance of a musical group.

For most tasks, some type of division of labor is possible. Heterogeneity can be an advantage in these cases providing that none of the subtasks assigned to low-ability members is critical for the success of the total group effort. The ideal group would be composed of specialists, each member having certain highly developed skills which the other members lack, as on a football team. Heterogeneity has effects similar to those of increased size: Potential productivity is usually boosted, but problems of organization and motivation may develop. When all members possess equal skills, who does what is relatively unimportant; however, with heterogeneous abilities, the problem of matching members with subtasks appropriate to their abilities becomes critical.

Many motivational problems can develop in

heterogeneous groups, especially when labor is divided. As a result of matching subtasks appropriately with abilities, some members may find themselves permanently stuck with boring or low-prestige jobs. If the differences in member ability are explicitly recognized, the less competent members may become jealous of the more competent members. The high-ability members, on the other hand, may become frustrated by the slowness of the low-ability members. Problems of fairness in the distribution of the work load are accentuated when members are of varying ability. The low-ability members may feel that they do not have to work very hard, since the high-ability members can always come to their rescue. Finally, the highly competent members may feel that they have provided more than their share of the work, and thus should have a greater-than-equal share of the group's rewards. Steiner (1972) suggests that losses due to organizational and motivational problems in heterogeneous groups are likely to be especially great when it is not clear what the different members' abilities are, when the pressures of time or status prevent the best possible matching of individuals and subtasks, or when certain subtasks are much more desirable than others.

Heterogeneity of Personalities. Research on the heterogeneity of personality traits suggests that dissimilar groups perform better. Several studies (Smelser, 1961; Fry, 1965; Moos & Spiesman, 1962; Ghiselli & Lodahl, 1958) have focused on the characteristic of dominance-submissiveness, with the general conclusion that heterogeneous groups are superior. The Ghiselli and Lodahl study further suggests that the best performance results from one member being appreciably more dominant than all the other members. It seems to facilitate group task effectiveness if one member can take charge and make necessary decisions and the other members are willing to accept his leadership. In a group composed entirely of nondominant people, nothing may ever be decided, while if all members have dominant personalities, the task may be neglected because of the resulting struggle for power.

Hoffman (1959) and Hoffman and Maier (1961) have provided evidence that general personality dissimilarity facilitates task performance. Subjects were first given a widely-used inventory which measures 10 relatively independent personality dimensions. They were then formed into heterogeneous or homogeneous groups based on their total distribution of personality traits. On a number of different problem-solving tasks, the dissimilar-personality groups did better. Hoffman and Maier suggest that heterogeneity of personality is associated with heterogeneity of problem-solving viewpoints. Different kinds of people are likely to approach a problem from different perspectives and to offer different alternative solutions. The greater the number of alternatives from which the group may pick, or the larger the number which can be combined, the better the potential group product.

However, while differing perspectives may promote group effectiveness, these different viewpoints must not be so diverse that members do not "speak the same language." Effective communication in groups is hindered not so much by disagreements, as by an inability to think about things in similar terms. Unless participants use words in the same way and use similar cognitive dimensions to evaluate objects, they may never understand just what they disagree about.

Cohesivensss and Performance

Is a more cohesive group more productive? In general, we can say yes, but there are important exceptions. As we have noted, a great deal of evidence supports the conclusion that the more cohesive a group, the more social influence it will exert on its members. The more members are attracted to a group, the more they will strive to follow group norms and achieve group goals (Lott & Lott, 1965).

However, while most task groups have norms of high productivity, others have norms of low productivity. In these cases a member's attraction to the group will be reflected in decreased rather than increased effort. Several laboratory experiments have manipulated both group cohesiveness and group production standards (Schacter, Ellertson, McBride, & Gregory, 1951; Berkowitz, 1954). These studies found that members were more influenced by low production norms in the high-cohesive groups than in the low-cohesive groups.

We can conclude that highly cohesive groups are more successful in achieving their goals than low-cohesive groups, but group goals may or may not include producing the best product.

Thus, we cannot advise people choosing co-members for our student research team whether to choose friends or strangers. Groups of friends may enjoy socializing so much that they never accomplish much on the task. Likewise, friends may not feel free to criticize each other's ideas. Friends may also resist the efforts of any member to exercise leadership. In a highly cohesive group which is more interested in friendly socializing than task accomplishment, a member who suggests getting down to work may be treated as a deviant and ridiculed or rejected.

Groupthink

One consequence of too great a level of cohesiveness in decision-making groups is that critical thinking will be replaced by what Janis (1972) has termed "groupthink." When groupthink occurs, argues Janis, loyalty to the group, its norms, and its past decisions replace the realistic considerations of alternatives. Groupthink is likely to appear during crisis situations when members of the group are experiencing severe stress. Another factor promoting groupthink is the sharing of the same set of values by all the group members. We have seen how, in both encounter and problem-solving groups, too much homogeneity can be harmful to the group's efforts by restricting the variety of viewpoints available.

The lack of conflict resulting from groupthink is not due to the usual group pressures for conformity. Members are not so much afraid of punishment for expressing deviant views; rather, they seldom have deviant views in the first place. Loyalty to the group results in the immediate approval of any proposal favored by the leader or the majority of the group. The emphasis on agreement and harmony prevents the careful weighing of pros and cons.

Janis has analyzed in great detail the deliberations of government leaders in situations where groupthink led to disastrous decisions, for example, the Vietnam War, the Bay of Pigs invasion, and the Pearl Harbor attack. He has identified eight primary symptoms of groupthink. Members of groups suffering from groupthink share an illusion of *invulnerability* which leads them to be overly optimistic. This feeling that "our side can't lose" causes members to disregard clear warnings of danger, as demonstrated by American officials ignoring many indications that Japan would attack Pearl Harbor. If a warning signal cannot be ignored, it can be explained away by means of various *rationalizations*. For example, the evidence that Japan would attack Hawaii was discounted by assuming that Japan's leaders would never start a war with the U.S. which they knew they could not win. Since groupthinking members believe that their group is inherently moral, the *morality* of its decisions never come into question. The enemy, and especially its leaders, are characterized in terms of *stereotypes*. The opposing leaders are assumed to be weak, stupid, and immoral. The enemy's weakness and lack of intelligence makes his defeat inevitable, while his lack of morality means he cannot be trusted in negotiations. *Self-censorship* is another characteristic of groupthink. Members tend to keep questions about the wisdom of the group's policies to themselves. Because of this reluctance to express doubts and the assumption that silence means agreement, the group suffers from an *illusion of unanimity*. Certain members may assume the role of *"mind-guards"* who protect the group from exposure to adverse information.

Janis offers a number of specific recommendations for preventing groupthink. The leader of the group should explicitly encourage criticism of policies and proposals. The establishment of several different policy and planning groups, all working on the same problem, enables each to serve as a check on the others. Group members should discuss the group's deliberations with the subordinates, who often have available information which their superiors lack. Outside experts should be invited to sit in on some of the meetings and offer their comments. One member should play the role of a "devil's advocate," arguing against the group even though he really agrees with it. Decisions can be made in stages, rather than made and then never reviewed or challenged.

LEADERSHIP

In our discussion of the various structures of groups, it was apparent that not all group members are equal in terms of their influence. In virtually all task and growth groups, as well as many social-friendship groups, one person assumes much more than his share of the duties of organizing, coordinating, planning, and decision making. "Leader" has been defined in a number of different ways by students of groups, but perhaps the most general and useful definition of a leader is *that group member who has the most influence on the other group members*. From this perspective, a group's leader may or may not have some official title or clearly recognized role; he and the other members may not even be aware that he is doing any leading. Although leaders appear in all types of groups, their roles are most clear in task groups. However, the research by Lieberman, Yalom, and Miles (1973b) provides some evidence for leadership effectiveness in growth groups.

Leadership in Encounter Groups

Lieberman, Yalom, and Miles (1973b) found all the varied functions of encounter-group leaders could be grouped into four general categories: emotional stimulation, caring, meaning-attribution and executive function.

Emotional stimulation refers to leader behavior which attempts to produce a direct response in the member to which it is directed. Challenging, confronting, and provoking would be examples. Another emotionally stimulating leader behavior was acting as a model to the members in expressing feelings. Emotional stimulation is a highly personalized function, in which the leader interacts as a fellow member, but at a more intense and deeper level than the other members.

The *caring* function involves expressions of love, concern, protection, warmth, and acceptance by the leader, and his encouragement of the other members to express similar positive feelings. When the leader is expressing caring, the participants feel that he is not just acting in a professional role but is genuinely concerned with them as persons.

When the leader engages in *meaning-attribution*, he is acting as a teacher—explaining, clarifying, interpreting, and giving meaning to the experiences of the members. Here the leader is offering insights, ideas, concepts, and values rather than expressing feelings, leading, or stimulating.

Executive functions involve what we usually think of as leadership behaviors—directing, guiding, managing. Establishing norms or rules, making decisions, and suggesting activities are all executive behaviors.

Lieberman et al. found that the most effective leaders were moderate in both stimulation and executive functions, high on caring, and high on meaning-attribution, especially if the meaning-attribution was directed toward individuals rather than the group as a whole. Thus, the effective leader was supportive both emotionally (caring) and intellectually (meaning-attribution).

Leadership in Task Groups

Our student research team can scarcely avoid questions of leadership. The group may resist naming one of themselves as the leader, but someone will eventually begin to exert the most influence. Thus, the fundamental problem of our group is not whether the group should be led, but rather how and by whom it should be led.

All groups are confronted with the question of who is to become the leader. Some groups may attempt to choose a leader on the basis of individual characteristics. The most dominant or competent member may have the leadership role placed upon him.

Another question involves how the leader is to exercise his influence. Should he take charge of the group and direct all its activities? Or should the leader act primarily as a friendly coordinator, keeping the group moving but without giving orders? Or should he perhaps let members "do their own things," and exercise leadership only when absolutely necessary?

A third set of problems concerns the different functions which leaders perform and how these functions are affected by aspects of the group's structure. Should the same person continue as leader throughout the life of the group? Or should the leader change as the group's situation changes? Can more than one person share the functions of leadership at the same time? Do different kinds of group situations call for different styles of leadership? These questions which the group must come to terms with parallel psychologists' differing conceptions of leadership. The various approaches to leadership are not necessarily incompatible; nor do they necessarily lead to contradictory predictions. However, they do represent contrasting methods of thinking about and studying leadership. Four approaches to the study of leadership derive from these different conceptions. They are (1) the *trait approach,* focusing on the individual characteristics of leaders; (2) the *style approach,* emphasizing how leadership is exercised and the effects on members of different leadership styles; (3) the *situational approach,* which considers the influence of structural factors on the emergence of particular persons as leaders; and (4) *the situational-style approach,* which specifies the most effective leadership style for particular situations. We will examine each of these four approaches.

The Trait Approach

The trait approach to leadership was popular until the end of World War II. Hundreds of studies attempted to find the relationships between various individual characteristics and leadership. We can conclude from these studies that leaders, compared to nonleaders, tend to be taller, more attractive in appearance, more intelligent, self-confident, psychologically healthy, dominant, extroverted, and sensitive to people (Gibb, 1969). The major problem with the trait approach has been that the relationships between traits and leadership have been very weak. No one individual characteristic predicts very well who will become a leader. Furthermore, specific traits are relevant only in certain groups and situations. For some groups, the usual relationships between individual characteristics and leadership may even be reversed. For example, Schrag (1954) found that leaders of prison inmates tended to be more psychologically disturbed than nonleaders, rather than less disturbed.

Two other methodological problems have plagued the trait approach. First, since these studies are correlational in nature, they do not explain much about why leadership tends to be associated with certain other characteristics. The direction of cause and effect between variables is unclear. Being self-confident, dominant, and extroverted may aid one in becoming a leader, but it also seems likely that becoming a leader should cause one to feel and act more self-confident, dominant, and extroverted. Another problem with some of the studies using the trait approach has been that the same persons rated both leadership and other traits. Thus, the relationships obtained may reflect mainly the raters' beliefs about what traits leaders are supposed to have. These methodological problems, together with the recognition that individual traits are not strongly associated with leadership across different situations, have caused a virtual abandonment of the trait approach.

The Leadership Style Approach

The leadership style approach is concerned not with what kind of people become leaders, but rather with how leadership is exercised by whoever happens to be the leader, and what the effects of different types of leadership are. Three fundamental styles of leadership have been identified: (1) autocratic, (2) democratic, and (3) laissez-faire. An autocratic leader centralizes power in himself and offers the other members little or no participation in the decision-making process. In this case, the effectiveness of the group is dependent on the effectiveness of the leader. A leader with a democratic style shares his power with the other members. Decisions are made by consensus or majority vote. Because of the greater member participation in decision making, satisfaction and motivation are likely to be high under democratic leadership. On the other hand, a democratically led group may be rather inefficient when quick decisions and immediate action are called for. A group doesn't have time to debate and vote when a crisis arises. The third type of leadership style, laissez faire, is perhaps best characterized as an absence of active leader participation. The laissez-faire leader is passive and lets the group make its own decisions. This nonparticipation of the leader often results in chaos as other members attempt to lead the group in different directions.

Lewin, Lippit, and White (1939) conducted a classic study of these three leadership styles. Rather than simply observe pre-existing groups which differed in leadership style, Lewin and his colleagues experimentally manipulated the type of leadership in groups of 10-year-old boys working on various hobby projects. Each adult leader was trained in all three leadership roles and leaders were rotated from one group to another every 6 weeks. In this way a particular style was not identified with only one particular leader, and each group was exposed to all three styles.

Autocratic leaders determined all policy, dictated techniques and activities, assigned tasks and work partners to group members, and were personal in their criticism and praise. Further, they remained aloof and impersonal from the group. The democratic leaders encouraged members to discuss and decide as a group on policy and steps toward goal attainment. They suggested alternatives, but did not give orders. Members were free to choose their own tasks and working companions. Democratic leaders tried to be objective in praise and criticism, and to be regular group members, at least in spirit. Laissez-faire leaders made no attempt to evaluate or regulate the group's activities, keeping their participation to an absolute minimum. They supplied information when asked, but otherwise left the group to itself as much as possible.

Various measures of group interaction were taken, with results showing that member behavior was affected markedly by the style of leadership. Laissez-faire leadership resulted in group behavior differing from that under democratic leadership. Less work was done in the laissez-faire groups, and the work was of poorer quality.

Democracy produced the highest group cohesiveness. The democratic groups also proved superior to the other two kinds of groups in that they achieved both general group goals—to complete the work projects and to have fun. By contrast, the autocratic groups achieved only task goals, and the laissez-faire groups only social goals. Although the autocratic groups spent more time working and produced a greater number of products, the quality of the work was superior under democracy. Moreover, the boys who participated in the democratically led groups exhibited greater maturity and motivation. When the adult leader left the room, the democratic groups kept on working, while the autocratic groups stopped working. Finally, in both work and play, the democratic groups exhibited a higher level of originality and creative thinking.

The autocratic groups experienced a great deal of negative feelings, which they sometimes expressed openly and sometimes kept hidden below the surface. Overt hostility and the destruction of property were common in two of the autocratic groups; in the others, frustration was expressed in less direct ways, as by dropping out of the group or "blowing off steam" immediately after a change to democratic or laissez-faire leadership. Autocracy was also characterized by greater dependence and less individuality than under democratic or laissez-faire systems.

Later work has tended to support the findings of Lewin, Lippit, and White. Both laboratory experiments (Preston & Heintz, 1949; Shaw, 1955) and field studies (Morse & Reimer, 1956) have confirmed that satisfaction is higher under democratic than autocratic leadership. The Morse and Reimer study also found that a democratic atmosphere resulted in higher productivity.

On the other hand, in some circumstances autocratic leadership can be more effective. Sanford (1950) and Haythorn et al. (1956) found that people with authoritarian personality types preferred highly directive leaders. And in a military organization, morale has been found to be highest under autocratic leaders (Scott, 1952).

The Situational Approach

The situational approach to leadership emphasizes the effects of task and structural variables in determining which members of the group will perform leadership functions. The assumptions of this orientation were expressed by Hemphill (1949): "There are no absolute leaders, since successful leadership must always take into account the specific requirements imposed by the nature of the group which is to be led, requirements as diverse in nature and degree as are the organizations in which persons band together" (p. 255).

There are several studies that illustrate how situational factors can influence who becomes a group leader. Seating position can place some individuals in a more favorable position to exert influence than others (Howells & Becker,

1962). Members who are on their own home territory are more influential (Martindale, 1971). Studies of communication networks (e.g., Leavitt, 1951) reveal that members in more centralized positions, who can control the flow of communication within the group, are likely to emerge as leaders. Bavelas and his colleagues (1965) showed how, by appropriate reinforcement, even a quiet member could be made to increase his talking rate and, consequently, his perceived leadership ability.

Bales (1953) has shown that not only the amount of communication, but also the specific type of communication which a member engages in will affect what leadership functions he assumes. Bales concluded that discussion groups tend to have not one leader, but two, each of whom specializes in particular kinds of communication. The task leader's comments are focused on getting a job done. He is the one who contributes opinions, suggestions, and information, and expresses disagreement. The social-emotional leader on the other hand, is concerned with maintaining smooth and harmonious interpersonal relations. His comments express solidarity, tension release, and agreement.

He also solicits suggestions, opinions, and information from the other members. Occasionally the same person may be able to fill both task- and social-leadership roles. For example, the democratic leader who encourages participation in decision making may be able to take on the task and social roles. Typically, however, these different functions are handled by different persons. Depending on the group's goals and needs at any particular time, either the task leader or the social leader may be more active.

The Style-Situational Approach

The style-situational approach refers to Fiedler's (1967) theory of leadership effectiveness. Fiedler attempted to integrate and extend the work of researchers in both the style and the situational orientations. His theory is the first to make specific testable predictions about what kind of leadership style (democratic or autocratic) will be more effective under given circumstances. Whether a task-oriented (autocratic) or an interpersonal-orientated (democratic) style is more effective is assumed to depend on the favorableness of the leader's situation.

Fiedler identifies a leader's style by means of questionnaire responses concerning the person's least preferred coworker (LPC). A high-LPC person (democratic) views his least preferred co-worker favorably and derives his major satisfaction in a group from successful interpersonal relationships. On the other hand, the low-LPC (autocratic) person sees his least preferred co-worker in unfavorable terms and is interested in successful task performance even at the risk of poor interpersonal relations among his fellow group members.

Fiedler has identified three factors which determine the favorability of the leader's situation: Leader-member relations, task structure, and leader position power. The most important component of situation favorability consists of the personal feelings of the members about the leader. The leader who is liked and respected needs no formal power; his attitudes influence the group more than those of a leader lacking member esteem. Therefore, a leader having good relations with group members is in a more favorable situation than one with poor relations, since the respected leader can act more confidently and decisively knowing that he has the loyal support of his members.

The second most important determinant of situational favorability for the leader is the degree to which the task is structured. The more clearly specified the task requirements (high structure) the more favorable the leader's situation. The task is structured to the extent that the goal is clear, there is a single path to the goal, there is only one correct solution or decision, and the solution is easily verified or proven correct.

The third factor influencing the favorability of the situation is the leader's position power. Position power refers to the degree to which the leader's position itself confers power upon him. The more legitimate authority the leader has and the more he is able to reward and punish the group members, the stronger his position power and the more favorable the situation is for him.

The situation is thus most favorable for the leader when he has the confidence of his followers, the task is highly structured, and he has a great deal of power. The situation is least favorable when his relations with the members are poor, the task is ambiguous, and his power is weak.

Fiedler predicted that the task-oriented low LPC leader would be most effective in situations which were either highly favorable or highly unfavorable. When the situation is favorable to the leader, he can manage, direct, and control the members without arousing their hostility. If things are going well, the group will not feel uncomfortable with the leader's directive behavior. In an unfavorable situation, on the other hand, strong direction is required to keep the group from falling apart.

If the situation is moderately favorable, interpersonal problems are likely to be important, and group members expect to be treated with consideration and respect. Here the warm, friendly, considerate high-LPC leader will be most effective.

Studies of natural groups have found fairly strong relationships between situational favorableness, leadership style, and group performance in the direction specified by the theory. Experimental studies have also supported the theory's predictions. Shaw and Blum (1966) demonstrated that leaders instructed to play a directive role were more effective in a highly favorable situation (high task structure), while leaders instructed to play a nondirective role were more effective when the situation was intermediate in favorability (moderate task structure). In another experiment (Chemers & Skrzypek, 1972), all three dimensions of situational favorability were manipulated. Groups of West Point cadets were assembled on the basis of previously administered sociometric questionnaires such that leader-member relations were either good or poor. Each group worked on both a structured task (converting blueprints from metric units to inches) and an unstructured task (discussion and policy recommendation). The leader's position power was manipulated by telling some groups that the leader would evaluate each member's performance and his ratings would affect their standing in the academy; other groups were given no such information. As Fiedler's theory predicts, relationship-oriented (high-LPC) leaders were more effective when the situation was intermediate in favorableness, while task-oriented (low-LPC) leaders were more effective when the situation was either quite favorable or quite unfavorable to them.

The strength of Fiedler's theory lies in its specification of the conditions under which different leadership styles will be most effective. The theory includes predictions which can be put to empirical test and which have been supported when so tested. The practical implications of the theory are great. Fiedler (1971) points out that industry and the military have spent millions of dollars to train people for leadership. Yet the effectiveness of such training programs is doubtful (Campbell, Dunnett, Lawler, & Weick, 1970). It is generally assumed that experience in being a leader makes one a more effective leader. However, Fiedler (1970) found no relationship between length of job experience and manager effectiveness.

Fiedler's theory suggests that rather than

relying on training or experience to produce effective leaders, organizations should devote more effort to matching the individual's leadership style to the needs of the situation. The relationship-oriented leader should be assigned to situations of moderate difficulty. The task-oriented leader should be placed in either very easy or very difficult leadership situations.

SUMMARY

Groups commonly make decisions which vary from the members' pregroup individual decisions. Sometimes such group decisions are riskier than individual decisions, and sometimes more cautious, depending on the cultural value aroused by the particular choice. When the risk (i.e., the probability and severity of negative consequences) is relatively small for the risky alternative, then riskiness is admired and groups will make riskier choices than individuals. However, when serious harm may result, then caution will be valued, and groups will be more conservative than individuals.

Another way in which groups may elicit more extreme responses is termed deindividuation. Highly deindividuated behavior is characteristic of violent crowds. Research has generally found that antisocial behavior in groups is fostered by anonymity, emotional arousal, and a loss of responsibility for one's actions. Under some conditions, however, a loss of identity can lead to norm-violating behavior which is positive and affectionate.

Group performance involves many factors. First, the mere presence of others may lead to a concern with being evaluated. This heightened arousal improves performance on easy or well-learned tasks, but interferes with performance on difficult or poorly-learned tasks. Groups usually produce better products than would their average members working individually. On tasks of moderate difficulty, where a division of labor is possible, groups may outperform even their best members. However, groups typically work at a slower rate than individuals. On brainstorming-type tasks, where a simple production of ideas is called for, members would be well advised to work independently initially and then pool their ideas.

Moderate-sized groups tend to be more productive than very large or very small groups. Potential productivity increases with size, but problems of organization and motivation also increase. Dissimilarity of member abilities has similar effects—the greater the variation in ability levels, the greater the potential of a group; but too much variation poses difficulties in coordination and satisfaction. Differing personalities, however, more often than not facilitate group effectiveness by providing a variety of perspectives on the task. Cohesiveness generally leads to greater conformity to group norms. However, group norms may encourage either high productivity or low productivity. Very high levels of cohesiveness may lead to "groupthink," in which critical, independent thinking is suspended in favor of maintaining a harmonious consensus.

Leadership, or influence in groups, has been studied from several different perspectives. The *trait approach* has been largely rejected because few personal qualities are strongly related to leadership across different kinds of groups. The *leadership style approach* distinguishes democratic, autocratic, and laissez-faire styles of leadership. One well-known study concluded that the laissez-faire style may result in member satisfaction, and the autocratic style may be effective in terms of performance, but only the democratic style maximizes both morale and productivity. However, some individuals and some situations call for an autocratic style. The *situational approach* assumes that leadership is determined by aspects of the task and the group structure.

Research analyzing communication suggests that groups commonly have two leaders, one who specializes in getting the job done and another who keeps people happy. Perhaps the most useful conception of leadership is Fiedler's *style-situational approach,* which speicifies when a task-oriented leader will be more effective and when a person-oriented leader will be more effective. The more respect and power a leader has, and the more structured the task, the more favorable is his situation. Task-oriented leaders do better when their situations are highly favorable or highly unfavorable; person-oriented leaders are more effective when their situations are moderately favorable.

SUGGESTED READINGS

Janis, I. *Victims of groupthink: A psychological study of foreign-policy decisions and fiascos.* Boston: Houghton Mifflin, 1972.

Janis analyzed virtually mountains of documents and interviews with government leaders to discover how high-level groups made poor decisions regarding the Pearl Harbor attack and the Bay of Pigs invasion, and good decisions regarding the Cuban missile crisis. Janis's groupthink theory provides one explanation of how even the most intelligent leaders can lead the country into disasters such as Vietnam or Watergate.

McGrath, J. E., & Altman, I. *Small group research: A synthesis and critique of the field.* New York: Holt, Rinehart and Winston, 1966.

McGrath and Altman summarize an attempt to build a classification system for organizing and synthesizing small group research. They then apply that system to a large sample of group studies and draw conclusions about relationships which have or have not been demonstrated. Chapters seven and eight in the book are especially recommended for their discussions of problems in the methodology of group research and the norms and practices of group researchers.

Shaw, M. E. *Group dynamics: The psychology of small group behavior.* New York: McGraw-Hill, 1971.

This book considers the issues and problems that have arisen in the study of groups and some of the solutions that have been offered. Shaw offers a comprehensive treatment of what we do and do not know about groups as a result of scientific investigation.

Steiner, I. D. *Group process and productivity.* New York: Academic Press, 1972.

Steiner tells "everything you always wanted to know" about task-group effectiveness. He provides a careful categorization of types of group tasks, and emphasizes the role of task demands in determining the effects of group size, heterogeneity, and reward systems. This book presents a well-reasoned theoretical synthesis of an area which has long suffered from a lack of integration of its wealth of research.

Stogdill, R. M. *Handbook of leadership.* New York: The Free Press, 1974.

Stogdill has abstracted, surveyed, and analyzed more than 3,000 books and articles to provide the most complete account available of what is known about leadership. A substantial bibliography of 150 pages brings together literally all published scientific research on leadership, and a complete name and subject index makes this volume the definitive reference tool for further work in this field.

Taylor, D. A. (Ed.). *Small groups.* Chicago: Markham, 1971.

Small groups is a collection of readings selected with the goal of providing the reader with a substantial sampling of the important studies on small groups. The various topical areas presented address issues in social psychology, sociology, and clinical psychology and should therefore encourage multidisciplinary interest.

PART FIVE

Social Issues and Applications

14. SOCIAL MOVEMENTS
  Introduction
  The Study of Social Movements
    Social movements and social change / The social psychology of social movements / Methods of study
  Three Contemporary Social Movements
    The student protest movement / The movement for an alternative culture / The women's liberation movement
  Conclusion
  Summary
  Suggested Readings

15. APPLIED SOCIAL PSYCHOLOGY
  Introduction
  Poverty
    The demography of poverty / The culture of poverty thesis—and its critics / Welfare dependency / Some conclusions
  The Black-White Thing
    The family / The schools

Black-White Interactions and Social Change
Some preliminary observations / Separatism versus integration
Summary
Suggested Readings

14
Social Movements

Barry McLaughlin

INTRODUCTION

In recent years the social sciences, and social psychology in particular, have been severely criticized by students, by governmental funding agencies, and, increasingly, by professionals themselves. There have been various types of criticisms—theoretical, methodological, and ethical. But overriding all other considerations is the contention that social scientists have lost the forest for the trees. Critics maintain that too much research is directed at topics of too little importance for the wrong reasons (e.g., Ring, 1967; Smith, 1972).

It is not our purpose to enter into this controversy here. We wish merely to argue that the critics of social science often overlook a large and growing body of research that indicates that social scientists are in fact concerned with issues of contemporary importance. This work can be conveniently assembled under the heading "research on social movements."

In this chapter we shall discuss research on three contemporary social movements—the student protest movement, the "hippie" movement, and the women's liberation movement. We recognize, of course, that other contemporary movements, such as the ecology movement, the encounter-group movement, and the "Jesus freak" movement, have also been studied by social scientists. But we feel that the three movements we shall focus on provide the most representative examples of the way in which social psychologists approach the topic of the study of social movements.

THE STUDY OF SOCIAL MOVEMENTS

What is a social movement? What distinctions can be made between different types of social movements? What theoretical concepts have been used by social psychologists in discussing social movements? What methods does a social psychologist use in investigating social movements? These are some of the questions we shall try to answer in this section. Implicit in this discussion is the contention that social movements are the best indicators of the social concerns of a society and consequently delineate the direction of impending social change.

Social Movements and Social Change

It is no easy task to define a social movement. There are certain characteristics that most authors writing on the topic tend to agree upon, but there are other characteristics that meet with little agreement. Most often, the author's theoretical or disciplinary orientation tends to color his definition of the field. Sociologists typically treat social movements within the context of collective behavior, whereas social psychologists orient their discussion more to the behavior of the individual participant. The sociologist C. Wendell King (1956), for example, identified what he felt to be the four distinguishing features of a social movement:

1. the promotion of social change,
2. an organization to achieve the goals of the movement,
3. a geographic scope transcending the local community, and
4. a degree of durability and persistence through time.

Another sociologist, Lewis M. Killian (1964), described a social movement as a collective attempt to promote or resist change characterized by:

1. the existence of shared values,
2. a sense of membership and participation,
3. norms as to behavior, and
4. a structure that involves a division of labor between leaders and followers.

Contrast these characteristics with those advanced by the social psychologist Muzafer Sherif (1970; Sherif & Sherif, 1969):

1. a social movement is a formative pattern of attempts toward change that develops in phases over time,
2. it is initiated through interaction among people prompted by a motivational base fed by persisting social problems,
3. carried by those directly affected and by others who join them,
4. developed through a declaration of gripes and a proclamation of platform and ideology,
5. for the purpose of bringing about or resisting change,
6. effected by means of appeals, agitation, episodes of collective action, and so forth.

While there are obvious points of agreement, sociological treatments tend to focus on the social movement as a collectivity with an organized structure where members share values and norms of behavior. The social psychologist focuses on individual personalities in social interaction, motivated to rectify a situation they perceive to be problematic. The social psychological point of view is put forth most forcefully by Hans Toch, who defined a social movement as "the effort by a large number of people to solve collectively a problem that they feel they have in common" (1965, p. 5).

Both points of view are necessary. An adequate treatment of a social movement obviously requires analysis of the movement as a collectivity, tracing its evolution over time, its structure, and the development of norms and values. At the same time, the motivational basis for individual membership deserves consideration, as well as the ways in which social interaction among the members affects the career of the movement. Most good authors manage to treat both aspects, although they may emphasize one or the other on the basis of their disciplinary allegiance.

What is of interest in the definitional debate is that all authors agree that social movements are concerned with social change (although there is disagreement as to whether counter-movements and movements resisting change deserve the label of social movements). The emphasis on social change originates in the recognition that social movements are directed at consciously reordering the social system in some fashion or other, to a greater or lesser extent. The movement is an indictment of society or of some particular aspect of the social system.

Social Change: Direct and Indirect. Some social movements work directly toward the goal of effecting change in governmental or institutional systems. Reform and revolutionary movements are usually of this sort. The target for the movement is the social order, and the movement is oriented specifically toward changing public policy. Such movements operate in the political sphere. They require for their success an ideological system and an organization focused on a program of demands, tactics, and strategies. The development of leadership and of an organizational structure allow the discontent of the membership to be mobilized into concerted political action. The classic revolutions of history and, more recently, the civil rights movement and the anti-war movement have been primarily political in their orientation, specifically directed against institutions and the agents of social control.

In contrast, some movements operate indirectly. They seek to change the social order, but they attempt to do so by changing individuals. Their focus is the personality of the participant, and the assumption is that when enough individuals change, a reordering of the social system will inevitably follow. Religious movements are typically of this sort. There is little or no concern with public institutions or new legislation; instead the conversion of the individual to a new way of life is the explicit goal of the movement. Ideology takes the form of a creed that is absolute and imperative. It is both a theology and an ethical code. What is of primary importance is not the social system, but personal life—one's own and that of one's associates (who are viewed as potential converts). The members strive for their own moral transformation and for the transformation of "nonbelievers."

The distinction between movements that operate directly to change the social system and those that operate indirectly by changing the lives of individual members is not always clear-cut. Successful political movements often place moral demands on their members, while many religious movements become entangled in attempts to change political institutions and the external social order. Usually, however, there is a definite orientation, discernible in the tactics and goals of the movement, that justifies calling it either a direct or an indirect social movement.

One last point should be made in this connection. An indirect social movement need not be moral or religious in any formal sense. The focus is on the transformation of individual personality. Contemporary counterculture (or better, alternative-culture) phenomena share this orientation with classic religious movements. Participants in this movement believe that what matters is not so much changing the rules of government or of other institutions; what is important is "changing people's heads."

Specific and General Social Movements. There is another distinction that is useful for our purposes. Some social movements have a highly developed organizational structure, involving a recognized and accepted leadership and a definite sense of participation among the members. The objectives and goals of the movement are clearly articulated in an ideology and program agreed upon by the participants. Such a movement we shall call a *specific* social movement (following Blumer, 1951). These may be directly or indirectly concerned with social change. They are specific in that they are highly structured with concrete programs, a formal leadership, definite ideology, and stated objectives.

On the other hand, some social movements have no organizational structure nor recognized leadership. There is no sense of membership nor any affiliation with specific organizations. Objectives and goals are poorly articulated and there is no formal ideology or program. Such a movement may be called a *general* social movement (Blumer, 1951). Again these movements may be directly or indirectly concerned with social change.

General social movements reflect cultural trends. They indicate gradual and pervasive changes in the values of people. Individuals may become sensitized in new directions, or they may come to experience dissatisfaction where before they felt none. The civil rights movement is a prime example of how people can come to develop a new image of themselves and of their rights and privileges. Other examples are the belief in free education, the emancipation of women, and increasing regard for children (Blumer, 1951). Often these movements develop into specific social movements, as occurred in the case of the civil rights movement. Dissatisfaction and the hope awakened by general social movements lead to movements with specific objectives and formalized structures.

The diffuse and uncoordinated nature of general social movements renders them less susceptible to study than are specific social movements. Most discussions, in fact, have been concerned with specific social movements. It is easier to deal with those cases where the leadership is established, the membership is recognized, and where there is a clearly defined belief system and normative structure. In some senses, however, general social movements are far more interesting. They signify the emergence of new values and new self-conceptions. They foreshadow the direction of social change and define social problems that beleaguer a society. A new perception, initially inchoate and obscure, becomes gradually sharp and defined. If a number of like-minded individuals share this perception, they may act collectively to alter their way of life.

To recapitulate, we have argued that, in spite of disagreement as to particulars, all authors regard social movements as instruments of social change. This concern with change may be direct, as is the case when the movement seeks to modify or overthrow a society's customary institutions and values, or it may be indirect, as is the case when the principal goal of the movement is to bring about change in the personality of individual participants (with the intent, eventually, of changing society). Second, a movement may be specific, when it has a clearly defined organizational structure, with a division of labor, and an ideology with precisely articulated norms and values. Or it may be general, when there is no clearly defined structure and when the ideology is vague and indeterminant. Both conceptual distinctions are, of course, based on continua and are not dichotomies, so that it may be difficult to categorize a given movement in these terms. Table 14-1 provides some examples (though even in the case of these "ideal types" there is room for debate).

The Social Psychology of Social Movements

A social psychological approach to social movements focuses on the individual member. The movement is viewed as the result of indi-

TABLE 14-1
Some Examples of Social Movements Based on the Direct–Indirect, Specific–General Distinctions

Nature of structure and ideology	Orientation toward social change	
	Direct	Indirect
Specific	French and Russian Revolutions Civil Rights Movement, 1960s Student Protest Movement, 1960s Women's Liberation Movement, 1970s	British Methodism Moral Rearmament Movement Alcoholics Anonymous
General	Early Stages Civil Rights Movement Early Stages Labor Movement Anticolonialism	Early Stages American Temperance Movement Early Stages of Religious Movements "Hippie" Movement

vidual needs and the behavior individuals engage in to satisfy their needs. From this perspective, social movements come about as a result of disenchantment with the existing state of things. There is a progressive weakening of the norms and values that bind the individual to prevailing social institutions and arrangements (Sherif & Sherif, 1969). Eventually the frustration and dissatisfaction individuals feel reaches the point where a movement develops.

A number of authors have noted, however, that frustration and dissatisfaction are relative concepts. In fact, individuals are not likely to evaluate themselves in absolute terms, but relative to the possessions, privileges, and rights of others. Relative deprivation has been one of the central theoretical concepts in discussions of social change (e.g., Merton, 1957; Pettigrew, 1964). Moreover, as authors concerned with revolutions have repeatedly pointed out, people are likely to rebel in situations of increasing economic prosperity (Brinton, 1952; Edwards, 1927) or, if there are economic reversals that precipitate the revolution, these come in the context of an extended period of economic and social development (Davies, 1962).

For a person to join a social movement, he must not simply be motivated to do so, he must feel that something can be done. This means that he must seek and find other people who share his frustration and dissatisfaction and who want to do something about it. There must be some hope of change through collective action. Ideology, at least in the sense of a nebulous vision of future possibilities, is crucial at this point. The ideology specifies what it is that the members are trying to achieve and what means are appropriate to reach that end.

Active involvement requires commitment on the part of the individual. Some authors see commitment to be the result of largely irrational forces and the psychological needs of the individual (Hoffer, 1951). Other authors point out that the membership may be fervently dedicated to the movement out of purely rational considerations (Toch, 1965). At any rate, the study of the commitment process is another important aspect of a motivational theory of social movements. On the individual level, commitment requires a personal "conversion" (defined by Toch as a turning point at which time the individual ceases to resist what he has wanted to believe for some time). At the group level, commitment requires interpersonal ties and loyalties that support and enforce norms and values.

Typically, the conversion process is apparently slow, the result of a gradual "incubation." There may be a dramatic precipitating experience, but this is usually merely the final episode in a series of disillusioning experiences. Sometimes there is no experience of change; the person simply slips into a new way of life and surrounds himself with new friends almost without being aware that he is doing so.

One's associates, who share the values of the movement, play an important role in securing individual commitment. The group acts to enforce normative conformity and doctrinal purity. Moreover, it provides consensual reinforcement, supporting the individual members in their beliefs. Certain individuals are critical since they provide leadership, formulate ideology, and devise tactics of action. In the early stages especially, the enthusiasm of the leader is a significant determinant of the motivation of his more hesitant followers.

These topics—relative deprivation, disillusionment, commitment, conversion, leadership, group interaction—have received the greatest amount of attention in social psychological treatments of social movements. It should be noted that such issues are central mainly during the initial stages of group membership. Toch has presented an excellent account of the process of disaffection and disengagement, but there has been relatively little attention given to the psychological processes operating during the stages of maintenance and institutionalization.

Methods of Study

So far we have dealt with conceptual and theoretical issues: we distinguished different types of social movements and discussed some theoretical constructs that have been used in social psychological accounts of social movements. Now we turn to the question of how to study social movements as historical or contemporary phenomena. At the risk of oversimplifying, we shall distinguish three separate methods of study—the historical-analytic, the nomothetic, and the idiographic.

The Historical-Analytic Approach. This approach attempts to place a social movement in its historical context and to analyze the movement in the light of the social, economic, and cultural conditions of the period. Such an analysis is directed at the causes of the movement—why it developed, why the members were attracted to the movement, and why the movement took the form that it did. The focus is on the motivational forces that influence the movement's development and the members' participation.

An example is Michael Walzer's (1963) account of the Puritan movement in seventeenth-century England. Walzer viewed Puritanism as a response of particular men in a particular historical setting to experiences of confusion, change, alienation, and exile. This social psychological perspective he contrasted to analyses based on Marxist or Weberian theories, which view Puritanism as a reflection of the interests of a rising economic class or the religious rationalization for unbridled capitalism. Instead, Walzer argued, Puritanism was a response to disorder and fear, a way of imposing order on an otherwise chaotic world.

A similar analysis was made by Hadley Cantril (1941) in his discussion of the kingdom of

Father Divine. Cantril traced the history of the movement and attempted to demonstrate the psychological functions the movement served for its members. He dealt specifically with the way in which the movement gave meaning and status to the believers, most of whom were poor blacks who had recently migrated to Harlem from the South. The kingdom was an escape from the realities of life and from extreme material hardship. It served as a protective microcosm shielding the members from the injustice and complexities of the external macrocosm.

Such analyses are typically more theoretical than empirical. They may stress the interaction of the movement and society and the effect of one on the other, or they may focus on the needs of the members and how these needs are satisfied by the movement. Of course such analyses can provide the basis for hypotheses that can be empirically tested (e.g., through questionnaires and interviews). When this happens, this approach begins to merge with either of the two following approaches.

The Nomothetic Approach. The distinction between a nomothetic and an idiographic approach was made popular in psychology by Gordon W. Allport (1961). The nomothetic approach stresses the general, the universal, or group norms. The idiographic approach emphasizes the specific, the individual, or the single case. The distinction is not always easy to maintain, but we shall use it to differentiate between large-scale studies that seek to establish through empirical means the characteristics of group members (nomothetic studies) and more clinical analyses based on a single movement or a detailed examination of a few members (idiographic studies).

There have been, for example, a large number of studies, which we would characterize as nomothetic, aimed at determining the personality correlates of student activism in the 1960s. Typically, these studies compare the attitudes, beliefs, family background, and intellectual abilities of young people who were active in political demonstrations against a comparable sample of young people who were not involved. Similar studies have been made, as we shall see shortly, of the personality characteristics of so-called "hippies," and of women actively involved in the women's liberation movement.

The primary goal of such studies is to describe the modal personality of the member of the movement—to provide through objective and systematic research an accurate, composite portrait of the participants in a specific social movement. Individuals may deviate considerably from the group's modal personality, yet these studies do tell us something about the nature of the movement, the population to which it directs its appeals, and perhaps something of the inner dynamics of the movement.

The Idiographic Approach. The idiographic approach emphasizes the unique features of the movement or of individual personalities of movement members. This is essentially the "case-study" method, where special attention is given to the dynamics of a particular movement or particular personalities.

There have been some interesting studies of contemporary millenarian movements that have been idiographic in this sense. The researchers usually act as participant observers in the movement, joining the cult as converts and interacting with the other members. Festinger, Reicken, and Schachter (1956), for example, studied an apocalyptic movement to determine how the members reacted to disillusioning (dissonance-arousing) experiences. Lofland investigated a small millenarian cult and presented an insightful analysis of the process whereby conversion occurred and was maintained (1966; Lofland & Stark, 1965).

Perhaps the classic studies of individual members of social movements are those of Kenneth Keniston. Keniston is a psychologist who has used the tools of his profession to investigate in detail the lives of individuals who were either alienated from society (1965) or actively involved in attempts to reform it (1968). His approach was the case-study method, involving the use of autobiography, detailed interviews, projective tests, and questionnaires. Keniston's aim was to determine regularities in life history, in thematic concerns as revealed in projective techniques, in values, and in interpersonal behavior patterns. He reported, for instance, that in his sample alienated students were estranged from their families, especially from their fathers, whereas activist youths were on good terms with their parents and did not differ from them in their values, but only in the extent of their commitment.

Keniston's studies are good examples of how the idiographic merges into the nomothetic. He started with the individual, but his data were used to reach general (nomothetic) conclusions about alienated and activist youth. Indeed, Keniston went beyond this. He also attempted to give historical perspective to his findings and to show how societal conditions and institutions have affected the lives of young people. In this sense his method is historical-analytic as well. Thus one author may use a number of methods to enrich and refine his analysis.

THREE CONTEMPORARY SOCIAL MOVEMENTS

In this section we shall turn to the three examples that we have selected as representative contemporary social movements—the student protest movement, the "hippie" movement, and the women's liberation movement. These movements are markedly different from each other in their development, their structure, and their goals. Nevertheless, many of the same questions have been asked about the three movements and the research we shall discuss is illustrative of how social scientists attempt to obtain objective and systematic information about these movements and their participants.

The Student Protest Movement

Few topics in the 1960s aroused such passionate interest as the student protest movement. Americans were sharply divided in supporting or condemning the aims and tactics of the student activists. Now, looking back on those days, it is easy to forget how charged the atmosphere was and how keenly people debated the issues. It is not surprising that contemporary accounts of the movement varied so considerably. In retrospect, with the data that are now available, a somewhat more dispassionate analysis is possible.

Youth and Social Change. The student protest movement was a movement of young people. In a sense it was a generational movement in that many (though obviously not all) members of the younger generation found themselves disenchanted with the decisions and policies of the older generation. The notion of a "generational" movement dates to Karl Mannheim (1952), who pointed out that members of the same generational cohort share a common location in the historical dimension of the social process. This is the result of what Mannheim called "the stratification of experience"—a phrase he used to refer to the way in which early impressions predominate and form a stratum that gives meaning to later experiences. These early impressions coalesce into a natural view of the world, a common consciousness that colors and modifies later strata of experience.

In periods of rapid social change, such as our own, the conflict between generations becomes especially acute. Young people today have unparalleled freedom and potentialities.

They have access to the new technology and to material goods that the previous generation sought eagerly to acquire. They lack, however, institutional structures and social identities appropriate to their view of the world. They are expected to fit into the structures and identities of the previous generation, yet their historical perspective is drastically different, not conducive to the statuses and roles they are offered.

In the eighteenth and nineteenth centuries the great social movements had as their focus the rising status of the working classes. The socialist movement, under various guises in different countries, was oriented toward socioeconomic issues and the plight of the worker. The result was revolutionary, political, and social change, as in Russia and China, or the institutionalization of reform, as in most Western countries. Today, however, as Turner (1969) has pointed out, the major constituencies for social movements are not socioeconomic classes, but age groups. In particular, it is the young upon whom the burden of adjusting to a rapidly changing social order falls most directly. Youth is the period when the most critical adjustments have to be made to the demands of society.

If one examines the major social movements of recent years, one finds that often they are movements of youth. The civil rights movement, for example, has changed its character drastically in the last ten years or so. The leadership is no longer in the hands of the middle-aged blacks; instead, the activists in recent years have been young blacks whose method of protest is more radical and extreme. The focus of the movement is now black identity and status. The older generation is left in an ambivalent state, sharing the goals of the younger generation, yet uncertain as to the means to use to reach those goals (Turner, 1969).

Similarly, the young were the predominant constituency in the anti-war movement of the 1960s. It was young people who had to pay the consequences in Southeast Asia of their elders' decisions. And although older people were also attracted to the movement, it was the young, mainly college students, who made the "anti-war movement" and the "student protest movement" synonymous.

The University and Dissent. It is not surprising that the university was the scene of dissent against the political system. It is here that one finds the most articulate members of society's youth. It is in the university that young people, in the midst of their prolonged "psychosocial moritorium" (Erikson, 1963), have the freedom and develop the critical skills to protest what they see to be the injustices of society (Habermas, 1970). In the early 1960s the focus of dissent was the university itself; in the late 1960s most protest was concerned with issues like ecology, racial policies, and above all the war in Vietnam.

Certainly not all students were involved in campus demonstrations and protest activities. In fact, activists were always a minority of the total student population (Horn & Knott, 1971). This does not mean that their impact was insignificant. While the majority of students were not members of activist organizations, sympathy for the activists was, in many cases, quite extensive. Nonetheless, it is a common misconception, based on distorted media accounts of student demonstrations, that to be a student in the 1960s was to be an anti-war activist.

Another misconception about student dissent is that campus protests were typically violent (Keniston & Lerner, 1971). In fact, violent protests involving either personal injury or property damage occurred on less than 7% of all campuses (Bayer & Astin, 1969). Most protests were peaceful and orderly, in spite of the stereotypes cultivated by the media and some politicians. Nor was violence tolerated by the university. According to one study (Bayer &

Astin, 1969), violent protests were followed by campus or civil court action in over 75% of the colleges where they occurred.

Studies of incidences of student protests indicate that the more prestigious the school, the more likely it was to have had activists (Astin, 1968; Keniston & Lerner, 1971). Schools with more selective admission policies, with traditions of academic excellence and freedom, were more likely to have experienced student protest (Keniston, 1967). These institutions Keniston called the protest-promoting institutions.

But the institution itself seems to have a negligible effect on student involvement in protest (Keniston & Lerner, 1971). The best evidence for this comes from Astin's (1968) study in which he controlled statistically for the characteristics of incoming freshmen. When this variable is held constant, there is no relationship between the characteristics of the institution and the incidence of protest activity. That is, it is the type of student body rather than the characteristics of the institution itself that relates to student protest activity.

The Activist Personality. Studies of activist youth in the 1960s indicate that those young persons who were most likely to engage in protest typically came from upper-middle class families. Their parents tended to be well educated, often in human service occupations (teachers, social workers). Their background was one of affluence and comfort (Flacks, 1967; Haan, Smith, & Block, 1968).

There is little support from these studies for the argument that student protest is a form of youthful rebellion against parental authority (Feuer, 1969). The political and ethical views of activist youths have been found to be highly similar to those of their parents (Flacks, 1967; Keniston, 1968). Parents are typically described as liberals rather than conservatives. In one study, for example, the large majority of the activists' fathers opposed bombing North Vietnam, whereas the large majority of the fathers of a comparable sample of students favored bombing North Vietnam at that time (Flacks, 1967). Indeed, the major difference between the political and social outlook of parents and activist offspring in these studies is that the children were more extreme than their parents (Keniston, 1968).

Another piece of evidence against the adolescent revolt hypothesis is the bond of identification between parent and child that was found to exist with respect to occupational preferences (Horn & Knott, 1971). Research indicated that the fathers of activists are more intellectually and socially than financially oriented, and that their offspring shared this orientation. Insofar as they identified with the world of work, activists typically preferred careers of service to careers directed at status or financial well-being. Again, the evidence suggests that, rather than rejecting parental values, activists shared them.

It should be pointed out, however, that there was a subgroup within the activist population for which there was some evidence of the rejection of parental values and of a sharp conflict between parents and child (Haan, Smith, & Block, 1968). While this group was a minority, its existence points up the necessity of maintaining awareness of the diversity and heterogeneity of personality types within the activist population.

Nor does the dominant impression of identification with parental values negate the intergenerational conflict hypothesis. The research findings indicate that by and large there was little evidence on the individual level for viewing the student protest movement as an extension of the Oedipal struggle between father and son. While identifying with their own parents, however, activists rejected the values of their parents' generation.

Research also indicates that, in the eyes of

their children, the parents of activists encouraged them to be independent and responsible. Discipline was described as lenient and based on reason rather than authority. Parents were seen to have encouraged self-expression and to have directed their children toward internally rather than externally defined goals (Haan, Smith, & Block, 1968).

Academic achievement was also valued in the activist home. Activists have been found to be academically superior to comparable samples (Flacks, 1967; Haan, Smith, & Block, 1968; Keniston, 1968). Activists did well on aptitude tests and were judged to be intellectually independent and inquiring. They valued education highly and tended to be oriented to social science and humanities—those areas of study that help to understand society and culture. They rejected the view that education is career-oriented as well as the view that knowledge is an end in itself. For most activists education had practical relevance—it helps one to understand oneself and one's fellow man.

Activists have also been found typically to hold a set of moral and ethical beliefs considered by Kohlberg (1970) to be representative of the highest level of ethical development (Haan, Smith, & Block, 1968). Whereas the majority of nonactivists were found to hold moral beliefs dictated by widely accepted conventions of what is right and wrong, the activists were found to base their moral outlook on explicitly reasoned and general moral principles.

Kerpelman (1970) administered a battery of tests measuring abilities, intelligence, personality characteristics, values, political activities, and political ideology to over 200 students from three types of institutions—a small liberal arts college, a private university, and a public university. He was able to divide his sample into two groups—activists and nonactivists—on the basis of their involvement in protest activities. Within each of these groups he distinguished left, middle-of-the-road, and right subgroups on the basis of political ideology. When these six groups were compared, Kerpelman found no differences between activists and nonactivists in emotional stability, responsibility, or intelligence. Activists were found to be more independent and more sociable than the nonactivists. The right activists and right nonactivists were more authoritarian than left activists and left nonactivists. These findings are important because they point up the necessity of distinguishing ideology and activism in comparing different subgroups of young people.

Kerpelman's study suggests that researchers may have exaggerated the differences thought to exist between activists and nonactivists. He found few differences between the two groups when he compared across institutions using quantifiable criteria for selection and distinguishing political ideology from political activism. Other investigators studying activism in the late 1960s also reported little difference between activist and nonactivist groups. These results, however, are most likely due to changes in the composition of the activist subgroups as the anti-war movement developed and began to include more diverse segments of the population.

Manhoff and Flacks (1971), for example, reported that the portrait of the activist that emerged from earlier studies—from upper-middle class professional families raised in permissive environments where the political outlook was liberal, where children were socialized to be concerned with problems of social justice, and where academic values were inculcated—no longer fit student activists in the late 1960s. The evidence suggested that recruits were being drawn from segments of the student population with different social backgrounds and family constellations. While the offspring of the liberal, educated, upper-middle class continued to play a role in the protest movement, an increasing proportion of the offspring of business men and of white- and blue-collar workers began to participate. The recruits reported far less parental acceptance of their life style and political views than was true of the veterans.

Manhoff and Flacks (1971) saw these trends as indicative of the development of a "collective consciousness" functionally equivalent to the "class consciousness" postulated by Marxism. They contended that an explanation of student activism based on family socialization theory becomes less adequate as the social base of the movement expands. Instead, they argued, attention should be focused on the hypothesis that a quasi-class consciousness has emerged among students, facilitated by the enormous concentration of young people in the universities and fostered by the general cultural and political crisis in American society.

The Activist in Historical Perspective. When one takes a broad view of student protest activity, one has a sense of *déjà vu*. Students protest activities are by no means unique to our time. There is a long history of student activism in almost all countries of the world. Feuer (1969) reviewed this history and concluded that such behavior is the inevitable consequence of the revolt of the young against the old. When the older generation makes a mistake that has serious consequences, it has lost its authority in the eyes of the young. Once this happens, the likelihood is that the latent Oedipal hostility of the young will become overt violence (Feuer, 1969).

Lipset (1972) has also stressed the recurrence of student protest activities. From the founding of America to the present day, student rebellions have been part of the national scene. Indeed, some earlier student revolts were far more violent than those of the last decade. Lipset saw student turmoil as a necessary concomitant of rapid social change, instability, or weak legitimacy of political institutions. Students, as a group, tend to be more sensitive to social conditions and have better opportunities to mount action aimed at change than other groups of the population.

Such analyses emphasize what present-day student activism has in common with student activism in the historical past. From this perspective what matters is not so much the specific constellation of events that led up to the protest as psychological tension between the young and the old or alienation in the face of rapid social change. Specific contemporary issues are not seen to cause, but to provide the occasion for student protests.

The analysis of Manhoff and Flacks (1971), on the other hand, placed much more stress on the uniqueness of the contemporary crisis—a crisis that they regarded as having to do with the impact of widespread affluence on the Protestant work ethic, changing patterns of child-rearing, and changing attitudes toward property, competition, and self-expression. In the 1960s there was a growing mistrust of the political system, arising out of the racial crisis and exacerbated by the war in Vietnam and by the failure of the political parties to recognize popular anti-war feeling. In addition, many young people experienced what they felt to be a bias against their cultural needs—their desire to experiment with new life styles, new values, and new identities. The draft was the most obvious barrier in the way of personal freedom, but this was only one of many ways in which young people felt "hassled" by the system. The delegitimation of political authority and the frustration encountered in the university in the search for relevance caused young people to turn to each other as sources of political and moral values and personal identity.

Authors stressing the uniqueness and importance of the contemporary student protest movement argue that the contemporary movement differs from those of the past because it occurred at a time in history when young people are demographically predominant in the whole population, when "youth" as a period of the life cycle encompasses an increasing number of years because of the amount of time required to train young people to take their place in the technological society, and when young people have growing economic and political power. According to this view, the emergence of a youth culture in America—a complex of language, music, fashion, and sentiment—has provided a collective generational identity that, in part at least, aids young people in attempting to resolve their personal crises of identity.

Student activism was one reaction to the crisis of the 1960s. This reaction was directed primarily at the political crisis and the failure of established agencies to bring about the changes necessary in the political system. There was another possible reaction, aside from that of apathy and adherence to the status quo, and that was withdrawal and despair of effecting change in the political domain. This reaction was directed primarily at the more general cultural crisis in American society.

The Movement for an Alternative Culture

It is not easy to characterize the nonpolitical protest movement of the 1960s and early 1970s. Stereotypes are readily available; its prototypical member was a bearded "hippie," addicted to oriental mysticism and psychedelic drugs and prone to short-lived experiments in communal living. Unfortunately such stereotypes are not very illuminating. They deal only superficially with the movement. The prime characteristic of the movement was that it sought to establish a cultural milieu radically different from the dominant cultural pattern in America. Like the student protest movement, it too was a movement of the young, yet it was not a movement aimed at political reform. As we mentioned earlier, it was essentially a movement concerned with "changing people's heads."

Both the political and the nonpolitical protest movements stem from radical discontent and aim at radical innovation. Theodore Roszak (1969) has argued that both movements share a similarity of sensibility, growing out of a mutual concern with alienation and the deadening of man's sensitivity to man. The theme that links the student activist to the hippie, he contended, is a concern with personalism. Both are part of what Roszak defined as the "counterculture" and form a continuum of thought and experience. At one end is the Freudian Marxism of Herbert Marcuse and the anarchism of Paul Goodman, at the other is the theological Freudianism of Norman O. Brown and the occult narcissism of Timothy Leary.

Nevertheless, there are considerable differences in orientation that distinguish political and nonpolitical protest movements. In terms of our earlier conceptual scheme, the political protest movement is a specific social movement that is directly concerned with social change; the nonpolitical protest movement is a general social movement indirectly concerned with social change. Because of these distinctions we shall avoid the use of the term "counterculture," which lumps both movements together, and shall speak instead of the movement for an alternative culture.

The Movement in Historical Perspective. Where and when did the movement originate? What were its historical antecedents and who were the figures that had the greatest impact on its development? Before attempting to answer these questions, we should point out that the movement for an alternative culture was amorphous and diversified. It is possible, however, to identify certain episodes and certain figures as influential in the movement's development.

The movement took shape in the mid-1960s. A new bohemian subculture developed and its members were christened "hippies" by Herb Caen, a San Francisco journalist. The term was picked up by the media and soon became a catchword describing the movement's various manifestations. Increasing numbers of young people were drawn to the movement as it received more publicity.

There are several identifiable precursors of the movement. On the West Coast in late 1959 and early 1960 Ken Kesey, a would-be novelist, was introduced to LSD as a volunteer subject in a psychology experiment. Soon he and the group around him, who became known as "The Merry Pranksters," were experimenting with the drug on their own. In 1964 they travelled across the country in a psychedelically painted bus to visit another group of devotees of hallucinogenic drugs. This group was formed around two former Harvard professors, Timothy Leary and Richard Alpert. The meeting took place at Millbrook, New York, where Leary had set up a retreat for his disciples.

The meeting of East and West was a significant event in the early days of the psychedelic revolution. Drugs had been part of the beatnik subculture of the 1950s, but they did not play the same role for the beats and the hippies. Jack Kerouac and his friends used drugs—marijuana, alcohol, and even heroin—as an enjoyable means of escape. The new movement used the psychedelics—especially LSD and mescaline—as a source of self-transcendence and enlightenment.

About this time another development was occurring, one with a far broader appeal and audience. In 1965, a newly formed San Francisco dance promotion group, The Family Dog, gave the first big rock dance (Gleason, 1969). Other groups developed—The Jefferson Airplane, The Grateful Dead, The Quicksilver Messenger Service. The music was more than entertainment: it carried the message of a cultural revolution and the artists were the spokesmen for the movement. They promoted the mystique of drugs, openness to experience, freedom, peace, and love.

One other development was the discovery of Zen and the mystic tradition of the Orient. Allen Ginsberg and Alan Watts were among the first to preach this gospel. Soon Indian gurus were travelling to America to spread the word. Meditation and the journey inward became preoccupations for many young people. Groups chanting the Hare Krishna appeared. The new religion was, above all, eclectic—there was no commitment to a specific doctrine. If it works for you, good; if not, find something else.

Psychedelics, "acid" rock, oriental mysticism—these were the manifestations of the new culture. Sympathetic observers viewed these developments as indications of the rejection of existing society and a search for new values and new life styles (Reich, 1970; Roszak, 1969; Slater, 1970). Slater's discussion of the "old" and the "new" cultures is an example. Slater argued that the core motivational features of the old culture is scarcity. As resources are limited, men must compete for them. The result is a Hobbesian ethic—every man against every other. Aggression is ritualized; psychopaths thrive. Inequality is made part of the system's structure. Everyone must work for his share of the material wealth; people who do not work deserve nothing. Status is a function of possessions. What one owns is more important than what one is.

The new culture reverses these values. Its adherents assume that human needs are easily satisfied and that the resources for doing so are plentiful. Competition is unnecessary, and work (especially work that is not creative) should be kept to a minimum. Since the good things of life are plentiful, there is no need for inequality. Everyone should share; what is mine is yours.

There are other differences between the two cultures. The ethic of the old culture results in a weakening of human ties. Things preempt people. One accumulates friends as one accumulates possessions, and with the same affect. Most personal relationships are superficial and trivial. People attempt to ward off loneliness by amassing new friends, but the result is an even greater personal isolation.

The new culture approaches human friendship in a drastically different way. One invests a great deal of emotion in one's friends. There is a confident belief in the power of love, so much so that utopian communities are established on this principle. In the new culture human social interactions are encounters governed by the implicit norms of trust, openness, and honesty.

Slater's portrait of the old and the new cultures is admittedly sketched in broad strokes. Neither culture presents a monolithic pattern. Adherents of the two cultures fall somewhere along a continuum, the extremes of which correspond to the ideal types Slater has described. Slater's analysis is, however, representative of a number of sympathetic commentaries written about the movement.

Other observers were less sympathetic. They saw the movement as simply old wine in new bottles—and not very good wine at that. Weggelaar (1969), for example, compared the "hippie" movement to three historical movements: the Dionysian rites of ancient Greece, the peyote worship of certain American Indian tribes, and witchcraft behavior. Each of these four "abnormalities" Weggelaar saw to be reactions to feelings of cultural uncertainty. In each case, he argued, the movement was a manifestation of group hysteria resulting from conflicts between feelings of freedom and the need for guidance.

Bennett Berger (1967) argued that today's hippies are merely one more manifestation of a bohemianism that dates to the nineteenth century. The ideology of this bohemian movement stresses freedom and love, emphasis on living for the moment, self-expression, and new ways of perceiving reality. There is nothing essentially new in the present movement; it simply carries on this tradition.

A more elaborate analysis is that of Nathan Adler (1968). He argued that the "hippie" personality constitutes a type that has emerged many times in history and that he referred to as the "antinomian" personality. It appeared first in the context of a theological metaphor system, where antinomianism designated those values and behaviors that challenged ecclesiastical authority. Subsequently, a similar configuration of values and conduct was articulated within the framework of a romantic metaphor system. Today the movement occurs in the context of a technological metaphor system.

The antinomian personality, according to Adler, recurs in specific stressful settings of social instability and crisis. It is a particular set of role behaviors that enables the individual to cope with cognitive, affective, and social strain. The antinomian values most the immediate and the sensual; he manipulates the visual world by means of fasting or drugs. Subjective and objective become undifferentiated; spatial and temporal boundaries are blurred; ecstasy is sought as a permanent state of consciousness.

Adler traced this pattern in the Gnostic heresies in Christian religious tradition. Gnostic cults stressed revelation, illumination, intuition, and a pantheistic fusion with nature. Membership in the cult was achieved by insight and personal purification. Its secular counterpart was the romantic movement with its assertion of the primacy of the intuitive, the emotional, and the inspirational. Both movements occurred in times when customary social and psychological assumptions were challenged. Both movements were reactions to alienation and personal estrangement.

According to Adler, the hippie represents the reemergence of the antinomian personality in today's technological society. The cultivation of intuition, immediacy, and self-actualization are reactions to social change that have occurred in other circumstances and in other historical eras. The hippie's search for utopia, for a world beyond immediate perception, and for mysticism and transcendence is an age-old quest in the history of the Western world. It is a specific mode of adaptation that has numerous antecedents. If this is understood one can find consistency and coherence in the many bizarre and diverse components of conduct that make up the new life style.

Adler's analysis, like Slater's and like similar analyses of the student protest movement, points up a fundamental limitation of what we earlier referred to as the historical-analytic approach—namely, that it becomes extremely difficult to resolve differences of opinion. In discussing both movements we are confronted with the question of whether there is anything unique about the situation in contemporary America that makes these movements unique or whether we are simply witnessing the repetition of ineluctable events acted out on the stage of history. Unfortunately, this question cannot be answered without resolving more basic issues such as the nature of historical determinism and personal freedom, topics that have been debated by great minds for centuries and that one can confidently predict will be debated for centuries to come.

The "Hippie" Personality Type. There is some problem about speaking in general of the "hippie" personality type. We shall return to this issue shortly. For the most part researchers use the term "hippie" to refer to young people in the 1960s and 1970s who have dropped out of high school or college, who live in communes of various sizes, and who are identified by their exotic and bizarre dress. Studies suggest that such young people come from predominantly upper-middle-class backgrounds and their parents come from the better-educated segment of society (Dobyns, 1969; Watts & Whittaker, 1968). Like the parents of college control groups, but unlike the parents of activists, the parents of the hippies tended to be in professional and white-collar occupations (engineers, business men) rather than in service occupations (teachers, social workers).

Hippies also did not differ from typical college students with respect to religious background, although the hippies themselves were quite different from the students in personal religious affiliation. While students tended to follow their parents along the lines of conventional religion, the hippies had rejected their parents' religious affiliation and were delving into mystical and esoteric religions, especially Oriental mysticism (Dobyns, 1969; Watts & Whittaker, 1968).

The street people in Watts and Whittaker's (1968) sample differed considerably from students in degree of estrangement from their parents. The hippie group had far less contact with their parents and expressed more disagreement with them on basic values. This contrasted not only with a random sample of students, but also with a sample of student political activists, who described their relations with their parents as warm and free of discord. This pattern of estrangement and rebellion from their parents has been found in other studies as well (Keniston, 1965; Nucci, 1974).

In comparing personality differences between the street people and Berkeley undergraduates, Whittaker and Watts (1969) found that the nonstudent population scored higher on tests designed to assess impulse expression—reflecting a need to seek gratification, to experiment with life and new experiences, and to express oneself freely. Hippie samples have also been found to be more introverted and intuitive than a comparable group of college students; the hippies scored higher on tests measuring creativity and are more independent (Dobyns, 1969). At the same time, however, the hippie groups were low on measures of impulse control and preferred to observe the environment passively rather than manipulate it actively. This suggests that their intellectual energies were turned inward and that they approached life on a passively sensuous, rather than on an actively intellectual basis. While introverted emotionality characterized the hippie groups, pragmatic rationality characterized student groups (Nucci, 1974; Whittaker & Watts, 1969).

Hippie groups also appeared less "healthy" than student groups. Students displayed more ego strength and tended to see themselves as actively in control of their own destinies (Nucci, 1974; Whittaker & Watts, 1969). In contrast, hippies were found to be low in ego strength and tended to see their fate determined by forces outside their control (Dobyns, 1969). One must remember, however, that the hippies were more likely to reject the larger culture's definitions of "healthy" personality and were more willing to acknowledge socially undesirable traits (Nucci, 1974).

Whittaker and Watts (1969) found that the street people in their sample were dramatically lower in authoritarianism than were a sample of Berkeley undergraduates, although the undergraduates were much lower than national norms. This finding is consistent with the rejection of current cultural values that typifies the hippie subgroup: The high authoritarian tends to be a defender of the status quo and conventional values; the low authoritarian tends to reject conventionality and to be attracted to the unusual and the esoteric. In general, hippies have been found to reject the syndrome of values associated with the Protestant ethic (Dobyns, 1969).

Cross, Doost, and Tracy (1970) compared the values of a group of hippies recruited from a commune with those of university students. Both groups were given a value scale devised by Rokeach (1969) that requires the subject to rank two sets of values—"terminal" values and "instrumental" values. Inner harmony, wisdom, world of peace, equality, and world of beauty were terminal values that the hippie group ranked significantly higher than the students. Self-respect, family security, sense of accomplishment, and national security were terminal values that the students ranked higher than the hippie group. Of the instrumental values, the hippies ranked honest and forgiving higher than the students, while the students ranked responsible, intellectual, capable, logical, and ambitious significantly higher than the hippies.

These findings are consistent with the literature on the movement and provide empirical evidence in support of the usual generalizations about hippies. Cross and his associates interpreted their data as indicating a rejection by the hippie group of values associated with the American academic environment. It seems likely, however, that the university is seen as a microcosm of society at large and that it is certain values of society that are being rejected.

We should note, however, that hippies have been found to differ from normal students on a relatively limited number of dimensions. Indeed, the similarities are more striking than the differences. Both groups place high value on freedom, love, happiness, and friendship. It is just that hippies tend to be more extreme in rating these values. Southern and Fry (1972) found that their samples of hippies and 1970 college students were more alike on measures of personality and values than either group was to measures on the same tests collected from a comparable college sample in 1960. These authors contended that hippies demonstrated in an exaggerated fashion the personality characteristics of contemporary college students.

On Studying the Movement for an Alternative Culture. The movement that we have been discussing here is quite different from the student protest movement or the women's liberation movement. It is a "general" as opposed to a "specific" social movement. There is no structure to the movement, no hierarchy of authority, membership is not clearly defined, the movement itself is multifaceted and diversified; many people are going in different directions. This makes the movement especially difficult to study.

This is compounded by the various personality types that are found in the movement and by the tendency of the mass media (and sometimes of researchers) to call everyone in the movement a "hippie." In fact, there are various types of hippies and various modes of "hippieness." Since one of the basic tenets of the movement is each person's right to "do his own thing," one does not find a single type of behavior that can be said to typify the hippie. There is a great deal of diversity, from the vagabond street freaks to hip entrepreneurs (Cavan, 1972).

This diversity and the fundamental amorphous quality of the movement make it especially difficult to research in a systematic way. The study of any social movement is problematic. One must select a representative sample, gain access to the participants, and ask relevant questions at an appropriate time. Each of these steps requires a major effort when dealing with a specific social movement; it is even more difficult to achieve these goals in the case of a general social movement. Sampling is troublesome in view of the many ways in which membership in the movement can be manifested. Gaining access and asking the right questions are especially difficult in the case of the movement we are discussing. Some researchers have argued that conventional techniques are impossible with hippie groups (Simon & Trout, 1967). There is resistance to intellectualizing and analyzing. The use of drugs makes interviewing suspect and possibly invalid. Investigators are sometimes seen as threats to the community and find it difficult to establish rapport. Occasionally, a group will make special efforts to convert outside observers, and they may succeed. Journalists and academic researchers who have set off to study hippie communes have been known not to return.

In addition to these problems, there is the difficulty of avoiding bias and being objective. Clinicians, who are likely to deal with "burnt-out cases," borderline schizophrenics, and emotionally disturbed persons, tend to have negative attitudes toward the movement. Researchers dealing with healthier groups generally are more positive. Thus while some clinicians have urged that the movement should be stamped out as soon as possible by the forces of law and order (e.g., Ball & Surowicz, 1968), some academic observers saw the movement as the only viable hope for America (e.g., Brown, 1969; Davis, 1967). Any movement that calls for a radical transformation of cultural values will invariably arouse antipathy on the part of some observers and a favorable reaction from others. The movement for an alternative culture has succeeded more than most in producing different reactions.

Another problem is that there are indications that the movement for an alternative culture, like the student protest movement in the late 1960s, has expanded its social base. In contrast to earlier studies where hippie subgroups were found to come predominantly from upper-middle-class backgrounds, Nucci (1974), studying hippies in the early 1970s, found that his sample of central California hippies came from the whole range of socioeconomic classes. This suggests that many of the generalizations about personality characteristics arrived at on the basis of early studies may not apply to the members of the movement a few years later.

These problems—the amorphous character of the movement, the difficulty of arriving at impartial and objective conclusions, and the changing character of the participants—are not necessarily insurmountable obstacles to research. The research of the investigators we have been discussing indicates that the movement can be studied. But to understand the implications of research one must keep in mind that the movement, like all movements, passes through different stages of development, and that the generalizations made at one point in time may not be valid at another. This is a topic that we shall return to at the conclusion of this chapter.

The Women's Liberation Movement

Of the three major contemporary social movements in American society the women's liberation movement is likely to have the greatest and most enduring impact. Curiously, however, this movement has been the least researched. The issues raised by various groups in the women's liberation movement have not been systematically analyzed in the social science literature, and there have been relatively few studies of the personality characteristics and values of participants in the movement. Nor have there been detailed analyses of the movement itself, of its development and of the changes that it is undergoing. In spite of this dearth of research, some observations are possible.

Women and Social Change. The most obvious generalization one can make is that in the last decade there has been a remarkable change in women's consciousness. There are numerous expressions of this change in consciousness, but the most important and far-reaching have to do with attitudes toward sex roles, attitudes toward work, and attitudes toward home and the family (Mandle, 1971).

Traditionally in American families girls are raised to be passive, dependent, and compliant, while boys are rewarded for displaying the opposite virtues (Maccoby, 1966). The girl is not expected to show initiative, to be responsible and self-sufficient. She is not prepared to take a place in a competitive society where self-confidence and assertiveness are critical to success. Instead, she learns from her parents, teachers, and peers that for a girl it is more important to be well-liked than to succeed (Hoffman, 1972). Indeed, there is evidence of a "fear of success" in women because the anticipation of success is accompanied by the anticipation of negative consequences through social rejection or loss of femininity (Horner, 1972).

Studies of role expectations indicate that women come to share our society's negative stereotype of themselves as conforming, dependent, and passive. Women judge themselves and other women to be less worthwhile, less intellectually capable, and less able to make important decisions than their male counterparts (Goldberg, 1968; McKee & Sherriffs, 1957). Both sexes consistently ascribe characteristics to men that are more positively valued than those ascribed to women. The positively valued masculine traits form a cluster of related behaviors which entail competence, rationality, and assertion; the positively valued feminine traits form a cluster reflecting warmth and expressiveness (Broverman et al., 1972). Since more feminine traits are negatively valued than are masculine traits, women tend to have a more negative self-concept in our society than do men. This negative self-image is a major barrier that women must overcome to succeed in those areas recognized as important by our society. One of the prime achievements of the women's liberation movement has been to make women aware of the sex role stereotypes that they have assimilated and of the sex role patterns and expectancies they are transmitting to their own children (DeLamater & Fidell, 1971; Mandle, 1971).

The second area where the movement has influenced women's attitudes is the area of work. The traditional American expectancy is that men occupy the more prestigeful and rewarding positions, while women hold the low-status and low-paid jobs. Even in the same occupational categories, there is evidence that women are paid less than men. In general, a woman in the United States who has a college degree can expect to earn slightly less than her male counterpart with a high school degree and over five thousand dollars a year less than a man with the same college degree—this in spite of the fact that over 40% of the women in the work force are the sole source of income for themselves or their families (Mandle, 1971).

A prime goal of the women's liberation movement has been the end of job discrimination and equal pay for equal work. Some progress has been made, especially in the universities where pressure from the Department of Health, Education, and Welfare has led to the appointment of an increasing number of qualified women. But if the goals of the movement are to be fully realized, equal pay is not enough. There is also the more insidious problem of the strain that a work role creates in terms of subjective feelings of anxiety and guilt due to having deviated from the normative role of a "good" wife and mother. Although there is evidence that an increasing number of women aspire to have work careers (Watley, 1969), to do so means in most cases taking on two roles that in our society are not easily reconciled—that of a working woman and that of a mother of a family.

This brings us to the third area where the women's liberation movement has had an effect on women's outlook—attitudes toward the family. In our society women are expected to fulfill themselves as mothers and homemakers. A woman must be a washerwoman, child psychologist, seamstress, cook, and so on, while at the same time providing the members of her family, especially her husband, with the emotional support they need to survive in an impersonal and technocratic society. This complex of roles is what is expected of her. Even when her children are in school, a woman continues to have family obligations. Eventually it becomes too late to change. Many women remain bored and unhappy, facing an empty future with apprehension. Their lives have been impoverished and their potential unfulfilled (Friedan, 1963).

A principal goal of the women's liberation movement is child care for women who choose working careers. In addition, members of the movement urge that family responsibilities—homemaking, raising children, and earning money—be shared by husband and wife. Some radical women's liberation groups have gone farther and espouse the abandonment of the family concept altogether. These women see the nuclear family as a type of institutionalized slavery. This position is probably too radical for most women, but the movement has definitely altered ways of thinking about the family. One researcher, for example, found that women with pro-women's liberation attitudes were far less eager to have children than were women whose attitudes were opposed to women's liberation, although the pro-liberation women ranked child rearing as more creative and expressed more personal interest in raising children (Lott, 1973).

These data are unfortunately illustrative of a conflict many women feel between traditional role expectations and the new consciousness resulting from the movement. At the present time the movement is ahead of the pace of social change. Day-care facilities are inadequate, vocational opportunities for women are still restricted, and part-time work schedules do not allow men and women to participate equally in their child's lives without losing their own professional skills and identities. As a result some women feel the most adequate solution is to sacrifice having a family in order to achieve personal satisfaction and a sense of personal identity, while other women argue that having children is an integral part of a woman's self-fulfillment. Unless the movement is effective in realizing its goals, many women, in their awareness of how things should be, will feel frustrated and embittered when confronted with how things are.

The Feminist Personality. Historically, the women's liberation movement has been a movement of well-educated, upper-middle-class women. This remains essentially true today (Mandle, 1971), although there is evidence that, like the other two movements we have discussed, the social base of the movement has changed in recent years as the movement expands.

Unfortunately, there have been relatively few studies of the background and personality characteristics of members of the women's liberation movement. There is some evidence that feminist women are more self-confident, more assertive, less affiliative, and more alienated in adolescence than comparable groups of women (Cherniss, 1972; Fowler & Van de Riet, 1972). Feminist women have also been found to be less authoritarian, more flexible, and more tolerant of ambiguity than control groups (Pawlicki & Almquist, 1973; Worell & Worell, 1971).

A persistent finding is that feminist and profeminist women score higher than control groups on measures of autonomy and self-control (Cherniss, 1972; Fowler & Van de Riet, 1972; Pawlicki & Almquist, 1973; Rychman et al., 1972; Sanger & Alker, 1972; Worell & Worell, 1971). This is not too surprising in view of the belief of women in the movement that women's low status in our society does not result from an innate inferiority but from socialization practices and institutionalized oppression.

Indeed it would seem that this variable—personal control and a sense of autonomy—is the major distinguishing personality characteristic of women in the movement and women with profeminist views when compared to other women. In one study, a comparison of feminist women and their peers failed to yield differences on some of the more salient political and feminist issues (Fowler, Fowler, & Van de Riet, 1973). The authors suggested that the variable "activism" could account for the differences that were obtained. And activism is no doubt related to a sense of fate control and the ability to influence the course of events (Rychman et al., 1972).

There is little known at the present time of the antecedents of this sense of personal control in women. In fact, there is in general little known about the personality development of women relative to what is known about male personality development. The research possibilities here are endless. With respect to our topic, what is needed are thorough studies of members of women's organizations, similar to those that have been conducted on (predominantly male) "hippies" and members of student protest groups.

Routinization and Commitment. Participation in the women's liberation movement is rather different from participation in the other movements we have been discussing. What we called the movement for an alternative culture was an amorphous "general" social movement; there were no organizations; everyone simply "did his own thing." In the student protest movement organizations tended to be ad hoc, set up to deal with specific events—strikes, demonstrations, peace marches, and so forth. Most of the members of the "movement" were spontaneous participants in these events.

The women's liberation movement is based upon organized groups of women. There is an extremely wide variety of these groups, from neighborhood "consciousness raising" groups to nationwide organizations. The largest and fastest growing of all women's groups is the

National Organization for Women (NOW). NOW has board members, a constitution, and over 700 chapters throughout the country. Founded in 1966, there were about 40,000 members in 1974. NOW is liberal but not radical, committed to realizing its goals through court action and legislative lobbying. Because of its size and influence, this group has come to typify the women's liberation movement in America.

Students of social movements have long contended that the idealism and the enthusiasm of the initial stages of a social movement are jeopardized when the movement becomes incorporated into an organization. The organization becomes an end in itself, organizational issues preempt the attention of the leadership, professionalism develops, and modes of recruitment are formalized. Weber (1922) wrote of the "routinization of charisma" and Michels (1911) proposed the "iron law of oligarchy" according to which conservative leadership is an inevitable result in organized movements. While recent research suggests that the problems of institutionalization are far more complex (Zald & Ash, 1966), the tendency toward routinization is one that confronts every social movement that develops large organizational units.

Many participants in the women's liberation movement are concerned about the way in which the movement has developed. The spontaneity and enthusiasm of the early days of the movement are endangered when the movement spawns organizations such as NOW. The mode of participation changes from consciousness raising to parliamentary debate. Leadership is no longer informal and local, but formally elected and national.

The more radical members of the movement fear that these developments will lead to cooptation. Quantitative goals may be attained (equal opportunity with equal pay, more child care centers), but without a qualitative change in American life. The question these women raise is whether women should strive for legislation that alters working opportunities without changing the fundamental conditions of our society that have led to inequality in the first place. For other women in the movement, however, there is no basic incompatability between specific and general goals.

One traditional way whereby social movements have maintained the enthusiasm and commitment of their members is through factionalism. Such a development allows for a diversity of goals through a diversity of means. This is the most likely line of development for the women's liberation movement. In spite of NOW's predominance, there are already a large number of different groups in the movement with different goals and different ideologies, and the number of these groups is increasing. These developments need not be regretted by advocates of the movement, since the presence of such variety is probably the best assurance of individual commitment.

CONCLUSION

Recently Kenneth Gergen (1973b) has raised the issue of whether it is possible for social psychology to formulate principles of behavior that remain valid over time. Briefly stated, Gergen's thesis is that social psychology is primarily an historical inquiry. Principles of human interaction cannot be developed over time because the facts on which they are based do not remain stable. Gergen argued that theoretical principles derived from recent social psychological research are not universal, but are firmly wedded to historical circumstances.

One of the examples Gergen cited was research on the student protest movement. He noted that the predictors of political activism in the early stages of the Vietnam war are different from those that successfully predicted political activism during later periods. He concluded that the evidence indicates that the factors motivating activism changed over time and that a theory of political activism built on the earlier findings would be invalidated by later findings.

Gergen's position raises a number of issues that we need not go into here. One critic feels that Gergen's argument is unduly pessimistic and overlooks numerous principles formulated in sufficiently abstract terms and based on evidence gathered from a range of evidence broad enough to establish the claim of their universality and transhistoricity (Schlenker, 1974).

With respect to the student protest movement the research that we have discussed does indeed indicate that the predictors of activism changed over the course of the movement. That is, as the movement grew and expanded, it attracted a new type of participant from a wider range of the student population. This tendency of the movement to broaden its social base as it grows and expands is most likely true of the "hippie" movement and the women's liberation movement as well. As in the student movement, there is evidence that the initial social base of the movement is the young, the upper-middle class, and the well-educated, but that in the course of time more members are attracted from other segments of the population.

That this development occurs is an interesting phenomenon in its own right and need not be seen as jeopardizing the possibility of achieving scientific understanding of such movements. It has long been recognized that different processes are at work at different stages in the development of a social movement (Gusfield, 1968; McLaughlin, 1969). There are changes in the type of leadership, in membership interaction, in the goals of the movement, in tactics, in ideology, and in recruitment procedures. Unfortunately, there has not been enough attention given in empirical studies of social movements to these developmental changes and their consequences.

Now that more social scientists are studying contemporary social movements, the data base is greatly expanding. We have more information than ever before about the participants in social movements. We know that member characteristics vary at different stages in the movement's development. But we know very little about modes of membership interaction at different stages, or about leadership characteristics, or about the determinants of movement success, or about the predictors of degree of commitment at different stages in the movement's career.

These and other aspects of social movements will doubtless receive more attention in the near future. What are particularly needed are studies that give due recognition to the fact that social movements are processes and not isolated events. An example is Hans Toch's (1965) study of the motivational processes that lead to attraction to and participation in social movements and of the factors which, in some cases, precipitate disengagement. In our terminology, Toch's study is an instance of the historical-analytic mode of analysis. The field awaits equally perceptive nomothetic and idiographic studies of the processes of affiliation and disaffiliation.

Finally, there should be some mention of the need for cross-disciplinary approaches to social movements. As we noted in the beginning of this chapter, the study of social movements is not exclusively the concern of social psychologists. It is a subfield of sociology as well. Adequate understanding of social movements means examination of the movement from a sociological as well as a psychological perspective. Sociologists tend to focus on social change, conflict, and the various types of collective behavior. This point of view is a necessary complement to the psychologist's emphasis on inner dynamics and personal interactions.

SUMMARY

A social movement is defined in social psychological terms as an effort by individual personalities in social interaction to rectify a situation they perceive to be problematic. Social movements may be directly concerned with social change in that they are oriented immediately toward changing social institutions, or they may be indirectly concerned with social change in that they aim first at changing individuals and only subsequently at changing society. Similarly, movements may be specific, with a clearly defined organizational structure, with a division of labor, and a precisely articulated ideology; or they may be general, with no clearly defined structure and a vague and indeterminate ideology.

We distinguish three approaches to the study of social movements. First, there is the historical-analytic approach, which attempts to place the movement in its historical context and to analyze the movement in the light of social, economical, and cultural conditions of the period. Second, there is the nomothetic approach, which is usually a large-scale study that seeks to establish empirically the characteristics of group members. The third approach is the idiographic, which is a more clinical, case-study examination of a single movement or of a few members. Often a single author will employ all three approaches, as was the case in Keniston's studies of alienated youth and student radicals.

The student protest movement of the 1960s was initially a movement of young people from upper-middle-class families attending some of the most prestigeful universities in the country. Studies indicate that these students by and large shared the values and political attitudes of their parents. As anti-war sentiments increased in the late 1960s, students from a broad range of institutions and backgrounds were assimilated into the protest movement. Many of the activists of the late 1960s came from different social backgrounds and experienced a different type of socialization process than was true of the veteran activists.

Another type of youth movement was the nonpolitical protest movement of the late 1960s and early 1970s. The characteristic of this movement was that it sought to establish a cultural milieu radically different from the dominant cultural pattern in America. Its espoused values were equality, brotherhood, personal trust, openness, and honesty.

Like student activists, most "hippies" came from upper-middle class backgrounds. But whereas the parents of student activists tended to be involved in service occupations (teachers, social workers), the parents of hippies tended to be in professional and white-collar occupations (engineers, businessmen). In contrast to activists and college students generally, hippies tended to have little contact with parents and disagreed with them on basic values. As the movement grew and expanded, it seems to have attracted members from a broader socioeconomic spectrum, with different background and different personality characteristics.

Studies of participants in the women's liberation movement reveal members to be more autonomous and self-confident than women generally. Feminists scored higher than comparable groups of women on various measures of personal control, suggesting that participants in the movement have a greater sense of fate control and feel they have more influence over the course of events than do other women. Little is known, however, about the antecedents of this sense of personal control.

The women's liberation movement is based on organized groups of women, varying in size from small neighborhood groups to large national organizations. The rapid growth of the movement has led to a crisis that often occurs in the development of specific social movements—the threat of routinization and bureaucratization. Fractionalism may prove to be the means whereby the enthusiasm and commitment of individual members is maintained.

SUGGESTED READINGS

Keniston, K. *Young radicals.* New York: Harcourt, Brace, and World, 1968.

An excellent case-study analysis of participants in the student protest movement. Keniston stresses the importance of socialization experience on subsequent development.

McLaughlin, B. (Ed.). *Studies in social movements.* New York: The Free Press, 1969.

A book of readings intended to provide a social psychological perspective to the study of social movements. It contains classic works in the area, including many cited in this chapter.

Smelser, N. J., *Theory of collective behavior.* New York: The Free Press, 1963.

An elaborate and rich theoretical formulation of the processes determining the nature and form of collective behavior. Smelser's analysis is applicable to social movements as well as to other types of collective behavior.

Toch, H. *The social psychology of social movements.* Indianapolis: Bobbs-Merrill, 1965.

A readable and perceptive account of the social psychology of participation in a social movement. Toch's discussions of the processes of conversion and disengagement are especially insightful.

15
Applied Social Psychology

Norman C. Weissberg

INTRODUCTION

Applied research in social psychology has focused on a myriad of both general and specific issues. For example, there is a growing literature that deals with one or another aspect of the criminal justice system in America, e.g., jury selection, jury decision making, eyewitness testimony, and police behavior. Another extensive body of material has focused on the impact of television violence on the frequency and kinds of aggression displayed following exposure to such violence. Also included under the rubric of applied social psychology would be research on such diverse topics as contraceptive use, civil disorders, poverty, the effectiveness of various forms of advertising, the selection of Peace Corps volunteers, race relations, student activism, sexual behavior, and social interaction in classroom settings. Volumes have been written on each of these topics, and no single essay can adequately cover them all. That being so, I have elected to focus on two social problems—poverty and race relations—and to try to convey some of what social psychology (and allied disciplines) have contributed to our understanding of them.

POVERTY

Despite the fact that poverty (no matter how defined) has been a persistent problem in the United States, it has exhibited a remarkable tendency to shift in and out of public consciousness. In this century, the consequences of the Great Depression were so profound and widespread that public attention was immediate and governmental action required in an effort to deal with the problems generated. Nonetheless, seven years later, in his second inaugural address, President Franklin Roosevelt spoke of "one-third of a nation ill-housed, ill-clad, ill-nourished." However, by the end of World War II and into the decade of the 1950s, poverty was once more a submerged issued. It burst again into public awareness with the publication in 1962 of Michael Harrington's *The Other America* and was made part of a publicly announced presidential concern in 1964 when President Johnson declared his "war on poverty." Since that time, many battles in the "war" have been and are now being fought; but a nation whose own official statistics proclaim that 25.5 million persons (12.6% of the total population in 1970) are living in poverty (U.S. Bureau of the Census, Current Population Reports, 1971) cannot complacently assume that the war is being won.

The Demography of Poverty

An appreciation of the scope of the problem of poverty in the United States is difficult to convey adequately in a few sentences. However, many of the assumptions made about the psychological characteristics of the poor and many of the strategies proposed to solve the "poverty problem" rest on misconceptions about both the distribution of poverty and the demographic characteristics of the low-income population. Before one can propose solutions, one ought to know what it is one is dealing with.

As I have already noted, the statistics indicate that some 12.6% of the population live in poverty. But the definition of what specific level of income serves as the boundary line between the poor and the nonpoor is quite arbitrary. Indeed, government statistics include a category of the "near poor" that, together with the official "poor" category, included some 35.7 million persons or about 17.6% of the population in 1970. For technical reasons that need not concern us here, most knowledgable observers agree that these numbers are underestimates. But more than this, if the number of persons who cannot provide for their needs is as large as I have been suggesting, then hunger and malnutrition must be fairly common. Though it may be difficult for some to accept, the facts are that hunger and malnutrition exist in every region of this country and that some 20% of all households subsist on "poor" diets as do more than one-third of all low-income households (Citizen's Board of Inquiry, 1968). Moreover, more recent data (U.S. Senate, 1973) indicate that 41 of the 50 States contain counties in which the poor are not being effectively reached by Federal food programs and in which, therefore, many poor persons are malnourished.

Granted, then, that poverty is widespread, just who are these poor people? Contrary to the usual image, the majority are white (69%), members of families (80%), the heads of which are predominantly male (63%), and are either under 18 or 65 and over (59.5%).[1] Moreover, 62% of the male heads of poor families worked at some time during 1970 (28% full time) while 43% of the female heads worked at some time during 1970 (7.6% full time). Note that this means that about 1.1 million heads of families who were classified as poor according to the conservative poverty line used by the government worked full time in 1970. Obviously, full time work did not pull these heads and their families out of poverty.

If the majority of the poor are white and live in families headed by a male, why has there been an emphasis on black, female-headed families in the media and elsewhere? Leaving aside reasons such as racism and political maneuvering, these distortions stem from the fact that while there are more white than black poor, a larger percentage of the black population (33.6) than of the white population (9.9) is poor. Similarly, while 12% of all U.S. families have a female head, among poor families the comparable statistic is 37%. Moreover,

---

[1] Unless otherwise indicated, the source for the statistics in this section is the U.S. Bureau of the Census, Current Population Reports (1971).

although the majority of both black and white families have a male head (69.5% and 90% respectively), poor black families are headed by a woman more often than are poor white families (57% and 30% respectively). Finally, while there are over two times as many white as black poor living in metropolitan areas and somewhat more white than black poor living inside central cities in these areas, 27% of all poor whites compared to 42% of all poor blacks live within these central cities.

Given, then, that about one in three blacks as opposed to one in ten whites is poor, that these black poor are more likely than their white counterparts to live in female-headed households, and that a larger percentage of the black than of the white poor live in the central cities, it is perhaps not surprising that the stereotype of the poor has at its core an image of a black family headed by a woman. After all, myths have been created out of flimsier substance than the difference between numbers and percentages. It remains true, however, that the audience to which these stereotypes are directed has been (and still is) quite ready to accept them. Moreover, opinion leaders (the mass media, politicians, both local and national) and some social scientists have been less than assiduous in attempting to counteract these myths (Billingsley, 1970; Herzog, 1970). Nonetheless, explanations of poverty and policies designed to reduce or to eliminate it must address themselves to the facts, not the myths.

The Culture of Poverty Thesis—and Its Critics

While probably not the first commentator to link the concepts of "poverty" and "culture," Oscar Lewis (1959, 1961, 1965, 1966, 1968) generally is acknowledged to have coined the phrase "culture of poverty." The culture of poverty (COP) thesis may best be described by quoting Oscar Lewis directly. Lewis' basic argument is that under certain specified conditions (e.g., a cash economy, production for profit, low wages) there emerges among major segments of the poor

> a way of life handed on from generation to generation along family lines. . . . It is a culture in the traditional anthropological sense in that it provides human beings with a design for living, with a ready-made set of solutions for human problems. . . . Once the culture of poverty has come into existence it tends to perpetuate itself. By the time slum children are six or seven they have usually absorbed the basic attitudes and values of their subculture. Thereafter they are psychologically unready to take full advantage of changing conditions or improving opportunities that may develop in their lifetime. (Lewis, 1966, pp. 3 and 5)

The "ways of life" and "designs for living" to which Lewis refers are described in the form of a set of "some seventy interrelated social, economic, and psychological traits" (Lewis, 1968, p. 5). Although Lewis stresses again and again that poverty (i.e., being poor) and the COP are distinct and separable, that the COP is present only among some of those who happen to be poor and emerges only under certain economic and social conditions, many of the traits he cites as characteristic of the COP seem more to reflect attributes associated with poverty than representative instances of a "design for living." Thus among the traits Lewis lists are the following: "relatively higher death rate," "lower life expectancy," "low level of education and literacy," "unemployment and underemployment," "low wages," "absence of savings," and "living in crowded quarters." As Valentine (1968) has noted, these phenomena can hardly be characterized as "a ready-made set of solutions for human problems." They are more appropriately understood as symptoms of poverty—problems in search of solutions rather than solutions themselves.

Similar difficulties are encountered when

one examines the remaining items on Lewis' list. Among these are: "the lack of effective participation and integration of the poor in the major institutions of the larger society"; the fact that those who live in the COP "do not belong to labor unions, are not members of political parties, generally do not participate in the national welfare agencies, and make very little use of banks, hospitals, department stores, museums, or art galleries"; they exhibit "a critical attitude toward some of the basic institutions of the dominant classes, hatred of the police, mistrust of government and those in high position"; "the absence of childhood as a specially prolonged and protected stage in the life cycle; early initiation into sex; free unions or consensual marriages; a relatively high incidence of the abandonment of wives and children"; "strong feelings of marginality, of helplessness, of dependence, and of inferiority"; and a "high incidence of maternal deprivation, or orality, and of weak ego structure; confusion of sexual identification; lack of impulse control; strong present-time orientation . . . ; sense of resignation and fatalism."

This depressing list includes attributes of the family structure and individual psychological characteristics of those who live in the COP as well as observations of the relationship between those who are caught in this subculture and the rest of society. But what this listing fails to provide is an assessment of the meaning of the observations recorded. For any of these traits to be taken as criterial of a COP it must be demonstrated that they are valued, sanctioned, prized, and transmitted by the family and other primary groups through the socialization process. In short, Lewis must document the assertion that these traits are normative; that they represent an effort to create and sustain an organized and coherent set of rules which govern behavior—a "way of life"—that is autonomous, i.e., that differs substantially from the "design for living" that is thought to be perpetuated by the "core" or dominant culture. It is important for Lewis to do this for, if he does not, there is a powerful alternative hypothesis that may be invoked to account for his observations, viz., that those traits that are central to the idea of a COP[2] represent no more than adaptations to social and economic circumstances over which the poor themselves have no control. In other words, these traits may be viewed as simply reflecting the fact "that the poor cognize and feel negatively about their position in the social structure" (Leeds, 1971, p. 254).

It may be well to identify more clearly some of the differences between these two hypotheses, which, for the sake of convenience, may be labelled the *cultural* hypothesis and the *situational* hypothesis (Gruber, 1972; Kriesberg, 1963, 1970; Leeds, 1971; Valentine, 1968).

The Cultural Hypothesis. At the core of the cultural hypothesis is the claim that the characteristics of the poor, i.e., their behavior patterns, values, attitudes, beliefs, and aspirations, constitute a coherent, organized system—a way of life—that is shared by those who live in poverty. More than this, the "system," once established, tends to become "internally perpetutated" or "self-contained," i.e., it is transmitted from one generation to the next in such a way as to lock the new generation into the same mold as the old. I take this to be what Lewis means when he says that young slum children, having absorbed the COP, are handicapped in their ability to respond to changing social conditions. One implication of this point of view is that the behavior patterns and personality attributes said to be characteristic of the poor may

---

[2]When I speak here of those traits that are "central" to the idea of a COP, I mean to exclude those features of Lewis' description that refer to symptoms of poverty such as crowded quarters, higher death rate, low level of education, and low wages. On the other hand, such traits as early initiation into sex, free unions, feelings of marginality, weak ego structure, and sense of fatalism I take to be central to Lewis' conception.

most effectively be changed by launching a frontal assault upon them; that is, by establishing social policies and governmental programs that directly encourage modifications in the behaviors, values, beliefs, and aspirations that are thought to be transmitted through the socialization process.

The Situational Hypothesis. At the core of the situational hypothesis is the assumption that the "design for living" in terms of which the poor are socialized is not markedly different from the design to which the nonpoor are exposed; however, the very real constraints imposed on the poor by virtue of their socioeconomic position may produce behavior patterns and/or value systems that differ from those observed among the nonpoor. But—and this is crucial—those differences that do exist do not reflect a commitment on the part of the poor to "a separate cultural design" (Valentine, 1968, p. 129); they are better conceived as ways of coping with the problems that engulf those in the lower strata of society (Rodman, 1964). The solutions achieved, no matter how inadequate they may be judged to be (and let us not lose sight of the fact that many of the solutions achieved by those in the middle and upper classes also often have been judged inadequate), are still responses to perceived and real conditions of life. One implication of this view is that it is the economic, social, and political conditions the poor confront that must be changed if changes are to be effected in behavior and values. Thus, governmental programs should be directed toward changing the social and material circumstances of the poor; behavioral and value changes will follow (cf. Gruber, 1972).[3]

A Consideration of the Two Hypotheses. Lewis himself has noted that the phrase "culture of poverty" is "catchy," and it should not be surprising that the cultural hypothesis has enjoyed more popularity than has the situational. However, very little empirical research has been conducted designed specifically to bring data to bear on the validity of these alternative hypotheses. Nonetheless, the COP thesis has not escaped serious criticism (Leacock, 1971; Leeds, 1971; H. Lewis, 1971; Roach & Gursslin, 1967; Valentine, 1968). Among the charges that have been levelled at Lewis' formulation are that the concept of culture has been misemployed, that the methods used to establish the existence of a COP have been faulty, that the data have been misinterpreted, and that the conclusions reached have been overgeneralized. It may be instructive to provide examples of the last two criticisms.

One of the observations Lewis records is that the poor tend to exhibit a "hatred of the police [and a] mistrust of government and those in high position." He interprets this characteristic set of attitudes as a part of the COP. An alternative interpretation is that these attitudes represent a realistic response to the social circumstances in which the poor live. Since Lewis provides no data in support of his cultural thesis, one cannot, at this time, definitively choose between these two interpretations. But I should like to argue here that the stiuational interpretation is at least plausible. First, I trust I need not convince readers that a lack of confidence in the police and a general disaffection with the overall political apparatus may be rooted in concrete experiences with specific representatives of these agencies. One need not be poor to believe that the actions of many of our national and local political leaders

---

[3]The notion that the problems of the poor will automatically disappear if fundamental changes are made in our social institutions is too simplistic. Past experiences and the relatively enduring personality dispositions they have produced affect the ways in which people respond to changing circumstances. This is not to say that the poor or anyone else cannot change; it is to say that such changes will not come about effortlessly and somehow magically simply because objective realities have changed (cf. Gurin & Gurin, 1970).

are not such as to inspire confidence and trust. With respect to attitudes toward the police and those in "high position," I invite readers to recall their experiences with a "police bust" on their own campuses or to talk to those who lived through such an experience. Many middle-class students and faculty exhibited, during these incidents, a "hatred of the police and of those in high position." And these feelings were justified by the participants on the grounds of what they saw, felt, heard, and experienced. Should it be surprising that many of the residents of low-income ghettos feel similarly and justify their feelings on the same grounds? Moreover, the greater persistence of these attitudes among the members of the poverty population than among the members of the middle class is explainable in terms of the persistence of the social conditions that breed these feelings in the first place. Little is experienced by the poor that would lead them to doubt the validity of these feelings, and much is experienced that reinforces them.

Another implication of the COP thesis is the notion that poor families choose public assistance (welfare) rather than work as a means of meeting their financial needs and that this choice is expressive of the values they hold rather than a response to constraints imposed upon them by the circumstances of their lives. However, the results of several studies (Goodwin, 1971; Kaplan & Tausky, 1972; Kriesberg, 1970) support the conclusion that external circumstances are more closely tied to the decision to work or to accept welfare than are internalized values. For example, Goodwin (1971) showed that the work orientations of both men and women on welfare were no different from the orientations held by the nonpoor. Moreover, there was no correlation between the strength of commitment to a work ethic and positive attitudes toward welfare assistance as a source of income. Similarly, Kriesberg's (1970) study of husbandless mothers supports Goodwin's findings. Neither a condemnatory attitude toward accepting welfare nor a negative attitude toward mothers working bore a significant relationship to whether earned income or public assistance benefits were used to support the family. Most predictive of this choice were the amount of secure, dependable income (e.g., social security, alimony, or pensions) the family had at its disposal and the number and age of the children. The interpretation of these relationships, buttressed by substantial supporting data, seems straightforward. If secure income is abundant, work is not necessary; if some dependable income is available, and the mother works, more money is earned than would be provided by public assistance benefits; however, if no secure income is being provided, then it is unlikely that she will be able to earn more than welfare payments alone would provide. If the mother has a number of children, and if one or more of these is preschool age, employment is quite difficult. Moreover, the more children there are, the greater the financial need; and while welfare payments increase with each additional child, wages do not. It appears, then, that external circumstances are more closely tied to the decision to work or to accept welfare than are internalized values.

Similar lines of argument may be advanced to account, in situational terms, for many if not most of the other characteristics Lewis includes in his list. For example, in his study of the marital and paternal relationships, employment patterns, sexual relationships, and friendship networks of a group of lower-class black men who frequented a streetcorner in Washington D.C., Elliot Liebow (1967) observed some of the same behaviors that usually are invoked as evidence for the existence of a COP. However, Liebow disavows this conclusion and writes of the men observed:

> His [i.e., the streetcorner man] behavior appears not so much as a way of realizing the distinctive goals and values of his own subcul-

ture, or of conforming to its models, but rather as his way of trying to achieve many of the goals and values of the larger society, of failing to do this, and of concealing his failure from others and from himself as best he can. (p. 222)

The second criticism of Lewis' thesis to which I am drawing attention is the charge that he has overgeneralized his limited empirical data. Lewis' own research was conducted primarily in certain areas in Mexico and Puerto Rico, and it was on the basis of observations recorded in these countries that he advanced the COP idea. While severe criticisms have been levelled at Lewis' insistence that his data support the inference that a COP is operating in the situations he describes, Lewis, nonetheless, has extrapolated his idea far beyond the specific contexts within which he worked. For example:

> This style of life [the COP] transcends national boundaries and regional and rural-urban differences within nations. Wherever it occurs, its practitioners exhibit remarkable similarity in the structure of their families, in interpersonal relations, in spending habits, in their value systems and in their orientation in time. (Lewis, 1966, p. 3)

In many ways, the assertions quoted above constitute a remarkable statement. What Lewis seems to be saying is that the force of the COP is so great that it washes out all of those structural and cultural variables that traditionally have been invoked to account for the variability observed in family structure, interpersonal relationships, and the like across regional and national boundaries. Thus, in two short sentences Lewis, the anthropologist, appears to have cast aside much of what the discipline of anthropology has taught us. However, rather than continue this line of argument (namely that Lewis' generalizations are unreasonable), I shall turn to some empirical evidence in support of my criticism.

Irelan, Moles, and O'Shea (1969) attempted a direct test of the hypothesis that poor persons from different cultural backgrounds exhibit marked similarities in values and attitudes. Eight "value orientations" (such as dependency, fatalism, social alienation, and the value placed on child autonomy) were identified and questions designed to tap these values were asked of the male heads of over 1150 intact poor families in California. Black-American, Anglo-American, and Spanish-speaking American families were represented in approximately equal numbers in the sample. Moreover, about half of each group were receiving welfare benefits while the other half were not on public assistance at the time of the interview. Answers to the various interview questions were analyzed separately for these two groups of respondents. Contrary to the COP thesis, the three ethnic groups did not, by and large, adhere to a common set of value orientations. Now it should be noted that a single piece of research neither confirms nor denies as broad a hypothesis as Lewis has put forward. Moreover, a number of criticisms may be levelled at Irelan et al.'s effort: (1) the fact that only the male heads of intact families were interviewed raises doubts as to whether the results may be generalized to female-headed households; (2) the absence of a control sample of nonpoor respondents for each ethnic group prevents one from comparing the relative similarity or dissimilarity of viewpoints between the poor and the nonpoor; and (3) the specific value orientations identified may not be the critical ones for the COP concept and/or the specific ways in which they were operationalized may not be adequate. However, despite these reservations, the degree of similarity of the value orientations studied across the three ethnic groups was not as great as the COP hypothesis implies.

In sum, then, while Oscar Lewis' hypothesis is intriguing, it remains a hypothesis in search of evidence rather than a hypothesis for which the evidence is compelling. It also is important to emphasize that I have not been trying to argue that the poor are no different from the middle class.[4] Rather, I have been trying to say that one must place whatever differences there are in perspective and not automatically assume that these differences reflect enduring personality characteristics that are relatively unresponsive to and relatively unaffected by the circumstances in which the poor find themselves.

Welfare Dependency

One segment of the poverty population that has found itself the target of considerable attention (usually adverse) is the "welfare poor." The conventional wisdom has it that those who are receiving public assistance are either lazy and will not work or Machiavellian and motivated solely by greed and a desire to cheat the system. By now the reader should be aware that such simple-minded shibboleths mask more than they reveal. Let us begin, then, by placing the welfare problem in perspective.

Being "on welfare" is not a label for a single state of affairs. Welfare assistance is extended to individuals and families under five major categories: Aid to Families with Dependent Children (AFDC); Assistance to the Blind (AB); Aid to the Disabled (AD); Old Age Assistance (OAA); and General Assistance (GA). The first category, AFDC, is the largest and contains some 75% of the welfare population. Although this is the group that usually is thought of when one refers to those on welfare, it ought not be forgotten that a substantial number of persons is being covered by these other forms of assistance.[5] In any event, the AFDC program was designed to provide assistance to needy, fatherless families with children under 18. In 1961, the Federal Government granted to the states the option of extending benefits to families in which there is an unemployed (male) parent. About half of the states have adopted this program (AFDC-UP).

To say that a family is receiving AFDC benefits does not mean that that household receives the same benefits no matter where it is located, nor does it mean that the income received is adequate to meet the family's needs. An analysis of the actual dollar amounts received by a typical AFDC family of four in 1971 reveals that, while there undoubtedly are those who cheat the system, the vast majority are not "doing well on welfare" (cf. U.S. Department of Health, Education, and Welfare, NCSS Report H-4 (71), 1971).

Moreover, the reader will be surprised to learn that most poor persons receive no welfare benefits. Only about 30% of all families below the poverty line receive public assistance. The "welfare poor," then, represent a minority of the poverty population, and whatever may be asserted about them may or may not also be applicable to the larger population. But why aren't more poor families receiving the benefits to which, theoretically, they are entitled? So far as I am aware, no one knows the answer to this question (cf. Moles, 1971). Speculation has centered on such variables as pride, ignorance, and bureaucratic indifference and arbitrariness. These undoubtedly are involved, but clearly more research is needed.

Empirical studies of the social-psychological correlates of welfare dependency are few.

---

[4] Reviews of some of these differences are contained in Allen (1970a, 1970b), Goodwin, (1971), Irelan (1968), and Weissberg (1970).

[5] About 2.9 million families representing 10.6 million recipients were receiving AFDC benefits in December, 1971. At the same time, some 4.1 million persons were receiving assistance through the four other programs (*Social Security Bulletin,* March, 1973).

Information on the demographic characteristics of recipients are available but rarely accompanied by psychological data. Moreover, even when such data are provided, the typical absence of any comparison groups (middle-class and/or nonwelfare poor respondents) makes the interpretation of these data quite difficult.

An exception to some of these inadequacies is a study by Stone and Schlamp (1971). These authors interviewed a sample of 600 AFDC-UP families and 600 nonrecipient families in California. The two sets of families were matched on income, ethnic distribution, and rural-urban residence. Since the 600 welfare families were drawn from among those receiving AFDC-UP benefits, these families, as well as the matched controls, were all male-headed. Thus, none of the families in the sample were representative of female-headed AFDC families. In addition to these 1200 families, 43 upper-middle-class families were administered the same questionnaire. Data on a large number of important topics were gathered, but here I will highlight only a small sample of them.

The families were classified into one of three groups based upon their welfare history: (1) those that never had received assistance (NOA); (2) those that had been receiving assistance for a short time (STA); and (3) a long-term assistance group (LTA). Two important psychological variables were assessed in this study, viz., psychological dependency and anomie. Attitude scales purporting to measure these concepts were constructed and administered to the husbands in these 1200 families. Not surprisingly, scores on these measures varied among the three subgroups classified on the basis of welfare history. In particular, the LTA group attained a higher mean score than did the NOA group on every subscale of the dependency measure. This pattern was repeated for the anomie scores. Similarly, the Spanish-speaking and black families had higher scores on these scales than did the white families. Moreover, the 43 upper-middle-class families scored lower than did the 1200 poor families on these same measures. While it would be fair to say that being on welfare for an extended period of time is correlated with anomie and psychological dependency, the interpretation of these relationships is far from clear.

First, whatever differences emerged were relatively small; we are not, then, talking about samples of persons with very divergent mean scores on a measure of psychological dependency. Second, granted that some of these differences attain statistical significance, Stone and Schlamp computed no measure of the strength of the association between their categories of welfare history and their measure of psychological dependency. One may assume, however, that the relationships are not as powerful as would be required to make strong predictive conclusions. A final complication is generated by virtue of the confusing responses of the NOA and LTA families to two additional attitude scales. Specifically, the husbands in the LTA families exhibited a stronger desire than did the NOA families to encourage autonomy in their children. But these same LTA fathers scored higher than did the NOA fathers on a scale purporting to measure the degree to which they foster dependency in their own children. Thus, the LTA fathers present a pattern in which they themselves are more psychologically dependent than the NOA fathers but, at the same time, appear to encourage both dependency and autonomy in their own children.

The presence of these rather weak and confusing relationships does not provide strong support for the argument that economic and psychological dependency are intitimately related. Nor do these data speak clearly to the question of cause and effect. That is, is psychological dependency to be thought of as an independent variable that, perhaps along with other personality characteristics, is causally implicated in the perpetuation of welfare dependency or does the causal chain run the other way, i.e., does continued economic dependency itself generate psychological dependency? It is also possible, and indeed likely, that the relationships we are trying to untangle here are highly complex and that the causal sequences are not as straight-forward as I have indicated above (cf. McGuire, 1973).

The preceding discussion dealt with psychological dependency as a correlate of economic dependency. Many other psychological characteristics have been assumed to be associated with the receipt of welfare assistance. Let us briefly examine one of these, viz., the educational and occupational aspirations welfare mothers have for their children.

A popular belief is that welfare mothers (and fathers) do not encourage their children to achieve educational and occupational success (as these are conventionally defined) and do not themselves value these kinds of achievements. These attitudes and values are then believed to help perpetuate an intergenerational cycle of poverty. As has been the case before, the available data do not support the conventional wisdom. For example, Moles (1965) found that over 90% of the children in his sample of public assistance families in Detroit believed that their mothers wanted them to complete college. Moreover, when the mothers themselves were asked whether they wanted their children to finish college, a larger percentage of "Yes" answers was obtained from those mothers who had been on welfare for an average of three years (50%) than from mothers drawn from a matched sample of low-income nonwelfare families (38%). Moles also included questions on occupational aspirations, and the results parallel those found for education. Thus, on the basis of this and other studies of both welfare families (Greenleigh, 1960; Podell, 1968; Raab, 1965) and low-income families in general (Kriesberg, 1970), it seems reasonable to conclude that the generally low level of actual achievement in the educational and occupational hierarchies that has been exhibited by the low-income (welfare) population is not due to a value pattern (in these domains) that differs markedly from that held by the more advantaged segments of our society.

Some Conclusions

The thrust of the argument presented in this section was that some of the presumed major social psychological correlates of poverty in general and welfare dependency in particular may, in fact, not be so closely associated with these statuses as one often has been led to believe. However, the research reported has been scanty. There is little doubt that poverty and welfare dependency induce certain psychological states in those who find themselves trapped by these circumstances and that these states differ from those engendered by virtue of middle class status. However, it is not at all clear that these states have been properly identified, that they become deep-rooted personality attributes that are relatively insensitive to changing circumstances,[6] that they play a causal role in the perpetuation of dependency both within and across generations, and that the distribution of these states is dramatically different within the lower and middle classes. Nonetheless, many of these doubtful assumptions underlie current laws and policies. For example, in 1971 the New York State Legislature voted into law a requirement that "employable" welfare clients report to State Employment Offices to receive their checks

---

[6] It is encouraging to note in this regard that psychologists have become increasingly disenchanted with the concept of personality traits and have come to recognize the central role that situational factors play in accounting for behavior (Mischel, 1973).

and to accept jobs or training offered them. Several dubious assumptions lay behind the enactment of this legislation. For example, one widespread feeling was that a substantial portion of the welfare caseload consisted of persons who could work and could find jobs but who preferred to collect their welfare checks instead. It was felt that the new law would clear the rolls of these "welfare cheats" and that the cycle of dependency could thus be broken. However, an analysis of the effectiveness of the law (U.S. Department of Health, Education, and Welfare, 1972) revealed that this and other goals were far from being reached. Not only were the number of "employables" a small fraction of the total caseload; but of the 23,000 clients willing to accept jobs, only about 7% were placed in positions that lasted four days or more. Moreover, after about three months, two thirds of these persons were no longer working. Evidence from a number of sources (Burnside, 1971; Rein and Wishnov, 1971) should have alerted policy makers to the fact that one cannot simply assume that the bulk of the welfare caseload (AFDC mothers) can be made to "work themselves off welfare" without providing the special services such a group requires. Even had that information not been available, one ought not launch a major and costly social change—especially one that has the potential to do more harm than good—without first weighing the consequences of that change. While there are a number of proposals designed to reform the welfare system and/or to eliminate poverty (including such plans as children's allowances, a guaranteed annual income, a negative income tax, guaranteed jobs, and work training and education), these schemes have yet to be tried out and their consequences assessed in a systematic fashion. An impressive array of arguments has been marshalled in support of all these plans; but the time surely has come when an action-oriented empirical approach should be adopted.

THE BLACK-WHITE THING

No chapter on applied social psychology can omit from consideration the vast literature on race and race relations. Books, articles, monographs, and essays pour onto the market as if from some vast cornucopia. The great bulk of this material focuses on black-white relationships (just as, in the days during and shortly after World War II, a substantial amount of professional attention was directed to a consideration of anti-Semitism) but other minorities (Asian-Americans, white ethnics, Chicanos, Puerto Ricans, American Indians) as well are now receiving deserved attention from the social science community. Nonetheless, I think it fair to say that it is the "black-white thing" that consumes most of the energies of the interested professional community and that is the "gut" issue confronting America today. Traditional treatments have focused on prejudice as an attitude, the determinants of such attitudes at both the individual and societal level, and, more rarely, the relationship between prejudice and discrimination. While such topics may be introduced as they become necessary, this discussion will be organized around two basic contexts: the *family* and the *schools*. Finally, a concluding section will be devoted to black-white interactions and social change.

The Family

Consider for a moment the image of the typical black family held by the (hypothetical) average middle-class white. The contrast between that image and the one held of the typical white family is stark. Significant features of the former, but not the latter, are likely to include: a poor husbandless mother, many children, some or all of whom are illegitimate, and, a father, who, if he is present at all, plays a very minor role in family decision-making. The family structure thus defined is held to be unstable.

Moreover, it is further alleged that a community largely composed of such families is unlikely to improve itself and indeed likely to generate a "tangle of pathology" that serves to reinforce its continued deterioration (Moynihan, 1965). How valid are these conceptions of the black family? I have identified three components of the stereotype—female-headed households, illegitimate children, and a matriarchal power structure—and shall consider each in turn.

Female-Headed Households. Only about 12% of all families in the United States in 1970 were headed by a female. Among white families, about 9% and among black families about 31% were female-headed. The majority of both black and white families, then, in terms of percentages as well as numbers, are headed by a male. And while there were more white (4.4 million) than black families (1.5 million) that were female-headed, such households were proportionately more often found among the black than among the white population. But these demographic facts and others that focus on trends over time (Farley and Hermalin, 1971) capture attention because female headship is assumed to have negative consequences for children raised in such family structures. However, rather than assume such a relationship, let us examine the evidence.

Data bearing on the question of the relationship between family composition and occupational and educational achievements have been provided by Duncan and Duncan (1969) and by Farley and Hermalin (1971). Their results support the conclusion that, for both whites and blacks, being raised in a female-headed household negatively affects both educational attainment and occupational achievement. However, while these effects were relatively modest, a comparison of whites and blacks who had grown up in an intact family and whites and blacks who had grown up in a female-headed family revealed that, for both comparisons, whites achieved higher occupational statuses than did blacks. This racial difference could not, of course, be attributed to differences in family-of-origin. Additional analyses showed that the occupational status differences between blacks and whites could not wholly be accounted for by educational differences associated with the fact that female-headed households are proportionately more often found among the black than among the white population; blacks suffer an occupational disadvantage, relative to whites, even when one controls for education and composition of the family-of-origin. More will be said about this point later. Finally, there is little evidence to support the oft-quoted assertion that family composition is intergenerationally transmitted (Duncan & Duncan, 1969; Heiss, 1972).

What, however, of the effects of father-absence on personality variables? First, I know of no studies that examine this question using adequate samples of both blacks and whites and that control for variables other than father-absence that may affect the dependent variable(s) under consideration. However, there are two studies that suggest that children reared in female-headed families may develop personality attributes that traditionally are judged to be undesirable.

Some years ago, Mischel (1961), working in the West Indies with two groups of young (8–9) black children from two different subcultures within those islands (Trinidad and Grenada), found that, within each group, children from father-absent families, as contrasted with children from families in which the father was present, tended to choose smaller immediate rewards more often than larger delayed rewards. It has been argued that the ability to delay immediate gratification for the sake of subsequent gratification with its potentially greater payoff is a crucial component in the setting of long-term goals, in the development of responsibility, and in the management of impulsiveness. Interestingly, Mischel found no relationship between father-absence and delay of gratification in his sample of older (11–14) children. His tentative interpretation of this last finding is that, with increasing age, the "trust" necessary for exhibiting delay of gratification behavior grows more out of the child's experiences outside the family than out of those experiences he encounters within the household.

One implication of this research is that the father serves as a model who exhibits and reinforces delay behavior in his children. But the meaning of delayed gratification in the context of the circumstances of the black family today must be considered before one leaps to the conclusion that blacks from father-absent families suffer an irreparable personality defect. First, as noted before, adequate research in this area is still wanting. Many variables have to be controlled and adequate samples employed before sweeping conclusions about the negative effects of father-absence can be made. Second, Mischel's own data suggest that experiences outside the family-of-origin or variations in child-training practices within the family over time may modify the impact of father-absence on delay of gratification. Third, to delay an immediate reward for the sake of a promised future reward requires that one have some confidence that the future reward actually will be received. The experience of many blacks in the United States, both subjectively and in terms of objective data (Duncan, 1969), may lead them to expect that the future reward may not be forthcoming. Thus, even if it were demonstrated that blacks suffer, proportionately more often than whites, from an inability to delay gratification, this state of affairs would need to be carefully interpreted in the light of the black experience. The problem may be less that of the pathology of the black family and more that of the pathology of the social conditions that induce or encourage the development of such expectancies in the first place. Indeed, rather than viewing a preference for immediate as opposed to delayed rewards as an instance of personality deficit, a growing body of research suggests not only that such preferences can be modified (Bandura & Mischel, 1965) but that they are more usefully conceived as situation-specific (Gallimore, Weiss, & Finney, 1974; Liebow, 1967; Miller, Riessman, & Segull, 1965).

The second study was based on interviews conducted with a representative sample of men in the United States (Schooler, 1972). No breakdowns by race were reported. Several specific areas of psychological functioning (e.g., authoritarianism-conservatism, ideational flexibility, distrust of others) were assessed in an effort to determine whether they were related to structural characteristics of the family-of-origin. Controls were employed for age, region of the country, father's education, rural residence as a child, religion, mother's working, and family size. Even with these controls, coming from a broken home was correlated with greater anxiety, more distrust of others, and less ideational flexibility. When the sex of the remaining parent was taken into account, those who grew up in female-headed families were more likely to be authoritarian and less likely to be ideationally flexible than the general population. But, as Schooler himself points out, these effects were all quite small.

In sum, while all the evidence is not yet in, it is reasonable to conclude that children who grow up in a female-headed household are slightly worse off (both in terms of education, occupation, and income and in terms of personality functioning) than children who grow up in intact families. However, not only is it unlikely that the structure of the family-of-origin has a strong independent impact on adult personality functioning, but the effects of race and other variables are likely to be much more significant than family composition in accounting for those differences that do emerge (Herzog & Sudia, 1968).

Illegitimate Children. Despite the fact that the majority of births in both the black (70%) and the white population (95%) were legitimate in 1968 (the latest year for which official government statistics are available), much has been made of the fact that, both in number and percentage, illegitimate births are more frequent among blacks than among whites. However, in assessing changes over time, the most meaningful statistic to examine is the birth rate.[7] In these terms, for nonwhites, both the legitimate and the illegitimate rate declined between 1960 and 1967; for whites, the legitimate birth rate also went down but the illegitimate rate went up (Farley & Hermalin, 1971). What shall we conclude?

First, it is an unalterable fact that the number of illegitimate children (both black and white) increased between 1960 and 1968. However, since the illegitimate birth rate among blacks went down during this period, the increase cannot be attributed to the fact that more unmarried black women were giving birth than ever before. Second, if one looks just at the number of illegitimate births, the absolute increase from 1960 to 1968 was greater for whites (72,000) than it was for blacks (42,000). Thus, while the number of illegitimate births has been and still is greater among nonwhites than among whites, the trend (as expressed both by the raw numbers and the birth rate) was in the direction of decreasing illegitimacy among blacks and increasing illegitimacy among whites. Nonetheless, this ought not be interpreted to mean that the black illegitimacy rate is insignificant; in 1970 it was four times that of the white rate (Sklar & Berkov, 1974).

However, pinpointing the reasons for changes in illegitimacy is a notoriously difficult undertaking. What is clear is that most traditional explanations (rising divorce rates, an increase in welfare payments, an increase in the number of AFDC families) are not valid (Cutright, 1971). Those who wish to reduce illegitimacy have at their disposal two major weapons: increasing the availability of abortion services and increasing the effective use of contraception among the unmarried population. The former has been shown to be effective in that the decline in the illegitimacy rate for both races between 1970 and 1971 clearly is attributable to the increased availability of legal abortion (Sklar & Berkov, 1974). Nonetheless, that this is not the complete answer is apparent from an analysis of changes in birth rates in California between 1971 and 1972 (Sklar & Berkov, 1973). This analysis revealed that despite the availability of legal abortion, many women were choosing unwed motherhood. Increasing the availability of effective contraception should also reduce the number of unwanted pregnancies but it is clear that, even if available, contraception often is not employed (Cutright, 1971, 1972; Whelan, 1974).

In sum, the black illegitimacy rate is high and poses a profound problem both for that population and for the society as a whole. However, illegitimacy is not a simple phenomenon and will not be solved by simple and simple-minded solutions.

Matriarchal Power Structure. The third component of the stereotype of the black family is that, in contrast to the white family, it is the wife who is the dominant figure and who exercises the major decision-making power over the family's affairs. This matriarchal structure is believed to be a consequence of the experience

---

[7]The birth rate is computed as the number of legitimate (or illegitimate) births per 1000 married women, 15–44 (or unmarried women, i.e., single, widowed or divorced, 15–44).

of slavery during which time slave masters systematically set about to disrupt and destroy the traditional nuclear family. The persistence of this state of affairs in modern society can be traced, in this view, to the fact that the black female has more employment opportunities than does the black male; her greater control of the economic resources available to the family then generalizes to reinforce her power in other domains within the family unit. Once such a power structure comes into being, it serves to further sustain the black male's feelings of emasculation and powerlessness (cf. Rainwater, 1966). Whatever the merits of this account (and, it should be noted, one or more parts of it have been criticized), the question to which I want to draw attention is whether or not it is a reasonable generalization to say that the pattern of female dominance and male subordination is typical for black families and atypical for white families.

Empirical research on this question has been scanty. One of the most sophisticated studies in this area was conducted by Ten Houten (1970, 1971) in Los Angeles County. Interviews designed to assess conjugal and parental power structures[8] were conducted with intact black and white families with children. The families were selected in such a way that they were matched for socioeconomic class and for the class level of the neighborhood in which they lived. Moreover, black families were interviewed by black interviewers and white families by white interviewers.

The data indicate that contrary to the thrust of the black matriarchy argument, an ideology of male dominance is more prevalent among blacks than among whites, lower-class black males do not wield significantly less power in family decision making than do husbands in the other race and class groups, and lower-class black families are least likely to be perceived as wife-dominated and most likely to be perceived as egalitarian.

The data bearing on parental power are more complicated and therefore more difficult to summarize. First, there were no racial differences with respect to whether the mother or father was perceived as having the prime responsibility for child rearing. To the extent that an ideology of maternal power in this domain exists, it is a function of class rather than racial differences. On the other hand, when interacting with their children, black mothers were perceived (by their children) to be more forceful than white mothers; but black fathers were not correspondingly perceived as weaker than white fathers. There was a significant class effect too such that higher socioeconomic-status mothers and fathers were seen as more dominant than their lower SES counterparts. The greater power of black mothers did not, however, result in the emasculation of the black male. This can be seen by noting that although the perceived power of the black mother increased eight percentage points when one considered middle-class as opposed to lower-class mothers, the same eight percentage point increase was observed for black fathers, thus maintaining the same disparity in power between black mothers and fathers in the two SES groups. For whites, the increase from low-

---

[8]The concept of "conjugal power" refers to the relative power of the husband and wife over decisions that affect the both of them and that bear on their relationship to each other. It has been assumed that the conjugal power structure of white families is one in which the husband is dominant and the wife submissive and that this role pattern is reversed for black families.

The concept of "parental power" refers to the relative power of the husband and wife over decisions that affect the ways in which their children are raised. It has been assumed that the parental power structure of white families is such that the husband makes the major decisions concerning the directions in which the child is to be socialized and the ways in which her/his activities are to be controlled and that this role pattern is reversed in black families.

er to middle class status was six percentage points for mothers and sixteen for fathers. Thus, as mothers' power increased among whites, fathers power increased at a much faster rate. However, the same disparity was not maintained between white mothers and fathers as one shifts attention from the lower to the middle class. If anything, the disparity between mothers and fathers for the two racial groups in the lower class is less than the disparity between the parents in the two racial groups in the middle class. While the white middle-class father is more directive than the black middle-class father, this does not mean that the black male is perceived as powerless. Rather, the balance of power seems to be more even across class lines for blacks than for whites.

While the data indicated that the vast majority of families in the entire sample exhibited a control pattern in which neither the mother's nor the father's power was disporportionate, some evidence for the matriarchy notion was provided by the fact that of the children in the sample families, those from lower-class black homes were least likely to perceive their fathers as setting rules intended to control their activities. Moreover, the disparity between the rule-making power of black lower-class mothers and fathers was greater than the corresponding disparity for any other group. Finally, with respect to the provision of concrete assistance to their children, black mothers were perceived as doing more than their white counterparts. But since no racial difference was found for fathers, the greater perceived resourcefulness of the black mother may be interpreted as a source of strength for the black family rather than as evidence for a role structure predicated on matriarchy.

Taken as a whole, the data provide no support for the black matriarchy notion. Only in the case of rule-making was there some evidence for a disparity between mother's and father's power. But even here the same high percentage (73%) of black and white lower-class parents were perceived as egalitarian. The data I have presented have come from a single study conducted in a single community. But data from three national samples (Hyman & Reed, 1969) support the findings reported by Ten Houten. Rather than providing evidence that black women, in contrast to white, exert extraordinary power within the family, these studies reveal that, in the main, black and white family patterns are quite similar and that the differences that do exist are "small and inconsistent" (cf. Mack, 1974).

Growing Up in a Black Family. In the preceding sections I examined components of the stereotype of the black family and took pains to question the validity of this stereotype. Nonetheless, growing up in a black family does have consequences. Up to this point, the burden of my remarks has been to deemphasize the sharp differences that are alleged to exist between black and white families. But differences do exist. While there are more whites than blacks living in poverty, a larger percentage of the black than of the white population is poor. Moreover, proportionately more black than white families are headed by a female and proportionately more black than white babies are born illegitimate. But above and beyond whatever consequences may ensue from these differences, being born black has independent effects on one's life chances. What does this statement mean?

To document the effects of discrimination on blacks is not so simple a task as one might assume. Everyone knows that such discrimination occurs and that it has tragic consequences; but to pin down precisely and quantitatively the nature of these effects and the mechanisms through which discrimination works to produce them is quite another matter. Systematic research on these questions only recently has been conducted, and there remain many unanswered questions. But enough is known to provide a thumbnail sketch of what has happened and still is happening.

The most sophisticated analyses of these issues have been published in book form by Blau and Duncan (1967) and by Duncan, Featherman, and Duncan (1972) and in a number of articles by these workers and their colleagues (cf. Duncan & Duncan, 1969, and Duncan, 1969). For example, Blau and Duncan report the not surprising statistics that blacks are less likely than whites to attain high educational levels and that they are likewise disadvantaged with respect to occupational attainment. They also confirm what others had noted previously, viz., holding educational level constant, whites attain higher status occupations than do blacks. But what they also show is that even when one imposes controls for the lower occupational status of the fathers of blacks relative to whites, for educational differences, and for differences in the status of one's first occupation, there is still a substantial difference in occupational achievement in favor of whites. Additional analyses (Duncan, Featherman, & Duncan, 1972) reveal that when one takes into account (i.e., statistically equates) the socioeconomic level of the family-of-origin, number of siblings, level of education, and occupational status, there is still a gap of over $1400 between the mean incomes of whites and blacks. Moreover, if one adds to the factors to be controlled the variable of "mental ability" (as indexed by scores on one or another test) and, as before, imposes controls for this difference between blacks and whites, one still finds a significant gap on earnings and occupational status (Duncan, 1969). This, then, is what it means to say that being born black has independent effects on one's life chances. It is not only the fact that, on the average, blacks start out from a less advantaged position than do whites; it is that even after all these disadvantages are taken into account, blacks still wind up behind whites. As Duncan (1969) has noted with respect to income:

> At least one-third of the income gap arises because Negro and white men in the same line of work, with the same amount of formal schooling, with equal ability, from families of the same size and same socio-economic level, simply do not draw the same wages and salaries. (p. 108)

The "cost of being a Negro" in our society is thus pervasive and cumulative. Those who argue that the "basic" race problem is really only a matter of differences in schooling, or ability, or socioeconomic level of the family-of-origin will have to explain how the data gathered by Duncan could come about. Perhaps on the other hand, Duncan has provided us with a good operational definition of what racial discrimination really means.

The Schools

One of the most important functions performed by the school system in our society is to educate children so that they are equipped with at least the minimal competencies necessary for "making it" in our urbanized, industrialized, technological society. To be sure, this is not the only function schools perform; but it is clearly one of their most central responsibilities. There is debate on whether or not the schools are discharging this responsibility adequately for white students, but there is ample evidence that blacks are being shortchanged. Earlier I noted that within any given level of educational attainment, blacks achieve lower status occupations than whites and that educational differences between blacks and whites cannot fully account for the disparity in income between the two groups. Thus the schools alone cannot be held responsible for the lower incomes of blacks, relative to whites, nor for their generally lower occupational achievements. But school does have an impact on these and other outcomes and is the context, moreover, for much of the debate on the issue of race and intelligence. Let us examine this context.

Preliminary Observations. Much of what is known about the public schools in the United States comes from one of the most massive social science documents ever produced, the "Coleman Report." Commissioned by Congress, this was a study designed to assess the degree to which there are inequalities in educational opportunities "by reason of race, color, religion, or national origin. . . ." The report iself was issued in 1966 and since then has served as a touchstone for any assessment of the relationship between race and education. Because of the large number of authors (Coleman, Campbell, Hobson, McPartland, Mood, Weinfield, & York, 1966), the report has become widely known simply as the "Coleman Report." I will use that label, as well as the abbreviation for the title of the report itself, EEOR,[9] in making reference to the document throughout this discussion. But a word of caution before I begin. The EEOR was based on interviews and tests administered to almost 600,000 students and their teachers, principals, and supervisors throughout the United States. The data presented often are quite complex and often entail sophisticated statistical analyses. More than this, the EEOR has been subjected to extensive criticism as to the quality of the data, the statistical operations performed, and the conclusions drawn by the authors (Marascuilo, 1967; Mosteller & Moynihan, 1972a; Pfautz, 1967; Sewell, 1967). I say all this to alert the reader to the difficulties one encounters in attempting to draw firm conclusions in an area as complex as this and to warn that many of the interpretations that have been drawn are to be understood as quite provisional.

What did the report show? First, the EEOR documented the fact that schools in the U.S. are racially segregated. The vast majority of white students attended schools that were predominantly white and the vast majority of black students attended schools that were predominantly black. Furthermore, it is clear that segregation has not abated since 1965. For example, in 1970 about 67% of all black elementary and secondary school students were attending schools in which over 50% of their classmates also were black. Moreover, 38% were attending schools in which between 95 and 100% of their classmates also were racemates (U.S. Bureau of the Census, 1973).

The second major finding of the EEOR, and one that generated a good deal of controversy, was that on the average, within regions of the country, there were no very striking differences between predominantly black and predominantly white schools on a wide variety of measures of school facilities and quality.[10] Still another finding was that blacks attain significantly lower scores than whites on a variety of measures of educational achievement (e.g., tests of verbal ability, reading comprehension, mathematics). Not only was this pattern found at the higher grades sampled (i.e., 9 and 12), but even at grade 1 there was a difference of at least one standard deviation between the scores of whites and blacks.

Finally, the most significant portion of the EEOR was devoted to an attempt to assess the relationship between academic achievement and a variety of school and nonschool (i.e.,

---

[9] The title of the report was "Equality of Educational Opportunity."

[10] Among the indicators of school quality that were assessed in this regard were: the presence or absence of a library and biology laboratory, the age of the school buildings, class size, student-teacher ratio, presence of specialty teachers (art, music, speech, etc.), and teacher's salaries.

family) influences. While the logic of a survey such as Coleman's makes it impossible unequivocally to infer cause and effect relationships, such a survey does provide an assessment of what variables are related to what other variables and an assessment too of the strength of the associations uncovered. If a strong relationship is discovered between two variables, there is still ambiguity with respect to the nature and direction of the causal link, if any, between them; but if no relationship is found, other things being equal, one has provided strong evidence that there is no causal link between them.

After controlling for a wide variety of family background factors, differences in school resources (e.g., equipment, teachers' salaries, staff training, pupil-teacher ratio) did not correlate with academic achievement. But if, on the whole, school resources do not make an independent contribution to achievement, what does? The data showed that home background factors (parents' education, number of siblings, reading material in the home, and so on) had the largest effect on both school-to-school and within-school variations in achievement in the early grades; smaller independent effects were found also for characteristics of the student body and teacher characteristics. Students' attitudes, particularly perceived control of the environment, had a strong effect on achievement in grades 6, 9, and 12. Since our interest primarily is on black-white differences in achievement, I will pursue next some of Coleman's findings relevant to this issue.

As noted before, it was found that, on the average, blacks attain lower scores than whites on a variety of tests of academic achievement and that this difference is substantial even in the first grade. This difference appears not so much because primarily black and primarily white schools have markedly different facilities but because blacks and whites come to school with different backgrounds in the first place. More than this, these family background factors not only serve as good predictors of differences in achievement between the races, but serve that function within the races as well. Parenthetically, these home background factors were more powerful predictors of test score differences among white than among black children.

Another variable relevant to black-white differences in achievement (after family background factors had been controlled) was the racial composition of a school. Several considerations must be kept clearly in mind when dealing with this issue. First, race and social class, while empirically correlated, must be kept distinct in these analyses. Second a distinction must be drawn between the overall racial composition of a school and the racial composition of individual classrooms within a school. What did the Coleman report find with respect to this issue?

First, students from lower social class homes had a poorer performance on tests of achievement than did students from more privileged homes. This was the case for both black and white students but differences in achievement were more affected by differences in individual social class for whites than for blacks. Now consider not individual social class but the social class composition of an entire school. Coleman found that the higher the social class level of the student body, the higher the achievement scores of individual students. This was true for both blacks and whites and for both higher and lower individual social class students within each racial group. But what of the racial as opposed to the social class composition of a school? The EEOR found that the effect of the racial composition of the school on individual achievement was practically zero when controls were imposed for the social class composition of the student body. What this means is that the finding that blacks achieve higher scores in majority white schools than they achieve in majority black schools is not so much a function of racial composition per se as it is a function of the fact that the students in majority white schools come from more advantaged backgrounds than do the students in predominately black schools. Additional analyses of Coleman's data by Mayeske, Okada, Wisler, Cohen, and Beaton (1972) support this conclusion.

Let us now look at the question of the relationship between achievement and the racial composition, not of the entire school, but of individual classrooms. Reanalyzing data gathered originally by Coleman and his colleagues, McPartland (1969) found that, for the ninth-grade black students and schools studied, the greater the proportion of white classmates, the higher the achievement scores of black students. Moreover, if one controls for family background differences and for percent white enrollment in the school as a whole, the positive effect of white classmates is not appreciably reduced. Thus, white classmates have a positive effect on black achievement independent of the overall racial composition of the school and of family background differences among the students. Cohen, Pettigrew, and Riley (1972), adding controls for parents' education and other variables, found essentially the same results for black students in grades 9 and 12 that McPartland reported. However, while the classroom racial composition effect is a real one, it should not be overinterpreted. While an increase in percent white classmates leads to a statistically significant increase in black achievement, the size of the effect is rather small. Thus, while there may be many arguments for classroom desegregation (to be discussed in a later section) it cannot be said that such a program will, of itself, lead to marked improvements in black achievement.

It remains to discuss briefly the final two factors Coleman studied, teacher characteristics and student attitudes. The EEOR data on teacher characteristics were so gathered that nothing could be said about the relationship between teachers and students within a school; the data bear only on the question of the relationship between differences in student achievement and differences in teacher characteristics among schools. This is important because one of the major overall findings of the Coleman report was that most of the differences in achievement, for both races, were found to lie within schools (Armor, 1972; Jenks, 1972; M. S. Smith, 1972). Another way of saying this is that the average differences in achievement from one school to the next were relatively small compared to the average differences in achievement that were found among students in the same schools.

What did Coleman find? First, he reported that differences among teachers on such characteristics as social class origins, race, scores on a test of verbal achievement, and educational level, contributed to differences in average verbal achievement levels among schools even after the individual family backgrounds of the students were controlled. He also concluded that teacher differences make more of an impact on blacks than they do on whites. Reanalyses of the data with more adequate controls (M. S. Smith, 1972) suggest that the link between teacher characteristics and achievement is less than Coleman reported and that the hypothesis that blacks are more sensitive to these differences than are whites is only very weakly supported by the data.

The final factor in this saga of the EEOR is student attitudes. Perhaps surprisingly, perhaps not, the variables that composed this factor (interest in learning, self-concept, and sense of control of the environment) had the strongest relationship to between-school differences in achievement of any of the variables studied in the survey. They accounted for more of the variation in achievement at grades 6, 9, and 12 than did either family background or school variables and, even when controls were imposed for family background differences among the students, this factor still maintained a significant relationship to achievement. Two points should be made here. First, both blacks and whites in the 12th grade exhibited rather high levels of self-esteem; moreover, the differences between the two groups on this variable were rather small. Second, whites and blacks do differ on the control of the environment measure. This concept refers to the degree to which one believes that what happens to oneself (i.e., what one can achieve) is primarily a function of one's own ability (internal control) or primarily a function of external events over which one has little control (external control). This concept was operationalized in the Coleman survey through the use of three questions, to which the children had to indicate whether they agree or disagree: "Good luck is more important than hard work for success;" "Every time I try to get ahead, something or somebody stops me;" and "People like me don't have much of a chance to be successful in life." Not only did blacks show less internal control than whites, but this "control of the environment" variable was a better predictor of academic achievement for blacks than it was for whites. (In contrast, the self-concept variable was a better predictor of achievement for whites than it was for blacks). These results persist even after one controls for family background differences.

An additional finding was that, for both racial groups, as the proportion of white enrollment in the school increased, the child's sense of internal control likewise increased. Several cautionary remarks should accompany this last, frequently cited, finding. First, the proportion of white enrollment in the school as a whole has been found to be more an index of social class level than of race per se. Second, since an increase in the proportion of white enrollment (or the proportion of students from more advantaged backgrounds) is associated with increases in achievement, variations in attitude may be a function of variations in achievement levels of the schools rather than a function of desegregation. Third, the absolute magnitude of this effect was quite small.

Some Conclusions. Having taken the reader through the complex findings contained in the EEOR relevant to the "black-white thing," what implications may be drawn from these data? First, it seems clear that traditional approaches to improving the ability of the schools to teach cognitive skills—spending more money on the physical plant or teacher's salaries or tinkering with the curriculum—have not and probably will not succeed. As Mosteller and Moynihan (1972b) have pointed out, this should not be interpreted to mean than "one can get behind in the teacher-salary market or let the buildings fall apart" (p. 42). But it does mean that if traditional manipulations and interventions are to be employed and if they are to have any chance of making an impact on achievement, they will have to be quite a bit more radical than anything that has yet been tried in the nation's schools. This is one of the important implications of the fact that the greatest variation in achievement occurred within schools. Second, one must come to grips with the fact that the best predictor of achievement in the elementary school grades was individual family background. It may well be that efforts to improve the academic achievement of black Americans should be directed toward improving their overall socioeconomic position rather than directed toward improving the schools themselves. This does not mean that one can ignore the question of school quality; it does mean that if the black-white achievement gap appears in the first grade, the schools themselves could not have contributed to that gap.

There is a growing body of evidence that mothers from different social class levels respond to their infants and young children in different ways and that at least some of these differences may be implicated in the differences in achievement between these groups when the children reach school age. In particular, the results suggest that social class differences are correlated with differences in the frequency of verbal interactions between mother and child (Tulkin & Kagan, 1972) or with differences in the "quality" of response to an infant's vocalization (Lewis and Wilson, 1972) or with the "richness" of the verbal environment in which the child is reared (Hess & Shipman, 1965). In each case, the differences that emerge favor the development of cognitive, particularly verbal, skills in the middle class child. The results provide one clue, then, as to why family background was so closely tied to verbal achievement in school. Black-white differences, in this view, arise primarily because blacks are more often found in the lower class. It should be emphasized, however, that the causal chain I have outlined above is highly speculative; a great deal more evidence (particularly from longitudinal studies that trace these childrens' careers from infancy through the elementary grades) is required before these ideas can be said to have validity.

But what then happens when these children with different levels of cognitive development reach school? M. S. Smith (1972) has advanced the hypothesis that these initial differences have an impact on the child's placement in ability groups in reading and mathematics and on the teacher's expectations of the kinds of work the child may be able to perform. Thus, instead of being overcome, these initial differences may be exacerbated by the school's tracking policies. Evidence that these initial disparities are not overcome has been provided by Vane (1966), who reported a correlation of .76 between 3rd- and 8th-grade achievement test scores. If this line of argument is true, it suggests that efforts should be made to educate parents to respond to their children in ways more conducive to the growth of cognitive skills and to build more flexibility into the tracking systems in use in the early grades. Also suggested by the argument that early experiences powerfully affect achievement is that preschool programs (e.g., Head Start, Sesame Street) should be strengthened. While the data on the effectiveness of these programs has been mixed, the overall results are encouraging enough (Ball & Bogatz, 1972) to warrant much greater efforts in this direction.

Finally, what are the implications for school integration? The effect on achievement of overall percent white enrollment in a school was found primarily to be a function of social class. That is, what a greater proportion of whites bring to a school is not so much their color as it is their social class background. Second, an increase in the proportion white in individual classrooms does have a positive effect on achievement independent of the effect of family background and of proportion of white enrollment in the school as a whole. Third, as the proportion of white enrollment in the school increases, so does the sense of "control of the environment." This latter variable was found to correlate with achievement. But for all of these relationships, the effects on achievement are rather small. Let us consider two issues here. The first is, assuming that integration at the school level has a positive effect on black achievement primarily through an increase in the socioeconomic level of the school population and that integration at the classroom level has an effect independent of family background, through what mechanisms is this effect achieved? The second issue is what benefits, other than improvements in cognitive skills, accompany desegregation?

One interpretation offered for why blacks achieve more in schools that are predominantly white is that, regardless of socioeconomic class, blacks who attend middle-class schools come from families that are more achievement-oriented than blacks that attend lower-class schools. What this interpretation says is that it is neither the social class level of one's schoolmates nor one's own class level (as traditionally measured) that is causally implicated in high achievement scores. Rather, the effect is due to a self-selection process such that certain types of black families with certain types of motivation send their children to middle-class schools. It is for this reason that blacks in such schools do better than blacks in lower-class schools. The EEOR does not contain data adequate for testing this interpretation and, while one study (Wilson, 1967) showed that blacks attending integrated intermediate schools had higher first grade mental maturity scores than their peers attending segregated schools, there does not seem to be systematic data that directly bear on the question of motivation.

More promising leads to the mechanisms that underlie the effect of desegregation on achievement come from the work of Cohen and Roper (1972) and Katz (1967, 1968). Katz (1968) has identified four situational factors that affect the performance of blacks in desegregated schools: social threat, social facilitation, lowered probability of success, and failure threat. A desegregated setting may be perceived as socially threatening (i.e., as generating expectations that one will be subject to harm or pain) because of white hostility (or rejection or indifference to attempts at social contact) and because of the predominance of white authority figures in the school. Such an expectation is likely to interfere with cognitive performance. On the other hand, if the desegregated atmosphere is one in which acceptance, friendliness, and approval are offered to blacks, a social facilitation effect may occur. This may operate in two ways. First, the generally higher achievement standards associated with predominantly white (i.e, middle-class) schools will be adopted by blacks as a response to their acceptance by whites. Second, encouragement from white teachers and schoolmates reassures blacks that they can perform as well as any other student, increases their desire to do so, and heightens the "rewardingness" of the approval that follows from successful achievement. The third factor is probability of success. If the black child feels unable to compete successfully with his white peers, this lowered subjective probability of success is likely to lead to a decline in his motivation to succeed. Finally, failure threat refers to the child's feeling that he will be subjected to severe disapproval if he does not succeed in the performance of some academic task. It follows, then, that as the child's subjective probability of success decreases, his/her fear of failure increases. Three of these four factors should interfere with performance while only one (based on acceptance, encouragement, support, and approval) should serve to facilitate performance.

The finding by McPartland (1969) that the positive effect of desegregation on achievement occurs at the classroom level begins, then, to make sense in the context of Katz's discussion of the social facilitation effect. For it is at the classroom level that cross-racial friendships are likely to emerge and in which a climate conducive to the operation of the social facilitation effect is likely to be present. The Coleman data are inadequate to test the hypothesis that differences in racial climate in the classroom are correlated with differences in achievement (Cohen, Pettigrew, & Riley, 1972), and there does not seem to be any research that directly tests this proposition. However, there are a number of studies that report data consistent with this specific hypothesis.

For example, reanalyses of Coleman's data by the U.S. Commission on Civil Rights (1967) showed that regardless of the social class background of the students and the social class composition of the school, the earlier the experience of an integrated classroom, the better the academic performance of 9th-grade black students. However, it would be incorrect to conclude that desegregated educational settings always lead to improved academic performance; the relationship should be positive only when there is an atmosphere of social acceptance. For example, if desegregation has variable effects depending on circumstances, then there should be more variability in the reading and mathematics scores of black students in schools in which more than half the students are white than in schools in which the proportion of white classmates is 50% or less. This is precisely what the EEOR found. Moreover, there should be situations in which the racial composition of the school should have no effect on achievement, and several studies have reported this finding (St. John & Lewis, 1971; Vane, 1966; Wilson, 1967). The data from these studies show that simply mixing blacks and whites in the same school or even in the same classroom is not a sufficient condition for improving the academic performance of blacks. To understand why this is so, one has to examine the psychological processes that operate in biracial settings. While much remains to be done along these lines, several promising leads have been established.

For example, in an early study, Katz and Benjamin (1960) assigned a series of performance tasks to biracial teams composed of two white and two black college students. The whites and blacks on each team were matched on a measure of intelligence, told that they had been placed together because of their similarity, and, through a deception, made to appear to attain the same scores (i.e., equal success) on the tasks. Nonetheless, blacks initiated fewer communications than whites, directed more of their communications to whites than to each other, tended to be more susceptible to influence by whites, and ranked whites as more competent on these tasks than their race-mates despite the fact that their objective performance was almost identical to that of whites. In these interracial situations, then, blacks tend to be compliant toward whites despite the fact that they believed they were equally intelligent and knew that they had performed the tasks equally well.

In a second study (Katz & Cohen, 1962), an attempt was made to increase the degree to which blacks would act assertively and autonomously in these biracial situations. Two kinds of training situations were compared. In one, "assertion training," blacks were given information that would aid them in solving the cognitive problems presented to the biracial teams for solution. In the "no training" condition, the information provided was not sufficient to enable them to offer solutions with great confidence. It was found that "assertion training" led blacks to express more confidence in their answers to a totally different set of tasks and to exert more influence on the team answer to these judgmental problems than blacks who had undergone the "no training" experience. But of equal importance, the influence exerted by those blacks who had been exposed to the "no training" manipulation was less than what it had been before. What these findings mean is that when blacks are compelled to achieve in the presence of whites (as in assertion training) they will be more assertive in a subsequent task. But when they are in the presence of whites and not forced to achieve (as in the no-training condition) they will be even more influenced by whites than before being required to interact with whites on a joint problem-solving task. All of this may be interpreted in terms of Katz's notion of "social threat." That is, black submissiveness in the presence of white companions may be understood as a response to the black's fear of white hostility.

In a follow-up study, Katz and Greenbaum

(1963) manipulated the amount of overt threat that blacks would experience in a same-race or different-race environment. Southern black college students individually performed a simple, nonthreatening task in the presence of an experimenter and a confederate of the experimenter who posed as another subject. In one condition, both were white and in another both were black. In addition, each subject was exposed to a condition of either high or low threat, created by announcing that the subject would receive either severe or mild electric shocks at random times during the performance of his task. In fact, no shocks ever were administered. It was found that when exposed to mild threat these black subjects achieved a better performance on their task when in the presence of whites than they did in the presence of blacks. But when severe shock was threatened, they performed better before an audience of their race-mates than they did before white companions.

The foregoing experiment indicated that under some conditions black college students will perform better in a biracial situation than in a setting in which all the participants are black. In an attempt to explore more fully some of the implications of this finding, Katz and his colleagues (Katz, Atchison, Epps, and Roberts, 1972) conducted still another study at predominantly black colleges in the South. The results support the following propositions: (1) in testing situations defined as involving the assessment of scholastic aptitude, black college students perceive white standards of performance as higher and more difficult to achieve than black standards; (2) they also perceive white test administrators as more capable than black examiners; (3) when placed in such testing situations and told that their performance will be evaluated relative to white standards, they achieve better scores with a black examiner than with a white; on the other hand, when told that they will be evaluated relative to black standards, they perform better with a white tester than with a black; and (4) the interpretation of the preceding result is that when failure is perceived as likely (as when white standards are employed), the presence of a high-status (white) evaluator interferes with performance. But when success is the more likely outcome (as when black standards are implied), the presence of a high-status (white) examiner facilitates performance.

What have these laboratory studies told us thus far? First, when interacting with whites in a situation requiring cooperative effort in the achievement of a goal, black college students adopt a submissive role and judge whites to be superior to themselves in intellectual performance. This was the case even when black and white partners had been matched on intelligence and when their objective performances were the same. Second, blacks can be made to act in a more influential manner, but still less assertively than whites, by forcing them to adopt a more dominant role in interracial interactions. Third, the mere presence of whites (without interaction with them) has an effect on black performance, but this effect interacts with other features of the situation, particularly how threatened the individual feels. Fourth, if the threatening aspects of biracial situations are minimized, black students perform better in the presence of whites than in the presence of their racemates (cf. Katz, 1973).

It should be noted that these laboratory data have been derived from studies of black college students. While children of primary school age may act differently, the existence of social threat and the negative consequences it has for black performance is, in all likelihood, a real pheonomenon that operates in classroom situations. If this is so, the question then becomes: How can one encourage blacks to act more autonomously and less submissively in interracial classroom environments and how can the threatening features of these settings be mitigated.[11] A recent study using black and white junior high school boys as subjects provides some clues (Cohen & Roper, 1972).

The authors begin by noting that the general cultural expectation that whites are more competent than blacks tends to infect interracial encounters between the races. Each participant carries around in his head expectations about his own and his cross-race partner's probability of success in the accomplishment of whatever task is at hand. Moreover, these expectations serve to create a self-fulfilling prophecy in which the lower-status member of the dyad (i.e., the black), assuming that he is less able than his higher-status partner (i.e., the white), behaves in such a way as to insure that he in fact will be less influential. The research conducted by Katz and his colleagues clearly supports this position. Cohen and Roper addressed themselves to the question of how to overcome or modify the negative effects of this set of expectations.

In the experiment this was accomplished by establishing training conditions designed to create expectations at variance with the general cultural assumption of black inferiority. Following the training, black-white interactions were observed as four-person teams (two blacks and two whites) played a game that required the team members to reach a consensus on the direction in which to move a playing piece on a game board. What is important about this is that the training conditions differed with respect to whether only the expectations of blacks were modified or whether the expectations of the participants from both races were influenced. In the first case, black students were made to feel competent and to display their competence in situations in which only fellow blacks were present; in the second case, these feelings of competence were created and displayed before the same white students with whom they were to be paired in the game that followed the training sessions. The results indicated that the effect of the training session designed to modify only black expectations was to preserve the pattern of white dominance and black subordination in the game. On the other hand, the training session that focused on the expectations of both races led to much greater involvement of and influence by blacks in the interracial game setting.

What are the implications of this study for school desegregation? First, it supports the contention that simply mixing whites and blacks in the same school or even in the same classroom is not alone a sufficient condition for modifying the expectations that each race has for itself and the other. In Katz's terms, social threat, fear of failure, and lowered probability of success are not likely to be modified markedly by such a procedure. Second, it also supports the argument that attempting to alter the expectations that blacks hold about their own performance potentials, without at the same time manipulating the expectations held by whites, is unlikely to result in major changes in black performance. It is difficult to see how this can be accomplished outside the context of desegregated classrooms. Thus, while desegregation is not a sufficient condition, it is a neces-

---

[11]The question assumes that interracial classroom environments should be encouraged. A critic might argue that since there is evidence that blacks can learn as well in segregated as in desegregated schools (Hansen, 1960; St. John & Lewis, 1971; Vane, 1966), one should abandon efforts to decrease segregation and concentrate instead on improving the quality of instruction in primarily black schools. While I am certainly in favor of improving the quality of instruction, I do not believe that efforts directed toward desegregation of the schools should be dispensed with. As I will argue, school desegregation has positive effects independent of scholastic achievement and, on these grounds alone, a strong case for desegregation can be made.

sary condition for intervention programs whose aim it is to overcome the feelings of inferiority with which many blacks approach interactions with whites. Now it would be the most blatant form of overgeneralization to say that these findings, derived from a laboratory study of small, task-oriented groups working cooperatively on a contrived game, can be applied directly to the school environment. But surely such data as Cohen and Roper provided are provocative, consistent with other available information and thinking, and worthwhile pursuing in more realistic settings.

With respect to the classroom itself, the threatening features of that environment can be mitigated by providing blacks with the kind of supportive atmosphere that benefits all students. However, to say that this should be done does not mean that it will be easy. Cohen and Roper have argued that there is a general cultural expectation that blacks are inferior and there is evidence that the nonverbal behaviors teachers direct toward students they believe to be "dull" signal less liking and approval than do the nonverbal behaviors they direct toward students they believe to be "bright" (Chaikin, Sigler, & Derlega, 1974). But more than this, Rubovits and Maehr (1973) have shown that white female education majors' reactions toward students labeled as "gifted" varied as a function of the race of the student. Specifically, compared to black students who had been labeled as "gifted," "gifted" white students received more praise, attention, and encouragement and were less often ignored. In fact, blacks who had been designated as "gifted" were subjected to more discrimination than were those blacks who had been labeled "nongifted." These findings do not encourage optimism with respect to the ways in which blacks will be treated in desegregated classrooms. But the solution lies neither in abandoning efforts at pupil desegregation nor in systematically matching the race of the teacher to that of the student;[12] what is crucial is to make teachers of both races more aware of their expectations and assumptions and to help them to modify their behavior.

Let us now turn to a consideration of the effects of desegregation on other than cognitive outcomes. While most of the research on the effects of desegregation has focused on academic performance, there is evidence that the positive benefits of such experiences are not restricted to the cognitive domain. Let us consider two such outcomes: attitudes and occupational achievement. With respect to the former, two studies are especially relevant. In the first (U.S. Commission on Civil Rights, Volume 2, Appendix C4), interviews were conducted with a sample of high school graduates, all of whom had attended the public schools in their community continuously since the first grade. Based upon the racial composition of their elementary schools, black and white students were designated as having had either a desegregated or a segregated experience. The data were presented only for black students. Among the more important findings were that those blacks who had attended desegregated schools were more likely than their race-mates who had attended segregated schools to: (1) be willing to send their own children out of the neighborhood to attend an integrated school; (2) say that they would be willing to live in an all-white neighborhood with its attendant difficulties if they could secure good housing there; (3) have white friends; and (4) be less suspicious of whites and more at ease in interracial settings.

---

[12]The evidence (Jencks, 1972; M. S. Smith, 1972; Summers & Wolfe, 1975) indicates that differences between schools in the achievement test scores of pupils of both races are not influenced by the percentage of white or black teachers in those schools.

The second study (U.S. Commission on Civil Rights, Volume 2, Appendix C5) was based on interviews with black and white adults in northern metropolitan areas. Again, the primary focus was on attitudinal differences between adults who attended desegregated as opposed to segregated schools. Black adults who attended desegregated schools, more often than their peers who attended segregated schools, preferred to live in a desegregated neighborhood, had children who were attending desegregated schools, had white friends, and had high self-esteem. Most of these findings held up after controls were applied for level of education and region of birth. Whites who attended desegregated schools were more likely than their racemates who attended segregated schools to have had a close black friend, to have had a black friend visit in their own home, to be living in a desegregated neighborhood, and to have more "liberal" racial attitudes in general.

Further support for this position comes from a study conducted by Brown and Johnson (1971) in England. These investigators found that white children more often attribute negative connotations to pictures of shaded figures than to pictures of white figures. This tendency was not present in 3- to 4-year-olds, increased substantially for the 5- to 8-year-old group, and decreased for those between 9 and 12. Brown and Johnson showed that the decrease occurred primarily for those children who attended schools in which there were a substantial number of "immigrant" children. While further research is needed in order to determine whether this decrease in prejudicial attitudes is real or merely a function of increasing sophistication on the part of the respondents from desegregated schools, the results are in accord with the previous findings from survey studies. If, then, one believes that the development of nonprejudiced racial attitudes is worthwhile, desegregated school experiences would seem to enhance this outcome.

However, the positive effects of desegregation on attitudes may take time to develop; moreover, they may not occur at all if desegregation is first encountered after elementary school age or if the experience itself is so threatening that what whites learn is to avoid blacks and what blacks learn is to avoid whites (cf. Carithers, 1970). For example, Silverman and Shaw (1973) found that there was very little interracial interaction during the first semester following desegregation at junior and senior high schools in Gainesville, Florida. However, there was some evidence that students' racial attitudes became more tolerant. Similarly, Shaw (1973) reported that students attending a desegregated elementary school indicated that they "most preferred to be with" members of their own race; on the other hand, when asked who they would "least prefer to be with," blacks rejected whites less frequently than would have been predicted if their choices had been governed by chance alone while the frequency with which whites rejected blacks was about that which would have been predicted by chance. With respect to cross-racial interactions, the frequency of such contacts was far below chance expectation. These and other data (Bartel, Bartel, & Grill, 1973) are not encouraging. But they serve to reinforce a point made earlier, viz., school desegregation is not, by itself, a panacea or magic solution for the racial problems that beset our society. Just as desegregation will have variable effects on achievement test scores depending on circumstances, so the effects on attitudes and interactions will be variable as well. Those charged with implementing desegregation programs devote a great deal of attention to the administrative and logistic details but very little attention to the human features of the situation. Perhaps if more and more effective programs within desegregated schools were implemented, such mixtures of blacks and whites would have more consistent and more positive outcomes.

But it is not only attitudes that are affected by interracial school contexts. Crain (1970) has shown that, as opposed to blacks who attended segregated high schools, blacks who attended integrated high schools are more likely to (1) hold "nontraditional" jobs, i.e., crafts, sales, and the professions—jobs in which blacks tend to be poorly represented and (2) have higher incomes and occupational prestige. These effects of integration persisted even after controls were applied for differences in the status of the family-of-origin and in family stability. Why should this be so? Crain provides data in support of the argument that one of the crucial mechanisms through which integrated schooling has these effects is that such schooling provides blacks with access to whites and through them to information about job opportunities. While this conclusion primarily is inferential, it is supported by other research. For example, Aldrich (1973) recently has shown that not only are white-owned businesses larger and more dominant than black-owned businesses in the ghettos of Washington, D.C., Boston, and Chicago, but that the white owners of these businesses "are more likely than black owners to hire employees from outside the area . . . [and to] hire white employees in greater proportion than the racial composition of the area would imply" (p. 1422). Aldrich also points out that the total employment resources of the ghetto are insufficient to support the labor force in the area. Thus, even were all blacks to be hired, the majority of the working force still would have to seek jobs outside the ghetto. As Crain suggests, then, the integrated school probably plays a significant role in providing the interracial associations necessary for making contact with employment opportunities outside the ghetto itself.

BLACK-WHITE INTERACTIONS AND SOCIAL CHANGE

Some Preliminary Observations

As I noted earlier, the "black-white thing" is a central issue confronting American society. However, although the focus is sharply on this issue, the principles and arguments have implications beyond the immediate case. That is, American society may be characterized as one in which there are a variety of conflicts between the dominant group in power and a number of minority groups (e.g., Chicanos, American Indians, Jews, Puerto Ricans, Asian-Americans), as well as one in which two minorities sometimes view themselves as pitted against each other (e.g., the Irish vs. the Italians, the Blacks vs. the Jews, the Puerto Ricans vs. the Blacks). To be sure, black-white conflicts are special because of the unique history of blacks in the United States and because of their high visibility. But intergroup conflict is not a narrow phenomenon; it is widespread and not restricted to confrontations across color lines (e.g., Northern Ireland, Biafra). While the referent for what I will be saying here is the black-white conflict in the United States, the reader should recognize that the perspective adopted may be applied to other forms of intergroup conflict.

Separatism versus Integration

Let it be noted at the outset that I believe that massive changes must be effected in our social institutions if the lot of the average black American is to be substantially improved relative to the advantages enjoyed by white Americans.[13] There is a great deal of data to support this

---

[13]This section leans heavily on Pettigrew's (1969b) provocative paper, "Racially Separate or Together?"

belief (Duncan, 1969), and I will not belabor the point here. The argument seems to focus less on the question of whether or not something needs to be done and more on the questions "how much?" and "how?" I will simply assert that a great deal must be done and proceed to discuss the question of "how" in the context of the debate over separatism versus integration.

It has become rather old-fashioned, even quaint, to argue today that we should strive toward the goal of an integrated society. Black integrationists are called "Uncle Toms" and white integrationists are pejoratively labelled "liberals." While the separatist philosophy correctly has highlighted a number of significant issues that the traditional integrationist philosophy swept under the rug, it is equally the case that unbridled separatism brings with it new problems that demand attention and analysis. Pettigrew (1969b) has pointed out that those who advocate black separatism advance three major assumptions in support of their position. The first assumption, which they share with white racists, is *"the comfortable assumption,"* viz., that both blacks and whites feel more at ease and less tense when surrounded by same-race peers than when interacting with members of the opposite race. The second assumption Pettigrew calls *"the white-liberals-must-eradicate-white-racism-assumption."*
The contention here is that sympathetic whites should address themselves to the white rather than to the black community. That is, since one of the central problems in our society is "white racism," whites should devote their energies to confronting their fellow whites on this issue and let blacks deal with the black community. The third assumption is that before blacks and whites can make contact with each other in such a way that each enjoys equal status, blacks must "gain personal and group autonomy, self-respect and power." This is called *"the autonomy-before-contact-assumption."*
The special value of Pettigrew's paper lies not in his identification of these themes but in the way in which he brings social-psychological research and theory to bear on the validity of each of these assumptions.

Consider "the comfortable assumption." There is no doubt that some discomfort and uncertainty typically are present in the initial phases of interracial contacts. But to argue that because there is discomfort interracial contacts should be avoided is not only to confuse cause and effect but to enhance the likelihood that such an awkward state of affairs will persist. The discomfort is a consequence of the widespread segregation along racial and class lines that exists in our society; the negative consequences of segregation will not be remedied by avoiding biracial situations. Moreover, as Pettigrew points out, racial isolation, whether self-imposed or artifically mandated, prevents the members of each racial group from learning about each other's basic humanity, i.e., about the problems, values, attitudes, beliefs, and anxieties they share. Not all interracial contacts, of course, lead to increased acceptance. Contacts between whites and blacks were probably at their height in the pre-Civil War South but did not lead to greater understanding between the races. We again appear to confront one of those situations in which the variable under consideration, interracial contact, is a necessary but not sufficient condition for producing positive cross-race feelings. But the fact that contact alone will not produce the desired result provides no warrant for asserting that contact is unneeded, undesirable, or unnecessary. After reviewing dozens of studies, Amir (1969) concluded that when the conditions are favorable (primarily equal-status contact in the pursuit of a common goal), contact does lead to a reduction in prejudice. The research discussed in the preceding section that dealt with the long-range positive attitudinal and behavioral correlates of the experience of early school desegregation likewise supports this point of view. An important caveat, however, is that even when positive changes do occur, they do not always generalize to other interracial contact situations. No one with any sophistication would argue today that mere contact between the races is a panacea; but, equally important, one ought not argue that racial isolation will lead to positive changes in the relationship between the races. That racial isolation may be more comfortable in the short run is not doubted. The question is, however, "What price comfort?" (Pettigrew, 1969b, p. 51).

Consider now the second assumption that whites should deal with white racism and blacks should deal with their own communities. This position seems to have been formed out of two observations. The first is that only fellow whites can deal effectively with white racism and the second is that some well-meaning whites, unintentionally or not, have manipulated and exploited some segments of the black community in such a way that their own needs and ends were served rather than the needs and ends of the people they claimed to be assisting. I believe the first observation to be wrong as a matter of empirical fact and the second to be insufficient to support the strategy being recommended.

Consider the issue of white racism. There is ample evidence that such racism exists both at the individual level and in its more pernicious form as institutionalized racism (Jones, 1972). But it would be incorrect to argue that whites are incurably racist or that their racism can be overcome solely by the actions of fellow whites. Several lines of evidence converge to support this conclusion. First, white attitudes have changed over time. For example, the percentage of whites who agreed that white and black students should attend the same schools increased from 30% in 1942 to 84% in 1972; among Southern whites the percentage rose from 2% in 1942 to 66% in 1972 (Hermalin & Farley, 1973).

To be sure, this finding ought not be overinterpreted. The general endorsement for school integration is highly qualified. Thus, most whites in Detroit, for example (approximately 90%), are opposed to busing to achieve this goal, and only about 35% agree that blacks would receive a better education in integrated classrooms (Hermalin & Farley, 1973). Many general attitudes, nonetheless, have changed. Thus, only 35% in 1952 agreed that it would make no difference if a black with the same income and education moved into their block, but in 1972 84% endorsed that position (Hermalin & Farley, 1973). As with the issue of school integration, questions directed toward specific issues related to residential integration show smaller proportions with favorable attitudes. Nonetheless, the direction of change over time is toward increasingly unprejudiced attitudes. Similarly, Campbell (1971) showed that there were either no changes or very minor changes between 1964 and 1968 in white receptivity to the idea that the federal government should insure fair employment practices and desegregated schooling. On the other hand, white approval for the right of blacks to live wherever they can afford to, for desegregation in general, and for equal access to public accomodations increased between 1964 and 1970. While the pattern of change is variable, the general direction is toward more positive racial feelings among the white population. These changes, of course, have not been fast enough or powerful enough or so sweeping that one can assert that white racism is on its way to being buried. Far from it. But the data also provide no comfort to those who argue that whites are intractable. Especially is this so when one looks at the data taking account of the respondents' age and education. With respect to such central racial attitudes as favoring interracial contact, perceiving blacks to be subject to much discrimination, and being sympathetic to black protests, education seems not to markedly have affected the proportion of those over 40 who subscribe to these views; however, for the pre-40 generation, those with some college experience more often hold these positive attitudes than do those with a high school education or less (Campbell, 1971). Now these shifts came about during a period of "confrontation and change" sparked, in large part, by the actions of blacks. These confrontations, moreover, were not directed at the black community but at whites. During this same time period, the frequency of cross-racial contacts, particularly as friends, increased. And there is evidence (Amir, 1969; Campbell, 1971; U.S. Commission on Civil Rights, 1967) that the more and the more equal the contact (as with friends), the more favorable interracial attitudes are likely to be. The evidence reported here, then, suggests that it would be folly for either blacks or whites to abandon their relationships with each other or actively to avoid such contacts altogether. Successful attacks on white racism cannot be achieved by whites alone; and racial isolation is more likely to lead to stronger negative attitudes than those that exist now.

Let us turn to the last of the three assumptions Pettigrew identified, the "autonomy-before-contact" assumption. Perhaps more than the others, this assumption requires some explication. An extreme form of this idea rejects altogether the notion of contact in the forseeable future. A less extreme position accepts the idea of contact between the races but relegates the contact to some dim time far in the future. For the present and for the next several years at least contact should actively be avoided (save where it is absolutely necessary) and an effort made instead to strengthen the ghetto, to develop black pride and a positive sense of identity, and to gain power and autonomy. While these are laudable goals, the strategy advocated for achieving them, viz., withdrawal, is unlikely to accomplish what is hoped for. As noted before, racial isolation is more likely to lead to a strengthening of white antipathy toward blacks and to a further reinforcing of those institutional arrangements (in schools, employment practices, and housing) that serve to restrict opportunities than to their opposites. Moreover, the notion that black ghettos can become economically autonomous from the rest of the society is a myth (cf. Aldrich, 1973). Black pride in a seperate ghetto is unlikely to provide more than short-run psychological satisfaction. First, the data contained in the Coleman Report show that a sense of control over the environment is more likely to be present in desegregated than in segregated schools. Second, the research of Katz and of Cohen and Roper show that developing a feeling of competence and displaying that competence before a black audience does not lead to competent performance in a subsequent task requiring interaction with whites. It seems unlikely that blacks will overcome their feeling that they cannot compete successfully against whites and white standards if they adopt a policy of withdrawal from contact with whites. Black pride and identity are important components in the process of social change, but they must be forged in interracial interactions if they are to play more than a symbolic role in this process.

Finally, let us address the question of how realistic it is to propose that immediate and direct desegregation remain the aim of those interested in social change. The argument that such a strategy is not feasible rests on two very real facts of life in contemporary America. The first is that in most large cities the proportion of the total population that is black has increased dramatically between 1950 and 1970 (Hermalin & Farley, 1973). The second fact supporting the argument that desegregation is unattainable is that a significant number of whites are opposed to it. For example, when white attitudes were assessed in a sample of 15 cities (Campbell, 1971), 56% agreed that blacks themselves were to blame for their generally inferior education, housing, and jobs; 67% believed that blacks were pushing too fast for what they want; and 84% believed that the riots in Newark and Detroit involved either "some planning" or definitely were "planned in advance."

Without denying the validity of these harsh realities, they do not convey the full story. Consider the growth of the black population in the cities. First, the data refer primarily to the very largest cities such as Boston, New York, Cincinnati, and New Orleans. The situation in the smaller cities is less bleak, and the demographic facts do not rule out integration in these places, e.g., White Plains, Berkeley, New Haven. Moreover, a sizeable minority (46%) of the black population in 1970 lived outside the central cities; and, of that number, 65% lived in nonmetropolitan areas. In short, as Pettigrew (1969b) has pointed out, the entire black population does not live in large isolated ghettos; they "reside in areas where racial integration is in fact possible in the short run were a good faith attempt to be made" (p. 62). Nor is racial integration impossible even in large urban areas. While the black population has increased in the central cities and remained at a fairly low stable level (4%) in the suburban rings, as Hermalin and Farley (1973) have noted, the marked underrepresentation of blacks in suburbia and their concentration in specific locales within the suburban ring is not primarily a function of the disparity in income between blacks and whites. If one compares whites and blacks who earn the same amount of money, at every income level, whites are overrepresented in the suburbs and blacks overrepresented in the central cities. Blacks can afford to live in the suburbs (although a larger proportion of blacks than whites cannot) and there is evidence (Campbell & Schuman, 1968; Schuman & Hatchett, 1974) that they prefer to live in desegregated neighborhoods. It is, then, primarily attitudes and institutional practices that block residential integration.

We come back to the question of how to overcome such feelings and actions. As noted before, it is not through isolation and withdrawal that this will be accomplished but through confrontation and the full authority of government. Racial integration does not mean that black pride, power, and people are to be abolished. It does mean that those locked into the ghetto be offered the opportunity to open the lock. At the same time, I agree with Pettigrew that those who choose to live in ethnic conclaves and those who are unable to leave even if they want to not be abandoned. Thus, while efforts to desegregate our neighborhoods and schools should be vigorously pursued, life in the ghetto must, at the same time, be made more livable. A "mixed integration-enrichment strategy" is needed. The enrichment programs must be carefully drawn and assessed in a systematic fashion so that they not lead to further racial isolation (as in the case of the massive public housing projects located in the heart of the ghetto); but it is this mixed strategy that holds the best hope for a future not saddled with the agonies of racial conflict that have been too much a part of the American tradition.

SUMMARY

Applied research is undertaken in order to provide at least a tentative answer to a socially relevant question. In social psychology, such research has focused on, among other things, the impact of exposure to television violence on the frequency and kinds of subsequent aggression, the correlates and consequences of student activism, the effectiveness of various forms of advertising, and so forth. This chapter focuses on two frequently studied social problems, poverty and race relations.

There are approximately 25.5 million persons known to be living in poverty in the United States; this statistic, grim as it is, is almost certainly an underestimate. Moreover, many of the conventional assumptions about the distribution of poverty and the characteristics of the low-income population are incorrect. For example, the majority of this population is white, are in families headed by a male, and are either under 18 or 65 and over.

A frequently cited explanation for the persistence of poverty is the "culture of poverty" thesis, i.e., the notion that poverty represents a "way of life" or "design for living" that is transmitted from one generation to the next. Support is marshalled here for an alternative explanation, viz., that the behavior patterns most often said to be exhibited by the poor represent adaptations to the social and economic circumstances in which they find themselves (the situational hypothesis). Most poor persons receive no welfare benefits. Furthermore, the "welfare poor" are shown to share many of the attitudes, values, and aspirations held by the nonpoor.

The misinformation concerning those in poverty is shown to have an impact on public policies designed to reform the system. The point is made that such policies must be based on facts, not myths, and that systematic, well-executed programs designed to assess the effects of such changes must be instituted.

Three components of the stereotype of the black family are female-headed households, illegitimate children, and a matriarchal power structure. The legitimacy of each assumption is severely questioned. For example, the majority of black families are headed by a male, the majority of births in the black population are legitimate, and there is no evidence that black women, in contrast to white, exert extraordinary power within the family.

On the other hand, growing up in a black family does have negative consequences. The effects of racial discrimination on one's life chances are profound, pervasive, and cumulative. Moreover, these negative effects persist even after one controls for initial disparities between the races on such variables as education and the socioeconomic status of one's family-of-origin.

With respect to academic achievement in school, black-white differences primarily are a function of differences between the races on such home background factors as parent's education, reading material in the home, and number of siblings. School desegregation has been found to have variable effects on academic achievement, depending on the circumstances that surround the experience. Clearly, simply mixing whites and blacks in the same classroom is not alone a sufficient condition for improving verbal and mathematical skills. On the other hand, continued segregation is unlikely to overcome those factors that interfere with black performance. Another argument in favor of desegreation is that it tends to promote positive interracial attitudes and higher levels of occupational achievement.

The philosophy that improvements in the lot of the average black American will take place only if blacks avoid contact with whites and establish their own power and autonomy (the separatist notion) is shown to be likely to lead to greater white antipathy toward blacks and to a further strengthening of those institutional arrangements that serve to restrict opportunities.

SUGGESTED READINGS

Allen, V. L. (Ed.). *Psychological factors in poverty.* Chicago: Markham, 1970.

    The papers in this volume, some of which present empirical findings and others of which review theoretical problems, all focus on a psychological approach to poverty. The articles themselves, for the most part, are not highly technical and are, therefore, quite readable.

Duncan, O. D. Inheritance of poverty or inheritance of race? In D. P. Moynihan (Ed.), *On understanding poverty*. New York: Basic Books, 1969.

A fairly technical discussion of the question of the extent to which poverty is intergenerationally transmitted. The negative consequences of being born black are shown to be greater than the negative consequences of coming from a low-income family. Well worthwhile the effort necessary to follow Duncan's analyses.

Goldschmid, M. L. (Ed.). *Black Americans and white racism*. New York: Holt, Rinehart & Winston, 1970.

A collection of 30 articles on various aspects of the problem of race relations in the U.S. Each of the seven chapters is accompanied by an introduction written by the editor, and the selections themselves cover virtually all of the major issues in this complex field.

Mosteller, F., & Moynihan, D. P. (Eds.). *On equality of educational opportunity*. New York: Random House, 1972.

A series of papers growing out of the Harvard seminar devoted to a study of the Coleman Report. Mosteller and Moynihan's introductory essay is a model of lucidity. The remaining 13 chapters vary greatly in the amount of sophistication they assume the reader to possess.

Valentine, C. A. *Culture and poverty*. Chicago: University of Chicago Press, 1968

A relatively short book by a working anthropologist devoted to a devastating critique of the "culture of poverty" concept.

References

Abelson, R. P. Modes of resolution of belief dilemmas. *Journal of Conflict Resolution,* 1959, *3,* 343–352.

Abelson, R. P. Computer simulation of "hot" cognition. In S. Tomkins and S. Messick (Eds.), *Computer simulation of personality.* New York: Wiley, 1963.

Abelson, R. P., & Lesser, G. S. The measurement of persuasibility in children. In C. I. Hovland and I. L. Janis (Eds.), *Personality and persuasibility.* New Haven, Conn.: Yale University Press, 1959.

Abelson, R. P., & Rosenberg, M. J. Symbolic psycho-logic: A model of attitudinal cognition. *Behavioral Science,* 1958, *3,* 1–13.

Abelson, R. P., & Zimbardo, P. G. *Canvassing for peace: A manual for volunteers.* Ann Arbor, Michigan: Society for the Psychological Study of Social Issues, 1970.

Adair, J. G. *The human subject: The social psychology of the psychological experiment.* Boston: Little, Brown, and Co., 1973.

Adair, J. G., & Epstein, J. Verbal cues in the mediation of experimenter bias. *Psychological Reports,* 1968, *22,* 1045–1053.

Adams, J. S. Toward an understanding of inequity. *Journal of Abnormal and Social Psychology,* 1963, *67,* 422–436.

Adams, J. S. Inequity in social exchange. In L. Berkowitz (Ed.), *Advances in experimental social psychology,* (Vol. 2). New York: Academic Press, 1965.

Adelson, J., & O'Neil, R. P. The growth of political ideas in adolescence: The sense of community. *Journal of Personality and Social Psychology,* 1966, *4,* 295–306.

Adler, N. The antinomian personality: The hippie character type. *Psychiatry,* 1968, *31,* 325–338.

Adorno, T. W., Frenkel-Brunswik, E., Levinson, D. J., & Sanford, R. N. *The authoritarian personality.* New York: Harper, 1950.

Aiello, R., Jr., & Cooper, R. E. Use of personal space as a function of social affect. *Proceedings of the 80th Annual Convention of the American Psychological Association,* 1972, *7,* 207–208.

Ajzen, K. Attitudinal vs. normative messages: An investigation of the different effects of persuasive communications on behavior. *Sociometry,* 1971, *34,* 263–80.

Ajzen, I., & Fishbein, M. The prediction of behavior from attitudinal and normative variables. *Journal of Experimental Social Psychology,* 1970, *6,* 466–87.

Aldrich, H. E. Employment opportunities for blacks in the black ghetto: The role of white-owned businesses. *American Journal of Sociology,* 1973, *78,* 1403–1425.

Alker, H. A. Is personality situationally specific or intrapsychically consistent? *Journal of Personality,* 1972, *40,* 1–16.

Allen, V. L. Situational factors in conformity. In L. Berkowitz (ed.), *Advances in experimental social psychology,* (Vol. 2). New York: Academic Press, 1965.

Allen, V. L. Effect of social support on fear of group sanction. Unpublished manuscript, University of Wisconsin, 1966.

Allen, V. L. Personality correlates of poverty. In V. L. Allen (Ed.), *Psychological factors in poverty.* Chicago: Markham, 1970. (a)

Allen, V. L. Theoretical issues in poverty research. *Journal of Social Issues,* 1970, *26*(2), 149–168. (b)

Allen, V. L., & Levine, J. M. Social support, dissent, and conformity. *Sociometry,* 1968, *31,* 138–149.

Allen, V. L., & Levine, J. M. Consensus and conformity. *Journal of Experimental Social Psychology,* 1969, *5,* 389–399.

Allen, V. L., & Levine, J. M. Social pressure and personal preference. *Journal of Experimental Social Psychology,* 1971, *7,* 122–124. (a)

Allen, V. L., & Levine, J. M. Social support and conformity: The effect of response order and differentiation from the group. *British Journal of Social and Clinical Psychology,* 1971, *10,* 181–184. (b)

Allen, V. L., & Levine, J. M. Social support and conformity: The role of independent assessment of reality. *Journal of Experimental Social Psychology,* 1971, *7,* 48–58. (c)

Allen, V. L., & Newtson, D. Development of conformity and independence. *Journal of Personality and Social Psychology,* 1972, *22,* 18–30.

Allport, F. H. The influence of the group upon association and thought. *Journal of Experimental Psychology,* 1920, *3,* 159–182.

Allport, F. H. *Social psychology.* Boston: Houghton Mifflin, 1924.

Allport, F. H. The J-curve hypothesis of conforming behavior. *Journal of Social Psychology,* 1934, *5,* 141–183.

Allport, F. H., & Hartman, D. A. The measurement and motivation of atypical opinion in a certain group. *American Political Science Review,* 1925, *19,* 735–760.

Allport, G. W. Attitudes. In C. Murchison (Ed.), *A handbook of social psychology.* Clark University Press, 1935.

Allport, G. W. *Personality: a psychological interpretation.* New York: Holt, 1937.

Allport, G. W. *The nature of prejudice.* Cambridge, Mass.: Addison-Wesley, 1954.

Allport, G. W. *Pattern and growth in personality.* New York: Holt, Rinehart, and Winston, 1961.

Allport, G. W. The historical background of modern social psychology. In G. Lindzey & E. Aronson (Eds.), *The handbook of social psychology* (Vol. 1). Reading, Mass.: Addison-Wesley, 1968.

Altman, I., & Haythorn, W. The ecology of isolated groups. *Behavioral Science,* 1967, *12,* 169–182.

Altman, I., Taylor, D., & Wheeler, L. Ecological aspects of group behavior in social isolation. *Journal of Applied Social Psychology,* 1971, *1,* 76–100.

American Psychological Association. *Standards for educational and psychological tests and manuals.* Washington, D.C.: American Psychological Association, 1974.

Amir, Y. Contact hypothesis in ethnic relations. *Psychological Bulletin,* 1969, *71,* 319–342.

Anderson, N. H. Averaging versus adding as a stimulus-combination rule in impression formation. *Journal of Experimental Psychology,* 1965, *70,* 394–400.

Anderson, N. H. Component ratings in impression formation. *Psychonomic Science,* 1966, *6,* 279–280.

Anderson, N. H. Application of a linear-serial model to a personality impression task using serial presentation. *Journal of Personality and Social Psychology,* 1968, *10,* 354–362. (a)

Anderson, N. H. Likableness ratings of 555 personality-trait words. *Journal of Personality and Social Psychology,* 1968, *9,* 272–279. (b)

Anderson, N. H. Integration theory and attitude change. *Psychological Review,* 1971, *78,* 171–206.

Anderson, N. H., & Farkas, A. J. New light on

order effects in attitude change. *Journal of Personality and Social Psychology,* 1973, *28,* 88–93.

Anderson, N. H., Lindner, R., & Lopes, L. L. Interaction theory applied to judgments of group attractiveness. *Journal of Personality and Social Psychology,* 1973, *26,* 400–408.

Appley, M. H. Derived motives. In P. H. Mussen & M. R. Rosensweig (eds.), *Annual review of psychology* (Vol. 21). Palo Alto, Cal.: Annual Review, Inc., 1970.

Ardrey, R. *The territorial imperative.* New York: Atheneum, 1966.

Argyle, M. *The psychology of interpersonal behavior.* Middlesex, England: Penguin, 1967.

Argyle, M., & Dean J. Eye contact, distance, and affiliation. *Sociometry,* 1965, *28,* 289–304.

Argyris, C. Some unintended consequences of rigorous research. *Psychological Bulletin,* 1968, *70,* 185–197.

Aries, P. *Centuries of childhood.* New York: Knopf, 1962.

Aristotle. *The rhetoric.* New York: Appleton-Century-Crofts, 1932.

Armor, D. J. School and family effects on black and white achievement: A reexamination of the USOE data. In F. Mosteller & D. P. Moynihan (Eds.), *On equality of educational opportunity.* New York: Random House, 1972.

Arons, S. Compulsory education: The plain people resist. *Saturday Review,* January 15, 1972, 52–57.

Aronson, E. Dissonance theory: Progress and problems. In R. P. Abelson et al. (Eds.), *Theories of cognitive consistency: A sourcebook.* Chicago: Rand McNally, 1968.

Aronson, E. *The social animal.* San Francisco: W. H. Freeman and Company, 1972.

Aronson, E., & Carlsmith, J. M. Effect of the severity of threat on the devaluation of forbidden behavior. *Journal of Abnormal and Social Psychology,* 1963, *66,* 584–588.

Aronson, E., & Carlsmith, J. M. Experimentation in social psychology. In G. Lindzey & E. Aronson (Eds.), *The handbook of social psychology* (Vol. 2). Reading, Mass.: Addison-Wesley, 1968.

Aronson, E., & Mills, J. The effects of severity of initiation on liking for a group. *Journal of Abnormal and Social Psychology,* 1959, *59,* 177–181.

Arsenian, J. M. Young children in an insecure situation. *Journal of Abnormal and Social Psychology,* 1943, *38,* 228–249.

Asch, S. E. Forming impressions of personality. *Journal of Abnormal and Social Psychology,* 1946, *41,* 258–290.

Asch, S. E. The doctrine of suggestion, prestige, and imitation in social psychology. *Psychological Review,* 1948, *55,* 250–276.

Asch, S. E. Effects of group pressure upon the modification and distortion of judgments. In H. Guetzkow (Ed.), *Groups, leadership, and men.* Pittsburgh: Carnegie Press, 1951.

Asch, S. E. *Social psychology.* Englewood Cliffs, N.J.: Prentice-Hall, 1952.

Asch, S. E. Opinions and social pressure. *Scientific American,* 1955, *193,* 31–35.

Asch, S. E. Studies of independence and conformity: I. A minority of one against a unanimous majority. *Psychological Monographs,* 1956, *70,* No. 9 (Whole No. 416).

Asch, S. E. The metaphor: A psychological inquiry. In R. Tagiuri & L. Petrullo (Eds.), *Person perception and interpersonal behavior.* Stanford, California: Stanford University Press. 1958.

Asch, S. E. Issues in the study of social influences on judgment. In I. A. Berg & B. M. Bass (Eds.), *Conformity and deviation.* New York: Harper & Row, 1961.

Astin, A. W. Personal and environmental determinants of student activism. *Measurement and Evaluation in Guidance,* 1968, 149–162.

Atkinson, J. W. The achievement motive and recall of interrupted and completed tasks. In D.C. McClelland (Ed.), *Studies in motivation.* New York: Appleton-Century-Crofts, 1955.

Atkinson, J. W. (Ed.). *Motives in fantasy, action, and society.* Princeton, N.J.: Van Nostrand, 1958.

Austin, W. *Theoretical and experimental explorations in expectancy theory.* Unpublished master's thesis, University of Wisconsin-Madison, 1972.

Austin, W., & Walster, E. Reactions to confirmations and disconfirmations of expectancies of equity and inequity. *Journal of Personality and Social Psychology* (in press).

Austin, W., & Walster, E. Equity and the law: The effect of a harmdoer's "suffering in the act" on assigned punishment and liking. In L. Berkowitz (Ed.), *Advances in experimental social psychology.* New York: Academic Press (in press).

Azrin, N., Hutchinson, R., & Hake, D. Extinction induced aggression. In L. Berkowitz (Ed.), *Roots of aggression*. New York: Atherton Press, 1968.

Back, K. W. Influence through social communication. *Journal of Abnormal and Social Psychology*, 1951, *46*, 9–23.

Backman, C. W., & Secord, P. F. The effect of perceived liking on interpersonal attraction. *Human Relations*, 1959, *12*, 379–384.

Backman, C. W., & Secord, P. F. The compromise process and the affect structure of groups. In C. W. Backman & P. F. Secord (Eds.), *Problems in social psychology*, New York: McGraw-Hill, 1966, 190–192.

Bailyn, L. Mass media and children: A study of exposure habits and cognitive effects. *Psychological Monographs*, 1959 (Whole No. 471).

Bain, A. *Mental science*. New York: D. Appleton & Co., 1868.

Bain, A. *The emotions and the will* (3rd ed.). London: Longmans Green, 1880.

Baldwin, A. L., Baldwin, C. P., Hilton, I. R., & Lambert, N. The measurement of social expectations and their development in children. *Child Development Monograph*, 1969, *34*, 4.

Bales, R. F. *Interaction process analysis: A method for the study of small groups*. Reading, Mass.: Addison-Wesley, 1950.

Bales, R. F. The equilibrium problem in small groups. In T. Parsons, R. F. Bales, & E. A. Shils (Eds.), *Working papers in the theory of action*. Glencoe, Ill.: Free Press, 1953.

Bales, R. F. Task roles and social roles in problem-solving groups. In E. E. Maccoby, T. M. Newcomb, & E. L. Hartley (Eds.). *Readings in social psychology* (3rd ed.). New York: Holt, Rinehart, & Winston, 1958.

Bales, R. F. *Personality and interpersonal behavior*. New York: Holt, Rinehart & Winston, 1970.

Ball, J. C., & Surawicz, F. C. A trip to San Francisco's hippie-land: Glorification of delinquency and irresponsibility. *International Journal of Offender Therapy*, 1968, *12*, 63–70.

Ball, S., & Bogatz, G. A. Summative research of Sesame Street: Implications for the study of preschool children. In A. D. Pick (Ed.), *Minnesota symposia on child psychology* (Vol. 6). Minneapolis: University of Minnesota Press, 1972.

Bandura, A. Social learning through imitation. In M. R. Jones (Ed.), *Nebraska symposium on motivation* (Vol. 10). Lincoln: University of Nebraska Press, 1962.

Bandura, A. Vicarious processes: a case of no-trial learning. In L. Berkowitz (Ed.), *Advances in Experimental Social Psychology* (Vol. 2). New York: Academic Press, 1965.

Bandura, A. *Principles of behavior modification*. New York: Holt, Rinehart & Winston, 1969.

Bandura, A., & Mischel, W. Modification of self-imposed delay of reward through exposure to live and symbolic models. *Journal of Personality and Social Psychology*, 1965, *2*, 698–705.

Bandura, A., Ross, D., & Ross, S. A. Vicarious reinforcement and imitative learning. *Journal of Abnormal and Social Psychology*, 1963, *67*, 601–607.

Bandura, A., & Walters, R. H. *Social learning and personality development*. New York: Holt, Rinehart and Winston, 1963.

Barber, T. X., & Silver, M. J. Fact, fiction, and the experimenter bias effect. *Psychological Bulletin*, 1968, *70*, 1–29.

Barclay, J. E., & Weaver, H. B. Comparative reliabilities and the ease of construction of Thurstone and Likert attitude scales. *Journal of Social Psychology*, 1962, *58*, 109–120.

Barker, R., Dembo, T., & Lewin, K. Frustration and regression: An experiment with young children. *University of Iowa Studies in Child Welfare*, 1941, *18*, 1–314.

Barnlund, D. C. A comparative study of individual, majority and group judgment. *Journal of Abnormal and Social Psychology*, 1959, *58*, 55–60.

Baron, R. A. Attraction toward the model and model's competence as determinants of adult imitative behavior. *Journal of Personality and Social Psychology*, 1970, *19*, 345–351.

Baron, R. A. Magnitude of victim's pain cues and level of prior anger arousal as determinants of adult aggressive behavior. *Journal of Personality and Social Psychology*, 1971, *17*, 236–243.

Baron, R. A. Aggression as a function of ambient temperature and prior anger arousal. *Journal of Personality and Social Psychology*, 1972, *21*, 183–189.

Baron, R. M. Attitude change through discrepant

action: A functional analysis. In A. G. Greenwald, T. C. Brock, & T. M. Ostrom (Eds.), *Psychological foundations of attitudes*. New York: Academic Press, 1968.

Bartel, H. W., Bartel, N. R., & Grill, J. J. A sociometric view of some integrated open classrooms. *Journal of Social Issues*, 1973, *29*(4), 159–173.

Barton, W. A., Jr. The effect of group activity and individual effort in developing ability to solve problems in first-year algebra. *Journal of Education Administration and Supervision*, 1926, *12*, 512–518.

Batchelor, J. P., & Goethals, G. R. Spacial arrangements in freely formed groups. *Sociometry*, 1972, *35*, 270–279.

Bateson, N. Familiarization, group discussion, and risk-taking. *Journal of Experimental Social Psychology*, 1966, *2*, 119–129.

Baumrind, D. Some thoughts on ethics of research: After reading Milgram's "Behavioral study of obedience." *American Psychologist*, 1964, *19*, 421–423.

Baumrind, D. Principles of ethical conduct in the treatment of subjects: Reaction to the draft report of the committee on ethical standards in psychological research. *American Psychologist*, 1971, *26*, 887–896.

Bavelas, A., Belden, T. G., Glenn, E. S., Orlansky, J., Schwartz, J. W., & Sinaiko, H. W. *Teleconferencing: Summary of a preliminary research project*. Washington: Institute for Defense Analyses, 1963.

Bavelas, A., Hastorf, A. H., Gross, A. E., & Kite, W. R. Experiments on the alteration of group structure. *Journal of Experimental Social Psychology*, 1965, *1*, 55–70.

Bayer, A. E., & Astin, A. W. Violence and disruption on the U.S. campus, 1968–1969. *Educational Record*, 1969, *50*, 337–350.

Becker, F. D. Study of spatial markers. *Journal of Personality and Social Psychology*, 1973, *26*, 439–445.

Becker, F. D., Sommer, R., Bee, J., & Oxley, B. College classroom ecology. *Sociometry*, 1973, *36*, 514–525.

Becker, H. Personal change in adult life. *Sociometry*, 1964, *27*, 40–53.

Beloff, H. Two forms of social conformity: Acquiescence and conventionality. *Journal of Abnormal and Social Psychology*, 1958, *56*, 99–104.

Bem, D. J. Self-perception: An alternative interpretation of cognitive dissonance phenomena. *Psychological Review*, 1967, *74*, 183–200.

Bem, D. J. *Beliefs, attitudes and human affairs*. Belmont, California: Brooks/Cole, 1970.

Bem, D. J. Constructing cross-situational consistencies in behavior: Some thoughts on Alker's critique of Mischel. *Journal of Personality*, 1972, *40*, 17–26. (a)

Bem, D. J. Self-perception theory, In L. Berkowitz (Ed.), *Advances in experimental social psychology* (Vol. 6). New York: Academic Press, 1972. (b)

Bem, D. J., & Allen, A. On predicting some of the people some of the time: The search for cross-situational consistencies in behavior. *Psychological Review*, 1974, *81*, 506–520.

Bem, D. J., & McConnell, H. K. Testing the self-perception explanation of dissonance phenomena: On the salience of premanipulation attitudes. *Journal of Personality and Social Psychology*, 1970, *14*, 23–31.

Bennett, E. B. Discussion, decision, commitment, and consensus in "group decision." *Human Relations*, 1955, *8*, 251–274.

Bennis, W. G., & Slater, P. E. *The temporary society*. New York: Harper & Row, 1968.

Benton, A. A. Accountability and negotiations between group representatives. *Proceedings of the 80th Annual Convention of the American Psychological Association*, 1972, *7*, 227–228.

Berelson, B. On family planning communication. *Demography*, 1964, *1*, 94–105.

Berg, I. A. Measuring deviant behavior by means of deviant response sets. I. A. Berg & B. M. Bass (Eds.), *Conformity and deviation*. New York: Harper & Row, 1961.

Berg, K. E. Ethnic attitudes and agreement with a Negro person. *Journal of Personality and Social Psychology*, 1966, *4*, 215–220.

Berger, B. Hippie morality—more old than new. *Transaction*, 1967, *5*, 19–20.

Berkowitz, L. Group standards, cohesiveness, and productivity. *Human Relations*, 1954, *7*, 509–519.

Berkowitz, L. *Aggression: A social psychological analysis*. New York: McGraw-Hill, 1962.

Berkowitz, L. Aggressive cues in aggressive behavior and hostility catharsis. *Psychological Review,* 1964, *71,* 104–122.

Berkowitz, L. (Ed.). *Advances in experimental social psychology* (Vol. 2). New York: Academic Press, 1965. (a)

Berkowitz, L. The concept of aggressive drive: Some additional considerations. In L. Berkowitz (Ed.), *Advances in experimental social psychology.* Vol. 2. New York: Academic Press, 1965, 301–329. (b)

Berkowitz, L. Some aspects of observed aggression. *Journal of Personality and Social Psychology,* 1965, *2,* 359–369. (c)

Berkowitz, L. Responsibility, reciprocity and social distance in help-giving. *Journal of Experimental Social Psychology,* 1968, *4,* 46–63.

Berkowitz, L. *Roots of aggression: A re-examination of the frustration-aggression hypothesis.* New York: Atherton Press, 1969. (a)

Berkowitz, L. Social motivation. In G. Lindzey & E. Aronson (Eds.), *The handbook of social psychology* (Vol. 3). Reading, Mass.: Addison-Wesley, 1969. (b)

Berkowitz, L. Reporting an experiment: A case study in leveling, sharpening, and assimilation. *Journal of Experimental Social Psychology,* 1971, *7,* 237–243. (a)

Berkowitz, L. The "weapons effect," demand characteristics, and the myth of the compliant subject. *Journal of Personality and Social Psychology,* 1971, *20,* 332–338. (b)

Berkowitz, L. Social norms, feelings and other factors affecting helping behavior and altruism. In L. Berkowitz (Ed.), *Advances in Experimental Social Psychology* (Vol. 6). New York: Academic Press, 1972. (a)

Berkowitz, L. *Social psychology.* Glenview, Illinois: Scott, Foresman, 1972. (b)

Berkowitz, L. Some determinants of impulsive aggression: Role of mediated associations with reinforcement for aggression. *Psychological Review,* 1974, *81,* 165–176.

Berkowitz, L., Corwin, R., & Heironimus, J. Film violence and subsequent aggressive tendencies. *Public Opinion Quarterly,* 1963, *27,* 217–229.

Berkowitz, L., & Friedman, P. Some social class differences in helping behavior. *Journal of Personality and Social Psychology,* 1967, *5,* 217–225.

Berkowitz, L., & Geen, R. G. Film violence and the cue properties of available targets. *Journal of Personality and Social Psychology,* 1966, *3,* 525–530.

Berkowitz, L., & Holmes, D. S. The generalization of hostility to disliked objects. *Journal of Personality,* 1960, *28,* 427–443.

Berkowitz, L., & LePage, A. Weapons as aggression-eliciting stimuli. *Journal of Personality and Social Psychology,* 1967, *7,* 202–207.

Berkowitz, L., & Rawlings, E. Effects of film violence on inhibitions against subsequent aggression. *Journal of Abnormal and Social Psychology,* 1963, *66,* 405–412.

Berlyne, D. E. *Conflict, arousal, and curiosity.* New York: McGraw-Hill, 1960.

Berlyne, D. E. Motivational problems raised by exploratory and epistemic behavior. In S. Koch (Ed.), *Psychology: A study of a science* (Vol. 5). New York: McGraw-Hill, 1963.

Berscheid, E., Boye, D., & Walster, E. Retaliation as a means of restoring equity. *Journal of Personality and Social Psychology,* 1968, *10,* 370–376.

Berscheid, E., Dion, K., Walster, E., & Walster, G. W. Physical attractiveness and dating choice: A test of the matching hypotheses. *Journal of Experimental Social Psychology,* 1971, *7,* 173–189.

Berscheid, E., & Walster, E. When does a harmdoer compensate a victim? *Journal of Personality and Social Psychology,* 1967, *6,* 435–441.

Berscheid, E., Walster, E., & Barclay, A. Effect of time on tendency to compensate a victim. *Psychological Reports,* 1969, *25,* 431–441.

Beswick, D. Theory and measurement of curiosity. Unpublished doctoral dissertation, Department of Social Relations, Harvard University, 1964.

Bettelheim, B. *Children of the dream.* New York: Macmillan, 1969.

Bickman, L. The effect of the presence of others on bystander intervention in an emergency. Unpublished doctoral dissertation, The City University of New York, 1969.

Bickman, L. The effect of another bystander's ability to help on bystander intervention in an emergency. *Journal of Experimental Social Psychology,* 1971, *7,* 367–379.

Bickman, L. Social influence and diffusion of responsibility in an emergency. *Journal of Experimental Social Psychology,* 1972, *8,* 438–445.

Biddle, B. J., & Thomas, E. J. (Eds.). *Role Theory.* New York: Wiley, 1966.

Billingsley, A. Black families and white social science. *Journal of Social Issues,* 1970, *26*(3), 127–142.

Blanchard, E. B. Relative contributions of modeling, informational influences, and physical contact in extinction of phobic behavior. Unpublished doctoral dissertation, Stanford University, 1969.

Blau, P. M. *Exchange and power in social life.* New York: Wiley, 1967.

Blau, P. M., & Duncan, O. D. *The American occupational structure.* New York: Wiley, 1967.

Blumer, H. Social movements. In B. McLaughlin (Ed.), *Studies in social movements.* New York: The Free Press, 1969.

Bochner, S., & Insko, C. A. Communicator discrepancy, source credibility, and opinion change. *Journal of Personality and Social Psychology,* 1966, *4,* 614–621.

Boden, M. Dissonance in the individual and in society. Unpublished paper, Social Relations Department, Harvard University, 1963.

Bogardus, E. S. Measuring social distance. *Journal of Applied Sociology,* 1925, *9,* 299–308.

Bogardus, E. S. Social distance and its practical implications. *Sociology and Social Research,* 1933, *17,* 265–271.

Bolles, R. C. *Theory of motivation.* New York: Harper & Row, 1967.

Bolt, R. *A Man for All Seasons.* New York: Random House, 1962.

Bolwig, N. Facial expression in primates with remarks on parallel development in certain carnivores, *Behavior,* 1964, *22,* 167–192.

Borgatta, E. F., & Bales, R. F. Sociometric status patterns and characteristics of interaction. *Journal of Abnormal and Social Psychology,* 1956, *43,* 289–297.

Borgida, G. National identity and the draft. *Journal of Clinical Child Psychology,* 1972, *1,* 8–9.

Bouchard, T. J., Jr. Personality, problem-solving procedure, and performance in small groups. *Journal of Applied Psychology,* 1969, *53,* 1–29.

Boyanowsky, E. O. Ingroup norms, retaliatory threat, and self-identity as determinants of discriminatory behavior. Unpublished doctoral dissertation, University of Wisconsin, 1970.

Boyanowsky, E. O., & Allen, V. L. Ingroup norms and self-identity as determinants of discriminatory behavior. *Journal of Personality and Social Psychology,* 1973, *25,* 408–418.

Bramel, D. Interpersonal attraction, hostility, and perception. In J. Mills (Ed.), *Experimental social psychology.* New York: Macmillan, 1969.

Brannon, R., Cyphers, G., Hesse, S., Hesselbart, S., Keane, R., Schuman, H., Vicarro, T., & Wright, D. Attitude and action: A field experiment joined to a general population survey. *American Sociological Review,* 1973, *38,* 625–636.

Bray, D. W. The prediction of behavior from two attitude scales. *Journal of Abnormal and Social Psychology,* 1950, *45,* 64–84.

Brehm, J. W. *A theory of psychological reactance.* New York: Academic Press, 1966.

Brehm, J. W. *Responses to loss of freedom: A theory of psychological reactance.* Morristown, N.J.: General Learning Press, 1972.

Brehm, J., & Cohen, A. R. *Explorations in cognitive dissonance.* New York: Wiley, 1962.

Brigham, J. C. Ethnic Stereotypes. *Psychological Bulletin,* 1971, *76,* 15–38.

Brinton, C. *The anatomy of revolution.* Englewood Cliffs, N.J.: Prentice-Hall, 1952.

Brislin, R. W., & Lewis, S. A. Dating and physical attractiveness: A replication. *Psychological Reports,* 1968, *22,* 976.

Brislin, R. W., & Olmstead, K. H. An examination of two models designed to predict behavior from attitude and other verbal measures. *Proceedings of the 81st Convention of the American Psychological Association,* 1973, 259–260.

Brock, T. C., & Becker, L. A. Debriefing and susceptibility to subsequent experimental manipulations. *Journal of Experimental Social Psychology.* 1966, *2,* 314–323.

Brock, T. C., & Buss, A. H. Dissonance, aggression, and evaluation of pain. *Journal of Abnormal and Social Psychology,* 1962, *65,* 192–202.

Brock, T. C., & Buss, A. H. Effects of justification for aggression in communication with the victim on post-aggression dissonance. *Journal of Abnormal and Social Psychology,* 1964, *68,* 403–412.

Broll, L., Gross, A. E., & Piliavin, I. M. Effects of offered and requested help on help seeking and reactions to being helped. Unpublished manuscript, 1973.

Bronfenbrenner, U. *Two worlds of childhood: U.S. and U.S.S.R.* New York: Clarion, 1972.

Broverman, I. K., Broverman, D. M., Clarkson, F. E., Rosenkrantz, P. S., & Vogel, S. R. Sex-role stereotypes and clinical judgments of mental health. *Journal of Consulting and Clinical Psychology,* 1970, *34,* 1–7.

Broverman, I. K., Vogel, S. R., Broverman, D. M., Clarkson, F. E., & Rosenkranz, P. S. Sex-role stereotypes: A current appraisal. *Journal of Social Issues,* 1972, *28,* 59–78.

Brown, B. The assessment of self-concept among four-year-old Negro and white children. In M. Deutsch, I. Katz, & A. R. Jensen (Eds.), *Social class, race, and psychological development.* New York: Holt, Rinehart, & Winston, 1968.

Brown, D. G. Sex-role preference in young children. *Psychological Monographs,* 1956, *70,* 14.

Brown, G., & Johnson, S. P. The attribution of behavioural connotations to shaded and white figures by Caucasian children. *British Journal of Social and Clinical Psychology,* 1971, *10,* 306–312.

Brown, M. E. Condemnation and persecution of hippies. *Transaction,* 1969, *6,* 33–46.

Brown, N. O. *Life against death.* Middletown, Conn.: Wesleyan University Press, 1959.

Brown, R. W. *Social psychology.* New York: The Free Press, 1965.

Bruce, R. S. Group judgments in the fields of lifted weights and visual discrimination. *Journal of Psychology,* 1935, *1,* 117–121.

Bruner, J. S. *On knowing.* New York: Atheneum, 1965.

Bruner, J. S., Shapiro, D., & Tagiuri, R. The meaning of traits in isolation and combination. In R. Tagiuri & L. Petrullo (Eds.), *Person perception and interpersonal behavior.* Stanford, California: Stanford University Press, 1958.

Bryan, J. H. & Test, M. A. Models and helping: Naturalistic studies of aiding behavior. *Journal of Personality and Social Psychology,* 1967, *6,* 400–407.

Buchwald, A. M. Verbal utterances as data. In H. Feigl & G. Maxwell (Eds.), *Current issues in the philosophy of science.* New York: Holt, Rinehart, & Winston, 1961.

Burdick, H. A. The relationship of attraction, need achievement, and certainty to conformity under conditions of a simulated group atmosphere. Unpublished doctoral dissertation. University of Michigan, 1955.

Burgess, E. W., & Wallin, P. Homogamy in social characteristics. *American Journal of Sociology,* 1943, *49,* 109–124.

Burgess, R. L. An experimental and mathematical analysis of group behavior within restricted networks. *Journal of Experimental Social Psychology,* 1968, *4,* 338–349.

Burnside, B. The employment potential of AFDC mothers in six states. *Welfare in Review,* 1971, *9*(4), 16–20.

Burtt, H. E. Sex differences in the effect of discussion. *Journal of Experimental Psychology,* 1920, *3,* 390–395.

Buss, A. H. *The psychology of aggression.* New York: Wiley, 1961.

Buss, A. H. Instrumentality of aggression, feedback, and frustration as determinants of physical aggression. *Journal of Personality and Social Psychology,* 1966, *3,* 153–162.

Buss, A. H., Booker, A., & Buss, E. Firing a weapon and aggression. *Journal of Personality and Social Psychology,* 1972, *22,* 296–302.

Byrne, D. Interpersonal attraction and attitude similarity. *Journal of Abnormal and Social Psychology,* 1961, *62,* 713–715.

Byrne, D. *The attraction paradigm.* New York: Academic Press, 1971.

Byrne, D., & Clore, G. L. A reinforcement model of evaluative responses. *Personality: An International Journal,* 1970, *1,* 103–128.

Byrne, D., Ervin, C. R., & Lamberth, J. Continuity between the experimental study of attraction and "real life" computer dating. *Journal of Personality and Social Psychology,* 1970, *16,* 157–165.

Campbell, A. *White attitudes toward black people.* Ann Arbor, Michigan: Institute for Social Research, 1971.

Campbell, A., Converse, P. E., Miller, W. E., & Stokes, D. E. *The American voter: An abridgement.* New York: Wiley, 1964.

Campbell, A., & Schuman, H. *Racial attitudes in fifteen American cities.* Ann Arbor: Survey Research Center, Institute for Social Research, The University of Michigan, 1968.

Campbell, D. T. The generality of social attitudes, Unpublished doctoral dissertation, University of California, Berkeley, 1947.

Campbell, D. T. The indirect assessment of social attitudes. *Psychological Bulletin,* 1950, *47,* 15–38.

Campbell, D. T. Factors relevant to validity of experiments in social settings. *Psychological Bulletin,* 1957, *54,* 297–312.

Campbell, D. T. Prospective: Artifact and control. In R. Rosenthal & R. L. Rosnow (Eds.), *Artifact in behavioral research.* New York: Academic Press, 1969.

Campbell, D. T., & Fiske, D. W. Convergent and Discriminant Validation by the Multitrait-Multimethod Matrix. *Psychological Bulletin,* 1959, *56,* 81–105.

Campbell, D. T., Kruskal, W. H., & Wallace, W. P. Seating aggregation as an index of attitude. *Sociometry,* 1966, *29,* 1–15.

Campbell, D. T., & Stanley, J. C. *Experimental and quasi-experimental designs for research.* Chicago: Rand McNally, 1966.

Campbell, J., Dunnette, M., Lawler, E., III, & Weick, K. *Managerial behavior, performance, and effectiveness.* New York: McGraw-Hill, 1970.

Cannon, W. B. *Bodily changes in pain, hunger, fear and rage* (2nd ed.). New York: Appleton, 1929.

Cantril, H. *The psychology of social movements.* New York: Wiley, 1941.

Cantril, H. The intensity of an attitude. *Journal of Abnormal and Social Psychology,* 1946, *41,* 129–135.

Cantril, H., Gaudet, H., & Hertzog, H. *The invasion from Mars.* Princeton, N.J.: Princeton University Press, 1940.

Carithers, M. W. School desegregation and racial cleavage, 1954–1970: A review of the literature. *Journal of Social Issues,* 1970, *26*(4), 25–48.

Carlson, A. J. *The control of hunger in health and disease.* Chicago: University of Chicago Press, 1916.

Carlson, R. Where is the person in personality research? *Psychological Bulletin,* 1971, *75,* 203–219.

Cartwright, D. The nature of group cohesiveness. In D. Cartwright & A. Zander (Eds.), *Group Dynamics.* New York: Harper and Row, 1968.

Cartwright, D. Risk taking by individuals and groups: An assessment of research employing choice dilemmas. *Journal of Personality and Social Psychology,* 1971, *20,* 361–378.

Cartwright, D., & Harary, F. Structural balance: A generalization of Heider's theory. *Psychological Review,* 1956, *63,* 277–293.

Cattell, J., & Brimhall, D. *American men of science* (3rd ed.). Garrison, N.Y.: Science Press, 1921.

Cavan, S. The class structure of hippie society. *Urban Life and Culture,* 1972, *1,* 211–238.

Chaikin, A. L., Sigler, E., & Derlega, V. J. Nonverbal mediators of teacher expectancy effects. *Journal of Personality and Social Psychology,* 1974, *30,* 144–149.

Chapman, A. J. Social facilitation of laughter in children. *Journal of Experimental Social Psychology,* 1973, *9,* 528–541.

Chapman, A. J. An electromyographic study of social facilitation: A test of the "mere presence" hypothesis. *British Journal of Psychology,* 1974, *65,* 123–128.

Chapman, L. J., & Chapman, J. P. Illusory correlation as an obstacle to the use of valid, psychodiagnostic signs. *Journal of Abnormal Psychology,* 1969, *74,* 271–280.

Chein, I. The problems of inconsistency: A restatement. *Journal of Social Issues,* 1949, *5,* 52–61.

Chein, I. Notes on a framework for the measurement of discrimination and prejudice. In M. Jahoda, M. Deutsch, & S. W. Cook, *Research methods in social relations.* New York: Dryden, 1951.

Chemers, M. M., & Skrzypek, G. J. Experimental test of the contingency model of leadership effectiveness. *Journal of Personality and Social Psychology,* 1972, *24,* 172–177.

Cherniss, C. Personality and ideology: A personological study of women's liberation. *Psychiatry,* 1972, *35,* 109–125.

Chertkoff, J. M., & Conley, M. Opening offer and frequency of concession as bargaining strategies. *Journal of Personality and Social Psychology,* 1967, *7,* 181–185.

Cheyne, J. A., & Efran, M. G. The effect of spatial and interpersonal variables on the invasion of group controlled territories. *Sociometry,* 1972, *35,* 477–489.

Christie, R. & Geis, F. L. *Studies in Machiavellianism.* New York: Academic Press, 1970.

Clark, K. B. *Dark ghetto.* New York: Harper & Row, 1965. (a)

Clark, K. B. Problems of power and social change: Towards a relevant social psychology. *Journal of Social Issues,* 1965, *21,* 5. (b)

Clark, R. D., III. Effects of sex and race on helping behavior in a nonreactive setting. *Representative Research in Social Psychology,* 1974, *5,* 1–6.

Clark, R. D., III, & Willems, E. P. Risk preferences as related to judged consequences of failure. *Psychological Reports,* 1969, *25,* 827–830.

Clark, R. D., III, & Word, L. E. Why don't bystanders help? Because of ambiguity? *Journal of Personality and Social Psychology,* 1972, *24,* 392–400.

Cline, V. B., & Richards, J. M. Accuracy of interpersonal perception—a general trait? *Journal of Abnormal and Social Psychology,* 1960, *60,* 1–7.

Clore, G. L., & Gormly, J. B. Attraction and physiological arousal in response to agreements and disagreements. Paper presented at the meeting of the Psychonomic Society, St. Louis, 1969.

Clore, G. L., & Johnson, C. Black-white interactions in a summer camp for children. Unpublished manuscript, University of Illinois, 1971.

Coch, L. & French, J. R. P. Overcoming resistance to change. *Human Relations,* 1948, *11,* 512–532.

Cohen, A. R. *Attitude change and social influence.* New York: Basic Books, 1964.

Cohen, D. K., Pettigrew, T. F., & Riley, R. T. Race and the outcomes of schooling. In F. Mosteller & D. P. Moynihan (Eds.), *On equality of educational opportunity.* New York: Random House, 1972.

Cohen, E. G., & Roper, S. S. Modification of interracial interaction disability: An application of status characteristic theory. *American Sociological Review,* 1972, *37,* 643–657.

Coleman, J., Hean, E., Peabody, R., & Rigsby, L. Computers and election analysis: The New York Times project. *Public Opinion Quarterly,* 1964, *28,* 418–446.

Coleman, J. F., Blake, R. R., & Mouton, J. S. Task difficulty and conformity pressures. *Journal of Abnormal and Social Psychology,* 1958, *57,* 120–122.

Coleman, J. S. *Community Conflict.* New York: The Free Press, 1957.

Coleman, J. S., Campbell, E. Q., Hobson, C. J., McPartland, J., Mood, A. M., Weinfeld, F. D., & York, R. L. *Equality of educational opportunity.* Washington, D.C.: U.S. Government Printing Office, 1966.

Collaros, P. A., & Anderson, L. R. Effect of perceived expertness upon creativity of members of brainstorming groups. *Journal of Applied Psychology,* 1969, *53,* 159–163.

Collins, B. E., & Guetzkow, H. *A social psychology of group processes for decision-making.* New York: Wiley, 1964.

Collins, B. E., & Raven, B. Group structure: Attraction, coalitions, communication, and power. In G. Lindsey & E. Aronson (Eds.), *The handbook of social psychology* (Vol. 4, 2nd ed.). Reading, Mass.: Addison-Wesley, 1969.

The Congressional Record, 88th Congress, Second Session, Vol. 110, No. 45, Washington D.C., March 12, 1964.

Cook, S. W., & Selltiz, C. A multiple-indicator approach to attitude measurement. *Psychological Bulletin,* 1964, *62,* 36–55.

Coombs, C. H. *A theory of data,* New York: Wiley, 1964.

Cooper, D. G. *The death of the family.* New York: Pantheon, 1970.

Corey, S. M. Professed attitudes and actual behavior. *Journal of Educational Psychology,* 1937, *28,* 271–280.

Cottrell, N. B., Wack, D. L., Sekerak, G. J., & Rittle, R. H. Social facilitation of dominant responses by the presence of an audience and the mere presence of others. *Journal of Personality and Social Psychology,* 1968, *9,* 245–250.

Cowdry, R. W., Keniston, K., & Cabin, S. The war and military obligation: Private attitudes and public actions. *Journal of Personality,* 1970, *32,* 1–13.

Cox, D. E., & Sipprelle, C. N. Coercion in participation as a research subject. *American Psychologist,* 1971, *26,* 726–728.

Crain, R. L. School integration and occupational achievement of Negroes. *American Journal of Sociology,* 1970, *75,* 593–606.

Crawford, J. L. Task uncertainty, decision importance, and group reinforcement as determinants of communication processes in groups. *Journal of Personality and Social Psychology,* 1974, *29,* 619–627.

Crawford, J. L., & Haaland, G. A. Pre-decisional information seeking and subsequent conformity in the social influence process. *Journal of Personality and Social Psychology,* 1972, *23,* 112–119.

Crawford, T. J. Beliefs about birth control: A consistency theory analysis. *Representative Research in Social Psychology,* 1973, *4,* 53–65.

Cronbach, L. J. Coefficient alpha and the internal structure of tests. *Psychometrica,* 1951, *16,* 297–334.

Cronbach, L. J. Processes affecting scores on "understanding of others" and "assumed similarity." *Psychological Bulletin,* 1955, *52,* 177–193.

Croner, M. D., & Willis, R. H. Perceived differences in task competence and asymmetry of dyadic influence. *Journal of Abnormal and Social Psychology,* 1961, *62,* 705–708.

Cross, H. J., Doost, R. M., & Tracy, J. J. A study of values among hippies. *Proceedings of the 78th Annual Convention of the American Psychological Association,* 1970, *5,* 449–451.

Crowne, D. P., & Liverant, S. Conformity under varying conditions of personal commitment. *Journal of Abnormal and Social Psychology,* 1963, *66,* 547–555.

Crutchfield, R. Conformity and character. *American Psychologist,* 1955, *10,* 191–198.

Cutright, P. Illegitimacy: Myths, causes and cures. *Family Planning Perspectives,* 1971, *3,* 26–48.

Cutright, P. The teenage sexual revolution and the myth of an abstinent past. *Family Planning Perspectives,* 1972, *4,* 24–31.

Dabbs, J. M., Fuller, J. P., & Carr, T. S. Personal space when "cornered"; college students vs. prison inmates. *Proceedings of the 81st Annual Convention of the American Psychological Association,* 1973, *8,* 213–214.

Dahrendorf, R. *Class and class conflict in industrial society.* Stanford, Calif.: Stanford University Press, 1959.

Darley, J. M., & Latane, B. Bystander intervention in emergencies: Diffusion of responsibility. *Journal of Personality and Social Psychology,* 1968, *8,* 377–383.

Darlington, R. B., & Meeker, C. F. Displacement of guilt-produced altruistic behavior. *Journal of Personality and Social Psychology,* 1966, *4,* 442–443.

Darwin, C. *The expression of the emotions in man and animals.* London: John Murray, 1872.

Dashiell, J. F. An experimental analysis of some group effects. *Journal of Abnormal and Social Psychology,* 1930, *25,* 190–199.

David, K. H. Generalization of operant conditioning of verbal output in 3-man discussion groups. *Journal of Social Psychology,* 1972, *87,* 243–249.

Davies, J. C. Toward a theory of revolution. In B. McLaughlin (Ed.), *Studies in social movements.* New York: The Free Press, 1969.

Davis, F. Why all of us may be hippies someday. *Transaction,* 1967, *5,* 10–18.

Davis, J. H. *Group performance.* Reading, Mass.: Addison Wesley, 1969.

Davis, J. H., & Restle, F. The analysis of problems and prediction of group problem solving. *Journal of Abnormal and Social Psychology,* 1963, *66,* 103–116.

Davis, K. W., & Jones, E. E. Changes in interpersonal perception as a means of reducing cognitive dissonance. *Journal of Abnormal and Social Psychology,* 1960, *61,* 402–410.

Davitz, J. R. The effects of previous training on postfrustration behavior. *Journal of Abnormal and Social Psychology,* 1952, *47,* 309–315.

Davitz, J. R., & Mason, D. J. Socially facilitated reduction of a fear response in rats. *Journal of Comparative Physiological Psychology,* 1955, *48,* 149–151.

Dean, L. R. Interaction, reported and observed: The case of one local union. *Human Organization,* 1958, *17,* 36–44.

DeFleur, M. L., & Westie, F. R. Verbal attitudes and overt acts: An experiment on the salience of attitudes. *American Sociological Review,* 1958, *23,* 667–673.

DeFleur, M. L., & Westie, F. R. Attitude as a scientific concept. *Social Forces,* 1963, *42,* 17–31.

DeFriese, G. H., & Ford, W. S. Verbal attitudes, overt acts, and the influence of social constraint in interracial behavior. *Social problems,* 1969, *16,* 493–504.

DeLamater, J., & Fidell, L. S. On the status of women: As assessment and introduction. *American Behavioral Scientist,* 1971, *15,* 163–171.

DeLucia, L. A. The toy-preference test: A measure of sex-role identification. *Child Development,* 1963, *34,* 107–117.

Del Vecchio, G. The problem of penal justice (imprisonment or reparation of damage). *Revista*

Juridica de la Universidad de Puerto Rico, 1959, 27 (Silving, Trans.).

Deutsch, M. Field theory in social psychology. In G. Lindzey & E. Aronson (Eds.), *The handbook of social psychology* (Vol. 1, 2nd ed.). Reading, Mass.: Addison-Wesley, 1968.

Deutsch, M. *The Resolution of Conflict.* New Haven, Conn.: Yale University Press, 1973.

Deutsch, M., Canavan, D., & Rubin, J. Effects of size of conflict and sex of experimenter upon interpersonal bargaining. *Journal of Experimental Social Psychology,* 1971, *7,* 258–267.

Deutsch, M., & Gerard, H. B. A study of normative and informational social influences upon individual judgments. *Journal of Abnormal and Social Psychology,* 1955, *51,* 629–636.

Deutscher, I. Words and deeds: Social science and social policy. *Social Problems,* 1966, *13,* 235–265.

Deutscher, I. Looking backward: Case studies on the progress of methodology in sociological research. *The American Sociologist,* 1969, *4,* 35–41.

Deutscher, I. *What we say/What we do: Sentiments and acts.* Glenview, Illinois: Scott, Foresman, 1973.

DeYoung, G. E., Cattell, R. B., Gaborit, M., & Barton, K. A causal model of effects of personality and marital role factors upon diary-reported sexual behavior. Paper presented at the 81st convention of the American Psychological Association, Montreal, 1973.

Diener, E., Westford, K. L., Diener, C., & Beaman, A. L. Deindividuating effects of group presence and arousal on stealing by Halloween trick-or-treaters. *Proceedings of the 81st Annual Convention of the American Psychological Association,* 1973, *8,* 219–220.

Diener, E., Westford, K. L., Dineen, J., & Fraser, S. C. Beat the pacifist: The deindividuating effects of anonymity and group presence. *Proceedings of the 81st Annual Convention of the American Psychological Association,* 1973, *8,* 221–222.

Dillon, W. S. *Gifts and nations.* The Hague: Mouton, 1968.

Dobyns, Z. P. A comparison of hippies and college students with respect to beliefs, attitudes, and personality. Unpublished Ph.D. dissertation, University of Arizona, 1969.

Dollard, J., Doob, L. W., Miller, N. E., Mowrer, O. H., & Sears, R. R. *Frustration and aggression.* New Haven, Conn.: Yale University Press, 1939.

Doob, L. W. The behavior of attitudes. *Psychological Review,* 1947, *54,* 135–156.

Dornbusch, S., Hastorf, A., Richardson, S., Muzzy, R., & Vreeland, R. The perceiver and perceived: Their relative influence on categories of interpersonal perception. *Journal of Personality and Social Psychology,* 1965, *1,* 434–440.

Dosey, M., & Meisels, M. Personal space and self-protection. *Journal of Personality and Social Psychology,* 1969, *11,* 93–97.

Driscoll, R., Davis, K. W., & Lipetz, M. E. Parental interference and romantic love: The Romeo and Juliet effect. *Journal of Personality and Social Psychology,* 1972, *24,* 1–10.

Druckman, D., Zechmeister, K., and Solomon, D. Determinants of bargaining behavior in a bilateral monopoly situation: Opponent's concession rate and relative defensibility. *Behavioral Science,* 1972, *17,* 514–531.

Duncan, B., & Duncan, O. D. Family stability and occupational success. *Social Problems,* 1969, *16* (3), 273–285.

Duncan, O. D. Inheritance of poverty or inheritance of race? In D. P. Moynihan (Ed.), *On understanding poverty.* New York: Basic Books, 1969.

Duncan, O. D., Featherman, D. L., & Duncan, B. *Socioeconomic background and achievement.* New York: Seminar Press, 1972.

Duncan, S., Rosenberg, M. J., & Finkelstein, J. The paralanguage of experimenter bias. *Sociometry,* 1969, *32,* 207–219.

Dunlap, K. *Civilized life.* Baltimore: Williams and Wilkins, 1934.

Durkheim, E. *Le suicide.* Paris: F. Alcan, 1897 (Translation, Glencoe, Illinois: Free Press, 1951).

Dymond, R. F. Personality and empathy. *Journal of Consulting Psychology,* 1950, *14,* 343–350.

Edwards, L. P. *The natural history of revolution.* Chicago: University of Chicago Press, 1927.

Efran, J. Looking for approval: Effects on visual behavior of approbation from persons differing in importance. *Journal of Personality and Social Psychology,* 1968, *10,* 21–25.

Efran, M. G., & Cheyne, J. A. Shared space: The cooperative control of spatial areas by two interacting individuals. *Canadian Journal of Behavioral Science,* 1973, *5,* 201–210.

Efran, M. G., & Cheyne, J. A. Affective concomitants of the invasion of shared space: Behavioral, physiological, and verbal indicators. *Journal of Personality and Social Psychology,* 1974, *29,* 219–226.

Ehrlich, H. J. Instrument error and the study of prejudice. *Social Forces,* 1964, *43,* 197–206.

Ehrlich, H. J. Attitudes, behavior, and the intervening variables. *American Sociologist,* 1969, *4,* 29–34.

Eisman, B. Some operational measures of cohesiveness and their correlations. *Human Relations,* 1959, *12,* 183–189.

Ekman, P., & Friesen, W. Origins, usage, and coding of nonverbal behavior. In E. Vernon (Ed.), *Communication theory and linguistic models in the social sciences.* Buenos Aires: DiTella, 1968.

Ekman, P., & Friesen, W. Constants across cultures in the face and emotion. *Journal of Personality and Social Psychology,* 1971, *17,* 124–129.

Ellsworth, P. C., & Carlsmith, J. M. Eye contact and gaze aversion in an aggressive encounter. *Journal of Personality and Social Psychology,* 1973, *28,* 280–292.

Ellsworth, P. C., Carlsmith, J. M., & Henson, A. The stare as a stimulus to flight in human subjects: A series of field experiments. *Journal of Personality and Social Psychology,* 1972, *21,* 302–311.

Elms, A. C. Role playing, incentive, and dissonance. *Psychological Bulletin,* 1967, *68,* 132–148.

Emerson, R. M. Power-dependence relations. *American Sociological Review,* 1962, *27,* 31–41.

Endler, N. S., & Hunt, J. McV. Sources of behavioral variance as measured by the S-R Inventory of Anxiousness. *Psychological Bulletin,* 1966, *65,* 336–346.

Engel, E. The role of content in behavior resolution. *American Journal of Psychology,* 1956, *69,* 87–91.

English, H. B., & English, A. C. *A comprehensive dictionary of psychological and psychoanalytical terms.* New York: Longmans, Green, 1958.

Epstein, Y. M., Suedfeld, P., & Silverstein, S. J. Subjects' expectations of and reactions to some behaviors of experimenters. *American Psychologist,* 1973, *28,* 212–221.

Erikson, E. H. *Young man Luther.* New York: Norton, 1958.

Erikson, E. H. *Youth: Change and challenge.* New York: Basic Books, 1963.

Erikson, E. H. *Ghandi's truth.* New York: Norton, 1969.

Eron, L. D., Lefkowitz, M. M., Huesmann, L. R., & Walder, L. O. Does television violence cause aggression? *American Psychologist,* 1972, *27,* 253–263.

Estes, S. G. Judging personality from expressive behavior. *Journal of Abnormal and Social Psychology,* 1938, *33,* 217–236.

Ettinger, R. F., Marino, C. J., Endler, N. S., Geller, S. H., & Natziuk, T. Effects of agreement and correctness on relative competence and conformity. *Journal of Personality and Social Psychology,* 1971, *19,* 204–212.

Evans, G. W., & Howard, R. B. Personal space. *Psychological Bulletin,* 1973, *80,* 334–344.

Exline, R. V. Explorations in the process of person perception: Visual interaction in relation to competition, sex, and need for affiliation. *Journal of Personality,* 1963, *31,* 1–20.

Exline, R. V. Visual interaction: The glances of power and preference. In J. Cole (Ed.), *Nebraska Symposium on Motivation* (Vol. 19). Lincoln: University of Nebraska Press, 1971.

Exline, R. V., Gray, D., & Schuette, D. J. Visual behavior in a dyad as affected by interview content and sex of respondent. *Journal of Personality and Social Psychology,* 1965, *1,* 201–209.

Exline, R. V., & Yellin, A. M. Eye contact as a sign between man and monkey. Paper read at the 19th International Congress of Psychology, London, England, 1969.

Eysenck, H. J. The validity of judgments as a function of number of judges. *Journal of Experimental Psychology,* 1939, *25,* 650–654.

Farley, R., & Hermalin, A. I. Family stability: A comparison of trends between blacks and whites. *American Sociological Review,* 1971, *36,* 1–17.

Faucheux, C., & Moscovici, S. Etudes sur la créativité des groupes: I. Tâche, situation individuelle et groupe. *Bulletin de Psychologie,* 1958, *11,* 863–874.

Feather, N. T. A structural balance model of communication effects. *Psychological Review,* 1964, *71,* 291–313.

Feldman, R. S., & Scheibe, K. E. Determinants of dissent in a psychological experiment. *Journal of Personality,* 1972, *40,* 331–348.

Felipe, N. Interpersonal distance and small group interaction. *Cornell Journal of Social Relations,* 1966, *1,* 59–64.

Felipe, N., & Sommer, R. Invasions of personal space. *Social Problems,* 1966, *14,* 206–214.

Ferguson, L. W. Primary social attitudes. *Journal of Psychology,* 1939, *8,* 217–223.

Feshbach, S. Aggression. In P. H. Mussen (Ed.), *Carmichael's manual of child psychology* (Vol. 2, 3rd ed.). New York: Wiley, 1970.

Feshbach, S., & Singer, R. D. *Television and aggression.* San Francisco: Jossey-Bass, 1971.

Festinger, L. Informal social communication. *Psychological Review,* 1950, *57,* 271–292.

Festinger, L. A theory of social comparison processes. *Human Relations,* 1954, *7,* 117–140.

Festinger, L. *A theory of cognitive dissonance.* Stanford, California: Stanford University Press, 1957.

Festinger, L. Behavioral support for opinion change. *Public Opinion Quarterly,* 1964, *28,* 404–417.

Festinger, L., & Carlsmith, J. M. Cognitive consequences of forced compliance. *Journal of Abnormal and Social Psychology,* 1959, *58,* 203–210.

Festinger, L., Reicken, H., & Schachter, S. *When prophecy fails.* Minneapolis: University of Minnesota Press, 1956.

Festinger, L., Schachter, S., & Back, K. *Social pressures in informal groups: A study of human factors in housing.* New York: Harper, 1950.

Feuer, L. *The conflict of generations.* New York: Basic Books, 1969.

Fiedler, F. E. *A theory of leadership effectiveness.* New York: McGraw-Hill, 1967.

Fiedler, F. E. Leadership experience and leader performance: Another hypothesis shot to hell. *Organizational Behavior and Human Performance,* 1970, *5,* 1–14.

Fiedler, F. E. *Leadership,* New York: General Learning Press, 1971.

Fillenbaum, S. Prior deception and subsequent experimental performance: The faithful subject. *Journal of Personality and Social Psychology,* 1966, *4,* 532–537.

Firestone, I. J., Kaplan, K. J., & Russell, J. C. Anxiety, fear, and affiliation with similar-state versus dissimilar-state others: Misery sometimes loves nonmiserable company. *Journal of Personality and Social Psychology,* 1973, *26,* 409–414.

Fishbein, M. The relationships between beliefs, attitudes and behavior. In S. Feldman (Ed.), *Cognitive consistency.* New York: Academic Press, 1966. (a)

Fishbein, M. Sexual behavior and propositional control. Paper presented at the Psychonomic Society meetings, 1966. (b)

Fishbein, M. Attitude and the prediction of behavior. In M. Fishbein (Ed.), *Readings in attitude theory and measurement.* New York: Wiley, 1967. (a)

Fishbein, M. A consideration of beliefs and their role in attitude measurement. In M. Fishbein, (Ed.), *Readings in attitude theory and measurement.* New York: Wiley, 1967. (b)

Fishbein, M. The prediction of behaviors from attitudinal variables. In C. D. Mortensen & K. K. Sereno (Eds.), *Advances in communication research.* New York: Harper & Row, 1973.

Fishbein, M., & Ajzen, I. Attitudes and opinions. *Annual Review of Psychology.* 1972, *23,* 487–544.

Flacks, R. The liberated generation: An exploration of the roots of student protest. *Journal of Social Issues,* 1967, *23,* 52–75.

Flanders, J. P., & Thistlethwaite, D. L. Effects of familiarization and group discussion upon risk-taking. *Journal of Experimental Social Psychology,* 1967, *5,* 91–98.

Ford, C., & Beach, F. *Patterns of sexual behavior.* New York: Harper & Row, 1951.

Fowler, M. G., Fowler, R. L., & Van de Riet, H. K. Feminism and political radicalism. *Journal of Psychology,* 1973, *83,* 237–243.

Fowler, M. G., & Van de Riet, H. K. Women today and yesterday: An examination of the feminist personality. *Journal of Psychology,* 1972, *82,* 269–276.

Franklin, B. In J. Bigelow (Ed.), *The autobiography of Benjamin Franklin.* New York: Putnam's, 1916.

Fraser, C. Group risk-taking and group polarization.

Paper presented at the European Association of Social Psychology Conference, Konstanz, 1970.

Fraser, S., Kelem, R., Diener, E., & Beaman, A. The Halloween caper: The effects of deindividuation variables on stealing. *Journal of Personality and Social Psychology,* in press.

Free, L. & Cantril, H. *The political beliefs of Americans: A study of public opinion.* New Brunswick: Rutgers University Press, 1967.

Freedman, J. L. Long-term behavioral effects of cognitive dissonance. *Journal of Experimental Social Psychology,* 1965, *1,* 145–155.

Freedman, J. L. Role playing: Psychology by consensus. *Journal of Personality and Social Psychology,* 1969, *13,* 107–114.

Freedman, J. L., Carlsmith, J. M., & Sears, D. O. *Social psychology* (2nd ed.). Englewood Cliffs, New Jersey: Prentice-Hall, 1974.

Freedman, J. L., Wellington, S. A., & Bliss, E. Compliance without pressure: The effects of guilt. *Journal of Personality and Social Psychology,* 1967, *7,* 117–124.

French, E. G. Motivation as a variable in work-partner selection. *Journal of Abnormal and Social Psychology,* 1956, *53,* 96–99.

French, J. R. P., Jr., & Raven, B. The bases of social power. In D. Cartwright (Ed.), *Studies in social power.* Ann Arbor: Institute for Social Research, 1959.

French, V. The strucutre of sentiments. *Journal of Personality,* 1947, *15,* 247–282.

Freud, S. The interpretation of dreams. In *The complete psychological works of Sigmund Freud* (Vol. 7). London: Hogarth, 1953. (1st ed., 1900.)

Freud, S. *Leonard da Vinci and a memory of his childhood.* (Tyson translation). New York: Norton, 1964. (Originally published, 1916.)

Freud, S. *Group psychology and the analysis of the ego.* London: International Psychoanalytic Library, 1922.

Freud, S. *Civilization and its discontents.* London: Hogarth, 1949. (Originally published, 1930.)

Freud, S. *Civilization and its discontents* (1930) (Strachey translation). New York: Norton, 1961.

Freud, S. The psychology of women. In J. Strachey (ed. and trans.), *New introductory lectures in psychoanalysis.* New York: Norton, 1933.

Freud, S. Femininity, lecture XXXIII. In *New introductory lectures on psychoanalysis.* New York: Norton, 1965.

Frey, R. L., Jr., & Adams, J. S. The negotiator's dilemma: Simultaneous in-group and out-group conflict. *Journal of Experimental Social Psychology,* 1972, *8,* 331–346.

Friedan, B. *The feminine mystique.* New York: Dell, 1963.

Frijda, N. H. Recognition of emotion. In L. Berkowitz (Ed.), *Advances in experimental social psychology* (Vol. 4). New York: Academic Press, 1969.

Fromm, E. Individual and social origins of neurosis. *American Sociological Review,* 1944, *9,* 380–384.

Fry, M. Justice for victims. In M. H. Rubin (Ed.), *Compensation for victims of criminal violence: a round table.* Atlanta, Ga.: Emory University Law School, *Journal of Public Law,* 1956, *8,* 155–253.

Gaertner, S. L. The role of racial attitudes in helping behavior. *Journal of Social Psychology,* 1975, *97,* 95–101.

Gaertner, S. L. Helping behavior and racial discrimination among Liberals and Conservatives. *Journal of Personality and Social Psychology,* 1973, *25,* 335–341.

Gaertner, S. L., & Bickman, L. The effects of race on the elicitation of helping behavior: The wrong number technique. *Journal of Personality and Social Psychology,* 1971, *20,* 218–222.

Gage, N. L., & Cronbach, J. J. Conceptional and methodological problems in interpersonal perception. *Psychological Review,* 1955, *62,* 411–422.

Gahagan, J. P. Social contact and communication in the prisoner's dilemma game. Paper presented at the Annual Meeting of the Eastern Psychological Association, 1970.

Gallatin, A., & Adelson, J. Legal guarantees of individual freedom: A cross-national study of the development of political thought. *Journal of Social Issues,* 1971, *27,* 93–108.

Gallimore, R., Weiss, L. B., & Finney, R. Cultural differences in delay of gratification: A problem of behavior classification. *Journal of Personality and Social Psychology,* 1974, *30,* 72–80.

Galton, F. Measurement of character. *Fortnightly Review,* 1884, *36,* 179–185.

Gamson, W. A. *Power and discontent*. Homewood, Ill.: The Dorsey Press, 1968.

Gardner, R. C., Wonnacott, E. J., & Taylor, D. M. Ethnic stereotypes: A factor analytic investigation. *Canadian Journal of Psychology*, 1968, *22*, 35–44.

Garfinkel, H. *Studies in ethnomethodology*. Englewood Cliffs, New Jersey: Prentice-Hall, 1967.

Garrison, R. J., Anderson, V. E., & Reed, S. C. Assortative marriage. *Eugenics Quarterly*, 1968, *15*, 113–127.

Gaylin, W. *In the service of their country: War resisters in prison*. New York: Viking Press, 1970.

Geen, R. G. Effects of frustration, attack and prior training in aggressiveness upon aggressive behavior. *Journal of Personality and Social Psychology*, 1968, *9*, 316–321.

Geen, R. G., & Stonner, D. Context effects in observed violence. *Journal of Personality and Social Psychology*, 1973, *25*, 145–150.

Geen, R., Stonner, D., & Kelley, D. Aggression anxiety and cognitive appraisal of aggression-threat stimuli. *Journal of Personality and Social Psychology*, 1974, *29*, 196–200.

Geller, S. H., Endler, N. S., & Wiesenthal, D. L. Conformity as a function of task generalization and relative competence. *European Journal of Social Psychology*, 1973, *3*, 53–62.

George, A. L., & George, J. L. *Woodrow Wilson and Colonel House: A personality study*. New York: John Day, 1956.

Gergen, K. J. *The psychology of behavior exchange*. Reading: Addison-Wesley, 1969.

Gergen, K. J. The codification of research ethics: Views of a doubting Thomas. *American Psychologist*, 1973, *28*, 907–912. (a)

Gergen, K. J. Social psychology as history. *Journal of Personality and Social Psychology*, 1973, *26*, 309–320. (b)

Gergen, K. J., Diebold, P., & Seipel, M. Intentionality and ability to reciprocate as determinants of reactions to aid. (In preparation)

Gergen, K. J., and Gergen, M. K. M. International assistance from a psychological perspective. In *1971 Yearbook of International Affairs* (Vol. 25). London Institute of World Affairs, 1971.

Gergen, K. J., Gergen, M. K. M., & Barton, W. H. Deviance in the dark. *Psychology Today*, 1973, *7* (5), 129–130.

Gesell, A. The ontogenesis of infant behavior. In L. Carmichael (Ed.), *Manual of child psychology*. New York: Wiley, 1954.

Gewitz, J. L., & Baer, D. M. Deprivation and satiation of social reinforcers as drive conditions. *Journal of Abnormal and Social Psychology*, 1958, *57*, 165–172. (a)

Gewitz, J. L., & Baer, D. M. The effect of brief social deprivation on behaviors for a social reinforcer. *Journal of Abnormal and Social Psychology*, 1958, *56*, 49–56. (b)

Ghiselli, E. E., & Lodahl, T. M. Patterns of managerial traits and group effectiveness. *Journal of Abnormal and Social Psychology*, 1958, *57*, 61–66.

Gibb, C. Leadership. In G. Lindzey and E. Aronson (Eds.), *The Handbook of social psychology* (Vol. 4, 2nd ed.). Reading, Mass.: Addison-Wesley, 1969.

Gibb, J. R. The effects of group size and of threat reduction upon creativity in a problem-solving situation. *American Psychologist*, 1951, *6*, 324.

Glass, D. C. Changes in liking as a means of reducing cognitive discrepancies between self-esteem and aggression. *Journal of Personality*, 1964, *32*, 531–549.

Gleason, R. J. *The Jefferson Airplane and the San Francisco sound*. New York: Ballantine, 1969.

Goffman, E. *The presentation of self in everyday life*. Garden City, New York: Doubleday, 1959.

Goldberg, P. Are women prejudiced against women? *Transaction*, 1968, *5*, 28–30.

Goldman, M. A comparison of individual and group performance for varying combinations of initial ability. *Journal of Personality and Social Psychology*, 1965, *1*, 210–216.

Goodall, J. van L. *In the shadow of man*. Boston: Houghton-Mifflin, 1971.

Goodmonson, C., & Glaudin, V. The relationship of commitment-free behavior and commitment behavior: A study of attitude toward organ transplantation. *Journal of Social Issues*, 1971, *27*, 171–183.

Goodwin, L. A study of the work orientations of welfare recipients participating in the work incentive program. Final Report. Submitted to: Office of Research and Development, Manpower Administration, Department of Labor. Washington, D.C., 1971.

Goranson, R. E., & Berkowitz, L. Reciprocity and responsibility reactions to prior help. *Journal of Personality and Social Psychology,* 1966, *3,* 227–232.

Gore, P. M., & Rotter, J. B. A personality correlate of social action. *Journal of Personality,* 1963, *31,* 58–64.

Gore, W. V., & Taylor, D. A. The nature of the audience as it effects social inhibition. *Representative Research in Social Psychology,* 1973, *4,* 18–27.

Gouldner, A. W. The norm of reciprocity: A preliminary statement. *American Sociological Review,* 1960, *25,* 161–178.

Green, B. F. Attitude measurement. In G. Lindzey (Ed.), *Handbook of social psychology* (Vol. 1) Cambridge, Mass.: Addison-Wesley, 1954.

Green, D. Dissonance and self-perception analyses of "forced compliance": When two theories make competing predictions. *Journal of Personality and Social Psychology,* 1974, *29,* 819–828.

Green, D. R. Volunteering and recall of interrupted tasks. *Journal of Abnormal and Social Psychology,* 1963, *66,* 397–401.

Green, J. A. Attitudinal and situational determinants of intended behavior towards Negroes. Doctoral dissertation, University of Colorado, 1968. (University Microfilms No. 68–2644.)

Greenleigh Associates. *Facts, fallacies and future.* New York: Greenleigh Associates, 1960.

Greenwald, A. G. On defining attitude and attitude theory. In A. G. Greenwald, T. C. Brock, & T. M. Ostrom (Eds.), *Psychological foundation of attitudes,* New York: Academic Press, 1968.

Gross, E. Symbiosis and consensus as integrative factors in small groups. *American Sociological Review,* 1956, *21,* 174–179.

Gross, N., McEachern, A. W., & Mason, W. S. Role conflict and its resolution. In H. Proshansky & B. Seidenberg (Eds.), *Basic studies in social psychology.* New York: Holt, Rinehart and Winston, 1965.

Gruber, M. The nonculture of poverty among black youths. *Social Work,* 1972, *17*(3), 50–58.

Guetzkow, H., Alger, C. F. Brody, R. A., Noel, R. C., & Snyder, R. C. *Simulation in international relations.* Englewood Cliffs, New Jersey: Prentice-Hall, 1963.

Gurin, G., & Gurin, P. Expectancy theory in the study of poverty. *Journal of Social Issues,* 1970, *26,* 83–104.

Gurnee, H. The effect of collective learning upon the individual participants. *Journal of Abnormal and Social Psychology,* 1939, *34,* 529–532.

Gusfield, J. R. The study of social movements. *International Encyclopedia of the Social Sciences.* New York: Collier-Macmillan, 1968.

Guthrie, E. R. *The psychology of learning.* New York: Harper, 1935.

Guttman, L. A basis for scaling qualitative data. *American Sociological Review,* 1944, *9,* 139–150.

Guttman, L. The problem of attitude and opinion measurement. In S. A. Stouffer et al., *Measurement and prediction.* Princeton, N.J.: Princeton University Press, 1950. Pp. 60–90.

Haan, N., Smith, M. B., & Block, J. Moral reasoning of young adults: Political-social behavior, family background, and personality correlates. *Journal of Personality and Social Psychology,* 1968, *10,* 183–201.

Habermas, J. *Toward a rational society: Student protest.* Boston: Beacon, 1970.

Hamblin, R. L. Leadership and crisis. *Sociometry,* 1958, *21,* 322–335.

Hansen, C. F. The scholastic performances of Negro and white pupils in the integrated public schools of the District of Columbia. *Harvard Educational Review,* 1960, *80,* 216–236.

Harding, J., Proshansky, H., Kutner, B., & Chein, I. Prejudice and ethnic relations. In G. Lindzey & E. Aronson (Eds.), *The handbook of social psychology* (Vol. 5, 2nd ed.). Reading, Mass.: Addison-Wesley, 1969.

Hare, A. P., & Bales, R. F. Seating position and small group interaction. *Sociometry,* 1963, *26,* 480–486.

Harford, R. J. Sex, room size, and topic intimacy as determinants of dyadic spacial configurations.

Unpublished master's thesis, University of Maryland, 1971.

Harlow, H. F. The nature of love. *American Psychologist,* 1958, *13,* 673–685.

Harlow, H. F. *Learning to love.* San Francisco: Albion, 1971.

Harrington, M. *The other America.* New York: Macmillan, 1962.

Harris, J. A. Assortative mating in man. *The Popular Science Monthly,* 1912, *80,* 476–492.

Harris, S., & Masling, J. Examiner sex, subject sex, and Rorschach productivity. *Journal of Consulting and Clinical Psychology,* 1970, *34,* 60–63.

Harrison, R., & Lubin, B. Personality style, group composition, and learning. *Journal of Applied Behavioral Science,* 1965, *1,* 286–301.

Hartley, E. L., & Hartley, R. E. *Fundamentals of social psychology.* New York: Knopf, 1952.

Hartshorne, H., & May, M. A. *Studies in the nature of character.* Columbia University Teachers College, Vol. 1: *Studies in deceit.* Vol. 2: *Studies in service and self-control.* Vol. 3: *Studies in organization of character.* New York: Macmillan, 1928–30.

Hartup, W. W., & Zook, E. A. Sex-role preference in three and four year old children. *Journal of Consulting Psychology,* 1960, *24,* 420–427.

Harvey, O. J., Hunt, D. E., & Schroder, H. M. *Conceptual systems and personality organization.* New York: Wiley, 1961.

Hastorf, A. H., & Cantril, H. They saw a game: A case study. *Journal of Abnormal and Social Psychology,* 1954, *49,* 129–134.

Hastorf, A. H., Richardson, S. A., & Dornbusch, S. M. The problem of relevance in the study of perception. In R. Tagiuri & L. Petrullo (Eds.), *Person perception and interpersonal behavior.* Stanford: Stanford University Press, 1958.

Hays, W. L. An approach to the study of trait implication and trait similarity. In R. Tagiuri & L. Petrullo (Eds.), *Person perception and interpersonal behavior.* Stanford: Stanford University Press, 1958.

Haythorn, W., Couch, A., Haefner, D., Langham, P., & Carter, L. The effects of varying combinations of authoritarian and equalitarian leaders and followers. *Journal of Abnormal and Social Psychology,* 1956, *53,* 210–219.

Heider, F. Social perception and phenomenal causality. *Psychological Review,* 1944, *51,* 358–374.

Heider, F. Attitudes and cognitive organization. *Journal of Psychology,* 1946, *21,* 107–112.

Heider, F. *The psychology of interpersonal relations.* New York: Wiley, 1958.

Heider, F. Perceiving the other person. In R. Tagiuri & L. Petrullo (Eds.), *Person perception and interpersonal behavior.* Stanford: Standord University Press, 1958.

Heider, F., & Simmel, M. An experimental study of apparent behavior. *American Journal of Psychology,* 1944, *57,* 243–259.

Heilbrun, A. B. Parental identification and college adjustment. *Psychological Reports,* 1962, *10,* 853–854.

Heingartner, A., & Hall, J. V. Affective consequences in adults and children of repeated exposure to auditory stimuli. *Journal of Personality and Social Psychology,* 1974, *29,* 719–723.

Heiss, J. On the transmission of marital instability in black families. *American Sociological Review,* 1972, *37,* 82–92.

Helson, H., Blake, R. B., & Mouton, J. S. Petition-signing as adjustment to situational and personal factors. *Journal of Social Psychology,* 1958, *48,* 3–10.

Hemphill, J. K. *Situational factors in leadership.* Columbus: Ohio State University Personnel Research Board, 1949.

Henchy, T., & Glass, D. C. Evaluation apprehension and the social facilitation of dominant and subordinate responses. *Journal of Personality and Social Psychology,* 1968, *10,* 446–454.

Hendrick, C., & Jones, R. A. *The nature of theory and research in social psychology.* New York: Academic Press, 1972.

Hermalin, A. I. & Farley, R. The potential for residential integration in cities and suburbs: Implications for the busing controversy. *American Sociological Review,* 1973, *38,* 596–610.

Herzog, E. Social stereotypes and social research. *Journal of Social Issues,* 1970, *26,* 109–125.

Herzog, E., & Sudia, C. E. Fatherless homes: A review of research. *Children,* 1968, *15*(5), 177–182.

Hess, R. D., & Shipman, V. C. Early experience and

the socialization of cognitive modes in children. *Child Development,* 1965, *36,* 869–886.

Hess, R. D., & Torney, J. V. *The development of political attitudes in children.* New York: Doubleday, 1968.

Hilton, I. Differences in the behavior of mothers toward first and later born children. *Journal of Personality and Social Psychology,* 1967, *7,* 282–290.

Hilton, I., Paul, H., Wajsman, G., Herscovic, F., Loew, R., & Chaplan, R. Sex differences in post-aggression retaliation. Unpublished mimeo, Yeshiva University, New York, 1974.

Hilton, I., & Singer, S. Mastery of the environment and post-aggression retaliation. Paper presented at the Eastern Psychological Association Meetings, Boston, Mass., 1972.

Hoffer, E. *The true believer.* New York: Mentor, 1951.

Hoffman, L. R. Homogeneity of member personality and its effect on group problem-solving. *Journal of Abnormal and Social Psychology,* 1959, *58,* 27–32.

Hoffman, L. R., & Maier, M. R. F. Quality and acceptance of problem solutions by members of homogeneous and heterogeneous groups. *Journal of Abnormal and Social Psychology,* 1961, *62,* 401–407.

Hoffman, L. W. Early childhood experiences and women's achievement motives. *Journal of Social Issues,* 1972, *28,* 129–155.

Hofling, C. K., Brotzman, E., Dalrymple, S., Graves, N., & Pierce, C. M. An experimental study in nurse-physician relationships. *Journal of Nervous and Mental Disease,* 1966, *143,* 171–180.

Hokanson, J. E. The effects of frustration and anxiety on overt aggression. *Journal of Abnormal and Social Psychology,* 1961, *62,* 346–351.

Hollander, E. P., & Julian, J. W. Contemporary trends in the analysis of leadership processes. *Psychological Bulletin,* 1969, *76,* 387–397.

Hollander, E. P., & Willis, R. H. Some current issues in the psychology of conformity and nonconformity. *Psychological Bulletin,* 1967, *68,* 62–76.

Holmes, D. S., & Appelbaum, A. S. Nature of prior experimental experience as a determinant of performance in a subsequent experiment. *Journal of Personality and Social Psychology,* 1970, *14,* 195–202.

Holmes, D. S., & Bennett, D. H. Experiments to answer questions raised by the use of deception in psychological research. *Journal of Personality and Social Psychology,* 1974, *29,* 358–367.

Holmes, J. G., Throop, W. F., and Strickland, L. H. The effects of prenegotiation expectations on the distributive bargaining process. *Journal of Experimental Social Psychology,* 1971, *7,* 582–599.

Homans, G. C. *Social behavior: Its elementary forms.* New York: Harcourt, Brace & World, 1961.

Hood, T. C., & Back, K. W. Self-disclosure and the volunteer: A source of bias in laboratory experiments. *Journal of Personality and Social Psychology,* 1971, *17,* 130–136.

Horai, J., & Tedeschi, J. T. Effects of credibility and magnitude of punishment on compliance to threats. *Journal of Personality and Social Psychology,* 1969, *12,* 164–169.

Horn, J. L., & Knott, P. D. Activist youth of the 1960's: Summary and prognosis. *Science,* 1971, *171,* 977–985.

Horner, M. S. Sex differences in achievement motivation and performance in competitive and non-competitive situations. Unpublished doctoral dissertation, University of Michigan, 1968.

Horner, M. S. Fail: Bright women. *Psychology Today,* November 1969, *3,* 6, 36–38.

Horner, M. S. Toward the understanding of achievement related conflicts in women. *Journal of Social Issues,* 1972, *28,* 157–176.

Hornstein, H. The effects of different magnitudes of threat upon inter-personal bargaining. *Journal of Experimental Social Psychology,* 1965, *1,* 282–293.

Horowitz, E. L. "Race" attitudes. In O. Klineberg (Ed.), *Characteristics of the American Negro.* New York: Harper, 1944.

Hovland, C. I. *Communication and persuasion.* New Haven, Connecticut: Yale University Press, 1953.

Hovland, C. I. (Ed.). *The order of presentation in persuasion.* New Haven, Connecticut: Yale University Press, 1957.

Hovland, C. I., & Janis, I. L. (eds.). *Personality*

and *persuasibility*. New Haven, Connecticut: Yale University Press, 1959.

Hovland, C. I., & Rosenberg, J. J. (Eds.). *Attitude organization and change*. New Haven, Connecticut: Yale University Press, 1960.

Howells, L. T., & Becker, S. W. Seating arrangement and leadership emergence. *Journal of Abnormal and Social Psychology*, 1962, *64*, 148–150.

Hull, C.L. *Principles of behavior*. New York: Appleton-Century-Crofts, 1943.

Hunt, J. McV. Traditional personality theory in the light of recent evidence. *American Scientist*, 1965, *53*, 80–96.

Hunt, P. J., & Hillery, J. M. Social facilitation in a coaction setting: An examination of the effects over learning trials. *Journal of Experimental Social Psychology*, 1973, *9*, 563–571.

Husband, R. W. Cooperative versus solitary problem solution. *Journal of Social Psychology*, 1940, *11*, 405–409.

Hyman, H. Do they tell the truth? *Public Opinion Quarterly*, 1945, *8*, 557–559.

Hyman H. Social psychology and race relations. In I. Katz & P. Gurin (Eds.), *Race and the social sciences*. New York: Basic Books, 1969.

Hyman, H., et al., *Interviewing in social research*. Chicago: University of Chicago Press, 1954.

Hyman, H. H., & Reed, J. S. "Black Matriarchy reconsidered: Evidence from secondary analysis of sample surveys. *Public Opinion Quarterly*, 1969, *33*, 346–354.

Hymer, S., & Atkins, A. L. The relationship between attitudes toward the women's liberation movement and modes of aggressive expression in women. *Proceedings, 81st Annual Convention, American Psychological Association*, 1973.

Hymer, S., Berman, A., Galper, R. & Fekete, A. A women's liberation movement scale. Unpublished manuscript, Yeshiva University, New York, 1972.

Inbau, F., & Reid, J. *Criminal interrogation and confessions*. Baltimore: Williams and Wilkins, 1962.

Insko, C. A. *Theories of attitude change*. New York: Appleton-Century-Crofts, 1968.

Irelan, L. M. (Ed.). *Low-income life styles*. Welfare Administration Publication Number 14. Washington, D.C.: Welfare Administration, Department of Health, Education, and Welfare, 1968.

Irelan, L. M., Moles, O. C., & O'Shea, R. M. Ethnicity, poverty, and selected attitudes: A test of the "culture of poverty" hypothesis. *Social Forces*, 1969, *47*, 405–413.

Izard, C. J. *The face of emotion*. New York. Appleton-Century-Crofts, 1971.

Jacobs, L., Berscheid, E., & Walster, E. Self-esteem and attraction. *Journal of Personality and Social Psychology*, 1971, *17*, 84–91.

Janis, I. L. *Victims of groupthink: A psychological study of foreign-policy decisions and fiascoes*. Boston: Houghton Mifflin, 1972.

Janis, I. L., & Feshbach, S. Effects of fear arousing communications. *Journal of Abnormal and Social Psychology*, 1953, *48*, 78–92.

Janis, I. L., & Field, P. B. A behavioral assessment of persuasibility: consistency of individual differences. In C. I. Hovland & I. L. Janis (Eds.), *Personality and persuasibility*. New Haven, Conn.: Yale University Press, 1959.

Janis, I. L. & Katz, D. The reduction of inter-group hostility: Research problems and hypotheses. *Conflict Resolution*, 1959, *3*, 85–100.

Jecker, J., and Landy, D. Liking a person as a function of doing him a favor. *Human Relations*, 1969, *22*, 371–378.

Jenks, C. S. The Coleman report and the conventional wisdom. In F. Mosteller & D. P. Moynihan (Eds.), *On equality of educational opportunity*. New York: Random House, 1972.

Jennings, H. H. *Leadership and Isolation*. New York: Longmans, Green, 1943.

Johnson, D. F. Compliance, deterrence and the need to save face. Paper presented at the Eastern Psychological Association Annual Convention, New York, 1971.

Johnson, D. F., & Pruitt, D. G. Pre-intervention effects of mediation vs. arbitration. *Journal of Applied Psychology*, 1972, *56*, 1–10.

Johnson, D. F., & Tullar, W. L. Style of third party intervention, face-saving and bargaining behavior. *Journal of Experimental Social Psychology*, 1972, *8*, 319–330.

Johnson, D. L., & Andrews, I. R. Risky-shift phenomenon tested with consumer products as stimuli. *Journal of Personality and Social Psychology*, 1971, *20*, 382–385.

Johnson, R. W., & Adair, J. G. The effects of systematic recording error vs. experimenter bias on latency of word associations. *Journal of Experimental Research in Personality,* 1970, *4,* 270–275.

Johnson, R. W., & Adair, J. G. Experimenter expectancy vs. systematic recording error under automated and non-automated stimulus presentation. *Journal of Experimental Research in Personality,* 1972, *6,* 88–94.

Johnston, J., & Bachman, J. G. *Young men look at military service.* Ann Arbor: Institute for Social Research, University of Michigan, 1970.

Joffe, N. F. Non-reciprocity among East European Jews. In M. Mead and T. Metraux (Eds.), *The Study of Culture at a Distance.* Chicago: University of Chicago Press, 1953.

Jones, E. E., & Davis, K. E. From acts to dispositions: the attribution process in person perception. In L. Berkowitz (Ed.), *Advances in experimental social psychology* (Vol. 2). New York: Academic Press, 1965.

Jones, E. E., and DeCharms, R. Change in social perception as a function of the personal relevance of behavior. *Sociometry,* 1957, *20,* 75–85.

Jones, E. E., & Gerard, H. B. *Foundations of social psychology.* New York: Wiley, 1967.

Jones, E. E., & Harris, V. A. The attribution of attitudes. *Journal of Experimental Social Psychology,* 1967, *3,* 1–24.

Jones, E. E., Kanouse, D. E., Kelley, H. H., Nisbett, R. E., Valins, S., & Weiner, B. *Attribution: Perceiving the causes of behavior.* Morristown, New Jersey: General Learning Press, 1972.

Jones, E. E., & Nisbett, R. E. The actor and the observer: Divergent perceptions of the causes of behavior. In E. Jones, D. Kanouse, H. Kelley, R. Nisbett, S. Valins, & B. Weiner (Eds.), *Attribution: Perceiving the causes of behavior.* Morristown, N.J., General Learning Press, 1972.

Jones, J. M. *Prejudice and racism.* Reading, Mass.: Addison-Wesley, 1972.

Jones, L. E., & Young, F. W. Structure of a social environment: Longitudinal individual differences scaling of an intact group. *Journal of Personality and Social Psychology,* 1972, *24,* 108–121.

Jones, R. A., Linder, D. E., Kiesler, C. A., Zanna, M., & Brehm, J. W. Internal states or external stimuli: Observers' attitude judgments and the dissonance theory–self-perception controversy. *Journal of Experimental Social Psychology,* 1968, *4,* 247–269.

Joseph, M. L., & Willis, R. H. An experimental analog to two-party bargaining. *Behavioral Science,* 1963, *8,* 117–127.

Jourard, S. M. *Disclosing man to himself.* Princeton: Van Nostrand, 1968.

Jung, J. Current practices and problems in use of college students for psychological research. *Canadian Psychologist,* 1969, *10,* 280–290.

Kagan, J. Acquisition and significance of sex-typing and sex role identity. In M. L. Hoffman & L. W. Hoffman (Eds.), *Review of child development research* (Vol. 1). New York: Russell Sage Foundation, 1964.

Kahan, J. P. Effects of level of aspiration in an experimental bargaining situation. *Journal of Personality and Social Psychology,* 1968, *8,* 154–159.

Kahn, L. A. The organization of attitudes toward the Negro as a function of education. *Psychological Monographs,* 1951, *65,* (13, whole No. 330).

Kaleta, R. J. Aggression intensity and femininity of the victim. Paper presented at the Eastern Psychological Association Meetings, Washington, D. C., 1973.

Kaplan, H. R., & Tausky, C. Work and the welfare Cadillac: The function of the commitment to work among the hard-core unemployed. *Social Problems,* 1972, *19,* 469–483.

Karlins, M., Coffman, T. L., & Walters, G. On the fading of social stereotypes: Studies of three generations of college students. *Journal of Personality and Social Psychology,* 1969, *13,* 1–16.

Katz, D. The functional approach to the study of attitude. *Public Opinion Quarterly,* 1960, *24,* 163–204.

Katz, D., & Kahn, R. L. *The social psychology of organizations.* New York: Wiley, 1966.

Katz, E. The two-step flow of communication: An up-to-date report on an hypothesis. *Public Opinion Quarterly,* 1957, *21,* 61–78.

Katz, I. The socialization of academic motivation in minority group children. In D. Levine (Ed.), *Nebraska symposium on motivation* (Vol. 15). Lincoln, Nebraska: University of Nebraska Press, 1967.

Katz, I. Factors influencing Negro performance in the desegregated school. In M. Deutsch, I. Katz, & A. R. Jensen (Eds.), *Social class, race, and psychological development,* New York: Holt, Rinehart, & Winston, 1968.

Katz, I. Experimental studies of Negro-White relationships. In L. Berkowitz (Ed.), *Advances in Experimental Social Psychology* (Vol. 5). New York: Academic Press, 1970.

Katz, I. Negro performance in interracial situations. In P. Watson (Ed.), *Psychology and race*. Chicago: Aldine, 1973.

Katz, I., Atchison, C. O., Epps, E. G., & Roberts, S. O. Race of evaluator, race of norm, and expectancy as determinants of black performance. *Journal of Experimental Social Psychology*, 1972, *8*, 1–15.

Katz, I., & Benjamin, L. Effects of white authoritarianism in biracial work groups. *Journal of Abnormal and Social Psychology*, 1960, *61*, 448–456.

Katz, I., & Cohen, M. The effects of training Negroes upon cooperative problem solving in biracial teams. *Journal of Abnormal and Social Psychology*, 1962, *64*, 319–325.

Katz, I., Glass, D. D., & Cohen, S. Ambivalence, guilt, and the scapegoating of minority group victims. *Journal of Experimental Social Psychology*, 1973, *9*, 423–436.

Katz, I., & Greenbaum, C. Effects of anxiety, threat, and racial environment on task performance of Negro college students. *Journal of Abnormal and Social Psychology*, 1963, *66*, 562–567.

Kaufmann, H. The price of obedience and the price of knowledge. *American Psychologist*, 1967, *22*, 321–322.

Kelly, G. A. *The psychology of personal constructs*. New York: Norton, 1955.

Kelley, H. H. The warm-cold variable in first impressions of persons. *Journal of Personality*, 1950, *18*, 431–439.

Kelley, H. H. Two functions of reference groups. In G. E. Swanson, T. M. Newcomb, & E. L. Hartley (Eds.), *Readings in social psychology* (Rev. ed.). New York: Holt, Rinehart and Winston, 1952.

Kelley, H. H. Experimental studies of threats in interpersonal negotiations. *Journal of Conflict Resolution*, 1965, *9*, 79–105.

Kelley, H. H. A classroom study of the dilemmas in interpersonal negotiations. In K. Archibald (Ed.), *Strategic interaction and conflict*. Berkeley, Calif.: Institute of International Studies, University of California, 1966.

Kelley, H. H. Attribution theory in social psychology. In D. Levin (Ed.), *Nebraska Symposium on Motivation* (Vol. 15). Lincoln: University of Nebraska Press, 1967.

Kelley, H. H. *Attribution in social interaction*. In E. Jones, D. Kanouse, H. Kelley, R. Nisbett, S. Valins, & B. Weiner, *Attribution: Perceiving the causes of behavior*. Morristown, N.J.: General Learning Press, 1972.

Kelley, H. H. The processes of casual attribution. *American Psychologist*, 1973, *28*, 107–128.

Kelley, H. H., Beckman, L. L., & Fischer, O. S. Negotiating the division of a reward under incomplete information. *Journal of Experimental Social Psychology*, 1967, *3*, 361–398.

Kelley, H. H. & Ring, K. Some effects of "suspicious" versus "trusting" training schedules. *Journal of Abnormal and Social Psychology*, 1961, *63*, 294–301.

Kelley, H. H., & Schenitzki, D. P. Bargaining. In C. G. McClintock (Ed.), *Experimental Social Psychology*. New York: Holt, Reinhart and Winston, 1972.

Kelley, H. H., & Thibaut, J. W. Group problem solving. In G. Lindzey & E. Aronson (Eds.), *The handbook of social psychology* (Vol. 4, 2nd ed.). Reading, Mass.: Addison-Wesley, 1969.

Kelman, H. C. Compliance, identification, and internalization: Three processes of opinion change. *Journal of Conflict Resolution*, 1958, *2*, 51–60.

Kelman, H. C. Processes of opinion change. *Public Opinion Quarterly*, 1961, *25*, 57–78.

Kelman, H. C. Human use of human subjects: The problem of deception in social psychological experiments. *Psychological Bulletin*, 1967, *67*, 1–11.

Kelman, H. Attitudes are alive and well and gainfully employed in the sphere of action. Presidential address to Division 8; American Psychological Association meeting, Washington, D. C., September 1971.

Kelman, H. C. The rights of the subject in social research: An analysis in terms of relative power and legitimacy. *American Psychologist*, 1972, *27*, 989–1016.

Kelman, H. C., & Baron, R. M. Determinants of modes of resolving inconsistency dilemmas: A functional analysis. In R. P. Abelson, E. Aronson, W. J. McGuire, T. M. Newcomb, M. J. Rosenberg, & P. H. Tannenbaum (Eds.), *Theories of cognitive consistency: A sourcebook.* Chicago: Rand McNally, 1968.

Kelman, H. C., & Lawrence, L. H. Assignment of responsibility in the case of Lt. Calley: Preliminary report on a national survey. *Journal of Social Issues,* 1972, *28,* 177–212.

Keniston, K. *The uncommitted: Alienated youth in American society.* New York: Harcourt, Brace & World, 1965.

Keniston, K. The sources of student dissent. *Journal of Social Issues,* 1967, *23,* 108–137.

Keniston, K. *Young radicals.* New York: Harcourt, Brace & World, 1968.

Keniston, K. Youth: A 'new' stage of life. *American Scholar,* 1970, *39,* 631–653.

Keniston, K., & Lerner, M. Campus characteristics and campus unrest. *The Annals of the American Academy of Political and Social Science,* 1971, *395,* 39–53.

Kerpelman, L. *Student activism and ideology in higher education institutions.* Washington, D.C.: U.S. Department of Health, Education, and Welfare. Office of Education, 1970.

Kiesler, C. A. Group pressure and conformity. In J. Mills (Ed.), *Experimental social psychology.* New York: Macmillan, 1969.

Kiesler, C. A., & Baral, R. The search for a romantic partner: The effects of self-esteem and physical attractiveness on romantic behavior. In K. Gergen & D. Marlowe (Eds.), *Personality and Social Behavior.* Reading, Mass.: Addison-Wesley, 1970.

Kiesler, C. A., Collins, B. E., & Miller, N. *Attitude change: A critical analysis of theoretical approaches.* New York: Wiley, 1969.

Kiesler, C. A., & Kiesler, S. B. *Conformity.* Reading, Mass.: Addison-Wesley, 1969.

Kiesler, C. Nisbett, R., & Zanna, M. On inferring one's belief from one's behavior. *Journal of Personality and Social Psychology,* 1969, *11,* 321–327.

Killian, L. M. Social movements. In R. E. L. Faris (Ed.), *Handbook of modern sociology.* Chicago: Rand-McNally, 1964.

King, C. W. *Social movements in the United States.* New York: Random House, 1956.

King, S. Encounter study assesses groups. *The New York Times,* February 12, 1973, p. 47.

Kinkade, K. A Walden-two experiment. *Psychology Today,* 1973, *6,* 8, 35.

Kinsey, A. C., Pomeroy, W. B., & Martin, C. E. *Sexual behavior in the human male.* Philadelphia: W. B. Saunders, 1948.

Kipnis, D. The effects of leadership style and leadership power upon the inducement of an attitude change. *Journal of Abnormal and Social Psychology,* 1958, *57,* 173–180.

Kipnis, D. Does power corrupt? *Journal of Personality and Social Psychology,* 1972, *24,* 33–41.

Klapp, O. E. *Collective search for identity.* New York: Holt, Rinehart and Winston, 1969.

Knight, H. C. A comparison of the reliability of group and individual judgments. Unpublished master's thesis, Columbia University, 1921.

Knowles, E. S. Boundaries around social space: Dyadic responses to an invader. *Environment and Behavior,* 1972, *4,* 437–445.

Knowles, E. S. Boundaries around group interaction: The effect of group size and member status on boundary permeability. *Journal of Personality and Social Psychology,* 1973, *26,* 327–331.

Koffka, K. *Principles of Gestalt Psychology.* New York: Harcourt, Brace, 1935.

Kogan, N., & Wallach, M. A. Group risk taking as a function of members' anxiety and defensiveness levels. *Journal of Personality,* 1967, *35,* 50–63.

Köhler, W. *Gestalt Psychology.* New York: Liveright, 1929.

Kohlberg, L. A cognitive-developmental analysis of children's sex-role concepts and attitudes. In E. Maccoby (Ed.), *The development of sex differences.* Stanford: Stanford University Press, 1966.

Kohlberg, L. Moral and religious education in the public schools: A developmental view. In T. Sizer (Ed.), *Religion and public education.* Boston: Houghton-Mifflin, 1967.

Kohlberg, L. Stage and sequences: The cognitive-developmental approach to socialization. In D. A. Goslin (Ed.), *Handbook of socialization theory and research.* Chicago: Rand-McNally, 1969.

Kohlberg, L. *Stages in the development of moral thought and action.* New York: Holt, Rinehart and Winston, 1970.

Kohlberg, L. Stages of moral development as a basis for moral education. In C. M. Beck, A. Crittenden, & D. Sullivan (Eds.), *Moral education: Interdisciplinary approaches.* Toronto: University of Toronto Press, 1971.

Kohn, M. L. Social class and the exercise of parental authority. *American Sociological Review,* 1959, *24,* 352–366.

Kohn, M. L. *Class and conformity: A study in values.* Homewood, Ill.: Dorsey Press, 1969.

Kohn, P. The concept of cognitive dissonance: A study in three tenses. Unpublished paper, Social Relations Department, Harvard University, 1962.

Komorita, S. S., & Barnes, M. Effects of pressures to reach agreement in bargaining. *Journal of Personality and Social Psychology,* 1969, *13,* 245–252.

Korte, C. Group effects on help giving in an emergency. Proceedings of the 77th Annual Convention of the American Psychological Association, 1969.

Kothandepani, V. Validation of feeling, belief, and intention to act as three components of attitude and their contribution to prediction of contraceptive behavior. *Journal of Personality and Social Psychology,* 1971, *19,* 321–334.

Krebs, D., & Baldwin, J. Reported in D. Krebs & P. Whitten, Guilt-edged giving—the shame of it all. *Psychology Today,* January, 1972, *5,* 50–78.

Krech, D., & Crutchfield, R. S. *Theory and Problems in Social Psychology.* McGraw-Hill, 1948.

Krech, D., Crutchfield, R., & Ballachey, E. *Individual in society.* New York: McGraw-Hill, 1962.

Kriesberg, L. The relationship between socio-economic rank and behavior. *Social Problems,* 1963, *10*(4), 334–353.

Kriesberg, L. *Mothers in poverty: A study of fatherless families.* Chicago: Aldine, 1970.

Kruglanski, A. W. Much ado about the "volunteer artifacts." *Journal of Personality and Social Psychology,* 1973, *28,* 348–354.

Kudirka, N. K. Defiance of authority under peer influence. Unpublished doctoral dissertation, Yale University, 1965.

Kuhn, T. S. *The structure of scientific revolutions.* Chicago: University of Chicago Press, 1962.

Kuusinen, J. Factorial invariance of personality ratings. *Scandinavian Journal of Psychology,* 1969, *10,* 33–44.

Laird, J. D. Self-attribution of emotion: The effects of expressive behavior on the quality of emotional experience. *Journal of Personality and Social Psychology,* 1974, *29,* 475–486.

Lambert, W. E., Libman, E., & Poser, E. G. The effect of increased salience of a membership group on pain tolerance. *Journal of Personality,* 1960, *28,* 350–357.

Lamm, H. Will an observer advise high risk taking after hearing a discussion of the decision problem? *Journal of Personality and Social Psychology,* 1967, *6,* 467–471.

Lamm, H., & Trommsdorff, G. Group versus individual performance on tasks requiring ideational proficiency (brainstorming): A review. *European Journal of Social Psychology,* 1973, *3,* 361–388.

Lana, R. E. Pretest sensitization. In R. Rosenthal & R. L. Rosnow (Eds.), *Artifact in Behavioral research.* New York: Academic Press, 1969.

Landis, B., & Tauber, E. S. *In the name of life.* New York: Holt, Rinehart and Winston, 1971.

Landis, C. The interpretation of facial expression in emotion. *Journal of Genetic Psychology,* 1929, *2,* 59–72.

Landy, O., & Sigall, H. Beauty is talent. *Journal of Personality and Social Psychology,* 1974, *29,* 299–304.

Lange, L. Neue Experimente über der einfachen Reaktion auf Sinneseindrucke, *Philosophische Studien,* 1888, *4,* 479–510.

Lanzetta, J. T., & Kleck, R. Encoding and decoding of facial affect in humans. *Journal of Personality and Social Psychology,* 1970, *16,* 12–19.

La Piere, R. T. Attitudes versus actions. *Social Forces,* 1934, *13,* 230–237.

Larson, K. S., Coleman, D., Forbes, J., & Johnson, R. Is the subject's personality or the experimental situation a better predictor of a subject's willingness to administer shock to a victim? *Journal of Personality and Social Psychology,* 1972, *22,* 287–295.

Lasswell, H. D. The structure and function of communication in society. In L. Bryson (Ed.), *Communication of ideas.* New York: Harper, 1948.

Latane, B. (Ed.). Studies in social comparison. *Journal of Experimental Social Psychology,* Supplement 1, September 1966.

Latane, B., & Darley, J. M. Group inhibition of bystander intervention in emergencies. *Journal of Personality and Social Psychology,* 1968, *10,* 215–221.

Latane, B., & Darley, J. M. Bystander "apathy." *American Scientist,* 1969, *57,* 244–268.

Latane, B., & Darley, J. M. *The unresponsive*

bystander: Why doesn't he help? New York: Appleton-Century-Crofts, 1970.

Latane, B., & Rodin, J. A lady in distress: Inhibiting effects of strangers on bystander intervention. *Journal of Experimental Social Psychology*, 1969, *5*, 189–202.

Laughlin, P. R., & Johnson, H. H. Group and individual performance on a complementary task as a function of initial ability level. *Journal of Experimental Social Psychology*, 1966, *2*, 407–414.

Lawton, M. P., & Goldman, A. E. Cigarette smoking and attitude toward the etiology of lung cancer. *American Psychologist*, 1958, *13*, 342.

Lay, C. H., & Jackson, D. N. Analysis of the generality of trait-inferential relationships. *Journal of Personality and Social Psychology*, 1969, *12*, 12–21.

Lazarsfeld, P. F. The logic and mathematical foundation of latent structure analysis. In S. A. Stouffer et al., *Measurement and prediction*. Princeton, New Jersey: Princeton University Press, 1950.

Leacock, E. B. Introduction. In E. B. Leacock (Ed.), *The culture of poverty: A critique*. New York: Simon & Schuster, 1971.

Leary, T. *Interpersonal diagnosis of personality*. New York: Ronald Press, 1957.

Leavitt, H. J. Some effects of certain communication patterns on group performance. *Journal of Abnormal and Social Psychology*, 1951, *46*, 38–50.

Le Bon, G. *The crowd*. London: Unwin, 1896.

Leeds, A. The concept of the "culture of poverty": Conceptual, logical, and empirical problems, with perspectives from Brazil and Peru. In E. B. Leacock (Ed.), *The culture of poverty: A critique*. New York: Simon & Schuster, 1971.

Leeper, R. A. A study of a neglected portion of the field of learning: The development of sensory organization. *Journal of Genetic Psychology*, 1935, *46*, 41–75.

Leper, M. On the relationship between attitudes and behaviors: An eclectic analysis. Unpublished Area Paper, Department of Psychology, Yale University, 1969.

Lerner, M. J., & Matthews, G. Reactions to the suffering of others under conditions of indirect responsibility. *Journal of Personality and Social Psychology*, 1967, *5*, 319–325.

Leventhal, G. S., Allen, J., & Kemelgor, B. Reducing inequity by reallocating rewards. *Psychonomic Sciences*, 1969, *14*, 295–296.

Levine, J. M., Saxe, L., & Ranelli, C. J. Extreme dissent, conformity reduction, and the bases of social influence. Unpublished manuscript, University of Pittsburgh, 1974.

LeVine, R. A. Culture, personality, and socialization: An evolutionary view. In D. A. Goslin (Ed.), *Handbook of socialization theory and research*. Chicago: Rand-McNally, 1969.

Levinger, G., & Schneider, D. J. Test of the "risk is a value" hypothesis. *Journal of Personality and Social Psychology*, 1969, *11*, 165–170.

Levy, L. H. Group variance and group attractiveness. *Journal of Abnormal and Social Psychology*, 1964, *68*, 661–664.

Levy, L. H. Awareness, learning, and the beneficent subject as expert witness. *Journal of Personality and Social Psychology*, 1967, *6*, 365–370.

Lewin, K. *Field theory in social science*. New York: Harper, 1951.

Lewin, K. Group decision and social change. In G. E. Swanson, T. M. Newcomb, & E. L. Hartley (Eds.), *Readings in social psychology* (Rev. ed.). New York: Holt, Rinehart, and Winston, 1952.

Lewin, K., Dembo, T., Festinger, L., & Sears, P. S. Level of aspiration. In J. McV. Hunt (Ed.), *Personality and the Behavior Disorders*. New York: Ronald Press, 1944.

Lewin, K., Lippit, R., & White, R. K. Patterns of aggressive behavior in experimentally created "social climates." *Journal of Social Psychology*, 1939, *10*, 271–299.

Lewis, H. Culture of poverty? What does it matter? In E. B. Leacock (Ed.), *The culture of poverty: A critique*. New York: Simon & Schuster, 1971.

Lewis, M., & Wilson, C. D. Infant development in lower-class American families. *Human Development*, 1972, *15*, 112–127.

Lewis, O. *Five families: Mexican case studies in the culture of poverty*. New York: Basic Books, 1959.

Lewis, O. *The children of Sanchez*. New York: Random House, 1961.

Lewis, O. *La Vida*. New York: Random House, 1965.

Lewis, O. The culture of poverty. *Scientific American*, 1966, *215* (4), 19–25.

Lewis, O. *A study of slum culture: Backgrounds for La Vida*. New York: Random House, 1968.

Lieberman, M. A., Yalom I. D., & Miles, M. B. *Encounter groups: First facts.* New York: Basic Books, 1973. (a)

Lieberman, M. A., Yalom, I. D., & Miles, M. B. Encounter: The leader makes a difference. *Psychology Today,* 1973, *6* (10), 69–72, 74, 76. (b)

Liebert, R. M., Smith, W. P., Hill, J. H., & Keiffer, M. The effects of information and magnitude of initial offer on interpersonal negotiation. *Journal of Experimental Social Psychology,* 1968, *4,* 431–441.

Liebow, E. *Tally's corner.* Boston: Little, Brown & Co., 1967.

Lifton, R. J. *History and human survival.* New York: Vintage, 1971.

Likert, R. A technique for the measurement of attitude. *Archives of Psychology* (140), 1932.

Linder, D. E., Cooper, J., & Jones, E. E. Decision freedom as a determinant of the role of incentive magnitude in attitude change. *Journal of Personality and Social Psychology,* 1967, *6,* 244–254.

Lindskold, S., Cullen, P., Gahagan, J., & Tedeschi, J. T. Developmental aspects of reaction to positive inducements. *Developmental Psychology,* 1970, *3,* 277–284.

Linn, L. S. Verbal attitudes and overt behavior: A study of racial discrimination. *Social Forces,* 1965, *44,* 353–364.

Lippmann, W. *Public opinion.* New York: Macmillan, 1922.

Lipset, S. M. *Rebellion in the university.* Boston: Little, Brown, 1972.

Little, K. B. Personal space. *Journal of Experimental Social Psychology,* 1965, *1,* 237–247.

Lofland, J., & Stark, R. Becoming a world-saver: A theory of conversion to a deviant perspective. In B. McLaughlin (Ed.), *Studies in social movements.* New York: The Free Press, 1969.

Lofland, J. *Doomsday cult.* Englewood Cliffs, N.J.: Prentice-Hall, 1966.

Loomis, C. P. Informal social systems and decision making. In J. L. Moreno (Ed.), *The sociometry reader.* Glencoe, Ill.: The Free Press, 1960.

Lorge, I. Prestige, suggestion, and attitudes. *Journal of Social Psychology,* 1936, *7,* 386–402.

Lorge, I., & Solomon, H. Individual performance and group performance in problem solving related to group size and previous exposure to the problem. *Journal of Psychology,* 1959, *48,* 107–114.

Lott, A. J., & Lott, B. E. Group cohesiveness, communication level and conformity. *Journal of Abnormal and Social Psychology,* 1961, *62,* 408–412.

Lott, A. J., & Lott, B. E. Group cohesiveness as interpersonal attraction: A review of relationships with antecedent and consequent variables. *Psychological Bulletin,* 1965, *64,* 259–309.

Lott, B. E. Who wants children? Some relationships among attitudes toward children, parents, and the liberation of women. *American Psychologist,* 1973, *28,* 573–582.

Lott, D. F., & Sommer, R. Seating arrangements and status. *Journal of Personality and Social Psychology,* 1967, *7,* 90–95.

Lowin, A., Walsh, J. A., Klieger, D. M., Sandler, B., & Wilkes, R. L. Are there any lasting effects of a deceptive manipulation? Unpublished manuscript, State University of New York, Albany, 1968.

Luchins, A. S. Primacy-recency in impression formation. In C. I. Hovland (Ed.), *The order of presentation in persuasion.* New Haven, Conn.: Yale University Press, 1957. (a)

Luchins, A. S. Experimental attempts to minimize the impact of first impressions. In C. I. Hovland (Ed.), *The order of presentation in persuasion.* New Haven, Conn.: Yale University Press, 1957. (b)

Luchins, A., & Luchins, E. Focusing on the object of judgment in the social situation. *Journal of Social Psychology,* 1963, *60,* 273–287.

Lund, F. H. The psychology of belief. IV. The law of primacy in persuasion. *Journal of Abnormal and Social Psychology,* 1925, *20,* 183–191.

Macaulay, J., & Berkowitz, L. *Altruism and helping behavior: social psychological studies of some antecedents and consequences.* New York: Academic Press, 1970.

Macaulay, S., & Walster, E. Legal structures and restoring equity. *Journal of Social Issues,* 1971, *27,* 173–187.

Maccoby, E. Sex differences in intellectual functioning. In E. Maccoby (Ed.), *The development of sex differences.* Stanford: Stanford University Press, 1966.

Maccoby, E. (Ed.). *The development of sex differences.* Stanford: Stanford University Press, 1966.

Maciejko, J. S. The effects of size and regularity of concession on negotiation. Paper delivered to the annual meetings of the Eastern Psychological Association, 1972.

Mack, D. E. The power relationship in black families and white families. *Journal of Personality and Social Psychology,* 1974, *30,* 409–413.

MacKenzie, B. K. The importance of contact in determining attitudes toward Negroes. *Journal of Abnormal and Social Psychology,* 1948, *43,* 417–441.

MacKinnon, D. W. Personality and the realization of creative potential. *American psychologist,* 1965, *20,* 273–281.

Mallick, S. K., & McCandless, B. R. A study of catharsis of aggression. *Journal of Personality and Social Psychology,* 1966, *4,* 591–596.

Malof, M., & Lott, A. J. Ethnocentrism and the acceptance of Negro support in a group pressure situation. *Journal of Abnormal and Social Psychology,* 1962, *65,* 254–258.

Mandle, J. Women's liberation: Humanizing rather than polarizing. *Annals of the American Academy of Political and Social Science,* 1971, *397,* 118–128.

Mangelsdorff, S. D. The effects of inequity and incentive on the helping behavior of idealists and pragmatists. Unpublished Doctoral Dissertation, University of Delaware, 1973.

Manhoff, M., & Flacks, R. The changing social base of the American student movement. *Annals of the American Academy of Political and Social Science,* 1971, *395,* 54–67.

Mannheim, K. *Essays on the sociology of knowledge.* London: Routledge and Kegan Paul, 1952.

Mantell, D. The potential for violence in Germany. *Journal of Social Issues,* 1971, *27,* 100–112.

Marascuilo, L. A. Review of equality of educational opportunity. *American Sociological Review,* 1967, *32,* 479–480.

Marcuse, H. *Eros and civilization.* Boston: Beacon Press, 1955.

Marks, E. S. Standardization of a race attitude test for Negro youth. *Journal of Social Psychology,* 1943, *18,* 245–278.

Marquis, D. G., & Reitz, H. J. Effect of uncertainty on risk taking in individual and group decisions. *Behavioral Science,* 1969, *14,* 281–288.

Marshall, J. E., & Heslin, R. Boys and girls together: Sexual composition and the effect of density and group size on cohesiveness. *Journal of Personality and Social Psychology,* in press.

Marston, W. M. Studies in testimony. *Journal of Criminal Law and Criminology,* 1924, *15,* 5–31.

Martens, R. Palmar Sweating and the presence of an audience. *Journal of Experimental Social Psychology,* 1969, *5,* 371–374.

Martens, R., & Landers, D. M. Evaluation potential as a determinant of coaction effects. *Journal of Experimental Social Psychology,* 1972, *8,* 347–359.

Martindale, D. Territorial dominance behavior in dyadic verbal interactions. *Proceedings of the 79th Annual Convention of the American Psychological Association,* 1971, *6,* 305–306.

Masling, J. Role-related behavior of the subject and psychologist and its effects upon psychological data. *Nebraska Symposium on Motivation* (Vol. 14). Lincoln: University of Nebraska Press, 1966.

Maslow, A. H. A dynamic theory of human motivation. *Psychological Review,* 1943, *50,* 370–396.

Mason, W. A. Socially mediated reduction in emotional responses of young rhesus monkeys. *Journal of Abnormal and Social Psychology,* 1960, *60,* 100–104.

Mason, W. A. Sociability and social organization in monkeys and apes. In L. Berkowitz (Ed.), *Advances in experimental social psychology* (Vol. 1). New York: Academic Press, 1964.

Masserman, J. Debatable conclusions. *International Journal of Psychiatry,* 1968, *6,* 181–182.

Masters, W. H., & Johnson, V. E. *Human sexual response,* Boston: Little, Brown, 1966.

Mauss, M. *The gift: Forms and functions of exchange in archaic societies.* Glencoe, Ill.: The Free Press, 1954.

Mayeske, G. W., Okada, T., Wisler, C. E., Cohen, W. M., & Beaton, A. E., Jr. On the explanation of racial-ethnic group differences in achievement test scores. Paper read at the 79th Annual Convention, American Psychological Association, Washington, D. C., 1971.

McArthur, L. A., Kiesler, C. A., & Cook, B. P. Acting on an attitude as a function of self-percept and inequity. *Journal of Personality and Social Psychology,* 1969, *12,* 295–302.

McClelland, D. C. The uses of measures of human motivation in the study of society. In J. W. Atkinson (Ed.), *Motives in fantasy, action and society.* Princeton, N.J.: Van Nostrand, 1958.

McClelland, D. C. *The achieving society.* Princeton, N.J.: Van Nostrand, 1961.

McClelland, D. C., Atkinson, J. W., Clark, R. A., & Lowell, E. L. *The acheivement motive.* New York: Appleton-Century-Crofts, 1953.

McClelland, D. C., & Friedman, G. A. A cross-cultural study of the relationship between children-training practices and achievement motivation appearing in folk tales. In G. E. Swanson, T. M. Newcomb, & E. L. Hartley (Eds.), *Readings in social psychology.* New York: Holt, 1952.

McClintock, C. G. Where there is smoke, there's smoke. *Contemporary Psychology,* 1973, *18,* 261–262.

McClosky, H. Conservatism and personality. *American Political Science Review,* 1958, *52,* 27–45.

McDavid, J. W. The sex variable in conforming behavior. Office of Naval Research Contract ONR-4008 (08), Technical Report No. 8, 1965.

McDavid, J. W., & Harari, H. *Social psychology: Individuals, groups, societies.* New York: Harper & Row, 1968.

McDavid, J. W., & Sistrunk, F. Personality correlates of two kinds of conformity behavior. *Journal of Personality,* 1964, *32,* 421–435.

McDowell, K. V. Violations of personal space. *Canadian Journal of Behavioral Science,* 1972, *4,* 210–217.

McGinnies, E., & Ferster, C. B. (Eds.). *The reinforcement of social behavior.* Boston: Houghton Mifflin, 1971.

McGrath, J. E., & Altman, I. *Small group research: A synthesis and critique of the field.* New York: Holt, 1966.

McGuire, W. J. Inducing resistance to persuasion: Some contemporary approaches. In L. Berkowitz (Ed.), *Advances in experimental social psychology* (Vol. 1). New York: Academic Press, 1964.

McGuire, W. J. Some impending reorientations in social psychology: Some thoughts provoked by Kenneth Ring. *Journal of Experimental Social Psychology,* 1967, *3,* 124–139.

McGuire, W. J. Personality and susceptibility to social influence. In E. F. Borgatta & W. W. Lambert (Eds.), *Handbook of personality theory and research.* Chicago: Rand McNally, 1968.

McGuire, W. J. The nature of attitudes and attitude change. In G. Lindzey & E. Aronson (Eds.), *The handbook of social psychology* (Vol. 3, 2nd ed.). Reading, Mass.: Addison-Wesley, 1969. (a)

McGuire, W. J. Suspiciousness of experimenter's intent. In R. Rosenthal & R. L. Rosnow (Eds.), *Artifact in behavioral research.* New York: Academic Press, 1969. (b)

McGuire, W. J. Attitude change: The information-processing paradigm. In C. G. McClintock (Ed.), *Experimental Social Psychology.* New York: Holt, Rinehart and Winston, 1972.

McGuire, W. J. The yin and yang of progress in social psychology: Seven koan. *Journal of Personality and Social Psychology,* 1973, *26,* 446–456.

McHugh, P. *Defining the situation: The organization of meaning in social interaction.* New York: Bobbs-Merrill, 1968.

McIntyre, A. Sex differences in children's aggression. *Proceedings of the 80th Annual Convention of the American Psychological Association,* 1972.

McKee, J. P., & Sherriffs, A. C. The differential evaluation of males and females. *Journal of Personality,* 1957, *25,* 356–371.

McLaughlin, B. (Ed.). *Studies in social movements.* New York: The Free Press, 1969.

McNemar, Q. Opinion-attitude methodology, *Psychological Bulletin,* 1946, *43,* 289–374.

McPartland, J. The relative influence of school and of classroom desegregation on the academic achievement of ninth-grade Negro students. *Journal of Social Issues,* 1969, *25*(3), 93–102.

McQuitty, L. L. Theories and methods in some objective assessments of psychological well-being. *Psychological Monographs,* 1954, *68,* No. 14 (Whole No. 385).

Mead, G. H. *Mind, self and society from the standpoint of a social behaviorist.* Chicago: University of Chicago Press, 1934.

Mead, G. H. *The philosophy of the act.* Chicago: University of Chicago Press, 1938.

Mead, M. *Sex and temperament.* New York: Morrow, 1935.

Mead, M. *Male and female.* New York: Morrow, 1967.

Menges, R. J. Openness and honesty versus coercion and deception in psychological research. *American Psychologist,* 1973, *28,* 1030–1034.

Merton, R. K. *Social theory and social structure* (Rev. ed.). New York: The Free Press, 1957.

Messick, S. J., & Kogan, N. Personality consistencies in judgment: Dimensions of role constructs. *Multivariate Behavioral Research,* 1966, *1,* 165–175.

Meumann, E. *Haus-und Schularbeit,* 1914. Cited in G. Murphy and L. B. Murphey, *Experimental social psychology.* New York: Harper, 1931.

Michels, R. *Political parties.* New York: Dover, 1959.

Michener, H. A., & Suchner, R. W. The tactical use of social power. In J. T. Tedeschi (Ed.), *The social influence process.* Chicago: Aldine-Atherton, 1972.

Middlebrook, P. N. *Social psychology and modern life.* New York: Knopf, 1974.

Milgram, S. Nationality and conformity. *Scientific American,* 1961, *205,* 45–51.

Milgram, S. Behavioral studies of obedience. *Journal of Abnormal and Social Psychology,* 1963, *67,* 371–378.

Milgram, S. Group pressure and action against a person. *Journal of Abnormal and Social Psychology,* 1964, *69,* 137–143.

Milgram, S. Liberating effects of group pressure. *Journal of Personality and Social Psychology,* 1965, *1,* 127–134. (a)

Milgram, S. Some conditions of obedience and disobedience to authority. *Human Relations,* 1965, *18,* 57–76. (b)

Milgram, S. Interpreting obedience: Error and evidence. A reply to Orne and Holland. In A. G. Miller (Ed.), *The social psychology of psychological research.* New York: Free Press, 1972.

Milgram, S. *Obedience to authority: An experimental view.* New York: Harper and Row, 1974.

Miller, A. G. Role playing: An alternative to deception? A review of the evidence. *American Psychologist,* 1972, *27,* 623–636.

Miller, G. A. *Psychology: The science of mental life.* New York: Harper and Row, 1962.

Miller, N. E. The frustration-aggression hypothesis. *Psychological Review,* 1941, *48,* 337–342.

Miller, N. E. Theory and experiment relating psychoanalytical displacement to stimulus–response generalization. *Journal of Abnormal and Social Psychology,* 1948, *43,* 155–178.

Miller, S. M., Riessman, F., & Segull, A. A. Poverty and self-indulgence: A critique of the non-deferred gratification pattern. In L. Ferman, J. Kornbluh, & A. Haber (Eds.), *Poverty in America.* Ann Arbor: University of Michigan Press, 1965.

Mills, J. Changes in moral attitudes following temptation. *Journal of Personality,* 1958, *26,* 517–531.

Milton, G. A. The effects of sex-role identity upon problem-solving skills. *Journal of Abnormal and Social Psychology,* 1957, *55,* 208–212.

Minor, M. W. Experimenter-expectancy effect as a function of evaluation apprehension. *Journal of Personality and Social Psychology,* 1970, *15,* 326–332.

Mischel, W. Father-absence and delay of gratification: Cross-cultural comparisons. *Journal of Abnormal and Social Psychology,* 1961, *63,* 116–124.

Mischel, W. *Personality and assessment.* New York: Wiley, 1968.

Mischel, W. Toward a cognitive social learning reconceptualization of personality. *Psychological Review,* 1973, *80,* 252–283.

Mixon, D. Behavior analysis treating subjects as actors rather than organisms. *Journal for the Theory of Social Behavior,* 1971, *1,* 19–31.

Mixon, D. Instead of deception. *Journal for the Theory of Social Behavior,* 1972, *2,* 145–177.

Moede, W. *Experimentelle massenpsychologie.* Leipzig: S. Hirzel, 1920.

Mogy, R. B., and Pruitt, D. G. The effects of a threatener's enforcement costs on threat credibility and compliance. *Journal of Personality and Social Psychology,* 1974, *29,* 173–180.

Moles, O. C. Child-training practices among low-income families. *Welfare in Review,* 1965, *3* (12), 1–19.

Moles, O. C. The relationship of family circumstances and personal history to use of public assistance. *Social Work,* 1971, *16* (2), 37–46.

Moore, O. K., & Anderson, S. B. Search behavior in individual and group problem solving. *American Sociological Review,* 1954, *19,* 702–714.

Moos, R. H. Sources of variance in responses to questionnaires and in behavior. *Journal of Abnormal Psychology,* 1969, *74,* 405–412.

Moos, R. H., & Spiesman, J. C. Group compatibility

and productivity. *Journal of Abnormal and Social Psychology,* 1962, *65,* 190–196.

Morgan, W. R., & Sawyer, J. Bargaining expectations, and the preference for equality of equity. *Journal of Personality and Social Psychology,* 1967, *6,* 139–149.

Morley, I. E., & Stephenson, G. M. Interpersonal and inter-party exchange: A laboratory simulation of an industrial negotiation at the plant level. *British Journal of Psychology,* 1969, *60,* 543–545.

Morley, I. E., and Stephenson, G. M. Formality in experimental negotiations: A validation study. *British Journal of Psychology,* 1970, *61,* 383–384.

Morse, N. C., & Riemer, E. The experimental change of a major organizational variable. *Journal of Abnormal and Social Psychology,* 1956, *52,* 120–129.

Moscovici, S., & Faucheux, C. Social influence, conformity bias, and the study of active minorities. In L. Berkowitz (Ed.), *Advances in experimental social psychology* (Vol. 6). New York: Academic Press, 1972.

Mosteller, F., & Moynihan, D. P. (Eds.). On *equality of educational opportunity.* New York: Random House, 1972. (a)

Mosteller, F., & Moynihan, D. P. A pathbreaking report. In F. Mosteller & D. P. Moynihan (Eds.), *On equality of educational opportunity.* New York: Random House, 1972. (b)

Mowrer, O. H. *Learning theory and personality dynamics: Selected papers.* New York: Ronald Press, 1950.

Moynihan, D. P. *The Negro family: The case for national action.* Washington, D.C.: U.S. Department of Labor, Office of Policy Planning and Research, 1965.

Mulder, M., & Stemerding, A. Threat, attraction to group and need for strong leadership. *Human Relations,* 1963, *16,* 317–334.

Mulder, M., and Wilke, H. Participation and power equalization. *Organizational Behavior and Human Performance,* 1970, *5,* 430–448.

Murdoch, P. Development of contractual norms in a dyad. *Journal of Personality and Social Psychology,* 1967, *6,* 206–211.

Murdoch, P., and Rosen, D. Norm formation in an interdependent dyad. *Sociometry,* 1970, *33,* 264–275.

Murstein, B. I. The relationship of mental health to marital choice and courtship progress. *Journal of Marriage and the Family,* 1967, *29,* 447–451.

Mussen, P. Early socialization: Learning and identification. In T. Newcomb (Ed.), *New directions in psychology III.* New York: Holt, Rinehart and Winston, 1967.

Myrdal, G. *An American dilemma.* New York: Harper & Row, 1944.

Neel, J. V. Lessons from a primitive people. *Science,* 1970, *170,* 815–822.

Nelson, E. Attitudes: I. Their nature and development. *The Journal of General Psychology,* 1939, *21,* 367–399.

Nemeth, C. A critical analysis of research utilizing the prisoner's dilemma paradigm for the study of bargaining. In L. Berkowitz (Ed.), *Advances in experimental social psychology* (Vol. 6). New York: Academic Press, 1972.

Newcomb, T. M. Autistic hostility and social reality. *Human Relations,* 1947, *1,* 69–86.

Newcomb, T. M. *The acquaintance process.* New York: Holt, Rinehart and Winston, 1961.

Newcomb, T. M. Attitude development as a function of reference groups: The Bennington study. In H. Proshansky and B. Seidenberg (Eds.), *Basic Studies in Social Psychology.* New York: Holt, Rinehart and Winston, 1965.

Nord, W. R. Social exchange theory: An integrative approach to social conformity. *Psychological Bulletin.* 1969, *71,* 174–208.

Nucci, L. The development of the hippie personality. Unpublished paper, University of California, Santa Cruz, 1974.

Nunnally, J. C. *Psychometric theory.* New York: McGraw-Hill, 1967.

Oliver, D. L. *A Solomon Island society.* Boston: Beacon Press, 1967.

Orne, M. T. On the social psychology of the psychological experiment: With particular reference to demand characteristics and their implications. *American Psychologist,* 1962, *17,* 776–783.

Orne, M. T. Demand characteristics and the concept of quasi-controls. In R. Rosenthal & R. L. Rosnow (Eds.), *Artifact in behavioral research.* New York: Academic Press, 1969.

Orne, M. T. Hypnosis, motivation, and the ecological validity of the psychological experiment. In W.

J. Arnold & M. M. Page (Eds.), *Nebraska Symposium on Motivation* (Vol. 18). Lincoln: University of Nebraska Press, 1970.

Orne, M. T., & Holland, C. H. On the ecological validity of laboratory deceptions. *International Journal of Psychiatry*, 1968, *6*, 282–293.

Orwell, G. *1984*. New York: Harcourt, Brace, 1949.

Osborn, A. F. *Applied imagination*. New York: Scribner's, 1957.

Osgood, C. E., Suci, G. J., & Tannenbaum, P. H. *The measurement of meaning*. Urbana: University of Illinois Press, 1957.

Osgood, C. E., & Tannenbaum, P. H. The principle of congruity in the prediction of attitude change. *Psychological Review*, 1955, *62*, 42–55.

Ostrom, T. M. The emergence of attitude theory: 1930–1950. In A. G. Greenwald, T. C. Brock, & T. M. Ostrom (Eds.), *Psychological foundations of attitudes*. New York: Academic Press, 1968.

Ostrom, T. M. The relationship between the affective, behavioral, and cognitive components of attitude. *Journal of Experimental Social Psychology*. 1969, *5*, 12–30.

Packard, V. O. *The status seekers*. New York: McKay, 1959.

Page, M. M. Demand characteristics and the verbal operant conditioning experiment. *Journal of Personality and Social Psychology*, 1972, *23*, 372–378.

Page, M., & Scheidt. R. The elusive weapons effect: Demand awareness, evaluation apprehension, and slightly sophisticated subjects. *Journal of Personality and Social Psychology*, 1971, *20*, 304–318.

Parry, H., & Crossley, H. Validity of response to survey questions. *Public Opinion Quarterly*, 1950, *14*, 61–80.

Parsons, T., and Platt, G. M. *The American university*. Cambridge, Mass.: Harvard University Press, 1973.

Passini, F. T., & Norman, W. T. A universal conception of personality structure? *Journal of Personality and Social Psychology*, 1966, *4*, 44–49.

Paulus, P. B., & Murdoch, P. Anticipated evaluation and audience presence in the enhancement of dominant responses. *Journal of Experimental Social Psychology*, 1971, *7*, 280–291.

Pawlicki, R. E., & Almquist, C. Authoritarianism, locus of control, and tolerance of ambiguity as reflected in membership and nonmembership in a women's liberation group. *Psychological Reports*, 1973, *32*, 1331–1337.

Peak, H. Attitude and motivation. In M. R. Jones (Ed.), *Nebraska Symposium on Motivation* (Vol. 3). Lincoln: University of Nebraska Press, 1955.

Pearson, K., & Lee, A. On the laws of inheritance in man: I. Inheritance of Physical characters. *Biometrika*, 1903, *2*, 372–377.

Perlmutter, H. V., & De Montmollin, G. Group learning of nonsense syllables. *Journal of Abnormal and Social Psychology*, 1952, *47*, 762–769.

Perls, F. *Gestalt therapy verbatim*. Lafayette, Calif.: Real People Press, 1969.

Perry, P. K. Election survey procedures for the Gallup Poll. *Public Opinion Quarterly*, 1960, *24*, 529–542.

Pessin, J. The comparative effects of social and mechanical stimulation on memorizing. *American Journal of Psychology*, 1933, *45*, 263–270.

Pessin, J., & Husband, R. W. Effects of social stimulation on human maze learning. *Journal of Abnormal and Social Psychology*. 1933, *28*, 148–154.

Pettigrew, T. F. *The profile of the American Negro*. Princeton, N.J.: Van Nostrand, 1964.

Pettigrew, T. F. Racially separate or together? *Journal of Social Issues*, 1969, *25* (1), 43–69.

Pfautz, H. W. Review of Equality of Educational Opportunity. *American Sociological Review*, 1967, *32*, 481–483.

Pfuetze, P. E. *Self, society, existence, human nature and dialogue in the thought of George Herbert Mead and Martin Buber*. New York: Harper, 1954.

Phares, E. J. Internal-external control as a determinant of amount of social influence exerted. *Journal of Personality and Social Psychology*, 1965, *2*, 642–647.

Piaget, J. *The moral judgment of the child*. London: Routledge & Kegan Paul, 1932.

Piaget, J. *The origins of intelligence in children*. New York: International Universities Press, 1952.

Piliavin, I. M., Rodin, J., and Piliavin, J. A. Good Samaritanism: An underground phenomenon? *Journal of Personality and Social Psychology*, 1969, *13*, 289–299.

Piliavin, I. M., & Scott, B. Police encounters with

juveniles, *American Journal of Sociology,* 1964, *70,* 206–214.

Piliavin, J. A. and Piliavin, I. M. Effects of blood on reactions to a victim. *Journal of Personality and Social Psychology,* 1972, *23,* 353–361.

Podell, L. *Fertility, illegitimacy, and birth control.* Preliminary Report Number 6. New York: Center for Social Research, City University of New York, 1968.

Poppleton, P. K., & Pilkington, G. W. A comparison of four methods of scoring an attitude scale in relation to its reliability and validity. *British Journal of Social and Clinical Psychology,* 1963, *3,* 36–39.

Porter, L., & Lawler, E., III. Properties of organization structure in relation to job attitudes and job behavior. *Psychological Bulletin,* 1965, *64,* 23–51.

Preston, M. G., & Heintz, R. K. Effects of participatory vs. supervisory leadership on group judgment. *Journal of Abnormal and Social Psychology,* 1949, *44,* 345–355.

Pruitt, D. G. Definition of the situation as a determinant of international action. In H. C. Kelman (Ed.), *International behavior: A social-psychological analysis.* New York: Holt, Rinehart and Winston, 1965.

Pruitt, D. G. Reciprocity and credit building in a laboratory dyad. *Journal of Personality and Social Psychology,* 1968, *8,* 143–147.

Pruitt, D. G. Choice shifts in group discussion: An introductory review. *Journal of Personality and Social Psychology,* 1971, *20,* 339–360. (a)

Pruitt, D. G. Indirect communication and the search for agreement in negotiation. *Journal of Applied Social Psychology,* 1971, *1,* 205–239. (b)

Pruitt, D. G. Methods for resolving differences of interest: A theoretical analysis. *Journal of Social Issues,* 1972, *28,* 133–154.

Pruitt, D. G., & Drews, J. L. The effect of time pressure, time elapsed, and the opponent's concession rate on behavior in negotiation. *Journal of Experimental Social Psychology,* 1969, *5,* 43–60.

Pruitt, D. G., & Johnson, D. F. Mediation as an aid to face saving in negotiation. *Journal of Personality and Social Psychology,* 1970, *14,* 239–246.

Pruitt, D. G., & Lewis, S. A. Development of integrative solutions in bilateral negotiation. *Journal of Personality and Social Psychology,* 1975, *31,* 621–633.

Raab, E. Toward the prevention of dependency. In *First Annual Report.* Sacramento, California: State Social Welfare Board, Department of Welfare, 1965.

Rabbie, J. M., Benoist, F., Oosterbaan, H., & Visser, L. Differential power and effects of expected competitive and cooperative intergroup interactions on intragroup and outgroup attitudes. *Journal of Personality and Social Psychology,* 1973, *30,* 46–56.

Rainwater, L. Crucible of identity: The Negro lower-class family. *Daedalus,* 1966, *95* (1), 172–216.

Rapoport, A. *Two-person game theory: The essential ideas.* Ann Arbor, Mich.: University of Michigan Press, 1966.

Raven, B. H. Social influence and power. In I. D. Steiner & M. Fishbein (Eds.), *Current studies in social psychology.* New York: Holt, Rinehart and Winston, 1965.

Raven, B. H., & French, J. R. P. Legitimate power, coercive power and observability in social influence. *Sociometry,* 1958, *21,* 83–97.

Raven, B. H., & Kruglanski, A. W. Conflict and power. In P. Swingle (Ed.), *The structure of conflict.* New York: Academic Press, 1970.

Raven, B. H., & Rietsema, J. The effect of varied clarity of group goal and group path upon the individual and his relation to his group. *Human Relations,* 1957, *10,* 29–44.

Reckman, R. F., & Goethals, G. R. Deviancy and group orientation as determinants of group composition preferences. *Sociometry,* 1973, *36,* 419–423.

Reed, E. W., & Reed, S. C. *Mental retardation: A family study.* Philadelphia: W. B. Saunders Co., 1965.

Reich, C. A. *The greening of America.* New York: Random House, 1970.

Rein, M., & Wishnov, B. Patterns of work and welfare in AFDC. *Welfare in Review,* 1971, *9*(6), 7–12.

Reitan, H. T., & Shaw, M. E. Group membership, sex-composition of the group and conformity behavior. *Journal of Social Psychology,* 1964, *64,* 45–51.

Resnick, J. H., & Schwartz, T. Ethical standards as

an independent variable in psychological research. *American Psychologist,* 1973, *28,* 134–139.

Riesman, D. *The lonely crowd.* New Haven, Conn.: Yale University Press, 1950.

Ring, K. Experimental social psychology: Some sober questions about some frivolous values. *Journal of Experimental Social Psychology,* 1967, *3,* 113–123.

Ring, K., & Kelley, H. H. A comparison of augmentation and reduction as modes of influence. *Journal of Abnormal and Social Psychology,* 1963, *66,* 95–102.

Ring, K., Wallston, K., & Corey, M. Mode of debriefing as a factor affecting subjective reaction to a Milgram-type obedience experiment: An ethical inquiry. *Representative Research in Social Psychology,* 1970, *1,* 67–88.

Roach, J. L., & Gursslin, O. R. An evaluation of the concept "culture of poverty." *Social Forces,* 1967, *45,* 383–392.

Robinson, J. P., Rusk, J. G., & Head, K. B. *Measure of political attitudes.* Survey Research Center, Institute for Social Research, 1968.

Robinson, J. P., & Shaver, P. R., *Measures of social psychological attitudes.* Survey Research Center, Institute for Social Research, 1969.

Rodman, H. Middle-class misconceptions about lower-class families. In A. B. Shostak & W. Gomberg (Eds.), *Blue-collar world: Studies of the American worker.* Englewood Cliffs, New Jersey: Prentice Hall, 1964.

Rokeach, M. *The open and closed mind.* New York: Basic Books, 1960.

Rokeach, M. Attitude change and behavior change. *Public Opinion Quarterly,* 1967, *30,* 529–550.

Rokeach, M. *Beliefs, attitudes, and values.* San Francisco: Jossey-Bass, 1969.

Rokeach, M., & Kliejunas, P. Behavior as a function of attitude-toward-object and attitude-toward-situation. *Journal of Personality and Social Psychology.* 1972, *22,* 194–201.

Rokeach, M., & Mezei, L. Race and shared belief as factors in social choice. *Science,* 1966, *151,* 167–172.

Rose, A. M. *Studies in reduction of prejudice.* American Council on Race Relations, 1948.

Rosen, B. C. Family structure and achievement motivation. *American Sociological Review,* 1961, *26,* 574–585.

Rosenberg, M. J. Cognitive reorganization in response to the hypnotic reversal of attitudinal affect. *Journal of Personality,* 1960, *28,* 39–63.

Rosenberg, M. J. When dissonance fails: On eliminating evaluation apprehension from attitude measurement. *Journal of Personality and Social Psychology,* 1965, *1,* 28–42.

Rosenberg, M. J. Psychological selectivity in self-esteem formation. In C. W. Sherif and M. Sherif (Eds.), *Attitude, ego-involvement, and change.* New York: Wiley and Sons, 1967.

Rosenberg, M. J. The conditions and consequences of evaluation apprehension, In R. Rosenthal and R. L. Rosnow (Eds.), *Artifact in behavioral research.* New York: Academic Press, 1969.

Rosenberg, M. J., & Abelson, R. P. An analysis of cognitive balancing. In M. J. Rosenberg, C. I. Hovland, W. J. McGuire, R. P. Abelson, & J. W. Brehm (Eds.), *Attitude organization and change.* New Haven, Connecticut: Yale University Press, 1960.

Rosenberg, M. J., Verba, S., & Converse, P. E. *Vietnam and the silent majority: The dove's guide.* New York: Harper & Row, 1970.

Rosenberg, S., & Olshan, K. Evaluative and descriptive aspects in personality perception. *Journal of Personality and Social Psychology,* 1970, *16,* 619–626.

Rosenhan, D. On being sane in insane places. *Science,* 1973, *179,* 1–9.

Rosenthal, R. *Experimenter effects in behavioral research.* New York: Appleton-Century-Crofts, 1966.

Rosenthal, R. Covert communication in the psychological experiment. *Psychological Bulletin,* 1967, *67,* 356–367.

Rosenthal, R. Experimenter expectancy and the reassuring nature of the null hypothesis decision procedure. *Psychological Bulletin,* 1968, *70* (6, Pt. 2), 30–47.

Rosenthal, R. Interpersonal expectations: Effects of the experimenter's hypothesis. In R. Rosenthal and R. L. Rosnow (Eds.), *Artifact in behavioral research.* New York: Academic Press, 1969.

Rosenthal, R. *On the social psychology of the self-fulfilling prophecy: Further evidence for Pygmali-*

on effects and their mediating mechanisms. New York: MSS Modular Publications, Inc., 1974. Mod. 53, 1–28.

Rosenthal, R., & Jacobson, L. *Pygmalion in the classroom: Teacher expectation and pupils' intellectual development*. New York: Holt, Rinehart, and Winston, 1968.

Rosenthal, R., Persinger, G. W., Vikan-Kline, L. L., & Mulry, R. C. The role of the research assistant in the mediation of experimenter bias. *Journal of Personality*, 1963, *31*, 313–335.

Rosenthal, R., & Rosnow, R. L. The volunteer subject. In R. Rosenthal and R. L. Rosnow (Eds.), *Artifact in behavioral research*. New York: Academic Press, 1969.

Rosenzweig, S. The experimental situation as a psychological problem. *Psychological Review*, 1933, *40*, 337–354.

Rosnow, R. L., & Aiken, L. S. Mediation of artifacts in behavioral research. *Journal of Experimental Social Psychology*, 1973, *9*, 181–201.

Ross, L. D., & Amabile, T. Investigations in the psychology of prediction. Unpublished manuscript. Stanford University, 1974.

Ross, L. D., Rodin, J., & Zimbardo, P. G. Toward an attribution therapy: The reduction of fear through induced cognitive-emotional misattribution. *Journal of Personality and Social Psychology*, 1969, *12*, 279–288.

Ross, M., & Shulman, R. F. Increasing the salience of initial attitude: Dissonance versus self-perception theory. *Journal of Personality and Social Psychology*, 1973, *28*, 138–144.

Roszak, T., *The making of a counter culture*. Garden City, N.Y.: Anchor Books, Doubleday and Co., 1969.

Rotter, J. B. Generalized expectancies for internal versus external control of reinforcement. *Psychological Monographs*, 1966, *80*, 1–28.

Rotter, J. B. Beliefs, social attitudes and behavior: A social learning analysis. In R. Jessor & S. Feshbach (Eds.), *Cognition, personality and clinical psychology*. San Francisco: Jossey-Bass, 1967.

Rubin, Z. Measurement of romantic love. *Journal of Personality and Social Psychology*, 1970, *2*, 265–273.

Rubin, Z. *Liking and loving: An invitation to social psychology*. New York: Holt, Rinehart, and Winston, 1973.

Rubovits, P. C., & Maehr, M. L. Pygmalion analyzed: Toward an explanation of the Rosenthal-Jacobson findings. *Journal of Personality and Social Psychology*, 1971, *19*, 197–203.

Rubovits, P. C., & Maehr, M. L. Pygmalion black and white. *Journal of Personality and Social Psychology*, 1973, *25*, 210–218.

Rychman, R. M., Martens, J. L., Rodda, W. C., & Sherman, M. F. Locus of control and attitudes toward Women's Liberation in a college population. *Journal of Social Psychology*, 1972, *87*, 157–158.

Saegert, S., Swap, W., & Zajonc, R. B. Exposure, context, and interpersonal attraction. *Journal of Personality and Social Psychology*, 1973, *25*, 234–242.

Saenger, G., & Gilbert, E. Customer reactions to the integration of Negro sales personnel. *International Journal of Opinion and Attitude Research*, 1950, *4*, 57–76.

Sample, J., & Warland R. Attitude and prediction of behavior. *Social Force*, 1973, *51*, 292–304.

Sampson, E. E. Birth order, need achievement and conformity. *Journal of Abnormal and Social Psychology*, 1962, *64*, 155–159.

Sampson, R. V. *The psychology of power*. New York: Vintage Books, 1968.

Sanford, F. H. *Authoritarianism and leadership*. Philadelphia: Institute for Research in Human Relations, 1950.

Sanger, S. P., & Alker, H. A. Dimensions of internal-external locus of control and the Women's Liberation Movement. *Journal of Social Issues*, 1972, *28*, 115–129.

Sarbin, T. R., & Allen, V. L. Role theory. In G. Lindzey & E. Aronson (Eds.), *Handbook of social psychology* (Vol 2, 2nd ed.). Cambridge, Mass.: Addison-Wesley, 1968.

Sarbin, T. R., & Coe, W. C. *Hypnosis: A social psychological analysis of influence communication*. New York: Holt, Rinehart, and Winston, 1972.

Sarnoff, I. Psychoanalytic theory and social attitudes. *Public Opinion Quarterly*, 1960, *24*, 251–279.

Sarnoff, I., & Katz, D. The motivational basis of attitude change. *Journal of Abnormal and Social Psychology,* 1954, *49,* 115–124.

Sarnoff, I., & Zimbardo, P. G. Anxiety, fear, and social affiliation. *Journal of Abnormal and Social Psychology,* 1961, *62,* 356–363.

Schachter, S. Deviation, rejection, and communication. *Journal of Abnormal and Social Psychology,* 1951, *46,* 190–207.

Schachter, S. *The psychology of affiliation.* Stanford, Calif.: Stanford University Press, 1959.

Schachter, S. Birth order, eminence and higher education. *American Sociological Review,* 1963, *28,* 5, 757–768.

Schachter, S. *Emotion, obesity and crime.* New York: Academic Press, 1971.

Schachter, S., Ellertson, N., McBride, D., & Gregory, D. An experimental study of cohesiveness and productivity. *Human Relations,* 1951, *4,* 229–238.

Schachter, S., Goldman, R., & Gordon, A. The effects of fear, food deprivation, and obesity on eating. *Journal of Personality and Social Psychology,* 1968, *10,* 91–97.

Schachter, S., & Gross, L. Manipulated time and eating behavior. *Journal of Personality and Social Psychology,* 1968, *10,* 98–106.

Schachter, S., & Singer, J. Cognitive, social, and physiological determinants of emotional state. *Psychological Review,* 1962, *69,* 379–399.

Schafer, S. *Restitution to Victims of Crime.* London: Stevens & Sons, Ltd., 1960.

Scheflin, A. E. Living space in an urban ghetto. *Family Process,* 1971, *10,* 429–450.

Scheflin, A. E. *Communicational structure: Analysis of a psychotherapy transaction.* Bloomington: Indiana University Press, 1973.

Scheibe, K. E. *Beliefs and values.* New York: Holt, Rinehart & Winston, 1970.

Schelling, T. C. *The strategy of conflict.* Cambridge, Mass.: Harvard University Press, 1960.

Schlenker, B. R. Social psychology and science. *Journal of Personality and Social Psychology,* 1974, *29,* 1–15.

Schmitt, D. R., & Marwell, G. Cooperation and inequity: Behavioral effects. (Unpublished manuscript), *1970.*

Schneider, D. J. Implicit personality theory: A review. *Psychological Bulletin,* 1973, *79,* 294–309.

Schoeninger, D. W., & Wood, W. D. Comparison of married and ad hoc mixed-sex dyads negotiating the division of a reward. *Journal of Experimental Social Psychology,* 1969, *5,* 483–499.

Schooler, C. Childhood family structure and adult characteristics. *Sociometry,* 1972, *35,* 255–269.

Schopler, J. Social power. In L. Berkowitz (Ed.), *Advances in experimental social psychology* (Vol. 2). New York: Academic Press, 1965.

Schrag, C. Leadership among prison inmates. *American Sociological Review,* 1954, *19,* 37–42.

Schuck, J., & Pisor, K. Evaluating an aggression experiment by the use of simulating subjects. *Journal of Personality and Social Psychology,* 1974, *29,* 181–186.

Schultz, D. P. The human subject in psychological research. *Psychological Bulletin,* 1969, *72,* 214–228.

Schuman, H. Attitudes vs. actions versus attitudes vs. attitudes. *Public Opinion Quarterly,* 1972, *36,* 347–354.

Schuman, H., & Harding, J. Prejudice and the norm of rationality. *Sociometry,* 1964, *27,* 353–371.

Schuman, H., & Hatchett, S. *Black racial attitudes: Trends and complexities.* Ann Arbor, Michigan, Institute for Social Research, 1974.

Schutz, W. C. *FIRO: A three-dimensional theory of interpersonal behavior.* New York: Rinehart, 1958.

Schutz, W. C. *Joy.* New York: Grove Press, 1967.

Scott, E. L. *Perceptions of organization and leadership behavior.* Columbus: Ohio State University Research Foundation, 1952.

Scott, W. A. Measures of cognitive structure. *Multivariate Behavioral Research,* 1966, *1,* 391–395.

Scott, W. A. Attitude measurement. In G. Lindzey and E. Aronson, (Eds.), *The handbook of social psychology* (Vol. 2, 2nd ed.). Addison-Wesley, 1969.

Sears, R. R., Maccoby, E., & Levin, H. *Patterns of child rearing.* Evanston, Ill.: Row, Peterson, 1957.

Sechrest, L. Situational sampling and contrived situations in the assessment of behavior. Unpublished manuscript, Northwestern University, 1965 (Mimeo).

Secord, P. F., & Backman, C. W. Personality theory and the problem of stability and change in individual behavior: An interpersonal approach. *Psychological Review,* 1961, *68,* 21–32.

Selcer, R. J., & Hilton, I. Cultural differences in the acquisition of sex roles. Paper presented at the American Psychological Association Meetings, Honolulu, Hawaii, 1972.

Sewell, W. H. Review of *Equality of Educational Opportunity. American Sociological Review,* 1967, *32,* 475–479.

Shannon, J., & Guerney, B., Jr. Interpersonal effects of interpersonal behavior. *Journal of Personality and Social Psychology,* 1973, *26,* 142–150.

Shaw, G. B. *Androcles and the lion.* Baltimore: Penguin Books, 1962.

Shaw, M. E. A comparison of individuals and small groups in the rational solution of complex problems. *American Journal of Psychology,* 1932, *44,* 491–504.

Shaw, M. E. A comparison of two types of leadership in various communication nets. *Journal of Abnormal and Social Psychology,* 1955, *50,* 127–134.

Shaw, M. E. Communication networks. In L. Berkowitz (Ed.), *Advances in experimental social psychology* (Vol. 1). New York: Academic Press, 1964.

Shaw, M. E. *Group dynamics: The psychology of small group behavior.* New York: McGraw-Hill, 1971.

Shaw, M. E. Changes in sociometric choices following forced integration of an elementary school. *Journal of Social Issues,* 1973, *29* (4), 143–158.

Shaw, M. E., & Blum, J. M. Effects of leadership style upon group performance as a function of task structure. *Journal of Personality and Social Psychology.* 1966, *3,* 238–241.

Shaw, M. E., & Costanza, P. R. *Theories of social psychology.* New York: McGraw-Hill, 1970.

Sherif, M. A study of some social factors in perception. *Archives of Psychology,* 1935, *27,* No. 187, 1–60.

Sherif, M. *The psychology of social norms.* New York: Harper, 1936.

Sherif, M. On the relevance of social psychology. *American Psychologist,* 1970, *25,* 144–156.

Sherif, M., Harvey, O. J., White, B. J., Hood, W. R., & Sherif, C. W. *Intergroup conflict and cooperation: The robbers cave experiment.* Norman. University of Oklahoma Book Exchange, 1961.

Sherif, M., & Hovland, C. I. *Social judgment, assimilation and contrast effects in communication and attitude change.* New Haven, Conn.: Yale University Press, 1961.

Sherif, M. & Sherif, C. W. *Social psychology.* New York: Harper and Row, 1969.

Shomer, R. W., & Centers, R. Differences in attitudinal responses under conditions of implicitly manipulated group salience. *Journal of Personality and Social Psychology,* 1970, *15,* 125–132.

Siegel, S., & Fouraker, L. E. *Bargaining and group decision making.* New York: McGraw-Hill, 1960.

Sigall, H., Aronson, E., & Van Hoose, T. The cooperative subject: Myth or reality? *Journal of Experimental Social Psychology,* 1970, *6,* 1–10.

Silverman, I. Role related behavior of subjects in laboratory studies of attitude change. *Journal of Personality and Social Psychology,* 1968, *8,* 343–348.

Silverman, I., & Shaw, M. E. Effects of sudden mass school desegregation on interracial interaction and attitudes in one Southern city. *Journal of Social Issues,* 1973, *29* (4), 133–142.

Silverman, I., & Shulman, A. D. A conceptual model of artifact in attitude change studies. *Sociometry,* 1970, *33,* 97–107.

Simmel, G. In K. H. Wolff (Trans.), *The Sociology of Georg Simmel.* Glencoe, Ill.: The Free Press, 1950.

Simon, C., & Trout, C. Hippies in college—from teeny-boppers to drug freaks. *Transaction,* 1967, *5,* 27–34.

Sistrunk, F., & McDavid, J. W. Sex variable in conforming behavior. *Journal of Personality and Social Psychology,* 1971, *17,* 200–207.

Sizer, N. F., & Sizer, T. R. Introduction. In J. M. Gustafson et al. (Eds.), *Moral education.* Cambridge: Harvard University Press, 1970.

Skinner, B. F. *Walden two.* New York: Macmillan, 1948.

Skinner, B. F. *Science and human behavior.* New York: Macmillan, 1953.

Skinner, B. F. *Beyond freedom and dignity.* New York: Knopf, 1971.

Sklar, J., & Berkov, B. The effects of legal abortion

on legitimate and illigitimate birth rates: The California experience. *Studies in Family Planning,* 1973, *4,* 281–292.

Sklar, J. & Berkov, B. Abortion, illegitimacy, and the American birth rate. *Science,* 1974, *185,* 909–915.

Slater, P. E. Contrasting correlates of group size. *Sociometry,* 1958, *21,* 129–139.

Slater, P. E. *The pursuit of loneliness: American culture at the breaking point.* Boston: Beacon Press, 1970.

Sletto, R. F. *Construction of personality scales by the criterion of internal consistency.* Minneapolis: Sociology Press, 1937.

Smelsor, W. T. Personality influences in social situations. *Journal of Abnormal and Social Psychology,* 1961, *62,* 535–542.

Smith, M. B., Bruner, J. J., & White, R. W. *Opinions and personality.* New York: Wiley, 1956.

Smith, M. B. Is experimental social psychology advancing? In L. Berkowitz (Ed.), *Advances in experimental social psychology* (Vol. 6). New York: Academic Press, 1972.

Smith, M. S. Equality of educational opportunity: The basic findings reconsidered. In F. Mosteller & D. P. Moynihan (Eds.), *On equality of educational opportunity.* New York: Random House, 1972.

Smith, S. Age and sex differences in children's opinions concerning sex differences. *Journal of General Psychology,* 1939, *54,* 17–25.

Smith, S., & Haythorn, W. W. Effects of compatibility, crowding, group size, and leadership seniority on stress, anxiety, hostility, and annoyance in isolated groups. *Journal of Personality and Social Psychology,* 1972, *22,* 67–79.

Snadowsky, A. Member satisfaction in stable communication networks. *Sociometry,* 1974, *37,* 38–53.

Snow, R. E. Unfinished Pygmalion. *Contemporary Psychology,* 1969, *14,* 197–199.

Social Security Bulletin (March), 1973, *36* (3). Department of Health, Education, and Welfare, Social Security Administration, Washington, D.C.

Solomon, R. L. Punishment. *American Psychologist,* 1964, *19,* 239–263.

Sommer, R. *Personal space: The behavioral basis of design.* Englewood Cliffs, N.J.: Prentice-Hall, 1969.

Sommer, R., & Becker, F. Territorial defense and the good neighbor. *Journal of Personality and Social Psychology,* 1969, *11,* 85–92.

Sorrentino, R. An extension of theory of achievement motivation to the study of emergent leadership. *Journal of Personality and Social Psychology,* 1973, *26,* 356–368.

South, E. B. Some psychological aspects of committee work. *Journal of Applied Psychology,* 1927, *11,* 348–368.

Southern, M. L., & Fry, V. F. Hippies and college students: Are they really different? *Psychological Reports,* 1972, *31,* 783–792.

Spencer, H. *Essays: Moral, political and aesthetic.* New York: Appleton & Co., 1874.

Spock, B. *Baby and child care.* New York: Pocket Books, 1957.

Staats, A. W. Experimental demand characteristics and the classical conditioning of attitudes. *Journal of Personality and Social Psychology,* 1969, *11,* 187–192.

Staats, A. W., & Staats, C. K. Attitudes established by classical conditioning. *Journal of Abnormal and Social Psychology,* 1958, *57,* 37–40.

Stang, D. J. Effects of interaction rate on ratings of leadership and liking. *Journal of Personality and Social Psychology,* 1973, *27,* 405–408.

Staples, F. R., & Walters, R. H. Anxiety, birth order and susceptibility to social influence. *Journal of Abnormal and Social Psychology,* 1961, *62,* 716–719.

Steiner, I. *Group process and productivity.* New York: Academic Press, 1972.

Stephan, F. F., & Mishler, E. G. The distribution of participation in small groups: An exponential approximation. *American Sociological Review,* 1952, *17,* 203–207.

Stern, W. *General psychology from the personalistic standpoint.* New York: Macmillan, 1938.

St. John, N., & Lewis, R. The influence of school racial context on academic achievement. *Social Problems,* 1971, *19,* 68–79.

Stollak, G. Obedience and deception research. *American Psychologist,* 1967, *22,* 678.

Stone, R. C., & Schlamp, F. T. *Welfare and working fathers.* Lexington, Mass.: Heath, 1971.

Stoner, J. A. F. A comparison of individual and group decisions involving risk. Unpublished master's thesis, School of Industrial Management, Massachusetts Institute of Technology, 1961.

Stoner, J. A. F. Risky and cautious shifts in group decisions: The influence of widely held values. *Journal of Experimental Social Psychology*, 1968, *4*, 442–459.

Storms, M. D. Videotape and the attribution process: Reversing actors' and observers' points of view. *Journal of Personality and Social Psychology*, 1973, *22*, 165–175.

Storms, M. D., & Nisbett, R. E. Insomnia and the attribution process. *Journal of Personality and Social Psychology*, 1970, *16*, 319–328.

Stouffer, S. A. *Communism, conformity and civil liberties*. New York: Doubleday, 1955. (Wiley Science Edition, 1966.)

Stricker, L. J. The true deceiver. *Psychological Bulletin*, 1967, *68*, 13–20.

Stricker, L. J., Messick, S., & Jackson, D. N. Evaluating deception in psychological research. *Psychological Bulletin*, 1969, *71*, 343–351.

Strickland, L. D. Surveillance and trust. *Journal of Personality*, 1958, *26*, 200–215.

Strodtbeck, F., & Hook, L. The social dimensions of a twelve man jury table. *Sociometry*, 1961, *24*, 397–415.

Sullivan, D. S., & Deiker, T. E. Subject-experimenter perceptions of ethical issues in human research. *American Psychologist*, 1973, *28*, 587–591.

Summers, A. A. & Wolfe, B. L. Which school resources help learning? Efficiency and equity in Philadelphia public schools. *Business Review*, February, 1975. Federal Reserve Bank of Philadelphia.

Summers, G. G. *Attitude measurement*. Chicago: Rand-McNally, 1970.

Sykes, G. M., & Matza, D. Techniques of neutralization: A theory of delinquency. *American Sociological Review*, 1957, *22*, 664–670.

Tarter, D. E. Attitude: The mental myth. *American Sociologist*, 1970, *5*, 276–278.

Taylor, D. W., Berry, P. C., & Block, C. Does group participation when using brainstorming facilitate or inhibit creative thinking? *Administrative Science Quarterly*, 1958, *3*, 23–47.

Taylor D. W., & Faust, W. I. Twenty questions: Efficiency of problem solving as a function of the size of the group. *Journal of Experimental Psychology*, 1952, *44*, 360–363.

Taynor, J., & Deaux, K. When women are more deserving than men: Equity, attribution and perceived sex differences. *Journal of Personality and Social Psychology*, 1973, *28*, 360–367.

Tedeschi, J. T. Threats and promises. In P. Swingle (Ed.), *The structure of conflict*. New York: Academic Press, 1970.

Tedeschi, J. T., & Bonoma, T. V. Power and influence: An introduction. In J. T. Tedeschi (Ed.), *The social influence processes*. Chicago: Aldine, 1972.

Tedeschi, J. T., Bonoma, T. V., and Schlenker, B. R. Influence, decision and compliance. In J. T. Tedeschi (Ed.), *The social influence process*. Chicago, Ill.: Aldine-Atherton, 1972.

Tedesco, J. F., & Fromme, D. K. Cooperation, competition and personal space. *Sociometry*, 1974, *37*, 116–121.

Teger, A. I., & Pruitt, D. G. Components of group risk taking. *Journal of Experimental Social Psychology*, 1967, *3*, 189–205.

Teichman, Y. Emotional arousal and affiliation. *Journal of Experimental Social Psychology*, 1973, *9*, 591–605.

Teichman, Y. Predisposition for anxiety and affiliation. *Journal of Personality and Social Psychology*, 1974, *29*, 405–410.

TenHouten, W. D. The black family: Myth and reality. *Psychiatry*, 1970, *33* (2), 145–173.

TenHouten, W. D. Errata: The black family: Myth and reality. *Psychiatry*, 1971, *34*, 224.

Terrill, R. The 800,000,000: China and the world. *The Atlantic*, January 1972, 39ff.

Thibaut, J. W. The development of contractual norms in bargaining: Replication and variation. *Journal of Conflict Resolution*, 1968, *12*, 102–112.

Thibaut, J. W. & Faucheux, C. The development of contractual norms in a bargaining situation under two types of stress. *Journal of Experimental Social Psychology*, 1965, *1*, 89–102.

Thibaut, J. W. & Gruber, O. L. Formation of contractual agreements between parties of unequal power. *Journal of Personality and Social Psychology*, 1969, *11*, 59–65.

Thibaut, J. W., & Kelley, H. H. *The social psychology of groups*. New York, Wiley, 1959.

Thibaut, J. W., & Riecken, H. W. Some determinants and consequences of the perception of social causality. *Journal of Personality,* 1955, *29,* 113–133.

Thibaut, J. W., & Strickland, L. H. Psychological set and social conformity. *Journal of Personality,* 1956, *25,* 115–129.

Thomas, K. (Ed.). *Attitude and behavior: Selected readings.* Baltimore, Maryland: Penguin Books, 1971.

Thomas, W. I., & Znaniecki, F. *The Polish peasant in Europe and America* (Vol. 1). Boston: Badger, 1918.

Thorndike, E. L. *The psychology of learning.* New York: Teachers College, Columbia University, 1913.

Thurstone, L. L. Attitudes can be measured. *American Journal of Sociology,* 1928, *33,* 529–554.

Tilker, H. Socially responsible behavior as a function of observer responsibility and victim feedback. *Journal of Personality and Social Psychology,* 1970, *14,* 95–100.

Tittle, C. R. & Hill, R. J. Attitude measurement and prediction of behavior: An evaluation of conditions and measurement techniques. *Sociometry,* 1967, *30,* 199–213.

Toch, H. *The social psychology of social movements.* Indianpolis: Bobbs-Merrill, 1965.

Tolman, E. C. *Purposive behavior in animals and men.* New York: Appleton-Century, 1932.

Tomkins, S. S. *Affect, imagery and consciousness: The positive affects* (Vol. 1). New York: Springer, 1962.

Torrance, E. P. Some consequences of power differences on decision making in permanent and temporary three-man groups. In A. P. Hare, E. F. Borgatta, & R. F. Bales (Eds.), *Small groups: Studies in social interaction.* New York: Knopf, 1955.

Triplett, N. The dynamogenic factors in pacemaking and competition. *American Journal of Psychology,* 1897, *9,* 507–533.

Tuckman, B. Developmental sequence in small groups. *Psychological Bulletin,* 1965, *63,* 384–399.

Tuddenham, R. D. The influence of a distorted group norm upon individual judgment. *Journal of Psychology,* 1958, *46,* 227–241.

Tuddenham, R. D. *Studies in conformity and yielding: A summary and interpretation.* Final Report, Office of Naval Research Contract NR 170-159, University of California, Berkeley, California, 1961.

Tulkin, S. R., & Kagan, J. Mother-child interaction in the first year of life. *Child Development,* 1972, *43,* 31–41.

Turner, C. W., & Simons, L. S. Effects of subject sophistication and evaluation apprehension on aggressive responses to weapons. *Journal of Personality and Social Psychology,* 1974, *30,* 341–348.

Turner, R. H. The theme of contemporary social movements. *British Journal of Sociology,* 1969, *20,* 390–406.

U. S. Bureau of the Census, *Current Population Reports,* Series P-60, No. 81, Characteristics of the low-income population, 1970. U. S. Government Printing Office, Washington, D.C., 1971.

U.S. Bureau of the Census, *Statistical Abstract of the U.S.,* 1973. Washington, D.C., 1973.

U.S. Commission on Civil Rights. *Racial isolation in the public schools* (Vols. I & II). Washington, D.C.: U.S. Government Printing Office, 1967.

U.S. Commission on Civil Rights, *Racial isolation in the public schools* (Vol. II, Appendix C4). Washington, D.C.: U.S. Government Printing Office, 1967.

U.S. Commission on Civil Rights, *Racial isolation in the public schools* (Vol. II, Appendix C5). Washington, D.C.: U.S. Government Printing Office, 1967.

U.S. Department of Health, Education, and Welfare, *NCSS Report* H-4 (71), Washington, D.C., 1971.

U.S. Department of Health, Education, & Welfare. Study of selected aspects of the 1971 New York State legislative provisions on public assistance employables. March, 1972.

U.S. Riot Commission Report. *Report of the National Advisory Commission on civil disorders.* New York: Bantom Books, 1968.

U.S. Senate. Select Committee on Nutrition and Human Needs. *Hunger—1973.* Washington, D.C.: U.S. Government Printing Office, 1973.

Valentine, C. A. *Culture and poverty.* Chicago: University of Chicago Press, 1968.

Vane, J. R. Relation of early school achievement to high school achievement when race, intelligence, and socioeconomic factors are equated. *Psychology in the Schools,* 1966, *3,* 124–129.

Van Hooff, J. A. R. A. M. The facial displays of the Catarrhine monkey and apes. In D. Morris (Ed.), *Primate ethology.* Chicago: Adline, 1967.

Vernon, P. E. Some characteristics of the good judge of personality, *Journal of Social Psychology,* 1933, *4,* 42–58.

Vinacke, W. E. Variables in experimental games: Toward a field theory. *Psychological Bulletin,* 1969, *71,* 293–318.

Vitz, P. C., & Kite, W. R. Factors affecting conflict and negotiation within an alliance. *Journal of Experimental Social Psychology,* 1970, *6,* 233–247.

Walker, M. Organizational type, rites of incorporation, and group solidarity: A study of fraternity hell week. *Dissertation Abstracts,* 1968, *29* (2-A), 689–690.

Walker, T. G. The decision-making superiority of groups: A research note. *Small Group Behavior,* 1974, *5,* 121–128.

Wallach, M. A., & Kogan, N. The roles of information, discussion, and consensus in group risk taking. *Journal of Experimental Social Psychology,* 1965, *1,* 1–19.

Wallach, M. A., Kogan, N., & Burt, R. Can group members recognize the effects of group discussion upon risk taking? *Journal of Experimental Social Psychology,* 1965, *1,* 379–395.

Wallington, S. Consequences of transgression: Self-punishment and depression. *Journal of Personality and Social Psychology,* 1973, *28,* 1–7.

Walster, E. The effect of self-esteem on liking for dates of various social desirabilities. *Journal of Experimental Social Psychology,* 1970, *6,* 248–253.

Walster, E., Aronson, V., Abrahams, D., & Rottman, L. Importance of physical attractiveness in dating behavior. *Journal of Personality and Social Psychology,* 1966, *4,* 508–516.

Walster, E., Berscheid, E., Abrahams, D., & Aronson, V. Effectiveness of debriefing following deception experiments. *Journal of Personality and Social Psychology,* 1967, *6,* 371–380.

Walster, E., Berscheid, E., & Walster, G. W. New directions in equity research. *Journal of Personality and Social Psychology,* 1973, *25,* 151–176.

Walster, E., & Prestholdt, P. The effect of liking on underrating or overrating another: Overcompensation or dissonance reduction. *Journal of Experimental Social Psychology,* 1966, *2,* 85–97.

Walster, G. W. The Walster *et al.* (1973) equity formula: A correction. *Representative Research in Social Psychology,* 1975, *6,* 65–67.

Walters, H. A., & Jackson, D. N. Group and individual regularities in trait inference: A multidimensional scaling analysis. *Multivariate Behavioral Research,* 1966, *1,* 145–163.

Walton, R. E., & McKersie, R. B. *A behavioral theory of labor negotiations.* New York: McGraw-Hill, 1965.

Walzer, M. Puritanism as a revolutionary ideology. In B. McLaughlin (Ed.), *Studies in social movements.* New York: The Free Press, 1969.

Warner, L. G., & DeFleur, M. L. Attitude as an interactional concept: Social constraint and social distance as intervening variables between attitudes and action. *American Sociological Review,* 1969, *34,* 153–169.

Warr, P. B., & Sims, A. A. A study of cojudgment processes. *Journal of Personality,* 1965, *33,* 598–604.

Warriner, C. K. The nature and functions of official morality. *American Journal of Sociology,* 1958, *64,* 165–168.

Watley, D. J. Career or marriage? A longitudinal study of able young women. *National Merit Scholarship Corporation Research Reports,* 1969, *5,* 1–16.

Watson, G. B. Do groups think more efficiently than individuals? *Journal of Abnormal and Social Psychology,* 1928, *23,* 328–336.

Watson, J. B. *Psychology from the standpoint of a behaviorist.* Philadelphia: Lippincott, 1919.

Watts, W. A., & Whittaker, D. Profile of a nonconformist youth culture: A study of the Berkeley non-student. *Sociology of Education,* 1968, *41,* 178–200.

Webb, E. J., Campbell, D. T., Schwartz, R. D., & Sechrest, L. *Unobtrusive measures: Nonreactive research in the social sciences.* Chicago: Rand-McNally, 1966.

Weber, M. *The Protestant ethic and the spirit of*

capitalism (T. Parsons, trans.). New York: Scribner, 1930. (1st ed., 1904.)

Weber, M. *The theory of social and economic organization.* Glencoe, Ill.: The Free Press, 1957. (Originally published, 1922.)

Weber, S. J., & Cook, T. D. Subject effects in laboratory research: An examination of subject roles, demand characteristics, and valid inference. *Psychological Bulletin,* 1972, *77,* 273–295.

Weggelaar, C. De hippies: Historische parallellen (The hippies: Historical parallels). *Nederlands Tijdschrift voor de Psychologie en haar Gensgebieden,* 1969, *24,* 329–349.

Weigel, R. H., Vernon, D. T. A., & Tagracci, L. N. Specificity of the attitude as a determinant of attitude-behavior congruence. *Journal of Personality and Social Psychology,* 1974, *30,* 724–728.

Weiner, B., Freize, I., Kukla, A., Reed, L., Rest, S., & Rosenbaum, R. Perceiving the causes of success and failure. In E. Jones, D. Kanouse, H. Kelley, R. Nisbett, S. Valins, B. Weiner, *Attribution: Perceiving the causes of behavior.* Morristown, N.J.: General Learning Press, 1972.

Weissberg, N.C. On DeFleur and Westie's "Attitude as a scientific concept." *Social Forces,* 1965, *43,* 422–425.

Weissberg, N. C. Intergenerational welfare dependency: A critical review. *Social Problems,* 1970, *18* (2), 257–274.

Weitz, S. Attitude, voice, and behavior: A repressed affect model of interracial interaction. *Journal of Personality and Social Psychology,* 1972, *24,* 14–21.

Welkowitz, J., & Kuc M. Interrelationships among warmth, genuineness, empathy, and temporal speech patterns in interpersonal interaction. *Journal of Counseling and Clinical Psychology,* 1973, *41,* 47–53.

Wells, H. G. *The war of the worlds.* New York: Heritage Press, 1964. (Originally published, 1898.)

Wertheimer, M. Untersuchungen zur Lehre von der Gestalt, II. *Psychologische Forschung,* 1923, *4,* 301–350.

Wheeler, L. *Interpersonal influence.* Boston: Allyn and Bacon, 1970.

Whelan, E. M. Compliance with contraceptive regimens. *Studies in Family Planning,* 1974, *5*(11), 349–355.

Whittaker, D., & Watts, W. A. Personality characteristics of a nonconformist youth subculture: A study of the Berkeley non-student. *Journal of Social Issues,* 1969, *25,* 65–89.

Whyte, W. H. *Street corner society.* Chicago: University of Chicago Press, 1943.

Whyte, W. H. *The organization man.* New York: Simon & Schuster, 1956.

Wicker, A. W. Attitudes *vs.* actions: The relationship of verbal to overt behavioral responses to attitude objects. *Journal of Social Issues,* 1969, *25,* 41–78. (a)

Wicker, A. W. Size of church membership and members' support of church behavior settings. *Journal of Personality and Social Psychology,* 1969, *13,* 278–288. (b)

Wicker, A. W. An examination of the "other variables" explanation of attitude-behavior inconsistency. *Journal of Personality and Social Psychology,* 1971, *19,* 18–31.

Willis, R. H. Two dimensions of conformity-nonconformity. *Sociometry,* 1963, *26,* 499–513.

Willis, R. H. The yes man, the no man, and the thinking man. *Personnel Administration,* November-December 1964, 6–12.

Willis, R. H. Conformity, independence, and anticonformity. *Human Relations,* 1965, *18,* 373–388. (a)

Willis, R. H. Making better use of the nonconformist. *Personnel Administration,* January-February, 1965, 6–15. (b)

Willis, R. H. The phenomenology of shifting agreement and disagreement in dyads. *Journal of Personality,* 1965, *33,* 188–199. (c)

Willis, R. H. Social influence, information processing, and net conformity in dyads. *Psychological Reports,* 1965, *17,* 147–156. (d)

Willis, R. H. Diamond Model of social response. In W. S. Sahakian (Ed.), *Social psychology: Experimentation, theory, research.* Scranton, Pa.: International Textbook Co., 1972.

Willis, R. H., & Hollander, E. P. An experimental study of three response modes in social influence situations. *Journal of Abnormal and Social Psychology,* 1964, *69,* 150–156. (a)

Willis, R. H., & Hollander, E. P. Supplementary note: Modes of responding in social influence situations. *Journal of Abnormal and Social Psychology,* 1964, *69,* 157. (b)

Willis, R. H., & Willis, Y. A. Role playing versus deception: An experimental comparison. *Journal of Personality and Social Psychology,* 1970, *16,* 472–477.

Wilson, A. B. Educational consequences of segregation in a California community. In U.S. Commission on Civil Rights, *Racial isolation in the public schools* (Vol. 2, Appendix C3). Washington, D.C.: U.S. Government Printing Office, 1967.

Wilson, J. R., Kuehn, R. E., & Beach, F. A. Modification in the sexual behavior of male rats produced by changing the stimulus female. *Journal of Comparative and Physiological Psychology,* 1963, *56,* 636.-644.

Wilson, R. W. *Learning to be Chinese: The political socialization of children in Taiwan.* Cambridge: MIT Press, 1970.

Winch, R. F. The theory of complementary needs in mate selection: A test of one kind of complementariness. *American Sociological Review,* 1955, *20,* 52–56.

Wishner, J. Reanalysis of "Impressions of personality." *Psychological Review,* 1960, *67,* 96–112.

Wispe, L., and Freshley, H. Race, sex, and sympathetic helping behavior: The broken bag caper. *Journal of Personality and Social Psychology,* 1971, *17,* 59–65.

Woodmansee, J. J., & Cook. S. W. Dimensions of verbal racial attitude: Their identification and measurement. *Journal of Personality and Social Psychology,* 1967, *7,* 240–250.

Woodworth, R. S. *Dynamic psychology.* New York: Columbia University Press, 1918.

Worell, J., & Worell, L. Supporters and opposers of women's liberation: Some personality correlates. *Proceedings of the Annual Convention of the American Psychological Association,* Washington, D.C., 1971.

Wrightsman, L. S., Jr. *Social psychology in the seventies.* Belmont, California: Brooks/Cole, 1972.

Wrightsman, L. S., Jr., O'Connor, J., & Baker, N. J. (Eds.). *Cooperation and competition: Readings on mixed-motive games.* Belmont, Calif.: Brooks/Cole, 1972.

Wyer, R. S. Category ratings as "subjective expected values." *Psychological Review,* 1973, *80,* 446–467.

Wylie, R. C. Children's estimate of their schoolwork ability as a function of sex, race and socioeconomic level. *Journal of Personality,* 1963, *31,* 203–224.

Yuker, H. E. Group atmosphere and memory. *Journal of Abnormal and Social Psychology,* 1955, *51,* 17–23.

Yukl, G. A. The effects of situational variables and opponent concessions on a bargainer's perception, aspiration and concessions. Unpublished manuscript, 1972.

Zajonc, R. B. Balance, congruity, and dissonance. *Public Opinion Quarterly,* 1960, *24,* 280–296.

Zajonc, R. B. Social facilitation. *Science,* 1965, *149,* 269–274.

Zajonc, R. B. The attitudinal effects of more exposure. *Journal of Personality and Social Psychology, Monograph Supplements,* 1968, *9,* 2. (a)

Zajonc, R. B. Cognitive theories in social psychology, In G. Lindzey & E. Aronson (Eds.), *The handbook of social psychology* (Vol. 1, 2nd ed.). Reading, Mass.: Addison-Wesley, 1968. (b)

Zajonc, R. B., Heingartner, A., & Herman, E. M. Social enhancement and impairment of performance in the cockroach, *Journal of Personality and Social Psychology,* 1969, *13,* 83–92.

Zajonc, R. B., & Sales, S. M. Social facilitation of dominant and subordinant responses. *Journal of Experimental Social Psychology,* 1966, *2,* 160–168.

Zald, M. N., & Ash, R. Social movement organizations: Growth, decay, and change. In B. McLaughlin (ed.), *Studies in social movements.* New York: The Free Press, 1969.

Zanna, M. P., Kiesler, C. A., & Pilkonis, P. A. Positive and negative attitudinal affect established by classical conditioning. *Journal of Personality and Social Psychology,* 1970, *14,* 321–328.

Zborowski, M. E., & Herzog, E. *Life is with people.* New York: Schoeken, 1952.

Zeller, A. F. An experimental analogue of repression. I. Historical summary. *Psychological Bulletin,* 1950, *47,* 39–51. (a)

Zeller, A. F. An experimental analogue of repres-

Zeller, A. F. An experimental analogue of repression. II. The effect of individual failure and success on memory measured by relearning. *Journal of Experimental Psychology,* 1950, *40,* 411–422. (b)

Zeller, A. F. An experimental analogue of repression. III. Effect of induced failure and success on memory measured by recall. *Journal of Experimental Psychology,* 1951, *42,* 32–38.

Zentall, T. R., & Levine, J. M. Observational learning and social facilitation in the rat. *Science,* 1972, *178,* 1220–1221.

Ziller, R. C., and Behringer, R. D. Assimilation of the knowledgeable newcomer under conditions of group success and failure. *Journal of Abnormal and Social Psychology,* 1960, *60,* 288–291.

Zimbardo, P. G. Involvement and communication discrepancy as determinants of opinion conformity. *Journal of Abnormal and Social Psychology,* 1960, *60,* 86–94.

Zimbardo, P. G. The human choice: Individuation, reason, and order versus deindividuation, impulse, and chaos. In W. J. Arnold & D. Levine (Eds.), *Nebraska Symposium on Motivation* (Vol. 17). Lincoln: University of Nebraska Press, 1969.

Zimbardo, P. G. Pathology of Imprisonment. *Society,* April 1972.

Zimbardo, P. G. Banks, W. C., Haney, C., & Jaffe, D. A Pirandellian prison. *New York Times Sunday Magazine,* April 8, 1973.

Zipf, S. G. Resistance and conformity under reward and punishment. *Journal of Abnormal and Social Psychology,* 1960, *61,* 102–109.

Name Index

Abelson, R. P., 173, 200, 206, 219, 220, 221, 222, 499, 501, 520, 531
Abrahams, D., 37, 38, 300, 538
Adair, J. G., 26, 36, 42, 499, 518, 519
Adams, J. S., 293, 336, 346, 368, 499, 513
Adelson, J., 99, 499, 513
Adler, N., 451, 452, 499
Adorno, T. W., 13, 139, 499
Aiello, R., Jr., 390, 499
Aiken, L. S., 34, 532
Ajzen, I., 148, 153, 155, 175, 184, 185, 211, 500, 512
Ajzen, K., 148, 499
Aldrich, H. E., 491, 494, 500
Alger, C. F., 39, 515
Alker, H. A., 181, 457, 500, 532
Allen, A., 194, 248, 264, 275, 277, 503
Allen, J., 293, 523
Allen, V. L., 87, 96, 311, 326, 327, 328, 329, 330, 331, 332, 333, 341, 470, 496, 500, 505, 532
Allport, F. H., 25, 157, 313, 314, 317, 500
Allport, G. W., 3, 9, 21, 146, 151, 152, 153, 156, 194, 326, 443, 500
Almquist, C., 457, 529
Alpert, R., 450
Altman, I., 387, 398, 433, 500, 526
Amabile, T., 239–78, 532
Amir, Y., 492, 494, 500
Anderson, L. R., 421, 508
Anderson, N. H., 206, 222, 257, 258, 276, 402, 500, 501
Anderson, S. B., 419, 527
Anderson, V. E., 287, 514
Andrews, I. R., 411, 518
Applebaum, A. S., 37, 517
Appley, M. H., 52, 501
Archibald, K., 520
Ardrey, R., 387, 501
Argyle, M., 253, 284, 501
Argyris, C., 31, 32, 501
Aries, P., 86, 501
Aristotle, 15, 285, 286, 501
Armor, D. J., 482, 501
Arnold, W. J., 529, 541
Arons, S., 100, 501
Aronson, E., 18, 21, 28, 29, 34, 36, 38, 45, 223, 224, 227, 228, 229, 354, 382, 402, 500, 501, 504, 508, 510,
514, 515, 520, 526, 532, 533, 534, 540
Aronson, V., 37, 38, 300, 538
Arsenian, J. M., 55, 501
Asch, S. E., 9, 10, 21, 147, 202, 203, 242, 243, 255, 256, 257, 258, 276, 310, 312, 316, 317, 321, 326, 327, 335, 336, 358, 501
Ash, R., 458, 540
Astin, A. W., 445, 446, 501, 503
Atchison, C. O., 487, 520
Atkins, A. L., 51–79, 63, 518
Atkinson, J. W., 70, 71, 501, 526
Austin, W., 293, 295, 306, 307, 501
Azrin, N., 56, 502

Bachman, J. G., 106, 519
Back, K. W., 35, 315, 358, 403, 406, 502, 512, 517
Backman, C. W., 154, 287, 300, 502, 534
Baer, D. M., 288, 384, 514
Bailyn, L., 95, 502
Bain, A., 152, 223, 502
Baker, N. J., 352, 540
Baldwin, A. L., 73, 502
Baldwin, C. P., 73, 502
Baldwin, J., 298, 522
Bales, R. F., 378, 391, 393, 394, 395, 430, 502, 505, 515, 537
Ball, J. C., 454, 502
Ball, S., 484, 502
Ballachey, E., 3, 146, 153, 154, 155, 331, 522
Bandura, A., 11, 58, 63, 87, 93, 94, 95, 109, 181, 305, 348, 475, 502
Banks, W. C., 113, 541
Baral, R., 301, 521
Barber, T. X., 42, 44, 502
Barclay, A., 294, 504
Barclay, J. E., 161, 502
Barker, R., 57, 502
Barnes, M., 363, 365, 522
Barnlund, D. C., 418, 502
Baron, R. A., 94, 124, 125, 134, 502
Baron, R. M., 326, 502, 520
Barron, F., 336
Bartel, N. R., 490, 503
Bartel, N. W., 490, 503
Barton, K., 178, 510
Barton, W. A., Jr., 418, 503

Barton, W. H., 414, 514
Bass, B. M., 501, 503
Batchelor, J. P., 390, 391, 503
Bateson, N., 410, 503
Baumrind, D., 27, 37, 503
Bavelas, A., 366, 393, 394, 430, 503
Bayer, A. E., 445, 503
Beach, F. A., 52, 89, 512, 540
Beaman, A. L., 414, 510, 513
Beaton, A. E., Jr., 482, 525
Beck, C. M., 521
Becker, F. D., 387, 392, 503, 535
Becker, H., 63, 503
Becker, L. A., 37, 505
Becker, S. W., 429, 518
Beckman, L. L., 362, 363, 520
Bee, J., 392, 503
Behringer, R. D., 344, 541
Belden, T., 366, 503
Beloff, H., 318, 338, 503
Bem, D. J., 11, 30, 39, 153, 154, 181, 194, 230, 231, 232, 233, 235, 248, 264, 272, 273, 275, 277, 503
Benjamin, L., 486, 520
Bennett, D. H., 37, 40, 517
Bennett, E. B., 315, 503
Bennis, W. G., 106, 503
Benoist, F., 402, 530
Benton, A. A., 368, 503
Berelson, B., 205, 503
Berg, I. A., 336, 501, 503
Berg, K. E., 147, 148, 503
Berger, B., 451, 503
Berkov, B., 476, 534, 535
Berkowitz, L., 32, 33, 34, 52, 58, 63, 95, 114, 115, 122, 123, 124, 142, 146, 153, 181, 294, 297, 311, 341, 346, 349, 425, 499, 500, 501, 502, 503, 504, 513, 515, 519, 520, 524, 525, 526, 528, 533, 534, 535
Berlyne, D. E., 52, 229, 504
Berman, A., 63, 518
Berra, Yogi, 93
Berry, P. C., 421, 536
Berscheid, E., 37, 38, 60, 288, 290, 294, 296, 300, 301, 308, 504, 518, 538
Beswick, D., 229, 504
Bettelheim, B., 70, 504
Bickman, L., 132, 133, 135, 137, 138, 504, 513

543

Biddle, B. J., 14, 505
Bigelow, J., 512
Billingsley, A., 465, 505
Blake, R. B., 193, 516
Blake, R. R., 331, 508
Blanchard, E. B., 94, 95, 505
Blau, P. M., 300, 479, 505
Bliss, E., 57, 513
Block, C., 421, 536
Block, J., 446, 447, 515
Blum, J. M., 431, 534
Blumer, H., 440, 505
Bochner, S., 201, 202, 505
Boden, M., 228, 505
Bogardus, E. S., 152, 153, 281, 505
Bogatz, G. A., 484, 502
Bolles, R. C., 52, 505
Bolt, R., 305, 505
Bolwig, N., 125, 505
Bonoma, T. V., 8, 353, 536
Booker, A., 33, 115, 124, 506
Borgatta, E. F., 393, 505, 526, 537
Borgida, G., 106, 505
Bouchard, T. J., Jr., 421, 505
Boyanowsky, E. O., 329, 330, 505
Boye, D., 61, 504
Bramel, D., 402, 505
Brannon, R., 145–98, 180, 191, 197, 505
Bray, D. W., 147, 505
Brehm, J. W., 224, 233, 306, 326, 505, 519, 531
Brigham, J. C., 148, 505
Brimhall, D., 72, 507
Brinton, C., 441, 505
Brislin, R. W., 148, 163, 301, 505
Brock, T. C., 37, 294, 503, 505, 515, 529
Brody, R. A., 39, 515
Broll, L., 297, 505
Bronfenbrenner, U., 81, 83, 88, 95, 102, 103, 104, 107, 109, 506
Brotzman, E., 120, 517
Broverman, D. M., 73, 455, 506
Broverman, I. K., 73, 455, 506
Brown, B., 44, 506
Brown, D. G., 73, 506
Brown, J. A., 490, 506
Brown, M. E., 454, 506
Brown, N. O., 14, 449, 506
Brown, R. W., 21, 52, 68, 71, 207, 223, 410, 506
Bruce, R. S., 418, 506
Bruner, J. S., 154, 208, 209, 247, 258, 506, 535
Bryan, J. H., 96, 506
Bryson, L., 522
Buchwald, A. M., 26, 506
Buck, R., 320

Burdick, H. A., 71, 506
Burger, W. G., 100, 101
Burgess, E. W., 287, 506
Burgess, R. L., 397, 506
Burnside, B., 473, 506
Burt, R., 410, 538
Burtt, H. E., 417, 506
Buss, A. H., 33, 62, 63, 114, 115, 118, 120, 121, 122, 124, 125, 134, 294, 505, 506
Buss, E., 33, 115, 124, 506
Byrne, D., 280, 281, 282, 283, 284, 285, 286, 302, 506

Cabin, S., 192, 508
Caen, Herb, 449
Calder, B., 197
Campbell, A., 157, 177, 178, 183, 184, 185, 493, 494, 495, 506
Campbell, D. T., 18, 24, 27, 36, 45, 47, 153, 155, 161, 166, 280, 281, 282, 283, 507, 538
Campbell, E. Q., 480, 481, 482, 483, 485, 496, 508
Campbell, J., 431, 507
Canavan, D., 41, 510
Cannon, W. B., 76, 507
Cantril, H., 139, 152, 154, 243, 309, 442, 443, 507, 513, 516
Carithers, M. W., 490, 507
Carlsmith, J. M., 18, 28, 29, 36, 38, 45, 126, 155, 225, 226, 232, 253, 325, 354, 501, 511, 512, 513
Carlson, A. J., 76, 507
Carlson, R., 35, 507
Carmichael, L., 92, 514
Carr, T. S., 390, 509
Carter, L., 429, 516
Cartwright, D., 222, 358, 359, 408, 409, 507, 513
Castro, F., 270
Cattell, J., 72, 507
Cattell, R. B., 178, 510
Cavan, S., 454, 507
Centers, R., 168, 534
Chaikin, A. L., 489, 507
Chaplan, R., 61, 517
Chapman, A. J., 416, 507
Chapman, J. P., 246, 507
Chapman, L. J., 246, 507
Chave, E. J., 156
Chein, I., 154, 155, 156, 173, 326, 507, 515
Chemers, M. M., 431, 507
Cherniss, C., 457, 507
Chertkoff, J. M., 365, 507
Cheyne, J. A., 389, 390, 507, 510, 511
Christie, R., 366, 507
Clark, K. B., 44, 150, 507, 508

Clark, R. A., 70, 526
Clark, R. D., III, 134, 135, 138, 411, 508
Clarkson, F. E., 73, 455, 506
Cline, V. B., 262, 263, 508
Clore, G. L., 283, 285, 286, 287, 506, 508
Coch, L., 359, 508
Coe, W. C., 311, 324, 532
Coffman, T. L., 245, 246, 519
Cohen, A. R., 147, 224, 306, 505, 508
Cohen, D. K., 482, 485, 508
Cohen, E. G., 485, 488, 489, 494, 508
Cohen, M., 486, 520
Cohen, S., 294, 520
Cohen, W. M., 482, 525
Cole, J., 511
Coleman, D., 112, 522
Coleman, J., 149, 508
Coleman, J. F., 331, 508
Coleman, J. S., 356, 480, 481, 482, 483, 485, 496, 508
Collaros, P. A., 421, 508
Collins, B. E., 147, 166, 235, 323, 403, 410, 508, 521
Conley, M., 365, 507
Converse, P. E., 177, 178, 183, 184, 185, 506, 531
Cook, B. P., 193, 525
Cook, S. W., 155, 162, 173, 507, 508, 540
Cook, T. D., 34, 36, 539
Coombs, C. H., 160, 508
Cooper, D. G., 106, 508
Cooper, J., 354, 524
Cooper, R. E., 390, 499
Corey, M., 38, 531
Corey, S. M., 147, 163, 187, 188, 508
Corwin, R., 95, 504
Costanza, P. R., 4, 10, 534
Cottrell, N. B., 416, 508
Couch, A., 429, 516
Cowdry, R. W., 192, 508
Cox, D. E., 31, 35, 508
Crain, R. L., 491, 508
Crawford, J. L., 394, 508
Crawford, T. J., 199–235, 212, 509
Crittenden, A., 521
Cronbach, L. J., 159, 261, 262, 263, 264, 272, 277, 509, 513
Croner, M. D., 331, 509
Cross, H. J., 453, 509
Crossley, H., 165, 185, 529
Crowne, D. P., 60, 509
Crutchfield, R. S., 3, 146, 153, 154, 155, 316, 327, 331, 332, 336, 338, 509, 522
Cullen, P., 352, 524
Cutright, P., 476, 509
Cyphers, G., 180, 191, 197, 505

Name Index 545

Dabbs, J. M., 390, 509
Dahrendorf, R., 358, 509
Dalrymple, S., 120, 517
Darley, J. M., 39, 128, 129, 131, 132, 134, 142, 147, 181, 509, 522
Darlington, R. B., 57, 509
Darwin, C., 250, 251, 252, 276, 509
Dashiell, J. F., 415, 509
David, K. H., 393, 509
Davies, J. C., 441, 509
Davis, F., 454, 509
Davis, J. H., 417, 418, 419, 509
Davis, K. E., 267, 268, 519
Davis, K. W., 294, 303, 509, 510
Davitz, J. R., 55, 57, 509
Dean, J., 253, 501
Dean, L. R., 165, 509
Deaux, K., 74, 536
DeCharms, R., 267, 268, 519
DeFleur, M. L., 147, 152, 164, 187, 188, 189, 509, 538
DeFriese, G. H., 165, 187, 189, 509
Deiker, T. E., 38, 536
DeJong, W. H., 239
DeLamater, J., 455, 509
DeLucia, L. A., 73, 74, 509
Del Vecchio, G., 306, 509
Dembo, T., 57, 362, 502, 523
DeMontmollin, G., 418, 529
Derlega, V. J., 489, 507
Deutsch, M., 10, 21, 41, 322, 328, 331, 354, 355, 356, 358, 369, 375, 506, 507, 510, 519
Deutscher, I., 161, 166, 168, 190, 197, 510
DeYoung, G. E., 178, 510
Diebold, P., 299, 514
Diener, C., 414, 510
Diener, E., 413, 414, 510, 513
Dillon, W. S., 298, 510
Dineen, J., 413, 510
Dion, K., 301, 504
Dobyns, Z. P., 452, 453, 510
Dollard, J., 56, 120, 510
Doob, L. W., 56, 120, 285, 510
Doost, R. M., 453, 509
Dornbusch, S. M., 244, 264, 510, 516
Dosey, M., 390, 510
Drews, J. L., 363, 530
Driscoll, R., 303, 510
Droba, 156
Druckman, D., 365, 510
Duncan, B., 474, 479, 510
Duncan, O. D., 474, 475, 479, 492, 497, 505, 510
Duncan, S., 43, 510
Dunlap, K., 204, 510
Dunnette, M., 431, 507

Durkheim, E., 18, 510
Dymond, R. F., 261, 510

Eagly, A. H., 235
Edwards, L. P., 441, 510
Efran, M. G., 284, 389, 390, 507, 510, 511
Ehrlich, H. J., 148, 158, 173, 511
Eisenhower, D. D., 178
Eisman, B., 401, 511
Ekman, P., 252, 277, 511
Ellertson, N., 425, 533
Ellsworth, P. C., 126, 254, 277, 511
Elms, A. C., 39, 511
Emerson, R. M., 355, 511
Endler, N. S., 331, 337, 511, 514
Engel, E., 243, 511
English, A. C., 311, 511
English, H. B., 311, 511
Epps, E. G., 487, 520
Epstein, J., 42, 499
Epstein, Y. M., 38, 511
Erikson, E. H., 69, 88, 445, 511
Eron, L. D., 95, 96, 511
Ervin, C. R., 283, 506
Estes, S. G., 261, 262, 511
Ettinger, R. F., 331, 511
Evans, G. W., 43, 254, 390, 511
Exline, R. V., 125, 252, 253, 284, 511
Eysenck, H. J., 418, 511

Faris, R. E. L., 521
Farkas, A. J., 206, 500
Farley, R., 474, 476, 493, 494, 495, 511, 516
Faucheux, C., 332, 368, 419, 511, 528, 536
Faust, W. I., 418, 536
Feather, N. T., 222, 511
Featherman, D., 479, 510
Feigl, H., 506
Fekete, A., 63, 518
Feldman, R. S., 96, 512
Feldman, S., 512
Felipe, N., 389, 391, 512
Ferguson, L. W., 155, 512
Ferman, L., 527
Ferster, C. B., 350, 526
Feshbach, S., 55, 60, 63, 96, 512, 518, 532
Festinger, L., 12, 29, 67, 150, 223, 225, 226, 232, 315, 322, 324, 325, 331, 345, 354, 358, 362, 443, 512, 523
Feuer, L., 446, 448, 512
Fidell, L. S., 455, 509
Fiedler, F. E., 430, 431, 512
Field, P. B., 206, 518
Fillenbaum, S., 31, 512

Finkelstein, J., 43, 510
Finney, R., 475, 513
Firestone, I. J., 403, 512
Fischer, C. S., 362, 363, 520
Fishbein, M., 148, 153, 155, 173, 175, 180, 184, 185, 211, 235, 500, 512, 530
Fiske, D. W., 162, 507
Fitzgerald, F. Scott, 255
Flacks, R., 446, 447, 448, 512, 525
Flanders, J. P., 410, 512
Forbes, J., 112, 522
Ford, C., 89, 512
Ford, W. S., 165, 187, 189, 509
Fouraker, L. E., 361, 534
Fowler, M. G., 457, 512
Fowler, R. L., 457, 512
Franklin, B., 295, 512
Fraser, C., 411, 512
Fraser, S. C., 413, 414, 510, 513
Free, L., 139, 513
Freedman, J. L., 39, 57, 155, 354, 513
Freize, I., 267, 539
French, J. R. P., Jr., 71, 323, 354, 356, 359, 508, 513, 530
French, V., 155, 513
Frenkel-Brunswik, E., 13, 139, 499
Freshley, H., 136, 540
Freud, S., 10, 13, 14, 15, 57, 63, 72, 87, 88, 93, 208, 381, 412, 513
Frey, L., Jr., 368, 513
Friedon, B., 456, 513
Friedman, G. A., 71, 526
Friedman, P., 349, 504
Friesen, W., 252, 278, 511
Frijda, N. H., 252, 513
Fromm, E., 69, 70, 513
Fromme, D. K., 390, 536
Fry, M., 306, 424, 513
Fry, V. F., 453, 535
Fuller, J. P., 390, 509
Funt, A., 36

Gaborit, M., 178, 510
Gaertner, S., 111–42, 137, 138, 140, 513
Gage, N. L., 261, 262, 263, 264, 277, 513
Gahagan, J. P., 352, 366, 513, 524
Gallatin, A., 99, 513
Gallimore, R., 475, 513
Gallup, G., 200
Galper, R., 63, 518
Galton, F., 284, 513
Gamson, W. A., 348, 514
Gardner, R. C., 155, 514
Garfinkel, H., 6, 14, 514
Garrison, R. J., 287, 514
Gaudet, H., 309, 507

546 Name Index

Gaylin, W., 106, 514
Geen, R. G., 57, 96, 122, 123, 504, 514
Geis, F. L., 366, 507
Geller, S. H., 331, 511, 514
Genovese, Kitty, 128, 131, 141
George, A. L., 88, 514
George, J. L., 88, 514
Gerard, H. B., 322, 328, 331, 347, 510, 519
Gergen, K. J., 28, 298, 299, 414, 458, 459, 514, 521
Gergen, M. K. M., 298, 414, 514
Gesell, A., 92, 514
Gewitz, J. L., 288, 384, 514
Ghiselli, E. E., 424, 514
Gibb, C., 427, 514
Gibb, J. R., 402
Gilbert, E., 164, 186, 187, 188, 190, 532
Ginsberg, A., 450
Glass, D. C., 294, 313, 416, 514, 516
Glass, D. D., 294, 520
Glaudin, V., 190, 514
Gleason, R. J., 450, 514
Glenn, E., 366, 503
Goethals, G. R., 390, 391, 399, 503, 530
Goffman, E., 14, 278, 514
Goldberg, P., 455, 514
Goldman, A. E., 175, 523
Goldman, M., 420, 514
Goldman, R., 76, 533
Goldschmid, M. L., 497
Goldwater, B., 203
Gomberg, W., 531
Goodall, J. L., 88, 514
Goodman, P., 449
Goodmonson, C., 190, 514
Goodwin, L., 468, 470, 514
Goranson, R. E., 349, 515
Gordon, A., 76, 533
Gore, P. M., 60, 515
Gore, W. V., 416, 515
Gormly, J. B., 286, 287, 508
Goslin, D. A., 109, 521, 523
Gouldner, A. W., 349, 515
Graves, N., 120, 517
Gray, D., 253, 511
Green, B. F., 156, 189, 515
Green, D., 233, 515
Green, D. R., 36, 515
Green, J. A., 189, 515
Greenbaum, C., 486, 520
Greenleigh & Associates, 472, 515
Greenwald, A. G., 155, 503, 515, 529
Gregory, D., 425, 533
Grill, J. J., 490, 503
Gross, A. E., 297, 393, 394, 503, 505

Gross, E., 398, 515
Gross, L., 77, 533
Gross, N., 14, 515
Gruber, C. L., 368, 536
Gruber, M., 466, 467, 515
Guerney, B., Jr., 394, 534
Guetzkow, H., 39, 410, 501, 508, 515
Guilford, J. P., 156
Gurin, G., 467, 515
Gurin, P., 467, 515, 518
Gurnee, H., 418, 515
Gursslin, O. R., 467, 531
Gusfield, J. R., 459, 515
Gustafson, J. M., 534
Guthrie, E. R., 11
Guttman, L., 146, 159, 160, 161, 281, 515

Haaland, G. A., 394, 508
Haan, N., 446, 447, 515
Haber, A., 527
Habermas, J., 445, 515
Haefner, D., 429, 516
Hake, D., 56, 502
Hall, J. V., 86, 516
Hamblin, R. L., 345, 515
Haney, C., 113, 541
Hansen, C. F., 488, 515
Harari, H., 313, 526
Harary, F., 222, 507
Harding, J., 154, 155, 158, 326, 515, 533
Hare, A. P., 391, 515, 537
Harford, R. J., 390, 515
Harlow, H. F., 52, 79, 86, 87, 88, 516
Harrington, M., 464, 516
Harris, J. A., 287, 516
Harris, S., 41, 270, 271, 272, 516
Harrison, R., 401, 516
Hartley, E. L., 154, 502, 516, 520, 523, 526
Hartley, R. E., 154, 516
Hartman, D. A., 157, 500
Hartshorne, H., 92, 516
Hartup, W. W., 73, 516
Harvey, O. J., 153, 403, 516, 534
Hastorf, A. H., 239–78, 243, 244, 264, 278, 295, 393, 394, 503, 510, 516
Hatchett, S., 495, 533
Hays, W. L., 258, 516
Haythorn, W. W., 387, 400, 429, 500, 516, 535
Head, K. B., 162, 531
Hean, E., 149, 508
Heider, F., 10, 12, 210, 224, 249, 265, 266, 267, 268, 278, 516
Heilbrun, A. B., 73, 516
Heingartner, A., 88, 417, 516, 540

Heintz, R. K., 429, 530
Heironimus, J., 95, 504
Heiss, J., 474, 516
Helson, H., 193, 516
Hemphill, J. K., 429, 516
Henchy, T., 313, 416, 516
Hendrick, C., 45, 516
Henson, A., 253, 511
Hermalin, A. I., 474, 476, 493, 494, 495, 511, 516
Herman, E. M., 417, 540
Herscovic, F., 61, 517
Hertzog, H., 309, 507
Herzog, E., 74, 465, 476, 516, 540
Heslin, R., 398, 525
Hess, R. D., 101, 109, 483, 516, 517
Hesse, S., 180, 191, 197, 505
Hesselbart, S., 180, 191, 197, 505
Hill, J. H., 363, 364, 524
Hill, R. J., 147, 161
Hillery, J. M., 416, 518
Hilton, I. R., 51–79, 60, 61, 66, 72, 73, 74, 502, 517, 534
Himmelfarb, S., 235
Hobbes, T., 15
Hobson, C. J., 480, 481, 482, 483, 485, 497, 508
Hoffer, E., 442, 517
Hoffman, L. R., 399, 424, 517
Hoffman, L. W., 455, 517, 519
Hoffman, M. I., 519
Hofling, C. K., 120, 517
Hokanson, J. E., 58, 517
Holland, C. H., 31, 119, 120, 529
Hollander, E. P., 311, 320, 330, 338, 341, 347, 517, 539
Holmes, D. S., 37, 40, 58, 504, 517
Holmes, J. G., 362, 517
Homans, G. C., 11, 285, 298, 300, 308, 517
Hood, T. C., 35, 517
Hood, W. R., 403, 534
Hook, L., 391, 536
Horai, J., 351, 352, 353, 517
Horn, J. L., 446, 517
Horner, M. S., 72, 73, 455, 517
Hornstein, H., 354, 356, 365, 517
Horowitz, E. L., 152, 517
Hovland, C. I., 200, 203, 204, 205, 206, 207, 229, 347, 499, 517, 518, 524, 531, 534
Howard, J., 406
Howard, R. B., 254, 390, 511
Howells, L. T., 429, 518
Huesmann, L. R., 95, 96, 511
Hull, C. L., 11, 518
Humphrey, H. H., 176, 177
Hunt, D. E., 153, 516

Name Index

Hunt, J. McV., 337, 511, 518, 523
Hunt, P. J., 416, 518
Husband, R. W., 415, 418, 518, 529
Hutchinson, R., 56, 502
Hyman, H. H., 146, 165, 173, 185, 188, 478, 518
Hymer, S., 63, 518

Inbau, F., 518
Insko, C. A., 147, 201, 202, 235, 505, 518
Irelan, L. M., 469, 470, 518
Izard, C. J., 251, 276, 518

Jackson, D. N., 34, 186, 258, 259, 523, 536, 538
Jacobs, L., 288, 518
Jacobson, L., 43, 45, 532
Jaffe, D., 113, 541
Jahoda, M., 507
James, W., 15
Janis, I. L., 55, 58, 206, 425, 426, 433, 499, 517, 518
Jecker, J., 295, 518
Jefferson, Thomas, 99, 203, 335
Jenks, C. S., 482, 489, 518
Jennings, H. R., 284, 518
Jensen, A. R., 506, 519
Jessor, R., 532
Joffe, N. F., 298, 519
Johnson, C., 283, 508
Johnson, D. F., 354, 363, 365, 367, 518, 530
Johnson, D. L., 411, 518
Johnson, H. H., 420, 523
Johnson, L. B., 464
Johnson, R., 79, 112, 522
Johnson, R. W., 42, 518, 519
Johnson, S. P., 490, 506
Johnston, J., 106, 519
Jones, E. E., 141, 248, 267, 268, 270, 271, 272, 278, 294, 322, 336, 347, 354, 405, 509, 519, 520, 524, 539
Jones, J. M., 493, 519
Jones, L. E., 405, 519
Jones, M. R., 502, 529
Jones, R. A., 45, 233, 516, 519
Joseph, M. L., 366, 519
Jourard, S. M., 37, 519
Julian, J. W., 347, 517
Jung, J., 35, 519

Kagan, J., 97, 484, 519
Kahan, J. P., 362, 519
Kahn, L. A., 155, 358, 519
Kahn, R. L., 358, 519
Kaleta, R. J., 62, 519

Kanouse, D. E., 278, 336, 519, 520, 539
Kaplan, H. R., 468, 519
Kaplan, K. J., 403, 512
Karlins, M., 245, 246, 519
Katz, D., 58, 208, 209, 358, 518, 519, 533
Katz, E., 346, 347, 519
Katz, I., 188, 294, 485, 486, 487, 488, 494, 506, 518, 519, 520
Kaufman, H., 29, 520
Keane, R., 180, 191, 197, 505
Kelem, R., 414, 513
Kelley, D., 57, 514
Kelly, G. A., 259, 520
Kelly, H. H., 11, 239, 240, 241, 268, 269, 271, 277, 278, 285, 322, 336, 349, 353, 354, 362, 363, 370, 418, 419, 519, 520, 531, 536, 539
Kelman, H. C., 26, 27, 28, 37, 39, 148, 203, 323, 326, 334, 520, 521, 530
Kemelgor, B., 293, 523
Keniston, K., 69, 86, 106, 193, 443, 444, 445, 446, 447, 452, 460, 461, 508, 521
Kerouac, J., 450
Kerpelman, L., 447, 521
Kesey, K., 450
Kieffer, M., 364, 524
Kiesler, C. A., 147, 166, 181, 193, 209, 233, 235, 301, 317, 326, 341, 519, 521, 525, 540
Kiesler, S. B., 317, 341, 521
Killian, L. M., 438, 521
King, C. W., 438, 521
King, S., 379, 521
Kinkade, K., 70, 521
Kinsey, A. C., 17, 318, 521
Kipnis, D., 305, 356, 521
Kissinger, H., 215
Kite, W. R., 366, 393, 394, 503, 538
Klapp, O. E., 106, 521
Kleck, R., 254, 521
Kleinhans, B., 377–433
Klieger, D. M., 37, 524
Kliejunas, P., 180, 531
Klineberg, O., 517
Knight, H. C., 418, 521
Knott, P. D., 446, 517
Knowles, E. S., 389, 521
Koch, S., 504
Koffka, K., 9, 521
Kogan, N., 259, 409, 410, 521, 527, 538
Kohlberg, L., 73, 74, 89, 91, 93, 98, 104, 447, 521
Köhler, W., 9, 521
Kohn, M. L., 60, 521

Kohn, P., 229, 339, 522
Komorita, S. S., 363, 365, 522
Kornbluh, J., 527
Korte, C., 132, 133, 135, 522
Kothandapani, V., 185, 522
Krauss, R. M., 21
Krebs, D., 298, 522
Krech, D., 3, 146, 153, 154, 155, 331, 522
Kriesberg, L., 466, 468, 472, 522
Kruglanski, A. W., 36, 323, 343, 348, 350, 375, 522, 530
Kruskal, W. H., 283, 507
Kuc, M., 405, 539
Kuehn, R. E., 52, 540
Kuhn, T. S., 8, 522
Kukla, A., 267, 539
Kutner, B., 154, 155, 326, 515
Kuusinen, J., 259, 522

Laird, J. D., 252, 522
Lambert, N., 73, 502
Lambert, W. E., 181, 522
Lambert, W. W., 526
Lamberth, J., 283, 506
Lamm, H., 409, 420, 421, 522
Lana, R. E., 30, 522
Landers, D. M., 416, 525
Landis, B., 70, 522
Landis, C., 251, 522
Landy, D., 295, 518
Landy, O., 203, 522
Lange, L., 146, 522
Langham, P., 429, 516
Lanzetta, J. T., 254, 522
LaPiere, R. T., 146, 149, 162, 163, 185, 187, 190, 522
Larson, K. S., 112, 522
Lasswell, H. D., 200, 522
Latane, B., 39, 128, 129, 130, 131, 132, 134, 142, 147, 181, 324, 509, 522, 523
Laughlin, P. R., 420, 523
Lawler, E. III, 402, 431, 507, 530
Lawrence, L. H., 334, 521
Lawton, M. P., 175, 523
Lay, C. H., 258, 523
Lazarsfeld, P. F., 160, 523
Leacock, E. B., 467, 523
Leary, T., 394, 449, 450, 523
Leavitt, H. J., 430, 523
LeBon, G., 412, 523
Lee, A., 287, 529
Leeds, A., 466, 467, 523
Leeper, R. A., 249, 523
Lefkowitz, M. M., 95, 96, 511
Lenin, 203
LePage, A., 32, 33, 34, 115, 124, 181, 504

548 Name Index

Leper, M., 168, 523
Lerner, M., 295, 445, 446, 521, 523
Lesser, G. S., 206, 449
Leventhal, G. S., 293, 523
Levin, H., 60, 533
Levine, D., 519, 520, 541
Levine, J. M., 309–41, 313, 327, 328, 329, 331, 332, 333, 500, 523, 541
LeVine, R. A., 85, 523
Levinger, G., 411, 523
Levinson, D. J., 13, 139, 499
Levy, L. H., 33, 38, 399, 523
Lewin, K., 4, 5, 10, 12, 15, 57, 112, 183, 195, 304, 315, 362, 428, 429, 502, 523
Lewis, H., 467, 523
Lewis, M., 483, 523
Lewis, O., 465, 466, 467, 469, 523
Lewis, R., 486, 488, 535
Lewis, S. A., 301, 369, 370, 371, 505, 530
Libman, E., 181, 522
Lieberman, M. A., 382, 402, 404, 406, 426, 524
Liebert, R., 363, 365, 524
Liebow, E., 299, 468, 475, 524
Lifton, R. J., 105, 524
Likert, R., 146, 156, 157, 158, 160, 161, 163, 281, 524
Linder, D. E., 233, 354, 519, 524
Lindner, R., 402, 501
Lindskold, S., 352, 524
Lindzey, G., 21, 500, 501, 504, 508, 510, 514, 515, 520, 526, 532, 533, 540
Linn, L. S., 186, 524
Lipetz, M. E., 303, 510
Lippitt, R., 428, 429, 523
Lippmann, W., 209, 524
Lipset, S. M., 448, 524
Little, K. B., 390, 524
Liverant, S., 60, 509
Lodahl, T. M., 424, 514
Loew, R., 61, 517
Lofland, J., 443, 524
Loomis, C. P., 285, 524
Lopes, L. L., 402, 501
Lorge, I., 335, 419, 524
Lott, A. J., 285, 288, 329, 330, 402, 403, 425, 524, 525
Lott, B. E., 285, 288, 402, 403, 425, 456, 524
Lott, D. F., 390, 524
Lowell, E. L., 70, 526
Lowin, A., 37, 524
Lubin, B., 401, 516
Luchins, A. S., 205, 331, 524
Luchins, E., 331, 524
Lund, F., 205, 524

Macaulay, J., 114, 142, 305, 306, 524
Maccoby, E., 60, 73, 79, 502, 521, 524, 525, 533
Maciejko, J. S., 365, 525
Mack, D. E., 478, 525
MacKenzie, B. K., 155, 525
Mackinnon, D. W., 88, 525
Maehr, M. L., 43, 44, 489, 532
Maier, M. R. F., 399, 424, 517
Makerenko, 102
Mallick, S. K., 57, 525
Malof, M., 329, 330, 525
Mandle, J., 455, 457, 525
Mangelsdorff, S. D., 112, 525
Manhoff, M., 447, 448, 525
Mannheim, K., 444, 525
Mantell, D., 119, 525
Marascuilo, L. A., 480, 525
Marcuse, H., 14, 449, 525
Marino, C. J., 331, 511
Marks, E. S., 161, 525
Marlowe, D., 521
Marquis, D. G., 411, 525
Marshall, J. E., 398, 525
Marston, W. M., 418, 525
Martens, J. L., 457, 532
Martens, R., 416, 525
Martin, C. E., 17, 318, 521
Martindale, D., 388, 430, 525
Marwell, G., 293, 533
Marx, K., 402
Masling, J., 31, 41, 516, 525
Maslow, A. H., 229, 525
Mason, D. J., 55, 509
Mason, W. A., 55, 68, 525
Mason, W. S., 14, 515
Masserman, J., 119, 525
Masters, J. C., 79
Matthews, G., 295, 523
Matza, D., 294, 536
Mauss, M., 298, 525
Maxwell, G., 506
May, M. A., 92, 516
Mayeske, G. W., 482, 525
McArthur, L. A., 193, 525
McBride, D., 425, 533
McCandless, B. R., 57, 525
McClelland, D. C., 18, 70, 71, 501, 526
McClintock, C., 46, 520, 526
McClosky, H., 139, 526
McConnell, H. K., 233, 503
McDavid, J. W., 313, 337, 339, 526, 534
McDowell, K. V., 389, 526
McEachern, A. W., 14, 515
McGinnies, E., 350, 526
McGrath, J. E., 398, 433, 526
McGuire, W. J., 11, 28, 29, 35, 148, 152, 155, 204, 205, 207, 235, 337, 472, 501, 520, 526, 531
McHugh, P., 14, 526
McIntyre, A., 61, 526
McKee, J. P., 455, 526
McKersie, R. B., 368, 375, 538
McLaughlin, B., 437–61, 459, 461, 505, 509, 524, 526, 538, 540
McNemar, Q., 162, 526
McPartland, J., 480, 481, 482, 483, 485, 497, 508, 526
McQuitty, L. L., 336, 526
Mead, G. H., 97, 109, 526
Mead, M., 59, 72, 519, 526
Meeker, C. F., 57, 509
Meisels, M., 390, 510
Menges, R. J., 37, 527
Merton, R. K., 441, 527
Messick, S., 34, 186, 259, 499, 527, 536
Metraux, T., 519
Meumann, E., 415, 527
Mezei, L., 165, 187, 189, 531
Michels, R., 458, 527
Michener, H. A., 346, 350, 527
Middlebrook, P. N., 155, 527
Miles, M. B., 382, 402, 404, 406, 426, 524
Milgram, S., 27, 29, 33, 38, 39, 92, 115, 116, 117, 118, 119, 121, 125, 134, 141, 142, 147, 312, 321, 333, 334, 337, 338, 341, 366, 413, 527
Miller, A. G., 23–48, 39, 48, 527
Miller, G. A., 201, 527
Miller, N., 147, 166, 235, 521
Miller, N. E., 56, 57, 120, 510, 527
Miller, S. M., 475, 527
Miller, W. E., 177, 178, 183, 184, 185, 506
Mills, J., 227, 305, 341, 402, 501, 505, 521, 527
Milton, G. A., 73, 527
Minor, M. W., 43, 527
Mischel, W., 194, 248, 263, 264, 277, 472, 474, 475, 502, 527
Mishler, E. G., 392, 535
Mixon, D., 39, 527
Moede, W., 313, 527
Mogy, R. B., 353, 527
Moles, O. C., 469, 470, 472, 518, 527
Mood, A. M., 480, 481, 482, 483, 485, 497, 508
Moore, O. K., 419, 527
Moos, R. H., 181, 424, 527
Moreno, J. L., 284, 524
Morgan, W. R., 366, 528
Morley, I. E., 366, 528
Morozov, Pavlik, 83, 84, 86, 103, 104
Morris, D., 538

Morse, N. C., 429, 528
Mortensen, C. D., 512
Moscovici, S., 332, 419, 511, 528
Mosteller, F., 480, 482, 497, 501, 508, 528, 535
Mouton, J. S., 193, 331, 508, 516
Mowrer, O. H., 52, 54, 56, 120, 510, 528
Moynihan, D. P., 474, 480, 482, 497, 501, 508, 510, 518, 528, 535
Mulder, M., 346, 358, 403, 528
Mulry, R. C., 45, 532
Murchison, C., 500
Murdoch, P., 368, 416, 528, 529
Murphey, L. B., 527
Murphy, G., 527
Murstein, B. I., 287, 528
Mussen, P. H., 87, 501, 512, 528
Muzzy, R., 244, 264, 510
Myrdal, G., 179, 184, 528

Nadar, R., 203
Natziuk, T., 331, 511
Neel, J. V., 85, 528
Nelson, E., 150, 528
Nemeth, C., 349, 360, 528
Newcomb, T. M., 12, 208, 241, 287, 501, 502, 520, 523, 526, 528
Newston, D., 330, 500
Nisbett, R. E., 141, 181, 248, 272, 274, 278, 336, 405, 519, 520, 521, 536, 539
Nixon, R. M., 105, 176, 216
Noel, R. C., 39, 515
Nord, W. R., 339, 528
Norman, W. T., 259, 529
Nucci, L., 452, 453, 454, 528
Nunnally, J. C., 156, 158, 160, 528

Occam, T., 155
O'Connor, J., 352, 540
Okada, T., 482, 525
Oliver, D. L., 298, 528
Olmstead, K. H., 148, 163, 505
Olshan, K., 248, 531
O'Neill, R. P., 99, 499
Oosterbaan, H., 402, 530
Orlansky, J., 366, 503
Orne, M. T., 24, 26, 30, 31, 32, 33, 34, 35, 39, 41, 119, 120, 147, 528, 529
Orwell, G., 310, 325, 529
Osborn, A. F., 420, 529
Osgood, C. E., 12, 153, 159, 215, 217, 218, 247, 529
O'Shea, R. M., 469, 518
Ostrom, T. M., 151, 155, 503, 515, 529
Oxley, B., 392, 503

Packard, V. O., 338, 529
Page, M. M., 32, 33, 38, 124, 529
Parry, H., 165, 185, 529
Parsons, T., 346, 502, 529, 539
Passini, F. T., 259, 529
Pate, M. A., 306
Paul, H., 61, 517
Paulus, P. B., 416, 529
Pavlov, I. P., 11
Pawlicki, R. E., 457, 529
Peabody, R., 149, 508
Peak, H., 347, 529
Pearson, K., 287, 529
Perlmutter, H. V., 418, 529
Perls, Fritz, 105, 529
Perry, P. K., 169, 529
Persinger, G. W., 45, 532
Pessin, J., 415, 529
Petrullo, L., 278, 501, 506, 516
Pettigrew, T. F., 441, 482, 485, 492, 493, 494, 495, 508, 529
Pfautz, H. W., 480, 529
Pfuetze, P. E., 98, 529
Phares, E. J., 60, 529
Piaget, J., 81, 89, 91, 93, 98, 529
Pick, A. D., 502
Pierce, C. M., 120, 517
Piliavin, I. M., 134, 135, 136, 138, 279, 297, 505, 529, 530
Piliavin, J. A., 134, 135, 136, 138, 529, 530
Pilkington, G. W., 185, 530
Pilkonis, P. A., 209, 540
Pisor, K., 34, 40, 533
Plato, 154
Platt, G. M., 346, 529
Podell, L., 472, 530
Polefka, J., 278
Pomeroy, W. B., 17, 318, 521
Poppleton, P. K., 185, 530
Porter, L., 402, 530
Poser, E. G., 181, 522
Prestholdt, P., 294, 295, 538
Preston, M. G., 429, 530
Proshansky, H., 154, 155, 326, 515, 528
Pruitt, D. G., 343–75, 346, 349, 353, 363, 365, 366, 367, 369, 370, 371, 372, 373, 375, 410, 411, 518, 527, 530, 536

Raab, E., 472, 530
Rabbie, J. M., 402, 530
Rainwater, L., 477, 530
Ranelli, C. J., 328, 523
Rapoport, A., 352, 530
Raush, H. L., 48
Raven, B., 323, 343, 348, 350, 354, 356, 358, 375, 403, 508, 513, 530

Rawlings, E., 122, 504
Reckman, R. F., 399, 530
Reed, E. W., 287, 530
Reed, J. S., 478, 518
Reed, L., 267, 539
Reed, S. C., 287, 514, 530
Reich, C. A., 450, 530
Reicken, H., 443, 512
Reimer, E., 429, 528
Rein, M., 473, 530
Reitan, H. T., 398, 530
Reitz, H. J., 411, 525
Resnick, J. H., 38, 530
Rest, S., 267, 539
Restle, F., 418, 419, 509
Richards, J. M., 262, 263, 508
Richardson, S., 244, 264, 510, 516
Riecken, H. W., 270, 537
Riemer, E., 429, 528
Riesman, D., 69, 338, 531
Riessman, F., 475, 527
Rietsema, J., 358, 530
Rigsby, L., 149, 508
Riley, R. T., 482, 485, 508
Ring, K., 37, 38, 353, 437, 520, 531
Rittle, R. H., 416, 508
Roach, J. L., 467, 531
Roberts, S. O., 487, 520
Robinson, J. P., 162, 531
Rockwell, G., 139
Rodda, W. C., 457, 532
Rodin, J., 130, 134, 135, 136, 138, 273, 274, 523, 529, 532
Rodman, H., 467, 531
Rokeach, M., 154, 165, 180, 187, 189, 453, 531
Roosevelt, F. D., 463
Roper, S. S., 485, 488, 489, 494, 508
Rose, A. M., 156, 531
Rosen, D., 368, 528
Rosenbaum, R., 267, 539
Rosenberg, M. J., 26, 30, 31, 43, 46, 173, 200, 208, 211, 212, 213, 221, 222, 229, 234, 499, 501, 510, 517, 520, 531
Rosenberg, S., 248, 531
Rosenkrantz, P. S., 73, 455, 506
Rosensweig, M. R., 501
Rosenthal, R., 24, 26, 40, 41, 42, 43, 44, 48, 507, 522, 526, 528, 531, 532
Rosenzweig, S., 26, 532
Rosnow, R. L., 34, 35, 48, 507, 522, 526, 528, 529, 531, 532
Ross, D., 94, 95, 502
Ross, L., 271, 274, 532
Ross, M., 197, 233, 532
Ross, S. A., 94, 95, 502
Roszak, T., 449, 450, 532

550 Name Index

Rotter, J. B., 60, 193, 515, 532
Rottman, L., 300, 538
Rubin, J., 41, 510
Rubin, M. H., 513
Rubin, Z., 284, 289, 532
Rubovits, P. C., 43, 44, 489, 532
Rusk, J. G., 162, 531
Russell, J. C., 403, 512
Rychman, R. M., 457, 532

Saegert, S., 86, 532
Saenger, G., 164, 186, 187, 188, 190, 532
Sahakian, W. S., 539
Sales, S. M., 416, 540
Sample, J., 148, 180, 532
Sampson, E. E., 66, 532
Sampson, R. V., 304, 532
Sandler, B., 37, 524
Sanford, F. H., 429, 532
Sanford, R. N., 13, 139, 499
Sanger, S. P., 457, 532
Sarbin, T. R., 87, 96, 311, 324, 532
Sarnoff, I., 14, 403, 532, 533
Sawyer, J., 366, 528
Saxe, L., 328, 523
Schachter, S., 53, 56, 66, 71, 72, 76, 77, 79, 181, 252, 273, 315, 402, 404, 425, 443, 512, 533
Schafer, S., 306, 533
Scheflin, A. E., 6, 387, 533
Scheibe, K. E., 81–109, 512, 533
Scheidt, R., 32, 33, 124, 529
Schelling, T. C., 350, 354, 365, 375, 533
Schenitzki, D. P., 370, 520
Schlamp, F. T., 471, 535
Schlenker, B. R., 353, 459, 533, 536
Schmitt, D. R., 293, 533
Schneider, D. J., 278, 411, 523, 533
Schoeninger, D. W., 363, 373, 533
Schooler, C., 475, 533
Schopler, J., 311, 349, 533
Schrag, C., 428, 533
Schroder, H. M., 153, 516
Schuck, J., 34, 40, 533
Schuette, D. J., 253, 511
Schultz, D. P., 25, 533
Schuman, H., 157, 179, 180, 191, 197, 495, 505, 533
Schutz, W. C., 70, 399, 400, 533
Schwartz, J. W., 366, 503
Schwartz, R. D., 35, 280, 281, 282, 538
Schwartz, T., 38, 530
Scott, B., 279, 529
Scott, E. L., 429, 533
Scott, W. A., 153, 154, 155, 156, 533

Sears, D. O., 155, 513
Sears, P. S., 362, 523
Sears, R. R., 56, 60, 120, 510, 533
Sechrest, L., 35, 280, 281, 283, 533, 538
Secord, P. F., 154, 287, 300, 502, 534
Segull, A. A., 475, 527
Seidenberg, B., 3–21, 515, 528
Seipel, M., 299, 514
Sekerak, G. J., 416, 508
Selcer, R. J., 74, 534
Selltiz, C., 173, 508
Sereno, K. K., 512
Sewell, W. H., 480, 534
Shakespeare, W., 15
Shannon, J., 394, 534
Shapiro, D., 247, 258, 506
Shaver, P. R., 162, 531
Shaw, G. B., 84, 86, 105, 534
Shaw, M. E., 4, 10, 396, 397, 398, 406, 418, 429, 431, 433, 490, 530, 534
Sherif, C. W., 403, 438, 531, 534
Sherif, M., 25, 314, 315, 347, 403, 438, 531, 534
Sherman, M. F., 457, 532
Sherriffs, A. C., 455, 526
Shils, E. A., 502
Shipman, V. C., 484, 516
Shomer, R. W., 168, 534
Shostak, A. B., 531
Shulman, A. D., 34, 35, 534
Shulman, R. F., 233, 532
Shuman, H., 157, 506
Siegel, S., 361, 534
Sigall, H., 34, 203, 522, 534
Sigler, E., 489, 507
Silver, M. J., 42, 44, 502
Silverman, I., 34, 35, 490, 534
Silverstein, S. J., 38, 511
Simmel, G., 299, 534
Simmel, M., 265, 516
Simon, C., 454, 534
Simons, L. S., 33, 537
Sims, A. A., 258, 538
Sinaiko, H., 366, 503
Singer, J., 53, 252, 273, 533
Singer, R. D., 96, 512
Singer, S., 60, 517
Sipprelle, C. N., 31, 35, 508
Sistrunk, F., 337, 339, 526, 534
Sizer, N. F., 105, 534
Sizer, T. R., 105, 521, 534
Skinner, B. F., 11, 70, 93, 111, 230, 534
Sklar, J., 476, 534, 535
Skrzypek, G. J., 431, 507
Slater, P. E., 106, 422, 450, 451, 452, 503, 535

Sletto, R. F., 146, 156, 535
Smelser, W. T., 424, 461, 535
Smith, M. B., 154, 209, 437, 446, 447, 515, 535
Smith, M. S., 482, 484, 489, 535
Smith, S., 73, 400, 535
Smith, W. P., 363, 364, 524
Snadowsky, A., 3–21, 397, 535
Snow, R. E., 44, 535
Snyder, R. C., 39, 515
Solomon, D., 365, 510
Solomon, H., 419, 524
Solomon, R. L., 54, 535
Sommer, R., 387, 389, 390, 391, 392, 503, 512, 524, 535
Sorrentino, R., 70, 535
South, E. B., 398, 535
Southern, M. L., 453, 535
Spencer, H., 306, 535
Spiesman, J. C., 424, 527
Spock, B., 81, 535
Staats, A. W., 33, 285, 535
Staats, C. K., 285, 535
Stang, D. J., 393, 535
Stanley, J. C., 24, 47, 507
Staples, F. R., 66, 535
Stark, R., 443, 524
St. Augustine, 15
Steiner, I. D., 70, 397, 421, 422, 423, 424, 433, 530, 535
Stemerding, A., 358, 403, 528
Stephan, F. F., 392, 535
Stephenson, G. M., 366, 528
Stern, W., 154, 535
Stevenson, A., 178
St. John, N., 486, 488, 535
Stogdill, R. M., 433
Stokes, D. E., 177, 178, 183, 184, 185, 506
Stollak, G., 27, 535
Stone, R. C., 471, 535
Stoner, J. A. F., 408, 409, 535, 536
Stonner, D., 57, 96, 514
Storms, M. D., 272, 274, 275, 536
Stouffer, S. A., 336, 515, 536
Strachey, J., 87, 513
Stricker, L. J., 34, 36, 186, 536
Strickland, L. H., 270, 322, 362, 517, 537
Strodbeck, F., 391, 536
Suchner, R. W., 346, 350, 527
Suci, G. J., 153, 159, 247, 529
Sudia, C. E., 476, 516
Suedfeld, P., 38, 511
Sullivan, D., 521
Sullivan, D. S., 38, 536
Summers, G. G., 156, 536
Surawicz, F. C., 454, 502

Name Index

Swanson, G. E., 520, 523, 526
Swap, W., 86, 532
Swingle, P., 530, 536
Sykes, G. M., 294, 536

Tagiuri, R., 247, 258, 278, 501, 506, 516
Tagracci, L. N., 195, 539
Tannenbaum, P. H., 12, 153, 159, 215, 217, 218, 247, 502, 520, 529
Tarter, D. E., 148, 163, 173, 190, 536
Tauber, E. S., 70, 522
Tausky, C., 468, 519
Taylor, D. A., 337–433, 387, 416, 418, 433, 500, 515
Taylor, D. M., 155, 514
Taylor, D. W., 421, 536
Taynor, J., 74, 536
Tedeschi, J. T., 8, 341, 351, 352, 354, 517, 524, 527, 536
Tedesco, J. F., 390, 536
Teger, A. I., 411, 536
Teichman, Y., 54, 56, 536
TenHouten, W. D., 477, 478, 536
Terrill, R., 101, 536
Test, M. A., 96, 506
Thibaut, J. W., 11, 270, 285, 322, 368, 418, 419, 520, 536, 537
Thistlethwaite, D. L., 410, 512
Thomas, E. J., 14, 505
Thomas, K., 198, 537
Thomas, W. I., 146, 537
Thorndike, E. L., 11, 537
Throop, W. F., 362, 517
Thurstone, L. L., 146, 156, 159, 160, 161, 199, 281, 537
Tilker, H., 125, 537
Titchener, E. B., 5
Tittle, C. R., 147, 161, 537
Toch, H., 438, 442, 459, 461, 537
Tolman, E. C., 11, 12, 537
Tomkins, S. S., 251, 499, 537
Torney, J. V., 101, 109, 517
Torrance, E. P., 419, 537
Tracy, J. J., 453, 509
Triplett, N., 313, 415, 537
Trommsdorff, G., 420, 421, 522
Trout, C., 454, 534
Tuckman, B., 384, 537
Tuddenham, R. D., 339, 537
Tulkin, S. R., 483, 537
Tullar, W. L., 367, 518
Turner, C. W., 33, 537
Turner, R. H., 445, 537

Valentine, C. A., 465, 466, 467, 497, 537
Valins, S., 278, 336, 519, 520, 539

Van de Riet, H. K., 457, 512
Van Hooff, J. A. R. A. M., 125, 538
Van Hoose, T., 34, 534
Vane, J. R., 486, 488, 538
Verba, S., 531
Vernon, D. T. A., 195, 539
Vernon, P. E., 260, 261, 262, 538
Vicarro, T., 180, 191, 197, 505
Vikan-Kline, L. L., 45, 532
Vinacke, W. E., 352, 538
Visser, L., 402, 530
Vitz, P. C., 366, 538
Vogel, S. R., 73, 455, 506
Vreeland, R., 244, 264, 510

Wack, D. L., 416, 508
Wajsman, G., 61, 517
Walder, L. O., 95, 96, 511
Walker, M., 402, 538
Walker, T. G., 418, 538
Wallace, G., 139, 176
Wallace, W. P., 283, 507
Wallach, M. A., 409, 410, 521, 538
Wallin, P., 287, 506
Wallington, S., 57, 538
Wallston, K., 38, 531
Walsh, J. A., 37, 524
Walster, E., 37, 38, 60, 279–308, 501, 504, 518, 524, 538
Walster, G. W., 279–308, 504, 538
Walters, G., 245, 246, 519
Walters, H. A., 259, 538
Walters, R. H., 58, 66, 87, 93, 109, 305, 502, 535
Walton, R. E., 368, 375, 538
Walzer, M., 442, 538
Warland, R., 148, 180, 532
Warner, L. G., 147, 538
Warr, P. B., 258, 538
Warriner, C. K., 178, 538
Watley, D. J., 456, 538
Watson, G. B., 418, 538
Watson, J. B., 4, 11, 538
Watson, P., 520
Watts, A., 450
Watts, W. A., 452, 453, 538, 539
Weaver, H. B., 161, 502
Webb, E. J., 35, 280, 281, 282, 283, 538
Weber, M., 71, 458, 538, 539
Weber, S. J., 34, 36, 539
Weggelaar, C., 451, 539
Weick, K., 431, 507
Weigel, R. H., 195, 539
Weiner, B., 267, 278, 336, 519, 520, 539
Weinfeld, F. D., 480, 481, 482, 483, 485, 497, 508

Weiss, L. B., 475, 513
Weissberg, N. C., 152, 463–97, 539
Weitz, S., 148, 539
Welkowitz, J., 405, 539
Wellington, S. A., 57, 513
Wells, H. G., 309, 539
Wertheimer, M., 9, 539
Westford, K. L., 413, 414, 510
Westie, F. R., 152, 164, 187, 188, 189, 509
Wheeler, L., 310, 341, 387, 500, 539
Whelan, E. M., 539
White, B. J., 403, 534
White, R. K., 428, 429, 523
White, R. W., 154, 209, 535
Whittaker, D., 452, 453, 538, 539
Whitten, P., 522
Whyte, W., 338, 379, 539
Wicker, A. W., 147, 168, 172, 190, 194, 197, 422, 539
Wiesenthal, D. L., 331, 514
Wilke, H., 346, 528
Wilkes, R. L., 38, 524
Willems, E. P., 48, 411, 508
Willis, R. H., 309–41, 366, 509, 517, 519, 539, 540
Willis, Y. A., 324, 540
Wilson, A. B., 485, 486, 540
Wilson, C. D., 483, 523
Wilson, J. R., 52, 540
Wilson, R. W., 101, 540
Winch, R. F., 399, 540
Wishner, J., 256, 540
Wishnov, B., 473, 530
Wisler, C. E., 482, 525
Wispe, L., 136, 540
Wolff, K. H., 534
Wonnacott, E. J., 155, 514
Wood, W. D., 363, 373, 533
Woodmansee, J. J., 155, 162, 540
Woodworth, R. S., 52, 540
Word, L. E., 134, 135, 508
Worell, J., 457, 540
Worell, L., 457, 540
Wright, D., 180, 191, 197, 505
Wrightsman, L. S., Jr., 155, 352, 540
Wundt, W., 5
Wyer, R. S., Jr., 211, 540
Wylie, R. C., 73, 540

Yalom, I., 382, 402, 404, 406, 426, 524
Yellin, A. M., 511
York, R. L., 480, 481, 482, 483, 485, 497, 508
Young, F. W., 405, 519
Yuker, H. E., 418, 540
Yukl, G. A., 362, 363, 365, 540

Zajonc, R. B., 12, 86, 229, 313, 415, 416, 417, 532, 540
Zald, M. N., 458, 540
Zander, A., 507
Zanna, M., 181, 209, 233, 519, 521, 540
Zborowski, M. E., 74, 540
Zechmeister, K., 365, 510
Zeller, A. F., 326, 540, 541
Zeno, 145
Zentall, T. R., 313, 541
Ziller, R. C., 344, 541
Zimbardo, P. G., 112, 113, 125, 142, 200, 222, 273, 274, 403, 412, 413, 414, 499, 532, 533, 541
Zipf, S. G., 356, 541
Znaniecki, F., 146, 537
Zook, E. A., 73, 516

Subject Index

AB (Assistance to Blind), 470
Achievement, 17–18, 70–73
  birth order, 66–67, 71–72
  correlated behaviors, 71
  dependence, 72
  economic growth, 71
  origins of, 71
  sex differences, 72–73
Acquiescence, 318, 338
Acquiescence effects, 158
Acquired drives, 52
Activist
  academic achievement, 447
  moral development, 447
  parental values, 446–47
  personality characteristics, 446–48
Actor, 14
Actor-observer effect, 272
Actual equity, 293, 294
AD (Aid to Disabled), 470
Adding model, 257
AFDC (Aid to Families with Dependent Children), 470, 476
AFDC-UP (Aid to Families with Dependent Children-Unemployed Male Parent), 470–71, 473
Affection compatibility, 400
Affective-cognitive consistency theory, 211–13
Affective dimension (attitudes), 154
Affective salience (attitudes), 154
Affiliation, 384, 402–403
  anxiety, 56, 59
  birth order, 66
  frustration, 59
Agent, *see* Representative
Agentic state, 334
Aggression (*see also* Hurting behavior), 59–60, 93–94, 95–96, 113–15, 115–27, 181
  ambient temperature, 124–25
  angry, 113–14, 112–24
  anonymity, 413–14
  anxiety, 59
  deindividuation, 413–14
  eye-contact, 125–27, 284
  feminist, 63–66
  frustration, 56–57, 59, 120–24
  guilt, 57–59
  instrumental, 114, 115–22

Aggression (*Cont.*):
  modeling, 93–94, 112–24
  personality, 58
  retaliation, 60–66
  sex differences, 60–63, 65, 66
  sex roles, 59–66
  stimulus cues, 32–34, 115, 122–24
  victim behavior, 125
Allies, 344, 357–58
Ally uility, 328
Altruism (*see also* Helping behavior), 57, 96–98, 114–15, 289–90, 297–98
  relationship, 297–98
  responses to, 297–98
Ambient temperature aggression, 124–25
Ambivalence (attitudes), 134
American dilemma, 179
Amish, 100–101
Anal stage, 13
Analysis of records, 17–18
Angry aggression, 113–14, 122–24
Anomie, 471
Anonymity
  aggression, 413–14
  antisocial behavior, 413–14
Anticathexis, 13
Anticipatory conformity, 318–19
Anticipatory socialization, 318
Anticonformity, 319, 320–21, 324, 325, 326, 329–30, 338
Antimonian personality, 451
Antisocial behavior
  anonymity, 413–14
  emotional arousal, 414
Anxiety
  affiliation, 55–59
  aggression, 59
  birth order, 66
  definition, 54
  dependency, 59
  fear, 54–56
  motivator, 54–56
  reduction, 273–74
Apparent fit, 172
Applied Social Psychology, 463–97
Arousal jag, 229
Arousal theory, 415–17
Asch-type situation, 316, 321, 335
Assertion constant, 218

Assertion training, 486
Assessor utility, 328
Assimilation, 267
Assumed similarity, 261–62, 264
Attachment behavior, 67–69, 86–87
Attitude change, 147, 155, 200–207, 311, 353–54
  consistency theories, 207, 209, 210–34
  one-sided argument, 204–205
  research methods, 199–200
  two-sided argument, 204–205
Attitude dimensions
  affective, 154–55
  centrality, 154
  cognitive, 154–55
  conative, 154–55
  connectedness, 154
  embeddedness, 154
  extremity, 154
  information support, 154
  intensity, 154–55
  magnitude, 154
  salience, 154
  valence, 154
Attitude measurement, 146–47, 150, 156–59, 166–67, 178–80, 182–83, 186, 190–91, 199–200
  acquiescence effects, 158
  behavior, 146–47
  closed-ended questions, 157
  connection effects, 186, 188–89
  forced-choice questions, 158
  measurement effect, 185–86, 188
  multiple-choice questions, 158
  open-ended questions, 157
  political polls, 156
  reliability, 161
  validity, 150, 161–62
Attitude scales, 17, 159–63
  Bogardus Social Distance, 281–82
  Comb's unfolding technique, 160
  common factor amplification, 159
  consensual method, 160
  construction, 159–61
  cumulative method, 160
  Guttman, 160–61, 281
  judgment method, 160
  Lazarsfeld Latent Structure Analysis, 160
  Likert, 157–58, 160–61
  multi-item, 173

554 Subject Index

Attitude scales (*Cont.*):
  psychophysical, 160
  scalogram, 160
  scoring, 159–60
  summative method, 160–61
  Thurstone, 156, 160–61
  Woodmanese and Cook scale of racial attitudes, 162
Attitudes, 145–98
  affective-cognitive consistency theory, 211–13
  affective dimension, 154
  affective salience, 154
  ambivalence, 154
  authority, 467–68
  balance theory, 213–15
  behavior, *see* Attitudes and behavior
  beliefs, 152–53, 154
  centrality, 154
  certainty, 155
  change, *see* Attitude change
  cognitive complexity, 154
  cognitive dissonance, 223–28
  competition, 176–79, 183, 186, 190
  congruence, 182
  congruity theory, 215–19
  connectedness, 154
  connection effects, 186
  consciousness, 155
  consistency, 161
  definition, 150–53, 166, 209
  degree of structure, 154
  differentiation, 154
  dimensions, *see* Attitude dimensions
  ego threats, 325–26
  expression, 166–67, 182–86
  extensity, 154
  extremity, 154
  family, 456
  flexibility, 155
  gradient of belief, 154
  intensity, 154, 183–84, 191, 192
  measurement, *see* Attitude measurement
  multiplexity, 154
  object, 211
  opinion, 153
  overtness, 154
  permeability, 154
  racial (*see also* Prejudice), 179, 191–92, 473–95
  reference groups, 208–209
  scales, *see* Attitude scales
  stability, 155, 183
  tenacity, 155
  theories, 151–55
  traits, 153

Attitudes and behavior, 146–50, 163–96
  congruence, 172–73, 175n, 180, 182, 186, 187, 188, 192
  constraints, 173–75, 175n, 180, 186, 188, 189, 190
  controversy, 146, 150, 162
  external explanation, 169–70
  perceived consequences, 169–70, 171
  personality characteristics, 192–93
  prediction, 180–83, 185, 190–95
  rewards, 193
  situational cues, 180–81, 186, 192
Attraction (*see also* Interpersonal attraction), 349, 356, 393, 401–402
  to groups, 383–84
Attractive communicator, 203–204
Attribution error, 271
Attribution theory, 264–74, 336
  causality, 265
  gestalt, 10
  inferences, 266
  prediction, 266, 271–72
Aufgabe, 146
Authoritarian, 453, 457, 475
  conformity, 336
  personality, 13
Authority, 344–45
Autistic hostility, 241
Autocratic leader, 428–39, 430
Autokinetic effect, 314
Autonomous state, 334
Autonomy before contact assumption, 494
Averaging model, 257–58

Balance theories, 213–15
Bargaining, 359–73
  communication channels, 366–67
  machiavellianism, 366–67
  need discussion, 367
Behavior
  artifactual, 30
  attitude, 146–50, 163–96
Behavioral intentions, 175, 180, 181, 191
Behaviorism, 11–12
Beliefs, 82, 154
  attitudes, 152–53
  definition, 210
  development, 83
  opinions, 154
Belief systems (*see also* Cognitive consistency theories), 207–34
  dynamics of change, 210–34
  functions, 205–209

Belief systems (*Cont.*):
  self-esteem, 208–209
  structure, 209–10
Best member effect, 418–19
Binding arbitration, 367
Birth order
  achievement, 66, 71–72
  affiliation, 56, 66
  anxiety, 56, 66
  dependency, 66–67
  education, 66
  popularity, 66
  suggestibility, 66
Bogardus Social Distance Scale, 281–82
Bolstering, 219
Boomerang effect, 319
Brainstorming, 420–21
Brainwashing, 204–205
Bridge, 6
Broken homes, 495
Buss aggression machine, 62
Byrnes Interpersonal Judgment Scale, 281, 282
Bystander inhibition, 130–37

Carrot-and-stick approach, 351
Categorizing data, 16
Cathexis, 13
Causal schema, 269
Causality, 265–66, 268
Central traits, 256–57
  context, 256–57
Centrality, 154
Certainty, 155
Character types, 69–70
  inner-directed, 69
  other-directed, 69–70
  tradition-directed, 69
Charismatic leader, 348
Cheating, 92, 164
Children
  illegitimate, 476, 478
  rearing, 100–101, 102
Choice Dilemmas Questionnaire (CDQ), 408–409, 410, 411
Choice shifts (*see also* Risky shift), 408–11
  cultural value theory, 410–11
  familiarization theory, 410
  leadership theory, 410
  occurrences, 411
  responsibility-diffusion theory, 409–10
Closed-ended questions, 157
Closure, 247
Clustering, 283
Coercive power (*see also* Influence, coercive), 324, 357, 359

Cognition, 12
Cognitive
  approach to person perception, 267–68
  category, 210
  complexity, 154
  consistency theory, see Cognitive consistency theories
  dissonance, see Cognitive dissonance
  dynamics, 12
  field theory, 12
  gestalt theory, 12
  interpersonal relations, 12
  maps, 12, 259
  orientation, 12–13
  stimuli, 53
  structures, 12
  theory, 18, 235–36
Cognitive-affective-conative model, 154–55
Cognitive consistency theories, 207–34
  affective-cognitive consistency theory, 211–13
  balance theory, 213–15
  Bem's self-perception theory, 230–34
  congruity model, 215–18
  consistency vs. curiosity, 229–30
  models of resolving belief dilemmas, 219–23
  theory of cognitive dissonance, 223–29, 232–34
Cognitive dimensions, 154–55
Cognitive dissonance, 12, 29, 223–29, 232–34, 325, 326, 353–54, 402
  cohesiveness, 402
  hedonic dissonance, 326
  moral dissonance, 326
  promises, 353–54
  threats, 353–54
Cohesiveness, 315–16, 389, 401–404
  cognitive dissonance, 402
  communication, 404
  compatibility, 400
  determinants, 402
  displacement of aggression, 402
  effects, 403
  encounter groups, 404
  goal attainment, 402
  group composition, 398–99
  group size, 377–78
  hostility, 402
  leadership, 402, 429
  measurement, 401–402
  productivity, 424–25
  severity of initiation, 402
  social comparison, 402
  threats, 402–403

Coleman Report, 480–82, 485, 486
Collecting on political debts, 349
Collective consciousness, 448
Collectivization, 102–104
Comb's unfolding technique, 160
Comfortable assumption, 492–93
Common effects, 267–68
Common factor amplification, 159
Communal living, 69–70
Communication
  amount, 392–94
  attraction, 393
  cohesion, 403
  leadership, 393, 429–30
  networks, see Communication networks
  reinforcement, 393–94
  type, 394
  verbal groups, 392
Communication networks, 394–97
  centralized, 396–97
  decentralized, 396–97
  leadership, 397
  status, 397
  task complexity, 396–97
  task groups, 396–97
Communicator
  characteristics, 200–204
  credibility, 202–204
  distance-attitude relationship, 202
Compatibility, 399–400
  affection, 400
  cohesion, 400
  control, 400
  inclusion, 400
Complexity, 12
Compliance, 34, 323, 325, 333, 354–55
  to promises, 354–55
  to threats, 354–55
Composition of groups, 397–99
Conative dimension of attitudes, 154–55
Concession, 360, 363
  rate, 365
Conditioned maturation, 87
Conflict spiral, 355–56, 357
Conformity, 309–41
  anticipatory, 318–19
  anticonformity, 319, 320–21, 324, 325, 326, 329–30, 338
  authoritarianism, 336
  class differences, 319
  congruence, 316, 318–19, 338
  counterconformity, 319
  cultural differences, 337–38
  delayed, 318–19
  ego strength, 336
  incidental, 310, 318
  intelligence, 336

Conformity (Cont.):
  J-curve hypothesis, 313–14
  leadership, 336
  measurement, 316–17
  movement, 316, 317–19, 338
  overconformity, 321
  producing agencies, 313
  responses, 316
  self-anticonformity, 320–21
  sex differences, 339–40
  stimulus ambiguity, 330–32, 333
  stimulus characteristics, 330–33, 337
  stimulus difficulty, 380–83
Congruence, 172–73, 175n, 180, 181, 186–89, 192
  implicit facts, 172
  indices vs. single measures, 173
  level of generality, 172
Congruity theories, 215–18
Conjugal power, 477
Connection effects, 186, 189
Consciousness of attitudes, 155
Consensual location method, 160
Consistency, 229, 248
Consistency of attitudes, 161
Constraints, 173–75, 175n, 180, 186, 188, 189, 190
Constructs, 259
Contact comfort, 52, 68
Contagion, 311
Content analysis, 17
Content-oriented, 202
Control compatibility, 400
Conventionality, 318, 338
Co-oriented power, 359
Correction for incredulity, 218
Counterconformity, 319
Countermeasures, 355–56
Covariation principle, 269
Credibility of threat, 350–51
Cross-sex identification, 73
Cross-situational consistency, 263–64
Cultural hypothesis, 466–67
Cultural value theory, 410–11
Culture of poverty, 465–70
Cumulative method, 160

Darwinian theory, emotion, 250–52
Data collection, 16–17
  interview, 17
  observation, 16
Debriefing, 27, 37, 40
  effectiveness, 40
Decentration, 89, 91, 98
Deception, 26–31, 36–37
  effects, 37
  incidence, 36–37

Decision making, 358–59
  tasks, 417–18
Defensive tactics, 364–65
Defensiveness, 361
Degree of structure, 154
Deindividuation, 112–14, 125, 411–15
  aggression, 413
  antisocial behavior, 412–14
  contributing factors, 113–14
  encounter groups, 415
  facilitating conditions, 412
  prosocial behaviors, 414–15
Delayed conformity, 318–19
Delegate, *see* Representative
Demand characteristics, 30, 32–33, 41
  sources, 41
Democratic leader, 428–29, 430
Dependency, 59, 66–67, 72, 338, 471–72
  achievement, 72
  anxiety, 59
  birth order, 66–67
  parental attitudes, 67
Desegregation, 489–91, 494–95
Desire to reach agreement, 361
Deviant behavior, 311, 314, 315–16
Deviation hypothesis, 336–37
Diamond model, 319–21
Differential accuracy, 262–63, 264
Differentiation, 12, 154, 219–20, 223
Discounting principle, 269
Discrimination, 146, 163, 455–56, 478
Displacement of aggression, 403
Displacement effect, 233
Dispositions, 153, 166, 241
Dissonance theory, *see* Cognitive dissonance
Distance-attitude relationship, 201–202
Distortion of action, 316
Distortion of judgment, 316
Distortion of perception, 316
Distributive orientation, 361, 363, 369, 371–72
Distributive tactics, 366, 367
Drive, 11, 52
Driving forces, 315
Dynamic approach, 10, 13
Dunlap's rule, 204

Eating behavior
  fear, 76
  time, 77
Ecologic validity, 31
Education
  birth order, 66
  family background, 481, 482–83
  race, 479–82

Education (*Cont.*):
  social class, 481
  socialization, 100–104
  U.S.S.R., 103–104
EEOR, *see* Coleman Report
Ego, 13
  strength and conformity, 336
  threats, 325–26
Einstellung, 205
Embeddedness, 154
Emotion, 53–54, 250–52, 414
  arousal and antisocial behavior, 414
  Darwinian theory, 250–52
  emotion-to-expression link, 250–51
  expression-to-perception link, 250–52
  labeling, 53–54
  learning theory, 251
  physiological stimuli, 53
Empathetic ability, 260
Empirical approach, 13, 15–18
Encounter groups, 379–82
  cohesion, 404
  composition, 399, 400–401
  deindividuation, 415
  effectiveness, 382
  goals, 379
  leader function, 426–27
  leaders, 381–82
  members, 380–81
  norms, 385
  stages of functioning, 380
Enculturation, 88
  vs. socialization, 97
Entity attribution, 269
Environmental difficulty, 267
Equality
  bargaining, 366
  norms, 366, 372
Equilibrium distance, 253
Equity theory, 290–302, 366
  actual equity, 293–94
  altruism, 296–99
  applications, 293–94
  exploitative relationships, 293–98
  inequitable relationships, 292–93
  intimate relationships, 299–302
  law, 304, 305–306
  norms, 346, 372
  psychological equity, 293–95
  responses, 294–96, 297–99
Ethnomethodology, 6, 14
Evaluation, 247, 248, 257
Evaluation apprehension, 31, 34, 44, 416–17
Expectancy effects, 24, 41–44, 45, 486–88, 489
  race, 486–88, 489

Expectancy effects (*Cont.*):
  sex differences, 41
  sources, 42
  teacher, 43–44, 489
Expectancy-value, 173
Expectation, 243
Experimental gaming, 352–53
Experimentation, 25
Expert power, 324
Exploitative relationships, 293–98
Expressive behaviors, 252–55
Expressive pathway, 251
Extensity, 154
External attribution, 266, 269, 270–71
External causality, 272
External explanation, 169–70
External validity, 18–19, 23
Externals, 60
Extinction learning, 11
Extremity, 154, 160
Eye contact, 125–27, 252–53, 284
  aggression, 125–27
  attraction, 284

Failure threat, 485
Fairness norms, 346
Fall-back position, 361, 362
Familiarization theory, 410
Family, 379, 456, 464–65, 474–76
  female-headed, 464–65, 474–76
  women, 456
Fear
  vs. anxiety, 54
  appeal, 55
  definition, 54
  eating behavior, 76
  as motivator, 55
  success, 455
Female-headed households, 474–76
  children, 474–76
  demography, 474
  educational achievement, 474
  occupational achievement, 474
Feminist personality, 457
Field, 5
Field experiment, 19
Field study, 18–20
  internal validity, 19
  vs. laboratory, 19–20
  mundane realism, 19
Field theory, 10–11
Filial attachment, 68–69
Fixed-alternative question, 157
Flexibility, 155
Forced-choice question, 158
Forced compliance, 225–26, 231–32
Formalistic error, 345–46
Forming stage (group development), 384

Freudian theory, 13, 335
Frustration, 55–57, 59, 109–10, 120–24
  affiliation, 59
  aggression, 56–57, 59, 120–24
  definition, 120
  motivator, 56–57
  reactions to, 109–10
  regression, 57
Functional approach, 6

GA (General Assistance), 470
Gate-keeper, 347
Generalization learning, 11
Generational movement, 444
Genetic viewpoint, 11
Genital stage, 13
Gestalt, 9–10, 12, 255, 335
Gradient of belief, 154
Group composition, 398–400, 422–24
  cohesiveness, 398–99
  complimentary, 399–400
  productivity, 422–24
  sex, 398–99
  similarity of members, 398–99
Group productivity, 417–23
  composition, 422–24
  vs. individual, 417–21
  size, 421–23
Group space, 388–90
  interpersonal attraction, 389
  invasion, 388–90
  spatial arrangement, 391–92
Group structure, 385–405
  dimensions, 386–87
  perception of, 404–405
Groups, 314–15, 322, 377–406, 407–15, 417–24, 425–26
  cohesiveness, 358–59
  composition, see Group composition
  definition, 377–78
  developmental stages, 384–85
  discussion, 314–15
  dynamics, 314–15
  family, 379
  growth, 378–79
  locomotion, 322
  norms, 314, 385
  performance, 415–26
  processes, 407–15
  productivity, see Group productivity
  social movement, 442
  space, see Group space
  structure, see Group structure
  territoriality, 387–88
  types, 377–79

Groups (*Cont.*):
  unanimity, 327
  verbal communication, 392–93
Groupthink, 425–26
  symptoms, 425–26
Guilt, 57–59
  inhibition of aggression, 57–58
  motivator, 57–59
  reactions, 57

Halo effect, 240–41, 247–48
Hedonic dissonance, 326
Hedonic relevance, 268, 271
Helping behavior (*see also* Altruism), 114, 127–40
  bystander intervention, 128–37
  instrumental, 114
  political ideology, 138–40
  victim characteristics, 134–40
Heuristic trial and error, 369, 371
"Hippie" (*see also* Movement for alternative culture), 449–55
  authoritarianism, 453
  personality, 452–53
  rejection of parental values, 452
  research methods, 453–55
  values, 453
Historical-analytical approach, 442–43
Holistic viewpoint, 13
Homosexuality, 246
Hostility
  cohesiveness, 402–403
  persuasibility, 206
Human relations workshop, 379
Hurting behavior (*see also* Aggression), 111–42
Hypnosis, 311

Id, 13
Identification, 87, 323, 348–49, 356, 383–84, 446–47
  groups, 383–84
  social mechanisms, 87
  student activists, 446–47
Illegitimate children, 476
Illusion of external constraints, 271
Imitation, 87, 93–96, 344, 348–49
  identification figure, 344, 348–49
  learning (*see also* Observational learning), 93–96
  socialization mechanism, 87
Implicit personality theory, 245–48, 258–59
  language, 259
  realism, 259–60
Impression formation, 9–10, 255–64
Imprisonment, 113

Incentive, 231–32
Incest taboo, 89, 92
Incidental conformity, 318–19
Incidental learning, 93
Inclusion compatibility, 400
Incongruity seeking behavior, 229
Incredulity effect, 202
Independence, 312, 317, 319–21
Individual norms, 314
Individual territory, 386–88
Individualistic orientation, 371
Inequity
  denial of responsibility, 294
  derogation of victim, 294
  exploitation, 306–307
  minimization of suffering, 294
  reciprocity, 298–99
  responses to, 294–96, 297–99, 306–307
  restoration of actual equity, 294
  restoration of psychological equity, 294
Influence (*see also* Interpersonal influence; Power)
  coercive, 344, 348, 350–51, 355–56
  co-oriented, 344, 347–48, 350
  expert, 344, 347
  independent, 323, 325
  informational, 327–28, 344, 346–47
  legitimate, 344–46, 357, 359
  negative, 325
  private-dependent, 324
  public-dependent, 323–24
  reciprocal, 344, 349–50, 356
  referent, 344, 348–49, 350, 356
  reward, 344, 350–05
  secondary effects, 325
Information power, 359
Information support, 154
Informed consent, 40
Initiation, 402, 490–92
Inner directed, 69
Inner observer variable, 240, 244
Innovation, 321
Instrumental responses, 59–67, 114–22
  aggression, 59–66, 114, 115–22
  dependency, 66–67
  helping, 114
  obedience, 115–20
Instrumental values, 453
Integrative bargaining, 368–72
Intelligence, conformity, 336
Intensity, 154, 191, 192
Interaction Process Analysis (IPA), 394
Internal attribution, 266–67, 269–70
Internal causality, 271–72

558 Subject Index

Internal validity, 18, 19, 23
Internalization, 323
Internals, 60
Interpersonal attraction, 280–308, 383
   attitudinal similarity, 286–87, 302
   definition, 280–81
   measurement, *see* Interpersonal attraction measurement
   theories, *see* Interpersonal attraction theories
   transituational reinforcers, 86–88
Interpersonal attraction measurement, 281–85
   Bogardus Social Distance Scale, 281
   Byrnes Interpersonal Judgment Scale, 281–82
   clustering, 283
   distance, 283–84
   eye contact, 284
   proximity, 283
   self-report questionnaires, 281
   sociometric, 284–85
Interpersonal attraction theories, 285–302
   equity theory, 290–302
   reinforcement theory, 285–89, 290–91
Interpersonal distance, 253–54
Interpersonal influence (*see also* Influence; Power), 309–41
Interpersonal judgment, 260–69
   accuracy, 260–64
   causality, 268–69
   process, 266
Interpersonal perception, 272–73
Interpersonal relations, 10, 12
Interpersonal simulation, 232–33
Interpersonal theory of personality, 394
Interviews, 167
Intimate relationships, 299–302, 303
Intuitive ability, 261
Iron law of oligarchy, 458

J-curve hypothesis, 313–14, 317
Joint limit, 362–63
Journals, 7
   Human Relations, 7
   Journal of Personality and Social Psychology, 7
   Journal of Social Issues, 7
   Sociometry, 7
Judgment method, 160

Known group method of validation, 162

Laboratory, 4, 18–20
   vs. field study, 19–20

Laissez-faire leader, 429
Language, 92, 244, 259
Law of effect, 11
Law of primacy, 205
Lazarsfeld Latent Structure Analysis, 160
Leadership, 336, 381–82, 393, 397, 402, 410, 426–32
   cohesiveness, 402, 429
   communication, 429–30
   communication networks, 397
   conformity, 336
   effectiveness, 430
   encounter groups, 381–82, 426–27
   methods, 427–29
   methodological approach, 427–32
   relationship oriented, 431
   task group, 427–32
   task oriented, 430–31
   theory, 410
Learning, 93–99, 335, 417–18
   imitation, 93–96
   incidental, 93
   observational, *see* imitation
   social role, 96–99
   tasks, 417–18
   theory, 335
Legitimate authority (*see also* Legitimate influence; Legitimate power), 118–19, 120, 431
Legitimate influence, 355
Legitimate power, 324, 334, 344–46, 357, 359
Legitimate threats, 354
Level of aspiration, 361–62, 363, 364
Lewinian field, 12
Libido, 13
Likert, 157–58, 160–61
Locus of control, 60
Logical error, 247–48

Magnitude, 154
Maintaining responses, 11
Malnutrition, 464
Mapping models, 320
Markets, 387
Matching hypothesis, 299–300
Maternal behavior, 67–69, 86–87
Matriarchal power structure, 476–78
Maturation, conditioned, 87
Measurement
   attitudes, 146–47, 150, 156–59, 166–67, 178–80, 182–83, 186, 190–91, 199–200
   cohesiveness, 401–402
   conformity, 316–17
   interpersonal attraction, 281–85
Measurement effect, 185–86, 188
Mediation, 367

Message effects, 204–206
Microsociology, 15
Misattribution, 271, 273–74
Models of decision making, 343
Molar approach, 9
Molecular approach, 9
Moral development, 89–91, 104–105, 107–108, 447
   activists, 447
   class differences, 91
   cultural differences, 91
   religious differences, 91
Moral dissonance, 326
Mother-child interaction, 66–67
Motives
   primary sources, 52
   secondary sources, 52
Movement, 317–18, 319
   conformity, 338
Movement for alternative culture, 449–52
   analysis, 450–52
   development, 449–50
   ideology, 450–51
Multiple-choice questions, 158
Multiplexity, 154
Mundane realism, 19
Mutual responsiveness, 373

Naive personality theory, *see* Implicit personality theory
Natural experiment, 19
Need discussion, 372–73
Need specific stimulation, 52
Negative influence, 322
Negativism, 312, 319
Negotiation, 360, 363
   time factors, 363
Nomothetic approach, 443
   vs. idiographic, 443
Nomothetic principles, 193–94
Non-common effect, 268
Nonconformity, 310–11, 312, 321
Nonverbal behaviors, 249–55
Normative function reference groups, 322
Normative influence, 322, 327
Norming stage, group development, 384
Norms
   bargaining, 368
   encounter groups, 385
   equality, 372
   equity, 346, 372
   fairness, 346
   following, 372
   following out of sense of obligation, 344–45
   formation, 314

Norms (*Cont.*):
  group, 385
  reciprocity, 349–50
  role theory, 14
  social, 314
  social responsibility, 346
  territoriality, 387
NOW (National Organization of Women), 457–58
Nurturance, 67–70

OAA (Old Age Assistance), 470
Obedience, 92, 115–20, 125, 147, 311, 333–34, 345–46
  agentic state, 334
  authority, 333–34
  autonomous state, 334
  criticisms, research, 119–20
  cultural differences, 333–34
  proximity effects, 117–18
  social support, 118–19
Observational learning, 94–96
  aggression, 95–96
  altruism, 96
  phobia, 94–95
Occam's razor, 155
Occupation, 455–56, 479, 491
  desegregation, 491
  race, 479, 491
  sex differences, 455–56
Open-ended question, 157, 168
Opinion, 153–54
  vs. attitudes, 153
Opposition behavior, 311
Oral stage, 13
Order of presentation, stimulus traits, 258
Other, role theory, 14
Other directed, 69, 70
Overconformity, 321
Overdifferentiation, 262, 272
Overtness, 154

Pact of ignorance, 32
Paradigm stage, theory, 8
Parental power, 477
Party identification, 177
Payoff structure, 352
Peer group, 68–70
  attachment, 68–69
Performing stage, 384
Permeability, 331
Person perception, 239–78
  cognitive approach, 12, 267–68
  cognitive processes, 242
  cultural differences, 242–43
  expectations, 243
  invariance of, 247–49
  language, 244

Person perception (*Cont.*):
  organization, 245
  stability, 247–49
  veridical, 242–44
Personal interaction, 6
Personal space, 253–54, 283–84, 386–92
  personal, 386
  physical environment, 390
  spatial arrangement, 391–92
  status relations, 390
  territory, 388–90
Personalism, 268, 271
Personality, 192–93, 336–37, 457
  attitudes, 192–93
  conforming, 336–37
  feminist, 457
Persuasibility, 206–207, 270
  hostility, 206
  self-esteem, 206–207
  sex differences, 206–207
  status effects, 270
Persuasion (*see also* Attitudes; Communicator), 315
Phallic stage, 13
Phenomenology, 5
Phobias, 94–95
Physical space, group, 386, 391–92
Physiological stimuli, 53
Placebo effect, 274
Political polls, 156
Political socialization, 101–104
Position power, 431
Post-decisional conflict reduction, 227–28, 232–33
Post-experimental interview, 26, 32–33
Poverty, 463–70
  culture of, 465–70
  demography, 464–65, 469, 471
  situational hypothesis, 466–67
  traits, 465–69
  values, 465–69
Power (*see also* Influence; Interpersonal influence), 305, 311, 323–25, 334, 343–59, 477
  coercive, 324–25, 359
  coordinated, 359
  group, 358
  informational, 358–59
  legitimate, 324, 334, 359
  parental, 477
  personal, 344
  punishment, 323–24
  reciprocal, 359
  referent, 324, 344, 349–50, 356, 359
  reward, 323–24, 359
Power balancing operations, 355
Powerful communicator, 203

Prebriefing, 38
Prediction, attribution theory, 271–72
Prejudice, 155, 163, 326, 329–30, 381, 489–90, 493–94
Primary effect, 205, 260
Primary drives, 52–53, 75–77
Primary socialization, 105–106
Primary sources, motivation, 52–53
Principle of Antithesis, 250
Principle of Minimum Effort, 221
Principle of Serviceable Associated Habits, 250
Prisoner's dilemma (*see also* Experimental gaming), 184, 185–86, 352–53
Private dependent influence, 324
Problem solving orientation, 361, 363, 369
Productivity, *see* Group productivity
Productivity, potential, 421–22
Prominent solutions, 365–66
Promises, 352–57
  compliance to, 354–55
  dissonance theory, 353–54
  vs. threats, 357
Proportionality effect, 201
Proposal, 360
Protestant ethic, 71
Proximity, 283
Psychoanalysis, 13–14, 355
Psychological equity, 293, 295
Psychological field, 5
Psychophysical method, 160
Psychosocial effects, 41
Public dependent influence, 323–25
Punishment, 11, 54, 324
  physical, 54
  power, 324
Puritanism, 442

Quasi-control group, 35
Quasi-stationary equilibrium, 315
Questionnaire, 17

Race
  attitudes, 179, 184, 188–89, 191–92, 282, 489–91
  conjugal power, 477
  education, 479–91
  family, 473–78
  helping behavior, 134–40
  illegitimate children, 476
  matriarchal power, 476–78
  occupation, 474, 479, 491
  parental power, 477
  poverty, 464–65, 469, 471
  teacher characteristics, 482
Rational calculation self-interest, 343
Reactance, 326

Subject Index

Realism, 259–60
Recency effect, 205, 260
Reciprocal power, 349–50, 356, 359
Reciprocal relations, 297
Reciprocity, 298–99
Reference groups, 208–209, 322
  attitudes, 208–209
  functions, 322
Referent power, 324, 344, 349–50, 356, 359
Regression, frustration, 57
Reinforcement, 11, 86
  social mechanisms, 86
  theory, see Reinforcement theories
Reinforcement theories, 11–12
  interpersonal attraction, 285–90, 290–91
  social exchange, 11
  social learning, 11
Relative deprivation, 441
Reliability, 161–62
Representative, 367–68
Research methods, 18, 25
Resistance to persuasion, 204–205
Resistance point, 361, 362
Resolving belief dilemmas, 219
Response
  definition, 11
  instrumental, 59–67
  traits, 256–58
Responsibility diffusion, 131–33, 134–35, 409–10, 422
Restraining forces, 315
Reward, 11
  attitudes, 193
  influence, 344, 350–51
  power, 323–24, 356
Risky shift phenomenon (see also Choice shifts), 407–11
Role
  expectation, 455–56
  learning, 94
  playing, 39–40, 87, 225
  taking, 98
  theory, 14, 311
Routinization of charisma, 458
Rules, 91

Salience, 143
Sampling, 36
Sanctions, 14
Scalogram method, 160
Secondary sources motivation, 53–59
  anxiety-fear, 54–56
  frustration, 56–57
  guilt, 57–59
Self-anticonformity, 320, 321
Self-attribution, 272–74
Self-credibility effect, 207

Self-esteem, 206–208
  belief systems, 208
  persuasibility, 206–207
Self-fulfilling prophecy, 488
Self-justification, 224–26
Self-perception theory, 230–34
Self-reinforcing quality, 348
Semantic differential, 158–59, 215–16
Sensitivity groups, 379
Separatism, 491–95
Set, 240, 248–49
Severity of initiation, 402
Sex
  differences, conformity, 349–50
  drive, 52–53
  group composition, 398–99
  roles, 59–63, 74–75
  typing, 73–75
Shape constancy, 247
Simplistic fallacy, 9
Situation favorability, 430–31
Situational approach, leadership, 427–30
Situational hypothesis, 466–67
Size constancy, 247
Social
  desirability, 168, 191, 267–68, 300–301
  enhancement, see facilitation
  facilitation, 25, 313, 415–17, 484–87
  goals, 67–75
  groups, 378–79
  identity, 85
  influence, 310
  inhibition (see also Bystander inhibition), 421
  justice, 304–305
  mechanisms, 86
  motivation, 51–79
  movements, see Social movements
  norms, 175, 317
  pressure, 147, 319–21, 332
  psychology, see Social psychology
  reality, 322
  reinforcers, 287–88
  role learning, 96–97
  stimuli, 7
  support, 118–19, 312, 326–30, 358
  threat, 485, 486–88
Social change, 439–42
  conversion, 442
  direct vs. indirect, 439–40
  relative deprivation, 441
Social movements, 437–61
  alternative culture, 449–52
  characteristics, 438
  definition, 438–39
  development, 441
  general, 439–40

Social movements (Cont.):
  group, 442
  "hippie," see alternative culture
  historical-analytic approach, 442–43, 452
  idiographic approach, 443–44
  nomothetic approach, 443
  psychological approach, 440–41
  sociological approach, 438–39
  specific vs. general, 439–40
  student protest, 444–49
  women's, 455–61
Social psychology
  applications, 7–8
  definition, 3–7
  empirical approach, 15–18
  sociology, 14
  theories (see also Theories), 12–27
Socialization, 81–109, 466–67
  behavior, 91–92
  China, 101
  collective ideals, 100
  content, 89–92
  cultural differences, 83–84
  definition, 81
  vs. enculturation, 97
  familiarity, 86
  language, 92
  monkeys, 88–89
  observational learning, 93–96
  political ideology, 99, 101–104
  processes, 87–89
  reinforcement, 86
  role-playing, 87
  U.S., 100, 105–107
  U.S.S.R., 102–104, 105
Sociogram, 284–85
Sociology, 14–15
Sociometric measure, 284–85
Sociometric technique, 401–402
Source, 343
Source credibility effect, 200–204
Source oriented, 202
Spatial arrangement, groups, 386, 391–92
Stability, 155
Stages, group development
  forming, 384
  norming, 384–85
  performing, 384
  storming, 384
Status
  communication networks, 397
  personal space, 390
  role theory, 14
Stereotypes, 59–60, 245–47, 259, 262–63, 264, 455
  accuracy, 262–63, 264
  sexual, 455

Stimulus, 11, 32
  elicited impulsive reactions, 32–34
  order of presentation, traits, 258
  social, 7
Storming stage (group development), 384
Student protest movement, 444–49, 459
Style approach, leadership, 428–29, 430
  autocratic, 428–29
  democratic, 428–29
  laissez-faire, 428–29
Style-situational approach, leadership, 430–32
Subjects
  apprehensive, 43
  attitudes, 38
  faithful, 31
  good, 30, 33
  negativistic, 31–32
  power deficiency, 26–27
  selection, 35–36
  self-esteem, 37–38
  socially desirable, 31
  volunteer, 35–36
Summated difference scale, 188–89
Summative method, 160–61
Superego, 13
Surrogate mothers, 52, 68
Surveillance, 351, 353–54

Tacit bargaining, 360
Tailoring, 264
Target, 344
  point, 361
Task groups, 378, 382–83, 391, 396–97
  communication networks, 396–97
  spatial arrangement, 391
  stages of functioning, 383
TAT (Thematic Appercention Test), 70
Teacher characteristics, 482
Teacher expectancy effects, 489
Teacher's pet phenomenon, 240
Television, aggression, 95–96
Telic continuum, 313
Terminal values, 453
Territoriality, 386–88
  markers, 387

Theories
  affective-cognitive-consistency, 211–13
  attitudes, 151–55
  attribution, 264–74, 336
  balance, 213–15
  cognitive consistency, 207, 209, 210–34
  cognitive dissonance, 223–29, 232–34
  congruity, 215–19
  cultural value, 410–11
  Darwinian, 250–52
  equity, 290–302
  familiarization, 410
  field, 10–11
  gestalt, 9–10, 12, 255, 335
  implicit personality, 245–48, 258–59
  interpersonal attraction, 285–302
  interpersonal theory of personality, 394
  leadership, 410
  learning, 11, 355
  naive personality, see implicit personality
  psychoanalytic, 13–14, 355
  reinforcement, 285–89, 290–91
  role, 14, 311
  self-perception, 230–34
  simple, 9
  social psychology, 12–27
  sovereign, 9
Threats
  capacity, 350
  cohesiveness, 402–404
  compliance to, 354–55
  countermeasures, 354–56
  credibility, 352, 353
  dissonance theory, 353–54
  intent, 350
  legitimate, 354
  magnitude, 352
  vs. promises, 357
  psychological cost, 354
Thurstone scale, 156, 160–61
Time
  eating behavior, 77
  negotiation, 363
Tradition-directed, 69

Traits
  adding model, 257–58
  approach, 427–28
  attitudes, 153
  averaging model, 257–58
  weighted model, 257–58
Transcendence, 220
Transitional reinforcers, 286–88
Typicality, 336

Ultimate goals, 361
Unity, 12

Valence, 154
Validity, 150, 154, 161–62, 163
  known group method, 162
  problem, 261, 263
Values, 82–86, 453
  conflicts, 84–85
  instrumental, 453
  purposes, 85
  terminal, 453
Voluntary commitment, 224
Voting behavior, 11, 169, 176–78, 183, 184–85
  party identification, 176–77

Weapons effect, 32–34, 115, 124
Weighted average model, 257–58
Welfare, 468, 470–73
  AB, 470
  AD, 470
  AFDC, 470
  AFDC-UP, 470
  demography, 471
  employment, 468, 472–73
  GA, 470
  OAA, 470
  recipient traits, 471–72
White racism, 492, 493–94
Withdrawal, 321
Women's liberation movement, 455–61
  scale, 63
Woodmanese and Cook scale of racial attitudes, 162

Zeigarnick phenomenon, 36